Cybertaxation

The Taxation of E-Commerce

Karl Frieden

CCH INCORPORATED
Chicago

Editorial Staff

Editor . . . . Sally Adams, J.D., LL.M.
Production . . . . Impressions Book and Journal Services, Inc.
Cover Design . . . . Sarajo Frieden Design
Index . . . . Lynn J. Brown

ISBN 0–8080–0450–6

CCH INCORPORATED
4025 W. Peterson Ave.
Chicago, IL 60646–6085
1 800 248 3248
http://www.cch.com

This book is dedicated to the memory of Mike and Evie,
and to Susan, Gabriel and Eva

About the Author

Karl A. Frieden is a partner with Arthur Andersen and is based in the firm's Boston office. He is a member of Arthur Andersen's global Tax, Legal, and Business Advisory E-Commerce Task Force. Prior to joining the firm, he was the Deputy General Counsel of the Massachusetts Department of Revenue.

Mr. Frieden consults regularly with leading-edge E-commerce businesses in the United States and abroad. Since the early days of Internet commerce in the mid 1990s, he has made presentations on E-taxation to business and tax conferences throughout the country. He has testified before the U.S. House of Representatives Commerce Committee on Internet tax-related issues. He was a member of the Steering Committee of the National Tax Association's Communications and Electronic Commerce Tax Project—the joint government/business project to develop uniform and simpler rules for the taxation of E-commerce.

Karl Frieden lives in Cambridge, Massachusetts, with his wife and two children.

Contents

Preface   *xi*

Acknowledgments   *xiii*

1 Global Taxation in the Age of the Internet   1

    The Transformation to an Internet Economy   3

    The Information-Age Economy   19

    The Global Expansion of Remote Selling   35

    The Tax Complexity of E-Commerce   46

    The Cutting-Edge Issues of Global Taxation   60

2 Sales and Use Taxation of E-Commerce   81

    The Primacy of State Sales and Use Taxes   81

    Taxation of Telecommunication Services   89

    The Taxation of Digital Commerce   101

    The Absence of a Uniform Sales Tax Base   116

    How to Source Sales   150

    Sales and Use Tax Simplification   183

3 State Income Taxation of the Internet   207

    Introduction   207

    The Traditional Apportionment Rule
        for Products and Services   208

    The Use of Market-State Sourcing Rules
        for Selected Service Industries   229

    Current Sourcing Rules for E-Commerce   238

    Special Taxes Applied to the Telecommunications
        Industry   249

4 Nexus, Remote Sellers, and the Internet 263

Introduction 263
De Minimis Physical Presence 272
Attributional Nexus 289
Corporate Nexus Issues 334
Future of Nexus Rules in an E-Commerce Era 341

5 Value Added Taxes and E-Commerce 359
Mike Loten and Jackie Hubbard

Introduction 359
Overview of Value-Added Taxes 363
Goods 372
Customs Duty 388
Services 393
Telecommunications Services 402
Electronic Delivery 408
Developments: The Political Debate 414

6 Federal and International Income Taxation
of E-Commerce 435
James M. Gannon and Jeffrey A. Weiss

Introduction to Cross-Border Direct Taxation 436
U.S. Treasury White Paper 439
Interaction of Tax Treaties and Statutory Law 442
Engaged in a U.S. Trade or Business:
  The Standard When There Is No Tax Treaty 446
Permanent Establishment under a Tax Treaty 454
Recent Developments: OECD Draft Proposal 460
Transfer-Pricing Issues 462
The Foreign Tax Credit 465
Classification of Income 468
Final Software Regulations 472
Source of Income 478
The Source Rules 482

Taxation of E-Commerce in Canada   492
Taxation of E-Commerce in Japan   497
Taxation of E-Commerce in the United Kingdom   504
Summary of Cross-Border Direct Taxations   514

Notes   517
Index   561

Preface

This book evolved out of my interest in the early 1990s in the taxation of telecommunications and on-line services, direct-marketing channels, cross-border transactions, and other forerunners of E-commerce. At that time, many businesses and governments were grappling with some of the emerging tax issues that are exploding today in conjunction with the Internet, albeit on a smaller and less visible stage.

Over the course of the last decade, I had the opportunity to address the issues arising from the collision of the new world of E-commerce and the old world of traditional tax systems, both as a government official representing the Commonwealth of Massachusetts and as a tax practitioner representing E-businesses at Arthur Andersen. These experiences have provided me with a dual public- and private-sector perspective on how the Internet age is likely to transform tax rules in the United States and abroad.

To adequately address taxation in the new economy, it is necessary to explore not only the technical tax issues but also the related political, economic, business models and technological developments. More than any other tax issue of the last half century, the taxation of E-commerce must be viewed within its broader social context. Given the dynamic character of the Internet, a thorough examination of taxation in the Internet age requires analysis not only of current tax issues but also of those issues likely to emerge as E-commerce grows tenfold in the next five years.

The primary topics that are covered in this book are transactional taxes applied to Internet purchases (sales and use taxes, value added taxes), income tax rules related to E-commerce, tax simplification, and the issue of nexus or jurisdiction to tax. Given the global nature of the Internet, this book focuses on taxes at all levels—local, state, federal, and international.

The audience for this book is not limited to tax practitioners. The book is aimed at businesses that need to understand the current (and future) tax rules that are likely to apply to Internet transactions, practitioners who need to provide advice to dot-coms and "click-and-mortar" companies, academics who want to teach law and accounting students about the intricacies of Internet taxation, and government officials who are trying to identify both the problems in the current tax rules and possible solutions to be applied to the new borderless and timeless Internet economy.

The purpose of this book is not to resolve the complex policy issues surrounding the taxation of E-commerce. That task, thankfully, is one that is best left to the U.S. Congress, state legislatures, and the business groups working with government on Internet tax-related issues. Rather, the goal here is to provide an in-depth discussion of both current and future tax issues related to E-commerce, focusing on the applicable rules, complexities, and problems of the current system, as well as the proposals from both business and government for changes in the future system.

While the state, federal, and international tax rules as applied to E-commerce are likely to change dramatically over the next decade, one can still benefit from a close examination of current tax laws and approaches. Although the direction of both E-commerce and government efforts to regulate and tax it cannot be fully anticipated, there is sufficient information available to provide both a guide to tax planning and compliance in the present and a window into the transformation of the tax sphere in the not-so-distant future.

Acknowledgments

I would like to thank Sally Adams, my editor at CCH, for her enthusiasm for this project and insightful suggestions and editorial comments throughout the process. I am also indebted to Allan Cohen of Arthur Andersen for his far-sighted support for E-commerce tax consulting dating back to 1995. In addition, Bill Curlee of Arthur Andersen offered early encouragement and support for this book project. I want to acknowledge Bud Gartland and all of the members of the state and local tax practice in Arthur Andersen's Boston office for their assistance over the course of this project. Special thanks to Rachel Craig and Lisa Cunningham for their help on all the administrative tasks, and to Roy Harrill for his assistance with the contractual and business arrangements. Sarajo Frieden's wonderful book cover has made this truly a family affair. I want to express my deep gratitude to my colleagues in Arthur Andersen who contributed chapters on value-added tax and international income tax: Mike Loten, Jackie Hubbard, Jim Gannon, and Jeffrey Weiss. Finally, I would like to acknowledge the support and love of my wife, Susan, and my two children, Gabriel and Eva, without whose (limited) patience I could never have completed this book.

In addition, the authors of chapter 5, Mike Loten and Jackie Hubbard, would like to thank Vanessa Marshall and Charlie Vaughan-Read for their considerable efforts in pulling together the information used in this chapter, and Juliet Wardle for her patience with the frequent requests to reshape and redraft the work as we pulled it together. The authors of chapter 6, Jim Gannon and Jeffrey Weiss, would like to thank our colleagues Deborah Anthony and Simon Ogle in London, Masaharu Umetsuji in Tokyo, and Craig A. Cowan and Deborah Ort in Toronto for their contributions to this effort.

1

Global Taxation in
the Age of the Internet

At the dawn of the 21st century, the age of the Internet is posing significant challenges to global tax systems. The nations of the world are entering a promising yet volatile electronic-commerce (E-commerce) realm that is characterized by a seamless, borderless, and timeless marketplace. The Internet is accelerating a number of trends that are laying the foundation for a new global economy, in which production and consumption become more mobile, dynamic, intangible, and multinational.

First, the shift from a manufacturing-based economy to a service-based economy has been reinforced by the explosive growth of the information technology industry. Second, the sharply falling costs of both transportation and communications—the so-called death of distance—have accentuated the development of an integrated global marketplace in which intermediate inputs and final products move more freely among states and nations. Finally, the growth of direct marketing and distance selling through mail order, telemarketing, television shopping networks, and most recently, Internet retailing has vastly expanded the proportion of "remote" commerce that can be conducted almost instantaneously between vendors based in one location and consumers in another.

These economic trends threaten to undermine the different local, regional, and national taxation formulas used by countries throughout the world. Nations traditionally created taxation rules to address sales of tangible property and locally or regionally based commerce—the then prevailing forms of business activity. This historical development is still reflected in the tax base reliance on property taxes on tangible or real property, as well as transactional and income tax rules primarily oriented toward sales of manufactured goods. It is obviously far easier to tax business activity that is locally based and involves the sale of tangible goods or property than it is to tax business activity that is mobile or multijurisdictional and which involves the sale of services or intangible property.

As the world has shifted toward a more service-based global economy, local and national governments have struggled to develop rules that more accurately reflect this type of business activity. However, the revamping of archaic tax rules threatens to be overwhelmed by the speed with which the Internet and E-commerce are changing the nature of the global marketplace. In the so-called new economy, physical properties matter less, distance disappears, and time collapses. The digital age—with its ability to create commerce between anyone, anytime, and anywhere—is placing an enormous strain on national and subnational government regulation, not the least of which is reflected in the global concern over the adaptability of current taxation rules to 21st-century commerce.

Put simply, it is much easier to impose a sales or transactional tax on the sale of an automobile at a local dealership than it is to tax the sale of digitized software or music to a consumer 10,000 miles away. Similarly, it is less difficult to impose an income tax on a vertically integrated business that operates primarily in one jurisdiction or region than it is to impose an income tax on a business that outsources product development, manufacture, and customer service to locations throughout the country or the world. And it is much simpler to impose a property tax on a manufacturing facility with an inventory of tangible goods than it is to impose a property tax on a movable computer server capable of storing and instantaneously delivering thousands of electronic goods or services.

This chapter considers the revolutionary changes in business models and consumption patterns associated with the Internet and the information age. This discussion is a necessary preface to the analysis of local, state, federal, and international taxation rules and how they are affected by the shift from an industrial-age economy to an information-age economy. Without understanding the pace and direction of technological and economic change brought on by the advent of the Internet and the expansion of E-commerce, it is not possible to reflect on or to comprehend the changes and adjustments that may be required in sales and use tax, value-added tax, corporate income tax, property tax, and other taxation systems utilized in the global economy.

The Transformation to an Internet Economy

The Phenomenal Growth Rate of the Internet

The Internet—the crowning achievement of the late 20th-century information age—has leaped into the world's consciousness during the second half of the 1990s. Prior to 1994 there was little public awareness of the Internet or its potential for revolutionizing commerce in the nations of the world. The growth of the Internet in the last six years of the 20th century has been nothing short of breathtaking. In the United States, the number of households that have access to the Internet increased from 0.2 percent in 1993 to 14 percent in 1996 to 37 percent in 1999. In terms of numbers of users, less than 1 million North Americans had access to the Internet in 1993 compared to 112 million users in the United States and Canada in 1999. Moreover, it is estimated that over one-half of all households in the United States will have Internet connections by the year 2002.[1]

Although the United States and Canada still account for more than one-half of all Internet users, the rest of the planet is catching up quickly. On a global basis the number of Internet users increased from about 3 million in 1993 to 200 million in 1999. By year-end 2000 an estimated 300 million people will be on-line. Within the first decade of the 21st century, an estimated 1 billion people will be connected to the Internet—or about one-sixth of the world's population. In the next five years the composition of the Internet population is likely to alter significantly, with over two-thirds of all users living outside of North America. Reflecting the increasingly international composition of the Internet, one-third of current users do not speak English (see figure 1.1).[2]

Figure 1.1. **The Composition of Internet Usage**
September 1999 (millions)
Total: 201 Million

Source: NUA Internet surveys.

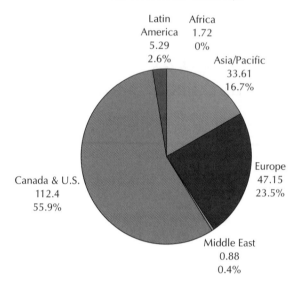

The rapid expansion of the Internet has undeniably taken place over an even shorter time frame than the adoption of other revolutionary technological breakthroughs. One measure of the pace of technological development is how long it takes a new invention to reach 25 percent of households in the United States. In this country electricity, the automobile, and the airplane all took 50 years to reach that threshold; radio and television took about 25 years; personal computers and cellular phones took less than 15 years. Once it was opened up for commercial use, the Internet reached the 25 percent penetration threshold in the United States in fewer than 10 years.[3]

Similarly, technological penetration on a global basis can be measured by how long it takes before 50 million consumers worldwide utilize the new invention. It took 38 years for radio to cross the 50 million threshold, 13 years for television to reach that mark, and 16 years for personal computers to achieve that goal. In comparison, it took the World Wide Web only four years to reach the threshold of 50 million consumers.[4]

The Digital World

So what is this new invention that has exploded across boundaries of time and space in the late 1990s? The Internet is a worldwide network of computers and other communications equipment linked by high-speed data lines and wireless systems that is being utilized as the center of a newly emerging global electronic marketplace. The Internet and its graphical subnetwork called the World Wide Web (the Web) enable millions of computers and other communication equipment using different hardware, operating systems, and software application programs to link to each other by a common protocol.

The Internet is on the verge of reinventing social and commercial relationships because it represents the convergence of three previously distinct communications channels: (1) data transmissions (associated with computers), (2) voice transmissions (associated with telecommunication services), and (3) video transmissions (connected with entertainment, cable, and television companies). It is not so much the amount of information on the Internet at any given point in time as it is the transforming ability to interconnect the world's businesses and people that gives the Internet its economic and social vitality. Indeed, according to one 1999 study all of the information on the Web—about three trillion bytes of information—could be fit onto about five thousand CD-ROMs and squeezed into a computer server smaller than the size of a bedroom closet.[5]

The Internet is the culmination of several decades of rapid progress toward a more fully digital world. In many ways digital technology appears to be a modest change in format; previously, telephone, audio, and video were transmitted in continuous waves using analog technology. In a digital age voice, audio, video, and data will be transmitted in a discontinuous flow of bits of zeros and ones. This rather basic change in format—the ability to transfer all data, pictures, voice, and music using the same protocol—provides for a fundamental simplification of all kinds of information used in commerce. This development in turn dramatically increases the efficiency of world commerce.

The Internet provides the critical link that facilitates the instantaneous and inexpensive movement of *bits* (electronic information) in a digital age. According to Nicholas Negroponte, the author of *Being Digital,* the world is at least partially transitioning from an economy based on the movement of "atoms" to one based on "bits." According to Negroponte, "The information superhighway is about the global movement of weightless bits at the speed of light." As the focal point of the digital revolution, the Internet is creating a significant increase in the "intangible" economy—which is made up of goods and services that never take the form of tangible goods. The Internet is also resulting in a substantial rise in the level of remote commerce—goods and services that are ordered and purchased by electronic means from anywhere in the world while delivered by tangible medium.[6]

North America has been in the forefront of this digital revolution. According to Forrester Research, by the end of the 10-year period between 1994 and 2003, nearly one-half of all households in North America will use personal computers, cellular telephones, and the Internet. By comparison, in 1994 less than one-third of all households had personal computers, less than one-fifth of all households had cellular phones, and less than one-twentieth of all households had Internet access. In Europe and Asia this trend is a few years behind the United States but is almost certain to catch up within the first decade of the 21st century (see figure 1.2).[7]

The Turning Point

The world's first programmable computer—the Electronic Numerical Integrator and Computer (ENIAC) was developed in 1946. It was 10 feet tall and 150 feet wide and performed up to five thousand operations per second. Today a laptop computer performs over 400 million instructions per second. In 1980 a telephone with copper wires could transmit one page of information per second. Today a tiny strand of optical fiber cable as thin as a human hair can transmit 90,000 volumes of an encyclopedia in one second.[8]

The Internet weaves together the major advances in both computer and communications technology. The predecessor to the Internet—the ARPANET—was created in 1969 by the U.S. Defense Department as a

Figure 1.2. **Digital Decade**

Source: Forrester Research, Inc.

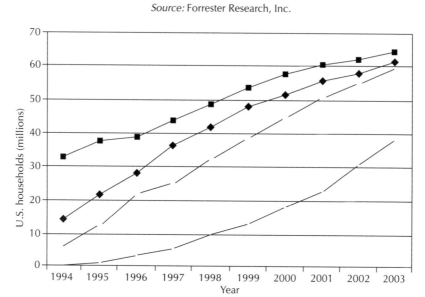

decentralized communications network that could continue to operate even in the event of a catastrophic military attack. The Internet created a common digital protocol, Transmission Control Protocol/Internet Protocol (TCP/IP), that could be used to connect computers that use different hardware and software programs.

Following its creation the Internet grew slowly for two decades—being used primarily by academic researchers around the United States. Two developments finally opened up the enormous untapped commercial potential of the Internet. First, in 1989 a British researcher named Tim Berners-Lee, working at CERN's European Laboratory for Particle Physics in Switzerland, developed the World Wide Web. The Web introduced two major innovations to the Internet: (1) it facilitated the use of multimedia video, pictures, and music—in addition to the data and text that was already available on the Internet; and (2) it used hypertext—a tool that allows users to highlight words or icons and move from these locations to related information that may be stored on a computer in another region of the world.

The second development occurred in 1993, when Marc Andreessen and his colleagues at the University of Illinois developed Mosaic, the multimedia Web browser. The Web browser made the Web more user friendly by allowing computer users to search efficiently for Web sites that contained certain specified information or images.

The cumulative impact of these two innovations transformed the Internet. The combination of digital communications, expanding bandwidth, a commonly accepted protocol, the mixing of graphics and data, and easy-to-use search mechanisms revolutionized the medium. By 1994 there were for the first time more commercial users of the Internet than academic users. Although other activities such as E-mail and Internet telephony use the Internet, the easy-to-use point-and-click interface of the Web is primarily responsible for the popularization of the Internet.

The Unlimited Potential of E-Commerce

E-commerce is generally defined as transactions that involve the exchange of goods and services by electronic means. *Direct* E-commerce involves goods and services that are both purchased and delivered by electronic or digital means. *Indirect* E-commerce involves goods and services that are purchased by electronic means but delivered in tangible form by common carriers or some other traditional form of delivery.

Although E-commerce previously expanded in other channels (e.g., corporate intranets and home shopping networks), the Internet is the most explosive and visible symbol of the multimedia linkage of data, audio, and video transmissions all in a single commercial pathway. In this information age the Internet vastly expands the potential to instantaneously purchase and/or transfer a wide range of goods and services among locations anywhere on Earth. The Internet removes barriers of time and geography, creating a virtual 24×7 world.

The rapid growth of Internet use did not initially lead to an explosive growth of E-commerce. In 1996, for instance, none of the top 15 most-visited Internet sites allowed for on-line shopping. These sites primarily focused on providing E-mail, on-line forums, information, and advertising. Three years later virtually all of the top Web-site destinations allowed for some form of on-line shopping. The trend toward E-commerce accelerated as more consumers came on-line and the pioneer Internet retailers experienced meteoric growth.

Companies in the United States recognized that on-line selling was not an optional distribution channel in the age of the Internet but rather a mandatory one. In 1998 24 percent of U.S. companies sold their products on-line; by 2000 an estimated 56 percent of U.S. companies will sell their products on-line. Another study estimates that by 2002 70 percent of the world's largest companies will use the Internet as a sales channel.[9] In 1999 a worldwide survey of five hundred large corporations conducted by the Economist Intelligence Unit and Booz Allen and Hamilton found that over 40 percent of the top executives believed the Internet would "transform" the global marketplace within three years. An additional 50 percent of the top managers believed that the Internet would have a "major impact" on the global marketplace within three years.[10]

Not surprisingly, these trends are reflected in the unprecedented projections for the growth of E-commerce. According to Forrester Research, on a worldwide basis, under optimistic scenarios, the trade of goods or services where the final order is placed over the Internet may reach as high as $3.2 trillion in 2003, or 5 percent of all global sales. Even under more conservative assumptions, E-commerce is likely to reach nearly $2 trillion in 2003. The rapidity of the worldwide expansion of E-commerce depends to a large degree on how quickly other advanced industrialized nations emulate the U.S. Internet-use rates. Forrester Research expects the United States to enter a "hyper-growth" phase of E-commerce in 2000, followed within two years by Canada, Britain, and Germany, and within four years by Japan, France, and Italy.[11]

Stock-Market Mania

The dramatic potential of E-commerce has not gone unrecognized by the stock and financial markets. Indeed, during the late 1990s Wall Street dramatically affirmed its confidence in the revolutionary potential of the Internet by causing dramatic run-ups in the valuations of a number of companies whose businesses centered around the Internet and E-commerce. For instance, the Hambrecht & Quist Internet Index, which encompasses more than 60 Internet-related stocks, rose by over 450 percent between April 1997 and January 1999. Individual Internet leaders experienced meteoric stock price appreciation. Over a 12-month period from mid 1997 to mid 1998, Amazon.com rose 1,063 percent, Yahoo increased by 679 percent, Lycos advanced by 677 percent, Excite rose by 635 percent, and America Online increased by 258 percent.[12]

The valuations of the leading Internet companies—almost all of which had been in business for less than five years—reached such dizzying heights in 1999 that they actually exceeded more traditional blue-chip competitors. For instance, in the spring of 1999, when Internet stocks peaked, Yahoo (created in 1994) had a market capitalization of $40 billion, or two times the valuation of the more-traditional media company Gannett (created in 1906) of $17 billion; Amazon.com's valuation reached $30 billion—10 times higher than Barnes & Noble's valuation of $2.7 billion; E-Trade (created in 1996) had a valuation of $10 billion—exceeding the valuation of Paine Webber (created in 1879) of $6.2 billion; Priceline.com (formed in 1997) had a valuation that reached $10 billion, or more than two times the valuation of United Airlines (formed in 1929) of $4.1 billion; and eBay (established in 1995) had a valuation of $22 billion—or more than 10 times the valuation of Sotheby (established in 1778) of $1.9 billion. Although these stock-market valuations fluctuated significantly in 1999, and some of the highfliers have fallen from their peaks, the overall trend clearly favors high valuation of cyber-businesses as compared with traditional brick-and-mortar stores. Indeed, the 279 Internet firms that went public in 1999 had a total market value of $148 billion at year end.[13]

From an international perspective companies in the forefront of the E-commerce revolution made huge strides between mid 1998 and mid 1999. Each year *Business Week* comes out with its ranking of the Global 1,000—those companies with the highest market valuations in the world. In 1999 19 of the top-50–ranked companies were businesses that were either wholly or substantially involved in the commercialization of the Internet. Among the largest gainers in 1999 were Cisco Systems, rising from 30th place to 9th place; America Online increasing from 229 to 20th place; IBM increasing from 13th place to 3rd place; MCI World-Com, rising from 71st place to 14th place; Nokia, increasing from 87th place to 38th place; Amazon.com, rising from unranked to 254; and eBay, gaining from unranked to 220 on the list. In fact, between 1989 and 1999, Microsoft rose from 539 to first place on the list.[14]

The Constraints on the Growth of E-Commerce

To be sure, there are constraints to the commercialization of cyberspace. A majority of households in the United States and the vast majority of households in the world do not have computers with which to access the Internet. Most households that do have Internet access do not have broadband connections, which means that their current use is limited by slow downloading speeds that do not have adequate bandwidth required for either efficient Web shopping or on-line enjoyment of pictures and video. Moreover, there are a myriad of other issues such as privacy, security, and affordability that need to be addressed before Internet commerce realizes its vast potential.

Nonetheless, such potential obstacles are likely to be overcome in the near future as E-commerce becomes accessible to the vast majority of the industrialized world's business and residential consumers. For business-to-business E-commerce there is already wide availability of broadband Internet access through work-related computer networks. For business-to-consumer E-commerce the expense and unavailability of computer terminals will be significantly offset by the use of other more widely available communication devices such as inexpensive network computers, televisions, and telephones for Internet access. Similarly, the problem of slow Internet connections will likely be overcome with rapid advances in cable, telephone, and satellite technology that will facilitate relatively inexpensive high-speed Internet access service into consumer residences. Other issues are likely to be resolved through government and/or business initiatives to make the Internet a safe and secure environment for E-commerce.

Consumer Information Appliances

To some degree the rate of use of the Internet will depend on the speed with which the Internet becomes accessible to communication devices other than the home computer. In the United States this is a modest problem—just over two-fifths of all households have home computers; in comparison, about two-thirds of all households have cable television and virtually all households have telephones and television sets.[15]

The limited availability of home computers is a much bigger problem outside the United States. On a worldwide basis, in 1996 there were over 2.3 billion communications units, including 1.36 billion televisions (211 million of which had cable television access), 743 million telephones, and 234 million computers. Even in more affluent nations in western Europe and Japan, less than 25 percent of all households have personal computers, and households with computers that currently are connected to the Internet tend to average under 10 percent. Thus, in the short term one of the keys to rapid growth of the Internet will be to provide access through the use of television sets or other widely available information appliances. Currently, 66 percent of the world's households have at least one television set.[16]

Resolution of the problem of access is close at hand, however—there have been major technological breakthroughs in the means by which the Internet can be accessed by nonbusiness customers. Whereas most consumers currently access the Internet through expensive home computers, in the near future Internet access will also be available by means of cable television, broadcast television, cellular telephones, cheaper network computers, and a variety of other communication devices.

Moreover, equipment manufacturers are beginning to mass-produce communications devices that can be used for several purposes at once. For instance, Web television sets, with connections to the Internet, will be able to provide not just television broadcast programs but also phone calls using a built-in speaker phone and on-screen caller ID, E-mail functionality, and other data and Web-related services. Cable television sets will be able to provide not only traditional cable television programming but also Internet access and other data services, video on demand, and phone service. Similarly, technology is already available that can use computer terminals to access the Internet and other data sources as well as to receive television and radio programming and use phone and fax services. So-called smart telephones are also being made that will use computer functionality and a screen so that they can facilitate downloads of Web databases, E-mail, and faxes and store information such as phone directories and calendars. Handheld computers that are pocket-size have the capability to store vast quantities of information and to provide wireless access to E-mail and the Web either directly or by hooking into cellular phones. Finally, other appliances such as pagers, bank automated teller machines (ATMs), and automobiles will also be equipped with computer technology and modems to facilitate access to data on the Internet.

The technological prowess of the next generation of consumer information appliances will lead to a convergence in functionality of telephones, television sets, desktop computers, and handheld computers. With already-available or soon-to-be-available technologies, consumers will be able to do the following: use voice-activated navigational tools in an automobile to provide directions to a destination; order meals or food delivery, or view fax or E-mail over a Web-connected picture phone; request video on demand over cable or telephone lines and choose from a library of thousands of movies; do home banking and pay home bills on a handheld computer while flying above the Pacific Ocean; access E-mail or the day's news through wireless Internet access on a handheld information appliance; invest and trade stocks over a home computer; shop for goods and services 24 hours a day from vendors located all over the world by using a Web TV screen; download individual songs or entire music albums off the Web and play them on a computer terminal with superb digital sound; and read books on a paperless electronic book storing hundreds of different volumes.

Not long ago, so-called intelligent information appliances were reserved for science-fiction books or fictional characters such as the detective Dick Tracy. For instance, speech-recognition software, which seemed somewhat far-fetched when the crew in the movie *2001: A Space Odyssey* (1969) communicated with the computer Hal, is now being commercialized by a number of companies such as IBM, Microsoft, Dragon Systems, and Wildfire Communications.

According to the research firm International Data Corporation, the global market for consumer information appliances is expected to increase from 13 million units and $4.6 billion in sales in 1999 to 56 million units and $15.3 billion in sales in 2002. Indeed, the demand for consumer information appliances of all types is so high—driven in large part by consumer interest in convenient and pervasive access to Web databases and service—that the use of these devices for Internet access may exceed the use of personal computers within four to five years. In 1999 94 percent of all Internet access was made by means of a personal computer. By 2002 only an estimated 64 percent of all Internet access will be done via a personal computer, with the remainder hooked up by Web TV, Web phones, and handheld computers.[17]

The Bandwidth Bandwagon

Bandwidth is a measurement of how much information can move from one location to another in a given amount of time. If the bandwidth is high, then voice, data, video, and audio can move quickly and clearly from one location to another. If the bandwidth is low, then access to Web sites, sound or picture feeds, or voice communications will be slow, inconsistent, or choppy.

The problem of inadequate bandwidth is primarily a problem for home, not business, use. Bandwidth limitations do not generally impact business-to-business commerce because most businesses have access to special fiber-optic lines or cable links that provide rapid Internet access and even allow for the movement of video and audio. Most also have access to telecommunications linkages with speeds of 1 to 1.5 megabits per second (mbps) or more. By comparison, most homes have dial-connections of only 28 or 56 kilobits per second (kbps). Thus, most business connections are twenty to fifty times faster than residential connections. In 1998 fewer than 1 percent of homes had the so-called broadband connections—with speeds of a 1 mbps or more.

Thus, a limiting factor to the rapid expansion of direct and indirect electronic commerce in U.S. households is the slow speed of transport of the "last mile" into the home. Once a residential user accesses a local or regional Internet service provider, the data travels on fiber-optic networks at much faster speeds—between 1.5 mbps and 274 mbps. These local or regional Internet service providers are connected to the national Internet service providers and the Internet backbone—where data travels at even faster speeds of 1.5 mbps to 2.5 gigabits per second (gbps). By 2002 the backbone connections could be as fast as 200 gbps.[18]

Low bandwidth creates problems both in slower access to Web sites and in the general impracticality of using the Internet to view or download audio or video information. Low bandwidth is much more of an obstacle for audio and video transmission, however, than it is for activities such as Web shopping, phone calls, or data transmission. For example, cellular phone calls require a bandwidth of about 10 kbps, minimal Web browsing requires about 28 kbps, traditional phone calls require about 64 kbps, minimal videoconferencing requires about 96 kbps, and minimal video transmissions require about one to six mbps. With regard to storage space, one megabyte of capacity can hold a 700-page book, 50 spoken words, five pictures, or just 3 seconds of video. A standard 28 kbps modem takes about 46 minutes to download a three-and-a-half minute video—compared with an 8 to 10 mbps modem that takes about eight seconds. Similarly, a 28 kbps phone-line modem takes 42 hours to download the three-hour movie *Titanic*—compared with a 10 mbps cable modem that takes about seven minutes.[19]

High Bandwidth Alternatives

There are currently a number of transmission channels vying for the opportunity to provide broad bandwidth service for residential use. These include cable companies using coaxial cable, telephone companies using digital subscriber line (DSL) technology to enhance the efficiency of traditional copper-wire lines, and satellite companies developing various wireless alternatives. In 1998 in the United States, only 2 percent of all on-line households (those with Internet access) had broadband connections.

According to Forrester Research, by 2002 about 16 million households in the United States, or about one-quarter of all on-line households, will have broadband connections to the Internet. About four-fifths of these households will obtain high-speed Internet access through cable modems. The remaining one-fifth of these households will receive high-speed Internet access through telephone modems and DSL technology. The cable and DSL connections may provide high-speed Internet access up to 50 times faster than today's standard 56 kbps modems.[20]

Cable Services.   In the short term the most promising channel for bringing broadband Internet access to nonbusiness, residential users in the United States is the coaxial cable lines used by cable television companies. Cable lines that currently provide cable television to about two-thirds of U.S. households can with modest investments be made two-way lines so as to facilitate Internet access and other data services. Cable lines are currently capable of being used for Internet access at downstream speeds of 1 to 5 mbps and upstream speeds of 33.6 kbps to 2.5 mbps.[21]

Cable lines are currently the least-expensive method for providing high-speed Internet connections, and cable companies are rapidly upgrading cable lines for two-way connectivity to facilitate both Internet access and phone service. In early 1999 most major cable companies had less than 2 percent of their customers hooked up with high-speed Internet access. The number of cable customers with high-speed Internet access is likely to increase from under 1 million in 1998 to 13 million in 2002.[22]

To be sure, cable Internet access is limited by the number of homes that currently have cable television access. In the United States only about two-thirds of homes have cable television, compared with over 95 percent of households that have telephone or broadcast-television connections. On a worldwide basis the limitation of Internet access over cable lines is even more definite. In Europe only about one-quarter of all households have cable television connections. In Asia, Africa, and Latin America, less than one-twentieth of all households have cable television connections. By comparison, about two-thirds of all of the world's households have regular broadcast-television access.[23]

DSL Phone Lines.   The second most promising channel for high-speed Internet access is digitally enhanced phone lines. Most of the major local telephone companies are beginning to offer DSL service to millions of their customers, particularly in the United States. Such DSL service, or a complementary technology—asymmetric digital subscriber line (ADSL), allows traditional phone companies to upgrade existing copper-wire phone lines in order to make the lines suitable for high-speed Internet access. As noted previously, DSL service is likely to account for about one-fifth of all broadband service in the United States in five years. On a worldwide basis there are more than three times as many households wired with copper telephone wires than there are households wired with coaxial cable from cable television companies.[24]

The advantage of DSL technology is that it relies on existing lines that already connect virtually all U.S. households, as well as a high percentage of households in many other nations. The DSL lines can provide bandwidths of 144 kbps to 8 mbps for downstream transmissions, and 64 kbps to 8 mbps for upstream transmissions. The disadvantage of DSL lines is that the up-front investment to upgrade the copper-wire lines to adapt them to digital traffic is costly, and thus the typical monthly charges to household users for broadband Internet access will be significantly higher than for cable access—at least in short term. Another disadvantage is that deployment of DSL technology is only viable for households within three miles of a central switching office of the telephone company—a constraint that currently limits DSL upgrades to approximately 50 percent of U.S. households. Finally, as of 1999 DSL technology generally provides less bandwidth than equivalent cable television systems.[25]

Wireless Services.   A final competitor for broadband Internet access is wireless technology. There are currently several satellite companies that sell wireless Internet access to households in the United States and other nations. Commercially available satellite service, for example, provides Internet access to households at downstream speeds of up to 400 kbps. Other satellite services provide downstream speeds of several megabits per second or more—although generally at prices that inhibit household users from participating. One of the advantages of wireless technology is that it does not require large capital investments to enhance the last mile of wires into residences. Instead, it relies on customers with satellite dishes, which receive transmissions from satellites circling the planet.

One of the disadvantages of current satellite systems, however, is the general unavailability of upstream Internet access. For the most part customers must use existing wire-phone systems with speeds of 28 kbps or 56 kbps for any upstream transmissions. Although upstream speed is less important than downstream speed because of the larger data transfer requirements of downloads of information, wireless connections are generally not yet as commercially attractive as wired connections.

Two-way broadband satellite service that is affordable for household use is at least several years away because the economic feasibility of various initiatives is still untested. Nonetheless, a number of competing satellite ventures such as Teledesic, Astrolink, Cyberstar/Skybridge, and Spaceway are planning to spend billions of dollars over the next five years to construct low-orbit satellite systems that could provide high-speed Internet connections of 1.2 mbps or higher at prices that would be competitive with phone or cable companies. Although these satellite systems may initially be focused on business use, they could very well provide high-speed access to residential households in the next decade.[26]

Moreover, combinations of wire and wireless systems may also emerge. Several start-up phone companies such as Winstar and Teligent, as well as established phone companies such as AT&T, are planning to use wire transmission for most of their network and use wireless for just the last one mile to the business or residential customer. Under these new systems voice or data would be transmitted from a satellite dish—but only for a short distance to a central office, which would then feed the information into a high-speed wire network. Indeed, AT&T already has plans for introducing Internet-ready cellular phones with speeds of 384 kbps.[27]

The bandwidth battle will evolve over the next five to ten years. Some of the constraints to immediate deployment of broadband are common to both phone and cable companies, including substantial infrastructure investment costs totaling in the tens of billions of dollars and prices to consumers two to five times what they are paying for slower Internet access. Other constraints are unique to particular technologies, such as slower service on cable systems if multiple users are on-line at once and the need for DSL phone-system users to be within three miles of a central switching office for the technology to work.

The battle between cable companies and phone companies to be the primary high-speed Internet service provider to households in the United States and elsewhere is evident in the continued high level of mergers and acquisitions in the telecommunications arena. Companies are consolidating at a rapid pace in order to obtain broader market coverage and to obtain adequate financing for the expensive infrastructure investments required for bringing broadband to residential households. In recent years a number of megamergers have occurred, including WorldCom's purchase of MCI, Bell Atlantic's purchase of rival NYNEX, and AT&T's purchase of cable company TCI and MediaOne.

Whether cable, phone, or wireless systems dominate or share the emerging broadband marketplace, the deployment of high-speed Internet access to households in the United States and other advanced industrialized countries is inevitable, whether high penetration rates occur in two, five, or ten years. Just as with advances in the speed of computer chips, the deployment of more-sophisticated telecommunications networks will continue to take place—spurred on by technological advances and consumer demand.

The Information-Age Economy

The maturation of the Internet as a global communications network will provide the capstone to the emerging preeminence of the information-based economy. An agriculture-based economy dominated world commerce up until the 19th century, whereas an industrial-based economy dominated world commerce in the 19th and 20th centuries. Beginning in the late 20th century, the information-based economy has begun to supplant both agricultural and industrial activities at the center of global commerce. In the process the provision of services has grown to over one-half of all economic activity in advanced industrialized nations, while the production of goods has slipped well below the one-half mark.

In the United States, for example, the information technology industry—which consists of computer hardware and software, telecommunication hardware and services, and broadcasting—is now the largest industry in the country. According to government statistics the information technology industry grew from 4.9 percent of gross domestic product in 1985 to 8.2 percent of gross domestic product in 1998. In recent years the information technology industry has been growing at nearly 15 percent per year, accounting for one-third of all real economic growth in the United States. In 1998 the information technology industry accounted for nearly $700 billion in commerce in the United States.[28]

With regard to business investment, the dominance of the information technology industry has been equally striking. In 1972 information technology spending as a share of total business investment equaled less than 10 percent in the United States. In 1997 information technology spending as a share of total business investment accounted for over 45 percent. Moreover, a federal government study predicts that by 2006 almost one-half of the U.S. workforce will be employed by businesses that produce information technology or are intensive users of it.[29]

On a global basis the information technology industry has also experienced explosive growth. In 1998 the information technology industry accounted for nearly $2 trillion in commerce on a worldwide basis. Between 1993 and 1997 the worldwide revenues of the information technology industry increased by over 40 percent. During those years certain subsectors experienced substantially more rapid growth. For instance, cable/satellite companies grew over 150 percent and wireless telecommunications companies expanded over 350 percent.[30]

Furthermore, the Internet-related economy has emerged from nowhere in the second half of the 1990s to take its place as a key component of the information technology industry. According to a recent study by the University of Texas Center for Research in Electronic Commerce, the Internet economy generated about $507 billion in 1999 in the United States alone, constituting a 68 percent growth from 1998. This study used a broad definition of the Internet economy to encompass not only E-commerce sales made over the Internet but also expenditures on infrastructure (e.g., Internet backbone providers and network hardware manufacturers), applications (e.g., search engine software and Web-enabled databases), and Web intermediaries (e.g., portals, on-line advertisers, and infomediaries) that facilitate Internet use. Thus, in just six years (since the emergence of the World Wide Web), the Internet economy exceeded the scale of more-traditional industries in the United States such as energy ($223 billion), automobiles ($350 billion), and airlines ($355 billion). Indeed, if the U.S. Internet economy existed as a part of a separate nation in 1998, it would already have constituted the 18th largest economy in the world.[31]

The growth of the information technology industry and the Internet economy has reinforced a preexisting trend toward the expansion of other largely service-oriented sectors, including banking, insurance, health care, education, transportation, retailing, personal services, entertainment, and publishing. In the late 1950s service industries accounted for less than 40 percent of gross domestic product in the United States. By the late 1990s service industries accounted for about 55 percent of gross domestic product in the United States.[32]

One key outcome of the information age is a vast expansion of goods and services that can be provided electronically—typically in digital format. Many services are already provided electronically, such as telecommunication services, television, radio and cable services, and many business-information services. Other services such as banking, insurance, medical services, repair services, and educational and training services are likely to have a significant increase in the share of such services provided by electronic and digital means.

Significant portions of the emerging digital economy will be composed of products that were once provided as tangible goods but which are now delivered as intangible electronic output. As a general rule, whatever goods or services that can be digitized or otherwise transferred electronically will find electronic commerce to be a fast and cost-effective way to reach consumers. Although the distribution of automobiles, food, and refrigerators will not occur electronically, other major business and personal-consumer items lend themselves to the digital age, including movies, magazines, books, computer software and services, photographs, music, newspapers, mail, and games (see table 1.1).

In the near future, digital or intangible goods and services will likely constitute only a minority of the economic output that will be in the

Table 1.1.   **The Digital Economy**

Computer software	Internet access services
Movies	Magazines
Books	Electronic bill payments
Music albums	Stock trading
Financial transactions	Newspapers
Video conferencing	Games
Educational and training materials	Business databases
E-mail	Remote medical diagnosis
Information services	Remote repairs
Bulletin boards and chat rooms	Home banking
Telecommunications	

forefront of E-commerce. The majority of goods and services that will be purchased over the Internet will continue to be delivered as conventional tangible goods (see discussion under "The Global Expansion of Remote Selling" in this chapter). Because, however, intangible goods and services typically create more complex income and transactional tax issues than does tangible output, the following discussion examines the primary categories of intangible (or potentially intangible) output in order to lay the proper foundation for the discussion of tax issues in subsequent chapters.

Telecommunications Services

Currently, the largest economic activity within E-commerce is telecommunications services. Telecommunications services, whether provided by traditional copper wires, coaxial cable, fiber-optic cable, wireless cellular telephones, or satellite, are the crucial transport mechanisms that carry voice, data, video, and other products to business and personal consumers. In the late 1990s, worldwide telecommunications services accounted for over $700 billion in revenues, with about one-quarter of that total occurring in the United States.[33]

Although telecommunications service has been one of the traditional mainstays of E-commerce—a forerunner of the digital world—the industry is in the midst of profound technological and economic change. The telecommunications industry is currently in the process of a fundamental shift from wire transport to wireless transport; from circuit-switching networks to packet-switching networks; and from voice transmission to data, video, and audio transmission.

The telecommunications industry is moving rapidly from a world of almost exclusively wire connections, to one in which wire and wireless transport mechanisms share the volume of traffic. A major element of the "anywhere, anytime" communications revolution is the enormous growth of wireless communications. The number of cellular phones in the United States increased from 1.6 million in 1988 to 66 million in 1998. Moreover, the number of cellular phones in the United States is expected to increase to 110 million in 2002. On a worldwide basis, it is expected that there will be over 400 million cellular phones in 2002—over one-quarter of all phones in the world.[34]

Another major change is related to Internet telephony. Internet telephony entails the use of the Internet and packet-switching technologies to carry voice and other telephone traffic. Instead of using traditional telephone circuit technology, in which a circuit must be kept open continuously between two parties on a phone call, Internet telephony utilizes packet-switching technology to transport voice or data signals by exclusively digital means. Voice signals are treated similar to other types of information—broken up into packets of digital bits with addresses—and sent over the Internet or over private data networks.

Internet protocol will prove particularly attractive for transporting the large amount of data that currently is transported over regular telephone channels. The transport of data or other information is not as affected by the constraints of real-time communications that impose a higher threshold of timeliness and quality on voice communications. Currently, about 8 percent of all long-distance calls in the United States and about 40 percent of all international calls from the United States carry fax communications. Moreover, while traditional voice traffic is growing at about 8 percent a year, data traffic (including faxes) is growing about 100 percent annually.[35]

Packet-switching networks have a number of cost advantages over traditional circuit-switching networks. First, the Internet's packet-switching technology can squeeze more voice or data communications into the same communications channel than can circuit-switched calls that inefficiently occupy entire open circuits. With a traditional circuit-switching network, an entire telephone channel is used for each voice, fax, or data communications. This format is akin to a truck driver reserving an entire highway lane for a single trip between Boston and New York. By contrast, a packet-switching network breaks voice and data into packets that can simultaneously use a communications channel, a format analogous to having many trucks and cars share a highway lane between the two locations. Moreover, the transport mechanisms themselves are more compact—typical voice circuits are 64 kilobits wide, whereas standardized packets are only 8 kilobits.

Second, new packet-switching networks have much larger capacities and more efficient equipment than older, more traditional circuit-switching networks, adding to the new technology's cost advantage. Finally, at least in the short-term, Internet traffic does not have the same regulatory burdens that are imposed on more traditional telephony. Internet transmissions are currently free from the access charges (at least in the United States) on the local portion of the calls that are imposed on long-distance voice telecommunications. Internet transmissions also avoid universal service charges and other special government fees or assessments that are imposed on traditional telephone calls.[36]

According to varying estimates, packet-switching networks are one-third to one-half cheaper than circuit-switching networks. Not surprisingly, according to some industry projections, Internet protocol networks or similar packet-switching technologies may account for 10 percent or more of all U.S. telephone traffic within four years.[37]

Television Services and Motion Pictures

Another large content-related type of E-commerce is the television industry. In advanced industrialized societies, people typically spend over one-third of their leisure time watching television. About one-fifth of the world's nearly 6 billion people own television sets, making television the most widely dispersed form of communications, exceeding even the reach of the telephone industry.[38]

Even though the television industry is already almost exclusively provided by electronic means, there are still fundamental changes occurring within the industry. One change is the movement toward cable and pay television, whereby most of the revenues are derived from subscription or program charges rather than advertising. On a worldwide basis, about one-fifth of households with televisions have access to cable television. In the United States, about two-thirds of households have cable television, and cable television revenues of approximately $40 billion a year now exceed advertising revenues earned by free broadcast television.

A second development is the transition to digital broadcasting. Historically, broadcast television was transmitted through analog transmissions. As a result of both technological developments and government regulation, however, digital broadcasting is likely to supplant analog broadcasting over the next decade. Digital broadcasting allows for better picture quality and for more channels per bandwidth (as many as four high-resolution digital channels for each analog channel). This trend is being enhanced by the rapid growth of direct satellite television. In 1998 over 8 million households subscribed to direct satellite television. By 2002 it is expected that nearly 20 million households will subscribe to satellite television. In 1994 virtually no households subscribed to satellite television. Direct satellite television has the capability of providing subscribers with over 500 channel choices—compared with approximately 50 to 75 for the typical cable system and about 15 for traditional broadcast television.[39]

A third trend is the creation of broadcasting channels transmitted over the Internet. Internet companies have developed a technology called *streaming,* which allows Web sites to provide real-time video and audio broadcasts to consumers over the Internet, rather than relying on traditional cable, radio, or television broadcasting. Streaming is different than Web TV, which uses a traditional television set to access data over the Internet. In 1998 one industry leader, Broadcast.com, was already providing customers with access to a wide range of programming, including nearly 400 radio stations, 40 television stations, sports broadcasts from over 400 college and professional sports teams, and other live programming. In 1998 an estimated 7 million U.S. visitors used the RealNetworks.com site for streaming media content each month, and another 2 million visited Broadcast.com's site. Web radio alone is expected to grow from a $21 million–business in 1998 to a $1.7 billion–business in 2004.[40]

Finally, there is likely to be a convergence over the next 5 to 10 years between the motion picture industry, the television industry and the Internet. Currently, the sale or rental of movie videos in the United States accounts for $17 billion a year, or nearly 60 percent, of the revenues that the movie studios make from their films. While there is increasing use of pay-per-view movie channels over cable television, the vast majority of video rentals and sales still take place at the nation's 28,000 video stores. However, the potential of "video on demand" over cable or Internet channels is likely to be realized in the near future. The video business is relatively inefficient compared with on-line consumption because it depends on customers appearing in person to pick up a consumer item that rents for about $4. Indeed, about one-quarter to one-fifth of all video-rental fees are for late charges. Clearly, electronic transmission via the Internet or cable television is a much more efficient distribution channel. With declining prices for cable operators to stream video and audio on a customized basis to consumers, the consolidation of home entertainment through expansive and up-to-date "video on demand" is inevitable.[41]

Advertising

The advertising industry is currently a nearly $200 billion business in the United States. While advertising is currently split between television, radio, newspapers, magazines, and direct mail, the Internet is likely to garner a small, but rapidly growing share over the next decade. Indeed, the major Web portals such as America Online, Microsoft Network, Yahoo!, Lycos, and At Home/Excite already have estimated audiences of 25 million or more, rivaling the audience size of the major television networks. These portals already are charging premium rates for companies to advertise on valuable "real estate" in cyberspace.[42]

The business model of the most-visited Internet sites is constantly evolving. Many of the sites were originally search engines and subsequently became portals with extensive graphic and data content. Currently, some of these sites are transforming themselves into Web malls or auction sites, selling goods and services of other vendors or of their own creation.

In addition, a new technology called *electronic ink* holds open the possibility of replacing traditional advertising posters or billboards with new, fully electronic signs. Electronic ink is made up of millions of tiny spherical microcapsules that enable the creation of "electronic" paper that displays electronic text that can be erased and re-created without discarding the paper. This futuristic technology could be combined with wireless technology, allowing information to be downloaded instantly onto electronic pages. If it becomes commercially viable, electronic ink will further blur the distinction between tangible advertising media and an intangible advertising service.[43]

Computer Software and Services

One of the major product categories with the most-significant potential for digital delivery is computer software. In 1998 worldwide sales of prepackaged (or canned) software totaled about $135 billion ($73 billion of which was in the United States). The sale of canned software is expected to increase to about $222 billion by 2002. The ease and speed of the electronic transfer of software virtually guarantee that this product category will be largely digitized over the next decade.[44]

Most computer-software vendors, whether they sell $1 million software to business customers or $100 software to nonbusiness consumers, are providing (or about to provide) purchasers with the option to receive the product by means of electronic delivery. As more residential consumers obtain broadband Internet access, the share of software delivered by electronic means will rise sharply. Software will be sent digitally to homes and businesses for unlimited use and will also be provided on vendor or third-party servers for more limited use.

Music

The music industry is another entertainment category that lends itself to digital delivery. In 1998 worldwide music album sales totaled $41 billion, about one-third of which were purchased in the United States. There are currently about 2 billion CDs sold worldwide each year and about 500 million tape cassettes. Each year about 30,000 albums are released. Worldwide music sales are expected to climb to about $48 billion in 2004.[45]

Once again, digital delivery promises to reduce the costs of manufacturing, distribution, and returns, which frequently account for 50 percent or more of total costs for record companies. Digital delivery could entail downloading entire songs or albums, or streaming songs to customers on a real-time basis. There are already several competing technologies such as MP3 and Liquid Audio that facilitate the downloading of songs or albums in the form of computer files. For instance, MP3 uses a compression technology that would allow a user to place the entire Beatles catalog onto one CD-ROM. Digitized songs could be played on special software built into computers or on pocket-sized portable players similar to a portable CD player.

Currently, the limited bandwidth of most Internet connections to residences creates a barrier to digitized music. Music albums hold large amounts of digital information—650 megabytes on just one CD—and therefore downloading just a single song can take as long as one-half hour on a typical modem. However, the fast broadband connections now being installed by cable companies and phone companies will facilitate the downloading of music. Mass customization is the likely outcome of the digital delivery of music. Instead of being required to purchase prepackaged CD-ROMs, consumers may be able to purchase their own selected bundles of songs. One company, MusicMaker, already allows customers to choose from over 30,000 different tracks and create their own customized CD-ROMs for a set price per song.[46]

In order to cope with the explosion of Internet-friendly technology currently available to download music from Internet sites, the music industry is scrambling to develop a standardized format for commercializing the digital delivery of music. A number of the largest record companies, such as Sony Music Entertainment and Universal Music, are working to create venues to sell single songs or albums over the Internet. The recording industry is trying to develop a standard technology that would permit the protection of copyrights and prevent the unauthorized copying or pirating of songs.[47]

Books, Newspapers, Magazines, and Information Databases

In 1998 an estimated $82 billion worth of books were sold worldwide. In the United States, where over one-quarter of these books are sold, the publishing industry sells about 2.3 billion books annually, nearly 80,000 of them new titles. Currently, about 45 percent of the cost of book sales is for inventory, shipping, and handling returns. Electronic transmission may become a very attractive alternative distribution channel.[48]

In addition, for those who do not like to read books on a standard computer or television screen, there are already handheld electronic books, such as RocketeBook and SoftBook, available for purchase. These electronic devices—only slightly larger than a typical book—can store 10 to 15 books and download them directly from on-line vendors. With technological advances these electronic books will undoubtedly hold hundreds of volumes and supplant a significant share of the tangible book-product market. In the short term electronic books will prove particularly popular among students, who purchase an estimated $5.5 billion in educational textbooks each year.[49]

Newspaper and magazine sales are also likely to become thriving on-line industries. The sale of newspapers is currently a $40 billion industry in the United States, and the sale of magazines is presently a $25 billion industry in the United States. Daily circulation of newspapers totals nearly 60 million, and circulation of the top 100 U.S. magazines exceeds 250 million. Both newspapers and magazines are already widely available in electronic format, although most such ventures are still experimenting with formulas for charging for on-line access.[50]

In the near future, it is likely that consumers will be able to customize their on-line newspapers or magazines based on the preselection of topics in which they are interested. Indeed, a number of information vendors such as Desktop Data have built fast-growing businesses based on selling customized on-line information in a format that maximizes the advantages of the Web. As early as 1996, this company allowed consumers to choose from 850 business news topics and then filtered 15,000 stories from 600 publications to provide individualized news briefings for paying customers.[51]

The sale of legal, medical, scientific, business, and other technical information to a largely business audience is a category of electronic services that is already widely commercialized. Business information services generate about $23 billion a year in the United States (over half of which is attributable to electronic information services). Global electronic information revenues are estimated at nearly $30 billion a year. Lexis-Nexis, CCH, and other brand-name information vendors provide huge databases that can be accessed electronically, with the option of downloading any specific content. The availability of sophisticated computer-search technologies and the daily updating of information make electronic distribution a particularly attractive alternative to information provided in tangible reports and databases.[52]

Educational Services and Job Training

Over $800 billion per year is currently spent on education (primary, secondary, and college) and job training in the United States. Over one-quarter of that amount is spent on college and university education. Clearly, there is a large potential for E-commerce growth if even a small fraction of this marketplace is supplanted or augmented by on-line training or schooling, videoconferencing, or educational software.[53]

The initial audience for more computerized distance learning is likely to be derived from nonresidential college students, continuing adult education courses designed for working people, and job-training programs. For instance, the market for adult education is growing rapidly in the United States. The number of participants in such programs increased from 23 million in 1984 to 76 million in 1995 and is projected to grow to 100 million by 2004.[54]

Similarly, business training is also being significantly reoriented by the growth of on-line training courses. In 1998 U.S. corporations spent about $60 billion on job training for their employees. While most corporate training is still instructor-led training, there has been a rapid growth in technology-based training with computerized software courses, video-conferencing, and on-line training expanding annually at rates of 40 percent and higher. It is estimated that the U.S. market for Web-based training programs will be over $6 billion by 2002.

College students make up another potential market for more digital learning programs. Nearly one-half of all college students are over 22 years old and do not live on or near campus. Many of these students have already made use of correspondence courses, videotape and audiotape instructional materials, and other forms of remote learning. Through the Internet schools will be able to provide more flexible distance learning through Web sites that have class-related information, the streaming of audio and video presentations to student's computers, bulletin boards, electronically downloaded instructional materials, and E-mail. According to one survey, educational software will serve about one-half of all students enrolled in community colleges and about one-third of all students enrolled in four-year institutions.[55]

Indeed, a growing number of schools are being established that provide services entirely by remote electronic means. One of the longest-standing distance-learning schools is the Open University of the United Kingdom. Since 1971 this school has provided off-site higher education to more than 2 million students by means of television, videotape, instructional materials, and other remote learning technology. The school is increasingly relying on the Internet to provide course materials and instruction to its far-reaching student body. In addition, the Open University is also planning on a major expansion in the United States in 1999.[56]

Jones International University near Denver, Colorado, is the first "virtual" university in the United States, operating entirely on-line with full accreditation. Other virtual universities that are opening their doors (or their portals) include Western Governors University, the Open University of the United States, and the California Virtual University. Many other traditional universities such as Duke and Stanford are rapidly expanding the availability of courses and programs provide on-line and off-site to meet the growing demand for flexible distance learning.

Financial Services

Another service industry that is ideal for digital commerce is the realm of financial services. In 1996 the banking, insurance, and security brokerage industries accounted for about $520 billion in gross domestic product in the United States. The financial-services sector has a lengthy history of using electronic means for exchanging data (e.g., credit-card transactions) and transferring monies (e.g., electronic funds transfers; bank check clearing).[57]

Although only a small minority of U.S. households currently use their personal computers to handle personal banking transactions, that is likely to change rapidly, with the vast majority of larger financial institutions now offering or developing personal computer banking products. In 1997 about 4.5 million households in the United States participated in on-line banking. By 2003 an estimated 26 million households in the United States will engage in on-line banking, or 25 percent of all U.S. households. Consumers are likely to use on-line banking for a number of activities, including obtaining account information, taking out loans, and paying bills.[58]

On-line origination of home mortgages is expected to increase sharply over the next few years. In the United States, approximately $1 trillion in home mortgages are issued each year—including new mortgages and refinancings. In 1998 less than 1 percent of home mortgages were originated on the Internet. By 2003 it is estimated that almost 20 percent of all mortgages will be originated on the Internet.[59]

Internet-based banking is likely to be enhanced by Web-based bill-payment services that can make consumer bill payment a largely paperless process. Currently, bill mailing, processing, and collecting costs U.S. vendors about $370 billion, or approximately $10 for each of the 37 billion bills sent out annually. By some estimates, about 60 percent of all first-class mail is used for sending bills. The vast majority of these payments still involve a multistep process of paper invoices and checks traveling through the mail between vendors, customers, and financial institutions.[60]

By contrast, in an electronic-payment system, a bill is sent electronically to a customer, the customer authorizes an electronic check, the customer's bank electronically transfers money from the customer's account to the biller's account, and the customer receives electronic monthly statements itemizing the payments. The widespread use of electronic bill payment, in conjunction with expanded on-line home banking, could save vendors 10 percent or more of the cost of bill processing and collection. One of the primary services likely to benefit from the use of electronic bill payment is telecommunications, with the number of households paying bills for phone service on-line estimated to increase from 1.6 million in 1998 to 10.8 million in 2003.[61]

Similarly, the use of Internet-based insurance services is likely to expand rapidly. Currently, about one-third of insurance policy costs is attributable to distribution costs, including commissions for insurance agents. On-line sales are much cheaper to make. By 2001 it is estimated that about $1 billion of insurance will be purchased over the Internet.[62]

Another financial service that is rapidly converting to an Internet-based business model is stock trading. In 1996 1.5 million investors used on-line brokerage accounts to trade stocks. In 1998 an estimated 5.3 million investors traded stocks on-line—using dozens of on-line brokers such as DLJ Direct, Quick & Reilly, Fidelity, and Schwab that offer quick, inexpensive trades, real-time quotes, and access to financial information on-line. On-line trades typically cost under $30 a trade compared to a traditional average of $80 a trade. By 2002 there will be an estimated 14 million on-line brokerage accounts. By that time on-line accounts will make up 25 percent of all retail trades and manage about $700 billion in assets.[63]

Other Digital-Business Categories

As an industry, health care accounts for approximately one-seventh of the U.S. gross national product. In 1996 national health care expenditures totaled about $1 trillion. Although health care services will generally continue to be delivered on-site at medical facilities, the potential now exists for transmission of high-quality medical images by electronic means to facilitate long-distance digital medical consulting. Indeed, a number of hospitals have already begun to use off-site medical specialists who provide diagnosis and advice based on electronically supplied patient information. This practice will be enhanced by the availability of patient lifetime health records on-line—so that medical professionals at any location can obtain access to detailed information about a patient's past medical history.[64]

The use of telemedicine is likely to be attractive for the treatment of patients who need home care visits. Patients in the United States currently receive about 500 million home visits a year from nurses and health care aides. The number of home-care visits will increase significantly over the first two decades of the 21st century with the graying of the American population. With advances in the use of remote monitoring equipment such as blood pressure cuffs, videoconferencing tools, and imaging machines, it may be possible to assist many of these patients by remote television monitors—at a much lower cost per patient.[65]

Product repairs and other types of customer services is another category that lends itself to digital delivery. The notion that a product could be repaired remotely over telephone lines may sound far-fetched, but such digital repairs are likely to be a rapidly expanding new business sector. In the near future, modern appliances such as washing machines, refrigerators, microwaves, and televisions will become "smart" appliances with computer chips imbedded in the products providing information to vendors over the Internet. With the emergence of virtual computing, diagnostic chips in a home appliance can be used to notify a manufacturer when a problem arises with the appliance, allowing the manufacturer to fix the problem remotely or to send out a repairman. Similarly, an automobile tune-up might be done remotely with electronic signals communicating with component parts. The computer software in appliances or equipment might also be modified remotely to allow the appliance to adapt to new conditions or provide new functionality.[66]

Customer support is also certain to be a major digital-related activity. Historically, much customer support was conducted by means of the telephone. The Internet will expand the potential of remote customer support, allowing not only direct E-mail or voice communication but also remote diagnostics and repairs. For example, approximately 10 percent of the overall costs of computer companies are related to customer service, with 200 million calls handled annually in the United States alone. Electronic product support may lead to significant efficiencies in time and cost of delivery.[67]

Another category that lends itself to digitization is gambling. In the United States alone, gambling in casinos, lotteries, horse races, and sports betting is an estimated $600 billion industry. For instance, in 1999 an estimated 2.5 million individuals bet on the NCAA March Madness basketball tournament through on-line betting—a number that is expected to reach 10 million by 2001. On-line betting could reach $2.3 billion by 2001—up from an estimated $300 million in 1998.[68]

Photography may also be altered completely by the digital revolution. It is now possible to replace traditional cameras and 35 millimeter film with digital cameras that use digital film. Digital film does not need to be developed but can simply be viewed on a computer or other monitor, with free copies sent to friends or relatives.

E-mail is the most common form of E-commerce. Nearly 90 percent of all on-line households regularly use the Internet for sending and receiving E-mail. In 1997 the U.S. Postal Service earned revenues of about $58 billion on the delivery of 190 billion pieces of mail. In that year, for the first time, more E-mails were sent than letters—at a considerably lower cost.[69]

The Global Expansion of Remote Selling

Along with the rapid expansion of direct E-commerce through goods and services sold and delivered electronically, the Internet is also facilitating an explosion of indirect E-commerce through goods and services purchased by electronic means but delivered in traditional tangible form. The meteoric rise of E-commerce and Web retailing is reinforcing the existing trend toward direct marketing and "remote" selling that has heretofore been propelled forward by the mail-order industry and television home-shopping channels.

Internet business-to-business sales and business-to-consumer sales are likely to result in a fundamental transformation in how consumers buy and sell goods and services, leading to a sharp decline in purely local commerce and a significant increase in multijurisdictional transactions and global trading. To a large degree, the local shopping mall will be supplanted by a virtual shopping mall that is open 24 hours a day, 7 days a week, and 52 weeks a year.

E-commerce is on the verge of revolutionizing both business-to-business and business-to-consumer sales by introducing a number of new business models for connecting suppliers and consumers. These models include on-line catalogs, virtual communities, portals, auctions, reverse auctions, subscription-based services, infomediaries, and aggregators.

NEW BUSINESS MODELS

On-Line Catalogs: Sites where ".com" retailers such as Amazon.com sell their products.

Virtual Communities: Sites that connect a targeted demographic, such as iVillage's focus on women.

Portals: Sites such as Lycos or Yahoo! that offer a variety of services such as calendar, news, E-mail, search engines, content, and shopping malls.

Auctions: Sites such as eBay that allow thousands of individuals and businesses to sell goods or services to the highest bidder.

Reverse Auctions: Sites such as priceline.com where buyers can name the price they are willing to pay for goods and services and try to be matched with a seller of such goods or services.

Subscription-Based Services: Sites such as CCH on-line where information or some other product is sold based on a monthly subscription payment.

Infomediaries: Sites such as Autobytel that provide specialized or industry-specific information on product quality, prices, financing, and so on, on behalf of producers of goods and services and their potential customers.

Aggregators: Sites such as Accompany where either buyers or sellers combine to increase their market power.

A whole new lexicon is developing around "E-business," which is broadly defined as the means to improve the exchange of goods, services, and information through the use of the Internet and other network-based technology. The Internet has vastly expanded the channels for communication between vendors and consumers, moving beyond the limitations of traditional channels such as face-to-face, telephone/fax, and mail.

The current projections for the growth of E-commerce are truly amazing. As noted previously, Forrester Research estimates that, on a worldwide basis, under an optimistic growth scenario, the trade of goods or services in which the final order is placed over the Internet may reach as high as $3.2 trillion in 2003, or 5 percent of all global sales. These estimates generally do not include purchases related to services (other than utilities) such as financial services, health services, educational services, transportation, and cable television services. Even under a more modest growth scenario, Forrester Research estimates that the low range of worldwide Internet commerce in 2003 will still total almost $1.8 trillion.[70]

The speed of the worldwide expansion of E-commerce depends to a large degree on how quickly other advanced industrialized nations emulate the U.S. Internet use rates. Forrester Research expects the United States to enter a "hyper-growth" phase of E-commerce in 2000, followed within two years by Canada, Britain, and Germany and within four years by Japan, France, and Italy. International Data Corporation estimates that, by the year 2003, nations outside the United States will account for about one-half of Internet-based commerce, up from one-quarter in 1998. The rate of expansion of E-commerce will also depend on public- and private-sector cooperation to make buying and selling over the Internet simple, secure, and internationally viable.[71]

In the United States Internet-based sales to both businesses and consumers are projected to increase from about $50 billion in 1998 to about $1.5 trillion in 2003 and to about $2.9 trillion in 2004. (As noted previously, these estimates generally do not include the purchase of services over the Internet.) Over 80 percent of this volume will be related to business purchases (see figure 1.3).[72]

These estimates may actually soon prove too conservative, as many projections of E-commerce sales have been in recent years. For instance, the University of Texas study projected U.S. Internet purchases of $102 billion in 1998, or nearly two times the level of the Forrester Research estimate. Similarly, a study by shop.org estimated that business-to-consumer commerce would total $36 billion in 1999, or nearly two times the level of the Forrester Research estimate.[73]

Figure 1.3. **Growth of Business-to-Business E-Commerce in the United States**

Source: Forrester Research.

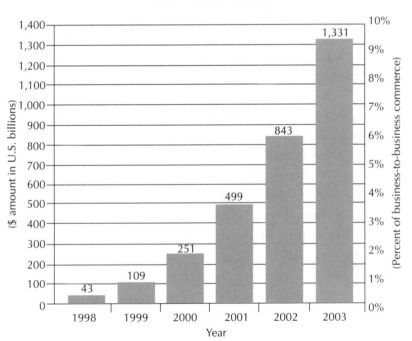

The meteoric growth of Internet commerce marks a continuation of a trend toward more remote selling of goods and services. In 1995 an estimated $219 billion of business and nonbusiness sales were placed in the United States by mail, phone, or electronically without the person ordering the product or service coming to the point of sale to place the order or the seller coming to the office or home of the purchaser. An additional $200 billion of business purchases were made over older electronic technology called electronic data interchange (EDI). The enhanced capabilities of the Internet to connect vendors and consumers in a user-friendly format hold the potential to dwarf the current impact of remote selling through mail order and similar means.[74]

The rapid growth of Internet commerce also reinforces the trend toward a more interconnected global economy. With the sharp declines in the costs of both communications and transportation during the 20th century, business location has become less important as a determinant of business success. Since the first half of the 20th century, the cost of ocean freight, air transport, satellite communications, and long-distance telecommunications have all dropped by over 80 percent. For instance, the price of a three-minute international phone call has dropped from about $50 in 1950 to about $1 today.[75]

The so-called death of distance caused by the falling costs of transportation and communication together with the growth of truly global companies with operations spanning the world have led to a dramatic increase in the scope of world trade. In 1978 world trade made up 9.3 percent of world gross domestic product. By 1998 world trade totaled $6.5 trillion, or 24.3 percent of world gross domestic product. In 2005 world trade is projected to grow to $11.4 trillion, or 28 percent of world gross domestic product. This rapid growth amounts to a three-fold increase in world trade's share of world gross domestic product over just a 25-year period.[76]

With E-commerce, businesses will be able to not only export goods and services to other nations but also directly and instantaneously communicate with foreign consumers without relying on domestic intermediaries. The tremendous efficiencies of Web commerce will create an environment in which both remote commerce and global trading will be mutually reinforcing.

Business Purchases over the Internet

In the United States business purchases from other businesses over the Internet are expected to increase from about $43 billion in 1998 to about $1.33 trillion in 2003 (and $2.7 trillion in 2004). As a percentage of business-to-business commerce, Internet purchases would increase from 0.4 percent in 1998 to 9.4 percent in 2003.[77]

The most commonly purchased items for businesses will be computer and electronics equipment, motor vehicles, petrochemicals, utilities, paper and office products, shipping and warehousing, and food and agriculture products. In 2003 in the United States, business commerce over the Internet is forecast to account for the following shares of these industries: computer and electronics equipment (39 percent), utilities (26 percent), shipping and warehousing (17 percent), motor vehicles (15 percent), petrochemicals (14 percent), paper and office products (6 percent), and food and agricultural products (3 percent).[78]

To be sure, thousands of businesses currently use EDI to purchase products electronically. However, EDI generally works only on more expensive private telecommunications networks. It is a rigid, closed system primarily used for transmitting purchase orders and invoices among parties according to existing contractual terms. By contrast, Internet commerce is based on an open system that any vendor or consumer can access. E-purchasing is part of a virtue value chain that is likely to transform the way in which businesses connect with each other. Internet commerce facilitates not only sales contracts but also other product information, inventory control, and customer service.[79]

Consumer Purchases over the Internet

Nonbusiness consumers in the United States are expected to increase their Internet-related purchases from about $8 billion in 1998 to about $144 billion in 2003. Within five years Web-related consumer purchases are likely to significantly exceed purchases made through mail order and other more traditional forms of direct marketing. In 1998 about 8.7 million U.S. households engaged in on-line shopping, averaging about $900 in purchases per household. By 2003 it is expected that nearly 40 million U.S. households will be engaged in on-line shopping, averaging about $2,700 in purchases per household.[80]

Moreover, business-to-consumer sales are likely to accelerate later in the first decade of the 21st century. For instance, in 2004 consumer Internet purchases are expected to rise to $184 billion, 30 percent more than in 2003, or 7 percent of all retail spending that year. According to a study by the Peppers and Rogers Group, total U.S. business-to-consumer sales (including both E-commerce and mail order) are expected to reach between $438 billion and $1.1 trillion by 2010. These remote sales would represent between 10 and 24 percent of all retail sales in this country.[81]

The growth in consumer on-line shopping is skyrocketing, driven by how fast, easy, and cheap on-line shopping can be. In the last six months of 1996, there were fewer than 1 million on-line purchases in the United States. In the last six months of 1997, that figure rose to about 14 million on-line purchases. In the last six months of 1998, there were about 56 million on-line purchases—a fourfold increase over one year earlier. Indeed, among households with Internet access, the number of on-line shoppers increased from 30 percent in 1997 to 47 percent in 1998.[82]

For nonbusiness purchasers, the most common items purchased over the Internet are likely to include travel, computer hardware and software, groceries, books, apparel, music, entertainment tickets, specialty gifts, and health and beauty supplies. According to Jupiter Communications, by 2002 nonbusiness commerce over the Internet will consist of the following purchases (listed by share of total on-line retail purchases): travel (29 percent), computer hardware and software (22 percent), books, music, and videos (14 percent), groceries (9 percent), apparel and accessories (7 percent), toys, consumer electronics, and specialty gifts (7 percent), entertainment tickets (4 percent), health and beauty products (3 percent), and miscellaneous categories (5 percent) (see figure 1.4). [83]

In relation to household consumption, the Internet will be tapping into some potentially enormous markets. For instance, in the United States the pharmaceutical market for prescription and over-the-counter drugs, vitamins, and health and beauty products totals about $170 billion

Figure 1.4.   **The Major Categories of Business-to-Consumer Internet Retailing (United States)**

Source: Jupiter Communications.

Travel	PC hardware
Grocery	Software
Books	Apparel and accessories
Ticketing	Specialty gifts
Music	Videos
Toys	Consumer electronics
Health and beauty	

and is already being targeted by on-line vendors such as Drugstore.com, PlanetRx, Soma.com, and Rx.com. The automobile market totals about $400 billion and is being pursued by a host of on-line vendors such as Autobytel.com, AutoConnect, Autoweb.com, AutoZone, and Carpoint. Other sizable U.S. markets for on-line shopping include the market for food and groceries, which totals about $480 billion; leisure-travel bookings market, which totals about $350 billion; the clothing and shoes market, approximately $265 billion; the consumer-electronics market, approximately $90 billion; the toy market, approximately $23 billion; and the flower market, approximately $15 billion.[84]

Convenience, Selection, Information, and Price

For consumers (both business and household), Internet commerce holds a number of significant advantages over traditional commerce, including convenience, a wider range of choices, availability of information, and competitive pricing.

Convenience

The Internet provides the ultimate in convenience, with product and service options available 24 hours a day by means of a home computer or television set. Shopping can be done in the comfort of the home, at any hour or on any day. The convenience factor is underscored in the advertisements for bid.com, which state simply, "shop naked." Three-fifths of Web consumers in fact report that they sometimes shop in their pajamas. Similarly, the recreational-equipment vendor REI reports that over one-third of its sales take place from 10:00 P.M. to 7:00 A.M.[85]

For activities such as food shopping, which typically requires three to five hours a week of household time, on-line shopping can accomplish the same task in less than one-quarter the time. On-line food shopping involves ordering food from an electronic shopping list and then having it delivered to the home by food merchants. Dozens of major supermarket chains are currently offering shoppers the option of on-line food purchases for either a modest monthly fee or delivery charge or free of charge for purchases above a certain amount. Food suppliers can eliminate a number of steps from the traditional food-supply chain, such as shipping from a warehouse to a store, stocking in a store, and removing outdated stock from a store, by using distribution centers solely meant for Internet food shopping.[86]

Choice

The Internet provides customers with a huge range of product choices—frequently far more than are available at any one retail outlet. For instance, Amazon.com carries about 3 million book titles in its on-line inventory, more than 15 times as many as the largest bookstore in the country, and more than one hundred times as many as the typical mall bookstore. Similarly, a large Web music retailer such as Cdnow carries about 250,000 album titles and 315,000 audio clips. Realtor.com lists about 1.1 million homes for sale at its Web site, or about 90 percent of all homes for sale in the United States. Drugstore.com opened for business in 1999 carrying nearly 19,000 items in its cyberinventory, ranging from prescription drugs to beauty products. EToys is offering over 4,500 different toys in its cyberinventory.[87]

Similarly, eBay, the Internet's leading person-to-person auction house carries on daily auctions that list more items than a typical auction house would sell in an entire year. During the last three months of 1998, eBay held auctions for almost 14 million items. On a typical day, eBay introduces 250,000 new items into its on-line catalog. It has about 3.8 million registered users worldwide and charges 5 percent of each transaction price. The company sells collectibles and antiques and will soon be expanding into markets for items such as cars and furniture. The success of variable pricing was evident in 1998, with about 15 percent of all consumer E-commerce spending applied to on-line auctions.[88]

Information

Web retailers provide business and household consumers with large amounts of information about products and services. For instance, on-line automobile stores can help consumers research and select a vehicle, locate a dealer with the best price, identify the best financing, insurance, and warranty options, and actually negotiate final terms for a purchase. Not surprisingly, it is estimated that the number of U.S. households engaged in Internet car shopping will rise from 2 million in 1998 to about 8 million in 2003. At the end of this five-year period, Web car shopping will affect about one-half of all consumer selection of vehicles, about one-third of all consumer selection of auto dealers, and about one-tenth of all consumer choices of car financing and insurance.[89]

Indeed, one of the fastest-growing business models on the Internet is that of the "infomediary." An infomediary provides a single site for consumers to buy from a range of sellers. The infomediary typically provides the consumer with access to neutral information on competitive prices and product information that would not be obtainable from a single vendor's site. The filtering of information is extremely important in connection with Internet buying because of the vast database that is easily accessed by any Web user.

There is also a tremendous potential to use Web retailing to customize information for specific consumer needs. For instance, a clothes retailer can store information on a customer's height, weight, clothes size, and style preferences and use this information to recommend the proper sizes when a customer orders a particular shirt, pants, suit, or undergarment. The information can also be used to demonstrate in real time how a selected garment will look on a particular consumer's body. Similarly, a cyber bookstore can store information on a particular consumer's book choices and then make recommendations on other titles that consumers with similar preferences have purchased. Many cyberstores are already greeting regular customers by name and sending them E-mails on new products or services based on their previous consumption preferences.

Price

Internet commerce can frequently undercut conventional commerce in terms of price competition. The Internet enables manufacturers (or at least wholesalers) to avoid the use of retailers or other intermediaries and sell directly to ultimate consumers. The Internet also has the potential for reducing transaction-processing costs for taking orders and billing. In addition, there is no need for Web retailers to maintain expensive inventories in retail outlets around the country. Cybervendors may also have a high volume of sales per Web site, allowing them to regularly discount items such as best-selling books, albums, tapes, and so on. These factors all contribute to significant potential savings through E-commerce.[90]

Some of the approaches to price competition are possible only because of the unique structure of the Internet. For instance, there are currently many brick-and-mortar wholesale clubs, such as BJ's Wholesale, Costco, and Sam's Warehouse Club, that buy products in bulk and sell them to club members at significant discounts. With Internet retailers, however, it is possible to actually adjust prices on a real-time basis to provide additional volume discounts. For instance, some Internet collective-buying companies, such as Mercata and Accompany, Inc., offer products at a specific price and then lower the price each time a certain number of buyers order the same product. As Mercata.com states in its advertisements, "By the time you read this, our prices will be out of date. (They'll be lower.)" In another example, the Internet retailer Buy.com uses software to search the Web on a daily basis to determine its competitor's prices. If prices are discovered that are lower than Buy.com prices for similar products, the proprietary search technology automatically reduces Buy.com's prices to below the lowest competitive price.

Amazon.com is perhaps the best-known example of a cyber retailer that has transformed a particular segment of the retail market by using the tremendous advantages that many Web retailers have over more traditional retail vendors. Since its inception in 1995, Amazon.com has evolved from no customers to 14 million customers in less than five years. By early 1999 Amazon.com's brand name was recognized by over one-half of the U.S. adult population. In 1999 the company garnered estimated sales of over $1 billion, a 1,000 percent increase over 1997. In its short life span, Amazon.com has become the nation's third-largest bookseller (of any type, not just cyberspace), trailing only Barnes & Noble ($2.7 billion in sales) and Borders ($2.3 billion in sales). However, Amazon.com maintains its sales volume from just one Web site, compared with over one thousand Barnes & Noble retail stores. The Web retailer's inventory turns over about 24 times a year; its more traditional competitor's rate is three times a year. Without retail locations Amazon.com avoids the need to carry $1.5 billion in assets and inventory that Barnes & Noble must maintain. Not surprisingly, the upstart Amazon.com, with a current growth rate in sales about 30 times higher than Barnes & Noble, has a market valuation of more than five times the industry leader. Amazon.com is in the process of extending its business model from books to record albums, pharmaceutical products, home repair products, computer games, and other products.[91]

The Tax Complexity of E-Commerce

The potentially serious impact of the expansion of the Internet and E-commerce on global tax structures has not gone unnoticed in the sphere of public finance. Indeed, in the late 1990s, no other single topic has dominated discussions among tax authorities in the advanced industrialized countries of North America, Europe, and Asia as much as the subject of how to adapt taxation systems to the emerging electronic and information age. It is likely that this issue has galvanized tax authorities across the world more than any other single issue in the 20th century.

The collision course of E-Commerce and taxation is caused not just by the enormous growth in use of the Web but also by the increase in business-to-consumer and business-to-business transactions. After all, the free Web sites that educate, inform, and entertain are not what create complex tax issues; rather, it is the flow of money, income, and sales that accompanies E-commerce.

While certain taxation issues such as mail-order sales, value-added tax (VAT) reform, and federal income tax simplification have had a significant impact on a specific tax category or on a particular nation's tax system, the taxation of the E-commerce cuts across national borders and tax types. The growth of E-commerce raises complicated issues regarding the taxation of multijurisdictional transactions and the sourcing of sales or income from services or intangible property transactions that are relevant to transactional (sales and use, VAT), income, gross receipts, and property taxes.

The complexity of E-commerce taxation is a reflection of five trends occurring within the burgeoning Internet economy. These include the rise in borderless commerce, the emergence of digital commerce, the hollowing out of the corporation, the explosion of real-time transactions, and the revolution of new business models.

Borderless Commerce

The Internet is a truly global phenomenon—influencing nations in North America, South America, Europe, Asia, Africa, and Australia. E-commerce does not respect geographical boundaries, and Internet transactions flow seamlessly across the globe. The rise in remote commerce will lead to an enormous increase in cross-border transactions and related taxation issues. Mail-order sales raised many of the same issues, but Internet commerce is expected to be five times larger than mail-order sales within five years.

Cross-border transactions have historically been one of the most problematic areas of taxation. The process of disintermediation, in which remote vendors sell directly to customers in other jurisdictions without the buffer of a wholesale distributor or retail outlet, will result in hundreds of thousands of entities dealing with taxes in additional states or countries for the first time. Both dot-coms and click-and-mortar companies will need to cope with tax rules in numerous additional jurisdictions. For instance, the number of small businesses in the United States (entities with revenues of less than $10 million) that transact business over the Internet is expected to increase from under 1,000 in 1996 to 400,000 in 2003.[92]

Thus, the exponential growth of remote commerce during the first decade of the 21st century is likely to lead to a significant increase in cross-border tax issues and controversies, particularly in relation to international income taxes, VATs, and sales and use taxes. Borderless commerce will expand both business tax compliance efforts in multiple new foreign jurisdictions and nexus and jurisdictional disputes over which states or nations can impose income or transactional taxes on Internet vendors.

Digital Commerce

As previously discussed, the Internet will accelerate the trend toward the digital economy. Direct E-commerce is composed of companies that sell goods and services that are both purchased and delivered by electronic or digital means. There is a wide variety of goods and services that can be digitized or otherwise transferred electronically to customers without the need for any form of more traditional physical delivery.

The vast expansion of the digital economy raises some of the most complex tax issues of the new information age. The digital economy will significantly increase tax controversies and compliance-related problems associated with income earned from services and intangibles. States and nations will have to grope with issues such as the characterization of income, the bundling of services and products, sourcing rules, transfer pricing, and the valuation of intangibles. The absence of tax rules adaptable to the digital economy will cut across both direct (income) and indirect (transactional) tax systems.

The Hollow Corporation

The Internet is also accelerating the trend toward "hollow" corporations with narrowly defined core competencies. In the information age, there is less need for vertical integration. Companies are more likely to narrowly define their core competencies and leave manufacturing. distribution, fulfillment, customer service, and other functions to third parties. In part this is because of the ease with which companies can enter into joint ventures, partnerships, outsourcing agreements, and other affiliations to bring products to market.

For instance, Cisco Systems, one of the shining stars of the Internet age, is primarily a virtual corporation. Cisco Systems sells many of the routers, circuits, and other equipment used to construct the infrastructure of the Internet. Over three-quarters of all Cisco Systems product orders are made on-line. Over two-thirds of all Cisco Systems manufacturing is outsourced to other companies. As a result, for a large percentage of its product sales, no Cisco employee ever comes into contact with either the customer or the actual product involved in a transaction.

An even more dramatic example of the virtual corporation is eMachines. This personal computer reseller sold 1.7 million computers globally in 1999, producing over $1 billion in revenue. Incredibly, the company used only 20 employees to conduct its business, relying on other entities for virtually all of its operational functions.

With the narrowing of core competencies, Internet businesses will frequently have more flexibility to relocate (or initially locate) their property and payroll in jurisdictions with more favorable income tax rules and rates. It is far easier to shift the location of computer servers, headquarter employees, or information technology personnel than it is to move around large factories. Thus, the emergence of the virtual corporation is going to put pressure on tax laws—particularly in the income tax arena—to develop new rules for apportioning the income of more mobile and dynamic businesses. In a complementary development, the Internet also places a premium on intangible values (such as brand names and customer information), leading to more tax compliance, planning, and litigation over the value and location of such intangibles.

Real-Time Commerce

The Internet also facilitates a significant increase in real-time, paperless transactions. This trend is likely to enhance the momentum toward tax compliance reengineering and automated tax solutions for transactional taxes. It will also increase the pressure on taxing authorities to simplify the substantive and procedural tax rules to make an automated system more workable and less costly.

During the 1990s the growing interest in the automation of sales and use tax or VAT compliance was part of a larger movement toward the use of enterprise resource planning (ERP) software to automate corporate-finance, distribution, and other operational functions. The explosion of E-commerce and the growth of Internet-based transaction processing for both business-to-business sales and business-to-consumer sales will accelerate the creation of a less paper-oriented environment in which electronic databases largely supplant filing cabinets filled with sales invoices and purchase orders.

Indeed, in the United States, a broad coalition of state and local government groups made a sweeping proposal to the federal Advisory Commission on Electronic Commerce (a commission created by the 1998 Internet Tax Freedom Act) for a "zero-burden" real-time compliance system for sales and use tax collections. The system would be at least partially government funded and rely on a technology-driven solution using third-party contractors to collect sales and use taxes on behalf of remote vendors.

Changing Business Models

Finally, the Internet is also fueling a revolution in business models that is creating new and challenging issues for state, federal, and international tax systems. The Internet is characterized not just by remote selling but by a range of evolving business models such as on-line auctions, reverse auctions, virtual communities, infomediaries, aggregators, and brokers. Traditional industries such as automobiles, clothing, book publishing, and pharmacies are being turned upside down by the potential of on-line retailing to replace conventional store purchases. Many manufacturers are being transformed into retailers; many conventional intermediaries such as wholesalers and distributors are disappearing or being replaced by new Web-based intermediaries.

These business models are significantly altering the landscape of interactions between suppliers, sellers, and buyers—creating many new tax issues. For instance, gift certificates are currently an $11 billion market in the United States. Prior to the Internet, gift certificates were primarily purchased at retail outlets. In the last two years, however, a number of Internet start-ups such as GiftCertificates.com and Giftpoint.com have begun to build an on-line marketplace for gift certificates. These entities buy the gift certificates from retail outlets at a discount and resell them over the Internet. Other Internet start-ups are specializing in creating an on-line market for gifts, providing consumers the opportunity to buy and deliver wine, flowers, golf-course privileges, four-star restaurant meals, and other goods and services to friends and relatives all over the world. The emerging business models for gift certificates and gift giving raise new and difficult tax issues regarding the identity of the actual retailer, the sourcing of consumption, the classification of the good or service sold, and the relevant sales price for transactional tax purposes.[93]

The Internet is reshaping the world economy, yet it is still in its infancy. Although there has been a tremendous growth in the number of users of the Internet, over 95 percent of the world's population of 6 billion still do not have Internet access. The levels of both business-to-consumer and business-to-business sales over the Internet have skyrocketed, yet they still represent less than 10 percent of anticipated sales in four years (from $129 billion in 1999 to $1.5 trillion in 2003). As a result, the business models that will be most successful are yet to be determined. Thus, even as new tax rules are adopted, they will have to remain flexible, capable of being revised or revamped in sync with changing technological, economic, and political needs.[94]

These five trends that have arisen from the growth of the Internet economy have transformed the landscape of tax policy in the United States and abroad. Since the mid 1990s there have been literally hundreds of study commissions, reports, and proposed or enacted regulations and legislation pertaining to the taxation of E-commerce. This flurry of activity has occurred both at the local and national levels in the United States and other countries.

Foreign Government Initiatives

On a global basis, the 29-member Organization for Economic Cooperation and Development (OECD)—made up of the nations with the leading economies in the world—has undertaken numerous activities since 1996 aimed at addressing the issue of E-commerce taxation. In 1996 the OECD Committee on Fiscal Affairs created a working group to study the issues related to the taxation of E-commerce. The European Commission also established a working group to determine its own position on Internet taxation.

In the European Union (EU) and elsewhere, most of the concern is with the impact of E-commerce on value-added taxes. In 1996 a European Commission report expressed the concern that "VAT is threatened in particular by the growing number of international services which use new technologies to locate taxable transactions outside the territorial scope of the common VAT-system."[95] A 1998 OECD report indicated that "problems concerning the application of consumption taxes are generally recognized as having more immediacy than the issues concerning direct taxation."[96]

A value-added tax is a tax on consumption that is applied at each stage of production and distribution. In effect, however, the tax burden is similar to that of a tax imposed on the final output sold to consumers because businesses are typically allowed credits for VAT paid at earlier input stages. All of the 29 OECD countries except for the United States have a value-added tax or a national-level consumption tax. Value-added taxes and other consumption taxes make up on average nearly one-third of the tax base in most advanced industrialized nations. As discussed in chapter 5, value-added taxes, like state sales and use taxes, raise particular problems because of the transactional nature of the tax. Moreover, unlike international direct taxes, value-added taxes are not harmonized around the world by international treaties that encourage or compel countries to conform their rules to those in other nations.[97]

The OECD and EU reports and discussions focus on a number of issues, including treatment of digital sales (as goods or services), sourcing of digital sales (to the location of the supplier or consumer), interjurisdictional transactions, tax simplification, and tax enforcement. Both organizations recognize that E-commerce is likely to lead to far-reaching changes in international tax rules. The European nations have expressed great concern over the potential for tax evasion created by electronic transactions across borders and continents.

The European Commission's preliminary positions are that (1) the existing VAT system can be adapted to E-commerce, (2) no new taxes such as a "bit tax" are required, (3) digital products should be treated as services, (4) all services supplied to a consumer in the EU should be subject to tax in the EU, regardless of origin, (5) countries should continue to use the system of consumer self-assessment for business-to-business transactions, and (6) compliance should be made as simple as possible.

U.S. Government Response

In the United States the federal government has made a significant effort to develop an E-commerce policy, including a strategy on both federal and state and local taxation issues. In December 1995 President Clinton created an Electronic Commerce Working Group. The working group represented a broad cross section of important government agencies, including the Office of Management and Budget, the National Economic Council, the U.S. Trade Representative, the Department of Treasury, the Department of Justice, the Department of Commerce, and the Federal Communications Commission. In December 1996 the Treasury Department issued a paper on the taxation of E-commerce entitled *Selected Tax Policy Implications of Global Electronic Commerce.* In July 1997 the federal working group released its final report, *A Framework for Global Electronic Commerce.* At the same time, President Clinton issued a presidential *Directive on Electronic Commerce.* The United States also collaborated with the EU, the OECD and numerous other individual nations and groups of nations on joint declarations on E-commerce. In November 1998 the Electronic Commerce Working Group issued its first annual report.[98]

Because the United States has no national-level sales tax or value-added tax, the federal government has focused primarily on the implications of E-commerce for federal income taxation and other international income tax systems. The government reports have emphasized a strong preference for dealing with E-commerce transactions within the current set of rules, without any new taxes. As President Clinton stated in his 1997 directive, "I direct the Secretary of the Treasury to work with State and local governments and with foreign government to achieve agreements that will ensure that no new taxes are imposed that discriminate against Internet commerce; that existing taxes should be applied in ways that avoid inconsistent national tax jurisdictions and double taxation; and that tax systems treat economically similar transactions equally, regardless of whether such transactions occur through electronic means or through more conventional channels of commerce."[99]

Accordingly, the federal government has expressed support for maintaining the principle of residence-based taxation in which each nation taxes all of the income of its domestic companies (less a credit for certain taxes paid abroad) and only the domestic source income of foreign companies. Similarly, the United States has backed the continued use of existing rules for determining jurisdiction over foreign companies (permanent establishment or engaged in business rules), for characterizing income (manufactured goods, services, royalties, etc.), and for sourcing income (to the location of the vendor, licensee, 50-50 split, etc., depending on the characterization of the economic activity).

The federal government has also recognized, however, that many of the preexisting concepts will need to be updated or modified to deal with the unique circumstances of E-commerce. Thus, permanent establishment concepts will need to address the importance of computer servers and Web sites in generating income. Characterization and source-of-income rules will need to analyze the explosion of digital commerce and whether it should be categorized as goods, services, or intangible property. Finally, federal income tax compliance rules will generally need to adapt to the growth of electronic money and the potential for anonymous and untraceable transactions that arise in connection with E-commerce.

Ironically, although the federal government has been highly visible in lobbying on a global basis for no new taxes on the Internet and for the application of preexisting rules to E-commerce, it has done very little to clarify how these preexisting rules will apply to the newly emerging Internet economy. For instance, the federal government in the late 1990s promulgated detailed regulations on the characterization and sourcing of income from the sale and license of software, but it has not clarified whether these new rules will apply to other forms of digital commerce such as music, video, and electronic information services. The federal government has also not provided a full explanation of how existing jurisdictional and sourcing rules can avoid uneven treatment of tangible and intangible transactions or eliminate the location of a computer server or Web site as a factor in determining income taxation.

The U.S. Congress also undertook several initiatives focused on Internet taxation. In 1996 a bipartisan Congressional Internet Caucus was formed with over one hundred members to address issues of Internet tax policy. In 1997 the Internet Tax Freedom Act (also known as the Cox-Wyden bill after its chief sponsors) was introduced in Congress. In October 1998 after one-and-a-half years of hearings, negotiations, and redrafting, the legislation was enacted by Congress and signed into law.[100]

The Internet Tax Freedom Act applies to state and local sales and use taxes for the period beginning on October 1, 1998, and ending three years later. The act addresses two major issues concerning Internet taxation. First, it prohibits the imposition of any new state or local sales or use taxes on Internet access or on-line services during this period. Second, the act prohibits the imposition of any multiple or discriminatory taxes on E-commerce. Generally, discriminatory taxes encompass taxes that are applied only to E-commerce but not to similarly situated goods or services that are not ordered and/or delivered electronically. Thus, a state could not impose a sales or use tax on the sale of canned software that is delivered by electronic means without imposing a similar tax (at an identical rate) on the sale of canned software that is delivered by conventional physical means. Similarly, a state could not impose a sales or use tax collection responsibility on a vendor that takes orders for products or services over the Internet without imposing a similar tax (at an identical rate) on a vendor that takes order for products or services by mail order.

The Internet Tax Freedom Act also created a 19-member Advisory Commission on Electronic Commerce. The law authorized Congress to appoint 16 members (8 from industry and 8 from state and local government), with the remaining 3 members coming from the executive branch (Department of Treasury, Department of Commerce, and the United States Trade Representative). The commission was charged with studying the complicated issues related to taxation of E-commerce and providing Congress with recommendations on future actions. While the federal commission was primarily directed to undertake a study of state and local taxes related to the Internet, the scope of its operations also included making recommendations on global taxation issues related to the Internet. As the statute set forth, the commission is charged with conducting "a thorough study of Federal, State and local and international taxation and tariff treatment of transactions using the Internet and Internet access and other comparable intrastate, interstate, or international sales activities."[101]

The Advisory Commission on Electronic Commerce has held public meetings and solicited testimony and written submissions from a wide variety of parties. The commission received nearly 40 different proposals from government, business, and other interested parties on tax reform related to E-commerce. With the creation of this commission, the issues of Internet taxation and remote commerce have been elevated to greater prominence than ever before, with corporate chief executive officers, presidential candidates, and state governors debating the merits of various proposals in meetings widely covered by both the business and political press. By statute, the commission is required to issue a report to the U.S. Congress with its recommendations by April 2000 (unless it receives an extension).

State and Local Government Initiatives

Although national governments in Europe, Asia, and North America have undertaken significant initiatives to formulate policies related to the taxation of E-commerce, perhaps no governmental bodies have expended as much effort or garnered as much political attention as state and local governments in the United States. These efforts have involved not just Congress but virtually every major state and local government group, including the National Governors Association, the National Conference of State Legislatures, the U.S. Conference of Mayors, the National League of Cities, the National Association of Counties, the Federation of Tax Administrators, the Multistate Tax Commission, and the National Tax Association.

In the United States the discussion of the taxation of E-commerce has centered on state taxes for a variety of reasons. First, subnational taxes are much more important in the United States than in most developed nations. State and local taxes account for over $700 billion in revenues in the United States—about 45 percent of all tax dollars raised in the country. Second, because the United States does not have a national value-added, sales, or property tax, issues that impact transactional or property taxes are of significant importance at the state and local level. This factor is of great importance because transaction taxes tend to be more complicated to administer than income taxes in relation to E-commerce business activities. Third, compared with other nations, there is a far greater number of subnational jurisdictions in the United States that have taxing authority. Along with the 45 states and the District of Columbia that currently impose sales or use taxes at the state level, there are approximately 7,500 counties, cities, towns, and special districts that also impose sales or use taxes on transactions occurring within their borders. This factor significantly increases the complexity of compliance with transactional taxes in the United States.[102]

The explosion of E-commerce has exacerbated the already-tenuous relationship between interstate commerce and the U.S. system of federalism. While the United States has the largest and most productive economy in the world, it also has a framework of intergovernmental fiscal relations that is among the most cumbersome in the world. Even before the commercialization of the Internet, state and local governments have chafed under legal restrictions placed on their ability to tax remote vendors without physical presence within their boundaries. Similarly, multistate businesses have reeled under the burden of complying with sales and use tax rules in hundreds or thousands of state and local jurisdictions. The advent of the information age has simply focused a bright spotlight on the need to reexamine both the legal restraints placed on taxing interstate commerce under the U.S. Constitution and the autonomy of state and local taxing authorities within U.S. federalism.

The urgency of the political and economic situation has resulted in one of the most concerted government-business tax reform efforts ever undertaken at the state and local levels in the United States. Under the auspices of the National Tax Association's (NTA) Communications and Electronic Commerce Tax Project, a group formed in 1997 consisting of 16 representatives from business groups, 16 representatives from state and local government, and 7 representatives from other groups. The membership of the group's steering committee included business representatives from a wide range of industries, including telecommunications, cable, financial services, Internet access, manufacturers, direct marketers, publishers, and computers. Similarly, the government members included representatives from all of the significant state and local broad-based and tax administration groups.

The NTA project created a number of working subcommittees, including committees on scope, situs and sourcing, tax base, tax rate, tax simplification, and telecommunications. The group met for a two-year period and issued a series of working papers. Although the group was unable to reach consensus on some of the more volatile political and legal issues, it did set forth a number of proposals on how to increase uniformity within sales and use tax rules and administrative procedures. The NTA project also discussed a potential political compromise between government and business on the taxation of E-commerce. Under this grand compromise, the states and localities would cede some of their sovereignty—agreeing to more uniform tax rules and administrative procedures and, most important, agreeing to abide by one tax rate per state. In exchange, the states and localities would be allowed to require remote vendors (i.e., vendors without physical presence) to collect sales and use taxes from consumers. Although the NTA project discussions concerning far-reaching changes in state and local sales and use and jurisdictional rules came to an impasse because of significant political differences between government and business participants, the unprecedented attention paid to this subject underlines the radical impact of E-commerce on state and local tax policy.

As discussed previously, the Internet Tax Freedom Act, enacted by Congress in 1998, is primarily focused on state and local taxes. Indeed, the Internet Tax Freedom Act represents a significant federal intrusion into state fiscal matters and taxation policy—an arena that the federal government has historically left to the discretion of the states and localities. The novelty of the federal action represents the depth of national government concern over arbitrary constraints being placed on E-commerce that could impede its growth.

The federal legislation has also heightened concerns of state and local governments that the fiscal autonomy that they have enjoyed historically within U.S. federalism was in danger of being preempted by federal action. Although the length of the moratorium is only three years, many state and local government representatives fear a more permanent federal intervention. Interest is particularly keen among local government officials who fear an erosion of their sales tax base, either through the loss of tax on Internet sales or through the removal of local option sales taxes as a whole as part of a political compromise. Both the U.S. Conference of Mayors (USCM) and the National Association of Counties (NACo) were very active in lobbying efforts over Internet taxation and the makeup of the Congressional Advisory Commission on Electronic Commerce. In fact, NACo and USCM filed a lawsuit to block the commission from meeting unless its membership was revised to reflect a balance between government and business representatives, as called for in the Internet Tax Freedom Act. According to past NACo president Randy Johnson, "It's great for commerce, but the Internet is not some kind of magic potion that immunizes an elite class of peddlers from collecting state sales tax. It should not be that way."[103]

The National Governors Association (NGA) has also been very active on the issue of Internet taxation. In 1998 the association supported passage of the Internet Development Act of 1998, which called for a simplified sales and use tax system and the elimination of multiple local sales tax rates in exchange for states being granted the authority to impose an expanded duty to collect sales and use tax on remote sellers.

In 1999 the NGA approved an amendment to the Internet Development Act of 1998 that calls for one rate per state, uniform definitions, *de minimis* rules to protect small businesses involved in E-commerce, and the imposition on remote sellers of an expanded duty to collect sales and use taxes.

A number of governors, both Republican and Democrat, have expressed fears over the possible erosion of the state tax base unless the problem of collecting taxes from remote vendors is solved. According to Governor Paul Patton of Kentucky, letting the sales tax questions go unanswered would create a "disruptive" chain reaction: "If we just sit back and leave everything the way it is, and we say that 'as long as the sale was an electronic transaction, we can't tax it,' . . . I think we're going to get a cascading effect that will be catastrophic."[104]

The key for many states and localities is not the taxation of digital commerce but the taxation of tangible goods ordered over the Internet. Ohio senate president Richard Finan, a Republican, stated in 1999: "We don't really care that much about taxing when you go on-line. We care about [the tax on] products. If we can't have the ability to collect that tax, we're going to die. Our schools are going to die. It's simply going to be a disaster for the states." Similarly, Harley Duncan, the executive director of the Federation of Tax Administrators, commented on the issue of the duty of remote vendors to collect sales and use taxes: "It seems to me that the forecasts for growth in electronic commerce are such that if this issue is not addressed in the near term, electronic commerce could effectively cripple the sales tax, and we need to be seriously concerned about its future in the state-local revenue structure."[105]

The Cutting-Edge Issues of Global Taxation

The deep concern exhibited by both government and industry over the impact of E-commerce on local, state, federal, and international taxation is attributable to the trends occurring within the Internet economy. The rise in borderless commerce, the emergence of digital commerce, the hollowing out of the corporation, the explosion of real-time transactions, and the revolution of new business models all exert pressure on traditional tax systems that were designed for a different era. Most taxing jurisdictions continue to use a mid-20th-century tax system—designed largely for manufacturers and vendors of tangible personal property—to tax a technologically advanced 21st-century service industry. Not surprisingly, these old tax rules are often ill-suited to taxing E-commerce.

The incompatibility of old tax rules and "new-economy" commerce is evident in the growing tension and friction within the tax world over the application of tax rules to leading E-commerce businesses. The complexity of adapting tax rules to E-commerce is manifest across tax types, including sales and use, VAT, gross receipts, income, and property taxes.

The Transition from Traditional Commerce to E-Commerce

In many jurisdictions the tax consequences can be dramatic for an individual company that engages in E-commerce whereas before it conducted business by more traditional means. Consider, for example, a computer software manufacturer ("taxpayer") is based in Massachusetts. The taxpayer has a network of sales representatives soliciting sales around the country who report to a sales office in Connecticut; and all its sales are shipped via U.S. mail to retail outlets around the country.

Under the traditional state and local tax rules on tangible commerce, the taxpayer only files *income* tax returns in Massachusetts and Connecticut. The activities of its sales representatives do not create income tax nexus for the taxpayer in other jurisdictions because they are protected pursuant to Public Law 86-272 (solicitation related to sales of tangible personal property). For income tax sourcing purposes, all of the taxpayer's sales to states other than Massachusetts and Connecticut will be sourced outside of Massachusetts and will not be subject to throwback in Massachusetts because the requirements of the Massachusetts throwback rule are satisfied. For sales tax purposes, the taxpayer will not be protected by Public Law 86-272 and will have a collection responsibility in most states (because the sale of canned software is considered taxable as the sale of tangible personal property by almost all states). In addition, the taxpayer will benefit from a number of favorable income tax (single sales apportionment, investment tax credit), sales tax (exemptions for machinery and materials used in manufacturing), and local property tax rules (exemptions for machinery used in manufacturing) that are available in Massachusetts only to businesses engaged in manufacturing tangible personal property.

However, a simple change in the method of delivery of the software would radically alter the taxpayer's state tax consequences. Assume that the taxpayer now delivers 100 percent of its sales of software electronically to its customers. In most jurisdictions the electronic transfer of software would be considered the sale of intangible property. Thus, in most jurisdictions the taxpayer now has an income tax filing responsibility because its network of sales representatives would, in all likelihood, no longer be protected by Public Law 86-272 (because the sales activity is no longer related to tangible personal property, e.g., a disk or magnetic tape). Moreover, for income tax sourcing purposes, because the sales of software electronically would probably be considered sales of intangible property, all of the taxpayer's sales will now be sourced back to Massachusetts (the state in which the income-producing activity occurs). This will result in a significant increase in the taxpayer's Massachusetts income tax liability.

With respect to sales tax collection responsibilities, the taxpayer would actually have fewer states in which it needs to collect and pay over sales and use tax. The sale of electronically transferred software is currently taxable in only about three-fifths of the jurisdictions because it is considered to be the sale of intangible property. Thus, the taxpayer would not need to collect and pay over sales taxes in certain jurisdictions in which the sale of canned software is only taxed in its tangible form.

Finally, the taxpayer may also become ineligible for certain income, sales (on purchases), and property tax benefits provided to manufacturers of tangible personal property. In this case, the taxing authorities might argue that these benefits are not available to a business that no longer manufactures and sells tangible personal property but instead fully or partially sells intangible property. Although this legal interpretation is not clear-cut, it could result in significant increases in the taxpayer's income, sales, and property tax liabilities in its home state.

Another issue that arises frequently with E-commerce is how to source goods and services that are used simultaneously in multiple jurisdictions. Traditionally, goods and services have been consumed in a single jurisdiction, and thus the notion of apportioning sales and use taxes or value-added taxes was unnecessary. With the explosive growth of interstate services, particularly in E-commerce, the apportioning of multijurisdictional transactions becomes more commonplace. Generally, with tangible personal property, transactional tax rules focus on the location where the product is delivered and a change of possession occurs. With E-commerce, the physical location of the actual information content may not be relevant. It is relatively easy to change the jurisdiction of the computer server that holds the digital product. Moreover, the consumer can access the information from a remote terminal without actually downloading the information. Thus, the relevant inquiry is likely to be the location where the consumer views the information (or in the case of a mobile consumer—the location where the consumer generally accesses the information).

For example, suppose a computer software company sells a multijurisdictional customer the right to use its software in 10 different states or countries. The computer software company then electronically transfers a single version of the software to a single server site—from which the software is accessed by the consumer's employees. Is the sale of the software taxable in just the single jurisdiction where the server is located? What if that jurisdiction does not tax software that is transferred electronically because it considers such a transaction to be the sale of nontaxable intangible property. Would a use tax or value-added tax be due in some or all of the other nine states or nations from which the purchaser's employees access the software? Does it matter if the software is sent to servers in all 10 jurisdictions? Does it make a difference if the software is hosted by the vendor or a third-party service provider and exclusively accessed remotely by the customer?

Given the complex, intangible, and multijurisdictional nature of E-commerce, taxation of the Internet touches on some of the most controversial and cutting-edge issues in state, federal, and international transactions. Although these issues predate E-commerce, they have become much more complex in the increasingly interconnected and constantly changing environment of E-commerce. These issues cut across tax types and national boundaries and need to be clearly understood both for purposes of complying with current tax rules and for adapting new tax rules to an Internet-age economy. The primary topics that will be discussed in more depth in subsequent chapters are transactional taxes applied to services, tax simplification, income tax rules related to E-commerce, special rules that apply to the telecommunications industry, and the issue of jurisdiction to tax.

Transactional Tax Issues Related to Services

State and local taxing authorities in the United States have traditionally had more difficulty applying sales and use or other transactional taxes to services or intangible property transactions than to tangible property transactions. The issue of whether the sales and use tax base should be extended to services has long been one of the most controversial policy debates in the state and local tax arena. Currently, a substantial minority of states tax a wide range of conventional and electronic services. Most states, however, still tax virtually no services (other than telecommunications services). In the last 15 years, only two states—Florida and Massachusetts—have made a large-scale effort to expand their tax base to include a wide range of services. Both efforts resulted in a political maelstrom, with the Florida legislation being repealed after six months and the Massachusetts legislation being repealed after three days.

Nonetheless, for most states and localities, the decision to pursue a policy in which goods and services are taxed, whether delivered as tangible property or as digital products, will require a significant expansion of the sales and use tax base to include electronic services. Aside from the explosive tax base issue, states and localities will also have to wrestle with a complex range of other issues. If the states continue to tax enumerated categories of electronic services (such as telecommunications or information services), they will have to cope with continuous ambiguities over what is taxable and what is exempt. For instance, is Internet telephony considered taxable telecommunications services or exempt Internet access services?

The states will also have to develop sourcing rules for determining which states should be allowed to tax a particular digital transaction. Should the sourcing rule be based on the state of consumption or the state of origin? What if the location of the customer is not known to the vendor in the ordinary course of business? What about sales to business customers that use the digital product simultaneously in multiple jurisdictions? Should such sales be apportioned?

Generally, the taxation of E-commerce under VAT rules presents less formidable obstacles than the U.S. equivalent transaction tax—the state and local sales tax. Unlike the U.S. framework, the VAT system does not have local jurisdiction transaction taxes, it does not have legal jurisdictional restrictions on imposing the tax on remote vendors with no physical presence in the customer's country, and it does not have a narrow tax base that exempts most digital transactions. However, the VAT policy makers must still resolve some of the same complex E-commerce issues as the states, including the following: Should the VAT be levied in the country of the supplier or the country of the consumer? Should the VAT be imposed on imports from nonregistered vendors to nonbusiness consumers? Should a digital transaction be treated as a supply of a good or a service? Where should sales of digital products that are used simultaneously by multiple users be sourced? And which party should the VAT be collected from?

Tax Simplification

As the economies of advanced industrialized nations have grown more complex, the burden of complying with tax laws has increased commensurately. Income tax laws have been loaded down with hundreds of different rules on classification of income, exemptions, deductions, and tax credits. Transactional tax laws have similarly become inundated with variations in tax bases, special exemptions, and differences in filing, reporting, and record-keeping requirements. The growth of service and intangible transactions may result in a significant increase in tax disputes, caused by the ambiguity in tax laws regarding such economic activities.

The explosion of E-commerce threatens to significantly increase the complexity of tax compliance. The expansion of remote commerce may result in a large increase in the number of vendors that need to comply with tax-filing requirements in multiple jurisdictions. The Internet will result in the removal of many intermediaries, leaving more entities exposed to compliance with laws in multiple jurisdictions. It will also result in a new breed of intermediary, particularly in the business-to-business sphere, that will be responsible for tracking back-office accounting and tax-collection data for hundreds of vendors in dozens of jurisdictions. To do so, the new intermediary will have to develop a solution that maintains accurate physical presence/nexus, product exceptions, and customer exceptions for each vendor.

Nowhere is the tax-simplification issue more potent than with regard to compliance with local sales and use tax rules in the United States. While the United States has only 50 states, it has nearly 90,000 local, county, and regional government units. Currently, approximately 7,500 cities, towns, counties, transportation districts, and other special local jurisdictions impose sales or use taxes on transactions occurring within their borders. About three-fifths of the states have localities that impose separate local sales and use tax rates.

It is not surprising that the debate over how to tax E-commerce has zeroed in on a reform that would limit the number of state and local jurisdictions that could impose a sales or use tax. Under the prevailing wisdom, the states would be limited to one rate per state, the revenues from which could be divided between a state and its localities as the particular state sees fit. As President Clinton observed in 1998, "We cannot allow 30,000 state and local tax jurisdictions to stifle the Internet, nor can we allow the erosion of the revenue that state and local governments need to fight crime and invest in education."[106]

However, the simplification of sales and use tax compliance through the restriction of tax rates and other uniformity proposals runs counter to the historic autonomy of states and localities under the U.S. federalism system. Any political compromise will require a resolution that replaces the large revenue stream that localities currently receive from local sales and use taxes—over $40 billion a year.[107]

Income Tax Issues Related to E-Commerce

The emergence of E-commerce also injects significant confusion and complexity into state, federal, and international income tax rules. Traditionally, income tax rules related to services and intangibles have created legal ambiguities and litigation, inconsistencies in the treatment of goods and services, and difficulties in identifying the location of income-producing activity. Moreover, the allocation of income (from both products and services) earned by multijurisdictional businesses is also one of the most complex fields in all of taxation. The vast expansion of E-commerce and borderless economic activity will undoubtedly reinforce this historical trend.

For instance, with regard to state income taxes, sales of goods are generally sourced (for sales factor purposes) to the location of the consumer. Conversely, sales of services or intangible property are typically sourced to where the vendor performs the income-producing activity. To the extent that physical goods are transformed into digital products and delivered electronically, the sourcing of income from such activities is likely to shift from a "market-state" approach to a "vendor-state" approach. Without any change in tax rules, this could result in very different tax outcomes depending solely on the method of delivery of a good or service. Moreover, identifying the costs of performance associated with E-commerce transactions may prove difficult. Should the server that holds the digital product and sends it to the customer be treated as the focal point for the income-producing activity, or should the taxpayer be required to analyze the location of all the underlying activity that led to the creation of the product? As previously indicated, vendors of digital products will no longer benefit from the jurisdictional protections afforded by the federal government to vendors of manufactured products and may have to file income tax returns in numerous additional states.

In relation to the sale of tangible goods, state income tax rules may have to be revised to reflect the greater mobility of many Internet vendors. New-economy enterprises with more narrow core competencies will frequently have much more flexibility to relocate property and payroll to jurisdictions with more favorable rates and apportionment rules.

There is likely to be pressure on states to use apportionment formulas that place more emphasis on the location of customers and less on the location of a business's property and payroll.

Similarly, with regard to federal and international income taxes, nations have historically used different rules for sourcing income earned from goods and income earned from services and intangibles. Income from services is generally sourced to where the service is performed, income from royalties is sourced to where the licensee uses the intangible property, and income from goods is sourced to where it is manufactured (or in some cases, split between the country of manufacturing and the country of consumption).

All of these rules predate the Internet, but they will take on a new layer of complexity with the rapid expansion of E-commerce. E-commerce transactions are likely to blur the boundaries between tangible and intangible goods and to exponentially increase the level of cross-border commerce. For instance, the U.S. government, after years of effort, recently released regulations that address some of these complex definitional and sourcing issues with regard to the software industry. However, with the rapid growth of E-commerce categories (other than software), it will be necessary to determine if these new rules similarly apply to other categories of digital services or if different rules apply.

In the international direct-taxation arena, countries will also have to reexamine the extent to which they want to rely on residence-based taxation (looking to the home country of the vendor), source-based taxation (focusing on the location of the vendor's operations), or market-based taxation (looking to where the customer uses the goods or services). Generally, nations use residence-based taxation—taxing all of the income of their own companies while allowing these companies a full or partial credit for taxes paid to other nations. In addition, nations tend to use source-based taxation for foreign companies—taxing them only on their income that is sourced to the particular jurisdiction. There are also a number of complex allocation of income rules used when a company has integrated operations in more than one country (arms-length accounting rules). The growth of E-commerce will undoubtedly put pressure on the framework of international direct taxation, exacerbating existing tensions between these different conceptual approaches and increasing the difficulty of identifying and monitoring the jurisdiction in which income-generating activity occurs.

Special Rules for the Telecommunications Industry

The digital era will also force taxing jurisdictions to reevaluate tax systems that apply different rules to special industries such as the telecommunications industry. For instance, in the United States, the telecommunications industry has historically been subjected to higher tax burdens than many other industries. Telecommunications companies are frequently subject to special property tax assessments, franchise fees, gross-receipts taxes, and sales tax rates that do not apply to other companies.

For instance, a 1999 study by an industry group, the Telecommunications Tax Task Force of the Committee on State Taxation (COST), determined that telecommunications companies are subjected to significantly higher effective tax rates and more burdensome administrative filing requirements than are general business corporations. The study found that the nationwide average effective rate of transactional taxes applied to sales of telecommunications services was nearly three times higher than the rate applied to sale of goods by general businesses. The study also concluded that telecommunications providers operating nationwide would have to file seven times more tax and related administrative returns than would similarly situated general business corporations.[108]

Although there may be a historic justification for imposing a disproportionate tax burden on telecommunications or other utility companies, the feasibility of maintaining unique tax rules on a special industry is eroding. First, the decline of the monopoly status of telecommunications carriers in an era of deregulation means that regulated companies are now competing with unregulated companies that may be subject to more beneficial tax rules. Second, voice telecommunications services are now being bundled with other services such as data, Internet access, and video—making it more difficult to isolate telecommunications services and subject them to a special tax burden. Third, with the arrival of Internet telephony that transmits voice communications using packet-switching technology, any distinction between telecommunication companies and providers of other digital services may disappear altogether.

The end result of these political, economic, and technological changes is that the maintenance of special industry rules for telecommunications will be more difficult to enforce and will create increasingly arbitrary and discriminatory outcomes. The likely result is that the special industry regulations will have to be modified or eliminated to reflect the changing dynamic of the information age. However, these changes will come haltingly, as many jurisdictions rely heavily on the tax revenue produced by special industry assessments and will want to replace such revenue streams before relinquishing special tax rules that apply to the utility industry.

Jurisdiction-to-Tax Issues

The issue of "jurisdiction to tax" or "nexus" is one that has traditionally been the source for much confusion and controversy among both subnational and national governments. Historically, this issue has been the subject of both extensive international negotiations over tax treaties and repeated U.S. Supreme Court decisions over state and local sovereignty. With the advent of E-commerce and the vast potential expansion of remote selling, the issue of jurisdiction to tax is becoming even more volatile.

Among state and local governments in the United States, the constitutional limitations on the ability of subnational government units to impose a sales and use tax collection responsibility on remote vendors is a major national political issue. Currently, states and localities cannot require remote vendors with no physical presence in the customer's state to collect sales or use tax from the customers on products shipped into the jurisdiction. State and local governments have sought relief from Congress for over one decade on this issue—beginning when it primarily affected their ability to collect sales and use tax from the mail-order industry. However, with E-commerce business-to-consumer sales expected to exceed mail-order-industry sales within five years and continue to grow rapidly after that, states and localities are expressing even more urgency to resolve this problem.

The estimates of potential loss of sales and use tax revenue from remote commerce in the United States vary widely. A study by Ernst and Young in 1998 estimated revenue losses from Internet remote sales at $170 million compared to revenue losses in that year from remote mail-order sales of $4.5 billion. By comparison, a report by Michael Mazerov of the Center on Budget and Policy Priorities estimated that sales and use tax revenue losses in the year 2003 would be about $10 billion from Internet remote sales and about $5 billion from mail-order sales.[109]

The high variability in the estimates of the potential revenue loss from remote commerce is largely due to the dependence of the studies on a number of assumptions about Internet revenue growth, composition of Internet sales, and tax-compliance patterns of businesses. For instance, the estimates can change significantly depending on assumptions on both the overall rate of growth of Internet sales and the composition of such sales (e.g., taxable products versus nontaxable services). Moreover, it is very difficult to predict either the percentage of business consumers that will voluntarily self-assess a use tax on Internet purchases or the proportion of Internet vendors that will voluntarily assume a multistate collection responsibility because of business operational needs (the desire to use consumer state stores or service providers) or in order to avoid protracted nexus litigation over *de minimis* links or possible use of agents in market states.

Although precision in the revenue estimates may not be possible, it is clear that many state and local governments believe that the very survival of the sales and use tax system is at stake if this problem is not resolved through federal legislation authorizing subnational governments to require remote vendors to collect the sales and use tax (even if the vendors have no physical presence in the customer state). State and local government officials continue to decry the unfairness of a system that imposes a sales and use tax collection responsibility on a small local retailer but not on a large remote vendor that blankets the state's residents with mass-media advertisements or with electronic solicitation through a preferential site on an Internet portal.

Nonetheless, while the states and localities await legislative relief from Congress, they are pursuing a variety of legal theories aimed at asserting their jurisdiction over companies with minimal physical presence in the customer state. Whereas many mail-order companies were able to operate in one jurisdiction, without the use of agents or affiliates in the market states, many E-commerce companies have more complicated organizational structures. These E-commerce companies frequently have affiliated retail stores, sales representatives, distribution and shipping centers, visits to suppliers, co-marketing agreements with unrelated in-state entities, or other third-party activities in the market states. In many circumstances it is difficult to isolate totally the E-commerce operations from the more traditional business operations—leaving the E-commerce entity vulnerable to having the physical presence of its affiliates or agents attributed to it—and thus subjecting the remote vendor to the market state's taxing jurisdiction. Thus, even though the states and localities have to date lost the judicial and legislative battle to impose collection responsibilities on remote vendors (based solely on economic presence), the subnational governments are engaged in widespread audits and litigation with multistate vendors over the limits of physical presence (either directly or through agents) in a customer state.

Similarly, for federal and international income tax rules, new issues are emerging over the concept of what constitutes a taxable connection with a sovereign nation. Although it is clear that the location of an office or a branch constitutes "doing business" or a "permanent establishment" resulting in a taxable presence in a foreign nation, it is not so clear whether a single or multiple computer servers in a foreign nation that are used for electronic solicitation or transaction processing or that store a vendor's products in electronic format would subject a remote vendor to the nation's income tax jurisdiction. E-commerce is likely to result in many different forms of business activity and business relationships with affiliates or other entities that will create considerable confusion with regard to income tax filing requirements.

For VAT purposes, the jurisdictional issue takes on a different form. There are no treaties that regulate the imposition of VAT on a worldwide basis. No jurisdictional constraints prohibit most countries from imposing VAT on foreign companies with no physical presence in the particular country. There are, however, significant enforcement issues. For instance, unlike U.S. sales and use tax rules, the VAT base generally includes all digital goods and services. Nonetheless, within the European community, value-added taxes are not currently imposed on sales of digital goods and services from a non-EU vendor to an EU nonbusiness consumer. This gap in the VAT regime is caused because the sale of such digital services is currently sourced to the vendor's location, not the consumer's location.

The EU countries are reconsidering this position and are likely to change the place of supply rules to focus on the location of the consumer, as is already the case with long-distance telecommunication services provided from outside the EU. However, even if this rule is changed, there will still be the added complexity of how to get non-EU vendors, many of whom will not have economic presence in the EU, to register as vendors and pay over the VAT tax. Unlike the import of goods into the EU, for which customs can be used to enforce the tax on the party importing the goods, no such compliance system is possible with electronic transactions, which are innately more difficult to identify and monitor.

In The Meantime . . .

It is abundantly clear that there are many complex tax issues relating to E-commerce that need to be addressed in the beginning of the 21st century. Indeed, governments across the globe are engaged in feverish activity to come up with new tax rules or a new tax regime to be applied to the unique characteristics and challenges of E-commerce.

The subject of Internet taxation is so white-hot that cybertaxation rumors regularly circulate over the Internet. For instance in June 1999, the U.S. Postal Service was forced to issue a press release branding as "completely false" rumors that were spreading throughout the Internet that claimed that the U.S. government was planning to levy a surcharge on E-mail usage. The rumors claimed that a per-message fee would be collected and given to the Postal Service to cover the $230 million in revenue the Postal Service might lose because people would use E-mail to send correspondence instead of letters through the traditional mail. The cyber-rumors quoted a proposed five-cents-a-message fee and even cited "Congressman Schnell" as a supporter (no such Congressman exists).[110]

Nonetheless, the taxation of E-commerce is not just a future issue, but a present reality. The vociferous political debate over the future design of global tax systems in the information age often obscures the fact that there are many existing rules that are currently applied—appropriately or not—to the taxation of E-commerce transactions. Currently, governments at all levels apply income taxes to E-commerce sales. In Europe and Asia governments also impose value-added taxes on virtually all E-commerce transactions. Even at the state and local level in the United States, virtually all states impose sales and use taxes on tangible products purchased over the Internet, and a substantial minority of states even impose sales and use taxes on certain categories of digital goods and services.

As the Internet continues to expand across the global business landscape, there is likely to be significant confusion over how to interpret and comply with traditional rules that are being applied to the emerging Internet-age economy. This uncertainty arises primarily with regard to jurisdictional and allocation rules affecting indirect E-commerce, as well as substantive tax and sourcing rules affecting direct E-commerce. The situation is exacerbated because many governments are refraining from issuing interim rulings or customized guidance while they attempt to come up with solutions on a grander scale.

In the short term, it is likely that the United States will remain the primary focal point for discussions concerning how to reform existing tax systems to adapt to the new realities of the Internet age. This outcome is due to the collision between the relatively advanced Internet economy in this country and the inordinately complex state and local tax system applied to multijurisdictional transactions.

The chaotic tax landscape in the United States is reflected in the enormous range of proposals submitted to the federal Advisory Commission on Electronic Commerce as possible solutions for rationalizing the state and local sales and use tax system in the age of E-commerce. These proposals encompassed no tax solutions, expanded nexus solutions, technological solutions, sales tax simplification, and telecommunications reform.[111]

Several proposals were made for eliminating taxes on tangible products purchased over the Internet. For instance, both Ohio Republican representative John Kasich and Virginia governor James Gilmore submitted proposals that would prohibit all sales and use taxes on business-to-consumer Internet transactions. Republican presidential candidate John McCain has made a "no tax" on the Internet position one of the centerpieces of his campaign. These proposals would move beyond simply relying on jurisdictional constraints to imposing collection duties on remote vendors and would actually eliminate existing taxes on goods or services acquired through E-commerce.

Conversely, several other proposals called for Congress to enact legislation that would permit states and localities to impose a sales and use tax collection responsibility on remote vendors, even if the vendors had no physical presence in the market state. These proposals were supported not only by governmental groups but also by brick-and-mortar retail trade associations such as the North American Retail Dealers Association. Alternatively, Democratic senator Ernest F. Hollings has introduced Senate Bill 1433, which would impose a 5 percent federal excise tax on all Internet retail sales transactions and then use a revenue-sharing model to return the revenues to the states.

Other proposals called for far-reaching changes in the taxes imposed on telecommunications companies; a vast simplification of the administrative and procedural rules applied to sales and use tax compliance, a new zero-burden sales tax collection system that would transfer filing responsibilities to "trusted third parties" using sophisticated tax software technology and shifting the costs of compliance to government; and a proposal for a significant expansion in nexus safe harbors provided to remote E-commerce vendors.

The Slow March of Tax Reform

It is unclear how long it will take before substantive tax reform occurs in the United States and abroad in relation to the challenges posed by the growth of E-commerce. It is likely that nations in Europe will adopt new rules before the United States—given the more contentious level of debate over state and local taxation of the Internet in the United States. The lack of clarity in the United States is reflected in the coverage that the initial meeting of the Federal Advisory Commission on Electronic Commerce received in June 1999. Some newspaper headlines highlighted the inevitability of taxation: "Panel: E-Commerce Levy Inevitable," "Get Ready for Internet Sales Taxes," "Tax-Free Web Goods May Become Thing of the Past." Other headlines highlighted the large gulf between the business and government Commission members: "Internet Panel Deeply Divided," "The Net Tax Commission Hits the Ground Arguing." Indeed, Republican House of Representatives majority leader Dick Armey posted a message on his Web page in response to the mixed news coverage of the initial meeting. He asserted, "I have noticed several disturbing news articles that say, among other things, that 'Tax-free Web goods may disappear.' . . . Not so fast. Only Congress can authorize one state to compel sellers in another state to collect Net taxes. And the American people would never stand for it. . . . We should take steps to immediately place a permanent moratorium on Internet taxation."[112]

The early disagreements among participants in the Advisory Commission on Electronic Commerce process have continued as the number of proposals before the Commission proliferate. While it is difficult to predict the outcome in the political arena, it seems unlikely in the short-term that the U.S. Congress will adopt (either on its own or on the Commission's recommendation) either a sweeping "no-tax" proposal that would eliminate current taxes on tangible goods ordered over the Internet or a far-reaching "pro-tax" proposal that would quickly expand the states' authority to require remote vendors to collect sales and use taxes based on an economic presence standard. Certainly, in the year 2000, a presidential election year, it is unlikely that any significant legislation will be enacted by the U.S. Congress on Internet taxation.[113]

The political dynamic could change if a compromise is reached between state and local governments and certain business groups that are not necessarily opposed to an extension of the duty to collect sales and use taxes (bricks and mortar retailers, telecommunications companies, and other entities that currently have to collect sales and use taxes because of extensive physical presence in some or all jurisdictions). The compromise could be shaped along the lines previously discussed: a radical simplification of sales and use tax rules and tax rates and other pro-business changes in exchange for the authority to require remote vendors (without physical presence) to collect sales and use tax.

Alternatively, different proposals could be packaged together so that —depending on the prevailing political environment—the result ended up tilted more heavily toward either business or state government positions. For instance, a business caucus within the Advisory Commission on Electronic Commerce issued a proposal in February, 2000 that would result in legislation more favorable to business interests. Under this proposal, the current Internet Tax Freedom Act moratorium would be extended for five years. During that period, the sales tax on both digitized goods and their non-digitized counterparts (books, music, etc.) would be prohibited. In addition, nexus safe harbors would be extended for both sales and use and income taxes for various market state activities; the sales tax on Internet access and the federal excise tax on communication services would be eliminated; disproportionate tax burdens on telecommunications companies would be modified; and state and local governments would be encouraged to draft and adopt a model Uniformity Act that radically simplified sales and use tax rules (both substantive and procedural). Toward the end of this period, a Congressional commission would be required to make a recommendation on the viability and desirability of extending the duty to collect sales and use taxes to remote vendors without physical presence in the market states.[114]

Even if the U.S. Congress does not enact any sweeping measures in the near future, it is likely that pressure will build for some solution as Internet sales increase and existing tax rules result in increased tax litigation, inconsistent treatment of tangible goods and digital products, and significant compliance burdens on businesses in the New Economy. An endorsement for a political compromise by the ACEC or a similar government-business group, however, would only begin the tax reform process. Any radical revamping of state and local jurisdictional and sales and use tax rules would likely require both Congressional approval and far-reaching state legislation—action steps that are almost certain to slow the process down. Moreover, any approach with a long-term phase-in would be open to Congressional modification or repeal during the intervening years, resulting in a cloud of uncertainty over the final outcome.

Thus, it is likely for the next few years (and perhaps longer) that E-commerce vendors will have to cope with a tax environment that lacks sufficient guidance on many of the critical issues of the Internet age. This will be evident across national and international borders, as well as among different tax types. There is likely to be considerable uncertainty over the application of jurisdictional issues, the determination of what is taxable and what is exempt, and the sourcing of income and transactions among states and nations.

Moreover, in the short term, the problem of dealing with the taxation of E-commerce will be exacerbated by quite different approaches taken by different levels of government and within different tax types. For instance, under state income tax rules and VAT rules, electronically delivered products such as software are generally treated as the sale of services or intangibles. Conversely, under federal income tax rules, electronically transmitted software is generally treated in the same manner as tangible goods. Finally, under state sales and use tax rules, the jurisdictions are split, with some states treating digital products as electronic services and other states treating them under the rules that apply to tangible personal property.

Similarly, with regard to the sourcing of digital products and services, there is a large variation among different tax systems. Under state sales and use tax rules, sales of digital products are generally sourced to the state of the consumer. Conversely, under federal income tax rules, sales of digital products are generally sourced to the state of the vendor (based on residency or income-producing activity). Finally, with value-added taxes and state income taxes, both market-state and vendor-state rules are used—depending on the industry type or the particular jurisdiction.

The emergence of the information age will have a profound impact on both global commerce and multijurisdictional taxation. The Internet—by transforming the business model for most of the world's industries—is compelling government to play catch-up with regulatory models or risk being dangerously out of sync. Unless governments revise tax statutes and regulations to address the unique challenges and problems created by E-commerce, the global tax systems may become hopelessly outdated—resulting in confusion, inconsistency, and even retarded economic growth.

2

Sales and Use Taxation of E-Commerce

The Primacy of State Sales and Use Taxes

Of all the global tax issues related to E-commerce, none has received more attention than sales and use tax issues in the United States. As discussed in chapter 1, the federal government–level Internet Tax Freedom Act, the federal Advisory Commission on Electronic Commerce, and the National Taxpayer's Association Communications and Electronic Commerce Tax Project have all focused primarily or exclusively on sales and use taxes (and related jurisdictional issues). While there has been a growing interest in the United States and in other OECD nations in federal and international income taxation issues and value-added tax issues, such focus has generally lagged behind consideration of sales and use taxes. Furthermore, much of the discussion of these other tax types has been framed in reference to the concepts under discussion in connection with sales and use taxes.

In the United States, the discussion of the taxation of E-commerce has been centered on state sales and use taxes for a variety of reasons. First, the United States has no national-level sales tax or other type of consumption tax. Among the OECD nations, only the United States has neither a national-level value-added tax nor a national-level sales tax. Only the state and local governments in this country have broad-based sales taxes. The federal government has sales tax–like excises on only a few goods and services, such as telecommunications and gasoline.

Second, transaction taxes such as the sales and use tax tend to be more complicated to administer than income taxes in relation to E-commerce business activities. Although both tax types raise difficult issues, transaction taxes generally require the collection of information on transactions for purposes of the payment of taxes on a monthly basis. By contrast, income taxes require the collection of information for purposes of an annual tax-filing requirement. In a world of instantaneous, intangible, and global transactions, compliance with transactional taxes places a more onerous burden on businesses involved with E-commerce. Moreover, transaction taxes are calculated on the basis of *gross* sales receipts, as compared with income taxes that are calculated on the basis of *net* income. Thus, for many start-up Internet companies that have not yet become profitable, transaction taxes are the only taxes that the companies have to concern themselves with.

Third, compared to other advanced industrialized nations, the sales tax in the United States is complicated by the large number of state, county, and local jurisdictions that impose sales and use taxes. Currently, 45 states and the District of Columbia impose sales or use taxes at the state level. Only five states do not impose a state sales and use tax: Alaska, Delaware, Montana, New Hampshire, and Oregon. In addition to the states, approximately 7,500 counties, cities, towns, transportation districts, and other special local jurisdictions impose sales or use taxes on transactions occurring within their borders.[1]

While the vast majority of localities follow state tax rules on what is taxable and how the tax is administered, a minority of jurisdictions require separate tax-return filings under their own unique set of rules. Moreover, even those local jurisdictions that follow state tax rules require vendors to collect information on the destination of the goods and services for purposes of compliance with the varying local tax rates. By contrast, in the European Union, there are only 15 countries and generally only 15 different national value-added tax rates. There are no local or county tax value-added tax rules or rates to be complied with.

Fourth, at the state level, the sales and use tax is the most important tax category in terms of revenue generation. In 1997, for example, state and local sales and use tax collections totaled approximately $170 billion.

State-level sales and use taxes are the single-largest overall source of state tax revenue, accounting for one-third of all state taxes. If special sales taxes on gasoline, liquor, and cigarettes are included, sales taxes account for nearly one-half of all state tax revenue. In 29 states, general sales and use tax collections (not including the special sales taxes) exceed personal income tax collections—the second-largest source of state tax revenue. By contrast, state corporate income taxes account for less than one-tenth of all state taxes.[2] (See figure 2.1.)

The Differences in State Sales Tax Bases

The complexity of sales and use taxation of E-commerce is caused not only by the multiplicity of jurisdictions and tax rates but even more so by the differences in tax bases among the jurisdictions. Historically, state governments have had virtually complete autonomy in determining what goods and services are subject to sales and use tax within their borders. The tradition of American federalism and states' rights dating back to the adoption of the U.S. Constitution has afforded each state the freedom of choice to determine tax rates and tax bases and to establish the propor-

Figure 2.1. **State Sales Tax Burden**

Source: U.S. Bureau of the Census, *Government Finances* (1996).

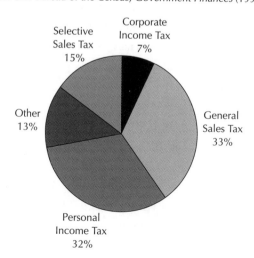

tional burden of different tax types, including sales and use tax, corporate income tax, personal income tax, property tax, and other levies.

To that end, a slight majority of states have relied more heavily on sales and use taxes than on other tax categories for state-revenue generation. Among the 46 jurisdictions (including the District of Columbia) with state-level sales and use taxes, the average of state tax revenues derived from the general sales tax is about 36 percent.[3] There are, however, large differences between the states with regard to reliance on sales and use taxes. These variations are caused by differences in state tax rates (ranging from 3 to 7 percent) and state tax bases.

Reliance on sales taxes is particularly high in the southwest states (Arizona, New Mexico, Oklahoma, and Texas), which average 43.6 percent reliance on sales tax, and in the far-western states (California, Hawaii, Nevada, and Washington), which average 43.5 percent reliance on sales tax. Conversely, reliance on sales taxes is lower than the norm in the middle-eastern states (Maryland, New Jersey, New York, Pennsylvania, and the District of Columbia), which average 26.3 percent reliance on sales tax, and in the New England states, which average 30.8 percent reliance on sales tax.[4]

In terms of tax base, there is an enormous variation in the range of goods and services taxed by different states. To be sure, there is uniformity in the sales tax base for certain goods and services. For instance, virtually all states impose sales and use taxes on most manufactured goods. Similarly, the vast majority of states do not impose sales and use taxes on prescription drugs, professional services, or financial services. However, with regard to a number of categories of goods and services such as food, clothing, and personal and business services,—there is a wide variety of state tax rules.

One measure of the breadth of a state's sales tax is the sales tax base measured as a percentage of total state personal income. The national average sales tax base is 48.8 percent of state personal income. States range from a high sales tax base of 106.9 percent in Hawaii to a low sales tax base of 27.6 percent in Rhode Island. Those regions with a higher-than-average sales tax base include the southwest states (Arizona, New Mexico, Oklahoma, and Texas), averaging 59.3 percent of state personal income, and the far western states (California, Hawaii, Nevada, and Washington), averaging 64.6 percent of state personal income. Conversely, those regions with a lower-than-average sales tax base include the mideastern states (Maryland, New Jersey, New York, Pennsylvania, and the District of Columbia), averaging 36 percent of state personal income, and the New England states, averaging 36.6 percent of state personal income.[5]

One major reflection of the breadth of state sales tax bases is the variation among states in the number of service categories taxed. Although virtually all states impose sales and use taxes on a broad range of tangible property transactions, there is much-greater disparity among states in the extent to which services are subject to tax. Most states impose a sales tax on certain personal, business, repair, and amusement services. However, some states tax a much-broader range of services. Hawaii, for example, taxes 157 different enumerated services; New Mexico taxes 152 different services; South Dakota taxes 141 different services; and New York taxes 74 different services. In contrast, California taxes only 18 different services, and Illinois taxes only 17 different services.[6] (See table 2.1.)

Table 2.1.   **State Sales Tax Base: Taxable-Service Categories**

	State	**Number of Taxable Services**
Broad Sales	Hawaii	157
Tax Base	Washington	154
	New Mexico	152
	South Dakota	141
	West Virginia	110
	Iowa	94
	Connecticut	87
	Texas	78
	Kansas	76
	New York	74
	Tennessee	71
	Mississippi	70
Medium Sales	Wisconsin	69
Tax Base	Arkansas	65

	State	Number of Taxable Services
Medium Sales Tax Base	Florida	64
	District of Columbia	63
	Wyoming	63
	Minnesota	61
	Pennsylvania	61
	Louisiana	60
	Arizona	57
	Utah	54
	Ohio	52
	New Jersey	50
	Nebraska	49
	Maryland	39
	Georgia	34
	Alabama	32
	Oklahoma	32
	South Carolina	32
Narrow Sales Tax Base	Idaho	29
	Michigan	29
	Missouri	28
	North Carolina	28
	Rhode Island	28
	Maine	27
	Kentucky	26
	North Dakota	25
	Vermont	23
	Indiana	22
	Massachusetts	20
	Montana	19
	California	18
	Virginia	18
	Illinois	17
	Colorado	14
	Nevada	11
	New Hampshire	11
	Alaska	1
	Oregon	0

Source: Federation of Tax Administrators, *Sales Taxation of Services: An Update.*

To a large degree, the current status of the sales taxation of E-commerce (particularly goods and services delivered by digital or other electronic means) coincides with the sales taxation of services. For the most part, the states that have traditionally taxed more categories of services are also the states that are currently taxing digital commerce. Those states are more likely to impose sales and use tax on telecommunications services, cable television services, electronic information services, data-processing services, and other categories that involve E-commerce.

Moreover, the vast majority of states impose sales and use tax only on those service categories that are specifically enumerated by statute. In contrast to the sales taxation of tangible personal property—whereby all goods are subject to tax with enumerated exceptions—services are typically taxed only if they are specifically listed in the statute. This method of determining the categories of taxable services by "inclusion" rather than "exclusion" adds to the confusion and lack of uniformity surrounding the sales taxation of E-commerce. In many states there is controversy over whether categories such as "telecommunications services" or "information services" apply to a range of digital or Internet-related services.

The sections that follow discuss the various sales and use tax issues related to the taxation of E-commerce. In particular, this chapter focuses on the following issues: (1) tax base issues related to telecommunications and other related transmission activities, (2) tax base issues related to various types of digital content, (3) tax base issues related to bundled services and input exemptions, (4) sourcing rules for digital services, and (5) sales tax simplification issues and initiatives.

In examining these issues, this chapter considers primarily the sales of goods and services that lend themselves to electronic delivery because these categories raise the most significant Internet-related sales tax issues. The chapter does, however, also discuss issues related to tangible property delivered by conventional means, particularly in relation to business input exemptions, parity issues between tangible goods and digital products, the bundling of tangible goods and electronic services, and sales and use tax simplification initiatives.

The Impact of the Internet Tax Freedom Act

Before analyzing the current status of state sales taxation of E-commerce–related business activity, it is necessary to consider the impact of the passage of the Internet Tax Freedom Act.[7] This federal legislation was passed in October, 1998, about one-and-a-half years after its introduction into Congress. Given the name of the legislation, it has been assumed by many affected parties that the legislation precludes any taxation of Internet-related businesses, at least for the duration of the bill's three-year moratorium. Actually, the legislation's impact is much narrower, basically limiting taxation of Internet access services, but not other categories of E-commerce. The final version of the Internet Tax Freedom Act varied significantly from the original version introduced by Senator Wyden and Representative Cox in March 1997. The original legislation imposed a broad restriction on "any tax" imposed "directly or indirectly" on the "Internet or interactive computer services."[8]

The Internet Tax Freedom Act applies to state and local sales and use taxes for the period beginning on October 1, 1998, and ending three years later. First, the act prohibits the imposition of any new state or local sales or use taxes on Internet access during this period. Under the legislation, Internet access is defined as "a service that enables users to access content, information, electronic mail, or other services offered over the Internet, and may also include access to proprietary content, information, and other services as part of a package of services offered to users. Such term does not include telecommunications services."[9] This moratorium would apply to any new or preexisting tax—except that the legislation has a grandfather clause that permits a sales or use tax on Internet access if the tax was generally imposed and actually enforced prior to October 1, 1998. Thus, under the Internet Tax Freedom Act, states are prohibited for the three-year period from imposing a new sales or use tax on Internet access or on on-line services such as America Online that are offered in conjunction with Internet access services.

The legislation does not, however, prohibit the imposition of new or preexisting sales or use taxes on other forms of E-commerce such as electronically delivered software, information, music, or other products sold as end products to ultimate customers. The legislation does not prohibit imposition of new or existing sales or use tax on business inputs such as services or equipment used by E-commerce businesses in producing their final outputs. In addition, it does not prohibit the imposition of new or preexisting sales or use taxes on products or services that are ordered over the Internet but delivered by means of conventional physical delivery (as long as existing jurisdictional requirements are satisfied). Under the new federal statute, the only protection afforded to businesses is that multiple or discriminatory taxes on E-commerce are prohibited.[10]

Discriminatory taxes generally encompass taxes that are applied only to E-commerce, not to similarly situated goods or services that are not ordered and/or delivered electronically. Thus, a state could not impose a sales or use tax on the sale of canned software that is delivered by electronic means without imposing a similar tax (at an identical rate) on the sale of canned software that is delivered by conventional physical means. Similarly, a state could not impose a sales or use tax collection responsibility on a vendor that takes orders for products or services over the Internet without imposing a similar tax (at an identical rate) on a vendor that takes order for products or services by mail order.

Taxation of Telecommunication Services

Sales or Use Tax on Transmission Activities

Although there is not yet widespread or uniform sales taxation of the information content that traverses the Internet, there is extensive sales taxation of the transport or transmission channels. Telecommunication services, whether by fixed-location phone or cellular phone, copper wire, cable, or satellite transmission, are subject to sales and use tax in the vast majority of jurisdictions. Similarly, telecommunications services, whether for basic residential service, basic business service, switching services (PBX, Centrex), or private-line services, are subject to sales and use tax in most jurisdictions.

Currently, telecommunication services are the largest source of revenue from E-commerce. As discussed in chapter 1, telecommunication services total nearly $200 billion in the United States and $700 billion worldwide. These totals include both wired and wireless transmissions. Wireless transmissions are taking an increasingly large share of the pie, predicted to reach over one-quarter of all transmissions within five years.

The vast majority of U.S. states impose a sales or use tax on telecommunications services that originate and terminate within a state's borders. Four-fifths of the states impose a sales or use tax on intrastate telecommunications. These states tax both local services and intrastate long-distance services. In addition, two-fifths of the states impose a sales or use tax on interstate telecommunications. These states tax both transmissions within the United States and transmissions that originate in the United States and terminate in some other country.

As a general rule, states that impose a sales or use tax on telecommunications services impose a tax for charges for *transport* of voice or information, not any separately stated charges for *information content* itself. For instance, in Massachusetts the sales and use tax is applied to "telecommunication services," defined as "any *transmission* of messages or information by electronic or similar means, between or among points by wire, cable, fiber optics, laser, microwave, radio, satellite, or similar facilities."[11]

Some states have special exemptions for certain types of "basic transmissions." For instance, a number of jurisdictions, including Michigan, Kansas, Ohio, and Oklahoma exempt interstate WATS or 800 services and private telecommunication services. Other jurisdictions, such as Massachusetts, exempt telecommunications services provided to residents. In general, most states impose a sales or use tax on services that are ancillary to telecommunications services, such as call forwarding, call waiting, call trace, caller ID, or voice mail.[12]

Enhanced Services

Although it is clear that local telephone calls, cellular communications, and most paging services constitute transmissions, it is less apparent whether certain additional or enhanced services constitute taxable telecommunications services. These include services such as Internet access, E-mail, electronic bulletin boards, facsimile services, packet switching, and ATM transactions. These services are similar to traditional telephone transmissions that connect two or more parties, but they generally involve some additional linkage or value added, such as temporary storage of messages on a computer server or a change in the protocol of the transmitted information. These services typically involve the transmission of data as compared to the transmission of voice. Given the novelty of some of these services, many states have not yet issued any clear positions on whether such value-added services will be subject to tax as telecommunications services. In these states businesses are left to speculate on the range of transmission activities included within the definition of telecommunications.

Narrow Definition

Many states have adopted a *narrow* definition of telecommunication services that excludes most enhanced services. Some states adhere to old federal regulatory distinctions between "basic" telecommunications services and "enhanced" telecommunications services. The Multistate Tax Commission (MTC) also used this dichotomy in its telecommunications regulation. Under these guidelines a "basic" transmission service such as a local or long-distance telephone call is a transmission between or among points without change in the form or content of the information sent and received. These basic services are essentially a pure transmission capability over a communications path that is virtually transparent in terms of its interaction with customer-supplied information. By contrast, an "enhanced service" is any service offered over a telecommunications network that (1) employs computer-processing applications that act on the format, content, code, protocol, or similar aspects of the subscriber's transmitted information; (2) provides the subscriber additional, different, or restructured information; or (3) involves subscriber interaction with stored information.[13]

States that adopt this approach for telecommunications services impose a sales or use tax on basic transmission services but not on enhanced or value-added services. For instance, Indiana, Illinois, and Kansas all have nearly identical exemptions from the sales or transactional tax on telecommunications, exempting "value-added services in which computer processing applications are used to act on the form, content, code, or protocol of the information for purposes other than transmission."[14]

Broad Definition

Other states use a broader definition of telecommunications services that encompasses certain value-added services as well as basic transmission services. For instance, the Tennessee Department of Revenue treats Internet access services as telecommunications services that are subject to sales tax. Under Tennessee law telecommunications is defined to mean "communication by electric or electronic transmission of impulses." Under this definition Tennessee ruled that Internet access clearly involves the "transmission of electronic messages across telephone lines." Tennessee chose not to make any distinctions based on computer processing or other protocol conversion.[15]

Similarly, Iowa (until a 1999 legislative change) used a broad definition of communications services that taxed such value-added services as Internet access and "packet switching." In this activity a telecommunications company does not create information but instead manipulates data received electronically from customers by converting it into "packets" and sending them at intervals, and by different routes, to their ultimate destinations. The packet-switching technology enhances the reliability and security of the electronic-data transmission.[16]

Other states tax some enhanced services such as telecommunication services while exempting other such services. For instance, South Carolina includes database access and E-mail within its definition of communications under the sales tax. However, it does not tax Internet access services. Massachusetts taxes facsimile services such as telecommunications services, but not other datalike services such as Internet access, E-mail, or computer on-line services.[17]

Internet Access Services

By far, the largest dispute over the breadth of sales and use taxes on telecommunication services has erupted over whether Internet access services should be subject to sales or use taxes (see table 2.2). Internet

Table 2.2. **Sales Taxation of Telecommunication, Internet Access, and Cable Television Services (Selected States)**

MAY 1999

State	Sales Tax on Intrastate Telecommunications	Sales Tax on Interstate Telecommunications	Sales Tax on Internet Access	Sales Tax on Cable-Television Services
California	No	No	No	No
Florida	Yes	Yes	No	Yes
Hawaii	No	Yes	Yes	Yes
Maryland	No	No	No	Yes
Massachusetts	Yes	Yes	No	No
Michigan	Yes	Yes	No	No
Missouri	Yes	No	No	No
New York	Yes	No	No	No
North Dakota	Yes	No	Yes	No
Ohio	Yes	Yes	Yes	No
Virginia	No	No	No	No
Wisconsin	Yes	Yes	Yes	Yes

access services are one of the fastest-growing segments of E-commerce and are projected to grow fourfold over the next four years. As of December 1999, eight states imposed a sales or use tax on Internet access services: Connecticut, Hawaii, North Dakota, Ohio, South Dakota, Tennessee, Texas (above $25), and Wisconsin.

Internet access is a service provided by several thousand companies that enables a customer to connect to Internet Web sites or to send mail or other data by means of the Internet. A traditional telephone call is facilitated by a circuit switch that keeps a line open between two points for a continuous voice transmission. By contrast, Internet access is enabled by a packet-switching technology that allows communication for a consumer using the TCP/IP—a communication protocol that enables messages broken up into packets and assigned Internet addresses to travel over the Internet. This technology allows communication between parties or Web sites, regardless of differences in hardware or software.

The transport service provided by Internet access providers to customers varies. Some provide no transmission services, relying on purchasing leased lines from other telecommunication providers or larger Internet service providers. Some Internet access providers have their own network of fiber-optic cables and merely contract with other telecommunications providers for access to the main Internet pipelines. Some Internet access providers such as cable companies provide transport services directly to the home or office. However, most Internet access providers rely on nonbusiness customers accessing a "point of presence"—a computer server owned or leased by the Internet access provider—through traditional local telephone service. Similarly, business customers frequently lease a private line from their offices to a local telecommunications carrier. Then they connect with the Internet access provider's server either through a private line leased by the customer or a private line that the Internet vendor leases from the telecommunications carrier.[18]

One indication of the confusion surrounding the imposition of sales or use taxes on Internet access services is the number of states that use different categories to tax this type of service. Several states, including North Dakota, Iowa (until 1999), and Tennessee, tax Internet access services as a communications or telecommunications service. On the other hand, other states tax Internet access services under some other category of taxable service such as a computer or data-processing service or an information service. For instance, Connecticut taxes Internet access charges as a computer or data-processing service. Texas taxed Internet access as an information service until it changed its law to exempt the first $25 per month of Internet.[19]

Some states have changed their positions not on the taxability of Internet access services but on what constitutes the appropriate taxable category of service. For instance, Texas initially imposed a sales or use tax on Internet access services under the category of "telecommunications services." However, it later reversed its position and imposed the tax on Internet access services under the category of "information services."[20]

Another indication of the difficulty states are having in determining whether the sales or use tax on telecommunications services applies to Internet access services is the large number of states that have reversed their positions on the taxation of this service category. Among the states that have made statutory changes or issued public written statements specifying that the sales or use tax on telecommunication services does not apply to Internet access services are Massachusetts, Florida, Missouri, the District of Columbia, Pennsylvania, and Iowa.

In Florida, for example, the Department of Revenue determined in 1995 that enhanced services such as E-mail and Internet access were taxable as telecommunications services under existing Florida sales tax law. The governor of Florida, however, established a commission to study the issue and delayed the effective date of taxation of such services until July 1, 1997. The Florida legislature subsequently enacted a statute that made the exemption of Internet access services, E-mail, computer-exchange services, and related on-line services permanent.[21]

Similarly, in Massachusetts the Department of Revenue announced informally in 1996 that Internet access services would be subject to the sales or use tax on telecommunications services. Subsequently, in 1997 it issued a technical information release declaring that there would be a moratorium on the enforcement of the tax on Internet access services. Finally, in mid 1997, the Massachusetts legislature enacted legislation that exempted Internet access services from the sales or use tax on telecommunications services—retroactive to September 1, 1990.[22]

The Department of Revenue in Missouri determined in a 1996 letter ruling that Internet access services were taxable as telecommunication services. However, without an intervening statutory change, it reversed course and stated in a 1997 letter ruling that such services were not subject to the sales and use tax. In Pennsylvania legislation was enacted in 1997 that repealed the sales tax on computer services—the category under which Internet access services had been taxed.[23]

Finally, a number of additional states that never specifically taxed Internet access services as a telecommunications service or some other taxable service category have enacted legislation or made policy pronouncements that such services are not taxable in their jurisdiction. For instance, California enacted the California Internet Tax Freedom Act to prohibit any new sales or use taxes on Internet services. Other states such as Washington clarified that Internet access services are not taxable under their sales tax statutes. The Washington legislation also prohibited any cities or towns from imposing sales or use taxes on Internet access—in response to legislation passed and then rescinded in one city that would have taxed Internet access only at the local level. New York recently clarified that Internet access services are neither a taxable telecommunications service nor a taxable information service. Similar legislative or regulatory actions occurred in Virginia.[24]

It is unlikely that any other single sales and use tax issue has garnered as much legislative and regulatory attention in recent years as the taxation of Internet access services. Moreover, as previously discussed, the U.S. Congress has also intervened in this arena—passing a three-year moratorium in 1998 on the imposition of any state or local sales or use taxes on Internet access. This moratorium would apply to any new or preexisting tax—except that the legislation has a grandfather clause that permits a sales or use tax on Internet access if the tax was generally imposed and actually enforced prior to October 1, 1998.

Internet Telephony

The recent emergence of Internet telephony has further muddied the definition of taxable telecommunication services. Internet telephony refers to voice transmissions that occur either in whole or in part by using packet switching rather than circuit switching in transporting the communication. The same technology that is used to break data up into packets and send the packets through the Internet can also be used to convert voice calls into packets that are shipped through the Internet and then reassembled at the call's termination point.

At first, such technology was limited because it could only be used in connection with voice traffic sent from a computer (with voice capabilities) to another similar computer. With technological advances, however, there is now widely available software that facilitates the use of Internet protocol for traditional voice calls between two parties using regular telephones. Indeed, this revolutionary technology is so attractive that it is estimated that Internet telephony will grow from $500 million in worldwide revenues in 1999 to $18 billion in 2004. Other studies suggest that 13 percent of all voice traffic will be conducted over the Internet or other data networks within four years.[25]

As discussed in chapter 1, Internet telephony has significant price advantages over traditional circuit-switching telephone networks. Although the voice quality is currently not as good for Internet telephone calls as for traditional analog telephone calls, the price differential and the rapid improvements in voice quality will ensure that Internet telephony gains a significant market share over the next decade.

As Internet telephony expands, state revenue departments and taxpayers will have to contend with the consequences for sales and use taxation. The issue of whether Internet telephony should be treated as taxable telecommunication services will be particularly acute among the four-fifths of the jurisdictions that currently do not tax Internet access.

In all likelihood, many jurisdictions will tax Internet telephony even if they do not tax Internet access services. The rationale for this approach is likely to be that it would be discriminatory and somewhat illogical to tax voice traffic that flows over traditional circuit-switching technology but then exempt the same transactions simply because packet-switching technology is used. As noted by the Federal Communications Commission (FCC) chairman William E. Kennard in 1998, "If you look at the characteristics of I.P. telephony and compare them to the characteristics of a traditional long-distance telephone call, functionally they are the same."[26]

Indeed, under certain definitions of Internet access, it would appear that Internet telephony could be treated in a different category. For instance, under the Internet Tax Freedom Act, "Internet Access" is defined as "a service that enables users to access content, information, electronic mail, or other services offered over the Internet, and may also include access to proprietary content, information, and other services as part of a package of services offered to users. Such term does not include telecommunications services."[27] Thus, under this act it would appear that if a consumer uses the Internet for voice communications, and not to access data or other information, then the transaction would not be subject to the three-year moratorium established by Congress.

In Pennsylvania the exemption from sales or use taxes for Internet access clearly does not encompass Internet telephony. In that state the statute clarifies that nontaxable Internet access does not include "the transport over the Internet or any proprietary network using the Internet protocol of telephone calls, facsimile transmissions or other telecommunications traffic to or from end users on the public switched network, if the signal sent from or received by an end user is not in an Internet protocol." Similarly, the definition of telecommunication services in Illinois would seemingly include Internet telephony, but not Internet access, as a taxable service. The Illinois definition exempts "value-added services in which computer processing applications are used to act on the form, content, code, or protocol of the information for purposes other than *transmission* [emphasis added]."[28]

On the other hand, certain definitions of Internet access focus almost entirely on whether the computer services are used that act on the "format, content, code, protocol or similar aspects of the purchaser's transmitted information." Under such a definition, Internet telephony may very well be exempt because it does involve computer processing (through packet switching) that acts on the format or protocol of the transmitted information.

Although the issue is raised most starkly with Internet telephony, there is also a categorization problem with other uses of Internet protocol or similar computer protocols for purposes other than accessing the Web. For instance, Internet protocol is frequently used for data and other nonvoice communication on a corporate intranet. A corporate intranet is a closed private network that links a number of corporate offices and/or corporate customers without using the public Internet. Companies typically conduct business such as information transfer, billing, inventory control, and so on, over such intranets using Internet protocol or some similar computer protocol to facilitate communications. Few states have issued any rulings interpreting whether vendors that provide such networks are selling taxable telecommunications services or some other nontaxable services.

The use of Internet protocol for data transfer or voice transmissions over VPNs is likely to expand rapidly. Virtual private networks typically combine the Internet's openness and low price with the higher performance, security, encryption, firewall, and authentication of private networks. The use of private networks will allow vendors to assert more control over routing and the quality of calls or other transmissions. Vendors will be able to use private networks as premium outlets for certain customers, charging a higher price in exchange for guaranteed and priority service. A number of telecommunications companies such as AT&T are making multibillion investments in ATM, frame relay, and other packet-switching networks to reduce their dependence on traditional circuit-switching networks.

The Slippery Slope

The determination of which services should be treated as taxable telecommunications services and which services should be treated as nontaxable enhanced services will continue to be a vexing one. The states are likely to attempt to use a variety of boundaries to differentiate between categories—with varying results.

For instance, some jurisdictions may try to draw a distinction between taxable voice and exempt nonvoice or data communications. To some extent, this might appear to divide services rationally based on the type of activity involved. However, this distinction would encounter problems because a significant share of currently taxable telecommunications services involves nonvoice facsimile services over regular phone lines or corporate data communications over private leased lines. Facsimile services, for example, currently account for about 8 percent of U.S. long-distance traffic and about 40 percent of international phone traffic originating in the United States.[29] Moreover, it may not be possible to distinguish between taxable voice Internet telephony and nontaxable nonvoice Internet access services when these services are provided to customers on a bundled basis.

Other states may try to draw a distinction between traditional circuit-switched telecommunications and new packet-switched telecommunications. This method of categorization would rely on dividing services based on the type of technology used in delivering the services. However, this dichotomy again breaks down because voice telephony would be taxed if it were transmitted over analog (or digital) circuit-switched lines, but not taxed if it were transmitted over digitized packet-switched lines. Similarly, certain types of information and data transmission would be taxed if delivered over dedicated high-capacity-transmission phone lines, but not over the public Internet network.

Other jurisdictions may try to draw a line between transport-related services and content-related services. This method of categorization may seem to divide services logically between the means used and the ends achieved. Ironically, even if a state includes most enhanced services within the definition of telecommunications services, it still may have to make some arbitrary distinctions between taxable *transmission* activities and typically nontaxable *information-content* services. For instance, a state could attempt to tax E-mail, computer bulletin boards, ATM transactions, and other value-added services as telecommunications services where the vendor was not actually supplying the information but rather was acting as a utility, connecting different customers or customers and third-party information vendors. This approach, however, would entail making a questionable distinction between a vendor who allowed a customer to connect directly with USA Today to purchase an electronic newspaper (a "utility") and one that resold the electronic newspaper that was downloaded onto the vendor's own computer (an "information provider"). Similarly, providing access to computer bulletin boards can involve solely connecting paying consumers (a utility-like activity) or supplying information to liven up the discussions (an information-provider–like function).

The boundary lines between taxable telecommunications and nontaxable enhanced services will be blurred even further as these services are increasingly performed by companies that offer one-stop, one-price shopping for a range of services. In the brave new world of telecommunications, both telephone companies and cable companies are beginning to offer bundled services that include telephone service, Internet access service, and cable television service. The intermingling of these services, frequently for one fixed price, will exacerbate the problems created by a statutory and regulatory slippery slope. (See discussion later in this chapter under "One Stop Shopping: The Bundling of Services.")

In addition, states that attempt to tax a hodgepodge of activities may also have a difficult time drawing the line between taxable and nontaxable value-added services. If offering E-mail is considered a taxable transmission activity, what about providing access to computer bulletin boards, which are largely a multiple-user E-mail–type arrangement? For example, New York has ruled that facsimile services are taxable telecommunications services and that bulletin-board services are taxable information services, but that Internet access services and customized message services offered by means of E-mail, fax, telex, packet switching, and hard-copy document delivery are nontaxable services.[30]

Finally, there are special problems for the two-fifths of states that impose a sales tax only on *intrastate* telecommunications, not on interstate telecommunications. Although it is clear that local or regional phone calls qualify as intrastate telecommunications, it is less clear whether E-mail or Internet access charges are within that definition. By their nature, such transactions can involve either intrastate or interstate communications. Nonetheless, certain states, such as North Dakota, that only tax intrastate telecommunication service still tax Internet access as a telecommunication service.[31]

The Taxation of Digital Commerce

Although telecommunications service is the largest category of the digital economy that is generally subject to sales and use tax, it is by no means the only category included within state and local sales tax bases. There is a large variation among states in the extent to which digital commerce is subject to sales and use taxes. These differences in tax incidence are generally attributable to significant differences in the breadth of sales tax bases, particularly with regard to the taxation of services. Overall, approximately three-fifths of the states tax canned software transmitted electronically, one-half tax cable television services, two-fifths tax 900-number services, one-quarter tax information services transmitted electronically, one-fifth tax custom software transferred electronically, and about one-seventh tax computer services. By contrast, 90 percent of all jurisdictions

(46 of 51 jurisdictions) tax similar transactions such as the sale of information or canned software when they are delivered by tangible medium (such as books, CD-ROMs, etc).[32] (See figure 2.2.)

Among the larger jurisdictions that tax a broad range of digital products and services are Connecticut, New York, Ohio, and Texas. Among the smaller jurisdictions that tax a broad range of digital products and services are Hawaii, the District of Columbia, New Mexico, and South Dakota. Most of these states tax all or most of the following digital goods and services: data processing, E-mail, computer bulletin boards, news and weather reports, credit reports, airline reservations, games, legal and medical databases, 900-number service, cable television, software downloads, and fax services.

Conversely, there are a number of jurisdictions that do not tax any digital goods and services. These states include Massachusetts, California,

Figure 2.2. **Taxation of Digital Products and Services**

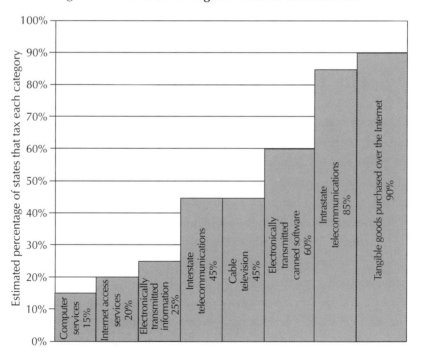

Georgia, Maryland, Michigan, and Missouri. In general, the states that currently do not impose sales taxes on any electronic services are those with narrower sales tax bases that include most tangible personal property transactions but few enumerated service categories. For instance, New Jersey has determined that information transferred electronically is not subject to sales tax because there is no tangible property involved in the transaction. Other states, such as California, that have issued regulations or rulings on this issue have also generally relied on the fact that the content that is transferred electronically is nontaxable intangible property, not taxable tangible property.

States vary as to whether they tax digital goods and services as an extension of sales tax imposed on tangible personal property or as a separate category of taxable services. The states also differ as to whether they tax all or just some subcategories of digital content. The particular state approach may be crucial for interpreting ambiguities or challenging possible overreaching of state tax rules.

Cable Television Services

One of the most commonly taxed categories of E-commerce content is cable television services. Historically, cable television services have been subjected to close government regulation, similar to the special treatment accorded to local and interstate telecommunications services. Cable television services were one of the first categories of electronically transmitted content to be taxed by numerous states. About half of the states currently tax cable television services.

Most states tax both basic service and premium-television services. For instance, Minnesota imposes a sales or use tax on all cable television charges, including "basic service, charges for premium service, and any other charges for any other pay-per-view, monthly, or similar television services." A few states such as Tennessee and Maryland, however, impose the sales and use tax only on premium services. For instance, Tennessee imposes the sales tax only on charges for cable television services in excess of the basic rate charge by the supplier. Thus, in that state only charges for premium or pay-per-view channels are subject to tax.[33]

Virtually all of the states that tax cable television impose the sales tax on all types of subscription television, whether it is transmitted via cable or satellite services. For instance, Rhode Island imposes a sales tax on "the furnishing of service for transmission of messages by telegraph, cable, or radio and the furnishing of community antenna television, subscription television, and cable television services." Similarly, Wisconsin imposes a sales tax on cable television system services, which are defined as "any facility which, for a fee, regularly amplifies and transmits wire, coaxial cable, lightwave, or microwave, simultaneously to 50 or more subscribers, programs broadcast by television or radio stations, or originated by themselves or any other party."[34]

A small minority of states have not yet updated their statutes to take into consideration the expansion of pay television by means of satellite transmission. For instance, Maine imposes a sales or use tax only on cable television services, not on satellite television services. Maine's statutory language was enacted before satellite-television services were offered as an alternative to cable television services.[35] This is particularly important as the market share of satellite-television services such as DirectTV expand rapidly. In 1998 about 8 million households subscribed to direct satellite television; that number is expected to increase to 20 million households by 2002.[36]

The Changing World of Cable Services

Sales or use taxes imposed on cable- and satellite-television services are almost exclusively imposed on audio or video programming, not on any other use of the cable systems, such as Internet access, electronic information services, or telephone calls. For instance, Texas imposes its sales or use tax on cable television services on "the distribution of video programming . . . and any audio portion of a video program." Similarly, Florida imposes a sales or use tax on any television system program service. It defines such service as "the transmitting by any means of any audio or video signal to a subscriber."[37]

Although these state tax rules might be extended to encompass not just traditional subscription television but also "video on demand," it is unlikely that the rules could be applied to other emerging uses of cable or satellite networks such as Internet access or interstate telephone calls. Indeed, the category itself, with the use of the word *television,* suggests that its impact is intended not for all services offered over cable systems but for television-like services. Some states, such as Connecticut, make it clear that their sales and use tax on cable television service applies only to "the one-way transmission of video programming."[38]

To be sure, many states tax Internet access or telecommunication services under other enumerated categories (as previously discussed). However, for the jurisdictions that do not impose sales or use tax on interstate telecommunications services (three-fifths of the states) or Internet access services (four-fifths of the states) under some other service category, it is unlikely that the sales or use tax on cable television services will be interpreted to cover the expanded services offered on cable systems.

Cable television has been a rapidly growing category of E-commerce for nearly two decades. Until recently, cable television has been offered largely free of any other cable-related electronic services, and thus, it has been a clearly defined category on which to impose sales and use tax. Moreover, unlike "free" broadcast television, cable television has traditionally been paid for directly by consumers in monthly fees rather than indirectly in advertising revenues. Thus, cable television has fit into the type of specific (and limited) category of E-commerce that states have tended to focus on for sales and use tax purposes.

The world of cable television systems, however, is in the earliest stages of a profound upheaval. Local cable systems are being viewed not just as a means of providing traditional television programming but also as a means of providing a broader gamut of digital services including video on demand, Internet access, Internet telephony, interactive games, and information downloads. The wide bandwidth of fiber-optic cable systems (in comparison to copper-wire telephone systems) and the ability to transform them from one-way systems into two-way transmission systems portends a dramatic transformation of the industry over the next decade. Indeed, it is estimated that cable modems with speeds one hundred times or more greater than the 28.8 kbp modems now connected to most home computers will be in over 13 million homes by the year 2002. Cable modems are expected to account for two-thirds to three-quarters of all broadband high-speed Internet access service to U.S. households in the near future. Cable systems will also be used extensively for local and long-distance telecommunications and data services.

If rules for the taxation of cable television are not revised, there is likely to be significant confusion in applying these rules to the more expansive content offerings of local cable systems. Some services such as television will be taxed, but other, nontelevision, offerings may be treated as exempt. Moreover, if these other services are bundled together with television services for a single fixed price, then taxation of cable services will become even more problematic.

Electronic Software Distribution

The state taxation of digital commerce is also commonplace in relation to electronic software transactions. Approximately half of the states impose a sales or use tax on the transfer of canned software by electronic means. Along with cable television services, electronic transfers of software are the most commonly taxed category of digital commerce (other than telecommunications). In large part this reflects concerted state efforts in the 1980s to clarify the taxation of canned and custom software. As a result of these statutory and regulatory efforts, many states, frequently inadvertently, addressed the taxation of software delivered electronically.[39]

States use varying rules to impose sales taxes on the electronic transfer of canned software. Some states tax the products as extensions of their rules on tangible personal property. In Texas, for example, the sale of canned software that is transmitted electronically is taxable as tangible personal property contained on "electronic media." In that state a computer program is defined as "a series of instructions sold as a completed program which are coded for acceptance or use by a computer system, and which may be contained in or on magnetic tapes, punched cards, printed instructions, or other tangible or electronic media." Similarly, in Illinois canned software that is transmitted electronically is taxable as tangible property. Under Illinois rules canned software is considered to be tangible personal property "regardless of the form in which it is transferred or transmitted, including tape, disc, card, electronic means, or other media."[40]

Other states tax electronically transferred canned software as the sale of taxable computer or electronic services. For instance, in Connecticut digitized software is taxable as a computer or data-processing service. Under Connecticut rules, "when a purchaser downloads software and a charge is made for such downloading and no tangible personal property is provided to the purchaser by the retailer and the software is delivered electronically, the charge is for taxable on-line access services, and not for the sale of tangible personal property."[41]

A number of states that tax the electronic transmission of software do not tax on-line content-related services in general. Illinois, for example, imposes a sales tax on the electronic transmission of software but does not tax the sale of electronically transmitted information services, data-processing services, or mainframe access and processing services. Generally, these states have specific language in their statutes or regulations that tax canned software in whatever form it is transferred but do not similarly treat other types of digitized information or computer services.

Virtually all of the states that do not tax electronically transmitted software treat such digital transmissions as nontaxable "intangible-property" transactions. Whereas all jurisdictions with sales taxes impose the tax on sales of canned software that is delivered in tangible form, over two-fifths of these jurisdictions exempt identical sales if the property is transmitted electronically. California, Maryland, Massachusetts, Missouri, South Carolina, and Utah are among the states that do not impose a sales tax on the electronic transmission of canned software. California, for example, will not tax canned software if it is transferred electronically from the seller's place of business to or through the purchaser's computer, and if the purchaser does not obtain possession of any tangible personal property, such as storage media, in the transaction. In carrying through with the distinction between taxable tangible transactions and nontaxable intangible transactions, California regulations provide that, even where the vendor goes to the buyer's location and transfers canned software from the vendor's disk, tape, or computer to the buyer's disk, tape, or computer without transferring title, possession, or control of tangible personal property, the transfer is not subject to tax.[42]

Thus, there is a large division among the states as to how they apply sales and use taxes to the electronic transmission of canned software. The inconsistencies among states is particularly evident with regard to the issue of whether digitally transferred software is categorized as *tangible property*, which most states tax, or *intangible property* or an *electronic service*, which most states do not tax. As discussed previously, almost all of the states that exempt digital transfers of canned software do so because they treat such a method of delivery as creating an intangible-property transaction. Conversely, the vast majority of states that tax the electronic distribution of software treat such transactions as taxable tangible-property sales.

Digital Transfers as Tangible Property

The notion that a digital transfer of software or some other commodity can be considered a "tangible-property" transaction is potentially at odds with traditional definitions of tangible property. For instance, according to *Black's Law Dictionary,* tangible property is defined as follows: "Having or possessing physical form. Capable of being touched and seen; perceptible to the touch; tactile; palpable; capable of being possessed or realized; readily apprehensible by the mind; real; substantial."[43] Similarly, the California tax code defines tangible property as "personal property which may be seen, weighed, measured, felt, or touched, or which is in any other manner perceptible to the senses."[44]

Where the issue has arisen, state courts and state revenue departments have gone both ways in ruling whether digital transfers of software constitute tangible-property transactions. For instance, in a letter ruling, South Carolina ruled that "computer software sold and delivered by electronic means . . . does not meet the definition of tangible personal property" and is not subject to the South Carolina sales/use tax. According to the ruling, "unlike computer software delivered in the form of a computer diskette or magnetic tape, computer software sold and delivered by electronic means cannot be seen, weighed, measured, felt, touched or is not otherwise perceptible to the senses. Accordingly, such computer software is an intangible."[45]

In an analogous situation involving the digital transfer of financial information, a Florida court similarly ruled that the electronic transmission of information was not taxable as the transfer of tangible property. The Florida statute defined tangible personal property as "personal property which can be seen, weighed, measured or touched or is in any manner perceptible to the senses." The court held in favor of the taxpayer that asserted that financial information and stock quotes provided to customers in the form of electronic signals appearing on a video-display terminal were intangible and thus not subject to tax as tangible personal property. The court found that the vendor's "images on a screen are not capable of being touched or possessed; they are transient and have no enduring existence."[46]

Conversely, the Louisiana Supreme Court ruled that the sale of canned software transferred electronically constituted the taxable sale of tangible property. The court focused on the fact that the software was on a tangible medium before it was transferred and was downloaded onto a tangible medium (a computer hard-disk drive) after it was transmitted. The Louisiana statute had language almost identical to that in Florida, defining tangible personal property as "personal property which may be seen, weighed, measured, felt or touched, or is in any other manner perceptible to the senses." However, the Louisiana court reached the opposite conclusion from the Florida court, stating "that the software can be transferred to various media, . . . Or even that it can be transferred over the telephone lines, does not take away from the fact that the software was ultimately recorded and stored in physical form upon a physical object."[47]

The divergent views on whether digital products should be classified as tangible or intangible personal property are compounded by the absence of clear statutory or regulatory language in many states regarding whether the jurisdiction applies the sales or use tax to canned software that is transferred electronically. A significant minority of jurisdictions do not have a clear statutory or regulatory position on how the state taxes digitally transferred software. These tend to be states that tax only tangible personal property and few, if any, service categories. In the absence of such language, state tax authorities and businesses alike are left to interpret vague language addressed more generally to what constitutes a "sale," "canned software," or "tangible personal property."

Many states such as Nevada, for example, have language that a "sale" means any "transfer . . . in any manner or by any means whatsoever, of tangible personal property." Other states, such as Kansas and Minnesota, have regulatory language that defines computer software to include all software or computer programs, "whether contained on tapes, discs, or other devices or materials." Other states, including Utah, have regulatory language that declares that the sale of software is subject to tax "regardless of the form in which the software is purchased or transferred."[48] Depending on the state, these ambiguous provisions are relied on as the basis for treating the electronic transfer of software as a taxable transaction involving tangible property, or are ignored by jurisdictions that determine the electronic transfer of software is a nontaxable transaction involving intangible property.

The Location of the Server

The use of a tangible-property category to tax the digital transfer of software is also likely to create issues when the software is sent to a server in another state and then accessed remotely in the taxing jurisdiction. For instance, if software is sent by a vendor electronically to California (which does not tax digital transfers) but accessed remotely by the customer's employees in Indiana or Minnesota (which do tax digital transfers), is a use tax due in the latter two states? Logically, the answer should be in the negative, because both states tax digital transfers of software under a tangible personal property category, and there has been no transfer of title or possession of the software in either of the two remote-access states. Conversely, if the state of remote customer access is one that taxes digital products under a service category, the outcome is probably different, because the taxation of services is not dependent on the transfer of title or possession of property.

Determining taxability of a digital product based on whether the property is actually located on a computer server in the customer's jurisdiction is not wholly without precedent. This outcome is analogous to situations where the location of certain property or personnel can transform a taxable *property* transaction into a nontaxable *service* transaction by removing the possession or control of the property from the customer. For instance, an Ohio court case made a ruling related to the taxation of an electric burglar-alarm system rented by a residential user. The burglar-alarm company offered the residential customer several alternative methods of service. Under one method, the vendor installed the alarm equipment (bells, wires, switches, etc.) on the customer's premises and an alarm bell went off in the event of any outsider intrusion onto the property. Under a second method, the equipment was installed on the customer's premises, but the alarm signal was connected to the vendor's central office. When the vendor received a signal that the alarm was going off, the vendor contacted the local police or sent out its own security personnel. The court ruled that the first method was taxable as the rental of tangible property. However, it ruled that the second method was a nontaxable service, that the property in the customer's location was just part of the remote-protection service offered by the alarm company (alarm services are not a taxable service category in Ohio).[49]

With changing business models in the digital world, however, any tax rule that is dependent on the location of a computer server will be problematic to enforce. Increasingly, software purchased by multistate businesses such as enterprise resource planning (ERP) software and other software used on an enterprise-wide basis is likely to be remotely accessed by many of the customer-business locations, either from a central customer server, the vendor's server, or some third-party application service provider that stores many different vendors' digital products. Indeed, many of the largest computer software companies have indicated that they plan to increase their product-hosting services, in part to respond to customer demand and in part to expand their installation, customization, consulting, and other information technology services. If taxation is based on the location of the server that holds the digital product, then this rule can be easily circumvented by moving the server to another jurisdiction.

Many of these ambiguous state rules are likely to lead to litigation. It does appear to be a stretch to suggest that the electronic transmission of software or other property in the form of a digital stream of zeros and ones is something that can be "touched, seen, or made perceptible to the senses." Even in those jurisdictions that have clear regulatory language, there may be legal disputes over whether a regulation that specifies that electronically transferred software is taxable as tangible personal property is consistent with narrower statutory provisions. For instance, in Alabama a regulation states that the sales or use tax on tangible property applies to the "transfer of canned software whether it is transferred to the purchaser in physical form, via telephone lines, or any other alternative form of transmission."[50]

Most of the state tax rules discussed previously address only the electronic transfer of canned software. There remains the issue of whether the electronic transfer of *custom* software is subject to tax. The outcome for this is likely to differ from the results regarding *canned* software because of the different approach that states take to these two products when they are delivered on a tangible medium. Whereas all states (with sales and use tax laws) tax canned software transferred on a tangible medium as taxable tangible property, only about one-quarter of the states similarly tax custom software when transferred on a tangible medium. In all likelihood, states will follow the rules set forth on the electronic transfer of canned software. A jurisdiction is likely to tax digitally delivered custom software only if the state taxes canned software transferred electronically and taxes custom software when transferred on a tangible medium.[51]

Electronic Information Services

Whereas about three-fifths of the states tax the electronic transfer of canned software, only about one-quarter tax the electronic transfer of information. The information category includes legal databases, such as Lexis/Nexis and CCH. It also includes other databases covering health care, topical news, stock quotes, financial information, and real estate listings. This information can be delivered to the consumer's server or accessed remotely from the vendor or a third party's server.

States use a number of different categories to impose sales and use tax on digitally transferred information. These include the following:

Information Service. Certain states treat the electronic transmission of information content as a taxable information service. The definition of information services in Washington D.C., for example, includes "the furnishing of general or specialized news or current information, including financial information, by printed, mimeographed, electronic, or electrical transmission, or by wire, cable, radio waves, microwaves, satellite, fiber optics." Texas has a nearly identical statutory provision.[52] New York imposes a sales tax on the receipts from the "furnishing of provision of an entertainment or of an information service . . . which is furnished, provided, or delivered by means of telephony or telegraphy or telephone or telegraph service (whether intrastate or interstate) of whatever nature, such as entertainment or information services provided through 800 or 900 numbers or mass announcement services or interactive information network services."[53]

Electronic Information Service. Ohio treats the electronic transmission of information content as a taxable electronic information service. Pursuant to Ohio law, an "electronic information service" means "providing access to computer equipment by means of telecommunications equipment for the purpose of either of the following: (1) examining or acquiring data stored in or accessible to the computer equipment; (2) placing data into the computer equipment to be retrieved by designated recipients with access to the computer equipment."[54]

Computer Service. Some states treat the electronic transmission of information content as a taxable computer service. Connecticut, for example, imposes a sales tax on computer and data-processing services that are defined as "providing computer time, storing and filing of information, retrieving or providing access to information."[55]

Sale of Tangible Personal Property. In certain states the electronic transmission of information content is treated as a sale of tangible personal property. For example, Iowa taxes digitally transferred information as tangible personal property—much the same way it treats digitally transferred software. According to the Iowa Department of Revenue, "the transfer of information electronically or by any other means is the sale of tangible personal property." The Department's rationale for this position is that such reformatted information is the "true item" being sought by the customer, and the electronically transferred information can be readily downloaded into a tangible form."[56]

Lease of Tangible Personal Property. The city of Chicago, Illinois, taxes the electronic transmission of information as the lease of tangible personal property if the information is accessed from a computer in Chicago. The transaction is taxable even if the database is stored on a computer out of state.[57] The majority of states, however, do not tax electronically transmitted information because they do not consider it to be taxable tangible personal property. Curiously, many states, such as Illinois and Minnesota, that tax the electronic transfer of software as the taxable transfer of tangible personal property do not take a similar position with the digital transfer of information.

Most states that tax digital information services do so under an enumerated service category. However, a small minority of states, including Colorado, Indiana, and Maine, take the position (at least informally) that the electronic transfer of information is taxable as the sale of tangible property. These states are vulnerable to disputes and possible litigation over their statutory interpretations—for similar reasons to the states previously mentioned that tax digital transfers of software as taxable tangible-property transactions.

Computer Services

Another category of electronic services that is taxed in a minority of jurisdictions is computer services. About one-seventh of the jurisdictions impose a sales or use tax on computer services. These states, including Texas, Ohio, Connecticut, New Mexico, the District of Columbia, and

South Dakota, impose a sales or use tax on a range of computer services. Texas, for example, imposes a sales or use tax on data processing services, which include word processing, data entry, data retrieval, data search, information compilation, and computerized data and information storage and manipulation.

In Ohio data processing services are also taxable. This category includes not only processing data for customers but also providing access to computer equipment to examine or acquire data. In Connecticut computer and data processing services are taxable, a category that includes providing computer time, storing and filing information, and retrieving or providing access to information. In the District of Columbia, data processing services are also taxable, including computerized data and information storage and manipulation.[58]

The states that tax computer services generally tax activities such as providing an EDI service for a customer so that it can facilitate communications with its vendors, consumers, and/or employees; providing a value-added network (VAN) for a customer so it can send data between multistate locations; providing data processing services; providing computer facilities management services; and providing computer-time-sharing services. *Computer services* is typically different than *electronic information services* because no data or information is provided by the vendor of computer services.

Many of these state tax rules have their origins in earlier provisions that imposed a sales or use tax on computer time sharing. Computer time sharing was a popular service in the years before desktop computers with large internal capacities were developed. In many jurisdictions sales or use tax was imposed on computer time sharing because it was considered the rough equivalent of the lease of tangible personal property (space on the computer). Subsequently, this taxable category was expanded to include the use of a vendor's computer servers and software for a customer's billing and order processing or for communications between a customer's various facilities.

Although certain states may exempt electronic services from taxation, such services may become subject to tax if tangible personal property is also received by the consumer as part of the transaction. For example, (1) the electronic creation of a home page may become taxable if accompanied by a hard copy on disk, (2) the electronic sale of canned software may be taxable if accompanied by the transfer of the software in a tangible medium, and (3) the electronic downloading of magazines and reports may be taxable if they are also provided in tangible form.

The Absence of a Uniform Sales Tax Base

The lack of uniformity of state and local sales tax bases, particularly with regard to telecommunications and electronic services, creates a number of problems. First, issues arise concerning whether a particular good or service is taxable, given ambiguities in definitions of different enumerated categories. This problem is exacerbated when taxable and non-taxable services are bundled together and sold for a single price. Second, there is an increased possibility for discriminatory taxation, with tax rules unduly favoring either tangible products or electronic services. Third, there are problems caused by a pyramiding of taxes, with inconsistent exemptions applied to business purchases resulting in taxes imposed both at the service-provider and retail-consumer level.

Tax Base Confusion

The absence of a uniform tax base creates confusion for both the government and taxpayers. A particular state may impose a sales tax on certain content-related electronic services but exempt other similar services from taxation. Unlike categories of tangible personal property whereby the general rule is taxability and the exemptions are carved out as exceptions, the general rule with services is nontaxability, with exceptions carved out for taxable categories. This method of determining a category of taxable services by inclusion rather than by exclusion leads to an inference that an activity is not taxable unless it fits squarely within a listed taxable category. Thus, with regard to services, questions frequently arise as to the definition of a service category and whether a particular service is properly included within such a taxable category.

As discussed earlier in this chapter, there are differences among telecommunication and enhanced service providers between *transport* and *content* services. As indicated, problems frequently arise in ascertaining whether a service is a taxable telecommunications service or a nontaxable Internet access, computer, information, or other similar service. These problems are particularly acute when data or other nonvoice communications take place over regular telecommunications channels.

Software versus Information Services

Although much of the legislative and regulatory debate in the late 1990s has focused on ambiguities and overlaps between telecommunications-related services, similar issues also arise in relation to other electronic or digital services. For example, given the large discrepancy between the number of states that impose a sales or use tax on electronically transferred software (about three-fifths of the states) and electronically transferred information (about one-quarter), the definition of what constitutes "software" becomes very important. A Web page or Web site is not typically thought of as software but could conceivably be regarded as such when it gets more complicated and more interactive with the user. Similarly, an encyclopedia is typically categorized as information, but might be considered software when it is sold as an interactive, multimedia CD-ROM.

Moreover, the definition of software varies among states. In Illinois computer software is defined as "all types of software including operational, applicational, utilities, compilers, templates, shells, and all other forms."[59] Texas defines software as "a series of instructions sold as a completed program which are coded for acceptance or use by a computer system and which are designed to permit the computer system to process data and provide results and information. . . . This definition includes computer game cartridges which allow certain games to be played on a television set through interaction with a computer or on home computers."[60]

With the rapid expansion of computerized training products, the distinction between software and information is likely to become even more confusing. When computer-led training products that teach various educational or job-related functions are provided to business customers on a tangible medium, it does not matter if they are classified as software or information because both are taxable as tangible personal property in the 46 jurisdictions with sales and use taxes. When these products are transferred electronically, however, the categorization issue becomes critical.

Are these computerized programs the sale of electronic information services because of the large amount of informational content provided on each training module? Or are these programs properly treated as the sale of electronically transferred software because of the source code functionality imbedded on each training module? Are the programs more likely to be treated as digital information services if the customer remotely accesses the programs from a vendor or third-party server and thus the source code functionality never is actually transferred to the customer? Moreover, what if the programs are offered by accredited educational institutions. Does the characterization of the training modules change, and do they become nontaxable educational services?

Information Services versus Computer Services

Problems also arise in distinguishing between *information services* and *computer services*. Once again, this can be an important distinction because fewer states tax computer services than tax information services. For example, if a state imposes a sales tax on computer services but not on information services, will the jurisdiction tax the downloading of information such as a magazine? Conversely, if a state imposes a sales tax on information services but not on computer services, will it tax the downloading of computer software or enhanced computer services such as E-mail, electronic bulletin boards, and Internet access? Similarly, if a state imposes a sales tax on data processing, will it include tax return preparation that may involve the use of computerized information?

Case law that has developed in states that tax a limited number of electronic services reflects the confusion that currently surrounds the application of sales and use tax to E-commerce. For example, Connecticut categorizes electronic services as either taxable computer and data-processing services or nontaxable information services. This leads to rather arbitrary determinations as to what is the true object of the transaction, from the buyer's perspective.

In *Hartford Parkview Ass'n. Ltd. Partnership v. Groppo,* the Connecticut Supreme Court held that a hotel that subscribed to a computer-based network that provided information concerning room reservations and availability worldwide was obtaining a nontaxable information service and not a taxable computer service. According to the court, the taxpayer's true object, or the "essence of the service," was to obtain reservation information, and the fact that a computer provided the information was "merely incidental" to the taxpayer's true object.[61]

Conversely, in *Cummings & Lockwood v. Commissioner of Revenue,* the Connecticut Superior Court determined that a law firm that subscribed to many information services, including Dialog Information Services, Information America, and NewsNet, was purchasing taxable computer and data-processing services. According to the court, this case could be distinguished from *Hartford Parkview Ass'n. Ltd. Partnership v. Groppo,* in which "the computer, although providing an efficient way of transmitting the information, was not necessarily the only means of transmitting the information," whereas in *Cummings & Lockwood v. Commissioner of Revenue,* the data and information were accessible only by computer, and the provision of the service required use of computers.[62]

In a 1993 letter ruling, the Connecticut Department of Revenue Services decided that marketing information provided to farmers through a computer constituted a taxable computer and data-processing service because the subscribers' true object was the convenience and accuracy of an immediately accessible database. The information consisted of market calls on grain and livestock, futures and option quotes from major exchanges, and weather and other information, which was updated throughout the day.[63]

Complex interpretative problems can arise with electronic services even in situations wherein a state taxes a wider range of digital products. For instance, in Ohio a particular service may constitute a taxable automatic data-processing, computer, or electronic information service or it may constitute an exempt professional or personal service, depending on the facts and circumstances. One factor to be considered in Ohio in classifying the particular service is whether the service involves a "degree of cognitive thought."[64]

In *Reuters America Inc. v. Tax Commissioner of Ohio,* the Ohio Board of Tax Appeals determined that media news services provided via computer did not constitute taxable automatic data-processing and computer services because the news and other information was gathered, edited, and journalized by Reuters' journalists worldwide in a fashion similar to the personal and professional services of "gathering, organizing, analyzing, recording, and furnishing" information for exempt credit reports per §5739.01(y)(2)(i) of the Ohio statutes.[65] The Reuters' monitor service, which provided a variety of data and information about financial and other subjects, including exchange data from 180 stock and commodity exchanges worldwide, was also determined to be an exempt personal and professional service rather than a taxable computer service.[66]

In *Amerestate, Inc. v. Tax Commissioner of Ohio,* the Ohio Supreme Court ruled that publishing of real estate sales information in reports and through a computer database was subject to tax because the taxpayer was providing objective information and not an interpretation or analysis of the information that would qualify the service as an exempt personal and professional service.[67]

Similar Statutes, Different Outcomes

Confusion is created not only by the determination of whether a particular service fits into a taxable or nontaxable category but also by divergent state interpretations regarding similar or identical statutory language. Connecticut, for instance, treats a service that links merchant computers with bank computers for purposes of credit-card authorization as a taxable computer and data-processing service. By contrast, Ohio has ruled that the same service is not taxable as automatic data-processing transactions because the company providing the linkage is merely acting as an electronic intermediary, while the bank is doing the actual data processing.[68]

Another example involves the disparate treatment of electronic information services in Massachusetts and New York, despite the nearly identical statutory language. In Massachusetts the definition of a "sale" includes "the furnishing of information by printed, mimeographed or multigraphed matter, or by duplicating written or printed matter *in any other manner.*" Based on this definition, Massachusetts will not tax the electronic transmission of information. The New York statute contains an identical definition of a sale. New York, however, taxes the electronic transmission of information.[69]

Confusion over New Web-Related Services

With regard to some of the newer Internet-related services, there is considerable confusion as to the application of preexisting categories of taxable services or tangible property to these E-commerce activities. For instance, does the creation of a Web site for use in conjunction with Internet retailing qualify as a graphic-design service, information service, data-processing service, or computer service, or is it some other type of service? What about charges for the hosting of the Web site by a third party?

Among states that tax a wide range of electronic services, there is a difference of approach on these issues. In Texas creation of a Web site is taxable as data-processing services if the customer is a Texas resident. According to the Comptroller's Tax Policy Division, because writing a home page normally involves word processing using a preexisting program and the addition of graphics, it would qualify as a taxable data processing service.[70] By the same token, charges for maintaining a Web page and for processing student data are taxable as data processing services.[71]

By contrast, in Connecticut the creation and maintenance of a Web site are not taxable as computer and data processing services. Under a Connecticut rule, taxable services do not include "services rendered in connection with the creation, development, hosting, or maintenance of all or part of a Web site which is part of the graphical hypertext portion of the Internet, commonly referred to as the World Wide Web."[72] In addition, charges for the creation, placement, or monthly maintenance of advertisements on the Internet are considered charges for nontaxable advertising services.[73]

It is also possible that the creation of a complex Web site could be treated as the sale of custom software—and taxed in those jurisdictions that tax such as service. If a vendor changes source code, not just machine-readable code, in creating a Web site, then the transaction could be treated as the sale of custom software. Arguably, charges for maintaining a Web site on a third party's computer server could constitute taxable lease payments related to tangible personal property. Would it make a difference if the company was paying for use of most or all of the third-party server? It is unlikely that a state would take this position, given that the Web site occupies less physical space than it does "cyberspace" on the computer's hard-disk drive. Or do these services qualify as a taxable computer service in those jurisdictions that impose sales or use taxes on such services?

Issues regarding the taxability of other service categories are likely to emerge as the Internet leads to additional novel products or to new ways of delivering old products. For instance, the "labor services" component of repair services is taxable in nearly half of the states. This category typically applies to labor services provided when an automobile or a video-cassette recorder is repaired in person at the vendor's or customer's location.[74]

Will these same rules apply when tangible personal property is repaired remotely by a person using a computer that is communicating with diagnostic computer chips imbedded in the tangible property? The statutes themselves provide little guidance but do not necessarily preclude the taxation of repairs conducted by remote means. For example, the New York statute enumerates as a taxable service category the following: "maintaining, servicing, or repairing tangible personal property, . . . whether or not the services are performed directly or indirectly by means of coin-operated equipment or by any other means, and whether or not the tangible personal property is transferred in the service." Likewise, Connecticut imposes the sales tax on "repair services to any electrical or electronic device including equipment used for purposes of refrigeration or air-conditioning."[75]

Although remote-repair services may sound far-fetched, they are likely to be a rapidly expanding new business sector. In the near future, modern appliances such as washing machines, refrigerators, microwaves, and televisions are likely to become "smart" appliances with computer chips imbedded in the products providing information to vendors over the Internet. With the emergence of virtual computing, diagnostic chips in a home appliance can be used to notify a manufacturer when a problem arises with the appliance, allowing the manufacturer to fix the problem remotely or send out a repairman. The computer software in the appliance could also be modified remotely to allow the appliance to adapt to new conditions or provide new functionality.[76]

Similarly, as more digital music becomes available for consumption over the Internet through different streaming or downloading technologies, will it be subject to tax as the sale of tangible personal property? Or will it somehow be shoehorned into an existing taxable service category such as a computer service or an information service? Once again, this is not a theoretical question; all indications point toward explosive growth in the sale of songs and music albums through electronic delivery in the next five years. By mid 1999 an estimated 4 million people were downloading music from the Internet each month, a fourfold increase over the year before.[77]

Finally, other categories of digital products will also emerge, such as the sale of photography delivered to consumers by exclusively digital means. Digital photography is already a commercially viable industry, and digital cameras are likely to become increasingly popular. Whether products such as digital pictures are subject to sales or use tax will depend at least initially on state interpretation of existing rules on tangible personal property. Will the states take the position that South Carolina has asserted: that digital photographs are not taxable because no transfer of tangible personal property has taken place? Or will they follow Louisiana's lead in the case *South Central Bell Telephone Company v. Barthelemy,* in which the court commented broadly on digital products: "[T]hat the information, knowledge, story, or idea, physically manifested in recorded form, can be transferred from one medium to another does not affect the nature of that physical manifestation as corporeal, or tangible."[78]

One-Stop Shopping: The Bundling of Services

The difficulty of distinguishing between taxable and nontaxable service categories is exacerbated when different service categories are bundled together and sold for a single price or charge per minute. For instance, a financial institution may provide nontaxable on-line banking services combined with taxable financial information services. Or a company may provide taxable telecommunication services combined with non-taxable computer services. Although the bundling of taxable and non-taxable categories occurs in connection with sales of tangible personal property (e.g., taxable automobile repair parts and exempt labor services), the overlap of taxable and nontaxable categories may be more difficult to unravel in connection with electronic services.

The problem of the bundling of services is particularly evident in the rapidly evolving telecommunications and data-services markets. Even if clear and uniform definitions could be developed to distinguish between various electronic services, this approach may be undermined by the rapid spread of services in which vendors will offer both telecommunications and enhanced data services on the same wired or wireless networks, frequently for a single fixed price. Until recently, electronic services were typically provided by separate vendors. Telephone companies provided voice communications, cable companies provided cable television, legal and business information services provided information and other data-related services, and Internet access providers provided Internet access services.

The explosion of new methods for expanding bandwidth, however, have created new opportunities for a range of companies to provide integrated transport and content services to customers. For instance, cable companies are beginning to offer new services in which they will provide residential end users with not just cable television services but also Internet access, voice services, facsimile services, and other data services. Cable modems can provide speeds up to 1.5 mbps, as much as 50 times faster than today's telephone modems.

In addition, AT&T is teaming together with the cable industry to offer a range of services over local cable lines to the home. AT&T already purchased Tele-Communications, Inc., the second-largest cable company in the country, and it has entered into joint ventures with other major cable companies such as Time Warner, Inc. AT&T's primary goal is to reenter the local telephone market. It currently controls about one-half of the $80 billion long-distance market, but it has not been providing local phone service since the 1984 federal antitrust suit was settled. Along with offering both local and long-distance phone service, AT&T will offer Internet access services, cellular telephone services, and other data services. With its current liaisons and joint ventures, it has the potential to directly reach over 40 percent of the nation's households through cable lines.[79]

Similarly, local telephone carriers are developing technology called digital subscriber lines or very high speed digital subscriber lines (DSL or VDSL). This technology enhances the bandwidth of existing copper telephone wires that are connected to most homes in the United States. With this technology telephone companies will be able to offer not just voice communications but also Internet access, data services, and even television services. The DSL lines are currently capable of speeds of 160,000 to 1.5 mbps—many times faster than today's typical telephone modems. Moreover, these speeds are likely to accelerate as the DSL technology continues to evolve.

The cellular telephone industry is also being revamped so that companies can offer both voice telecommunications and data services over these wireless channels. A new technology called Wireless Application Protocol (WAP) is spreading rapidly throughout the world, enabling cellular phone customers to use their phones to access stock quotes, E-mail, and other data from the Internet. Motorola estimated that one-half of the 200 million cell phones that will be sold worldwide in 2000 will be equipped with WAP browsers.[80]

Other companies are offering a range of wireless electronic services using Web TV networks. Under one such scheme, satellite companies and other wireless vendors would provide broadcast television, Internet access, and other data services to homeowners who will use regular televisions that have been fitted with special equipment to take advantage of the potential of satellite television services and data services. Customers would have the benefit of accessing such services on their television sets, even if they did not own a computer. Other channels such as DirecPC provided by Hughes Network Systems rely on wireless transmissions of Internet access to a customer's home computer.

In addition, other channels to residential homes similarly promise the capability of offering a range of services to the home. Many electric utilities have fiber-optic networks that run alongside the utility rights of ways. These networks were previously used for communications purposes. Now, utilities are entering into joint ventures with other communication companies to use these valuable lines to provide an integrated voice, data, and video service to nonbusiness customers. Similarly, new companies such as Qwest Communications and older companies such as Sprint are investing tens of billions of dollars in new fiber-optic networks to facilitate the provision of voice, facsimile, video, data, and Internet access on a single, extremely fast, packet-switching network.

Although only a small number of residences are currently equipped with broadband cable, telephone, or wireless capabilities, this number will increase dramatically over the next five years. Forrester Research estimates that the number of homes in the United States with broadband will reach 20 percent by 2003. Broadband is likely to be supplied primarily by cable and DSL in the short term.

All of these new communication channels will expand the potential for one-stop shopping by consumers. The enormous bandwidth of the new technology will allow households to use the variety of voice, data, and video services all at the same time over just one wired or wireless link. While these developments herald an exciting new era for nonbusiness customers in the United States, they also create additional complexities for state tax laws. The newly integrated services will guarantee that it will be much more difficult to distinguish between transport and content. Depending on their business plans, vendors will offer these services for either a single bundled price or for a number of separately stated prices. Where these services are offered for a bundled price, it will be difficult to apply existing sales and use tax laws, especially when some of the categories of services are taxable and some are exempt. In some cases the vendor will not even be able to distinguish the volume of particular services being used over the single communications channel. For instance, if a vendor provides both Internet access and Internet telephony, it may not be possible to distinguish which packets are being shipped as data and which packets are being shipped as voice transmissions.

The extent to which prices for services are bundled will depend largely on competitive strategy, not technological limitations or tax base categorization. For instance, there may be considerable pressure to provide services for a single bundled rate or the same rate per minute so as to reduce customer switching. The cost of acquiring new customers is one of the largest expenses of any of the large communications companies, as customers switch much more frequently than in the past in response to aggressive new pricing plans. The bundling of services in one easily understood package provides the vendor with the opportunity to both make money from each of the services and reduce the chance of the customer switching to another company. Where quality differences between vendors are not obvious, pricing strategies take on more importance. Indeed, the bundling strategy lies at the heart of the campaign AT&T introduced in early 1999 to charge a single 10 cents per minute for all long-distance calls, whether made over home phone lines or a wireless mobile phone. To join the AT&T program, customers must pay a fixed monthly fee. For a higher fixed monthly fee, the customers can receive 150 hours of Internet access as well. (See table 2.3.)

Government Deregulation

The blurring of the medium and the message is being reinforced by drastic changes occurring on the political and economic landscape. The Telecommunications Act of 1996 brought to an end the government regulation that has maintained barriers between local and long-distance

Table 2.3.   **Bundled Services: Local Phone, Long Distance Phone, Internet Access, Cable Television, Other Data Services**

Transmission Channel	Type of Vendor
Coaxial cable	Cable company
Digital subscriber line	Local telephone company
Wireless application protocol	Cellular-phone company
Web television	Television or satellite companies

telephone, cable television, broadcasting, and wireless services. The act led to a flurry of restructurings, mergers, and product changes among telecommunications companies, broadcasters, and other information age entities.

Similarly, the FCC approved new rules in September 1996 to make it easier for electric and gas companies to enter into telecommunications fields such as telephones and cable television. These new rules allow public power utilities to use their expansive in-house fiber-optic cable and other communications networks to provide phone and television transmissions to customers. This is a particularly significant development because these utilities have a ready-made market of millions of customers for their traditional services.[81]

The deregulation of the telecommunications industry is making it more difficult (for tax purposes) to separate transmission, enhanced services, and content-related services. For example, with cable television, for which one provider has traditionally supplied both transmission (coaxial cables) and basic content services (television), the states have generally not attempted to separate the bundled services. They have typically either taxed both of these services (as cable television services) or neither of these services. It remains to be seen what tax authorities will do to cope with a broader range of vertically integrated companies providing both transport and content services.

The convergence of services fostered by government deregulation is accelerating because of the dysfunctionality of many current rules separating the different types of companies. For instance, in the United States, local phone companies are currently allowed to charge long-distance companies access charges for using the local phone network for originating and terminating long-distance calls. However, as of midyear 1999, no such access charge may be charged to Internet access companies. This is creating a hardship for local phone companies because Internet access calls typically average two to four times the length of regular voice telecommunications. In other parts of the world, such as Europe where there are different regulatory rules and Internet access charges are assessed per minute of use even for the "local loop," Internet access is frequently twice as expensive as it is in the United States.[82]

Traditional Approaches for Taxing Bundled Services

The state taxing authorities have two traditional methods for dealing with the taxation of bundled services (or property), in which part of the transaction involves a taxable category and part relates to a nontaxable category. First, many states use an approach called the *object of the transaction,* in which the bundled product or service is treated as one composite output, not two combined products. Under this approach a state may categorize a business activity as a nontaxable service even if it contains certain taxable inputs. Alternatively, other states use a *separate statement* approach that requires vendors to clearly delineate on invoices taxable services from nontaxable services or risk that the entire transaction will be subject to sales and use tax.

Object of the Transaction

Under an object-of-the-transaction approach, the bundled product or service is treated as one transaction, either wholly taxable or fully exempt. Many electronic information vendors, for example, allow customers to access their database through "free" local-access telephone calls. These telephone calls are facilitated by the purchase and resell of leased telecommunications channels. However, in many jurisdictions the object of the transaction is deemed to be a nontaxable electronic information service, not a taxable telecommunications service. The telecommunications service is treated as an input, not an output. Because many more jurisdictions tax telecommunications services than electronic information services, this categorization results in a lower incidence of taxation of such services.

In Massachusetts a purchaser of telecommunications services is considered to be the reseller of such services only if the purchaser does not itself use or consume the telecommunication services as an input in its own services. If a purchaser of telecommunications services is a participant in the transaction, such as the originator or recipient of the telephone call, then the purchaser will not be considered to be the vendor of taxable telecommunication services. Thus, in the case of a vendor of an information service, if it purchases a telecommunications channel that is used by a customer to reach the vendor's remote database, the vendor will be the recipient of the telephone call, and therefore not considered the vendor of taxable telecommunications services.[83]

Similarly, in New York transaction fees received by a company for electronic banking services performed through ATMs were not subject to sales and use tax because the telecommunication services necessary to perform the transaction were incidental to the company's electronic-banking services. In connection with ATM services used for clearing credit-card or bank-card charges with the cardholder's bank, the vendor of the electronic-banking services would typically purchase telecommunications lines as an input to a multistate operation.[84]

The New York Department of Taxation and Finance has taken a similar position with nontaxable Internet access services. Under New York tax rules, ancillary products and services provided by an Internet access vendor to its customers, such as personalized daily electronic newsletters, the ability to create customized Web sites, and E-mail service, for which the customers pay no additional charge, are considered incidental items that do not make the Internet access services taxable.[85]

Similarly, the federal Internet Tax Freedom Act defines Internet access as "a service that enables users to access content, information, electronic mail, or other services offered over the Internet, and may also include *access to proprietary content, information, and other services as part of a package of services offered to users* [emphasis added]."[86]

Separate Statement

Alternatively, state taxing authorities impose a "separate statement" rule that requires vendors to separate taxable services from nontaxable services or have the entire sales transaction subjected to sales and use tax. Under such an approach, the transaction is treated as having two outputs—not one output. If a taxable and nontaxable service are provided together, then the entire transaction is taxable—unless the taxable portion is separately stated on the invoice from the nontaxable portion.

In Texas, for example, a taxable information service is defined as information that is gathered, maintained, or compiled and made available by the provider of the service to the public. In determining the tax base, the statute provides that "unrelated services," such as consultation and training, shall be subtracted. However, if a purchaser pays a single charge for both taxable services and unrelated services, a bright-line test is used. If the taxable portion is more than five percent of the total charge, then the entire charge is taxable. A provider can overcome this test if it separately states the charge for the taxable service at the time the transaction occurs. This separately stated charge must be reasonable and supported by the provider's books.[87]

Similarly, in Alabama, although electronically transmitted information services are not subject to the sales/use tax, amounts that are paid to rent data-receiving equipment are subject to tax. If the rental charge is not billed separately, the entire amount received from the purchaser is treated as taxable proceeds from the rental of tangible personal property.[88] In Connecticut the electronic filing of a tax return is a taxable computer and data-processing service, but the preparation of a return is a nontaxable service. If a tax-return preparer delivers a completed return to someone else to transmit, the transmitter is providing the taxable service, and a tax applies to the charge for the filing service. If instead, the return preparer transmits the return itself, the entire charge, including return preparation, is taxable unless the charges for preparing the return are separately stated.[89]

In the same vein, North Dakota has a broad category of taxable "communication services." Under the North Dakota tax rules, a communication service includes a computer service that allows a subscriber the means of communicating by computer or electronically with others, such as by Internet access service, bulletin board service, or other interactive service. The North Dakota rule clarifies that the sale of electronically transmitted information is generally not subject to tax. However, under the North Dakota rule, "where the charge to the subscriber of the electronically transmitted information service includes charges for the communication service, the total charge is subject to sales tax."[90]

The state administrative rule that imposes a sales or use tax on the entire bundled service, unless the nontaxable portion is separately stated, may run afoul of the recently enacted Internet Tax Freedom Act. As previously noted, the federal act imposes a three-year moratorium on the taxation of Internet access services that applies to all states that did not tax such services at the time the Act was enacted. However, what happens if an Internet access service is bundled together with traditional telephone services and sold for a single price? If a state taxes telephone services but not Internet access services, should the entire service be taxable because the Internet access portion is not separately stated on the invoice to the customer? Can a state tax administrative rule override a federal substantive tax rule? According to Walter Hellerstein, a leading state tax law commentator:

> Since federal law is clearly the "supreme Law of the Land, . . . any Thing in the . . . Laws of any State to the Contrary notwithstanding," and federal law in the form of the Internet Tax Freedom Act bars states from taxing Internet access, one may certainly contend that, even in the absence of separate statement, a state may not impose a tax on Internet access despite the fact that it was sold for a "bundled" charge with taxable telecommunication services. The Internet Tax Freedom Act fails to provide any guidance on this troublesome question.[91]

With digital services, the combination of different electronic services is increasingly commonplace. For instance, many on-line commercial services, such as America Online, charge a flat monthly fee for a range of electronic services. These services typically include E-mail, electronic bulletin boards, chat rooms, newspaper or magazine news, sports news, an electronic marketplace, and Internet access services. Similarly, as discussed previously, many telecommunication companies now provide bundled services, including telecommunications and other data services. The determination of whether part or all of such transactions are taxable may depend on which rule the state imposes. If the state uses the object-of-the-transaction rule, then the entire transaction will be either taxable or exempt. If the state uses the separate statement rule, then the transaction may be taxable in its entirety or partially exempt, depending on how the vendor invoices the customer.

All or Nothing

The problems created by ambiguities in categorization of taxable and nontaxable electronic services are typically avoided only in states that tax either virtually all electronic services or no electronic services. Thus, in states such as Hawaii, South Dakota, and Texas, which tax a broad range of services, most telecommunications and electronic services are taxable and thus fewer disputes arise over what is a taxable service and what is an exempt service. (Of course, a broad base does not eliminate, and is likely to increase complexity over, other issues such as the sourcing of digital services, as will be discussed later in the chapter.)

For example, in Texas the state tax rules enumerate a variety of over-lapping taxable service categories. Taxable service categories include telecommunications services, information services, and data-processing services. Texas also taxes the electronic transfer of software under a broad definition of the sale of tangible property. Indeed, the state reversed an earlier determination that Internet access services were subject to sales tax as "telecommunications services" and asserted that such services were taxable as "information services." However, because the state imposed a sales tax on both telecommunications and other electronic services, Internet access services could be more easily included under either one of the categories. (Subsequently, Texas passed legislation to exempt Inter-net access services under $25.)[92]

Conversely, in states such as California, Virginia, and Maryland, which use a narrow sales tax base, such problems do not arise. These states do not tax telecommunications or electronic services of any kind. They do not impose a sales or use tax on intrastate or interstate telecommuni-cations services, do not tax any electronic services, and do not attempt to tax any digitized transactions such as the electronic transfer of software as the taxable transfer of tangible personal property. Thus, there is little confusion in these states on whether particular E-commerce transactions are subject to tax.

Discrimination between Tangible Goods and E-Commerce

Together with ambiguity over whether a particular good or service is taxable, a second problem with the lack of uniformity in the sales tax base is the increased possibility for discriminatory taxation, with tax rules either unduly favoring tangible products or favoring electronic services. It is a standard principle of both legal systems and economics that similarly situated goods and services should be treated alike or discriminatory rules or price distortions will occur.

The potential for discriminatory taxation against E-commerce transactions has been a major focal point of U.S. government efforts to regulate the taxation of E-commerce. In July 1997 President Clinton directed the secretary of treasury to work with state and local governments, and with foreign governments, to achieve agreements that prevent discriminatory taxation against E-commerce transactions. Clinton called for rules "that will ensure that no new taxes are imposed that discriminate against Internet commerce; that existing taxes should be applied in ways that avoid inconsistent national tax jurisdictions and double taxation; and that tax systems treat economically similar transactions equally, regardless of whether such transactions occur through electronic means or through more conventional channels of commerce."[93]

According to a November 1998 report of a U.S. government working group on E-commerce, the federal government has made a concerted effort to thwart any discriminatory taxation of the emerging digital economy. As stated in the government report, "to ensure that growth of this promising medium is not stunted by duplicative or discriminatory taxation, the Administration has worked domestically and internationally to ensure fair tax treatment of transactions using the Internet or other electronic means."[94]

As discussed earlier, the Internet Tax Freedom Act—enacted in October 1998—also addressed the issue of discriminatory taxation toward E-commerce. During the three-year moratorium period extending until September 2001, the legislation prohibits states and localities from imposing discriminatory sales or use taxes on E-commerce. Discriminatory taxes generally encompass taxes that are applied only to E-commerce, not to similarly situated goods or services that are not ordered and/or delivered electronically. Thus, a state could not impose a sales or use tax on the sale of a game such as Monopoly that is delivered by electronic means without imposing a similar tax (at an identical rate) on the game when delivered by conventional physical means at a department store. In the same manner, a state could not impose a sales or use tax on digitally transferred stock quotes if it did not impose a sales or use tax on stock quotes purchased on a tangible medium. Finally, a state could not impose a sales or use tax on the sale of books that are ordered over the Internet (but delivered by conventional means) without imposing a similar tax on books ordered by mail order or at a retail store.

In reality, there is very little current discrimination against E-commerce in the United States. Despite widespread fears over the taxation of the digital economy, it is difficult to identify instances whereby electronic goods are taxed and their tangible counterparts are exempted. Likewise, as discussed in chapter 4, even without the Internet Tax Freedom Act, the jurisdictional rules as applied to goods or services ordered over the Internet are currently no different than the nexus requirements for similar products and services purchased through more traditional channels.

Newspaper and Magazine Exemptions

Existing discrimination against E-commerce is mostly accidental. In some states, for example, exemptions that are available for sales of tangible personal property may not apply when the transaction is conducted electronically. Generally, these differences reflect the fact that the exemptions were typically developed with reference to sales of tangible personal property, not services. Thus, in many states, sales and use tax rules have not been updated to create a parity of treatment between vendors of tangible property and services. For example, about two-fifths of the states exempt purchases of magazines and about three-quarters of the states exempt purchases of newspapers from the sales or use tax. However, most of these states have not addressed the issue of whether similar information is exempt when delivered electronically (assuming the state has a sales tax on electronic information services).[95]

In Connecticut, for example, the sales tax generally does not apply to sales of newspapers and magazines.[96] However, electronically transmitted newspapers and magazines generally do not qualify for this exemption. Even in this instance, there is likely no per se discrimination because the tangible and electronic products are actually delivered in different formats.[97] By contrast, New York has specifically extended its sales tax exemption for newspapers and periodicals to electronic transmissions of these products. However, the exemption only applies to instances wherein the vendor electronically transmits the entire edition or issue of the newspaper or periodical, with or without the advertising included in the paper edition or issue.[98]

Sales tax exemptions involving newspapers or magazines are complicated because many states restrict these exemptions to items sold by subscription or delivered to the home, not encompassing similar items purchased at newsstands. Moreover, it is not always clear what constitutes a "magazine." For instance, there is considerable litigation in various states over whether real estate guides, business newsletters, and similar publications constitute exempt magazines or taxable information services. Finally, with electronic transmissions, consumers may not purchase individual newspapers or magazines, but just specific articles on certain topics that have been preselected by "business radar" or some similar form of "pull" technology. Thus, the absence of an exemption for the electronic transmission of news information may create disparate treatment as compared with tangible newspapers, rather than discriminatory treatment.

Training or Educational Services

In other instances, consumers of digital products may be taxable where comparable nondigital services are exempt. For example, the $60 billion-a-year corporate training industry is being transformed by the emergence of the Internet as a vehicle for transmitting information to corporate employees. On a wide-scale basis, instructor-led training is being supplanted or replaced by Web-based training. With Web-based training the training process is automated, and employees at remote locations are educated on new topics, not in classroom settings, but with multimedia, interactive training software modules that typically can be accessed over the Internet. It is estimated that the U.S. market for Web-based training will exceed $6 billion by 2002. A similar change is likely to affect higher education, whereby classroom learning may be augmented by computerized education provided by "virtual" learning centers. Indeed, this trend is being propelled forward by the growth in distance-learning programs. The International Data Corporation has estimated that the number of

U.S. students in distance-learning programs will increase from 710,000 in 1998 to 2.23 million in 2002, totaling nearly 15 percent of all students.[99]

In this instance there is no per se discrimination. If identical training or educational materials were assembled in tangible form, they would similarly be taxable. However, the Internet has essentially transformed a training service (taxable in a few jurisdictions) or an educational service (taxable in virtually no jurisdictions) into a digital product that may be taxable in more, or at least different, jurisdictions (as the sale of electronic information services).

Other Related Categories

As discussed further in chapter 4, there has been some talk of basing *jurisdiction-to-tax* or *nexus* rules on the presence of a Web site on a computer server in a state or the presence of an "agent" who hosts a remote vendor's Web site in the state. Indeed, the Multistate Tax Commission, in some of its working drafts on jurisdictional rules for sales and use taxes, listed several Web mall- and agency-related activities that might result in nexus for remote vendors. However, few states to date have issued any rulings or taken any public positions that would suggest any aggressive or novel approaches to nexus that would single out E-commerce vendors and have a possible discriminatory impact. Moreover, as long as such new tax rules focus on the physical presence of a server or agent *inside* the customer state and satisfy the *Quill Corp. v. North Dakota* decision's physical-presence threshold, these new rules might not violate the specific definition of a discriminatory tax set forth in the Internet Tax Freedom Act. The Internet Tax Freedom Act limited its focus to discrimination created by new jurisdictional rules related to Web sites and computer servers located *outside* the customer state.

Finally, there are some services that are only offered electronically, such as computer services (and even telecommunications services). Do the states that impose a sales or use tax on these services violate the provisions of the Internet Tax Freedom Act that prohibit a "discriminatory" tax that "is not generally imposed and legally collectible by such State or such political subdivision on transactions involving similar property, goods, services, or information accomplished through other means"?

There is certainly some ambiguity in the act as to whether it was intended to impose its strictures on services that had no physical-world counterpart. As a technical matter, however, because such services would likely be taxable when offered over non-Internet electronic channels (such as corporate Intranets or the normal telephone network), as well as over the Internet, these tax base categories would likely not violate the antidiscrimination provisions of the federal act.[100]

Internet-Specific Tax Proposals in Other Nations

To be sure, there have been other targeted or discriminatory tax rules that, if not enacted, have at least been part of the public dialogue over E-commerce. For instance, there was some considerable discussion in Europe in the mid 1990s of creating a "bit tax." A bit tax is a levy on E-commerce that would be based on the volume of digital information per unit of time transmitted electronically. The bit tax was originally developed by Canadian economist Arthur Cordell in 1994. The tax generated interest from Luc Soete, an economist who served as the chairman of a European Community advisory panel on information technology issues. The tax was originally proposed at a rate of 1 cent per megabit. However, after the tax received widespread criticism as unwieldy and burdensome to E-commerce, the concept was officially rejected by the EU in 1997.

Similarly, in 1997 German officials announced plans to impose a tax on businesses that have Internet-capable personal computers. Under the proposal Germany would impose a tax of roughly $555 per year for every one hundred personal computers with Internet connections that had the capability of running either video or audio. The tax would be an extension of the existing levies on German owners of radios and televisions. These existing fees are used to support the country's two public broadcasting networks. The proposal to tax Internet-connected personal computers—at the time numbering about 6 million in Germany—was conceived after if was determined that Internet personal computers operate similar to televisions because they are capable of receiving audio and video. Germany subsequently backed off from the proposal to extend the "TV tax" to the Internet.[101]

In 1999 a United Nations agency issued a report that recommended global taxes be imposed on Internet E-mails. The United Nations Development Program called on governments to introduce legislation that would require Internet users to pay a tax of the equivalent of one U.S. cent on every one hundred E-mails. The report's authors noted that, if such a tax was in place in 1996, it would have generated $70 billion. The authors suggested that the new tax dollars be used to provide assistance to developing nations. However, after a public outcry, the United Nations agency backed away from the proposal within one week and stated it has "no plans" or authority to levy taxes on anyone.[102]

With these notable exceptions, worldwide organizations and individual foreign countries have generally steered clear of proposing new taxes or duties on the Internet or E-commerce. Instead, they have focused on how to apply existing indirect taxes (value-added taxes) and direct income taxes to E-commerce.

Thus, the Internet Tax Freedom Act is perhaps best viewed not as a prohibition against widespread *existing* discrimination against E-commerce but as a curb against any *future* discrimination against E-commerce. By enacting the act by a wide voting margin, the U.S. Congress made an important political statement that it would not tolerate any newly enacted laws that imposed novel theories to discriminate against the fast-growing Internet and E-commerce spheres.

Preferential Treatment of E-Commerce

The relative absence of discrimination against E-commerce transactions should not be surprising given the historical roots of the sales tax. The sales tax in the United States, dating back to the 1930s, was imposed initially on tangible personal property. Only in subsequent decades, and only in a minority of jurisdictions, was the sales tax extended to cover certain service or intangible property transactions. Because most jurisdictions that tax digital transactions do so under legal rules aimed at taxing services and not goods, the slow growth of states with broad sales tax bases covering services has likewise limited the number of jurisdictions that tax electronic transactions.

As can be seen from the previous discussion of the variations in the sales and use tax base among different states related to a range of digital goods and services, it is clear that preferential tax treatment—to the extent it exists—is generally accorded to E-commerce activities over tangible goods and services. Thus, canned software on a tangible medium is taxable in all 46 jurisdictions with a sales or use tax, whereas digitally transferred software is only taxable in about one-half of these states. Likewise, information services provided on a tangible medium are taxable in all 46 jurisdictions with a sales or use tax, whereas electronic information databases are taxable in only about one-quarter of these states.

Other emerging forms of digital commerce are also likely in the short run to have similar tax base outcomes. Electronic books purchased at bn.com's Web site are likely to be subject to sales or use tax in far fewer jurisdictions than tangible books purchased at Barnes & Noble bookstores. And electronically delivered music albums are likely to be subject to sales or use tax in far fewer states than music purchased at Tower Records.

Different Media Used for Motion Pictures

The variation in state and local sales tax bases not only sometimes results in favoring digital transactions over traditional tangible transactions but also creates other inconsistent outcomes, with disparate treatment of similarly situated economic activities. For instance, motion pictures are viewed and purchased by consumers in a variety of ways. These include attendance at movie theaters, viewing on network television, viewing on cable television or pay per view, purchasing a videotape, and renting a videotape.

Globally, there are large differences between nations in the consumption patterns related to motion pictures. Remarkably, revenues from movie theaters make up less than 50 percent of overall revenues in virtually all industrialized nations. In many countries, including the United States, Australia, and Japan, video rentals and purchases make up more than half of total consumer expenditures on movies. In other nations, including the United Kingdom, France, and Spain, pay-per-view revenues account for the largest single category of consumer expenditures on movies.[103]

Indeed, in 1996 overall revenues from subscription television (cable television and direct-broadcast television) in the United States exceeded revenues (from advertising) for broadcast television. This trend is likely to accelerate with the introduction of new recording devices that allow viewers to more easily record multiple programs and movies for later viewing and even to skip advertisements with rapid 30-second fast-forward tools.

With regard to motion pictures, the clear trend is toward larger market share for pay-per-view movies. The growth of expansion of cable-industry bandwidth, the rapid growth of direct broadcast satellite television (DBS), and the emergence of digital television significantly enhance the ability of the entertainment industry to provide consumers with near video-on-demand. Digital transmission occupies less bandwidth capacity than analog transmission (due to compression techniques) and thus allows DBS systems to offer multiple movies on demand akin to a hotel video service.

Nonetheless, state sales and use taxation of motion picture sales reflects inconsistent tax rules depending on the method of delivery. All 46 jurisdictions with sales and use taxes impose the tax on the sale or rental of videotapes—treated by the states as the sale of tangible property. Approximately half of the states tax subscription-television services transmitted by cable or satellite, including any pay-per-view charges for motion pictures. By contrast, only about one-fifth of the states impose sales or use taxes on tickets purchased at movie theaters. In addition, less than one-tenth of the states tax free television. "Free" television is, of course, not without cost. However, the costs of free television are recouped not by charging subscribers but by charging advertisers. Only two states (New Mexico, Hawaii) currently impose a sales or use tax on advertising services.[104]

Pyramiding of Taxes

The absence of uniformity among states in the breadth of sales and use tax bases also creates the potential for the pyramiding of transaction taxes with taxes sometimes imposed both on business inputs and business outputs. One distinguishing factor of state sales taxes in the United States is the frequency with which the taxes are applied to business purchases. According to one estimate, about two-fifths of all sales and use tax revenues arise from sales of goods and services to businesses.[105]

The potential for double taxation arises when businesses such as retailers or service businesses buy taxable inputs such as computer equipment, office furniture, or telecommunications services. These business inputs are generally subject to tax, and there is no credit mechanism for subtracting these costs from total tax liability on taxable sales to customers. Thus, a pyramiding of taxes results because a sales or use tax is imposed on both inputs and outputs.

By contrast, the value-added tax system used in much of the rest of the world for imposing consumption-based taxes specifically precludes the taxation of business inputs except in cases where business output is exempt. Most countries use the "credit invoice" value-added tax. Under this methodology VAT taxes are imposed on businesses at each stage of production. However, the business can then offset its total tax liability by taking a credit for taxes paid on business inputs.

Ironically, the absence of universal sales tax exemptions for business inputs disproportionately affects service industries such as digital commerce and E-retailing. This is because service industries such as retail or telecommunications historically have had few input exemptions whereas the tangible-goods industries such as manufacturing or agriculture have traditionally been afforded extensive input exemptions.

Input Exemptions for Manufacturing and Services

Nearly three-quarters of the states currently allow exemptions from sales tax for purchases of materials and machinery used in the manufacturing process. Thus, most states exempt the raw materials that are incorporated in goods to be manufactured or that are used and consumed in the manufacturing process. Likewise, most states exempt factory equipment that is purchased for use in manufacturing products.[106]

By comparison, only about one-quarter of the states provide input exemptions for telecommunications companies. Among the states with broad exemptions for equipment used in telecommunications are Indiana, New Jersey, Ohio, Pennsylvania, Virginia, and West Virginia. For instance, Ohio provides a broad sales tax exemption for tangible personal property and services used directly and primarily in transmitting, receiving, switching, or recording any interactive, two-way electromagnetic communications, including voice, image, data, and information, through the use of any medium including, but not limited to, poles, wires, cables, switching equipment, computers, and record-storage devices and media. The Ohio exemption would cover both equipment used by telephone companies and information-services companies.[107]

By contrast, other states, including New York, Michigan, North Carolina, and Wisconsin, have narrower exemptions for equipment used in providing telecommunications services. For instance, New York provides a limited sales tax exemption primarily for telephone central-office switching equipment and related station apparatus. The New York law only provides an exemption for telephone companies. Moreover, it does not exempt other related network equipment such as transmission systems (repeaters, wire) or switches.[108]

Even fewer states provide input exemptions for nontelecommunications service industries such as cable, Internet access, or digital information services. For instance, in 1996 New Jersey extended its input exemption for telecommunications providers to encompass broadcasting equipment such as transponders, microwave dishes, and transmitters and receivers used by cable and satellite-television service providers.[109]

Conversely, Massachusetts provides input exemptions for certain E-commerce businesses, but not for the telecommunications industry. In Massachusetts inputs such as materials and machinery used in the operation of commercial radio broadcasting, television transmission, and cable television transmission are exempt from sales and use tax. This tax exemption applies even though the output of these industry segments are not subject to sales and use tax. However, inputs used in the operation of telecommunication services are not exempt from sales and use tax in Massachusetts, even though the output of this industry is subject to sales and use tax.[110]

However, given the changing nature of the cable industry, it is not clear whether the current exemption in Massachusetts will cover all activities conducted by a cable company. The exemption is specifically designed to encompass equipment used for cable television transmission. If the cable system is used for Internet access or telephone service, the exemption may not apply.

In some circumstances sale-for-resale exemptions are used to fill in the cracks and exempt inputs used in providing various electronic services. However, resale exemptions have limited use because most electronic services consist not of a series of sales between a manufacturer, wholesaler, distributor, and retailer but of a series of value-added steps in which a direct resale is inapplicable. In these cases the more appropriate exemption is a broader input exemption or component-services exemption. However, few states use such exemptions—at least outside the manufacturing or agriculture industries.

Many jurisdictions, for example, will not allow an Internet access provider to give a resale exemption for telecommunication services purchased for use as part of the Internet access service. The reasoning of these states is that Internet access is a value-added computer service (protocol conversion, E-mail services) and not merely the resale of telecommunications transmission channels. Thus, in Pennsylvania: "Telecommunication charges incurred by an Internet service provider to deliver Internet access to its subscribers are subject to tax. Local, toll or long distance telephone charges incurred by a subscriber to transmit signals from a computer to the Internet service provider are subject to tax." The Pennsylvania rule reiterates that there is no sale-for-resale exemption when an Internet service provider purchases telecommunication services, "regardless of whether the cost of the telecommunication services is separately stated on the invoice to the enhanced telecommunication service provider's customer." [111]

Similarly, Connecticut does not allow a resale certificate for telecommunication services purchased and used by a vendor of computer or data processing services. Connecticut's rationale is that the vendor of computer services is not reselling the telecommunications services but is using such services as an input in its computer services. The absence of a resale or component-services exemption leads to a pyramiding of the tax, because Connecticut taxes both telecommunications services and computer services.[112]

In some cases the use of a sale-for-resale exemption can be quite confusing—applying to certain transactions involving a particular good or service but not to other transactions involving the same good or service. For example, suppose a company owns fiber-optic cables and leases them to a telecommunications carrier for use in providing telecommunication services. In this scenario the lessor might lease one-half of the fiber-optic cables as part of a "dark" fiber transaction requiring the telecommunications vendor to install electronics equipment so as to activate the transmission capacity. The lessor might lease the other half of the fiber-optic cables as part of a "lit" fiber transaction with already installed electronic equipment allowing the telecommunications carrier to immediately access the transmission capacity. When purchased by the lessor, the portion of the fiber-optic cable that is leased as dark fiber is exempt because the lessor will "resale" these fibers to a telecommunications company. However, the portion of the fiber-optic cable that is leased as lit fiber is not likely to be exempt when purchased by the lessor because this portion of the fiber will be used by the lessor itself as a telecommunications service provider leasing available capacity to another telecommunications provider. Unless the state has an input exemption for telecommunications providers, the latter purchase is not a purchase for resale, but rather is a value-added purchase used for provision of a different type of service by the lessee.

Thus, in the vast majority of states, there are no exemptions for inputs used in most E-commerce-related businesses such as telecommunications, cable television, information services, computer services, Internet access, and so on. In these states companies typically pay sales or use tax when they purchase their fiber-optic cables, computer switches and routers, and other E-commerce-related equipment. To the extent many states tax these outputs, double taxation can result.

The problem of double taxation is not unique to E-commerce. Indeed, taxation of both inputs and outputs is commonplace in most retail and nonmanufacturing commercial-business sectors. However, the absence of uniform input exemptions will have a significant impact on E-commerce because such commerce typically involves the sale of services, not the sale of property. Generally, there are few input exemptions for entities whose output involves the sale of services.

Digital Manufacturing

With the expanding digital economy, there may also be a gradual withering away of the exemption for inputs used in manufacturing. In most states the input exemption for materials and machinery used in manufacturing is provided only where such production factors are used directly and exclusively (or at least predominantly) in the manufacture of tangible property to be sold. If materials and machinery are used to produce products that are shipped in digital form, not in tangible form, then such input exemptions arguably no longer apply. For instance, a book publisher may lose the exemption for its printing presses if it transfers some or all of its books electronically because it will not be considered to be using the equipment exclusively for producing tangible personal property. Similarly, a software maker may lose the exemption for its equipment if it transfers its product in digitized format instead of duplicating it and sending it to customers on a tangible medium such as a CD-ROM.

Some states have updated their statutes to extend input exemptions to "digital" manufacturing. For instance, Michigan recently broadened its exemption for business inputs used in publishing to encompass equipment used in electronic desktop publishing. Ohio recently enacted legislation that provides a 25 percent refund of any Ohio sales and use tax paid to a vendor for purchases of qualified equipment used to provide electronic information services. Minnesota provides an exemption for machinery used in providing electronic information services, but not for machinery used in conjunction with Internet access services—because the latter does not involve charges for access to an on-line computerized data-retrieval system as required by the Minnesota statute.[113] Similarly, Missouri has ruled that the manufacturing exemption applies to an electronic information service provider's purchase of equipment. The Missouri Supreme Court ruled that the exemption applies even if the output is intangible because "what comes out of the system is clearly different than from what went into it."[114]

Given the complexity of E-commerce, however, even in states that update their statutes to provide input exemptions for certain forms of digital manufacturing, there are likely to be conflicts over the scope of the exemption. For instance, in 1998 New York amended its sales tax statute to provide an exemption for the purchase of "computer system hardware used or consumed directly and predominantly in designing and developing computer software for sale." More recently, New York extended this exemption to include computer system hardware used or consumed directly and predominantly in providing the service, for sale, of designing and developing Internet Web sites. These provisions will now exempt equipment used to create Web sites or to produce software that is sold to customers, whether it is delivered in a tangible format or sent electronically. It is not clear, however, whether this exemption will encompass equipment that is purchased for use in producing application software that is not sold or delivered to customers but is hosted by the vendor and provided to customers on a remote access, fee-for-service basis.[115]

Vertical versus Horizontal Equity

States that have modernized or liberally applied their manufacturing input exemptions are the exception. By and large, most states have not amended their statutes or regulations to provide a parity of treatment between traditional manufacturing and digital service providers. Thus, there does seem to be a significant amount of disparity in the rules related to E-commerce and other service-related businesses. However, the unequal treatment revolves around the inadequacy of input exemptions, not the inequality of output taxation.

This outcome is most ironic. The Internet Tax Freedom Act and other similar political measures focus almost entirely on horizontal equity—the treatment of various tangible and electronic product *outputs.* The three-year federal moratorium does nothing to regulate vertical equity—the treatment of various business *inputs* that are used in producing tangible and electronic goods and services. As a result, in this arena inputs used in creating tangible goods are frequently given preferential tax treatment over inputs used in creating digital products or in facilitating E-retailing.

The Internet Tax Freedom Act specifically prohibits multiple taxation of E-commerce. However, the act defines pyramiding in such a way as to limit its prohibition to situations related to horizontal inequity. Multiple tax is defined as "any tax that is imposed by one state or political subdivision thereof on the same or essentially the same E-commerce that is also subject to another tax imposed by another state or political subdivision thereof (whether or not at the same rate or on the same basis), without a credit (for example, a resale exemption certificate) for taxes paid in other jurisdictions." Thus, the prohibition on multiple taxation, like the moratorium on discriminatory taxation, focuses exclusively on horizontal equity, not vertical equity. The federal rule precludes taxing digital goods and services in more than one jurisdiction, but it does not restrict a state's authority to pyramid taxes by imposing a sales or use tax burden on successive levels of value-added service or production.[116]

To be sure, in many instances electronic services are not treated as taxable outputs, and thus, subjecting some or all of their business inputs to sales and use taxation may not be unfair. However, in many other instances, both the inputs and the outputs will be subject to sales and use tax, resulting in a pyramiding of the tax base.

Sales Tax Base Reform

The current sales and use tax rules in most states are characterized by favorable treatment accorded to digital products over tangible goods, and preferential treatment accorded to manufacturing inputs over service- or retail-industry inputs. Indeed, economists who analyze the U.S. sales and use tax system frequently observe that a more efficient and fair system would be fostered by broadening the sales tax base to treat similarly situated tangible goods and digital products alike (the horizontal dimension) and simultaneously narrowing the sales tax base to exempt both inputs used in manufacturing and service industries (the vertical dimension).[117]

The approach favored by many economists is analogous to the method used by most foreign countries with regard to the value-added tax. The European Union, for example, defines taxable services broadly, encompassing virtually all E-commerce activities—thus, telecommunications services, electronic software transfers, electronic information services, Internet access, and similar digital services are all subject to the value-added tax. Moreover, in a value-added tax framework, virtually all business inputs are exempt, typically through a credit mechanism that allows businesses to take a credit for value-added taxes paid on business inputs. Advocates of this approach do not necessarily favor a value-added tax system for the United States, but rather a retail sales tax system that imposes taxes only on the ultimate nonbusiness consumer.

Adoption of any such system for sales and use tax in the United States, however, would require significant changes that may be politically unachievable. On the one hand, business groups and voters are likely to resist any major expansion of the sales and use tax base to encompass digital goods and services. Although base broadening might create more uniformity in application of sales and use taxes, it is likely to be perceived as either a tax increase or a constraint on the growth of the Internet. In a period of economic prosperity and relatively high state tax collections, most state governments are likely to be reluctant to enact new laws that would be perceived as tax increases.

Conversely, state and local governments are likely to oppose any major contraction of the sales and use tax base to eliminate all or most business inputs from taxable categories. As already discussed, given the current level of sales taxation of business inputs in the United States, any such changes might cause a shrinkage in sales and use tax revenues totaling billions of dollars.

A more likely outcome is that individual states will make changes on a piecemeal basis. Some states may extend the sales and use tax to encompass digital products if the same goods are taxed when delivered as tangible property. Other states may broaden business input exemptions, particularly in relation to business purchases that are exempt when used in connection with the manufacture of tangible goods. However, broadscale sales tax reform is less likely, in the short-term, given both the level of public support for tax-free Internet commerce and the heavy reliance of state and local governments on business-to-business input sales. Indeed, given the complexity of taxing digitized products, there is likely to be considerable support at the state and federal levels for exempting from sales tax, even if temporarily, some or all digitized goods and services.

How to Source Sales

Assuming that a category of electronic goods or services is taxable in a particular state, there still needs to be a determination with regard to which jurisdiction a particular transaction should be sourced to for purposes of sales and use tax jurisdiction. For example, if a telecommunications vendor connects two parties in two different states, should the call be sourced to the state of origination or termination? Does it matter which state the call is billed to? Similarly, if an information vendor allows a customer in another jurisdiction to electronically access a database in the vendor's state, should the transaction be sourced to the vendor's state where the information is accessed or the consumer's state where the information is read?

These sourcing rules are particularly vexing with electronic services because the transactions are frequently instantaneous and multistate. With E-commerce, a vendor can be located physically in one jurisdiction, the product or service can be stored on a computer server in a second state, the consumer can reside in a third state, the consumer can access the information from a fourth state, and a financial intermediary or other third-party contractor can facilitate the transaction in a fifth state. Which state (or states) has the jurisdiction to tax the transaction? The nature of E-commerce increases the likelihood that the location of the consumer will be more difficult to determine or that more than one jurisdiction may lay claim to the transaction for sales and use tax purposes.

This is another issue that has not been addressed or resolved by the federal Internet Tax Freedom Act or similar state tax legislation. For the millions of daily transactions involving telecommunications, digital software, electronic information, cable television, and other categories are currently subject to tax in some or most jurisdictions, this issue has to be wrestled with on a monthly basis as sales and use tax returns are filed.

Where there are no clear-cut rules, taxpayers are left to guess at the appropriate sourcing rule or rely on informal (and nonbinding) advice from the tax authorities.

Although some states have set forth guidance on where to sources sales of services, many other states have a policy void, with no public pronouncements on how to source various digital transactions. Many states do not tax services and therefore have never been required to develop rules for sourcing the sale of digital products or services. Other states tax primarily locally based services such as dry cleaning, amusement parks, athletic clubs, hotel rooms, entertainment tickets, motor vehicle repair, construction services, secretarial services, barber shops, parking lots, landscaping, and janitorial and property maintenance services, where both the location of the vendor's performance and the place of the customer's beneficial use are in the same jurisdiction.

Market- (Consumer-) State Sourcing Rules

The general sourcing rule used in sales and use taxation of tangible products is to tax a transaction where the consumer takes possession of the product. The so-called destination rule is imposed under either the sales or use tax. The sales and use tax has traditionally been viewed as a tax on consumption, and thus sales are sourced to the jurisdiction to which the product is destined for use or consumption.

Typically, it does not matter where a sales contract is negotiated, or even where the title to a good is transferred. The key factor is the jurisdiction in which the consumer takes possession of the product. Thus, in an interstate mail-order sale, the transaction is subject to tax in the state in which the taxpayer receives the product, not the state from which the vendor ships the product. From a technical perspective, the sale may occur in the ship-from state because title in the good typically transfers at that point. Nonetheless, almost all states have a sales tax exemption for products for which the consumer takes possession outside the jurisdiction. In that case, a use tax is imposed in the state in which the customer takes possession and presumably consumes or uses the product.[118]

In the case of services, including electronic services, there is not necessarily a taking of possession equivalent to the purchase of goods. However, a similar rule is frequently used that sources the sale or use of a service to the jurisdiction in which the purchaser consumes or enjoys the benefit of the service. This rule approximates the rule for goods by focusing on the place of consumption, not the place of production or the place of formal passage of title, as the appropriate taxing jurisdiction.[119] Connecticut, for example, generally sources services to the location at which the services are used. Likewise, Pennsylvania sources services based on where they are delivered and predominantly used. Services delivered to consumers in Pennsylvania are generally considered to be predominantly used in Pennsylvania; services delivered to locations outside the state are deemed to be predominantly used outside the state and are not subject to sales or use tax.[120]

In several states rules have been established in relation to repair services that specify that such services are sourced to the location at which the customer enjoys the benefit of the service. For instance, in South Dakota a service is sourced to the location where the customer has the "beneficial use" of the property. In that state it was determined that the beneficial use of the property takes place not where the vendor performs the repair but at the location where the customer has the right to use and enjoy the property. Similarly, in New York repair services are taxable only if the property is delivered to a purchaser in the state—regardless of where the repair was performed.[121]

The adoption of a market-state rule is particularly evident in those states that have addressed the multistate sourcing of electronic services. For instance, Connecticut uses a market-state rule to source the sales of on-line access to any type of computerized information or computer database or network, whether the transmission of information is one-way or interactive. Connecticut applies the same rule to sourcing sales of Internet access, E-mail, electronic publications, bulletin boards, or other electronic services, whether the information is downloaded or just used on a read-only basis. Under the Connecticut rule, the sale of electronic services is sourced to Connecticut if "the purchaser's computer terminal with respect to which the service is rendered is located in Connecticut." In the case of mobile computer equipment, the sale is sourced to Connecticut if "the home base of the mobile computer is located in Connecticut."[122] Likewise, pursuant to a District of Columbia regulation, information services that are "sold and delivered by the vendor to locations outside the District" are exempt from sales tax. And Texas exempts an information service or a data processing service "to the extent it is used outside Texas."[123]

With regard to Internet access services, several other states have developed sourcing rules that tend to look to where the consumer is located. In Iowa Internet access charges are sourced to the location of the subscriber. In Tennessee Internet access charges are sited to the location where the subscriber accesses the Internet service provider's service. In Texas Internet access charges are exempt to the extent the services are for use outside the state.[124]

For telecommunication services, states typically use a two-out-of-three test for determining which state is the appropriate taxing jurisdiction. This rule results in a transaction being sourced where it is consumed, either at the point of origination or the location of termination of a phone call. In Massachusetts, for example, if a telecommunications (1) either originates or terminates in a jurisdiction and (2) is charged to a service address or billed to an address in that jurisdiction, then the sale is sourced to that jurisdiction.[125] A service address is defined as the location of the equipment at which a purchaser originates or receives the telecommunications service. This rule derived from the U.S. Supreme Court case *Goldberg v. Sweet*.[126]

Vendor-State Sourcing Rules

Although most states that have taken a clear statutory or regulatory position use a market-state rule, a minority of states use a vendor-state rule based on where the service is performed. These jurisdictions use a vendor-state rule either for all services or, more typically, for at least some services that do not lend themselves to a market-state solution.

Minnesota, for example, sources the sales of all taxable services where the service is performed. If the service is performed in more than one state, it is sourced to Minnesota if the greater portion of the service is performed in Minnesota. Arkansas also sources the sale of repair services to the state where the service is performed, even if the property is then delivered to the customer out of state. Similarly, New Mexico sources the sale of professional and personal services to the place where the services are performed; if the services are performed in more than one state, the receipts are prorated based on the portion of the services performed in the state.[127]

The use of a sourcing rule for the sale of a service based on the location where the vendor performs the service is analogous to the cost-of-performance rule used for income tax purposes for sourcing the sales of service or intangible property. Although there are a few states that have this rule, it is unclear whether these states would use a similar rule when sourcing electronic services. Indeed, Minnesota uses the *Goldberg v. Sweet* rule for sourcing interstate telecommunication services—looking to the location where the customer originates the service.

Texas is one of the only states that, at least initially, took a vendor-state position in relation to sourcing the sale of digital products. A 1996 ruling issued by the Texas Comptroller of Public Accounts, for example, addressed the taxability of information sales made over the Internet. The taxpayer in the ruling maintained a server location in Texas and sold taxable information services. In the case of information that was directly downloaded by out-of-state customers from the Internet, the taxpayer was required to collect tax on the sale because the information was considered "picked up" at the server location in Texas. Texas took a similar position with the electronic sale of canned software. If the software was located on a Texas server and accessed by an out-of-state purchaser, then it was subject to sales tax in Texas. The rationale for this position was that the transaction is akin to a consumer taking possession of a CD-ROM in Texas.[128] After considerable criticism of the antibusiness impact of its rulings, however, Texas reversed field and clarified that it would only tax these digital products to the "extent of use" by the customer in Texas.

States are reluctant to adopt a vendor-state rule for digital services because it risks discouraging businesses from locating in a jurisdiction. It is very easy to remove a computer server and related operations from a jurisdiction. If a state bases its state tax-sourcing rules on where digital information is stored, then a vendor will be tempted to move its operations to a different state that sources sales based on the customer's location.[129]

Tangible Products

As discussed previously, a market- or destination-state rule is also the norm with the interstate sales of tangible goods. For instance, if a compact disc player or winter jacket is purchased by mail order and shipped by a vendor in one state to a consumer in another state, the sales or use tax is typically imposed by the destination state.

However, even with tangible goods, there are exceptions to the general rule, when a vendor-state rule is used to simplify tax collection. Many states, for example, have a rule for gifts of flowers that are purchased by customers in one state to be delivered to friend or relative in another state. These states typically impose the tax at the vendor's location where the customer places the order, not in the state where the flowers are delivered. The rationale for this approach is that the gift is being paid for in the initial vendor's jurisdiction, and thus, it may be impractical to collect the tax in the donee's state. For example, in Michigan a tax regulation states: "On all orders taken by a Michigan florist and telegraphed to a second florist, either in Michigan or to a point outside of the state, the florist taking the order is liable for the tax." In California a tax regulation states: "Tax applies to amounts charged by florists who receive orders for the delivery of flowers, wreaths, etc. to points outside this state and instruct florists outside this state to make the delivery." Conversely, in these states, the sales or use tax does not apply to amounts received by in-state florists who make deliveries in the state pursuant to instructions received from out-of-state florists.[130]

In addition, in some states a vendor-location rule is also used for local sales and use tax collection purposes on intrastate sales of tangible goods. For instance, in California the county sales tax is imposed on products shipped from a vendor's location in the state to a consumer's location in the state based on the location of the customer. By contrast, the local sales tax is sourced based on the vendor's shipping location.

Prepaid Phone Cards

Although vendor-state rules are not commonly used in relation to sourcing the sale of electronic or telecommunications services, there are special situations whereby some states will use these rules, particularly when it significantly simplifies sales tax compliance. For instance, the sale of a prepaid long-distance telephone card may be treated as the sale of the card itself (i.e., tangible personal property) or the sale of a service (i.e., telecommunications). If the sale of the card is treated as the sale of tangible personal property, the sale is sourced to the vendor's retail location. If the sale of the card is treated as the sale of a service, it is sited to the location where the consumer uses the telecommunications service.

A prepaid telephone calling card is a debit card that entitles the purchaser to the right to use a predetermined amount of telecommunications time. The cards are sold directly to consumers through retail outlets, given to consumers for free in conjunction with a promotional campaign associated with the purchase of some other goods or service, or sold at a premium as collector cards with pictures of famous persons or places embedded on the card. The card can be used for local or long-distance phone service. A consumer dials an 800 number, provides a personal identification number (PIN) listed on the card, and then enters the desired telephone number. Once a call has been completed, amounts or units are debited from the card, until the total value is used up and the card expires.

Prepaid telephone cards became popular in Europe and Asia in the 1970s and 1980s. During the 1990s, prepaid telephone calling cards exploded in popularity in the United States, with market sales expected to total $3 billion by the year 2000.[131] The cards are popular among consumers for a number of reasons, including convenience and cost as compared to operator-assisted calls; certain rate discounts; and occasional use as part of promotional campaigns in which the cards are given to consumers for no charge.

The prepaid cards provide a convenient method for consumers to make phone calls (particularly when they are traveling), but they create significant administrative problems for vendors. To begin with, the cards are typically distributed through a chain of vendors. Although telecommunications carriers sometime retail cards directly to consumers, the cards are more frequently sold through a distribution chain that includes a telecommunications carrier, telecommunications reseller, distributor, and retail outlet.

This distribution chain creates problems with regard to collection of sales or use tax that are unique to this industry. First, the retail vendor does not typically know where the telecommunications services are used. Thus, if the retail vendor is required to collect the sales tax based on the location of consumption of the end service, it will be unable to do so. Moreover, it is generally not administratively feasible for the telecommunications carrier that places and monitors the call to provide the information to the retail outlets. Similar issues arise if the final vendor is a bank or other company using the cards as part of a promotional campaign.

Second, the telecommunications carrier does not typically know the final retail sales price because the cards are marked up each step along the distribution chain. Thus, if the telecommunications carrier is required to collect the sales tax based on the final retail sales price (as compared to the wholesale price), it will be unable to do so. As compared with the sale of a typical product at a retail store, there is generally no one phone-card vendor that knows both the location of use and the final retail sales price.[132]

Not surprisingly, states have conflicting sales and use tax rules that apply to the sale of prepaid phone cards. Initially, a large majority of states treated the purchase of prepaid phone cards as the sale of telecommunication services and taxed it at the time and location of use. A minority of states imposed a sales or use tax on the retail purchase of the cards and taxed it at the time and location of purchase of the card itself.[133]

Those states that tax phone cards only when they are used typically exempt the purchase of the cards as the purchase of an intangible right for the future use of a telecommunications service. For instance, Pennsylvania taxes only the actual usage of the phone cards, not the purchase of the phone cards. According to the Pennsylvania rule, "The sale of prepaid telephone calling cards, which allow the holders of the cards to use a predetermined number of minutes or set dollar amount of a telecommunications service, are not subject to Pennsylvania Sales Tax. The sale of the cards are considered to be the sale of a right to future telecommunication services and not a sale of tangible personal property." Similarly, the sale of prepaid phone cards is not taxable under Connecticut law. The telecommunications services rendered when the cards are used to make calls either originating and terminating within Connecticut or originating within Connecticut and terminating outside Connecticut are subject to tax in Connecticut. The tax is based on the full sales price of the telecommunications service that would have been paid without the use of a prepaid phone card, and it should be charged to the user by debiting the amount of tax from the prepaid units remaining on the user's card.[134]

However, in the last two years, given the practical difficulty of the point-of-consumption approach, an increasing number of states take a vendor-state–oriented approach and now tax the cards at the point of sale of the card from the retail outlet. For instance, Washington treats the sales of prepaid long-distance telephone cards as taxable retail sales. The Washington Department of Revenue presumes that the retail sales tax applies if the customer makes the purchase of the card in Washington or the card is delivered by the seller to the customer in Washington. The place of sale for local sales tax purposes will be the location at which the retailer transfers possession of the card to the customer, not where the customer actually uses the telecommunications service.[135]

By early 1999 over half of the states that tax telecommunications services had adopted the point-of-sale approach. A number of states, including the District of Columbia, Kansas, Louisiana, Minnesota, Mississippi, Utah, Vermont, Wisconsin, and Wyoming, switched their positions from using a point-of-consumption approach to using a point-of-card-purchase approach. Furthermore, the federal government has also adopted this approach for purposes of taxing prepaid telephone calling cards under the 3 percent federal excise tax on telecommunications.[136]

Most of the states that use the point-of-sale sourcing rules define the sale of the card as the sale of tangible personal property, not the sale of telecommunication services. For instance, states such as Arizona, Kansas, Mississippi, and Oklahoma categorize the sale of phone cards as the sale of tangible personal property.[137] Arguably, if the sale of phone cards is defined as the sale of tangible personal property, then states that don't impose sales or use taxes on telecommunication services could still tax phone cards under the more general tangible personal property category. Indeed, Alabama has taken this position—imposing a sales tax on phone cards at the point of sale, even though Alabama does not otherwise tax intrastate or interstate telecommunications services.[138] California—a state that does not tax telecommunication services—has taken an even more curious position. California imposes the sales and use tax on a phone card only if it is purchased for its collectibility rather than for future telephone service. According to the California ruling, "For example, an individual may purchase a card because it includes a graphic representation of a famous person or a 'classic' automobile. In this case, the true object of the transfer is the card itself, not the telephone service."[139]

Thus, even in the realm of pure transmission services, without any bundling of Internet access, E-mail, information, or other enhanced services, questions arise as to how a sale should be characterized and sourced. Should the sale of a prepaid telephone card be treated as the sale of tangible personal property and thus taxed at the time and location at which the vendor transfers the card to the purchaser? Or should the sale of a telephone calling card be treated as the sale of intangible rights to future telecommunication services and thus taxed at the time and location of the consumer's use of the telecommunications services? The approach that a state takes can alter the gross sales price and the jurisdiction in which the tax is due. Moreover, because more states tax tangible property than tax telecommunications services (particularly interstate telecommunications services), the vendor-state point-of-sale method can actually lead to a tax being collected even in jurisdictions that do not tax telecommunications services.

In the near future, the phone-card issue is likely to repeat itself in a larger arena as these debit cards get merged together with other "smart cards" used for purchasing a variety of goods and services. In these instances there will be further complications in administering sales and use tax laws and choices to be made between point of sale and point of consumption rules.

800 Numbers

Another type of telecommunication service that creates sourcing problems is toll-free 800 numbers. An 800 number is an *inbound service*—paid for by a business that allows the customers or employees to call the business from other regions of the country for no charge. Typically, a business is charged a flat fee for an unlimited number of calls from specified geographic regions. The call may be made by a customer to order a product from a mail-order company, confirm hotel or travel reservations, or request customer service on a product defect. The call may also be initiated by an employee who is using a toll-free number to call back to the home office while traveling for business reasons. The phone bank that receives the call may be operated by the retailer, by a company that is performing remote technical assistance on a contract basis, or by the employer. Indeed, more than one phone bank may be involved. The phone banks may be located at corporate headquarters or at some other site in a different jurisdiction.

Over the last three decades, 800 numbers have proliferated as businesses find them to be a convenient way to communicate with customers or employees. Toll-free calling originated in the United States in 1967. Thirty years later, in the United States alone, about 100 million toll-free calls are made daily to more than 8 million 800 numbers. Between 1993 and 1996, the number of toll-free telephone numbers quadrupled. By the late 1990s, advances in world communications systems allowed companies to use a single toll-free number for global commerce. In many ways toll-free numbers were a precursor to the Internet as a means to facilitate global communication and commerce.[140]

With regard to 800 numbers, states tend not to use a market-state sourcing rule, instead relying on a vendor-state–oriented rule or exempting the transactions entirely. For instance, some states such as Massachusetts source these calls to the location of the phone banks operated by the retailer or other vendor. Although this entity is not the vendor of the telecommunications service, it is also not the ultimate consumer who initiates the phone call. Many other jurisdictions, such as Ohio, Michigan, Minnesota, and Tennessee, currently exempt these calls altogether—

perhaps so as not to discourage businesses that use phone banks from locating in their state.

States generally do not use a market-state approach because of the complexity of its application—where the originators of the telephone call are not charged for their usage of the telecommunications channel. Although records are generally maintained of where the originators of the calls are located, it is much easier to charge the calls to the location of the retailer or other purchaser of the 800 service's phone banks.[141]

Where Is Waldo?

Another problem that frequently arises in sourcing E-commerce transactions is identifying the location of the consumer. Even though many states will site sales of electronic services to the place at which the consumer uses the service, this location may not be readily identifiable by the vendor. With respect to sourcing sales of E-mail and similar services, siting the sale is complicated by the fact that a consumer's computer may not be permanently located in one jurisdiction but may instead be moving between jurisdictions (especially with the increased use of laptop computers). Similar problems arise with wireless telecommunications such as cellular phones, pagers, or personal communications networks. Increasingly, wireless phones, handheld digital assistants such as Palm Pilots, and minicomputers will operate as mobile digital platforms, used not only for voice communications but also for sending or receiving E-mail and faxes or connecting to the Internet. By its nature this equipment typically is used by mobile consumers who generally are not in any fixed location. Vendors may know where the billing address of their customer is, but they may not know where the use of the service occurs.

Furthermore, for many Web transactions, the vendor may be unaware of the state in which the consumer resides (and in which the product or service is used). Web addresses, such as consumer@aol.com, do not typically identify the state of the customer's residence or commercial domicile. This additional information may be in a vendor's database, in a third party's database, or unknown. Even if a vendor knows the state in which the consumer resides, it may not know the actual city or county for purposes of complying with local sales or use tax rules. For state taxation of E-commerce to remain viable, states may need to require transactional information reporting that includes the location of the consumer's street billing address and/or the location of the use of the service.

An additional issue may also arise in determining the jurisdiction(s) in which the taxable use of the property/service occurs where the electronic product or service is stored on a vendor or third party's server in one jurisdiction but used by the consumer in a different jurisdiction. The tendency to store both the data and application software at a remote location is likely to increase with the advent of network computers and Java "applets." This new technology allows consumers to access data and application software from a remote server on an as-needed basis, thereby reducing the need for large computer memory. Under such circumstances, is the relevant inquiry to determine use where the consumer is located or where the server is located that holds the electronic information or software that is being accessed by the consumer?

Roaming Charges

A good example of information-age complexity over the location of the consumer arises with wireless telecommunications such as cellular telephones and digital personal communications service. For instance, a cellular telecommunication involves a mobile telephone, a group of radio transmitters (cell sites), and a switching office. A cellular transmission is carried by radio wave to the cell site in the cell in which the call originates. The cell site then transmits the communication to a mobile telephone switching office. This computer switch then transmits the message by wireless or wired channels to the destination of the recipient.

The creation of sourcing rules for wireless telecommunications is complicated by several factors. First, there is no fixed service address for the origination of a wireless phone call because of the mobility of wireless telephone callers. Second, the customer's home telecommunications carrier does not always know in which cell site or locale a transmission originated. This information may be held only by another service provider with whom the home carrier has a "roaming" agreement. Third, a wireless communication may actually encompass more than one jurisdiction if the originator of the call travels (by automobile) through several locations while the call is in process. The sourcing of roaming charges for cellular phone calls may grow more complex with the so-called one-rate plans now being offered by telecommunications carrier that may charge only one rate, regardless of the location of the caller. Under these plans, from an operational perspective, there will be no need for another provider to supply the billing vendor with information on the roaming portion of the call because it will not be reflected in a higher price to the ultimate consumer.[142]

Nonetheless, most jurisdictions currently take the position that companies need to comply with rules for actually identifying the jurisdiction of roaming calls and sourcing the transactions accordingly. For example, in Pennsylvania roaming calls are sourced to the state in which the caller originates the telephone call, not to the subscriber's home jurisdiction. According to a Pennsylvania tax rule, "If the mobile telephone switching office or similar facility first receiving the telecommunication is outside the subscriber's assigned service area (that is, the subscriber is "roaming"), the service address is deemed to be the location of that mobile telephone switching office or similar facility."[143]

The Formulation of Sourcing Rules for an Internet Economy

To date, the most-detailed discussions about how to source E-commerce transactions for sales and use tax purposes occurred as part of the uniformity efforts undertaken by the National Tax Association's Communications and Electronic Commerce Tax Project. Ultimately, this group failed to reach a broad consensus on how to proceed. Despite the absence of a final comprehensive recommendation, however, the group did explore a number of key issues related to the development of sourcing rules for both nonbusiness and business purchases. Moreover, the group set forth a number of possible solutions for sourcing E-commerce transactions. Although these proposals may not survive the federal or state legislative process intact, they provide a useful framework within which to consider both the problems and possible solutions to the E-commerce taxation puzzle.[144]

There is broad support among both business and government groups that any sourcing rules for digital products and services need to balance the government's interest in taxing transactions that occur within its borders with the business community's interest in having sourcing rules that are not unduly burdensome. The sourcing rules need to be straightforward enough that (1) consumers can understand them and (2) vendors can comply in good faith without being vulnerable to intrusive audits. The rules must recognize the special characteristics of E-commerce transactions, such as the difficulty in obtaining timely information on the location of the consumer. Finally, the sourcing rules, to the extent possible, should treat similar goods and services in the same manner, regardless of the method of product delivery or the channel of product marketing.

Generally, the NTA project participants supported a market-state sourcing rule. The project's steering committee approved a resolution that stated: "Transactions should be sourced only to the state level; sourcing to a sub-state level should not be required. Transactions should be sourced to the state of use or destination to the extent that adequate information is available in a practical, unobtrusive and efficient manner. Transactions for which such information is not available should be subject to one or more default rules, to be developed."[145]

If a market-state sourcing rule is adopted in an information-age economy, it is likely to be based on a rough approximation of where actual consumption occurs and not necessarily require a determination of the actual place of consumption. There is broad agreement among both government and business groups that sourcing rules related to E-commerce should require the sourcing of sales to the state level only, without requiring that transactions be sourced to the city, county, or local district level. (See section later in this chapter, "One Sales Tax Rate per State.") These rules should also rely on sources of information readily available to vendors on a real-time basis. A vendor should be able to rely on information available to it during the normal course of an E-commerce transaction. The vendor should not be required to take extraordinary measures to examine information it might have in its files or to obtain information from an independent third party.

With regard to sales of *tangible goods* ordered over the Internet, there is generally a "ship-to" address that is available to determine the destination jurisdiction to which the sale should be sourced. This information is typically available to the seller in the normal course of business, whether the transaction involves a business or nonbusiness customer. Therefore, sales and use tax compliance for the large share of E-commerce transactions that involve delivery of tangible goods by means of traditional common carriers will vary little from current sales tax compliance practices. However, there may be an operational need for a seller to use tax software or some other technological solution to ensure that the proper tax amounts are recorded—on a real-time basis if necessary—on the credit-card authorization or other form of payment that is used.

With regard to the sale of *digital products and services delivered on-line to business customers,* the seller will generally have information available at the time of the transaction of the actual destination of the goods or services. For business-to-business transactions, information will be more readily available than for business-to-consumer transactions, based on the likelihood of existing business relationships between the parties. Thus, information to be used to source the transaction to the state of destination may be available from pretransaction contractual agreements or post-transaction billing arrangements.

Sales and use tax compliance in relation to business-to-business transactions can be facilitated in part by allowing a liberal use of direct-pay permits that enable the purchaser (who certainly has the requisite information on the place of consumption) to self-assess the use tax on its purchases of digital goods and services. A direct payment solution will be particularly useful in conjunction with business customers who consume digital products or services simultaneously in multiple jurisdictions (see "Problems with Multiple-User Products" later in this chapter). In the event that information on the location of consumption is unavailable to the vendor, then the seller may be able to rely on the rules set forth in the following section for nonbusiness customers, such as the use of a billing address as a proxy for the state of destination. In business-to-business transactions, the vendor will almost always have information relating to the customer's normal billing address or customary place of business.

The Unique Issues of Nonbusiness Consumers

The most difficult issues relating to the development of sourcing rules for E-commerce revolve primarily around the sale of digital products and services delivered on-line to nonbusiness customers. In the case of business-to-consumer transactions, the actual destination of a product delivered electronically to a customer may not be known to the vendor at the time of the transaction. In such cases the seller may be allowed to use a default rule and source the sale to the customer's normal billing address. Although the billing address will not always coincide with the destination state where the nonbusiness consumer uses the electronic product, the billing-address state is a useful proxy for where consumption actually occurs. As compared to an actual destination rule employed with tangible products, a billing-address rule is simpler to use and generally results in the same outcome for personal consumption. The seller will typically be able to determine the billing address of a nonbusiness customer from information the seller (or a third-party intermediary) has collected from the consumer for purposes of marketing, technical support, or credit-card processing.

One of the most contentious issues in the sourcing debate concerns what the vendor should do in the event that the billing-address state is not readily available to the seller in the normal course of a transaction. This situation could arise because a third-party intermediary has the information and is not required or not willing to share it with the vendor. It could also arise because the customer uses some form of electronic payment such as digital cash payments to create a truly anonymous transaction whereby neither the state of destination nor the billing address of the customer is known to either the seller or to the financial intermediary in the regular course of business.

One possibility that was widely discussed by the NTA project was to create a default rule to be followed in the event that a sale of digital products could not otherwise be sourced (with a good-faith effort on the part of the vendor) to either the state of destination or the state of the

customer's billing address. Several alternatives were set forth as part of a
default regime. Under one scenario a "throwback" approach would be
used that would assign the sale to the origin state (i.e., the state of the
seller). Under a second alternative, a "throw-around" rule would be used
that would assign the sales to the other states in which the vendor has
customers based on some formula. Under the throwback rule, the sales
made to unknown or unknowable destinations would be assigned to the
state of origin of the sale or to the state of the vendor's principal place
of business or commercial domicile. Under the throw-around rule, the
sales made to unknown or unknowable destinations would be apportioned to the jurisdictions in which the seller makes sales with a known
destination or billing address.

To its advocates, a default rule would help sellers by providing certainty on how to deal with situations for which the destination of a
product being sold could not be determined; it would also help governments by ensuring that all transactions would be subject to some form of
sales tax, regardless of the sufficiency of information available on the customer's location. To its critics, a default rule might be administratively
burdensome to comply with. Each alternative has its drawbacks. A
throwback rule might create economic distortion by either discouraging
vendors from locating in certain high-tax states or encouraging sellers to
locate in low-tax (or no-tax) states. A throw-around rule would require
difficult administrative decisions to be made over what tax rate to apply
and how to distribute the revenues. A throw-around rule would also
result in revenues being distributed to a jurisdiction that may have had
no connection to the underlying transaction.

Lingering Issues

While it is possible to set forth in theory a general framework of workable rules for sourcing E-commerce transactions, there will be a myriad
of details to be worked out in application. Many of these issues are interconnected and will depend on the resolution of other key tax rules. For
instance, if "one rate per state" is adopted on a near-universal basis, then
many of the sourcing issues will become much more manageable. Similarly, whether default rules (such as throwback or throw-around rules) are

needed or workable will depend to a large degree on the extent to which the Internet will generate sales to unknown or unknowable destinations, a fact that is not discernable at this early stage in the development of E-commerce.

There are a number of other issues that would need to be resolved—either up-front or on a trial-and-error basis. Should a seller that makes sales of digital products to business customers always have an obligation to determine the actual destination of use? At what point is it reasonable for the seller to simply source the transaction to the business customer's billing address? With regard to vendors who make sales of digital products to nonbusiness customers, will they be responsible for sourcing the sale to the actual state of destination if it is known to them (or least appears somewhere in their records)? What level of effort will be required of a vendor to determine the customer's billing address if it is unknown to them? Will a safe harbor be available to a vendor if it uses a throwback or throw-around method after making a good-faith effort to determine the customer's billing address? Should gift transactions use special rules and be sourced to the location of the purchaser, not the location of the recipient of the gift? What about transactions for which a customer pays with a check and may be unfamiliar with the sales tax situsing rules?

There are also a number of issues related to third-party intermediaries that will need to be addressed. Do the financial intermediaries have sufficient information available to provide the vendor with the location of the billing address? If they do not, should additional responsibility (perhaps with compensation) be placed on the financial intermediaries to build into Secure Electronic Transaction (SET) or other electronic credit-card technologies the requirement to collect such jurisdictional information? Will credit-card companies be required by law to collect and share information on a consumer's billing address or other location?

Given the level of uncertainty and complexity surrounding E-commerce sales tax sourcing rules, any system that is created will likely need to be modified and adjusted after it is implemented. There are simply too many unanswered questions and unforeseeable economic and technological developments to design a system that can anticipate all the various needs of both government and business. Much will depend on whether a uniform set of rules is developed at the national level or whether individual states begin to experiment with cutting-edge rules on their own.

Problems with Multiple-User Products

An additional problem created by the digital economy is the need to source sales of electronic services to business customers where there are multiple users in numerous locations of the same product or service. The vast expansion of digital products facilitates the real-time multistate consumption of goods and services. For instance, a business can purchase online access to a legal information database such as CCH or to a medical information database. The business purchaser can pay the vendor for the right to have employees in numerous jurisdictions simultaneously access the product.

There are numerous methodologies available for providing multijurisdictional access to digital products. An information database could be accessed at the vendor's server based on information requests or searches by the consumer ("pull" method). Alternatively, the information may be streamed on a daily (or hourly) basis to the consumer's server based on certain categories of information customized for the consumer ("push" method). The database could also be located on one or multiple servers of some third party that is in the business of hosting multiple-vendor databases or other on-line products. The customer's employees could access the data remotely over the Internet or over an extranet.

In addition, the database product could be shipped electronically to the customer's location and updated by the vendor on a periodic basis. The consumer might choose to have the database stored on one central server and accessed over a company intranet. Alternatively, the consumer could choose to have the database stored on multiple servers at different company locations and accessed over numerous local-area networks. This could be accomplished by having the vendor send the database electronically to multiple customer sites. Or it could occur if a customer took electronic delivery of a master disk at one location with the contractual right to duplicate the disk for use at other customer locations.

This vast potential for multiple-user products arises not just with electronic information databases but with software, computerized training modules, music, and other similar digital products, as well. For instance, a business might purchase ERP software such as SAP or People Soft. The canned software can be electronically transmitted to a central server of the business customer. From that server, the employer may have employees in multiple jurisdictions use the software over a corporate intranet for purposes of inventory control, sales orders, manufacturing operations, and other similar functions.

Alternatively, the customer could have the vendor or some other third party host the software and have the customer's employees access the software over the Internet. The outsourcing of digital storage sites is a growing trend, fueled in large part by the movement toward outsourcing information technology functions in general. This development is akin to the widespread outsourcing of other back-office, accounting, or computer service functions by financial institutions, mutual-fund companies, and other service businesses. This trend will increase the likelihood that multiple-user sourcing rules will need to be used with multijurisdictional business customers.

When a business consumer uses a digital product in multiple jurisdictions, the question arises as to whether the sale should be sourced to one jurisdiction or apportioned among a number of jurisdictions? Should the sourcing rule be different depending on whether the digital product is located on the vendor's server, on a third party's server, on the consumer's central headquarters server, or on the consumer's regional servers? Does it matter if a pull or a push methodology is used?

The whole notion of apportionment of a sales or use tax transaction is relatively novel. *Apportionment* is a concept that typically arises in conjunction with state income taxes. For purposes of determining the share of income to be taxed in each jurisdiction, an apportionment formula is used that divides the income between jurisdictions based on factors such as labor, property, and sales receipts. However, this process occurs only on an annual basis. By contrast, with sales and use tax transactions, sales are typically sourced on a transaction-by-transaction basis, not on an apportioned aggregate basis. Moreover, sales and use taxes are imposed on the transactions occurring each month, not on accumulated transactions taking place annually.

Multiple Purchases of Tangible Property

To be sure, multiple sales to one business customer already occur frequently in connection with tangible property transactions. For instance, a package-delivery service such as Federal Express or United Parcel Services might purchase five thousand motor vehicles from a large automobile manufacturer and have them delivered to all 50 states. Or a large retailer such as Wal-Mart or Toys "R" Us might order a thousand computers for use as cash registers in retail locations throughout the country.

Nonetheless, these transactions are generally much easier to allocate among the states. Typically, the products are shipped directly to the ultimate destinations (e.g., the regional package-delivery headquarters or the local retail-store branch). In that case the sales tax on the transaction is allocated based on the ultimate destination of the goods, much as it would be if a thousand individuals made the purchases separately.

Alternatively, the products are shipped to a central distribution center of the purchaser and then allocated out to the specific geographic regions as the demand arises. In that case either the tax is due entirely in the first jurisdiction or, if there is a temporary storage exemption in the warehouse state, a use tax is due when the products are first used in the jurisdiction where they are placed into service. In either situation there is no occasion whereby the product is consumed by a purchaser in a location other than where the product is physically located. A delivery truck or cash register is used only where such a product is physically located. This makes it much easier to track the state of ultimate destination and use.

Multiple Users of Digital Products

By contrast to the multiple sales of tangible property, a digital product such as software or electronically transmitted information can be purchased and used simultaneously in multiple jurisdictions across the country or even across the world. With the declining cost of telecommunications, a customer can just as easily access the product remotely from the vendor's server or one or several of its own remote servers, as it can have the product delivered to a server or computer terminal in each of the locations at which its employees will use the product. Thus, with digital products there is much more variation as to how and where a product is consumed.

The multistate use of digital products not only raises issues different than those connected with tangible products but also raises issues unique to services. Traditionally, most services were locally based, such as beauty shops or parking lots. To the extent services were multistate in character, such as investment banking services or legal services, the services tended not to be taxable in most jurisdictions and therefore did not require sourcing rules.

Given the nature of the digital economy, state and local governments may not have the option to source digital products used in multiple locations or jurisdictions in the same way that they would source multiple sales of tangible personal property to the same customer. This is because there will generally not be a digital database or product physically downloaded at the location or jurisdiction of each of the customer's employees who are using the product.

In lieu of basing the sales tax on the actual physical location of each of the digital products, the state and local governments may have to come up with an alternative sourcing scheme. One possibility is to apportion the sales tax based on the location of the customer's employees who use the product. Another option is to source the sale to the location(s) of the server where the customer remotely accesses the product (either at the vendor's location or the customer's location). A third option is to source the sale to the commercial domicile, principal place of use, or the billing address of the business customer.

There may not be a constitutional bar to developing an all-or-nothing rule that sources the sale to one jurisdiction, such as the jurisdiction of primary use by the customer. Based on its decisions in *Goldberg v. Sweet* and *Oklahoma Tax Commission v. Jefferson Lines,* the U.S. Supreme Court seems to have established the legal right of a state to impose a sales tax on the entire charge for an interstate service if some of the service is performed in the taxing state and the customer is billed for the service in the taxing state. With respect to the interstate provision of telecommunications services, the Court has held that a state in which an interstate telephone call originates or terminates has the right to tax a customer's purchase of that call as long as the call is billed or charged to a service address within the taxing state. In the area of interstate transportation services, the U.S. Supreme Court recently upheld Oklahoma's imposition of a sales tax on the sale of a bus ticket purchased in Oklahoma for interstate travel originating in Oklahoma.[146]

Although a state may not be required to apportion interstate digital services, it may decide to do so because the alternative is sometimes even less attractive. Apportionment can lead to administrative problems in determining the exact locations in which the customer uses a product. The seller may know (from a contract) how many of the customer's employees are allowed to access a digital product. However, the seller will not necessarily know in which jurisdictions these employees are located—unless this information is supplied by the customer.

Nonetheless, using an all-or-nothing sourcing rule can lead to some major disincentives for business. If a state decides to source a sale to the vendor's location if the database resides on the vendor's computer, then the state might discourage E-commerce vendors from locating within its borders. If a state decides to source a sale to the customer's commercial domicile or other primary location, it similarly may penalize a company for headquartering in the state, even though most of its employees and product use might be outside the state. Moreover, if the state looks solely to where the server(s) that holds the digital property is located, the rule can be easily subverted because it is relatively easy to shift the location and jurisdiction of a server that is used to store a digital product.

The NTA project explored the problem of sourcing sales of multiple-user products but ultimately backed away from any recommendation because of a division among its members as to the most appropriate solution. One solution that was discussed by the NTA project called for apportionment of the sales among the states in which the users are present according to some reasonable, supportable basis. The presumption was that such information was either available to the vendor in the regular course of business or that the purchaser could provide such information. Business customers that purchase electronic products that will be used in multiple points could provide a disclosure form to the vendor detailing the states in which the product will be used, as well as the amount of use, for purposes of deriving an apportionable sales tax to each state. Alternatively, in lieu of the vendor collecting and paying over the tax to the state, the purchaser would have the option to elect a direct-pay mechanism in which the purchaser would self-assess the use tax in each of the relevant market states. An expanded use of the direct-pay concept, which is usually reserved for manufacturers, could coincide nicely with some of the unique characteristics of E-commerce.[147]

Current State Positions

A small minority of states—made up from the ranks of states that currently tax electronic services—have already developed sourcing rules that require or allow a vendor to apportion sales if the consumer uses the digital product in more than one jurisdiction. Most of these modernized tax rules have developed in relation to the sales taxation of electronic information services or computer services. For instance, in the District of Columbia, electronic information services used in more than one jurisdiction are apportioned to the District of Columbia based on the pro rata share of use in the district. According to the District of Columbia rule, "Information services performed or delivered outside of the District for use within other jurisdictions as well as for use within the District shall be subject to a prorated share of the District use tax, provided that no sales tax was required to be paid on that prorated share to the other jurisdiction."[148]

Even if the information is delivered initially to a server outside of the District of Columbia, it is still partially taxable in the district if a sales tax has not been imposed on the portion of the transaction in the jurisdiction where the server is located. According to the District of Columbia rule, "Information services performed, purchased, or delivered outside of the District but subsequently brought into the District for use or consumption shall be subject to the District use tax, provided that no sales tax was required to be paid to the other jurisdiction."[149]

Similarly, in Texas if an information service (or a data processing service) is used by a customer's locations both within and without Texas, then the service is not taxable in Texas to the extent that it is used outside of Texas. If a multistate customer asserts that the information will be used both within and without the state, then the customer must provide the vendor with an exemption certificate in lieu of the tax. Once this direct-pay–like certificate has been given to the vendor, it becomes the customer's responsibility to report the tax to the various states for that portion of the information services used in each state. A vendor that accepts a certificate in good faith is relieved of any responsibility for collecting and remitting tax in transactions to which the certificate applies.[150]

Under the Texas rule, it does not make a difference whether the information is stored on a server in Texas or at a location in another state. The apportionment of the sales tax is based solely on the pro rata use of the information service in Texas. Under the Texas rule, a multistate customer may use any reasonable method for allocation that is supported by business records. Under the Texas regulation, "The customer's books must support the assignment of the service to an identifiable segment of the business, the determination of the location or locations of the use of the service, and the allocation of the taxable charge to Texas."[151]

Texas has a similar rule for the apportionment of sales tax between local jurisdictions for purposes of the local sales and use tax. It is one of many states that have city, county, transit authority, and/or special district sales taxes. If a customer uses an electronic information service in multiple local jurisdictions within Texas or in multiple local jurisdictions inside and outside of Texas, then the customer must use an exemption certificate and self-assess the tax in each local jurisdiction—based on the percentage of the service used in each local jurisdiction.[152]

Likewise, under New York tax rules, if information services are provided by electronic means to a consumer both inside and outside of New York, then the sales tax is apportioned. Under the New York rule, the "tax for reports delivered by electronic means should be allocated according to the number of client offices within and without New York that have access to the electronic reports."[153]

Many other states that tax electronic goods and services, including Ohio, South Carolina, and South Dakota, do not have specific rules to deal with situations whereby a product is delivered to a single location for use by multiple consumers in multiple locations. For instance, Ohio has no specific sourcing rule, only an ambiguous general rule. Under the Ohio rule, "(a) The provision of automatic data processing services or computer services in this state for a consideration for use in business is a sale; and (b) The receipt of the benefit of these services in this state for use in business constitutes a use."[154] In Ohio and other similar states, business consumers are left to either guess what the right result is or rely on informal (and nonbinding) advice from state tax authorities.

If states do not adopt direct-pay certificates for this type of situation, then what is the responsibility of the vendor for determining where the business customer actually uses the digitized product? Does the vendor have to inquire before the transaction is completed? What if the customer does not provide the locational information—is the vendor off the hook, and can the state only audit the customer? This problem is exacerbated when the vendor hosts the digitized product—because the vendor may not have the option of sourcing the whole sale to the state to which it initially sends the digital product.

Sourcing Software versus Information Services

Similar issues arise with sourcing sales of software that are sold to customers who use the products in multiple locations. However, unlike sales of information services, most jurisdictions do not have any rules for the apportionment of sales of electronically transmitted software. Part of the explanation for this may be that until recently software was less likely than information to be delivered electronically to one location but used remotely from a number of other locations. Another explanation for this outcome, however, is that states generally use a different sales tax base category for taxing the sale of digitized software. Although most states that tax digitized information do so under a service category that includes sales of electronic information services, most states that tax digitized software do so under the state rules governing sales of tangible personal property. As discussed previously, most of these states treat electronically transferred software as if it were still the sale of tangible personal property.

The states that tax the electronic transfer of canned software as a taxable sale of tangible property typically do not have a special sourcing rule for circumstances whereby the software is accessed by a consumer in multiple jurisdictions. In the absence of a special sourcing rule, these states will most likely use sourcing rules that are applied to other types of tangible personal property. Thus, if the software is delivered initially to a server in a state that taxes the electronic transfer of software, that state is likely to impose the sales tax on the entire transaction regardless of whether the software will be accessed remotely and used in other jurisdictions. If the software is delivered initially to a server in a state that does not tax the electronic transfer of software, other states may not tax the transaction at all.

As a result of this dichotomy, it is quite possible that states may not apportion sales of digitally transferred software even though they would apportion sales of digitally transferred information. If the state is treating a digital transfer as if it were tangible personal property, then the transfer of title and possession of the product becomes more important. Software that is accessed remotely never has a transfer of title or possession in the taxing jurisdiction. This explains why a state may tax the entire transaction if the software is sent to a server in the state but none of the transaction if the software is accessed remotely from a server in another state. This is also consistent with the notion of a use tax on tangible personal property, which is typically only imposed on the use, storage or consumption of tangible personal property delivered into a state after it has been purchased in another state.

Although this outcome may derive logically from the use of a category of tangible personal property to tax digitized software, it still leads to some of the problems already discussed, whereby a sourcing rule is based on the location of a server, not the location of consumption. Thus, a transaction might be fully taxable if the software sent to a server in a jurisdiction that taxes digital transfers, even if only one-quarter of the use of the software occurs in the host state. Conversely, the transaction may not be taxed at all if the software is sent electronically to a server in a state that does not tax electronic transfers but is primarily accessed remotely from states that tax digitized software (but only as the transfer of tangible personal property).

Texas is one of the few states that has issued a ruling on this fact pattern, and its ruling is consistent with the foregoing analysis. Texas taxes electronic transfers of software as the sale of tangible personal property. The state will tax all of a multistate transaction if the software resides solely on a Texas server, and none of the transaction if the software resides on a server in another state and is never downloaded onto a server in Texas.[155]

To confuse matters, what would be the outcome if the software is sent simultaneously to several states, or if the software is sent to the server(s) of a third-party hosting service that happens to be in the jurisdiction where the customer is headquartered. The vendor may not even know what jurisdiction(s) in which the third-party server is located. Even if the vendor knows the location of the third-party server, is the transaction fully taxable in that state even though possession and title to the property does not necessarily pass to the customer? Clearly, states that tax electronic products as tangible personal property will have to grapple with whether to use an all-or-nothing approach or an apportionment sourcing rule.

Secondary Users or Beneficiaries

Another problem with the apportionment of multistate sales of services arises when it is not possible or practicable to determine the location of the ultimate use of the digitized product. For instance, an information vendor might sell an on-line stock-brokerage company access to an electronic database that contains financial information and stock quotes. The business customer may have the financial information shipped electronically to its central server in one jurisdiction and also to a backup server in another jurisdiction. Next, the information may be shipped to regional servers used by the business customer's employees in additional jurisdictions. Finally, the information database may be open to access (for free or a separate charge) as part of a bundle of services offered to the stock-brokerage company's own customers at multiple locations throughout the country or even throughout the world. In that case the stock-trading company (the business purchaser) itself may not be able to make a reasonable estimate of where the digital products are being used or where it is getting the benefit of the information service.

A similar situation can arise with the use of leased telecommunications lines. Where leased telecommunications lines are used by a lessee to provide a regional or nationwide digital network, it may be difficult to determine which consumer's use is relevant for sales and use tax purposes. For instance, where a vendor of Internet access or on-line services leases telephone lines from a telecommunications carrier and uses them to provide free local access to the residential purchasers of the Internet access service, should the purchase of the leased lines be sourced to the location at which the Internet access company has its central communications center or to the multiple locations at which the ultimate consumers access the Internet access company's points of presence?[156]

There are analogous situations for which the apportionment of multistate services, both those delivered electronically and those delivered in person, is complicated because of the lack of clarity of where the benefit of the services is delivered. While year-end apportionment of income is commonplace for corporate income taxes, it is still relatively unusual for transactional sales and use taxes. For instance, if a state imposes sales taxes on legal, investment, or other professional services, it may decide to apportion the tax based on where the service is used. This can be problematic if the service is used in multiple jurisdictions. Thus, if a law firm draws up a pension plan for a multinational business client, the gross receipts from that activity could be apportioned based on the percentage of that client's employees that work or reside in the taxing jurisdiction.

While this calculation is possible to make, it is very different from the usual sales or use tax calculation which is based on the consumption of a product or service in just one jurisdiction. Indeed, in 1990 Massachusetts drew up regulations to interpret its short-lived sales tax on professional (and other) services, to provide vendors and consumers with a "rough-justice" alternative to a transaction-by-transaction apportionment rule. Under this alternative, for sales tax purposes, a vendor could site its sales to a particular multistate client based on its annual gross receipts from

taxable sales to the client multiplied by the client's corporate apportionment percentage in the taxing jurisdiction. Although this method was
inexact, it was determined to be better than the alternative, which was to
source the whole sale to the commercial domicile of the customer.

General Observations on Market-State versus Vendor-State Sourcing Rules

It is clear that the creation of sourcing rules for a digital economy will be
an arduous and frustrating task. No one set of rules is likely to prove
ideal, and therefore, a considerable amount of experimentation can be
expected. It is probable, however, that the basic foundation will be built
around market- or destination-state sourcing rules that focus on the
location of consumption or use, not on vendor-state sourcing rules that
focus on the location of the remote seller. While vendor-state rules may
be used for specific types of activities (e.g., phone cards) or even for specific industries (e.g., broadcasting), their more-widespread use is likely to
be limited for both practical and political reasons.

Since the mid 1990s, a number of state tax-related groups and individuals have addressed the issue of how to source sales of telecommunication services, digital goods, and services and other forms of E-commerce.
Most of these efforts have focused on developing uniform rules that rely
on sourcing sales to the location of the customer (or market state). In
1995 the Information Highway State and Local Tax Study Group (composed primarily of large telephone, cable, and wireless companies) issued
a position paper on the taxation of telecommunications and information
services. The paper set forth a framework that called for parity between
vendors that sell digital products and vendors that sell similar tangible
products. The paper strongly advocated that the telecommunications
industry should be "taxed in the same manner and at the same level as
other commercial and industrial businesses." Although the paper did not
specifically address sales tax sourcing rules, the clear implication was that
states should use the same destination-based rules that were used in conjunction with tangible property sales.[157]

Similarly, in late 1996 the Interactive Services Association (made up of a number of leading computer and telecommunication companies involved in on-line computer services) issued a report on cybertaxation. The report addressed a broad range of sales and use tax issues primarily focused on the approach that should be taken toward the taxation of Internet access services and other on-line computer services. Although sales tax sourcing issues were not the group's primary focus, the report did express a preference for attribution to the consumer's billing address as a proxy for the consumer's service address.[158]

In the spring of 1997, Walter Hellerstein, a leading state-tax authority, wrote a paper that set forth a market-state approach to situsing E-commerce sales. Hellerstein's initial proposal called for a reverse engineering of the collection issue, with vendors generally required to collect sales tax in the jurisdiction of the consumer regardless of the vendor's level of physical presence in the consumer state. Obviously, this proposal would require congressional legislation to override the constraints placed on states by the *Quill Corp. v. North Dakota* decision. The Hellerstein proposal generally advocated a market-state rule—sourcing E-commerce sales to a state if the consumer's billing address were in that state. For situations whereby the consumer's billing address could not be determined, a throwback rule would source the sales to the state of the vendor's principal place of business, assuming that state imposed a sales or use tax on the applicable category of E-commerce.[159]

Finally, as previously discussed, the most visible and prolonged effort to formulate uniform rules for sourcing sales related to E-commerce has been made by the NTA's Communication and Electronic Commerce Tax Project. Although this group did not adopt any final conclusions, it passed a resolution that supported a state-of-use or destination approach to sourcing sales of digital goods and services.[160]

The primary reason for the strong support for a market-state–based system derives from its consistency with traditional sales tax sourcing rules (governing sales of tangible personal property), which look to the location of consumption for siting purposes. The market-state approach also has the advantage of treating the sale of digital goods and services in the same manner as the sale of similarly situated tangible property.

The market-state rule does, however, have some disadvantages compared to the vendor-state rule. First, if sales are sourced to the vendor state, there is no *Quill Corp. v. North Dakota* or constitutional nexus problem. The vendor state already has the constitutional authority to require the seller to collect sales or use tax in the state of origin. Second, if the state-of-origin rule is used, then there need be no burdensome administrative rules on how to identify the state of consumption or, as an alternative, the location of the consumer's billing address. Likewise, there is no need to develop rules for sourcing sales that involve multiple users because these sales are all sourced back to the state of origin.

Indeed, on the basis of administrative simplicity and constitutional fidelity, the vendor-state rule does have some supporters, particularly in the broadcasting and high-technology industries. Moreover, in other countries that use a VAT system, the issue of market-state versus vendor-state sourcing is by no means settled. Although the VAT countries generally use a destination-state system, there are many instances in which they also source transactions to the seller's jurisdiction. As will be seen in chapter 5, the VAT countries are still wrestling with how to source digital services as well.[161]

It is quite possible that states may not rely solely on either the market-state rule or the vendor-state rule. As noted, there may be a number of situations for which a vendor-state rule is the appropriate solution, for example, in relation to phone cards, gift transactions, or similar situations for which a destination rule would impose too much of an administrative burden.

Nonetheless, the vendor-state approach has certain weaknesses that most likely rule it out as a general solution for sourcing E-commerce sales. First, there is the issue of identifying the vendor state. While this may seem obvious, there may be a choice between the state of incorporation of the vendor, the location of the vendor's commercial domicile, the location at which the vendor principally manages its E-commerce business, and even the location of the vendor's computer server that hosts the E-commerce business. Depending on the particular method chosen, there will also be a disincentive to locate the vendor's operations in a state with a higher sales tax rate, even if virtually all of the vendor's customers were located in other states. The possibility would also arise for certain states to create a favorable environment for E-commerce vendors by exempting them from tax (or from the imposition of a vendor-state rule), thus creating widespread avoidance of the sales tax.

Even more problematic is that a vendor-state rule used solely for digital transactions would create a dual sourcing system that would source sales of digital goods and services differently than similarly situated tangible goods. For instance, the sale of canned software delivered on a tangible medium would be sourced to the state of consumption, whereas the sale of canned software delivered electronically would be sourced to the state of origin. Depending on the relative tax rates in the two jurisdictions, this dual system would discriminate against one of the forms of commerce. A vendor-state rule would also lead to economic distortion, with sellers potentially changing their method of delivery to derive the most favorable tax result.

Sales and Use Tax Simplification

The emergence of E-commerce is not only raising novel issues related to *substantive* sales and use tax rules, but it is also heightening awareness of the cumbersome, complex, and in many cases, unworkable sales and use tax *procedural* rules. Simplification of sales and use tax compliance has long been a rallying call for multistate businesses, and the climate for change has never been more fertile. On the one hand, businesses are generally unwilling to consider the adoption of uniform rules for requiring remote vendors to collect sales and use tax on E-commerce transactions without a vast simplification of the sales and use tax compliance rules. On the other hand, the states and localities are so afraid of the erosion of the sales tax base caused by remote vendors engaged in E-commerce that they are willing to contemplate radical simplification of state and local tax autonomy in exchange for a liberalization of nexus rules so that such rules apply to vendors without physical presence in the consumer's jurisdiction.

As already discussed, sales and use tax compliance in the United States is complicated by the number of local jurisdictions that impose sales and use taxes. Currently, approximately 7,500 states, cities, towns, counties, transportation districts, and other special local jurisdictions impose sales or use taxes on transactions occurring within their boundaries. The estimated breakdown by type of jurisdiction is as follows: states (46), cities (4,696), counties (1,602), and other jurisdictions including school districts and special districts (1,113). The approximately 7,500 jurisdictions with tax rates make up less than 10 percent of the approximately 87,000 state and local government units in the United States. Currently, about three-quarters of the jurisdictions with state-level sales taxes also have local-level sales and use taxes (see table 2.4).[162]

Although the vast majority of localities with sales and use taxes adhere to state tax rules for determining what is taxable and how the tax is administered, a minority of jurisdictions require separate tax-return filings under their own unique local sales tax rules. For instance, localities in Alabama, Arizona, Colorado, and Louisiana impose home-rule sales taxes. In these jurisdictions local rules may vary from state tax rules and separate returns must be filed to report local sales and use tax collections.

Even in those jurisdictions that follow state tax rules and allow local taxes to be collected and paid over as part of a state tax return, vendors must still comply with a myriad of local tax rates. For example, in New York the combined state and local sales and use tax rates range from 4 percent to 8.5 percent, depending on the local and county jurisdiction; in Oklahoma the combined state and local rates range from 4.5 percent to 10.5 percent; in Kansas the combined state and local rates range from 4.9 percent to 7.4 percent.

Some jurisdictions even have different state-level rates depending on the type of goods or services subject to tax. Alabama, for instance, imposes a general rate of 4 percent on most goods and services. However, it imposes a rate of 2 percent on sales of automobiles, a rate of 1.5 percent on sales of manufacturing and farm equipment, a rate of 3 percent on food products sold through vending machines, and a rate of 2 percent on the rental of linens and garments. Similarly, Mississippi has a general sales tax rate of 7 percent on most goods and services but imposes a rate of 3 percent on farm tractors, a rate of 1.5 percent on

Table 2.4.   **States with Local Sales Taxes (as of May 1999)**

States*	Total State and Local Sales Tax
Alabama	4–10%
Alaska	1–7%
Arizona	5–8.8%
Arkansas	4.625–8.625%
California	7.25–8.5%
Colorado	3–10%
Florida	6–7.5%
Georgia	5–7%
Idaho	6–7%
Illinois	6.25–9%
Iowa	5–7%
Kansas	4.9–7.4%
Louisiana	5.8–9.7%
Minnesota	6.5–7.5%
Missouri	4.225–7.975%
Nebraska	4.5–6.0%
Nevada	4.250–7.250%
New Mexico	5–6.938%
New York	4–8.5%
North Carolina	6%
North Dakota	5–7%
Ohio	5.5–7%
Oklahoma	4.5–10.5%
South Carolina	5–7%
South Dakota	4–6%
Tennessee	7–8.75%
Texas	6.25–8.25%
Utah	5.75–7.75%
Virginia	4.5–4.5%
Washington	7.0–8.6%
Wisconsin	5–6%
Wyoming	4–6%

*Total = 32.

manufacturing machinery, a rate of 8 percent on wholesale sales of food to be used in vending machines, a rate of 3.5 percent on construction services, and a rate of 3 percent on admissions to publicly owned coliseums and auditoriums.[163]

Indeed, it generally requires a computer program simply to keep up with the changes in state and local sales tax rates. Since 1990 5,856 jurisdictions have either changed their tax rates or added new sales tax rates. In 1998 alone a total of 579 jurisdictions changed existing tax rates or added new sales tax rates. Over 95 percent of these rate changes were at the city, county, and special district levels. Thus, multistate taxpayers shoulder the administrative burden of keeping track of all of these changes in jurisdictions where they have a filing obligation.[164]

Over the last 20 years, states and localities have significantly increased their reliance on sales taxes. In 1998 the average state sales tax rate was 5.109 percent, the average county rate was 1.519 percent, and the average rate charged by cities was 1.623 percent. This resulted in a record-high average combined rate of 8.251 percent (for jurisdictions with all three tax types). By comparison, in 1981 the average combined state and local sales and use tax was 6.515 percent. (See table 2.5.)[165]

The sales and use tax filing requirements imposed by taxing jurisdictions create substantial filing burdens on multistate taxpayers. First, corporations must ensure that they are registered for sales and use tax collection in all of the states in which they have nexus. Second, businesses must monitor rate and tax base changes in all of these jurisdictions, keep track of exemptions, and ensure that the proper filings are made in a timely manner. These requirements can be quite cumbersome, particu-

Table 2.5.   **Growth of State and Local Sales Tax Rates 1981–1998 (in percent)***

	State	County	City	Combined
1981	4.101	1.153	1.261	6.515
1990	4.945	1.339	1.528	7.812
1998	5.109	1.519	1.623	8.251

Source: Vertex, Inc. *Vertex Tax Cybrary.*
*Average rates for jurisdictions with each level of tax.

larly for companies that do business in most state and local jurisdictions. AT&T, for example, files 39,912 state and local tax returns annually. That total number amounts to one return filed every 3.12 minutes.[166]

The sales and use tax compliance burden is exacerbated by the vast differences in procedural rules between the states. There are significant differences not only in tax rates and in the breadth of the sales tax base but also in registration rules, filing requirements, exemption-certificate utilization, voluntary disclosure, and other procedural requirements.

Historically, simplification of sales and use tax compliance has been inhibited by the system of federalism in the United States. Aside from certain constitutional restrictions on state and local taxation, jurisdictions are free to enact their own rules and regulations. Because each state and local jurisdiction engages in this process independently, there is currently little incentive for any state to conform its legislation and policies to that of any other state. The result is a virtually incoherent system of state and local sales and use procedural rules that imposes substantial compliance burdens on taxpayers.

Age-Old Problem

The problems associated with multistate sales and use tax compliance are not new. Indeed, there have been numerous attempts in recent decades to simplify sales and use tax procedural rules. These initiatives have generally centered on promoting more uniformity among the states in terms of tax returns, audits, information collection, exemption requirements, and other procedural rules. For the most part, however, these governmental and business efforts have failed to stem the tide of complexity that has swept over multistate sales and use tax compliance.

For example, in 1965 the Willis Commission made a report to the U.S. Congress on state taxation of interstate commerce. The report detailed numerous problems with sales and use tax compliance and recommended either a limitation of the expansive jurisdictional standards imposed on out-of-state sellers or a major simplification of sales and use tax compliance rules. Among the primary concerns were the 2,300 different jurisdictions that were imposing sales and use tax, as well as the lack of uniformity of forms and rules. According to the report, "interstate sellers would be exposed to severe compliance difficulties if they were required to account for interstate sales to all customers in each taxing locality."[167]

Thirty-five years later few of the Willis Commission recommendations have been adopted. During this period, however, the number of local jurisdictions imposing sales and use taxes has nearly tripled. Moreover, in the intervening years, multistate businesses and state and local governments have engaged in a continuous battle over the jurisdictional requirements and procedural rules imposed on out-of-state vendors.

The jurisdictional battlefield has been framed around several significant U.S. Supreme Court decisions that placed restrictions on a state's ability to impose a sales or use tax collection responsibility on out-of-state vendors. In 1967 the Supreme Court issued its decision on the limits of a state's authority under the U.S. Constitution to impose a sales or use tax on an out-of-state mail-order company that had no physical presence in the jurisdiction of its consumers. In *National Bellas Hess, Inc. v. Department of Revenue,* the Court held that it was unconstitutional under both the Due Process and Commerce Clauses of the U.S. Constitution for states or localities to impose sales and use tax collection obligations on businesses that did not have an in-state physical presence.[168] According to the Court, although Congress can enact legislation to correct deficiencies in the Commerce Clause, the Due Process Clause is outside of the scope of matters regulated by Congress.

In the 1980s, despite the Court's decision in *National Bellas Hess, Inc. v. Department of Revenue,* the states began to once again broaden their nexus standards and move away from the physical-presence requirement. For instance, in 1984 the MTC withdrew its five-factor nexus standard based on physical presence and replaced it with a new broad nexus standard based on economic presence in the customer's jurisdiction—above a *de minimis* level. The states believed that the U.S. Supreme Court, if given the opportunity, would overturn the *National Bellas Hess, Inc. v. Department of Revenue* decision.

In 1992, however, the Court in *Quill Corp. v. North Dakota* affirmed its earlier decision that a state could not impose a sales and use tax filing obligation on a seller that had no physical presence in the state. Although the Supreme Court followed its earlier precedent, it did so in a way that elevated the constitutional significance of multistate sales and use tax compliance rules. The Court reversed itself on one key element of its earlier decision—the notion that the imposition of a collection responsibility on a vendor with no physical presence in the consumer's state violated the Due Process Clause of the Constitution. The Court stated that an out-of-state company with a significant customer base in a state could be required to collect sales and use tax in a state, even without physical presence, without violating the Due Process Clause. However, the Court still sided with the multistate taxpayer—concluding that a broader economic presence nexus standard was still unconstitutional under the Commerce Clause, in large part because neither the states nor the U.S. Congress had ever established a more simplified and uniform system of sales and use tax compliance.

Rising Pressure for Reform

While efforts to simplify the sales and use tax compliance system have historically met with failure, there are several factors currently at work that hold the potential for changing the political equation. First, the explosion of E-commerce is threatening to erode the sales tax base far more than mail-order sales in the past. As discussed in chapter 1, E-commerce–related sales are expected to far exceed mail-order sales within the next five years. This reality creates far more urgency for the states and localities to devise a compromise solution or risk a significant erosion of their sales tax base.

Second, the *Quill Corp. v. North Dakota* decision has opened up the possibility that Congress, or perhaps the states acting on their own initiative, could overcome Commerce Clause objections to imposing a duty to collect on remote vendors with only economic presence in the customer's jurisdiction. To rectify this problem, however, it will be necessary to significantly simplify the sales and use tax compliance system. This dual reality has compelled states and localities to take simplification initiatives much more seriously.

In the late 1990s, a number of government and business projects have been initiated in an effort to simplify state and local sales and use tax compliance. For instance, the MTC formed a Sales Tax Simplification Planning Committee. This committee, which is made up of professionals from both the public and private sectors, is focused on providing the MTC with solutions for simplifying sales taxes. The current recommendations involve the easing of sales tax administrative burdens, to the extent realistically possible, by creating uniformity among the rules, regulations, procedures, and policies promulgated by each state. The ideas suggested have been divided into four main categories by the committee: (1) broad policy simplification, (2) compliance simplification, (3) audits and appeals, and (4) education and communication.[169]

The NGA has also addressed sales tax compliance in an effort to create a "simplified 21st-century state sales tax system. The NGA believes a new and simplified sales and use tax system would reduce costs and administrative burdens for businesses and consumers, provide U.S. companies with a competitive advantage in the global marketplace, and provide a tool for states to create equity between mainstream businesses and remote sellers. In 1998 the NGA endorsed legislation that would make sweeping changes to state and local tax rules. First, it proposed that there be only one tax rate per state on all taxable E-commerce and mail-order purchases. The NGA also recommended the creation of a system of uniform definitions for goods and services that may be taxed, allowing states to choose whether to tax the uniformly defined goods and services within their boundaries. The new sales and use tax system would also improve the administration of sales and use taxes by promoting uniform registration, tax returns, remittance requirements, and filing procedures.[170]

The NTA's Communications and Electronic Commerce Tax Project also embarked on a serious effort to achieve some government and business consensus over necessary administrative reforms to the sales and use tax compliance system. Over the course of a number of meetings in 1998 and 1999, the NTA project members analyzed and debated numerous proposals for a major overhaul of state and local procedural sales tax rules. Under one widely discussed scenario, the duty to collect sales and use tax would be extended to remote vendors with economic presence above a certain minimal threshold in the customer's state, the sales and use tax compliance system would be drastically simplified with the adoption of one sales tax rate per state for all commerce, and the compliance system would be further made workable by the adoption of a number of uniformity and simplification proposals related to tax returns, registration requirements, exemption certificates, tax base definitions, and so on. Without reaching agreement on any grandiose tax reform proposal, the NTA did publish a series of working papers and a final report that at least evaluated the strengths and weaknesses of various administrative reform proposals.

More recently, the Federal Advisory Commission on Electronic Commerce—created by the U.S. Congress in 1998 to examine the global and U.S. issues related to the taxation of E-commerce—has undertaken a study of the issue of sales tax simplification. The Federal Internet Tax Freedom Act authorized the commission to examine model state legislation that would "provide uniform definitions of categories of property, goods, service, or information subject to or exempt from sales and use taxes." To that end, the commission has held hearings and solicited public comments and papers on possible means to simplify the sales and use tax compliance system in the United States. Participants in this effort include state governors, corporate chief executives, and top federal government officials.[171]

These government and business initiatives have created a substantial momentum toward simplification of the U.S. sales and use tax system. At no point in the last quarter century has there been more of a groundswell in favor of both minor and radical reform of state and local sales tax rules. Nonetheless, substantial political hurdles remain as the participants attempt to balance business's need for drastic simplification with government's desire to impose collection responsibilities on remote vendors.

One Sales Tax Rate per State

The single most important reform that has been recommended for simplifying sales and use tax compliance is to replace the current system of a multiplicity of tax rates within one state with a single sales tax rate per state. This would involve having one tax rate per state rather than having separate and distinct taxes at the state, county, and local level. The multiple-rate structure is an issue in about three-quarters of the states, where there is not only a state-level sales or use tax rate but also a wide variety of local rates. As long as there are multiple tax rates in many jurisdictions, a multistate vendor will need to comply with not only the 46 state jurisdictions that impose a sales or use tax but also with some or all of the additional 7,500 local jurisdictions that impose a sales or use tax on transactions within their borders.

The prevalence of local rates imposes a number of administrative burdens on multistate vendors. First, the vendors must obtain information on the destination of the sale not just based on the customer's state but also on the customer's locality. This can be particularly difficult with intangible products ordered over the Internet. Second, the vendor must keep track of nearly 700 local tax rate changes a year, rather than fewer than 10 state tax-rate changes a year (or purchase software that performs this function). Third, the vendor must file tax returns that break out the sales tax collected for each state and local taxing jurisdiction.

The one-rate-per-state proposal raises a number of important issues that need to be resolved before such an idea could be implemented. One primary issue is whether the single rate per state applies to all commerce or just to remote commerce. The NTA project, subject to its general position that "nothing is agreed to until everything is agreed to," approved a resolution in favor of a single rate per state on *all* commerce. The NTA project recommended: "There should be one tax rate per state which would apply to all commerce involving goods or services that are taxable in that state. Provision must be made to ensure protection and equitable distribution of revenues to local jurisdictions. The details of how to encourage or require states, local governments, and businesses to participate in this new system need further study." The NGA, on the other hand, proposed legislation in 1998 that would enact one rate per state, but only for remote commerce.[172] If the one-rate proposal is applied to only remote commerce, it could lead to discriminatory treatment of main street retailers who must collect all local taxes. If the one-rate proposal is applied to all commerce, it would provide more equality between vendors but also place greater stress on state-local government revenue-sharing arrangements, given the larger tax base at stake.

Second, there are a number of options for how the single rate would be determined. One option is to use the lowest combined tax rate collected statewide. Another option is to impose a blended rate, which involves determining a blended rate for the local jurisdictions and adding it to the state rate. Yet another option involves applying a new rate determined by the legislature of each state. Each of these options creates its own set of problems, and is objected to by some constituency. For example, a uniform rate that is lower than the combined rate currently imposed by a jurisdiction is objected to by localities, as it may result in budgetary shortfalls. Additionally, localities may face problems paying for existing debt, such as bond issues, to which sales and use tax revenue is already pledged. The extent of the shortfalls will depend on what the new rate is applied to. If the lower rate applies to all transactions, the shortfall will be substantially greater than if the lower rate only applies to remote or electronic transactions. Reciprocally, if the uniform rate were higher than the current rate, businesses would object because the increased rate would potentially have a negative impact on business.

Third, the imposition of statewide uniform rates would also reduce the autonomy of local governments. Cities and counties would no longer be able to increase the sales tax rate to fund local projects, such as sports stadiums, educational facilities, and municipal public works. In addition, when faced with an unexpected budgetary shortfall, cities and counties would not be able to increase sales and use taxes to raise additional revenue. This inflexibility could create significant hurdles for localities that have relied on local sales tax revenues to relieve pressure on local property tax rates. Serious consideration would also have to be given to how to replace local sales tax revenue streams that were pledged to repay long-term debt used for public works construction. Indeed, in some states, such as California, a one-rate system could not be implemented without a change in that state's Constitution.

The impact of the one-rate-per-state proposal would be felt both on an individual locality basis and in the aggregate. As noted previously, in many states the local rates vary significantly between jurisdictions. For example, in Chicago, Illinois, the aggregate tax rate is 8.75 percent (6.25 percent state rate, 1.5 percent Cook County rate, and 1 percent city of Chicago rate). In other parts of Cook County, there is no city rate, and thus the aggregate rate in those localities is 7.75 percent. In other parts of Illinois, there are no county or city rates, so the total sales tax rate is 6.25 percent. A one-rate plan would eliminate all of these differences but also reduce the flexibility of local and county jurisdictions.

Moreover, on an aggregate basis, local sales taxes make up about 10 percent of all local tax receipts and are the second-largest local tax source (after property tax). Of the 200 cities in the United States with populations over 100,000, 116 impose retail sales taxes. In addition, 37 more of these largest cities are located in counties or special districts that have retail sales taxes. In recent years local tax revenues in the United States from local sales tax collections totaled about $40 billion. Under a one-rate proposal, localities would have to come up with alternative sources of revenue, the state would have to reimburse the localities, or total local revenues would shrink.[173]

Thus, while in principle there is broad support for the dramatic change in state and local federalism that would be caused by the elimination of local sales tax rates, in practice there are many formidable obstacles to the implementation of this proposal. Complicated issues regarding information reporting to the localities, state government revenue sharing, bond authority contractual arrangements, and state constitutional law would need to be resolved. Indeed, the political and administrative problems associated with the one-rate proposal are leading many government officials to favor a state government funded, technology-driven compliance solution that might simplify the collection process enough to obviate the need for a one-rate plan (see Real-Time Approach). As one local government official noted in 1999, the "single-rate cure may be worse than any disease suggested."[174]

Uniform Sales and Use Tax Base

A second major simplification reform involves creating more-uniform definitions of categories of tangible property or services that are included or excluded in the sales tax base. The digital economy has significantly increased the complexity of determining what is taxable and what is exempt under current state and local sales tax rules. The lack of uniformity among states in defining taxable goods and services has been prevalent throughout the 70-year history of the sales tax in the United States. However, with the vast expansion of E-commerce, there is likely to be a sharp proliferation of disputes over statutory ambiguities, bundling of taxable and nontaxable services, and input exemptions.

In recognition of this looming problem, the NTA project evaluated the utility of various existing federal and international product and service classification systems to determine their usefulness for purposes of U.S. sales and use tax base definitions. The NTA project surveyed the United Nations Centralized Product Classification Scheme, the World Customs Organization's Harmonized Commodity Description and Coding System, the North American Industrial Code System, and the Bureau of Labor Statistics Expense Categories. Generally, the NTA project group found these other classification systems too cumbersome or too oriented toward "goods" to use as the basis for a uniform system of sales tax categories. However, the group noted that the United Nations system and a pending U.S. Census Bureau classification scheme were the most promising in terms of providing a base on which to construct a similar uniform classification structure for sales and use tax bases.[175]

The simplification of the sales and use tax base requires balancing the preservation of a state's right to determine the breadth of its sales tax base with the need to establish a system that is not unduly burdensome for a remote vendor to comply with. Ultimately, even if a more uniform classification scheme is adopted by the states, its utility will be somewhat diminished as long as the states continue to adopt widely varying sales tax bases and to enact significant numbers of exemptions for business, political, and social rationales.

As already noted, states in the northeastern part of the United States have sales tax bases that are typically one-third to one-half smaller than states in the western part of the country. In addition, many states tax fewer than 25 service categories, while other states tax over a hundred service categories. Even with more-uniform definitions, the use of widespread exemptions creates more ambiguities and more overlaps between taxable and nontaxable goods and services. The hodgepodge nature of many state sales tax bases also increases the likelihood of issues arising over the bundling of products and the pyramiding of taxes.

Ironically, the value-added tax used extensively abroad in lieu of a retail sales tax has far greater uniformity with regard to its tax base. For instance, although some nations within the European Community have their own definitions of certain product or service categories, most definitions are determined on a continent-wide basis, with few differences among nations. Of course, this outcome is enhanced in VAT countries by extremely broad tax bases that exclude far fewer items (especially among service categories) than U.S. state and local sales taxes.

In the United States, such an approach would require significant sales tax base broadening, particularly for states that currently tax few or no service categories or digital-products categories. Such base broadening would certainly appeal to those who believe that products should be subject to the same tax rules regardless of whether they are delivered in tangible or electronic form. In many jurisdictions, however, such wide-scale tax-rule changes are likely to create considerable political controversy, given both the checkered history of recent state initiatives to broaden the sales tax on services and the level of public support for tax-free or tariff-free Internet commerce.

Uniform or Simpler Administrative Procedures

Another major focus of sales tax simplification is to create more uniformity among states in the use of vendor registration forms, sales and use tax returns, and exemption certificates. Traditionally, states (and to some extent localities) have used their own formats for each of these administrative requirements. The uniqueness of each state to procedural formats has created a significant paperwork burden for multistate taxpayers, particularly those that have operations in the majority of states. Typically, a taxpayer must use different forms in each state, with customized information requirements, different filing frequencies, and different record-keeping requirements. These varying filing requirements have made multijurisdictional sales tax compliance a burdensome, paper-intensive, and time-consuming activity. The disparate rules and formats have also inhibited efforts to accelerate the electronic filing of registration forms and sales and use tax returns.

As with some of the other components of sales tax simplification, the reform of procedural and filing requirements has broad support among both business and government constituencies. The MTC, the Federation of Tax Administrators (FTA), National Taxpayers Association Electronic Commerce Tax Project, and other groups have developed numerous administrative uniformity proposals. However, unlike some of the other more politicized issues within the sales tax arena, the adoption of more-uniform administrative rules encounters fewer implementation obstacles.

For instance, the MTC developed a *uniform multijurisdictional exemption form,* which has now been adopted by 36 jurisdictions. This certificate is designed to be used for both exempt sales for resale and exempt purchases for use in activities such as manufacturing. This uniform certificate is used by purchasers that do business in numerous states, allowing them to give a seller only one resale certificate for multiple states.

Similarly, the FTA, in conjunction with a business-government task force, has developed a model regulation to establish uniform procedures for the use of *direct-pay permits.* Traditionally, direct-pay permits have been used by purchasers who are unable to determine at the time of purchase whether a purchase will be used in an exempt manner. Many states permit purchasers of large quantities of goods and services to pay tax directly to the state, when and if the goods purchased are used in a taxable transaction. Taxpayers who are allowed to do this receive direct-pay permits from the state. Vendors are not obligated to collect sales and use tax from these purchasers once the vendor has received the direct-pay permit. The purchaser, however, is responsible for self-assessing use tax and remitting it to the state.

About two-thirds of the states currently allow purchasers to use direct-pay permits. The use of such permits, however, is typically limited by cumbersome and constraining state tax rules. The FTA model regulation would create more uniformity in state administrative rules on direct-pay permits and allow for many more vendors to use them. There is a growing consensus that direct-pay permits may be useful in conjunction with E-commerce to facilitate the apportionment of multiple use of a good or service, to enhance compliance with procurement-card purchases, and to use in connection with managed-use tax audits.

Another uniformity initiative involves developing *uniform sales tax registration forms.* One recommendation generally supported by both the NTA project group and the MTC task force is to provide a multistate registration process at the national level, including standardized forms, allowing taxpayers to provide one stream of information for all the states in which they need to register.[176]

There have also been a number of proposals made to simplify *sales and use tax return filings.* The MTC task force recommended that all returns filed within a state be uniform, including format, descriptions, information requested, and placement of information. Another suggestion involved eliminating home-rule jurisdiction reporting, so that the state would administer all levels of sales and use tax reporting using one return. In addition, the group proposed that returns filed by type or category, such as sales, rentals, and consumer use, be eliminated. Instead, all sales categories would be included on one return, thereby requiring only one return for each reporting jurisdiction. Compliance burdens could also potentially be reduced by requiring less-frequent filings (either quarterly or annually), with a minimum filing threshold. Finally, the MTC group proposed allowing electronic filing and payment in all states. However, the differences among states in the breadth of the tax base and use of sales tax exemptions make it more difficult to create uniformity in sales and use tax returns than in some of the other administrative areas.[177]

Another favorite target of supporters of sales tax simplification is the audit and appeals process. Even more than income tax audits, companies find sales and use tax audits and appeals extremely paper intensive, time consuming and expensive. Sales and use taxes are, by nature, transaction oriented and very fact specific. Whereas income tax audits and disputes are likely to focus on legal interpretations, sales tax disputes are more likely to center on factual issues such as the location of a purchaser, the proof of a customer's tax-exempt status, or the use of purchased equipment within a manufacturing process.

Once again, there are a number of administrative reforms to the audit and appeals process that are currently under consideration or being implemented by the states. One of the most important procedural changes that many states are adopting involves *managed-compliance audits* for determining use tax liability on purchases of materials and equipment used by companies in the conduct of their business. Managed audits typically involve a process whereby a company uses a statistical sampling method to determine the percentage of its purchases that are taxable and then applies that percentage to all of its purchases to derive a monthly use tax liability.

Managed audits are particularly useful in industries in which some purchases are exempt (such as machinery and materials used in manufacturing) and other purchases are taxable (such as office and administrative expenses or purchases of services). This reform proposal literally turns the audit process on its head, with the taxpayer performing the audit and the state reviewing the results. Moreover, the audit is generally conducted to determine a tax liability going forward, not just to determine any additional tax liability owed in a prior tax period.

This methodology can result in significant time and money savings for both taxpayers and government. For taxpayers, managed audits relieve companies of the need to determine whether purchases are taxable or exempt on an item-by-item basis for literally thousands of expense accounts. In lieu of such determination, the taxpayer merely gives its vendors a direct-pay permit and calculates the tax based on its statistical sample. This methodology also lends itself to procurement-card purchases when keeping track of taxability on a transaction-by-transaction basis is impractical.[178]

Another program that has been widely adopted to simplify the audit and assessment process involves *voluntary disclosure* by taxpayers of previous tax liabilities. The vast majority of states have now adopted voluntary-disclosure programs that allow taxpayers to approach the state and voluntarily report past liabilities, typically in exchange for a limitation of prior year liabilities to three or four years and a waiver of all related penalties.

These programs are particularly useful in connection with taxpayers who may have had minimal physical presence with a jurisdiction and never collected sales or use tax from customer in the jurisdiction. Many states are currently taking a more aggressive position toward taxpayers who have no permanent employees or office in a state but who have some periodic physical presence through sales representatives or repair activities. Without a voluntary-disclosure program, taxpayers who come forward to resolve past liabilities face exposure for any years for which they have not filed tax returns, sometimes going back 5, 10, or 15 years, because there is no statute of limitation for nonfilers.

Reform of the Tax-Collection Process

Aside from consideration of individual uniformity or simplification proposals to address specific elements of the state and local sales tax administrative process, there has also been an increasing level of discussion of more sweeping reforms that would result in a fundamental transformation of the current system. For instance, the NTA project evaluated two such reforms—a base state tax administration approach and a real-time tax-administration approach.

The primary aim of these proposed reforms is to significantly reduce the costs of compliance with sales and use tax collection systems so that remote vendors would be more likely to voluntarily collect use taxes on Internet-based and other direct-marketing transactions. While these proposals are still largely in the design stage, they tend to focus either on reducing the number of state taxing authorities that a multistate taxpayer has to report to (the base-state system) or reducing the cost of compliance through a state-subsidized technological solution (the real-time approach).

The costs of collecting and remitting sales and use taxes can be very high, particularly for small and medium-sized companies. The primary categories of compliance costs are return filing costs, point-of-sale equipment costs, customer service and training, credit-card fees on sales taxes included in the amount charged by customers, and keeping track of rate and tax base changes. A 1998 study by the Washington Department of Revenue found that costs of compliance on a single-state basis ranged from 1 percent of sales tax collected for a large company to 3.7 percent of sales tax collected for a medium-sized company to 7.2 percent of sales tax collected for a small company.[179]

A 1999 study by Ernst and Young looked at the potential costs for remote vendors selling goods to consumers in multiple jurisdictions. The study found that the compliance burden for a large company ($10 million or more in sales) ranged from an estimated 8 percent of sales tax collected for a business selling in 15 states to 14 percent of sales tax collected for a business selling in 46 states. For a medium-sized company ($750,000 in sales) the compliance burden ranged from an estimated 33 percent of sales tax collected for a business selling in 15 states to 48 percent of sales tax collected for a business selling in 46 states. For a small company ($250,000 in sales) the compliance burden ranged from an estimated 54 percent of sales tax collected for a business selling in 15 states to 87 percent of sales tax collected for a business selling in 46 states.[180]

The measurement of compliance costs is based on a number of assumptions, making these studies somewhat controversial. Indeed, the Ernst and Young study has been criticized by the author of the Washington state study for utilizing unrealistic assumptions that inflate the compliance burden. Nonetheless, while studies may differ on the relative costs of compliance, there is widespread agreement that the costs of multistate sales tax collections are a major disincentive to voluntary compliance by remote vendors particularly smaller or medium-sized companies. To be sure, slightly more than half of the states currently provide an allowance to vendors for the collection and administration of the sales tax. These *vendor-compensation* rules allow sellers to offset, at least in part, the cost of sales tax compliance by taking a percentage allowance against sales taxes otherwise due. However, the current vendor-compensation allowances are small, typically reimbursing less than 5 percent of vendor-compliance costs.[181]

Base-State System

Under a base-state system, a multistate vendor would limit its contacts on most elements of tax administration (e.g., registration, return filing, tax payments, and audit) to only one state, its base state. The base state would generally be the state in which the vendor has its commercial domicile or its principal operations. The taxpayer would collect sales and use tax from customers in any state where it does business but only report these tax collections to the base state. The base state would then be responsible for providing information, tax payments, and auditing functions on behalf of all of the other jurisdictions in which the vendor is taxable. A base-state system is currently used for fuel tax collections from multistate transportation companies.

Proponents of the base-state approach believe it would lead to a significant reduction in paperwork and administrative burden for multistate vendors whose compliance activities would be limited to dealing with a single state, a single tax return, and a single audit procedure. Critics of the base-state approach believe that it would be impractical outside of the fuel tax arena. These critics note that state tax laws vary considerably among jurisdictions and that it would be impractical for one state to interpret and enforce the laws of other jurisdictions.

Real-Time Approach

Another concept that garnered attention from state tax administrators is a real-time tax-administration system. Under a real-time approach, state and local governments would contract with third parties in the private sector to develop and install software for sales tax administration into the software used for E-commerce transactions. This software could include rules for each state on product and service taxability, sourcing of sales, tax rates, and tax-return-compliance procedures. Under this system taxes would be collected as part of electronic transactions on a real-time basis. Vendors would be relieved of tax-collection responsibilities, and governments would look to private-sector contractors to develop and administer the system.

Indeed, in November 1999 a broad coalition of state and local government groups made a proposal to the Advisory Commission on Electronic Commerce for a zero-burden real-time compliance system. This proposal was supported by the so-called Big Seven of state and local government groups, including the National Governors' Association, the National Conference of State Legislatures, the National Association of Counties, the National League of Cities, the U.S. Conference of Mayors, the Council of State Governments, and the International City/County Management Association.[182]

This proposal would create a system that would be funded and certified by state governments, and which could be used by remote vendors at much lower compliance costs. Government would pay for all the costs of the system, which would be based on a technology-driven solution using a "trusted third party" (TTP) rather than the vendors for collection of sales and use taxes. For instance, the TTP could be credit-card companies that calculate, collect, and pay over the taxes on behalf of multiple vendors.

While the rapid expansion of E-commerce and electronic transactions between buyers and sellers clearly opens up new possibilities for automating tax compliance, a real-time tax administration system suffers from a number of obstacles that may make its use impractical, at least for the foreseeable future. As with the base-state approach, the sheer complexity of the sales and use tax system may make it impractical for a third-party vendor(s) to take responsibility for tax compliance that involves inconsistent state tax rules and taxpayers in widely varying industries. Other difficult issues would also have to be resolved, including residual liability of the vendors, financial feasibility for the third-party contractors, and record-keeping requirements.

Tax Software Automation

Even if real-time tax administration by third parties is not widely adopted, the accelerating automation of the sales tax process is likely to have a profound effect on sales and use tax compliance. Increasingly, multistate vendors themselves are using tax software solutions such as Vertex or Taxware to help them comply with complex sales and use tax laws. These tax software programs are used both to determine what sales and purchases are taxable and to generate all necessary returns. The programs are customized to fit a particular company's products, customers, and locations. Any sales invoices sent to customers can be routed through the software to determine if the transaction is taxable, and at what rate, typically based on a ship-to address. The tax software also improves the flow of information on the back end, ensuring that data flows from the financial accounting system (billing and purchasing) or the Web-based transaction processing system to the return, allowing for a more automated sales and use tax-return filing process.

The trend toward automation of sales and use tax compliance is part of a larger movement toward use of sophisticated ERP software such as SAP, BAAN, People Soft, J.D. Edwards, and Oracle to automate corporate-finance, distribution, and other operational functions. The explosion of E-commerce is likely to accelerate this process. In particular, the growth of Internet-based transaction processing for both business-to-business sales and business-to-consumer sales is likely to result in a less paper-oriented business environment in which electronic databases largely supplant filing cabinets filled with sales invoices and purchase orders.

Summary

In the current environment, it is possible that significant sales and use tax administrative reforms will be enacted, either on a state-by-state basis or by means of federal legislation. There is more support now for simplification of the sales and use tax compliance system than at any time in the last quarter century. To a large degree, the simplification of sales and use tax compliance is now viewed as a precondition to any extension of state authority to impose a collection responsibility on remote vendors—particularly those involved with E-commerce.

Some of the reforms, such as the use of uniform exemption certificates or the acceptance of managed-use tax audits, will continue to spread rapidly on a state-by-state basis. For other more consequential changes, however, even with widespread public/private sector support, there remain significant political obstacles. For instance, the one-rate-per-state plan is widely supported as a means to simplify the current structure from one of 7,500 different tax rates to a system with, at most, 50 different tax rates. Nonetheless, any meaningful implementation of this proposal is likely to lead to significant controversies in state and local intergovernmental finances. Moreover, there is a strong likelihood that this reform will not be accepted on a widespread basis until the politically volatile issue of a remote vendor's sales and use tax collection responsibility is resolved.

There are similar political and administrative problems that are likely to slow down efforts to provide more guidance on substantive sales and use tax issues related to E-commerce. There is almost universal acknowledgment on the part of both government and business that current sales tax rules do not adequately address the Internet economy. Nonetheless, progress in creating more consistency and clarity on tax base definitions, the characterization of electronic products, the sourcing of digital sales, the sourcing of multiple-use products, the bundling of taxable and nontaxable services, the updating of input exemptions, and other E-commerce–related tax issues is likely to be retarded by the technical complexity of many of the problems and the political controversy over many of the solutions.

A high-level congressional commission—the Advisory Commission on Electronic Commerce—is actively evaluating the problems and potential solutions to the E-commerce puzzle. It is certainly possible that this group will recommend, and the U.S. Congress will enact, legislation that will result in significant reform of the nation's sales and use tax laws. However, in the current political environment, progress in developing a new set of workable substantive and administrative sales tax rules adapted to E-commerce is likely to be plodding. Although it is too early to predict the outcome in the political arena, it is quite possible that the current deadlock between business and state and local government will drag on, a victim of the complexity of the issues and the lack of consensus for any particular set of tax reforms.

Thus, for the next several years (and perhaps longer), it is likely that both governments and businesses will have to cope with a state and local sales tax system that lacks adequate guidance for many of the critical issues of E-commerce. Once again, this is not a problem that has been addressed or resolved by the federal Internet Tax Freedom Act or recent state tax legislation. For the millions of daily E-commerce transactions involving telecommunications, digital software, electronic information services, cable television, and other categories that are currently subject to tax in many jurisdictions, the application of current tax rules has to be wrestled with on a monthly basis as sales and use tax returns are filed. Where there are no clear-cut rules, taxpayers are left to guess at the appropriate rules or rely on informal (and nonbinding) advice from the tax authorities.

One of the great strengths of the United States is its system of federalism that allows states and localities to exercise significant autonomy in developing their own solutions to economic and political issues occurring within their geographic boundaries. However, this system can prove unwieldy when dealing with an emerging information-age economy that is characterized by instantaneous, intangible, and borderless E-commerce transactions. The balancing of traditional state and local government interests with the exploding new world of E-commerce is likely to be a challenging political conundrum.

3

State Income Taxation
of the Internet

Introduction

Virtually all of the discussion of state taxation of E-commerce has been focused on the impact of sales tax on this rapidly emerging industry. The efforts of the NTA's Communications and Electronic Commerce Tax Project, the federal Internet Tax Freedom Act, and the National Governor's Association's (NGA) legislative proposals have all been concerned with limiting or rationalizing the impact of sales taxes on E-commerce. This focus on transactional taxes has been mirrored at the national and international levels, wherein governments have been primarily engaged in discussing the impact of indirect taxes such as value-added taxes on E-commerce, with relatively little focus on direct taxes such as national corporate income taxes.

Given the complexity of imposing transactional taxes on revolutionary new technologies and the large share of state revenue accounted for by sales taxes, this primary focus is not surprising. However, the lack of attention paid to the impact of state corporate income taxes on E-commerce has left relatively intact an aging system of income taxation of tangible property, services, and intangibles—somewhat ill-suited for a modern 21st-century economy. These tax rules are frequently inadequate to deal with E-commerce issues related to characterization of income, apportionment of income, location and value of property, sale of intangible assets, and the maintenance of parity between tangible and electronic goods and services.

This benign neglect of income taxation rules is ironic given that virtually all states impose income taxes on E-commerce activity (including digital products), whereas only a minority of states impose sales taxes on most digital goods and services. In addition, constitutional or practical constraints that restrict the imposition of sales or use tax collection responsibilities on vendors that do not have physical presence in the state of their customers generally do not apply to income taxation. Vendors (at least in their state of commercial domicile) cannot avoid income taxation of their E-commerce–related activity based on the absence of nexus with the customer's state because income taxation rules generally source the income where the vendor is located, if the vendor is not taxable in the customer's jurisdiction.

To analyze the current issues surrounding the income taxation of E-commerce, it is necessary to understand the traditional rules that have been applied to the taxation of income from service activity and intangible property. Historically, states have applied a two-pronged approach to sourcing income from sales of manufactured goods and services. Typically, sales of goods have been sourced (for sales-factor purposes) to the location of the customer, while sales of services have been sourced to the location of the vendor. As this chapter will discuss, this dichotomy has generally carried over into modern-day income tax rules, with sales of tangible property such as canned software sourced to the customer's location, whereas sales of intangible property such as digitally transferred software or information are sourced to the vendor's location.

The Traditional Apportionment Rule for Products and Services

In determining taxable income for corporate income tax purposes, most jurisdictions employ an apportionment formula generally comprised of a payroll factor, a property factor, and a sales factor. These factors are calculated for each state and the ratio of the combined factors in the state constitutes the taxpayer's apportionment ratio in a particular state. For instance, after calculating the apportionment formula, a company may determine that its business activities are 40 percent in a particular jurisdiction. This percentage is then applied to the entity's total taxable income and multiplied against the state's corporate tax rate to calculate the company's tax in that jurisdiction.

This method of calculating taxable income in a particular state is significantly different than the rules employed for determining taxable income for federal income tax or foreign income tax purposes. At the national level, countries typically use a residence-based taxation scheme in which the "home" country taxes all of an entity's income, less a credit for taxes paid to other jurisdictions. As will be discussed in chapter 6, this method uses credits and arms-length adjustment rules rather than apportionment formulas for dividing income between jurisdictions.

For state apportionment purposes, the sales (or receipts) factor is the most important factor because it is double weighted in most jurisdictions. This means that one-half or more of the apportionment formula for identifying how much income was earned in a jurisdiction will be determined by where the sales are sourced. Indeed, in a growing minority of jurisdictions such as Iowa, Nebraska, Texas, Illinois, and Massachusetts, the sales factor is the only factor used. In these states the apportionment formula does not include the payroll or property factor at all but relies exclusively on the sales factor.[1]

In addition, the sales factor is typically the most critical factor for analysis because the legal rules applied to determining where sales should be sited tend to be more variable and inconsistent among different jurisdictions than the rules applied to the other two factors. Although the calculation of the taxpayer's payroll and property factors tends to be straightforward—typically divided among the taxpayer's physical locations—the calculation of the sales factor can result in a number of more-complex factual or legal determinations. This is particularly true with receipts from E-commerce activity that can be categorized as either the sale of goods or the sales of services or intangible property. (However, see the discussion later in this chapter on issues related to intangible property for purposes of the property factor.)[2]

The Sales Factor

The sales factor generally reflects two different approaches to sourcing income. Sales of tangible personal property such as automobiles, refrigerators, and fast food are generally sourced to where the customer is located (the destination- or market-state rule). Sales of services such as law firms, travel agencies, and telecommunications are generally sourced to where the income-producing activity is performed based on the costs of performance (the vendor-state rule).

Both rules derive from the original Uniform Division of Income for Tax Purposes Act (UDITPA). The UDITPA guidelines were developed by the National Conference of Commissioners on Uniform State Laws and approved by the 66th Annual Conference in 1957. The purpose of this act was to provide a uniform method for apportioning the income of a multistate corporation among the various states. The UDITPA rules have been adopted either in their entirety or in part by a majority of the states. The act set forth rules for allocating nonbusiness income and apportioning business income. Many of the rules originated from the so-called Massachusetts three-factor apportionment formula, which many states had already adopted in the first half of the 20th century.

Under UDITPA, the sales factor is defined as "a fraction, the numerator of which is the total sales of the taxpayer in this state during the tax period, and the denominator of which is the total sales of the taxpayer everywhere during the tax period."[3] This act sets forth the following definitions of market-state and vendor-state rules.

The Market–State Rule: For purposes of UDITPA, sales of tangible personal property are within the taxing state if:

(a) the property is delivered or shipped to a purchaser, other than the United States Government, within this state regardless of the f.o.b. point or other condition of the sale; or

(b) the property is shipped from an office, store, warehouse, factory, or other place of storage in this state and (1) the purchaser is the United States Government or (2) the taxpayer is not taxable in the state of the purchaser.[4]

The Vendor–State Rule: Sales other than sales of tangible personal property are in the taxing state if:

(a) the income-producing activity is performed in this state; or
(b) the income-producing activity is performed both in and outside this state and a greater proportion of the income-producing activity is performed in this state than in any other state based on costs of performance.[5]

Where the vendor and the consumer are in the same jurisdiction, the vendor-state rule and the market-state rule have identical outcomes. In this case, the location of the vendor's income-producing activity and the place of the property or service's destination are the same. However, where the vendor and the consumer are in different jurisdictions, then the two rules lead to opposite results. With the market-state rule, the sales are sourced to where the customer is located; in the vendor-state rule, the sales are sourced to where the vendor is performing the related income-producing activity.

Sourcing Rules for Sales of Tangible Property

For indirect E-commerce, whereby goods are ordered over the Internet but delivered by more traditional means, the characterization and sourcing rules will generally treat tangible products in the same way as before. Thus, for sales-factor purposes, sales will be sourced to the location of the purchaser, regardless of the method by which the product is ordered. Similarly, the property and payroll factors will be determined by the location of the company's offices, facilities, and employees.

One major change, however, is that businesses selling tangible property over the Internet will typically have more flexibility to locate their factors of production, such as property and payroll, in different jurisdictions so as to minimize state income taxes. As previously discussed (see chapter 1), the Internet is accelerating the trend toward "hollow" corporations with more narrowly defined core competencies. With E-commerce, there is less need for companies to be vertically integrated. Many of the business models associated with the Internet are designed for an entity that manages sales of products to consumers over a Web site, with many of the manufacturing, product delivery, accounting, and customer-service functions outsourced to other companies. In part this is because many dot-com companies are start-ups. In part, it is because of the ease with which companies (including brick-and-mortar entities) can enter into joint ventures, partnerships, outsourcing agreements, and other affiliations to bring products to market.

This business model significantly increases the potential for a business to restructure its operations and locate its facilities in a manner that minimizes state income tax payments. With the narrowing of core competencies, Internet businesses will frequently have the flexibility to relocate (or initially locate) their property and payroll in jurisdictions with more favorable income tax rules and rates. It is far easier to shift the location of computer servers, headquarter employees, or information technology personnel than it is to move around large facilities or factories. Thus, the emergence of the virtual corporation is going to put pressure on taxing authorities to develop new rules for apportioning the income of more mobile and dynamic businesses.

Most of the discussion in this chapter revolves around sales of digital products because of the significant difficulties in applying existing rules to the new digital economy. In analyzing differences in state corporate income tax rates and apportionment rules, however, it is important to remember that companies that sell traditional tangible products will also be affected by the enormous variation of state income tax bases, rates, and rules. Although the property, payroll, and sales factors may be applied in much the same manner as before to these entities, the changing business models fostered by the growth of the Internet will nonetheless inject significantly more complexity and inconsistency into the application of preexisting rules to vendors of tangible products.

Sourcing Rules for Sales of Digital Content

With regard to E-commerce, most of the difficult income tax issues arise in connection with direct E-commerce—by which goods and service are both ordered over the Internet and delivered by electronic means. In this context difficulties arise in characterization of income, sourcing of income, and differential tax treatment accorded to tangible goods and electronic products.

For corporate income tax purposes, states generally have not taken a position on whether sales of electronically transferred software, data, books, or other digital content will be considered the sale of tangible personal property or the sale of services/intangible property. Given the rapid growth of E-commerce and digital products, it is somewhat surprising that few states have provided guidance on such a fundamental income-characterization issue. However, states have tended to focus on sales tax issues or have been reluctant to address E-commerce issues at all until they gain a fuller appreciation of the dynamics of this revolutionary new business model.

In the absence of specific statutory or regulatory guidance, taxpayers must rely on informal discussions with state tax authorities or on ambiguous provisions in the current law. Some states may categorize digital content as the sale of tangible personal property, assuming that the same products are considered tangible property when sold in nondigital retail sales. This is analogous to the treatment accorded by some states to electronic software distribution. To the extent that digital-content sales are treated as sales of tangible personal property, they will be sourced according to the usual market-state destination rule—where the customer is located.

It is likely, however, that most states will characterize electronic goods and services as the sale of services or intangibles. States will adopt this intangible classification using the same reasoning applied most frequently to digital transactions for purposes of sales and use tax law—that the electronic content does not have a physical form and cannot be seen, measured, or touched so as to qualify as tangible property. Because the UDITPA category is all-encompassing—"sales other than sales of tangible property"—the logical conclusion under existing statutes is that any tangible property such as business information or music albums that is delivered in an electronic or intangible format should be included in this residual classification. This treatment is also consistent with the position most states have taken with the forerunner of the electronic age—telecommunication services, which are not treated as tangible property.

To the extent that such sales are considered sales of services or intangible property, they will generally be sourced (for sales-factor purposes) under the UDITPA vendor-state rule. In a small number of states, such as Minnesota, Georgia, Iowa, and Maryland, sales of intangible property or services are sourced to the jurisdiction in which the consumer is located. In these states the sourcing rule is based on where the benefit of the service/intangible is received (similar to the market-state rule for products). In the vast majority of states, however, sales of digital content (that are treated as services or intangible property) will be sourced to the place where the vendor is located. In these states the sourcing rule will look to where the income-producing activity is performed, based on the vendor's costs of performance.

The Income-Producing Activity Rule

Under the vendor-state rule, if all of the income-producing activity is conducted in one state, then the sales are sourced to that state. Thus, the vendor-state rule can be one that is easily complied with if a vendor does not have decentralized operations. This is especially evident where the vendor's operations and income-producing activities are centralized but the vendor's services or intangible property are used by customers in multiple jurisdictions. Under these circumstances, for sales-factor purposes, the vendor need only keep track of its own operations, not the locations of its customers.

However, if the vendor's income-producing activity is performed in more than one state, then there are two different rules that are used by the states, depending on their statutes, the "all-or-nothing" rule or "pro rata allocation."

All-or-Nothing Rule. Both California and Massachusetts law provide that sales of services/intangibles occur within the state if the income-producing activity is performed in the state. If the income-producing activity is performed both within and outside of the state, then the sale will be taxable in the state if a greater proportion of the income-producing activity is performed in the state than in any other state, based on the costs of performance.[6]

Pro Rata Allocation. Connecticut taxes services based on the percentage of the costs of performance that were accrued within the state. Accordingly, even if a majority of the costs of performance was in another state, Connecticut will still seek to tax part of the service.[7] Texas apportions service receipts to the location where the service is performed. If services are performed inside and outside Texas, such receipts are Texas receipts on the basis of the fair value of the services rendered in Texas.[8]

To some extent, the all-or-nothing rule can simulate the pro rata rule if a business has activities in different jurisdictions that are relatively distinct. This is particularly true in jurisdictions that have a narrow definition of "income-producing activity." For example, in Massachusetts income-producing activity is defined as follows: "[A] transaction, procedure, or operation directly engaged in by a taxpayer that results in a separately identifiable item of income. In general, any activity whose performance creates an obligation of a particular customer to pay a specific consideration to the taxpayer is an income-producing activity."[9]

For instance, if a business separately serves a set of customers in one state and a different group of customers in a second state, then the taxpayer will be treated as if it has two distinct income-producing activities, and the sales will be apportioned the same under either the all-or-nothing or the pro rata rule. However, if a business has an integrated business activity that has costs related to manufacturing, research and development, and customer service spread across several jurisdictions, there will be a different outcome under these two tests.

In addition, the vendor-state income-producing activity rules differ among states in the types of costs that are included within the calculation. In some states only direct costs related to activities of the vendor's employees are included in the calculation; in other states both direct costs and indirect costs are used in determining the jurisdiction with the greater proportion of activities related to the transaction.

Direct Costs of Performance. In most states, such as California and Massachusetts, the location of the income-producing activity is determined only by direct costs. California defines direct costs as any costs that have a clearly identifiable beneficial and causal relationship to the services performed.[10]

Indirect Costs of Performance. Other jurisdictions, however, include both direct and indirect activity in the definition of income-producing activity. For financial accounting purposes, indirect costs include those costs that cannot be associated with a particular business operation in an economically feasible manner. These include overhead costs such as insurance, company-wide legal fees, and interest on loans. Indirect costs also typically include work performed by third parties. For instance, in New York receipts from services performed in New York will be allocated to New York, whether the services were performed by employees, agents, or subcontractors of the taxpayer, or by any other persons.[11]

The Application of the Income-Producing Activity Rule to Multistate Services

The application of the income-producing activity rules are relatively straightforward in the case of personal or business services, such as hairdressing, construction, machinery repair, or health care, that typically involve business services performed where the individual customer or the customer's property is located. In these situations it is not difficult to identify which income-producing activities of the vendor's employees are responsible for creating the revenue stream. Moreover, such services are typically performed in one jurisdiction, and thus there is little need to compare costs of performance in multiple jurisdictions.

However, income-producing activity rules become more confusing when they involve multistate services, such as financial services, legal services, or telecommunication services. For instance, with regard to a loan to an out-of-state business, the income-producing activity may involve solicitation, investigation, negotiation, approval, and administration of the loan. A number of these steps may occur in different jurisdictions. Under an all-or-nothing rule, it may be troublesome to determine where the preponderance of contacts occurred. Under a pro rata rule, it may be difficult to calculate the relative portion of the activities that occur in each jurisdiction.[12]

The income-producing activity rules also become more complex when they involve the sourcing of intangibles, such as trade names or licenses of technology. In these instances it may be unclear what the relevant income-producing activities are. If a company licenses the right to use certain computer software to a licensee for use in its manufacturing business, what are the vendor's costs of performance? Are the relevant income-producing activities the headquarter costs related to the contract between the licensor and licensee; or the research and development that created the technology; or perhaps the costs of assisting the licensee in effectively installing and using the licensed software?

Under an all-or-nothing rule, it may be difficult to identify in which jurisdiction the majority of the licensor's costs of performance occurred. Under a pro rata rule, it is similarly problematic to calculate the relative portion of the activities that occur in each jurisdiction. Moreover, until it is determined which of the vendor's income-producing activities are relevant to the particular income stream, no progress can be made in sourcing the sales.

Lack of Guidance on the Relevant Costs

With regard to identifying the appropriate income-producing activities and costs of performance, there is very little guidance available from the vast majority of states that have adopted the UDITPA vendor-state rule for sourcing the sales of services and intangibles. First, a taxpayer must determine the relevant revenue stream. If there is more than one separately identifiable service or intangible property transaction, then the income-producing activity test must be used for each such transaction.

Next, the taxpayer must identify the relevant income-producing activities related to such an item of income to determine which jurisdiction has the greater proportion of such activities (assuming the use of the standard all-or-nothing rule). It is possible that a state might use either a broad or narrow definition of income-producing activity, with quite potentially different end results. For instance, a broad definition would encompass all functions necessary to provide a particular service. Under a broad definition, a company that provides telecommunications services might include activities related to solicitation of customers, billing, collections, maintenance costs, operational costs, and leasing access lines. Under a narrow definition of income-producing activity, a telecommunications provider might only include those activities integrally connected with actually providing the service, such as initiating and terminating the call and providing access lines, but not maintenance fees or order-processing costs.

Finally, a taxpayer may also have to ascertain what are the relevant direct costs of performance to be used in measuring where the income-producing activity takes place. The MTC regulations define costs of performance as "direct costs determined in a manner consistent with generally accepted accounting principles and in accordance with accepted conditions or practices in the trade or business of the taxpayer." However, there is no official Generally Accepted Accounting Principle (GAAP) rule for identifying the direct costs for the performance of services, leading to possible confusion on this factor as well.[13]

E-Commerce–Related Activities

The problems with sourcing the sales of intangibles or services that involve multistate vendor activity or multifaceted income-producing activities are quite evident with regard to sourcing the sales of digital content, such as business information or canned software. As with financial services, the relevant vendor income-producing activity can occur in multiple jurisdictions. The frequent impracticality of using these income-producing activity and cost-of-performance sourcing rules is evident when one analyzes their application in specific product categories within E-commerce.

For instance, with the electronic sale of legal information, some of the information can be created in one jurisdiction, contracts for the purchase of additional information can be negotiated in a second jurisdiction, the information can be catalogued and edited in a third jurisdiction, and the information can be stored for access by customers on a computer server in a fourth jurisdiction. Whether using an all-or-nothing approach or a pro rata rule, there will be problems associated with determining the location of the income-producing activity.

Similar problems arise with the electronic distribution of software. For instance, with the sale of canned software transferred electronically, is the income-producing activity the development and creation of the software, the manufacture or duplication of the software, or the transmission of the software from a company-owned computer server? Should all of these costs of performance be considered in determining the location of the income-producing activity related to the sale of canned software? If the jurisdiction used a market-state rule, instead of a cost-of-performance rule, these issues would never arise, as the only relevant inquiry would be determining the location where the consumer uses the canned software.

The various functions associated with digital product development can easily occur across state and national boundaries. For instance, a company could have its headquarters in Massachusetts, research and development facilities in New York, software engineers writing source code in India, customer-service personnel in South Dakota, and its production facilities in New Hampshire. Moreover, with digital products, there may be no manufacturing function because the product can be stored on a main server and downloaded from there by multiple customers or sent to a consumer that then makes extra copies itself.

The difficulty in using cost-of-performance rules is also evident with a more traditional form of E-commerce: telecommunications services. Do the relevant costs of performance include the headquarter offices, the circuit-switching equipment, the transmission lines, or the decentralized sales offices? With modern telecommunications technology, interstate telephone calls are instantaneously and continuously routed through a complex network of copper-wire lines, fiber-optic cables, satellite transponders, and other equipment. An effort to identify the precise costs of performance can be extremely difficult.

In addition, it is necessary to determine whether different income-producing activities, such as long-distance calls, local calls, voice mail, and other ancillary services, need to be segregated and costs of performance calculated separately for each one. All of these issues complicate the determination of how sales revenue from telecommunications services should be sourced under the cost-of-performance rule. The California Franchise Tax Board commented in conjunction with a draft telecommunications regulation: "There are extraordinary pragmatic problems with trying to identify specific costs associated with specific receipts. Under [existing cost-of-performance rules], each separate item of income must be examined to determine its associated income-producing activity and costs of performance. Sellers of telecommunications and information provider services can have literally billions of charges. . . . Requiring telephone companies to identify costs of performance for each call is a monumental, if not impossible, burden on the telephone industry, and an equally great burden on the taxing agencies to audit and verify."[14]

To be sure, many E-commerce transactions may involve the transmission of digital content by a vendor whose research, marketing, manufacturing, headquarters, Web site, and other related activities are all located in one jurisdiction (and frequently in one building). In these instances the cost-of-performance rules are simple to administer and the vendor-state rule easy to comply with.

Nonetheless, the electronic age increases exponentially the potential for businesses to operate on a multistate or global basis, with far-flung operations connected by wire or wireless telecommunications and computer linkups. Furthermore, the location of the Web site or server that stores or transmits the digital content for the consumer's use can be located virtually anywhere. If location of the server becomes important (e.g., because of a high tax burden), the Web site can easily be switched to a different domestic jurisdiction or overseas. Any sourcing rule that focuses on the vendor's costs of performance runs the risk of being subverted by taxpayers that plan their operations accordingly, or being detrimental to taxpayers that do not seek to relocate their servers or similar facilities.

Finally, there is very little guidance available for taxpayers on how to apply the income-producing activity test and the costs of performance rule to E-commerce–related business activities. Few states have made any effort to spell out how these rules work outside the telecommunications arena. Thus, taxpayers are left in most jurisdictions with ambiguity both as to how E-commerce activities are to be characterized (tangible or intangible property) for state income tax purposes and as to how such activities are to be sourced for sales-factor purposes if it is necessary to apply vendor-state rules.

The Vendor-State Disincentive

In addition to the problem of identifying and locating the relevant income-producing activities, the vendor-state rule also is burdened by a second structural flaw. By its nature the income-producing activity test tends to source sales of services or intangibles to the state of the vendor's commercial domicile, or at least the state where the vendor's primary business activities are located. Under the more common all-or-nothing variation of the income-producing activity rule, sales of multistate services or intangibles are sourced solely to the vendor state even if that state has less than a majority of the related costs of performance, but more such costs than any other single state. As a result, the taxpayer may end up with a disproportionately higher tax in its state of commercial domicile.

In this regard the vendor-state rule used for purposes of the sales factor is potentially in conflict with the historic role of the sales factor within the three-factor apportionment formula. The traditional purpose of the sales factor has been to reflect the contribution of the market state to the production of income (i.e., where the consumer is located), whereas the payroll and property factors are more indicative of where the vendor is located.

To the extent that the sales factor does not reflect the location of the consumer, the apportionment percentage of the domiciliary state will be increased, as the payroll and property factors already account for the location where the costs of performance are incurred. This may create a disincentive for the vendor to locate in the domiciliary state, as compared to a state that uses a market-state approach, as the following example illustrates.

Company A sells its software by means of a tangible medium, while Company B sells its software on-line. Both companies are located in the same state and have payroll and property factors of 100 percent in that state, but zero customers in the state. In a typical state (with a double-weighted sales factor—i.e., one-half of the apportionment formula), Company A, whose sales are sourced on a destination basis, would apportion 50 percent of its income to the home state (assuming no throwback of sales), while Company B, whose sales are sourced on a cost-of-performance basis, would apportion 100 percent of its income to the home state.

The Variation in State Corporate Income Tax Rates and Apportionment Rules

If all states had the same reporting requirements (unitary versus separate return), tax rates, apportionment rules, and throwback sales rules, then the differences between states with regard to how the states source income from services or intangible property would matter less. Assuming uniform rules, then a company whose commercial domicile was in a jurisdiction with a vendor-state sales factor rule would simply pay more tax in its home state, but this would be offset by similar savings in the state where its customers are located. Conversely, a company whose commercial domicile was in a jurisdiction with a market-state sales factor rule would pay less tax in its home state, but this would be balanced by additional taxes it would pay in states where its customers were located.

However, there have traditionally been huge differences among the states with regard to state tax rates and rules applied to interstate commerce. For instance, over two-thirds of the states are separate return jurisdictions in which corporations file a tax return separately reporting the income of each entity that is doing business in the jurisdiction. Conversely, about one-third of the states are unitary jurisdictions, in which corporations must file a combined return reporting the income and apportionment factors of all related corporate entities, whether the entities are separately doing business in the taxing jurisdiction. Other states, such as New York, are generally separate return jurisdictions but can require unitary combination reporting under certain circumstances.

In terms of state corporate income tax rates, a number of states have top corporate income tax rates of 5 percent or less: Alabama (5 percent), Colorado (5 percent), Mississippi (5 percent), South Carolina (5 percent), Texas (4.5 percent), and Utah (5 percent). Many other states have top corporate income tax rates of 9 percent or more: Alaska (9.4 percent), District of Columbia (9.975 percent), Iowa (12 percent), Massachusetts (9.5 percent), Minnesota (9.8 percent), New Jersey (9 percent), North Dakota (10.5 percent), Pennsylvania (9.99 percent), Rhode Island (9 percent), Vermont (9.75 percent), and West Virginia (9 percent). Moreover, about one-third of the states have graduated rates that vary according to the level of corporate income (e.g., Alaska, 1 to 9.4 percent; Arkansas, 1 to 6.5 percent; Iowa, 6 to 12 percent). Finally, many other states, including Texas, Massachusetts, Pennsylvania, and Ohio, have net worth or statewide property taxes in addition to the state corporate income tax (see table 3.1).[15]

Similarly, with apportionment ratios, about one-half of the states use double-weighted sales factors (i.e., one-half of the apportionment formula), with the payroll and property factors each accounting for one-

Table 3.1. **Differences in State Income Tax Rules (Selected States)**

State	Unitary or Separate Return	Tax Rate	Apportionment Formula
Alaska	unitary	1–9.4%	three-factor
California	unitary	8.84%	three-factor (double-weighted sales)
Colorado	unitary	5%	three-factor or two-factor (sales, property)
Florida	separate return	5.5%	three-factor (double-weighted sales)
Iowa	separate return	6–12%	single sales factor
Ohio	separate return	5.1–8.5%	three-factor (double-weighted sales)
Texas	separate return	4.50%	single sales factor
Utah	unitary	5%	three-factor

Source: CCH, *Multistate Corporate Income Tax Guide (1999).*

quarter of the apportionment formula. However, many states still use the more traditional apportionment formula with the sales, payroll, and property factors each accounting for one-third of the apportionment formula. Finally, an increasing number of states, including Texas, Nebraska, Iowa, Massachusetts, and Illinois, use a single sales-factor formula, with the sourcing of gross receipts accounting for the entire apportionment formula.[16]

With regard to throwback sales rules, many states with market-state sales factor rules operate effectively like states with vendor-state rules because of the impact of throwback sales rules. A corporation that makes sales to customers in a state in which the corporation is not subject to tax will generally be required under a market-state rule to throw back or source such sales to the vendor state, or at least the state from which the property is shipped. Conversely, sales of services/intangible property are generally not subject to the throwback sales rules because all such sales are sourced to the vendor's location in the first place.[17]

Thus, if a corporation is making interstate sales of digital content from one state and does not have a physical presence in the other states where its customers are located, it may have the same state tax apportionment under either the vendor state or the market-state rule— through the use of a throwback sales provision. However, the lack of uniformity between states prevents the throwback sales rule from equalizing the treatment of vendors in vendor-state and market-state jurisdictions. Only about one-half of the states have throwback sales rules. In the other states, vendors will effectively not be taxed in their home states on sales to customers in other states, even if the corporation is not subject to tax in the state where the customer resides (see table 3.2).

As a result of the broad differences between states with regard to state tax rates, apportionment formulas, unitary or separate-reporting rules, and throwback sales rules, vendors can be subject to significantly different tax consequences depending on the tax rules within their state of domicile. In some circumstances this can be beneficial to a corporation—when, for example, the vendor is located in a state with low corporate tax rates and a market-state rule for digital-content sales without a complementary throwback sales rule. However, in the majority of states

Table 3.2.   **States with Throwback Sales Rules**

Alabama	Mississippi
Alaska	Missouri
Arkansas	Montana
California	Nebraska
Colorado	New Hampshire
District of Columbia	New Mexico
Hawaii	North Dakota
Idaho	Oklahoma
Illinois	Oregon
Indiana	Texas
Kansas	Utah
Maine	Vermont
Massachusetts	Wisconsin

with a vendor–state rule for sourcing sales of services or intangibles, vendors may find themselves at a competitive disadvantage compared with their counterparts in other jurisdictions. This is particularly true of vendor states with an above-average corporate tax rate. This tax disadvantage can put pressure on a company to relocate some or all of its functions to a jurisdiction with a more favorable tax climate.

In the extreme such corporations can face double taxation on their sales. For example, assume a company is principally located in a jurisdiction that uses a vendor–state rule for sourcing sales. If this company makes sales to customers in some states that use a market–state rule, then it will be subject to double taxation on its sales (assuming it has a physical presence in the market state). The entity will pay tax on its interstate sales in its home state based on the costs of performance rule, and it will pay tax on some of the same sales in the market states based on the market-sale rule.

One additional factor needs to be emphasized. With the rapid expansion of the digital economy, many manufactured goods that have traditionally been delivered as tangible property are now capable of being delivered electronically or as intangible property. Whereas the physical delivery of manufactured goods is almost always sourced based on the market-state rule, the electronic delivery of manufactured goods is typically sourced based on the vendor-state rule. Thus, the potential distortion of apportionment factors where the vendor-state rules is used not only affects new companies engaging in E-commerce or other service industries but also affects existing manufacturing companies that begin to ship their products electronically to customers.

The Discomfort with the Original UDITPA Sourcing Rules for Services

The problems associated with using a vendor-state rule for sourcing the sales of services and intangibles are not of recent origin. Indeed, the framers of the UDITPA rules were well aware of the shortcomings of using the income-producing activity/cost-of-performance rule for such business activities.

At the time many states used a pro rata cost-of-performance rule for sourcing receipts from services. Under this rule revenues from services were sourced to a state (for sales factor purposes) to the extent the services were performed in the state. As noted previously, when UDITPA was adopted, the drafters adopted the income-producing activity rule— but based on an all-or-nothing principle. Thus, sales of services were sourced entirely to the state in which more of the costs of performance took place than in any other single state, even if this jurisdiction constituted the location of only a minority of the overall costs of performance.

Most of the policy discussions relating to the adoption of the UDITPA rules in the 1950s focused on sales of tangible goods, given the historic dominance of manufacturing, mining, farming, and merchandising in the U.S. economy. Indeed, the UDITPA rule adopted for purposes of sourcing sales of services and intangibles does not even refer to these economic activities but rather uses the more indirect phrase, "sales other than sales of tangible personal property."

The drafters of the UDITPA rules were aware of the problems with the all-or-nothing cost-of-performance rule, but they could not come up with any better rule to apply to services and intangibles. To limit the impact of the rule, and because some states already had separate rules for certain service industries, the drafters excluded a number of important service industries from the rule's application. These industries included financial institutions, electric and gas utilities, insurance companies, transportation companies, and telecommunication companies. The drafters also expected states to adopt special industry regulations or to use the adjustment or relief provisions of UDITPA to cope with unusual business activities.[18]

As individual states began to adopt the UDITPA rules, however, the taxing jurisdictions typically did not incorporate the language that excluded the application of the vendor-state rule to specific service industries. Most states adopted these rules for all economic activities within the state and thus, by default applied the vendor-state rules to all service industries and intangibles. Other states, such as Massachusetts, adopted most of the UDITPA principles without formally adopting the UDITPA rules or subsequent MTC regulations and thus did not exclude the application of the vendor-state rule to these specific service industries.

To be sure, in the late 1950s and early 1960s, the vendor-state rule caused fewer problems because of the makeup of the U.S. economy. The manufacturing and farming industries were still the dominant economic sectors and constituted most of interstate economic activity. The service industries, while expanding, were still largely local or regional in nature. Many of the major service industries, such as banking, telecommunications, and electric utilities, were required by government regulation to operate in a single jurisdiction or at least to operate separate affiliates in each jurisdiction. Thus, the import of multistate service industries and the issues raised with sourcing the income of such industries was less apparent.

Moreover, in the early postwar era, the world of E-commerce was in its nascent stages. The computer had only recently been invented. The early computers took up the space of an entire room to provide less computing power than one of today's laptop computers. There was no software computer industry. Televisions were just being introduced into U.S. households, and radio was still the dominant form of mass communications. The early stages of development of the ARPANET, which eventually became the Internet, were still more than a decade away. Long-distance phone calls were expensive, and the audio quality was inferior. Satellites were in the experimental stage, and the notion of vast

telecommunications and information networks relying in part on satellite feeds was still in the realm of science fiction.

The Growth of the Service Economy

Over the last four decades, the growth of the service sectors in the
United States has far outpaced the growth of the manufacturing and
farming industries. For instance, in the late 1950s, goods-producing jobs
in manufacturing, construction, and mining made up about 40 percent
of total private-sector employment in the United States. At that time
service-producing jobs in transportation, finance, retail trade, and other
miscellaneous services made up about 60 percent of all private-sector
jobs. By the mid 1990s, goods-producing jobs had dropped to 18 percent
of all private-sector employment, while service-producing jobs had risen
to 82 percent. While, in aggregate numbers, manufacturing job growth
remained essentially flat over that period, service sector jobs grew by
nearly 300 percent. During this period, while the goods-producing sectors added about 3 million jobs, service-producing sectors added over 50
million jobs in the United States.[19]

Moreover, the deregulation of major industries, such as telecommunications, electricity and gas, transportation, and banks, led to an enormous proliferation in multistate economic activity related to the service
sector. The deregulation of the telecommunications industry occurred
largely because of the landmark AT&T decision in 1984 and the Telecommunications Act of 1996. The deregulation of the banking industry
occurred because of changes in federal and state banking laws in the
1970s and 1980s. Finally, the deregulation of the electricity industry took
place because of changes in state utility laws in the 1990s.

The expansion of multistate and global service businesses has been
reinforced by tremendous advances in telecommunications and computer technology. The world has become "wired" from end to end, with
increases in telecommunications bandwidth, computer storage capacity,
and interconnectivity of tens of millions of computers resulting in the
phenomenal advance in human technology known as the Internet. This
has enabled vendors and consumers throughout the world to connect
and interact in commercial transactions that were unimaginable 20 years
before.

As a corollary to the growth of the services industries, wealth created by intangible property also became a more important component of the U.S. economy. This was in large part due to the technological revolution sweeping the country that accompanied advances in computer technology and the sciences. For instance, between the late 1950s and mid 1990s, the number of patents and trademarks issued per year nearly tripled. This has led to a significant increase in the amount of income earned from licensing intangibles, such as patents, trademarks, trade names, and copyrights.[20]

The value of mergers, acquisitions, and divestitures has also increased significantly during the post–World War II era. For instance, in the early 1980s, U.S. merger and acquisition activity totaled in the range of $100 billion to $150 billion in value per year. By the late 1990s, U.S. merger and acquisition activity totaled in the range of $500 and $900 billion in value per year. This has also resulted in significant increases in income from the sale of intangibles, such as corporate goodwill, intellectual property, and corporate stock.[21]

E-commerce has indeed begun to blur the distinction altogether between the goods-producing industries and the service sector. As discussed in chapter 1, many products that were formerly associated with the goods-producing sector of the economy are now becoming part of the service-producing sector of the economy. Thus, canned software, music albums, books, newspapers, and other information-age products can now be provided to consumers as intangibles rather than as goods that need to be manufactured. This development will undoubtedly accelerate the economy's shift toward the service-producing sector.

The Use of Market-State Sourcing Rules for Selected Service Industries

The shift to a more services-based economy has not gone unrecognized by state tax policy makers. While the predominant sales factor sourcing rule used by the states for the sale of services or intangibles has remained the vendor-state rule, there has been a significant shift toward developing market-state rules for apportioning income earned by fast-growing multistate service industries and for apportioning income attributable to licensing intangible property. Indeed, in recognition of the limitations of the income-producing activity rule and the possible disincentives to locally based businesses resulting from its application, an escalating number of states have moved selectively toward sourcing receipts from the sale of services to where the consumer is located.

A small number of states, including Minnesota, Iowa, Maryland, and Georgia, have completely revamped the income-producing activity rule to source receipts from all sales of services to the jurisdiction in which the service is consumed. In general, however, most states have replaced the income-producing activity rule only for selective industries. These industries include primarily financial institutions (banks, mutual funds, securities brokerage firms), media companies (broadcasting, publishing), transportation companies (airlines, railroads, ship transport, pipelines, motor carriers), and telecommunications companies (see figure 3.1).[22]

Financial Institutions

The regulations promulgated by MTC in regard to apportionment of income for financial institutions or similar market-state rules have been adopted by nearly one-half of the states. These rules were finalized in 1994 after nearly a decade of discussions between the states and the banking industry. Although representatives of state government and the banking industry could not agree on topics such as nexus rules or the definition of financial institutions subject to the new apportionment rules, they did reach agreement on a far-reaching change in the apportionment rules as applied to banks.

The MTC regulation has over 20 new sourcing rules for financial institutions. The vast majority of these rules use a market-state approach for sales-factor sourcing rules based on where the customer or property is located. Under the new MTC financial-industry rules, the numerator of the receipts factor, for receipts from credit-card receivables, includes interest from receivables if the billing address of the cardholder is in the state. The numerator of the receipts factor, for interest received from

Figure 3.1. **Service Industries:**
Jurisdictions with Market-State Rules

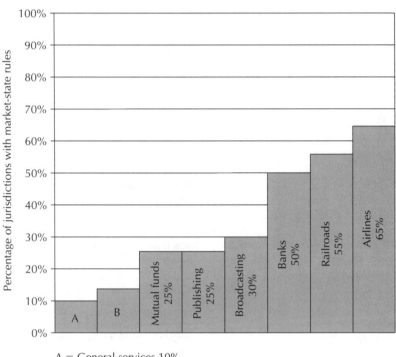

A = General services 10%

B = Telecommunications 15%

loans secured by real property, includes interest or loans secured by real property if the property is located within the state. The numerator of the receipts factor, for interest received from unsecured loans, includes such interest if the borrower's mailing or billing address is located in the jurisdiction (in the case of nonbusiness borrowers) or if the borrower's commercial domicile is located in the jurisdiction (in the case of business customers). (See table 3.3.)[23]

Each of these new rules focuses on the activities of the customer, not the activities of the lender. Under the UDITPA vendor-state rules previously used in many of these jurisdictions, all of these sales would have been sourced to the location of the vendor's income-producing activity, not the borrower's consumption-related activity. If the vendor and the

Table 3.3.   **Multistate Tax Commission Sourcing Rules for Financial Institutions**

Activity	Receipts Attributed
Leases	
Lease of real property	Where property is located
Lease of tangible personal property	Where property is first placed in service
Lease of transportation property	Where the property is used, or where property has principal base of operations
Loans	
Loans secured by real property	Where the property is located
Consumer loans not secured by real property	Where the customer is regularly billed
Commercial loans not secured by real property	Where the borrower maintains its commercial domicile
Sale of loans secured by real property	Ratio based on where the properties are located
Sale of consumer loans not secured by real property	Ratio based on where the customers are regularly billed
Sale of commercial loans not secured by real property	Ratio based on where the borrowers maintain their commercial domicile
Loan servicing fees for servicing another entity's secured or unsecured loans	Where the nonbusiness customer is regularly billed or the commercial borrower maintains its commercial domicile
Credit Cards	
Credit, travel, and entertainment cards	Where the cardholder is regularly billed
Merchant discount income	Where the merchant maintains its commercial domicile
Credit-card issuer's reimbursement fees	Ratio based on where the cardholders are regularly billed
Sale of credit-card receivables	Ratio based on where the cardholders are regularly billed
Other Services	
Other services	Where the greater proportion of the income-producing activity is performed, based on costs of performance
Investment and Securities	
Investment and trading activities	Ratio based on regular place of business where day-to-day investment or trading decisions are made

customer were located in the same jurisdiction, the outcome would be the same under either set of rules. However, where the vendor and customer are located in different jurisdictions, the vendor-state rule would source sales to the vendor's location, whereas the market-state rule would typically source sales to the customer's location.

The new MTC financial-institution regulations also revise the property factor used for determining the apportionment factors for banks. Under the traditional UDITPA property factor, only real property and tangible personal property are included in the property-factor calculations. Under the new MTC financial-institution formula, certain kinds of intangible property such as loan receivables and credit-card receivables are also included in the property-factor calculations. The rules for sourcing intangible property focus on the jurisdiction in which the financial institution has primarily conducted its business relating to the credit-card or loan customers. This vendor-state orientation is consistent with the typical focus of the property factor. While the new MTC regulations broaden the property base to include both tangible and intangible property, both types of property continue to be sourced to where the vendor is located.

Mutual-Fund Industry

With the expansion of the mutual-fund industry in several states, new rules have developed on sourcing sales of these types of financial companies. In approximately one-fifth of the states, including Massachusetts, Texas, New York, and New Jersey, new market-states rules have been adopted for companies selling management and other services to or on behalf of a regulated investment company (mutual funds). These rules generally source the sales of the mutual-fund-management companies based on where the customers of the mutual fund are located rather than where the services are provided.

In some states, such as Massachusetts, a highly favorable single sales factor is used, with all sales sourced to the customer's location. In Massachusetts—home to many of the nation's largest mutual funds—the singles sales factor, when combined with a market-state sourcing rule and no throwback of sales, leads to a low corporate apportionment ratio. This formula encourages the mutual-fund companies to expand their operations in Massachusetts, because payroll and property additions are not taken into account in determining Massachusetts income subject to tax.

Transportation Industries

Many states have special industry regulations for transportation industries, especially ones that involve interstate transit. For instance, three-quarters of the states have special industry regulations for motor carriers, three-fifths of the states have special industry regulations for airlines, half of the states have special industry regulations for railroads, one-quarter of the states have special industry regulations for pipelines, and one-quarter of the states have special industry regulations for ship transport. The special industry regulations for transportation companies are generally adapted from model MTC regulations for these types of companies. The MTC model regulations were adopted in the following years: railroads, 1981; airlines, 1983; and trucking companies, 1989. All of these regulations adopt a market-state-like approach, apportioning sales based on the location of customers or the pro rata level of market-state activity. For instance, the special industry regulation on apportioning the income of airline companies uses a receipts factor that divides sales according to the percentage of airline departures from one state's airport over the total number of departures from all airports. The special industry regulation on apportioning the income of motor carriers uses a receipts factor that divides sales according to the percentage of miles traveled by mobile property in the state over the total number of miles traveled in all states. These formulas vary from the UDITPA income-producing activity test both because they focus on the location of activities involving customers and because they involve pro rata, not all-or-nothing, tests for dividing sales between jurisdictions.

Broadcasting and Publishing

One-fifth of the states have also promulgated special industry regulations in connection with the apportionment of income of publishers and broadcasters. Once again, these regulations are largely derived from

MTC model regulations for the publishing and broadcasting industries. Both regulations use a market-state approach instead of a vendor-state approach in connection with sourcing advertising revenues under the sales factor. The MTC broadcasting regulation was promulgated in 1990. The MTC publishing regulation was promulgated in 1993.

For instance, the special regulation for the publishing industry provides that the numerator of the sales factor includes gross receipts from the sale of advertising according to the ratio that the taxpayer's in-state circulation of purchasers and subscribers of its printed materials bears to its total circulation of purchasers and subscribers everywhere.[24]

Similarly, the special regulation for the broadcasting industry provides that the numerator of the sales factor for a television or radio station includes gross receipts from the sale of advertising according to the ratio that the taxpayer's in-state viewing/listening audience bears to its total viewing/listening audience everywhere.[25] With a cable television system, the numerator of the sales factor is based on the ratio of subscribers in one state to subscribers everywhere.

The publishing and broadcasting regulations both ignore vendor-state factors such as headquarters or sales-force costs of performance and instead focus on the location of customers, in this case, the nonpaying customers of most media companies. Although it is not always clear where a broadcaster's audience is located, the taxpayers can rely on third-party information from published rating services for making this calculation.

Telecommunications Industry

Finally, about one-fifth of the states have promulgated special industry regulations for apportioning the income of telecommunications companies. Although most states still source sales of telecommunication services using the cost-of-performance rule, the jurisdictions with special industry rules, including Florida, Georgia, Iowa, Kentucky, and North Carolina, use market-state rules that source sales based on where the telecommunications customer is located, not necessarily where the telecommunications vendor incurs most of its costs.

Among states that use market-state rules, there is some variation on how the location of the consumer is determined. There is no MTC special industry regulation for telecommunications companies. Some states use the consumer's billing address, while others use where the calls originate. For example, in Florida sales of telecommunications are sourced to the state if the call originates or terminates in Florida and the service is charged to a Florida customer. In Kentucky gross receipts for telecommunications services are taxable in the state if they are billed to a customer in Kentucky.[26]

In addition, several states, such as Arkansas, Connecticut, Missouri, and New York, use a pro rata vendor-state rule. These states still rely on an income-producing activity test for sourcing sales by telecommunication companies. However, unlike the majority of UDITPA states that use all-or-nothing cost-of-performance rules that source sales to the single state that has the greatest proportion of the costs of performance, these states apportion sales based on the percentage of a vendor's activities. To the extent that a vendor's physical operations such as offices, telecommunications lines, and service centers are distributed among the states in proportion to where its consumer reside, the pro rata vendor-state rules will approximate the market-state sourcing rules.

For instance, in Missouri, taxable income for telephone companies that operate interstate lines includes all income arising from sources within Missouri. This includes receipts from all service rendered wholly within Missouri, as well as revenue from service using only corporate facilities in Missouri. If services are rendered using both in-state and out-of-state facilities, the taxable income includes the proportion of such income as the mileage involved in Missouri bears to the total mileage involved over the company's lines everywhere.[27]

License Revenue from Intangible Property

In addition to adopting special industry regulations for service industries, many states have also adopted special sourcing rules for royalty revenues that derive from the licensing of intangibles. As discussed previously, the UDITPA vendor-state rules typically apply to sales other than sale of tangible personal property. Thus, most states use the income-producing activity rule for sourcing business income from patents, copyrights, trade secrets, trade names, and other types of intangible property.

However, in recent years about one-quarter of the states, including Alaska, Colorado, Connecticut, Florida, Massachusetts, New York, and Texas, have adopted market-state rules for sourcing income from intangibles for sales-factor purposes. For instance, in Massachusetts gross receipts from the licensing of intangible property are sourced to Massachusetts if the property is used by the licensee solely in Massachusetts. If the licensee uses the intangible property in more than one state, the gross receipts from licensing are sourced to the state that has the greatest proportion of use by the licensee. The Massachusetts regulation gives several examples of use, including use of patents in a manufacturing process and the retail display of a trade name.[28]

One impetus for the new market-state rules for sourcing income for intangible property has been taxpayers that are commercially domiciled in a state that do not want royalty income to be sourced back to their headquarters' state. In these situations the use of a vendor-state rule increases the taxation of manufacturers who may license technology or a trade name to entities in other states or countries and yet are required to source the sales revenue from such licenses to the home state.

Ironically, the interest in adopting market-state rules for sourcing revenue from the license of intellectual property has also come from state governments, particularly as a corollary to the expansion of the so-called *Geoffrey* nexus rule. Under the *Geoffrey* rule—established in a South Carolina court case involving the Toys "R" Us trade name (Geoffrey the Giraffe), numerous states have asserted jurisdiction over out-of-state companies that have no physical presence in the state but have intangible property such as trade names or trademarks that are licensed to customers for use in the state.[29] Licensors of intangible property frequently have no property or payroll in the licensee's state. Therefore, if a state does not adopt a market-state rule sourcing royalty income from the license of an intangible to the state where the licensee uses the property, then the state may be successful in asserting jurisdiction over an out-of-state company but end up with no tax liability because the taxpayer has no property, payroll or sales in the state under the typical UDITPA vendor-state rules.

Currently, about one-half of the states have adopted rules that extend the state's taxing jurisdiction to companies that license intangible property to licensees within their borders. Among the states adopting a *Geoffrey*-like nexus rule are Florida, Maryland, Massachusetts, Missouri, New Jersey, and Tennessee.

Current Sourcing Rules for E-Commerce

While there has been a significant shift among the states toward market-state sales-factor sourcing rules, this has occurred almost entirely on an industry-by-industry basis. Only a few states use market-state rules for all service industries. Thus, with regard to E-commerce transactions involving sales of digital information, music, software, video, and other products and services, the vast majority of states still use the vendor-state approach for such E-commerce revenue streams. The absence of market-state rules applied to E-commerce is explained by the fact that these types of transactions do not fit neatly into any of the existing service categories that have been addressed by special industry regulations. Digital transactions are generally tangible property sales that have been transformed into electronic transmissions by the emerging Internet-based economy. Thus, these emerging industry segments have never been separately addressed as service categories.

While there have been special industry regulations developed for some related industries such as telecommunications, broadcasting, and publishing, these regulations generally do not extend to E-commerce transactions. The regulations tend to focus on more traditional activities that predated the digital economy. For instance, the special industry regulations on telecommunications typically cover basic transmission-type services and not Internet access, digitized products, or other fast-expanding E-commerce products and services. Similarly, the special industry regulations related to publishing typically focus on traditional businesses that publish information on a printed media, and not publishers who use electronic media for disseminating news and receiving advertising revenue.

Finally, the special industry regulations on broadcasting generally cover television, radio, and cable television broadcasting, but not other uses of the airwaves or cable networks for transmitting information, video, and other digitized products. However, there is some ambiguity in the special industry regulation on broadcasting because the MTC regulation defines a broadcaster as "a business entity that derives advertising revenue from the dissemination of audio or visual programming by an electronic signal conducted by wireless transmission or by wires, lines, coaxial cables, wave guides, fiber optics, or other conduit of communication."[30]

Thus, if a cable television provider that receives at least some of its income from advertising revenue broadens its services to include Internet access and sale of digitized movies, these services could be subject to the sourcing rules of the broadcasting regulation, at least in the states that adopt these rules. Similarly, an Internet service provider that derives revenues from both advertising and the sale of an on-line service (that includes some audio or visual programming) could also be subject to the broadcasting industry regulations, even though the intent of the regulations was originally to cover just the traditional broadcasting media.

However, even if certain digital service providers are made subject to the special industry regulation for broadcasting, the result will not vary much from the vendor-state rules used by most states. This is because the special industry regulation for broadcasters has market-state rules only for advertising revenue. Other revenue, including revenue from the electronic sale and delivery of digital products and services, is sourced under the regulations under the traditional income-producing activity test. Thus, the special industry regulation is just a hybrid, with market-state sourcing rules for advertising revenue and vendor-state sourcing rules for other types of revenue.

The Market-State Jurisdictions for All Service Categories

As already noted, there are a handful of jurisdictions that use a market-state sourcing rule for all service businesses. These states, which include Iowa, Minnesota, Georgia, and Maryland, include in the numerator of the sales factor the amount of receipts in proportion to the benefit received by the recipient in the state. Thus, in each of these states, digital transactions would be sourced (for sales factor purposes) according to the location of the customer, not the location of the vendor.

For example, in Iowa all gross receipts are includable in the numerator of the receipts factor if the recipient receives all of the benefit of the service in Iowa. If the recipient of the service receives some of the benefits of the service in Iowa, then the gross receipts are includable in proportion to the benefit of the service received in Iowa. Similarly, in Minnesota receipts from the performance of services must be attributed to the state where the services are received. If intangible property is used in more than one state, the receipts must be apportioned to Minnesota in proportion to the amount of use in Minnesota. In Georgia, receipts are attributed to that state if they are from "business done within this state." Gross receipts are sourced to Georgia "if the receipts are derived from customers within this state or if the receipts are otherwise attributable to this state's marketplace."[31]

The Property Factor

Although the discussion so far has focused almost entirely on the issues raised in conjunction with sourcing sales for purposes of the *sales factor,* it is worth briefly mentioning some related issues involving the *property factor.* Typically, the property factor in most states is concerned solely with the location of the tangible and real property of the vendor. In this regard E-commerce businesses generally do not raise any special issues in terms of administrative compliance. However, to the extent that the digital economy increases the number of businesses that sell intangible property, instead of tangible products, there may be some novel issues that arise in relation to the property factor.

For instance, companies selling digital products may have much less inventory than traditional manufacturers, because there is little need to stockpile products that are easily stored as files on a computer server. E-commerce companies may also have less need for factory equipment because many products will be duplicated electronically or simply downloaded from a master file by the consumers. Thus, tangible property may diminish in importance for many digital age companies—raising questions about the utility of a property factor that focuses almost exclusively on tangible, not intangible property. Finally, if a company's entire catalog of products resides on a computer server, how will such property be valued for property factor purposes? If such intangible property is taken into consideration in apportioning a company's income, then the whole inventory can easily be moved to another jurisdiction and placed on a different computer server.

Thus, the rise of E-commerce may lead to a reexamination of the role of the property factor in corporate apportionment formulas. If corporate tangible assets shrink in value in relation to intangible assets, then states may have to consider adding intangible property to the property factor (as has been done with the MTC bank tax apportionment formula), or scrapping the property factor altogether (as has been done in states with single sales factors).

Tangible-Product Rules

As previously noted, companies that sell tangible products over the Internet frequently have significant flexibility in how they structure their business and where they locate their factors of production such as property and payroll. Many of the business models associated with the Internet are designed for an entity that manages sales of products to consumers over a Web site, with many of the manufacturing, product delivery, accounting, and customer-service functions outsourced to other companies.

The Internet business model is likely to place additional pressure on states that have higher tax rates or less-attractive apportionment formulas than comparable states. For instance, an Internet retailer may have more ability to move out of a high tax jurisdiction than a traditional brick-and-mortar company. A company that does not own expensive (and hard-to-move) in-state production or distribution facilities may determine that it is worthwhile to move its Web site and office support staff to another jurisdiction to lower its future income tax liability.

Similarly, an E-business may be more attracted to a jurisdiction with a single sales factor (and no throwback sales rule) than to a state with the traditional three-factor formula. For this reason, the modest trend toward a single sales factor apportionment formula for state corporate income tax purposes may receive additional impetus given the favorable climate it creates for entities that primarily have customers in other jurisdictions.

Future Consideration of Market-State Rules

To date, few states have even addressed whether a market-state approach should be considered for the sales of goods and services related to the digital economy. The most notable exception to this inaction was California, which proposed, and then rescinded, a sweeping special industry regulation for sourcing sales from companies involved with various segments of E-commerce. While this proposed regulation is no longer under consideration, it does provide a useful example of the types of rules that might be adopted as part of a special industry regulation on digital commerce. Indeed, in October 1997, while the draft regulation was still under consideration, the MTC used one of its annual government-industry meetings to discuss the pros and cons of the California proposal. In 1997 the California Franchise Tax Board, after nearly two years of effort, released a draft regulation on apportionment for telecommunications, subscription television, Internet access, and electronic information services. This regulation would have replaced the vendor-state income-producing activity sourcing rules for E-commerce-related activities with market-state–oriented sourcing rules.[32]

This draft regulation provided new sourcing rules not only for traditional telecommunications and subscription-television services but also for Internet access services and electronic information services. For the purposes of this regulation, an electronic information service was defined to include "providing information or entertainment for a charge by means of telecommunications including through access to the "Internet."[33] This catch-all category would have likely encompassed most categories of digital content, including on-line services, and electronic transfers of information, music, software, and similar products. Under the draft regulation, gross receipts from the furnishing of *telecommunications services* would generally be sourced to the state if the call was intrastate, or if the call was interstate and it either originated in the state or was received in the state and was billed to a customer in the state. Gross receipts from interstate private telecommunications services (where a subscriber has exclusive or priority use of a communications channel) would generally be apportioned between the states based on either separately billed segments or the ratio of termination points (where information can enter or leave the telecommunications network) in the state to total termination points.

Under the draft regulation, gross receipts from providing *electronic information services* or *Internet access services* would generally be sourced to the state in which the information is received by the customer or to the state at which the Internet access connection point of the customer is located. Where the information is simultaneously received or the Internet access is simultaneously provided at multiple connection points in more than one state, the gross receipts would be apportioned based on the percentage of connection points in each state. Where the exact location of the customer's equipment at which the information is received or the Internet access is provided cannot be determined, then there are several presumptions that would be used for sales-factor sourcing, including the location of the local telephone exchange or of the customer's billing address.

Similarly, gross receipts derived from *advertising* in connection with subscription-television services, electronic information services, or Internet access services would be sourced based on the ratio of customer billing addresses in the state to total customer billing addresses. These rules parallel the market-state rules in the MTC broadcasting industry regulation.

Thus, the income from all five types of revenue—telecommunications service, subscription-television service, electronic information service, Internet access service, and advertising revenue—would be sourced using market-state rules that focus on the location of the consumer. Where a customer consumes an E-commerce service simultaneously in multiple jurisdictions, an apportionment formula would be used for dividing the revenues based on the number of termination or connection points in each jurisdiction.

In the event that the vendor is not taxable in the jurisdiction of the consumer, several *throwback sales* rules would be used. For telecommunications services, receipts would be thrown back to a state if the customer's billing address was in that state. For electronic information services and Internet access services, receipts would be thrown back to the state of the customer's billing address, assuming the vendor is taxable in that state. If the location of the consumption of the service cannot be identified, or the location of the customer's billing address cannot be determined, the receipts would be thrown back based on a ratio of property and payroll used by the vendor in developing the service. Finally, advertising revenue would be thrown back to the state of the vendor's commercial domicile. Thus, the throwback sales rules reflected a variety of solutions adapted to the particular income stream. If the California proposal had been adopted by the state, the throwback sales rules would have attracted considerable attention. First, throwback sales rules are typically used with sales of tangible property, not sales of services. Second, even with regard to sourcing tangible property sales, only about one-half of the states use throwback sales rules.

The draft regulation also proposed several changes to the property factor. First, outerjurisdictional property, such as satellites and undersea transmission cables, that is not located in any one particular jurisdiction but is used for telecommunications or electronic services would be included in the property factor and sourced based on the ratio of property within the state used in providing such service to property everywhere. In addition, the value of certain intangible property, such as licenses granted by the FCC, would be included in the property factor. Such licenses would be sourced based on the ratio that the population within the geographic area in the state covered by the license bears to the total population covered by the license.

The California draft regulation clearly represented a sweeping set of new rules for sourcing income from telecommunications and other E-commerce–related business activities. Several industry representatives charged that the proposed regulation was unnecessary, premature, impractical, and overly complex. They argued that the current vendor-state rules were still workable with perhaps some minor revisions. The California Franchise Tax Board apparently accepted these critiques and terminated the draft regulation project in January 1998.[34] At that time, Dean Andal of the Franchise Tax Board described the draft regulation as "a solution trying to find a problem."[35]

While California decided not to proceed with promulgating a market-state rule for sourcing income from telecommunications and other electronic services, the state has nonetheless veered from a strict enforcement of the UDITPA vendor-state all-or-nothing rule for telecommunications companies. According to Michael Brownell, the principal author of the California Franchise Tax Board's draft regulation on income tax sourcing rules for E-commerce:

> [T]he Franchise Tax Board, in consultation with the telephone industry, has developed ad hoc practices under section 25137 for the industry, reflected in the department's Multistate Audit Technique Manual. Under those practices, ... interstate and international calls are assigned to California in the ratio of the 'net plant facilities' in California used in the call. The rationale for this ratio is that net plant facilities is a reasonable proxy for the costs used in the call. However, even the ad hoc practices of the department are difficult to apply in practice, because of the difficulty in identifying the specific 'net plant facilities' used in the call, because of continuous rerouting of telephone calls in the system. At best, these values can only be approximated.[36]

In effect, California has informally adopted a pro rata cost-of-performance rule for sourcing the sales of telecommunication services.

Problems with the Use of Market-State Rules for E-Commerce

There has been a clear trend over the last two decades of state adoption of market-state rules for sourcing income of selected service industries. This trend has been uneven, with broader adoption of market-state rules in certain industries, such as transportation and banking, than in other industries, such as publishing, broadcasting, and telecommunications. Nonetheless, the trend has been continuous and has even accelerated in recent years.

Nonetheless, the inclination of many jurisdictions to replace vendor-state rules with market-state rules does not mean that the newly adopted market-state rules have been free of administrative problems. These rules—while more akin to the rules used for sourcing sales of tangible property—raise a number of potentially troublesome issues, such as problems related to nexus over the vendor in the customer state and the administrative complexity of identifying the location of the customer state. Indeed with regard to E-commerce activities, the absence of wide-spread consideration of market-state rules may reflect a caution that arises from unfamiliarity with how these rules would apply to a fast-growing and technologically complex new industry.

First, unlike vendor-state rules, a taxing jurisdiction does not always have nexus over a business in the state where the business's customers are located. Under traditional corporate nexus criteria, a state cannot impose a corporate income tax filing responsibility on an out-of-state company based solely on economic presence, the presence of the vendor's customers in a state. Thus, a pure market-state solution is not always possible. This explains why market-state solutions to sales-factor sourcing are frequently accompanied by throwback sales rules. With a vendor-state income-producing activity rule, there is no problem with asserting nexus over a taxpayer with operations in the taxing jurisdiction.

Second, a market-state solution can frequently be more complicated than a vendor-state rule. For a business with some or most of its costs in its state of commercial domicile, it is relatively easy to determine which state to source its sales using the UDITPA all-or-nothing income-producing activity rule. While a vendor-state rule may create an economic disincentive to expand operations in a company's home state, it is not necessarily difficult to administer. Assuming some or all of a company's revenue streams are attributable primarily to operations in the state of commercial domicile, then the sales factor is 100 percent in that state and zero in any other state with the identical sourcing rule.

Unlike with a market-state rule, there is no need in a vendor-state rule to identify precisely where a company's customers are using its services. Whether a company's customers are located in 5 jurisdictions or 25 jurisdictions does not change the outcome. Even if it is difficult to identify a customer's location, because of the use of a Web address and/or the involvement of a financial intermediary in the transaction, nothing changes. In each instance the taxpayer need merely focus on its own operations and other information within its control for determining the proper sourcing of its receipts for income tax purposes.

The vendor-state rule can be significantly easier to implement in connection with a multistate business customer. Unlike sales and use tax, there is no concept of direct payment with regard to income tax filing responsibilities. In contrast to sales and use tax, there is no opportunity to have a customer assume responsibility for sourcing sales related to its transactions with the vendor by using information in the customer's control concerning where services are being consumed. Whether a customer uses a particular digital service simultaneously at 20 connection points around the country does not affect the sourcing rule. All sales are sourced under the vendor-state rule based on the vendor's activities, not the customer's activities.

Thus, although market-state rules for service activities more closely parallel the treatment of similarly situated tangible goods, such rules frequently create other administrative problems. In particular, market-state rules regarding E-commerce can raise issues relating to nexus with the market-state jurisdiction and administrative complexity relating to locating where the actual consumption or market-state activities occur.

In this regard it is interesting to note that market-state rules designed for E-commerce activities may be novel with regard to sourcing sales for *income tax purposes,* but they are much more commonly used for sourcing sales for *sales tax purposes.* Thus, the unique rules set forth in the draft California regulation for sourcing sales of telecommunications and digital products for income tax purposes are strikingly similar to the rules discussed by the NTA Communications and Electronic Commerce Tax Project for sourcing E-commerce sales for sales tax purposes. As discussed in chapter 2, the NTA project focused primarily on market-state solutions for sourcing sales of digital goods and services. It also wrestled with similar administrative issues relating to identifying the location of customers, apportioning digital sales involving consumption by numerous persons in multiple locations, and even exploring some form of a throwback rule.[37]

Indeed, it is quite possible that the development of new income tax sourcing rules for E-commerce may become intertwined with efforts to establish new sales tax sourcing rules. If more states enact laws with specific market-state sourcing rules for sales tax purposes, it may become easier for the same states to use a similar approach for income tax purposes. To the extent that states use similar approaches for both tax types, it may reduce the administrative burden of complying with the new rules.

Into the Future

For the foreseeable future, multistate businesses will undoubtedly have to cope with state taxing authorities that use two different sets of rules. Some jurisdictions will continue to use vendor-state rules for sourcing income from E-commerce activities. Other jurisdictions will switch to market-state approaches for sourcing income from E-commerce. This outcome parallels the situation that exists for other service industries, with a mix of vendor- and market-state rules coexisting side by side.

Moreover, with sales and use taxes, a jurisdiction can avoid these complexities by narrowing the sales tax base to exclude certain electronic and digital products and services. With income taxes there is no such flexibility because income from virtually all goods and services is subject to tax, regardless of whether it is attributable to sales of tangible products or electronic services. While few states subject financial services or computer services to sales and use tax, virtually all states impose income taxes on such services. For purposes of income taxes, the issue for states is not *whether to tax* the digital economy, but *how to tax* such goods and services.

If all states used a vendor-state solution in connection with relatively uniform tax rates, apportionment formulas, and other tax rules, the vendor-state solution might work quite well. Unfortunately, as indicated, there is a huge variation among states in tax rates, apportionment formulas, sales-factor sourcing rules, and throwback sales rules. Because there is a long tradition in U.S. federalism of state autonomy over state tax regimes, it is unlikely that the differences in state tax rules will disappear in the near future.

In states that have higher corporate income tax rates, there will be pressure to consider switching from vendor-state rules for sourcing E-commerce–related business activity to market-state rules. Otherwise, businesses may pay a penalty for expanding operations in their state of commercial domicile. This is particularly true for companies that are in the process of switching from delivering their products via a tangible medium to delivering their products electronically. With the advent of the Internet and the growth of the digital economy, it will become commonplace for certain tangible personal property to be delivered electronically in digital format (software, videos, music albums, business information, books, etc.). Under existing rules sale of such products would be sourced to the market state when they are delivered in tangible form, but to the vendor state when they are delivered in digital form. The application of the income-producing activity rule to the digital economy may create a significantly higher tax burden in the vendor's state of commercial domicile. This development is likely to lead to increasing pressure to replace this vendor-state rule with the market-state rule—not just in special industries but across the entire spectrum of service businesses.

Nonetheless, as previously indicated, there are also many difficulties associated with using a market-state rule for E-commerce–related activities. Given the complexities associated with either solution, it is likely that states will proceed cautiously in the next few years. While more states may attempt to adopt market-state rules for sourcing E-commerce revenues, there will likely be considerable experimentation with different formulas in an effort to develop a system that is administratively workable and that also creates tax parity between tangible and digital products.

Special Taxes Applied to the Telecommunications Industry

In considering the state income taxation of economic activity related to E-commerce, it is also important to understand the special rules that have developed in relation to the taxation of the utility industry (telecommunications, electric and gas utilities, transportation companies). Although this discussion focuses only on the telecommunications industry, the issues are similar with regard to other utility-type industries. Historically, utility taxation has only encompassed a portion of E-commerce—those companies engaged in basic telecommunications transmission. Other companies such as computer, television, entertainment, and information businesses have not been subject to these special rules that tax—and frequently disproportionately tax—public utility companies.

As previously discussed, a minority of states use special industry income tax regulations for sourcing the sales of telecommunications companies. The special rules applied to telecommunications companies, however, include not only different income tax sourcing rules but also different state- and local-level gross receipts tax rules, property tax rules, sales taxes, franchise fees, license taxes, utility user's fees, telephone user's surcharges, state regulatory fees, and other assorted levies. There are also special federal level taxes such as the federal excise tax on communications and the Universal Service Fund.

Historically, these special industry rules developed because of the regulated monopoly status of most telecommunications and electric utility companies. Special tax regimes were developed to impose additional fees on these entities and in some cases to compensate localities for providing the utilities with valuable rights-of-way on public lands. With the deregulation of the telecommunications industry and the emergence of the Internet, however, the application of these rules has caused considerable confusion. The deregulation of the industry has not been accompanied by the revamping of the taxes tied to the special regulatory status of the industry. It is unclear if separate tax regimes for telecommunications companies will survive the proliferation of unregulated competitors and diversified business activities.

There are currently a variety of activities carried on by telecommunications and related E-commerce companies. These include:

- Wireline services, including local telephone, toll service, additional telephone service, 800/900 transmission service, and WATS provided by copper wires or fiber-optic cables.

- Wireless services, including cellular telephone, personal-communication services (PCS), mobile radio, beepers/paging, and radio dispatch provided by means of satellites, microwaves, or radio waves.
- Computer-related and other services, including E-mail, Internet access, data transmission, data processing, facsimile (fax) service, packet switching, Web hosting; Web retailing.
- Television and video programming, including television and radio broadcasting, cable television service, and direct-broadcast satellite service.

Historically, special utility industry taxation has applied only to those activities traditionally carried on by local exchange carriers and interstate exchange carriers, generally the wireline or wireless service categories. However, as telecommunications companies diversify and begin to offer more services related to digital content and other nontraditional activities, states with special industry rules are faced with several relatively unpleasant choices.

The states can maintain a narrow definition of telecommunications and impose special industry taxes and fees on any regulated or unregulated companies that provide traditional wire and wireless voice-transmission activities. The states can expand the definition of telecommunications to encompass a broader range of Internet and computer services provided by both traditional telecommunications companies and their nonregulated competitors. Alternatively, the states can attempt to impose special industry taxation on all of the business activities of certain entities, such as local exchange carriers or long-distance carriers, opting not to tax the unregulated competitors of these entities.

As the following sections show, none of these options may be viable over the medium term, raising questions about the survival of special industry tax rules on the telecommunications industry in an environment of revolutionary technological change.

Gross Receipts Taxes

While virtually all states impose income taxes on business entities, many states also impose gross receipts taxes on telecommunication providers.

Gross receipts taxes differ from net income taxes in that they are imposed on gross, rather than net income. They generally differ from sales taxes because they are imposed on the vendor, not on the consumer, and apply to all levels of economic activity, not just to retail sales. Gross receipts taxes typically use a lower tax rate than income taxes (e.g., 1 to 6 percent) because they are imposed on gross revenues, not net revenues.

A handful of states, including Washington, Indiana, and Delaware, impose gross receipts taxes on all business organizations. However, most states with gross receipts taxes impose them only on telecommunications companies or other regulated industries. These states use gross receipts taxes either in addition to or in lieu of net income taxes. Some states use gross receipts taxes in lieu of other taxes such as local property taxes.

In 1997 approximately 20 states imposed gross receipts taxes on some type of telecommunications services. In several states, including New York, Ohio, Rhode Island, and South Dakota, some or all telecommunications providers are subject to gross receipts taxes in lieu of state income taxes. In other states, including Delaware, Florida, Indiana, Maryland, Montana, Pennsylvania, and South Carolina, some or all telecommunications providers are subject to both corporate income taxes and gross receipts taxes.[38]

There are major differences and inconsistencies in the current application of gross receipts taxes to telecommunications companies. Statutory and regulatory definitions that determine what types of telecommunications companies and services will be subject to tax vary significantly from jurisdiction to jurisdiction. For example, in many states gross receipts taxes apply only to public utilities. Therefore, whether telecommunications service providers are subject to the tax depends on the definition of public utility. In other states gross receipts taxes apply to all telecommunication providers, regardless of whether they are regulated utilities.

In most states with gross receipts taxes, the tax base includes only intrastate revenues. Approximately 20 states impose the gross receipts tax on intrastate revenues of telecommunications companies. Within these states the gross receipts tax applies to the intrastate earnings of all local exchange carriers. However, only about two-thirds of these states impose the gross receipts tax on the intrastate revenues of interstate exchange companies. Moreover, only about one-third of these states impose the gross receipts tax on an allocated portion of the interstate and international revenues of interstate exchange companies. Finally, only one-fifth of these states impose the gross receipts tax on cable television revenues.[39]

The inconsistent tax rules are indicative of significant differences in approaches among the states. For instance, in New York a 4.25 percent gross receipts tax applies to all local telephone receipts while a 3.5 percent tax applies to nonlocal, interstate, and international telecommunication services. Moreover, in New York the gross receipts tax applies only if more than 50 percent of a company's gross receipts are derived from the sale of telecommunication services. In Pennsylvania a 5 percent gross receipts tax applies only to providers of intrastate services. In Florida a 2.5 percent gross receipts tax applies to intrastate, interstate, and international telecommunication services. In Ohio a 4.75 percent gross receipts tax applies only to local exchange carriers.[40]

There are also wide variations in the types of services subject to the gross receipts taxes. For instance, in Pennsylvania the gross receipts tax base is narrow. The Pennsylvania tax base includes almost all wireline services, but no wireless, cable television, or computer-related services. In New York the gross receipts tax base is in the middle. The New York tax base includes wireline and wireless services, but not computer-related or cable television services. By contrast, the gross receipts tax base in Ohio is quite broad. The Ohio tax base includes virtually all wireline, wireless, cable television and computer-related services.[41]

Internet-Related Telecommunications Services

The states with gross receipts taxes are also struggling to determine whether new Internet-related telecommunications services are subject to the tax. A number of states, including Alabama, Florida, and New York, have reversed earlier positions and determined that Internet access services are not subject to the state's gross receipts tax. A similar issue is now arising with Internet telephony. Internet telephony refers to voice transmissions that occur either in whole or in part by using packet switching rather than circuit switching in transporting the communication. The same technology that can be used to break data up into packets can also be used to convert voice calls into packets that are shipped over the Internet and then reassembled at the call's termination point. Not surprisingly, states are having a difficult time determining if such packet-switched voice services are subject to the gross receipts tax, particularly in jurisdictions that tax wireline and wireless telephone services but do not tax Internet access services.

In many ways the ambiguities and inconsistencies that are arising in relation to state gross receipts taxes on telecommunications services parallel similar issues that are emerging with regard to state and local sales and use taxes. However, those states with gross receipts taxes must deal with an additional issue—the narrow or wide application of the tax to categories of companies such as local exchange carriers, interstate exchange carriers, regulated companies, and unregulated companies. By contrast, sales and use tax issues generally arise only with regard to the breadth of the tax base, not the classification of the vendor.

Even if clear and uniform definitions could be developed to distinguish between various electronic services, this approach may be undermined by the rapid spread of services in which vendors will offer both telecommunications and enhanced data services on the same wired or wireless networks, frequently for a single fixed price. Until recently, electronic services were typically provided by separate vendors. Telephone companies provided voice communications, cable companies provided cable television, legal and business information services provided information and other data-related services, and Internet access providers provided Internet access services. However, the explosion of new channels for reaching household consumers has created new opportunities for a range of companies to provide integrated transport and content services to customers.

In an era of economic and technological convergence, it will be particularly difficult to maintain separate tax rules for companies providing telecommunication or computer-related services. As discussed in chapter 2, both telecommunications companies and cable television companies are beginning to offer bundled services that encompass telephone service, data services, Internet access services, and cable television programming. Similarly, both local exchange carriers and long-distance carriers are entering each other's markets for local and long-distance telecommunications. Moreover, thousands of unregulated companies are now competing with the traditional telephone and cable companies for transmission and content-related telecommunication services.

The changing economic, technological, and competitive landscape will place increasing pressure on states to reform their gross receipts tax statutes. Between 1986 and 1996 the number of states with gross receipts taxes on telecommunications companies dropped from 30 to 20. This trend is likely to continue over the next decade. The lack of clarity and inconsistency in various state approaches to entity classification and tax base breadth under existing gross receipts taxes is likely to accelerate, threatening the survival of the remaining gross receipts taxes as applied to telecommunications companies.

Property Taxes and Telecommunication Providers

Another tax type for which there is frequently a disparity between the treatment of telecommunications companies and more traditional businesses is the local property tax. Many state and local governments impose property taxes on telecommunication utilities both on a broader asset base and at higher rates than similar taxes assessed on nonutility businesses.

One major factor in the imbalance in property tax treatment of telecommunications companies is the breadth of the asset base that is subjected to tax. States frequently use a unit valuation method for assessing the property of telecommunications companies and other regulated utilities. This method effectively includes in the property tax base not just real and tangible personal property but also intangible property such as licenses, good will, and so on. Currently, 14 states apply special property taxes to the intangible value of telecommunications companies. Thus, for utility taxation purposes, the property tax base commonly represents the apportioned market value of an enterprise, not just the value of its tangible assets.[42]

In many states a disproportionate property tax burden is also placed on telecommunications companies because of higher assessment rates imposed on telecommunications companies than on other commercial or industrial companies. In states such as Alabama, Kansas, Louisiana, Mississippi, Ohio, Oklahoma, and Tennessee, the personal property of telecommunications companies is subject to higher assessment rates than similarly situated property of other commercial or industrial companies.[43]

The net result of these factors is that many telecommunications companies pay substantially more in local property taxes than do other nonutility companies. Indeed, state and local government property tax assessments on telecommunications companies have resulted in a number of lawsuits across the country. In particular, telecommunications companies have litigated against the inclusion of intangibles in the property tax base. For instance, in Oregon a wireless carrier brought suit over the inclusion of the value of its personal communication service licenses in its property valuation. Similarly, in California several court cases in the early 1990s that were won by the taxpayers caused the state Board of Equalization to reduce the assessed value of 40 cellular companies by $600 million to avoid the inclusion of intangible property in the property tax base.[44]

Franchise Fees and Other Special Charges

Another special levy that is imposed on telecommunications companies in many jurisdictions is a local franchise fee. Historically, franchise fees have been imposed on telecommunications companies, cable television companies, and other utilities by local governments as a means of compensating the local governments for use of public rights-of-way. Traditionally, telephone and cable companies needed to use public lands for the placement of their pipes, poles, and cables. In exchange for granting these private businesses an easement to public streets, highways, and other land, the municipal governments levy a franchise fee. Typically, franchise fees are imposed as a percentage of gross receipts.[45]

Although franchise charges are generally characterized as fees, not taxes, they raise many of the same issues as do special tax assessments on telecommunications companies. Cities and towns must determine the base on which the fees are to be assessed and whether such fee base includes not just telephone or cable television revenues but other types of income as well. Moreover, while franchise fees can be readily applied to utilities that enjoy a local monopoly, they are more difficult to use in a competitive, deregulated industry where there are multiple channels of access to local consumers. For instance, franchise fees have limited usefulness with regard to direct-broadcast satellite companies or wireless telephone companies that do not generally need public rights-of-way in order to reach their customers.

There are a number of other special assessments that are imposed on telecommunications entities (or their customers) in various jurisdictions. These include the following:

- Public Utility Commission (PUC) charge. This is a fee imposed on users of regulated services in order to finance the operational costs of the local or state regulatory body.
- Business and occupation tax. This privilege or license tax is imposed on a telecommunications provider for the privilege of doing business in the taxing jurisdiction.
- Utility users tax. This tax is a charge imposed by certain local jurisdictions in lieu of a local sales tax, typically assessed as a percentage of a customer's telephone bill.
- Universal service fund surcharge. This surcharge is imposed on telecommunication providers for the purpose of making basic telecommunication services affordable to low-income people.

Finally, while the federal government in the United States does not typically impose sales or transactional taxes, it does impose a telecommunications excise tax of 3 percent. This tax is imposed on all local, intrastate, and interstate telecommunications services and collected by the vendor from the consumer. Although the federal tax rules are still evolving, this tax is generally not imposed on Internet access or other computer or content-related services.

The Cumulative Impact of Special Taxes and Fees Imposed on Telecommunications Companies

The numerous special assessments imposed on telecommunications providers and their customers lead to a crazy quilt mixture of taxes and fees that frequently differ significantly from the assessments imposed on other business corporations. Among the states and localities, there is no single pattern of taxation of telecommunications companies. There are frequently differences in tax rates and taxable bases as compared with other business corporations.

In Massachusetts, for example, a utility corporation pays a tax equal to 6.5 percent of its net income, as compared to the tax imposed on other business corporations of 9.5 percent of net income.[46] However, a utility corporation must pay substantially higher property taxes than other corporations because machinery used in producing telecommunications is not exempt from the local property tax whereas machinery used in manufacturing is exempt from the local property tax.[47]

In California the taxation of telecommunications companies is comprised of the corporate franchise (income) tax, property taxes, franchise fees, utility user taxes, and various surcharges that fund special social programs only tenuously related to telecommunications services. The property tax is highlighted by a bifurcation between property values established by the State Board of Equalization (state-assessed property) and those set by the county assessor (locally assessed property). Franchise fees paid by cable companies are charges for the privilege of engaging in specialized services as well as for the right to use public rights-of-way to lay their cables.[48] The utility user tax is a locally assessed gross receipts tax collected by telecommunications companies from their consumers. This tax has no ceiling and can also be levied on the consumption of electricity, gas, water, sewer, and cable television service.[49]

In Ohio the state imposes a gross receipts tax on telecommunications companies in lieu of a corporate income tax. The local governments impose a personal property tax on telecommunications companies, at substantially higher rates than for nonutility companies. A study in 1995 found that Ohio's telephone companies pay 50 percent more state and local tax than similarly situated nontelecommunications companies. In that year taxation of the utility industry generated $385 million in taxes, compared with $243 million had this sector been treated as regular business corporations.[50]

The cumulative impact of all of the special taxes, fees, differential tax bases and rates, and valuation methods imposed on the telecommunications industry is that telecommunications companies generally have a much higher overall tax and administrative burden than do other business corporations. For instance, a 1999 study by an industry group, the Telecommunications Tax Task Force of the Committee on State Taxation (COST), found that the nationwide average effective rate of transactional taxes applied to sales of telecommunications services was nearly three times higher than the rate applied to the sale of goods by general businesses (18.15 percent versus 6.31 percent). (The telecommunications taxes include the state and local sales tax, the federal communications excise, and various special assessments imposed on telecommunication companies.)[51]

The COST study also determined that, because of the range of transactional taxes imposed on telecommunications companies, there are approximately 687 different state and local tax bases that a telecommunications company must keep track of, compared with an estimated 184 different tax bases for general business corporations. In addition, the study concluded that telecommunications providers operating nationwide would have to file annually 55,748 tax and related administrative returns, compared to general business corporations that would have to file 7,237 returns.[52]

The Future of Utility Taxation

The rapid growth of E-commerce represents a fundamental challenge to decades-old state tax policies that treat telecommunications companies differently—and typically less favorably—than other business entities. To a large degree, regulatory, technological, and economic changes have eroded the special status of telecommunications companies. These changes have both resulted in a more competitive marketplace and led to a proliferation of utility and nonutility companies selling a wide range of telecommunications and enhanced services to customers.

In 1984 antitrust litigation resulted in the breakup of the Bell system. Prior to 1984 AT&T supplied local and long-distance telecommunications service to the vast majority of U.S. businesses and households. After the breakup a large number of new competitors, both large and small, entered into the telecommunications marketplace.

In addition, in 1996 Congress enacted the Telecommunications Act of 1996, which brought to an end the government regulation that has maintained barriers between local and long-distance telephone, cable television, broadcasting, and wireless services. The effect of the Telecommunications Act is already being reflected in various restructurings and mergers resulting from telecommunications, broadcasting, and information technology entities entering into each other's businesses. As a result, a new group of telecommunications companies is emerging. These are frequently highly diversified companies that either on their own or through alliances offer a full menu of electronic services including local and long-distance telephone service, cellular phone service, Internet access, data services, and cable television.

In this dynamic environment, state tax statutes that attempt to tax telecommunication utilities differently than their nonutility counterparts may become an endangered species. State taxing schemes that rely on the special status of utilities are likely to unravel given both competitive and regulatory challenges to the local monopoly status of many telecommunications utilities.

Nonetheless, a complete overhaul of special taxes imposed on telecommunications companies will probably take a number of years. A complete overhaul of federal, state, and local taxes applied to telecommunications companies would need to eliminate or simplify industry specific taxes and levies (such as the 3 percent federal telecommunications excise), reform property tax rules, increase sales tax exemptions for business inputs used by telecommunications companies, and create more-uniform tax base categories and sourcing rules.

The evolutionary nature of tax-rule changes will reflect, in part, the complexity of existing schemes and the need to derive alternatives before the current system is scrapped. The pace of change will also reflect the large dollars at stake. States and localities will have to scramble to replace the revenues from special assessments on telecommunications companies that in many cases contribute a significant share of state and local tax revenue.

4

Nexus, Remote Sellers, and the Internet

Introduction

Because many E-commerce transactions involve sales made by remote sellers, a key element in considering sales or use tax collection responsibilities and income tax filing obligations will be a company's nexus with the taxing jurisdiction. Even if the transaction is otherwise subject to a sales or use tax, if the vendor has no nexus (sufficient contacts or connections) with the taxing jurisdiction, then the vendor has no obligation to collect or remit the sales or use tax.[1] Similarly, even if the vendor is earning income from transactions with customers in the taxing jurisdiction, the vendor will have no income tax filing responsibility unless it has nexus with the taxing jurisdiction.

The determination of the boundaries of a state's authority to impose taxes on out-of-state companies has become an increasingly contentious battlefield between the states and multistate enterprises. The state tax field is overflowing with new or evolving theories for extending a state's taxing jurisdiction to remote sellers, including slight physical presence, attributional nexus, intangible-property presence, and economic presence.

Even before the Internet revolution took off, a nationwide survey found that over one-third of top financial and tax executives believed that nexus uncertainty was their primary state tax concern, outweighing other more traditional issues, such as sourcing of corporate income and state tax audits.[2] The explosion of E-commerce has exacerbated state/ business conflicts over nexus issues, by both increasing the number of remote vendors and creating a myriad of new fact patterns that raised novel jurisdictional issues.

General Principles

In order for a state to impose a tax on an interstate transaction, the tax-payer must have sufficient nexus with the state under both the Commerce Clause and the Due Process Clause of the U.S. Constitution. Under the Due Process Clause, there must be some *minimum connection* between a state and the person, property, or transaction it seeks to tax. Under the Commerce Clause, a tax is valid only if it is applied to an activity having a *substantial nexus* with the taxing state. Whereas the Due Process Clause is historically focused on issues of fundamental fairness, the Commerce Clause is concerned with possible burdens placed on interstate commerce by tax rules and procedures.[3]

Generally, a state needs to establish jurisdiction over both the *transaction* and the *taxpayer* in order to impose a sales or use tax or income tax. The requirement for transactional nexus is based on the need for a connection between the state and the business activity subject to tax. The requirement for presence nexus is grounded in the need for a connection between the state and the taxpayer (or tax collector, in the case of a use tax). This chapter focuses primarily on nexus issues related to the *taxpayer*.

Sales and Use Tax Nexus versus Income Tax Nexus

In general, the rules for determining nexus for purposes of the sales and use tax and the corporate income tax are the same. For both tax types, physical presence of the taxpayer's employees or property will typically create a taxable connection with the state. For both tax types, as well, an agent that performs certain types of activities in the market state on behalf of an out-of-state vendor can create nexus.

There are several important distinctions, however, between sales and use tax nexus rules and income tax nexus principles. With regard to sales and use tax nexus, the U.S. Supreme Court has ruled that some form of physical presence is needed to establish nexus. In *Quill Corp. v. North Dakota* (hereafter referred to as *Quill*), the issue was whether a state could require a company that solicited sales only by mail-order catalogs to collect use tax on sales made into the state.[4] The U.S. Supreme Court ruled that the Commerce Clause barred North Dakota from requiring an out-of-state mail-order company to collect and pay use tax on goods sold to North Dakota customers when the company had no outlets, sales representatives, or other significant property in the state.[5]

For corporate income tax purposes, there is no such precedent. The Supreme Court has not yet ruled whether physical presence is a precondition to establishing state tax jurisdiction over a remote vendor. Thus, there remains the theoretical possibility, at least for service-related transactions, that mere economic presence or intangible-property presence would be sufficient to create an income tax filing responsibility.[6]

By contrast, corporate income tax nexus rules provide a certain measure of protection for sellers of tangible personal property that is not similarly provided for sales and use tax nexus purposes. In 1959 Congress enacted Public Law (PL) 86-272, which creates a safe harbor from state income taxation for multistate companies that meet certain criteria. Under PL 86-272, a state may not subject a foreign corporation to a tax on or measured by net income derived within the state from interstate commerce if the "only business activities within such State by or on behalf of such foreign corporation" are the solicitation of orders for sales of tangible personal property, whereby the orders are sent outside the state for approval or rejection and are filled by shipment or delivery from a point outside the state.[7]

The protection afforded by PL 86-272, however, was designed for an era when the predominant economic activity was the manufacture and distribution of tangible personal property. In fact, PL 86-272 only protects sellers of tangible personal property. Accordingly, it does not protect solicitation activity related to the sale of services or intangible property, including E-commerce. Thus, if a software company begins to distribute some of its products electronically (not on tangible media), it may lose the protection of PL 86-272. If such a company has a nationwide network of salespersons who solicit sales on its behalf, it could conceivably be subject to income tax in numerous jurisdictions even if just a modest portion of its output is sold electronically. Mere solicitation is not a protected activity if the sales involve both sales of tangible property and intangible property.

Overlap of Sales and Use and Income Tax Nexus

The focus in this chapter is primarily on sales and use tax nexus issues. Most of the current debate revolves around this particular tax type, in part because of the large share of all state and local taxes that is attributable to sales and use taxes and the ability of many remote vendors to avoid a sales and use tax collection responsibility. Our attention is also riveted to transactional tax nexus because these taxes are trustee taxes: owed by customers but collected on their behalf by vendors. Thus, if a company takes an aggressive position on a nexus issue related to sales and use taxes, it risks paying a tax assessment on revenues that were not its own original liability. By contrast, when a company ignores a potential income tax filing responsibility, it is gambling on its own liabilities and risking, at most, additional interest and penalties.

Nonetheless, when addressing issues related to sales and use tax nexus, it is important to remember that many of the same issues affect income tax nexus rules. For instance, both *de minimis* rules and attributional nexus rules, discussed at length in this chapter, are applicable to income tax nexus as well as to sales and use tax nexus.

The Growth of Internet Marketing

The issue of the jurisdiction of a state (or locality) to impose a sales or use tax collection responsibility on a remote vendor has been a contentious one for decades, initially inflamed by the growth of direct marketing through mail-order catalog sales. With the explosion of E-commerce, the issue of "jurisdiction to tax" will become even more volatile. As noted in chapter 1, the ability of remote vendors to reach consumers in other states has significantly expanded with the emergence of information-age technologies. In particular, the Internet represents a fantastic increase in the ability of vendors and customers to communicate and conduct business transactions in a user-friendly format without ever having to rely on face-to-face interactions.

Under the *Quill* precedent, remote vendors are not required to collect sales and use taxes as long as they do not have physical presence in the customer's location. Vendors are allowed to reach customers through media and billboard advertisements, direct mail, mail-order catalogs, and Web sites without incurring a sales or use tax collection responsibility.

In the next five years, E-business sales are expected to far exceed sales from other forms of direct marketing, such as mail-order sales. The current projections for the growth of E-commerce are astounding. According to Forrester Research, on a worldwide basis, Internet sales (business-to-business and business-to-consumer) will range from $1.8 trillion to $3.2 trillion. In the United States, Internet-based sales are expected to climb from $280 billion in the year 2000 to $1.5 trillion in 2003. By comparison, an estimated $219 billion in mail-order sales were made in the United States in 1995.[8]

With regard to business-to-consumer transactions, Internet retail sales in the United States are expected to increase from $18 billion in 1999 to $144 billion in 2003—a four-year growth rate of 800 percent (see figure 4.1). By contrast, mail-order sales are expected to increase from $57 billion in 1999 to only $72 billion in 2003—a four-year growth rate of 25 percent. Moreover, Internet retail sales in the United States are expected to increase to $184 billion in 2004—a five-year growth rate of 1,000 percent.[9]

Moreover, there is a vast and fast-growing population of businesses that engage in Internet retailing. Along with major Internet retailers, an estimated 30,000 small businesses—entities with revenues of less than $10 million—made sales over the Internet in mid 1999. This constituted an increase from only 200 such companies in 1996. It is projected that 400,000 small businesses will be engaged in Internet retailing in the United States by 2003.[10]

The difficulty of requiring remote vendors to collect sales or use tax is primarily associated with business-to-customer sales, not business-to-business sales. With regard to business-to-consumer sales, the transactions

Figure 4.1. **A Comparison of the Growth of E-Commerce
to Mail-Order Consumer Retail Sales**

Sources: Forrester Research, *USA Today.*

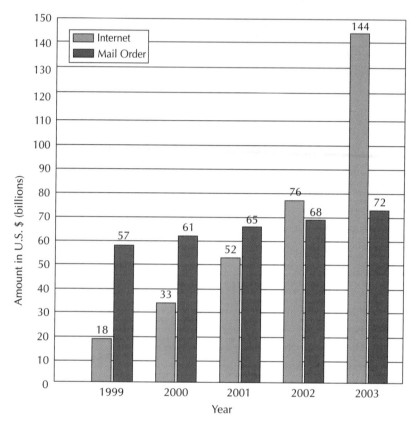

are generally taxable. If the remote vendor does not collect the tax, then the tax is typically uncollectable because most nonbusiness consumers do not self-assess use tax, and it is not practicable (or desirable) for states to audit such persons.

With regard to business–to–business sales, the transactions themselves are frequently exempt and thus present less of a problem to state tax collectors. These business–to–business transactions are often not subject to tax because they are sales of products or services for resale, or sales of products used in a manufacturing or other similar activity where inputs are exempt from sales tax.

Nonetheless, many business-to-business transactions are subject to sales or use tax because there are many categories of business purchases or inputs that are not exempt from sales or use tax. For instance, the purchase of accounting software by a hotel, the acquisition of cash registers by a retail store, and the purchase of telecommunications services by a financial institution are typically subject to sales or use tax. Indeed, as discussed in chapter 2, it has been estimated that about two-fifths of all sales tax collections are derived from business-to-business transactions. Thus, the problems associated with the inability of states to require remote vendors to collect sales and use tax are exacerbated by the enormous projected growth of business-to-business transactions in future years.

However, certain factors reduce the likelihood that business-to-business taxable sales will avoid taxation. First, unlike retail consumers, business purchasers are much more likely to self-assess the use tax to avoid future interest and penalties if they are audited by state tax authorities. Second, state taxing authorities are much more likely to audit and assess business purchases (where no tax has been paid) because governments expend significantly higher resources and manpower to audit business entities than to audit individual households.

The Organizational Structure of E-Retailers

To be sure, not all (or even most) E-retailing operations avoid physical presence in the customer states, thus circumventing a sales and use tax collection responsibility. Many Internet retailers collect sales or use taxes in their customer's jurisdictions.[11] These companies establish and maintain a physical presence in market states for a number of reasons. Some entities, such as Eddie Bauer or The Gap, have retail stores in most jurisdictions and may want to take advantage of these local outlets for distribution, returns, marketing, and other similar operational purposes.

Likewise, drugstore.com uses its part owner Rite Aid's 3,800 stores nationwide to facilitate same-day pickup of medications ordered over the Internet. AutoNation, the nation's largest new car dealership chain, uses its existing 400 stores for home delivery of vehicles purchased from its Web site. Circuit City allows customers the choice of picking up their

Web purchases at local retail outlets or having their products directly shipped to their homes. Gateway sells most of its computers through mail order and Internet channels, but it maintains 164 stores across the country so that its customers can try out its computers before making a purchase. Other start-up dot-com companies may want to establish a network of sales representatives or service personnel in market states to facilitate marketing, vendor relations, customer service, or some other operational needs.[12]

Nonetheless, a large number of Web retailers establish organizational structures that do not require physical presence in customer states. These include newly created dot-com companies such as eToys and Buy.com. They also include more conventional businesses such as Barnes & Noble (bn.com) and Wal-Mart (Wal-Mart.com) that set up separate Internet subsidiaries. These operational structures are frequently chosen not to avoid sales and use tax collection responsibilities but to minimize operational costs. With a Web-retailing business model, it is generally possible to operate from only a few locations and save the expense of using market-state retail locations, service providers, or intermediaries.

The limited geographical presence of an Internet vendor's primary facilities is augmented by a significant reliance on unrelated third parties to perform shipping, distribution, and other operational functions. For instance, many Internet retailers use third-party fulfillment centers or distributors, such as Fingerhut Business Services, Inc., Keystone Fulfillment, Inc., Ingram, or Tech Data, to simplify shipping and back-office processing. Fingerhut Business Services, Inc., handles processing and shipping for start-ups such as eToys and existing giants such as Levi Strauss.[13]

According to Forrester Research, Web retailers will ship approximately 230 million packages in 1999, mostly during the holiday season. Many larger Internet companies will ship more than a thousand packages daily. The largest dot-coms may ship over 50,000 packages a day in the holiday months of November and December. For new companies the use of fulfillment centers or third-party distributors helps avoid the expense of setting up their own warehouse, distribution, or shipping facilities. For existing companies, in-house warehouse and shipping facilities are generally equipped to send inventory in bulk to retail stores, not to send individual orders to single households. For these companies, distributors provide an efficient channel to ship goods to Web purchasers and also to perform real-time back-office functions such as processing orders or handling customer-service calls. Alternatively, many Internet retailers contract with the original manufacturers to drop ship the products directly to the consumers.[14] These arrangements help the dot-com companies avoid the expense of costly distribution and shipping facilities. While the third-party contractors are generally chosen for operational purposes, their use by Internet retailers also allows these vendors to limit their physical presence and avoid costly sales and use tax collection responsibilities (see discussion in chapter 2).

The organizational structure and geographic presence of Internet retailers is not a static landscape, but rather a constantly evolving scenario. As operational needs change, many Internet retailers may opt for using customer-service, fulfillment and shipping centers, promotional activities, repair facilities, and other in-state persons or property in market states. These activities may create a physical presence for the E-retailers in market states and thus, a sales or use tax collection responsibility.

Current Nexus Issues

The rapid expansion of direct-marketing channels through mail order or Internet Web sites has significantly restricted the ability of states to collect sales or use taxes on in-state purchases from out-of-state vendors. Instead of eliminating nexus issues relating to out-of-state vendors, however, the *Quill* decision has effectively shifted the inquiry from whether economic presence alone is enough to create a tax collection responsibility to whether the out-of-state vendor has some modest links to the customer state—either through its own employees or through third-party contractors—that satisfy the substantial nexus requirement of the Commerce Clause.

Indeed, the search for these links, and the disagreements over their existence or import, has created a veritable minefield for remote vendors to wade through as they generate customers in other jurisdictions.

Among the most contentious issues are those related to *de minimis* safe harbors, agency nexus, and affiliate nexus. The growth of E-commerce will significantly increase the number of government-business disputes over whether an out-of-state vendor has physical presence in a market state through occasional visits, third-party repair or other service contracts, the presence of affiliate corporations, or some other connection with the jurisdiction.

Finally, newly created Internet companies are likely to have significantly more jurisdictional issues than already-established mail-order companies. Start-up dot-coms frequently need to make visits to other jurisdictions to set up supplier networks, arrange for advertising, engage in various forms of co-marketing with other business partners, and attend conferences or trade shows. Dot-coms may also feel more pressure to engage in in-person marketing or solicitation in consumer states to build up brand-name recognition and awareness of their Web sites. By contrast, mail-order companies typically have established brand names, existing advertising contracts, and well-developed supplier networks and distribution channels that require minimal contacts with major market states.

Therefore, a full exploration of nexus as it relates to E-commerce requires an examination of the developing law surrounding *de minimis* nexus, agency nexus, affiliate nexus, and other similar concepts. Although these categories have been present for several decades, E-commerce is injecting them with new importance and, as discussed below, many new variations.

De Minimis Physical Presence

Introduction

Under the standard set by the *Quill* case, a vendor does not have a sales or use tax collection responsibility unless it has physical presence in the jurisdiction of the customer. Under the traditional physical presence standard for nexus, a vendor with employees, equipment, or other property in the state will have sufficient nexus for sales and use tax purposes.

In order to have nexus in a taxing jurisdiction, a taxpayer need not have an office in the taxing jurisdiction. For instance, the presence of sales representatives, technicians performing occasional repair or installation services, and the provision of on-site technical advice or support can create nexus for both corporate income and sales and use tax purposes. Similarly, a computer software company that sends its representatives into a taxing jurisdiction to conduct business activities such as the design and creation of a home page may also be creating nexus in the taxing jurisdiction.

De Minimis Exception

The U.S. Supreme Court has determined that a certain *de minimis* level of physical presence will not create nexus for an out-of-state corporation. For instance, in the *Quill* case involving sales and use taxes, the Supreme Court ruled that nexus could not be based on a slightest presence test. The Court stated, "Although title to a few floppy diskettes present in a State might constitute some minimal nexus . . . we expressly rejected a slightest presence standard of constitutional nexus." Similarly, in *William Wrigley, Jr. Co. v. Wisc. Dept. of Revenue,* a case involving income taxes, the Court ruled that nexus could not be established based on *de minimis* contacts with the State.[15]

The problem with applying the *de minimis* safe harbor is that it is unclear how much physical presence of either employees, representatives, or property will exceed the constitutionally permissible threshold and thus impose a filing responsibility on an out-of-state vendor. To date, a variety of statutes, regulations, and court cases have addressed the issue, but there is no definitive guidance from the U.S. Supreme Court on the boundaries of the *de minimis* safe harbor. Moreover, most states provide no clear guidance on the issue, leaving state tax administrators and multistate taxpayers to fend for themselves, using a case-by-case approach.

A Narrow View of the *De Minimis* Safe Harbor

In a number of situations, state courts or taxing authorities have determined that an out-of-state vendor has nexus, based on a very narrow interpretation of the *de minimis* threshold. For instance, in a 1995 Texas ruling, a vendor whose presence in the state was limited to three training sessions of two to three day's duration each was found to have nexus in Texas for sales and use tax purposes. In this case the vendor was a computer retailer headquartered in Florida. The vendor sold hardware, licensed software, and provided telephone technical support to customers in Texas. The out-of-state retailer asserted that it did not have nexus under Texas law and, alternately, if it did have nexus under Texas law, that it did not have it under the *Quill* precedent. In its ruling the Texas comptroller distinguished this case from *Quill* in that the out-of-state vendor in this case had physical presence in Texas arising from sending its employees into Texas to hold three two- to three-day training sessions. The comptroller held that training in Texas by vendor's employees combined with the licensing of software constituted substantial nexus.[16]

Similarly, in New York the courts have held that nexus is created by a very modest amount of physical presence. The New York Court of Appeals, in *Orvis Co., Inc. v. Tax Appeals Tribunal* and *Vermont Information Processing, Inc. v. Tax Appeals Tribunal,* held that sporadic visits by a mail-order company's sales personnel for the purpose of soliciting orders from retailers and that occasional visits by a computer software and hardware developer's personnel to install software, train employees, and correct difficult or persistent problems were both sufficient to satisfy the substantial nexus standards of the *Quill* case.[17]

In *Orvis Co. Inc. v. Tax Appeals Tribunal,* employees who did not live in New York visited customers at least 12 times over a three-year period. In *Vermont Information Processing v. Tax Appeals Tribunal,* the taxpayer's personnel made 30 to 40 trips into New York over a period of three years. The New York Court of Appeals held that, while a physical presence of the vendor is required under *Quill,* it need not be substantial. Rather, the presence must be more than a slightest presence and may be manifested by the presence in the taxing state of the vendor's property or the conduct of economic activities in the taxing state performed by the vendor's personnel or on its behalf.[18]

The Illinois Supreme Court adopted the "demonstrably more than slightest presence" test in the 1996 case *Brown's Furniture, Inc. v. Wagner.* While that case involved a fact pattern involving continuous physical presence 942 deliveries by the out-of-state retailer to consumers in Illinois over a 10-month period, the court quoted approvingly the New York court decision in *Orvis Co. Inc. v. Tax Appeals Tribuna*.[19]

Cases involving the *de minimis* standard also arise in conjunction with the imposition of income taxes. A 1997 Michigan case determined that the presence of a sales representative in a customer state for two weeks a year was sufficient to establish nexus. Magnetek was a Michigan manufacturer with sales to various states. Under Michigan law sales made to states in which the taxpayer is not taxable are considered Michigan sales for the purpose of the state's single-business tax. To avoid liability it is not necessary that the taxpayer be actually taxed on those sales, just that the taxpayer's activities in those states constitute a sufficient physical presence to make the taxpayer susceptible to taxation in those states under the Commerce Clause.[20]

Magnetek's sales managers went to their target states for a minimum of two weeks every year. The Michigan Court of Appeals held that the activity of independent sales representatives was sufficient to establish nexus with those states (and thus avoid the throwback of sales to Michigan). The court held that the appropriate test was that enunciated by the New York Court of Appeals in *Orvis Co. Inc. v. Tax Appeals Tribuna*.[21]

Michigan is one of the few states that has set forth specific rules on the boundaries of the *de minimis* safe harbor. Michigan's interpretation of the *de minimis* rule is quite narrow. Under the Michigan rule, an out-of-state seller must collect Michigan use tax when it has one or more employees resident or temporarily present in Michigan engaged in any activity (other than certain protected activities). An employee temporarily present in Michigan for two days will create nexus.[22]

Indeed, the Michigan position is similar to the approach advocated by a number of states under the auspices of the MTC. In the mid to late 1990s, the MTC organized a public participation working group of business and government representatives to try to develop a model constitutional nexus guideline for application of a state's sales and use tax to out-of-state businesses. After several years of discussions and draft proposals, the MTC working group ceased its efforts because of significant differences of opinion between the government and business representatives.

In January 1998 the government participants issued their last revised draft nexus guidelines. This draft proposal, like several of the earlier government representative pronouncements, reflected the opinions of the majority of state representatives to the project. It makes clear that many states adhere to a very narrow definition of the *de minimis* safe harbor.[23] The draft takes the position that nexus can be created by the temporary presence of one or more employees where the "temporary presence is significantly associated with the ability of the out-of-state business to establish and maintain the market in the taxing state with respect to the sale for which the possible use tax collection duty may be imposed." The draft indicates that the presence of an employee (or agent) for an average of two days per year to solicit sales or engage in repair services is sufficient to exceed the *de minimis* safe harbor.[24]

The MTC draft states that a remote seller's presence is *de minimis* when that "presence either does not exceed a slightest presence or is inadvertent." "Slightest presence" is defined in the guidelines in a minimalist fashion: "Although not easily stated in objective terms, presence of the out-of-state business does not exceed a slightest presence when the collective judgment of disinterested observers would conclude the presence is a frivolous basis upon which to support a finding of nexus." "Inadvertent" is defined as not reflecting a "conscious" choice. A conscious choice exists when "the presence arises from a regular and systematic business practice, the pursuit of an established company policy on a continuing basis, an affirmative decision of management, or a step taken to assist in the establishment and maintenance of a market in the taxing State."[25]

While a regulatory position such as that set forth in the Michigan ruling (or the MTC's draft guidelines) could still be challenged in court as unduly restrictive under the *Quill* precedent, it at least establishes the boundaries of what an aggressive state position of the *de minimis* role would be on audit or in litigation.

A Broader View of the *De Minimis* Safe Harbor

Other states have applied a more generous interpretation of the *de minimis* safe harbor, allowing out-of-state vendors to conduct more activity in the customer state without triggering nexus and a sales and use tax filing responsibility. In some of these jurisdictions, the permissible activity in the customer state was still relatively modest, at least to the extent of the facts presented in the particular case.

For instance, a 1996 Florida Supreme Court ruling rejected a state nexus claim over an out-of-state vendor based on a slight presence in the state. This case involved Share International (Share), a Texas mail-order vendor of chiropractic supplies that had no offices or employees in Florida. Share sold its products via direct-mail solicitation out of its principal offices in Texas. For three days each year, the company's president and vice president attended a seminar conducted by a related party in Florida, at which Share's products were displayed and sold. The Florida Supreme Court held that this did not create substantial nexus with the state for purposes of collecting use tax on the company's mail-order sales. The court found that the presence at the seminar did not further the company's exploitation of the consumer market in Florida because the attendees, mostly from other states, all had preregistered for the seminar. The once-a-year visits to Florida by the corporation's president and vice president were found to be merely a slight presence. The *Quill* substantial nexus standard was interpreted by the court as demanding an ongoing continuous physical presence in the state.[26]

Similarly, in a 1986 Pennsylvania case, the state court ruled that L.L. Bean, the well-known Maine mail-order company, did not have nexus with Pennsylvania despite several connections to the state. L.L. Bean generally conducted business with Pennsylvania customers only through mail-order catalogs shipped to in-state residents, as well as media advertisements in the state. However, L.L. Bean employees also made infrequent visits to supplying manufacturers in Pennsylvania to discuss problems concerning past and future shipments. In addition, L.L. Bean's employees made several trips to Pennsylvania to discuss the company's relationship with a clothes outlet chain, which it used for reselling its returned merchandise and discontinued products, in order to advise this retailer on display techniques, to police L.L. Bean's trademark, and to check on the accuracy of L.L. Bean's own accounting practices. However, the Pennsylvania court did not deem these activities sufficient to create taxable nexus in Pennsylvania.[27]

In yet another case, a 1995 Arizona court decision recognized a much broader *de minimis* safe harbor, allowing in-state presence for more than three weeks per year. In that case, Care Computer, a Washington corporation, was engaged in the business of selling and leasing computer hardware, licensing computer software, and providing computer training to nursing homes nationwide. During the audit period in question, Care Computer's contacts with Arizona consisted of a sales representative's annual visit, approximately 21 days of customer training per year by non-resident personnel, and approximately 180 mail-order sales transactions generating around $385,000 of Arizona income. Care Computer also had two personal computers in the state for seven months. These computers were subject to lease purchase agreements. The company did not have an office, warehouse, or storage facility in Arizona, maintained no business address there, and had no permanent employees there. The Arizona Board of Tax Appeals held that the foregoing factors were not sufficient to establish substantial nexus. The board stated that, "[t]o have substantial nexus, . . . a business must have more than just a large number of sales and occasional visits of personnel."[28]

Even in New York, where the courts have set forth one of the narrowest *de minimis* exceptions in the country, at least one administrative judge ruling has taken a more flexible approach, holding that no nexus was created by 20 vendor visits into the state over a three-year period. This 1996 case involved NADA Services, a Delaware corporation that distributed several publications in New York. This company sold subscriptions to its publications through its relationship with its corporate parent, the National Automobile Dealers Association, and by including mail-back cards in the publications.[29] NADA's contacts with New York, which included 20 trips by its employees to the state during the audit period, were found by the court to be inconsequential in effect, unrelated to the matter at hand, and therefore, insufficient to establish nexus for Commerce Clause purposes. The contacts with New York that were found inadequate were for the purposes of consulting with independent contractors located in New York who were retained by NADA to solicit display advertising for one of its publications, obtaining information for articles in NADA's publication, serving as an honorary judge at an awards ceremony, and attending numerous educational seminars concerning various aspects of publishing and journalism. In addition, the court ruled that occasional visits to New York by independent contractors hired by NADA to solicit advertising for its publications did not exceed the slightest physical presence test.[30]

Statutory Ambiguity

Most states have not specifically addressed the *de minimis* safe harbor by statute or regulation. Unlike the income tax nexus issue regarding what activities exceed *solicitation* for purposes of the PL 86-272 safe harbor, for which many states have issued detailed guidance, few states have attempted to clarify the boundaries of the *de minimis* exception.

Many states rely on very broad language, such as what is constitutionally permissible, to define what constitutes sales and use tax nexus. This language not only offers little guidance but on its face provides little protection for out-of-state vendors. For instance, an out-of-state vendor has a sales and use tax filing responsibility in Massachusetts if it exploits "the retail sales market in the Commonwealth through any means whatsoever, including, but not limited to, salesmen, solicitors or representatives in the Commonwealth." In Texas a retailer is engaged in business "if the retailer otherwise does business in the state."[31]

Similarly, in Ohio substantial nexus with the state exists when the seller regularly has employees, agents, representatives, solicitors, installers, repairpersons, salespersons, or other individuals in the state for the purpose of conducting the business of the seller. In addition, substantial nexus with the state exists when the seller has *any other contact* with the state that would allow the state to require the seller to collect and remit use tax under Section 8 of Article I of the Constitution of the United States.[32]

Is There a Safe Harbor for Certain Types of Activities?

Along with the problem of defining a bright-line test for purposes of the *de minimis* safe harbor, there is also the issue of whether certain types of vendor activities in a customer state (above a *de minimis* threshold) may be permissible because they do not create "substantial nexus" from a constitutional perspective.

For instance, several U.S. Supreme Court cases have made it clear that physical presence in the market state related to certain *presales* activities such as solicitation of sales or gathering of relevant market information creates sales and use tax nexus (assuming these activities exceed a *de minimis* safe harbor). However, the Court has not yet ruled on whether physical presence relating to other types of *after-sales* activities in the market state such as making repairs or providing customer service or ancillary activities such as meetings with suppliers similarly create sales and use tax nexus for a remote vendor. (See detailed discussion of presales activities and after-sales activities in the section on "Attributional Nexus.")

In particular, a good argument can be made that certain types of ancillary activities that are unrelated to creating and maintaining a marketplace in the customer state for the vendor's products or services will not create nexus for a remote vendor (or alternatively will require a greater level of physical presence before creating a collection responsibility). For instance, an Internet vendor may send employees into a market state to meet with suppliers or distributors, attend board-of-director meetings, assist in a lawsuit, meet with third-party contractors, attend training seminars, or negotiate a single large transaction. Arguably, none of these activities are related to making sales to customers in that particular state but are more focused on the remote vendor's overall business operations.

Support for a limited safe harbor for certain types of physical presence can be found in the U.S. Supreme Court cases issued to date on nexus-related issues. The cases emphasize the importance of purposeful business activity directed toward the market state. As the Court stated in *Tyler Pipe Industries, Inc. v. Washington State Department of Revenue,* "the crucial factor governing nexus is whether the activities performed in this state on behalf of the taxpayer are significantly associated with the taxpayer's ability to establish and maintain a market in this state for the sales."[33]

Similarly, the MTC, in its most recent sales and use tax nexus guidelines issued in 1998, followed closely the analysis set forth in *Tyler Pipe.*

These draft guidelines, while not finalized or binding on the states, generally reflect the position of numerous state departments of revenue that were working with the MTC as part of a government-business working group focused on defining the constitutional parameters of sales and use tax nexus.

In its 1998 draft nexus guidelines, the MTC placed significant emphasis on temporary physical presence in the market state that is "significantly associated with the ability of the out-of-state business to establish and maintain the market in the taxing state." The draft guidelines state that such activities include "solicitation and marketing directed to in-state persons, including market research for sales to be made into the taxing state; product fulfillment activities, including delivery, distribution, installation, training, testing, and consultation; repair services that are on behalf of the out-of-state business; and customer adjustment services, including handling of complaints and returns. Other activities include providing the seller with information about the market, including product performance, competing products, pricing, market conditions, and trends; existing and upcoming products; customer financial status; and other critical local information." Notably, these guidelines do not identify any supply-side or other ancillary activities unrelated to establishing and maintaining a market as creating nexus for an out-of-state retailer.[34]

Moreover, some states have established statutory or regulatory safe harbors for out-of-state vendors engaged in similar types of activities. Under a Michigan rule, for example, if an out-of-state seller is not conducting activities to establish or maintain a market in Michigan and its contacts in Michigan are limited to certain types of protected activities, then the contacts are generally presumed not to create nexus. The following are types of protected activities (nexus safe harbors) identified by Michigan:

- meeting with in-state suppliers of goods or services
- attending occasional meetings
- holding recruiting or hiring events
- attending a trade show at which no orders for goods are taken and no sales are made

Furthermore, state courts in several jurisdictions have ruled for the tax-payers in nexus-related cases, at least in part because of the type of activities being conducted by the out-of-state retailers in the state. As previously discussed, activities such as visits to suppliers (the *L.L. Bean* case) and consultations with independent contractors, participating in an awards ceremony, and attending educational seminars (the *NADA Services* case) were found to be inadequate for purposes of establishing nexus with the market state. Similarly, in a 1989 Maryland case, *Matthew Bender & Co., Inc. v. Comptroller of the Treasury,* the court held that visits to a supplier did not create nexus for the out-of-state vendor.[35]

Nonetheless, despite the lower nexus risk created by certain types of market-state activities by a remote vendor, there is no certainty that states will refrain from challenging such activities or, if challenged, that the tax-payer's position will prevail in litigation. The vast majority of states have not spelled out specific safe-harbor boundaries related to supply-side or other ancillary physical presence. The MTC has only issued a draft regulation that even if finalized is not binding on the states. Moreover, if given the opportunity, it is possible that the U.S. Supreme Court will go beyond its dicta in *Tyler Pipe* and base a finding of nexus on broader categories of physical presence in the customer state. Indeed, there is language in a 1977 U.S. Supreme Court case, *National Geographic Society v. California Board of Equalization,* that suggests that the taxpayer's link to the state need not be directly related to the solicitation or sale of goods or services (although the level of the taxpayer's physical presence in this case was high). Finally, even if the *de minimis* threshold is higher for certain activities than for others, there is likely a level of physical presence above which even these other nonmarketing or solicitation activities will create nexus and a sales and use tax collection responsibility for an out-of-state vendor.

Conclusion

In the absence of a U.S. Supreme Court determination of what constitutes *substantial nexus,* the standard for the *de minimis* safe harbor will vary from state to state. There is still considerable debate over whether the *de minimis* threshold is exceeded by incidental or sporadic activity or whether it requires a more significant or continuous presence. If physical presence for creating substantial nexus requires regular and systematic contacts, what exactly does this mean? Although occasional, irregular, unplanned, aberrational visits may be *de minimis,* what about a regular annual visit, for purposes of solicitation of business from significant customers, that only lasts one week?

Until the U.S. Supreme Court addresses more fact patterns or the states provide clearer guidance, there will remain great uncertainty over the scope of the *de minimis* safe harbor. Are two weeks of presence by a sales representative sufficient to create nexus for sales and use tax purposes? What about one week or three weeks? What about only three days of presence of multiple individuals to negotiate a major sales transaction? If employees perform installation or maintenance work in the customer's state, is nexus created if they do it once? How about two or three times in a one-year period?

Moreover, does it matter what type of activity is being conducted? Are fewer days required if the activity is presales marketing or solicitation activity as compared to if the activity is postsales repair, customer service, installation, and so on? What if the vendor's activity is related to ancillary activities, such as attending board-of-director meetings or meeting with third-party contractors? Could any of these activities create nexus and a sales and use tax collection responsibility? A clear answer does not yet exist for most of these questions. Fact patterns will need to be resolved on a case-by-case basis.

These *de minimis* issues have been present for a number of years in relation to traditional commerce. However, E-commerce, with its vast expansion of remote vendors, is likely to significantly increase the level of disputes over whether a vendor's presence in a customer state is protected by a *de minimis* safe harbor.

De Minimis **Property**

Questions regarding *de minimis* activities arise not only with the presence of employees or agents in the taxing jurisdiction but also with the location of certain kinds of property in the state. E-commerce increases the frequency with which remote vendors may have a modest amount of property in a market state, such as inventory at a fulfillment house or freight forwarder, licensed software used by customers, bank accounts, a Web site on a server in the state, points of presence maintained by a tele-communications company, or transitory property moving through a jurisdiction to its destination point. In each of these instances, the issue arises as to whether the remote vendor's property creates a taxable presence in the customer state or is protected by the *de minimis* exception.

Inventory in a Market State

The growth in the use of fulfillment houses and freight forwarders by Internet vendors and other remote vendors creates the potential for nexus at these distribution and shipping points. Typically, a fulfillment house is a third party hired by a vendor to store its goods at certain convenient distribution points and then ship the goods when the remote vendor receives an order. The seller can either send property from its own inventory to the intermediary or have a manufacturer forward goods directly to the fulfillment house. The seller generally owns the property while it sits in the warehouse of the fulfillment house. The fulfillment house may also hold packaging with the vendor's labeling and may place the goods in the packaging before shipment.

A fulfillment house is typically not structured to function as either a reseller or a drop shipper. Unlike a reseller, the fulfillment house never takes title to property that it subsequently ships. Unlike a drop shipper, the fulfillment house does not ship its own product on behalf of another retailer. Rather, a fulfillment house operates as an independent contractor for a remote vendor, holding products in its warehouse or distribution facility and then shipping them to customers designated by the retailer. In many cases a fulfillment house may perform other functions such as quality control, repackaging, billing, tax calculations, and collections.

Because a fulfillment house typically holds a substantial amount of property of a retailer on a short-term, but continuous basis, it is likely that the location of the remote vendor's inventory in the customer state would create nexus (above a *de minimis* level) in many states. Alternatively, some states may treat the fulfillment house as the agent of the remote vendor creating agency nexus for the retailer in the jurisdictions where the fulfillment house holds inventory and ships on behalf of the remote vendor.

Similar situations arise where companies maintain a steady supply of semiprocessed goods at a third-party contractor's location in another state. The out-of-state vendor may send unfinished products to a contractor so that some additional processing or manufacturing function can be performed or repairs can be made. It is likely that many states would consider the storage of such property, even if it were solely for a transitory business purpose, to create nexus for the out-of-state manufacturer.

However, some states such as New York have passed laws that encourage outside vendors to use third-party contractors in the state. These laws typically provide a nexus safe harbor for the maintenance of property at a third-party contractor's physical location in the state. For instance, New York's corporate nexus rules state that a company shall typically have nexus with the state if it holds property that is stored or warehoused in the state. In 1997 New York amended its regulation to exempt property that was stored on the premises of a fulfillment service. New York defined "fulfillment services" to mean any of the following services: "(a) the acceptance of orders electronically or by mail, telephone, telefax or internet; (b) responses to consumer correspondence or inquiries electronically or by mail, telephone, telefax or internet; (c) billing and collection activities; or (d) the shipment of orders from an inventory of products offered by sale by the purchaser."[36]

Leased or Licensed Property

With the vast expansion in the use of computer software, issues also arise concerning whether the licensing or leasing of software that is physically located at a customer's site in a market state causes nexus to arise for an out-of-state software company. Generally, companies that license software in perpetuity and maintain no control over the software are considered to have sold the software and thus are not treated as owning property in the customer state. The licensing is viewed more as the maintenance of legal rights in the intellectual property, not an indication that a leasing arrangement has been entered into.

However, the result may be different if the software is not sold but is licensed or leased to a customer for a fixed period of time, such as three years. In this case the software company is more likely to be viewed as maintaining ownership of the property and, in many states, the software company may be treated as having nexus. This fact pattern is analogous to one involving a company that leases other kinds of property such as automobiles, tractors, office equipment, computer, and so on. In a traditional leasing arrangement, the lessor would typically be treated as having nexus in any physical location where its property is principally located or situated.

In *Quill*, the U.S. Supreme Court ruled that software that was licensed or leased to a customer in the market state did not create nexus for the out-of-state mail-order company. However, the Court appeared to base its decision on the fact that the number of leased software applications did not exceed a *de minimis* threshold. According to the Court in a footnote to this decision, "[a]lthough title to a few floppy diskettes present in a State might constitute some minimal nexus . . . [the Court] expressly rejected a 'slightest presence' standard of constitutional nexus." Accordingly, the Court concluded that Quill's licensing of the software in that case did not meet the substantial nexus requirement of the Commerce Clause. In light of the footnote in the *Quill* decision, it is likely that some states will argue that the presence of licensed software creates nexus, especially if the volume of software is substantially more than a few disks.[37]

Indeed, in 1998 the Texas comptroller ruled that the leasing and licensing of software programs by a Minnesota company to 20 to 30 Texas customers per year creates sales and use tax nexus for the out-of-state company. Kansas made a similar ruling related to income tax nexus (although the out-of-state company also had a small amount of physical presence in Kansas that year.).[38]

This issue may take on added importance as software is increasingly licensed to consumers not for use in perpetuity but for a limited time, such as a one- to three-year period. Under these circumstances, the actual software can be delivered to the customer's location, stored on the vendor's server, or stored on the server of some third-party contractor.

The ownership of property in a market state also arises in connection with the practice of many on-line companies or computer-service companies to give away thousands or tens of thousands of free copies of software to be used by consumers in accessing the on-line company's service. Similar issues are beginning to develop with digital categories such as time-limited Digital Video Disc (DVD) or other time-constrained electronic products. In each of these cases, the question arises as to whether the ownership of various properties in a market state, without any other physical presence, creates nexus for an out-of-state vendor.

Other E-Commerce Property Issues

In an E-commerce era, nexus-related issues also develop in relation to other categories of physical property such as computer servers or routers, Web sites, leased lines, and other equipment that are used to facilitate multistate commerce in an electronic age. In each instance a business must try to determine whether these nontraditional, and frequently sporadic, links with a market state create the potential for sales and use or income tax nexus. Connecticut, for example, has had a protracted legal battle with America Online over whether that company has nexus with the state. The state Department of Revenue Services claims that America Online had sufficient nexus based on the company's extensive network of computer modems, either owned or leased, that are present in Connecticut, as well as every other state.[39]

The issue of whether these modems constitute tangible property used in a trade or business, and thus create nexus for America Online, is as yet unresolved by the courts. Nevertheless, many large Internet service providers or electronic information vendors have a similar fact pattern because they rely on thousands of routers or computer servers spread throughout the country to facilitate dial-in service for a nationwide network of consumers.

Similarly, with the rapid spread of company Web sites on the Internet, there has been considerable speculation as to whether Web sites or Web shopping malls located on a computer server in a state create a taxable connection for the Web vendor. Under some theories these Web sites may be considered to be either physical property in a state or the lease of part of an in-state computer server for purpose of operating a Web site. To the extent the Web site is located on a vendor's own computer server or on a computer server in the vendor's state of commercial domicile, any possible nexus-related issues may be irrelevant because the vendor will have nexus with the state based on the in-state location of its headquarters office and the presence of its employees. On the other hand, if the Web site is located on a third party's computer server in another jurisdiction, then possible nexus-creating contacts with the market state must be explored.

Generally, the presence of a Web site by itself is likely to constitute a *de minimis* physical presence for an out-of-state vendor. However, the presence of an in-state third party that hosts the Web site and may perform other transactional processing-related functions on behalf of the remote vendor raises possible issues of agency nexus. These issues are in the following section.

Other similar nexus-related issues arise in connection with telecommunications companies. For instance, many business customers of telecommunications companies lease telephone lines from such companies to connect business locations in multiple states or to facilitate on-line customer networks. As a result, some states may take the position that these leased lines constitute the rental of tangible personal property in the market states, thus creating nexus for the business customer. A closer examination of these transactions, however, reveals that these so-called leases do not mean that a business customer has the exclusive right to use certain telecommunication channels running between states. Rather, these contracts provide business customers with guaranteed bandwidth to meet their interstate needs, while stopping short of providing the customers with the use of specified telephone lines. Thus, if a state did attempt to impute the rental of specific in-state telephone land lines to a business customer, it would likely be unsuccessful.

As with *de minimis* issues related to the presence of employees or agents of the vendor in the customer state, the *de minimis* issues related to property are also likely to surge with E-commerce. All of these issues illustrate that, even with the vastly expanded ability of companies in one jurisdiction to sell to customers in other jurisdictions without the need for offices or full-time employees, there are frequently links of some type with the market state that need to be identified and evaluated for their possible nexus-creating risks. Moreover, as with *de minimis* issues related to the presence in the market state of employees or independent contractors, the *de minimis* issues related to the presence of property will generally be characterized by the absence of definitive state laws or court cases, leaving the remote vendor to comply with jurisdictional issues largely in a vacuum.

Attributional Nexus

As previously noted, the U.S. Constitution requires that some substantial link or connection exist between a state and the person, property, or transaction it seeks to tax. This legal requirement is known as *substantial nexus,* and it exists when an out-of-state vendor has a physical presence of employees or tangible property in the market state. In addition, state taxing authorities have also asserted that an out-of-state corporation can have nexus based not only on its own activities but also on the in-state activities of an agent or affiliate. This theory of nexus is known as *attributional,* or *agency,* nexus, and it is based primarily on principles of agency law. According to the attributional-nexus theory, nexus exists between a state and an out-of-state entity when an in-state person or corporation acts as an agent representing the interests of its out-of-state principal. Under the theory of attributional nexus, even if a corporation *itself* does not have sufficient presence in a taxing jurisdiction, the jurisdiction may assert nexus over the remote vendor by attributing the presence or activity of another person or entity to the corporation.

The U.S. Supreme Court sanctioned the theory of attributional nexus based on agency law in several cases, including *Scripto, Inc. v. Carson* (1960) and *Tyler Pipe Industries, Inc. v. Washington State Department of Revenue* (1987). In *Scripto, Inc. v. Carson,* the Court held that Florida could require an out-of-state seller to collect use tax on orders solicited on its behalf in Florida by independent contractors. Scripto, the seller, which was based in Georgia, had 10 independent contractors conducting continuous local solicitation in Florida who forwarded the resulting orders from Florida to Georgia for shipment of the ordered goods. The Court found that the only incidence of the sales transaction that was not in Florida was the acceptance of the order, a fact that was not enough to persuade the Court that the taxpayer did not have sufficient contacts with Florida. In addition, the Court held that, although the salespeople were not regular paid employees of the taxpayer but were instead independent contractors by agreement between the parties, "such a fine distinction is without constitutional significance. The formal shift in the contractual tagging of the salesmen as 'independent' neither results in changing his local function of solicitation nor bears upon its effectiveness in securing a substantial flow of goods into Florida." On these facts the Court found that there was an "exploitation of the consumer market" by the taxpayer and held that requiring the taxpayer to register and collect use tax was not unconstitutional.[40]

In *Tyler Pipe Industries, Inc. v. Washington State Department of Revenue,* the Supreme Court reaffirmed its holding in *Scripto, Inc. v. Carson* that, as a matter of law, a showing of sufficient nexus can be made without regard to whether the in-state sales representatives are independent contractors or agents of the taxpayer. In this case the taxpayer did not have any activity in Washington except for independent contractors who were paid to solicit sales. These independent sales representatives performed, on a daily basis, substantial activities for the taxpayer, including calling customers and soliciting orders; improving the taxpayer's name recognition and goodwill in Washington; gathering information about the Washington market relating to product performance, competition, and pricing; analyzing customer financial liability; and providing information on upcoming construction projects. The Court held that "the crucial factor governing nexus is whether the activities performed in this state on behalf of the taxpayer are significantly associated with the taxpayer's ability to establish and maintain a market in this state for the sales." It found that the activities of the taxpayer's sales representatives adequately supported the state's assertion of jurisdiction to impose its wholesale tax on the taxpayer because the activities were necessary for the maintenance of the taxpayer's market and the protection of its interests.[41]

Although the theory of attributional nexus has been sanctioned by the U.S. Supreme Court for nearly 40 years, its use has accelerated over the last decade. This is largely a response to the *Quill* case, which restricted the states' ability to impose a sales or use tax collection responsibility on remote vendors solely on the basis of economic presence. With the growth of remote commerce, the state taxing authorities have frequently turned to theories of attributional nexus (and affiliate nexus, discussed later in this chapter) to limit the impact of the *Quill* decision on the state's ability to compel out-of-state vendors to collect sales and use tax. This trend is likely to be reinforced by the rapid expansion of E-commerce—with the many new links that it creates between remote sellers and market-state independent contractors.

Level of Control

One issue that arises with attributional nexus cases is the level of control required by a vendor over another person or corporation to establish an agency relationship. In general corporate law, agency is established by two critical elements: (1) an agent has the authority to act on behalf of the principal, and (2) an agent acts on behalf of the principal and is subject to the principal's control. In tax cases, however, the courts have generally taken a very relaxed view of what constitutes an agency relationship. For instance, in *Tyler Pipe Industries, Inc. v. Washington State Department of Revenue,* the crucial factor governing agency was whether the activities performed in the state on behalf of the taxpayer were significantly associated with the taxpayer's ability to establish and maintain a market in that state for its sales. In tax cases the courts have frequently focused not on how strict the principal's control is over the third party but what role the third party plays in establishing and maintaining a marketplace for the principal.

Similarly, in California, for a representative to be considered as operating under the authority of an in-state retailer, it is not necessary for the retailer to supervise or control the details of the work of the representative. The statutory phrase "under the authority of" refers to any relationship pursuant to which any power whatsoever is delegated by the out-of-state retailer to its California representative.[42]

Nonetheless, states frequently have differing positions over the level of control required to constitute an agency relationship and create attributional nexus for an out-of-state vendor. For instance, in a series of cases involving mail-order book clubs use of in-state representatives, the state courts have differed sharply on whether the representatives created an agency relationship. These cases generally involved an out-of-state mail-order book club that had no employees in the market state. In order to market its books, the book club would mail catalogs to teachers, who were under no obligation to order any merchandise or to obtain orders from students. The catalog generally contained order forms, which the teachers and other school personnel distributed to students. The teachers would then collect the order forms and distribute the books to students. The teachers were not typically paid for their efforts but did receive bonus points based on the size of their orders, which could be used to obtain merchandise from a catalog.

In Kansas and California, the courts held that the teachers were acting as agents of the book club and imposed a sales and use tax collection responsibility on the out-of-state book club. Both states held against the taxpayer, even though there was no express contract between the book retailer and the contracts. For instance, the Kansas Supreme Court held that agency may be expressly created or may arise by inference based on the relationship of the parties. In addition, an implied agency relationship may exist notwithstanding either a denial of the agency by the alleged principal or a lack of mutual understanding of the agency between the parties. The teachers were considered to be the implied agents of the retailer because they undertook to sell the books to the students, and the retailer accepted orders and payments and shipped merchandise to the teachers for distribution to the students.[43]

By contrast, the state courts in Michigan, Ohio, and Arkansas held that the use of the teachers, without more, did not establish a substantial nexus with, or physical presence in, the customer state for the out-of-state book club. In these states the courts held that the relationship between the retailers and the teachers did not satisfy traditional definitions of agency, which include the ability of the agent to act on behalf of the principal and an element of control by the principal. For instance, the Michigan Court of Appeals held that the relationship between teachers did not satisfy the traditional definition: the teachers were not the taxpayer's agents because there was no indication that the teachers had the authority to bind the retailer; the retailer had no control over the teachers; and the teachers were under no obligation to participate in the retailer's program.[44]

The Type of Third-Party Activity

There is also considerable controversy over what types of third-party activities can create attributional nexus for out-of-state vendors. The U.S. Supreme Court cases have focused almost exclusively on third-party solicitation activities in the market state on behalf of the out-of-state vendors. This has left unresolved whether other actions by independent contractors such as performing installation, repairs, legal work, and marketing may also create attributional nexus.

After-Sales Activities

One particularly contentious arena has been whether after-sales activities by third parties can create attributional nexus. In 1995 the MTC issued a nexus bulletin, 95-1, which was endorsed by about one-half of the states. The bulletin took the position that contracting with a third party to provide in-state warranty repair services creates nexus for the remote seller for both corporate income and sales or use tax purposes. According to the MTC bulletin, "the provision of in-state repair services provided by a direct marketing computer company as part of the company's standard warranty or as an option that can be separately purchased and as an advertised part of the company's sales contributes significantly to the company's ability to establish and maintain its market for computer hardware sales in the State."[45]

Although the MTC bulletin did not address the provision of other after-sales services, the bulletin's logic could conceivably apply to services other than repair services. For example, the provision of training or technical support by a third-party independent contractor could also lead to nexus for a computer company. Similarly, the provision of repair services for vendors of other products such as furniture or consumer electronics could create nexus under the bulletin's logic.

California, which originally supported the MTC's position in *Bulletin 95-1*, later recanted. In an amendment to its nexus regulation, the California Board of Equalization set forth the new policy: "A retailer is not 'engaged in business in this state' based solely on its use of a representative or independent contractor in this state for purposes of performing warranty or repair services with respect to tangible personal property sold by the retailer, provided that the ultimate ownership of the representative or independent contractor so used and the retailer is not substantially similar."[46]

In a 1999 Maryland court case, *Furnitureland South, Inc. and Royal Transport, Inc. v. Comptroller,* the state court imposed a use tax collection responsibility on an out-of-state furniture retailer that had no physical presence in the state, but which used a common carrier to handle both in-state delivery and certain other after-sale functions such as the setup and repair of furniture, returns, and the collection of accounts. The court determined that the furniture vendor's use of this trucking company amounted to "a large scale, continuous and systematic exploitation of the Maryland furniture market and created nexus for the out-of-state vendor. However, the court's decision in this case may have been influenced by a substantial institutional overlap between the furniture vendor and the trucking company, including the provision of original financing, shared office space, and intermingled advertising.[47]

Proponents of an expansive notion of attributional nexus rely on broad dicta in U.S. Supreme Court cases such as *Tyler Pipe Industries v. Washington State Department of Revenue.* In that case the Court cited with approval the state court's analysis that "the crucial factor governing nexus is whether the activities performed in this state on behalf of the taxpayer are significantly associated with the taxpayer's ability to establish and maintain a market in this state for the sales."[48] However, U.S. Supreme Court cases such as this one have generally been limited to third-party solicitation activity and not to other types of third-party services such as providing infrastructure support or postsale services such as repairs. The few reported cases that have involved after-sales activities have typically involved situations in which *employees,* not *independent contractors,* performed the services in the market state. Thus, many critics within the business community have argued that the states have significantly overstepped the constitutional boundaries with the agency nexus provisions set forth in the MTC *Nexus Bulletin 95-1.*[49]

This nexus controversy is even more important because the position on agency nexus related to after-sales activities set forth by many of the states in the MTC bulletin encompasses both sales and use and income taxes. Whereas PL 86-272 provides a safe harbor for income tax filings for multistate companies whose only presence in a state involves solicitation activities, it provides no such protection for after-sales activities. Whereas after-sales activities in a market state would clearly constitute nexus if performed by an employee, the issue remains whether the same activities would create nexus for income tax purposes if performed by an independent contractor. The list of activities that fall outside the scope of solicitation in PL 86-272 is quite extensive and encompasses actions such as making repairs, providing maintenance, collecting delinquent accounts, investigating creditworthiness, installing products, training, handling customer complaints, carrying samples, monitoring in-state retailers, and replacing damaged or unsalable inventory.[50]

The use of third parties to handle after-sales activities such as installation, training, customer service, and repairs is likely to arise frequently for E-commerce vendors. This is particularly true of start-up dot-com companies that have no existing distribution or servicing network and will frequently rely on third parties to perform these functions in market states. Moreover, warranty services will frequently involve a greater level of complexity than that contemplated in MTC *Nexus Bulletin 95-1.* Many Internet retailers do not directly enter into contractual arrangements with third-party repair companies to provide warranty-related services for their customers. Instead, they contract with warranty service companies such as WarrantyNow and RevBox that are in the process of establishing nationwide networks of repair shops. For instance, WarrantyNow has entered into fulfillment arrangements with 60,000 repair companies in the United States. WarrantyNow sells its product warranties to Internet retailers, who in turn resell the warranties to their customers. It is unclear whether the signatories of MTC *Nexus Bulletin 95-1* would extend their legal position to encompass Internet retailers that did not themselves enter into arrangements with third-party agents engaged in customer state repairs but instead relied on other warranty services to establish a repair network.[51]

There are relatively few state tax rulings on most of the novel theories of attributional nexus discussed here. Because state tax law on constitutional nexus issues generally evolves on a case-by-case and state-by-state basis, it is likely to be a number of years before taxpayers have clarity on what positions the different states are taking on nexus related to the after-sales activities conducted on behalf of vendors by third parties. Moreover, until the U.S. Supreme Court rules on such third-party activities or the federal government enacts preemptive legislation, the constitutional validity of various state positions on attributional nexus will remain unclear. Unfortunately for remote sellers, despite the lack of clarity in nexus rules, the burden falls on the vendors if it is subsequently determined that after-sales activities create nexus.

Presales Activities

Another contentious arena for nexus involves whether presales activities other than solicitation can create agency nexus. It is clear from *Scripto, Inc. v. Carson* and *Tyler Pipe Industries, Inc. v. Washington State Department of Revenue* that *in-person* solicitation activities, whether conducted by an employee or an independent contractor, result in a sales or use tax collection responsibility for an out-of-state vendor. Such prohibition on the performance of solicitation activities by third parties may extend to situations wherein a third party has a physical presence in the customer's state even though the third-party contractor is not directly interacting in person with customers on a one-to-one basis. For instance, the Illinois Department of Revenue ruled in 1995 that an out-of-state vendor that hired an Illinois-based marketing company to solicit customers around the country by telephone had nexus with Illinois because of the presence of the telemarketer in the state. California has ruled that an out-of-state vendor that not only advertises on a California television station, but uses the in-state station for receipt of orders over an 800 telephone line and through a mailbox at the station, has nexus in the state because of the presence of its agent in California.[52]

The prohibition on third parties performing solicitation activities on behalf of an out-of-state vendor is sometimes extended to sales-type activities even if they do not formally involve soliciting or taking orders. For instance, an Ohio court ruled that an out-of-state manufacturer had nexus with the state because it hired an independent contractor in the state to ensure that Ohio retailers maintained adequate stock levels of its products, to coordinate sales meetings, to set up product promotions, to provide training, to hire new independent retailers, and to provide samples to end users. Even though the manufacturer's representative was not authorized to and did not directly solicit sales orders for the manufacturer, the third party's presence was attributed to the out-of-state vendor because the representative's role was clearly to support the sales activities of the independent Ohio retailers on behalf of the manufacturer.[53]

Conversely, it is relatively clear from *Quill* and other court cases that media advertisements on television and radio and in newspapers do not create nexus for out-of-state retailers. These more-general marketing activities are probably exempt because the third-party contractor (e.g., the television station or newspaper) has no physical presence in the customer state or, if it does, its activities are passive in nature and not specifically directed toward soliciting sales in the market state.

What about other presales activities? For instance, what if a third party is hired by an out-of-state vendor to do general marketing activities, such as posting advertisements in public spaces, handing out flyers in downtown business sections, setting up information tables with general product displays, or handing out sample products or inexpensive gifts emblazoned with the product logo? Do some of these activities create agency nexus because they are similar to solicitation activities and are intended to establish and maintain a marketplace for the remote vendor in the customer's state? Or are these actions more comparable to advertising activities and thus fall within a safe harbor for such third-party contracts?

Unfortunately, there is very little guidance in either state tax rules or state tax cases on presale activities outside the realm of solicitation. On the one hand, such activities are different than protected advertising activities because these presale marketing activities typically involve in-person actions by third parties in the market state. On the other hand, these activities are different from prohibited solicitation activities because they are not aimed at individual interactions with possible customers for the purpose of initiating a product purchase.

Although few states have express provisions that deal with these types of in-person marketing activities, the language of many state sales and use tax jurisdictional provisions is sufficiently broad to encompass marketing-type activities as well as solicitation activities. For instance, a number of states, including Michigan, Ohio, Florida, and Illinois, have a laundry list of different activities that create nexus for sales and use tax purposes, but they also have a catchall provision that allows the state to impose a sales and use tax collection responsibility on out-of-state sellers to the extent permitted by the U.S. Constitution. However, because the U.S. Supreme Court has not issued rulings on presale fact patterns other than solicitation activities, it is difficult for a remote vendor or a state taxing authority to determine the types of activities that are constitutionally permissible.[54]

Many other states have provisions relating to sales and use tax jurisdictional requirements that appear to be more limiting and to focus on third-party activities such as solicitation and selling. For instance, the California statute includes within the definition of retailer "any retailer having any . . . agent . . . operating in the state under the authority of the retailer . . . for the purpose of *selling,* delivering, installing, assembling, or the *taking of orders* for any tangible personal property [emphasis added]".[55] The Indiana statute similarly identifies nexus-creating activity in relation to an agent under the authority of a retail merchant that "sells, delivers, or takes orders" of tangible personal property in the state.[56] Based on discussions with state tax authority officials in various states, however, it is clear that interpretations of these jurisdictional statutes vary widely. Some states assert that most marketing-type activities will create agency nexus, while other states acknowledge that there may be a difference between prohibited third-party solicitation activities and permissible in-person, third-party marketing activities.

The MTC has tentatively set forth a more-assertive state tax position that would make no distinction between third-party solicitation and marketing activities in terms of their impact on the creation of nexus for out-of-state retailers. In its draft 1998 sales and use tax nexus regulation, the MTC and a number of member states support the position that agency nexus could be created by a third-party representative that conducts business in the market state on behalf of the out-of-state company that was "significantly associated with the ability of the out-of-state business to establish and maintain a market in the taxing state."

The MTC draft uses the phrase "significantly associated with the ability of the out-of-state business to establish and maintain the market" in a way that makes it clear that it is meant to encompass both marketing and solicitation activities. The phrase refers to business activities that include "activities that (i) involve contact with the customer or potential customer in the capacity as a customer or potential customer or (ii) involve the collection of information that pertains to the market in the taxing State or to information about a customer or potential customer that furthers the business of the out-of-state business with respect to the customer or potential customer in the capacity of a customer or potential customer." The draft regulation states that such activities consist of (1) solicitation and marketing directed to in-state persons, including market research for sales to be made into the taxing State; (2) product fulfillment activities, including delivery, distribution, installation, training, testing, and consultation; (3) repair services on behalf of the out-of-state business; and (4) customer-adjustment services, including handling of complaints and returns. Other activities included providing the seller with information about (a) the market, including product performance, competing products, pricing, market conditions, and trends; (b) existing and upcoming products; (c) customer financial status; and (d) other critical local information.[57]

Once again, in the absence of clear guidance, out-of-state vendors are not provided with any clear checklist of the type of presales marketing activities they can conduct through a third party in a customer state without creating attributional nexus and a sales and use tax collection responsibility. From the published and informal opinions of state taxing authorities, it is clear that there is a wide range of state tax rules and opinions on this subject. As a result, until the federal and state courts clarify this issue, there is likely to be uneven and inconsistent enforcement of state tax rules on activity conducted by third parties in the market state. Moreover, until the U.S. Supreme Court issues more rulings, it will remain uncertain where the line between permissible advertising and marketing activities ends and impermissible solicitation or other nexus-creating activities begins.

Do Web Sites and Electronic Partnerships Create Agency Nexus?

New Business Models

The Internet has created new business models involving remote vendors and third parties in customer states that raise novel issues regarding agency nexus. Many of these new business models involve an Internet retailer that has electronic links to a business in the customer's state. These electronic connections can consist of a third party that actually hosts the Internet retailer's Web site in the customer's state or a third party that links its own Web site and customer base to the out-of-state retailer's Web site. The commercial links may also involve a third party in the customer's state that conducts electronic order processing, billing, credit-card authorization, collections, tax accounting, or some other transaction processing function for the Internet retailer.

These myriad combinations between on-line businesses are a fundamental feature of E-commerce. The Internet facilitates practically limitless relationships between businesses selling goods and service on-line and other businesses that electronically solicit customers to shop at the on-line vendor's Web site, frequently in exchange for a commission for each sale that is engendered.

Electronic marketing deals often involve an E-retailer purchasing on-line advertising or other links to its Web site from a Web portal such as Yahoo!, America Online, Microsoft Network, Lycos, or @Home/ Excite. These Web portals have monthly audiences that generally range from 15 million to 40 million people. Alternatively, an E-retailer may enter into agreements with other on-line sites with more specialized audiences such as iVillage, CBS Sportsline, GeoCities, ESPN Sports Zone, and USA Today. Finally, many Web retailers enter into arrangements with hundreds or thousands of smaller Web sites known as affiliates. These Web sites feed traffic to the Internet vendor in exchange for commissions or discounted products.

There are also other common forms of electronic partnerships. For instance, Web auction houses list products of other vendors and sell the products to the highest bidders in exchange for commission fees and listing fees. Many Web malls sell the products and services of other vendors on their sites, either based on an agency relationship or as a sale for resale. Unlike more traditional supply chains with E-commerce, it is frequently difficult in these cases to determine who is the retailer of record and who is the intermediary. There are also other Internet companies that perform a variety of back-office billing, accounting, and collection functions for Internet vendors.

With the growth of E-commerce, the level of Web advertising is expected to increase dramatically in the next five years. Forrester Research has estimated that Web advertising spending will increase from $2.8 billion in 1999 to $22 billion in 2004.[58] These on-line arrangements with third-party Web sites can involve significant levels of expenditures for E-businesses. For instance, in 1998 Amazon.com spent about $50 million in advertising and paid another $50 million to America Online, Yahoo!, and MSN to bring customers to its site. A bank, First USA, agreed to pay America Online up to $500 million over five years to be the exclusive marketer of credit cards on America Online's various personal finance channels, AOL.com, CompuServe, Digital City, and other America Online properties. The contract provides not only for preferential and exclusive advertising and links to First USA but also for on-line payment of bills and balance updates. On average, on-line retailers spent $26 on marketing and advertising per sale in 1998, compared with their physical counterparts, who spent only $2.50 per sale.[59]

Although costs for these business deals can be high, such arrangements can be very lucrative in terms of increases in sales volumes. For instance, Barnes & Noble, the world's largest bookseller, embarked on an aggressive campaign in 1997 and 1998 to catch up with Amazon.com in the on-line retailing of books. Through its Internet subsidiary, Barnesandnoble.com, the company paid about $10 million a year for four years to be America Online's exclusive bookseller. It also entered into similar agreements with other Web sites such as CBS Marketwatch, USA Today, and CNN. Barnes & Noble expects these on-line partnerships that funnel potential purchasers to its Web site to account for one-quarter to one-third of all of its on-line revenues. Similarly, 1-800-FLOWERS.com is paying America Online $25 million for four years to be its exclusive florist. The company expects this deal to result in $250 million in sales over the four-year period. The little-known telephone company Tel-save.com has added 1.5 million subscribers, primarily through its exclusive $100 million contract with America Online.[60]

Protected Advertising Activities

It is clear from *Quill* and other U.S. Supreme Court cases that media advertisements on television, radio, and in newspapers do not create nexus for out-of-state retailers. This is true regardless of the size of the media contracts or the power of electronic media to reach consumers and influence their consumption habits.

In the *Quill* case, the North Dakota use tax rule that was overturned had a very low threshold of media penetration that created nexus for an out-of-state retailer. As the Court noted, "On its face, North Dakota law imposes a collection duty on every vendor who advertises in the State three times in a single year. Thus, absent the *Bellas Hess* rule, a publisher who included a subscription card in three issues of its magazine, a vendor whose radio advertisements were heard in North Dakota on three occasions, and a corporation whose telephone sales force made three calls into the State, all would be subject to the collection duty. What is more significant, similar obligations might be imposed by the Nation's 6,000-plus taxing jurisdictions."[61]

Thus, in the *Quill* case, the Supreme Court reaffirmed the rule in *National Bellas Hess, Inc. v. Department of Revenue* (hereafter referred to as *Bellas Hess*) that established a bright-line physical-presence requirement for a state to assert jurisdiction over an out-of-state vendor. In effect, the Court held that a taxpayer should be able to reach customers in a market state without sales and use tax collection responsibility, as long as it avoids physical presence of employees or agents in the market state.

On-Line Solicitation

What, then, of on-line advertising on Web portals, popular Web destinations or Web affiliates? Does a Web site that advertises the goods or services of an Internet retailer create attributional nexus for the retailer in the jurisdiction where the Web site is located?

First of all, it is clear that Web marketing, like mass-media marketing, involves the use of electronic means to advertise goods and services to consumers. The fact that the former occurs on the Internet and the latter occurs on television, radio, newspapers, or other channels makes no difference in terms of a state tax safe harbor protection.

Unlike media advertising, however, Internet advertisements frequently take the form of electronic solicitation as well as electronic advertisement. Given the differences in technology, the Internet with its hypertext markup language (HTML) lends itself to instantaneously connecting customers who are viewing advertisements on third-party sites with the Internet retailers themselves. Any Web vendor is simply a click away for an interested consumer. Most Internet banner ads or other forms of Web advertising are designed so that an interested consumer can click on the advertisement and be instantly transported to the Web retailer's Web site for purposes of either gaining additional information or for completing sales transactions. This is roughly equivalent to reading a newspaper or watching television and being able to purchase a product simply by touching the paper or television screen.

Moreover, unlike media advertisements that are typically paid for on a per-minute flat fee, Web advertisements on third-party Web sites are frequently paid for not only on a flat-fee basis (based of the number of viewers) but also on a commission sales basis. With the Internet it is possible not only to advertise and solicit sales simultaneously but also to track the hits or purchases by consumers who have linked from one Internet site to another and then compensate the third-party advertiser on the basis of a percentage of sales dollars derived from the Internet traffic.

At present, the most common current method of payment is similar to the traditional media model—to charge for Web ads based on the number of viewers of the advertisement—cost per thousand impressions. Many analysts are predicting, however, that most Web advertisements over the next few years will shift to a pay-for-performance standard, with payment based at least partially on cost per click, cost per sale, or cost per lead. The Internet Advertising Bureau estimates that about 50 percent of all current Web advertising contracts include some element of performance-based pricing.[62]

Remote Access to Electronic Solicitation

To be sure, the fact that Web advertising frequently connects interested consumers directly with vendors does not mean that the third parties facilitating sales on behalf of these remote Internet retailers create agency nexus for such vendors. To begin with, in those jurisdictions in which consumers can merely access the electronic advertisements, and neither the Web retailer nor the third-party advertiser has physical presence (either via a computer server or other presence), there is no nexus over the Web retailer directly or through the actions of the third party because there is no physical presence in the customer's state.

This outcome clearly falls within the *Quill* case ruling. It is also dictated by provisions within the Internet Tax Freedom Act passed by the U.S. Congress in 1998. Under the Internet Tax Freedom Act, an Internet access provider, on-line service provider, or other Web mall may not be deemed to be an agent of a remote seller for determining tax collections obligations solely as a result of "the display of a remote seller's information or content on the out-of-State computer server" of such third-party Web intermediary or "the processing of orders through the out-of-State computer server" of such third-party Web intermediary.[63]

The emphasis in this federal act is on out-of-state computer server, so that this provision clearly protects any vendor if the third-party intermediary's computer server is located outside of the customer's state. Thus, assuming the third party's Web site is in only one state, the Internet retailer need not be concerned about attributional nexus deriving from the actions of the third party in the other 49 states.

This outcome is constant, regardless of the scale or success ratio of the electronic advertising or marketing. Even if the advertising reaches hundreds or thousands of consumers in the market state who make purchases through downlinks from the third-party intermediary's site to the Internet vendor's Web shopping site, there is still no physical presence in the customer state and thus no nexus for the out-of-state vendor. Under these circumstances Internet-based advertising will not create a sales or use tax collection responsibility for an out-of-state vendor, whereas several part-time sales representatives physically located in the customer state for part of the year will satisfy the physical presence test and create nexus for the remote Internet retailer.

Interestingly, a few court cases have addressed this issue, but only in relation to nontax issues. The issue of jurisdiction over Internet companies based solely on access to Web sites or Web servers has arisen in a number of nontax cases. These cases typically involved whether it was constitutional under the Due Process Clause of the U.S. Constitution to impose a state's jurisdiction over a company whose only in-state presence consisted of access by in-state customers to an out-of-state Web site. The cases have typically involved lawsuits related to trademark infringement or similar intellectual property litigation. The courts have actually ruled in both directions on these cases although their precedential value for sales tax nexus cases is limited because of the absence of Commerce Clause considerations.[64]

Third-Party Web Site or Intermediary Located in the Customer's State

What about a situation wherein the third-party intermediary has its server in the customer's state and has a Web site on such server that is the location of an electronic advertisement for the out-of-state vendor? Does the physical presence of the third party create a sales and use tax nexus for the out-of-state Internet retailer on the basis of some notion of agency nexus? A similar issue can arise when the in-state Web mall hosts the actual Web site of the out-of-state Internet retailer. The Internet Tax Freedom Act does not address this issue. That legislation only provides protection for third-party advertising that is located on a server outside of the customer's state.

As previously noted, electronic marketing by an in-state Web mall or other Web intermediary typically involves more than just media advertising. It also involves directing traffic over the Web site to the out-of-state retailers Web site for purposes of encouraging the review and/or purchase of the remote vendor's products or services. Thus, Internet marketing arrangements (at least in the host state of the Web intermediary) appear to emulate unprotected in-person solicitation activities because of the physical presence of the third-party intermediary and the use of solicitation-like links to the out-of-state retailer. Although the solicitation itself is not in person as it is in the attributional nexus cases, such as *Scripto Inc. v. Carson* and *Tyler Pipe Industries, Inc. v. Washington State Department of Revenue,* could some combination of electronic solicitation and physical presence of the third party's operations create a similar outcome?

The MTC, in its 1996 draft of *MTC Constitutional Nexus Guidelines for Application of Sales and Use Tax to an Out-of-State Business,* initially took the position that a third-party Web server in the customer state linking to an out-of-state retailer could create nexus for such out-of-state Web retailer. The MTC provided the following example: "Corporation A is an out-of-state business with respect to State 1. Corporation A directs business to State 1 through a World-Wide Web page. Corporation A hires Corporation B, an Internet cybermall service that is not an in-state person of State 1 for purposes of linking Corporation A's Web page on a host computer located in State 1, whose uses Corporation B licenses." Under these facts, the MTC determined that the out-of-state retailer, Corporation A, had nexus in State 1 because it used a third party's host computer located in that state to establish and maintain a market in State 1. However, in a later draft the MTC deleted this example stating that it had "temporarily deferred the example(s) to allow for further examination."[65]

Texas also initially took the position in 1996 that an in-state third-party server that hosted the Web site of an out-of-state retailer created nexus for the remote vendor. Texas concluded that the in-state service provider that hosted the Web site acted as the agent of the out-of-state company in helping it to establish a market in Texas. However, after reconsideration Texas later reversed its position.[66]

The biggest weakness of the argument that nexus is created by means of electronic marketing by an in-state entity on behalf of an out-of-state retailer is that the Web-related activity is neither in person nor necessarily directed at local customers. Most of the U.S. Supreme Court cases on attributional nexus appear to place a strong emphasis on an out-of-state vendor that uses an in-state entity in furtherance of purposeful business activity directed toward the market state. As the Court stated in *Tyler Pipe Industries, Inc. v. Washington Department of Revenue,* "the crucial factor governing nexus is whether the activities performed in this state on behalf of the taxpayer are significantly associated with the taxpayer's ability to establish and maintain a market in this state for the sales."

Generally, Web marketing is directed at a national or international consumer marketplace, not at a local marketplace. That a Web mall is located in a particular jurisdiction is almost irrelevant to the local marketplace because consumers can just as easily access the Web site from 1,000 miles away as from 10 miles away.

Another indication of the importance of purposefully directing an agent's activity toward the local marketplace can be found in the explanation for a state's position to adopt MTC *Bulletin 95-1* on third-party warranty repair services in the customer state. According to the MTC bulletin, "the provision of in-state repair services provided by a direct-marketing computer company as part of the company's standard warranty or as an option that can be separately purchased and as an advertised part of the company's sales contributes significantly to the company's ability to establish and maintain its market for computer hardware."[67] Although it is not clear what would happen if this issue were tested in the courts, a number of states have passed legislation stating that the presence of the third party's server in the state is not enough to create attributional nexus for an out-of-state retailer. Some examples are detailed in the following section.

Taxpayer-Friendly Rulings

In 1997 California adopted regulations that protected Web malls from being treated as agents for nexus purposes. The regulation states:

> The use of a computer server on the Internet to create or maintain a World Wide Web page or site by an out-of-state retailer will not be considered a factor in determining whether the retailer has a substantial nexus with California. No Internet Service Provider, On-line Service Provider, internetwork communication service providers, or other Internet access service provider, or World Wide Web hosting services shall be deemed the agent or representative of any out-of-state retailer as a result of the service provider maintaining or taking orders via a Web page or site on a computer server that is physically located in this state.[68]

In a similar case, New York issued a legal ruling in 1997 that clarified that in New York nexus is not created solely by placing an advertisement on a New York server or by doing business through a New York–based Internet service provider. Oklahoma adopted a comparable position by regulation.[69]

Most states, however, have not yet taken a position on this issue. Although it is likely that other states would avoid imposing nexus under these circumstances, there are no guarantees. From a public-policy perspective, most states may not want to discourage out-of-state retailers from entering into contracts with in-state Web intermediaries. Moreover, because it is so easy to move computer servers to different jurisdictions, any policy that bases a nexus determination on the location of a computer server is likely to be easily frustrated. Finally, the link to an out-of-state retailer may actually reside not on a single computer server but on multiple computer servers of the third-party Web intermediary. Frequently, the Internet vendor will not even know the location of the intermediary's servers, thus making compliance with any aggressive agency nexus policy highly problematic.

Does Local Market Orientation Matter?

Will the outcome be any different if a third party that advertises or electronically solicits on behalf of an Internet retailer has a Web site in the customer's state that is targeted exclusively or primarily to that state's customers? Does this mean that the third-party activity is more likely to be found to be helping the out-of-state retailer establish and maintain a market in the customer's state?

In Illinois, for example, the nexus statute takes a tough stance in an analogous situation whereby a broadcaster, publisher, cable television operator, or television shopping system directs advertising toward a primarily in-state audience. According to the Illinois statute, an out-of-state retailer has nexus with Illinois if it enters into a contract with a third-party broadcaster or publisher for the purpose of "soliciting orders for tangible personal property by means of advertising which is disseminated primarily to consumers in Illinois and only secondarily to bordering states." The Illinois statute has similar language in relation to a cable television operator and a television shopping system.[70]

It is not clear, however, that Illinois is enforcing these statutory provisions or, if it does, whether such enforcement would stand up to court scrutiny. U.S. Supreme Court decisions such as in *Quill* clearly create a safe harbor for out-of-state vendors that use advertising to reach an in-state audience. If the state is allowed to treat an in-state media company or newspaper as the agent of the out-of-state retailer simply because the broadcaster or publisher reaches a local market (such as a city-based newspaper) and not a national market, this would severely weaken the Court's safe harbor protection. It is likely that the Court protection extends to all electronic or third-party advertising, whether it is directed toward a local or national audience.

Indeed, in a 1997 California case, *JS&A Group, Inc. v. State Board of Equalization,* the state court held against the government in a similar situation. In that case an out-of-state mail-order company's only contacts with California derived from entering into advertising contracts with California and local cable television companies. The State Board of Equalization contended that these local companies created agency nexus for the remote seller. The court ruled against the state taxing authority, stating that such contracts did not create physical presence for the out-of-state vendor because advertising was a protected activity under the U.S. Supreme Court precedents. The court noted that the television companies did not solicit or receive any commission or other compensation based on sales of the out-of-state retailer.[71]

Third-Party Affiliates or Associates Program

The problems created by the presence of a server hosting the Web site advertisement or solicitation is exacerbated by the widespread use of affiliates or associates programs. Affiliates are individuals or businesses that have Web sites that link electronically to another larger Web site that is engaged in Internet retailing. The smaller affiliate sites typically have banner ads or buttons that can be clicked on to bring a consumer to the Web retailer. Many of these affiliates are simply individuals or small businesses with a Web site that makes recommendations on certain books or music albums to buy and then hooks an interested party up directly with an Internet retailer.

Affiliates generally enroll to be conduits of consumers to a larger Web retail site by electronically agreeing to contractual terms set forth at the Internet vendor's Web site. Affiliates typically receive some financial benefit for soliciting sales on behalf of the Internet retailer, ranging from free or reduced-cost products to commissions of 1 to 15 percent.

The use of affiliates by many Web retailers is extensive, with certain large Internet retailers using thousands or even tens of thousands of affiliates. Thus, the likelihood is that any Internet retailer with affiliates has entities with physical locations in every state that solicit sales electronically on behalf of the Internet vendor. Moreover, unlike larger advertising sites such as Internet portals, smaller Web sites owned by most affiliates may actually be targeted narrowly, reaching only a local or statewide audience.[72]

Do such affiliates create nexus for an Internet retailer, given the pervasiveness of the Web marketing/solicitation taking place? Should Web affiliates be treated as if they were multilevel marketing schemes that conferred nexus on out-of-state vendors or treated more like advertisers that don't actually own or sell the product and don't create attributional nexus for out-of-state vendors? Does it matter that the affiliate's in-state presence is primarily electronic-based and does not rely on in-person solicitation of sales? Is the state's case strengthened if the affiliate performs certain services related to maintaining the hyperlink such as customizing and updating the web site? The use of multiple, smaller Web sites located collectively in all jurisdictions certainly poses a more difficult legal issue than the use of large, nationally directed sites typically located in only one or several jurisdictions.

However, if state taxing authorities or courts ever determined that such affiliates created attributional nexus for affected Internet retailers, they would be effectively creating an economic-presence test, given the ubiquitous use of affiliates and associates in the Internet business model. It is quite possible that, in the current favorable political environment for Internet businesses, most states will refrain from pursuing a theory of nexus based on the presence of numerous small in-state companies with electronic links to an out-of-state Internet retailer. State legislatures may also create additional safe harbors for such Web retailers to avoid basing jurisdictional standards on Web site or Web server presence in the market state. Even if some states litigate this issue, they may lose in the courts because of the significant differences between prohibited *in-person* solicitation and other kinds of *electronic* solicitation.

Where the Third-Party Intermediary Performs Other Services

Although it seems unlikely under current judicial precedent that agency nexus will be created by an in-state company that hosts an out-of-state retailer's Web site, or electronically solicits customers on behalf of the remote vendor, this is not necessarily the case with an in-state company that performs other Web-related functions on behalf of the out-of-state vendor. Suppose, for example, that a third party hosts a Web site for an out-of-state retailer. What if the third party not only charges the out-of-state company for hosting services but also charges for certain other back-office functions such as invoicing, billing, and collections. What if the in-state third-party vendor provides other services for the out-of-state Internet retailer such as credit-card authorization or fraud detection? Do these activities performed in the market state on behalf of the out-of-state company create agency nexus?

The California regulation that provides a safe harbor for third parties located in California that host Web sites for out-of-state retailers actually goes a step further and states that no Internet service provider or other Web company located in California "shall be deemed the agent or representative of any out-of-state retailer as a result of the service provider maintaining *or taking orders* via a Web page or site on a computer server that is physically located in this state [emphasis added]."[73] However, the California regulation does not address other situations, such as when the California-based company not only takes orders but also performs other transaction processing or accounting services for the out-of-state Internet retailer.

Connecticut, more explicitly, has ruled that Web site providers may be agents for out-of-state Internet vendors. According to a 1998 Connecticut policy:

> Companies that maintain Web sites for sellers of tangible personal property may sometimes perform other services for the sellers, such as billing the sellers' customers, collecting payments from the customers or otherwise acting as agents for the sellers in connection with sales. A seller of tangible personal property will not be a Connecticut seller . . . merely because the company that maintains its Web site is physically located in Connecticut. However, if a company that maintains a Web site for an out-of-state seller of tangible personal property performs services for the seller in addition to maintaining the seller's Web site, such as billing or collecting and remitting payments for the seller, and the company does so from a physical location in Connecticut, the seller of tangible personal property will be a Connecticut seller by virtue of having an agent located in Connecticut performing services in connection with its sales.[74]

Analogous situations have arisen in other states relating to more traditional commerce. As already mentioned, the Illinois Department of Revenue ruled in 1995 that an out-of-state vendor that hired an Illinois-based marketing company to solicit customers around the country by telephone had nexus with Illinois because of the presence of the telemarketer in the state. Illinois also ruled that an out-of-state retailer using an in-state answering service to which certain calls from customers ordering products were routed also had nexus with the state. Finally, California has ruled that an out-of-state vendor that not only advertises on a California television station but also uses the in-state station for receipt of orders over an 800 telephone line and through a mailbox at the station has nexus in the state because of the presence of its agent in California.[75]

Many of these precedents involve a third party with physical presence in the market state actually performing activities such as a phone bank or receipt of actual orders on behalf of the out-of-state entity by means of an in-state workforce. Would the result be different if the billing or credit checks all took place automatically without any human intervention? If such electronic-based activities were deemed to create attributional nexus for the out-of-state retailer, this would lead to many practical implementation problems because the location of a Web server and related back-office functions could generally be moved relatively easily to another jurisdiction where a different outcome might be obtained.

Moreover, in the case of a large Internet service provider or Internet portal that provides various Web-related services to an Internet vendor, it is possible that the electronic activities are carried out not just in one location but in multiple locations (or backup servers) around the country. In that case it may not be practical to assign any possible nexus-creating activities to a particular state, thus complicating any application of agency-nexus principles.

To the extent that any of these in-state third parties are treated as the agents for the out-of-state retailers, the state is likely to impose a collection responsibility on both the out-of-state retailer and the in-state agent. Under traditional sales and use tax principles, state tax officials are generally authorized to treat an agent who solicits sales or performs other functions on behalf of a principal as jointly liable for the collection of sales and use tax. For instance, in Massachusetts the definition of retailer includes the following persons: "Every salesman, representative, peddler or canvasser who, in the opinion of the commissioner, it is necessary to regard for the efficient administration of this chapter as the agent of the dealer, distributor, supervisor or employer under whom he operates or from whom he obtains the tangible personal property sold by him, in which case the commissioner may treat and regard such agent as the retailer jointly responsible with his principal, employer or supervisor for the collection and payment of the tax imposed by this chapter."[76]

Thus, at the present time, the state tax rules related to in-state activities by a third party that extend beyond mere electronic advertising and soliciting are very unclear. The vast expansion in the use by Internet vendors of electronic billing services, credit-card authorization companies, tax collection intermediaries, and other similar entities will likely continue unabated, accompanied by considerable uncertainty over any potentially damaging agency nexus-creating activities.

Web Auctions

Another common situation that arises with Internet retailing involves Web auction sites. Among the better-known Web sites for auctions are eBay.com, Onsale.com, and Bid.com. Web auctions are similar to in-person auctions in that the auction house serves as an intermediary between sellers and buyers. However, the entire auction occurs on-line, without the physical presence of any buyers, sellers, or live auctioneers.

In a typical scenario, the Web auction house registers sellers and verifies certain information about them, lists the items for sale, promotes the auction items through advertising or other means, charges sellers a commission fee of 1 to 5 percent of the selling price, notifies winning bidders of the total cost, including shipping, and in some cases, provides buyers with a guarantee up to a certain dollar limit in the event that a product purchased is defective or not received. The Web auction house does not actually hold any of the auction inventory or collect the sales price from the consumer. Instead, shipping and payment are arranged directly between the seller and the buyer.

Web auctions are expected to be one of the fastest growing segments of the Internet. On-line auction transactions are estimated to increase from $1.4 billion in 1998 to about $19 billion in 2003. Over that five-year period, the number of on-line shoppers participating in such auctions is projected to increase from 9 million to 40 million households. The number of items offered for sale is truly breathtaking. For instance, eBay, the Internet's leading auction house, carries on daily auctions that list more items than a typical auction house would sell in an entire year. On a typical day, eBay introduces 250,000 new items into its on-line catalog.[77]

Once again, the issue will arise as to whether these Web auction houses serve as the agent for the sellers. Are they agents that are authorized to act on behalf of principals in concluding on-line sales? Should agency that is created electronically be treated any differently than in-person agency? Even if the auction houses are treated as agents, does this matter in any state other than where the auction houses have their physical operations and server? Unlike the typical agency scenario, the principals here (the sellers) sometimes have physical presence in the market state, but the purported agents (the auction houses) typically do not.

In 1999 New York issued a ruling in favor of the taxpayer in a case involving an on-line auction house based in New York. This case involved sotheby's.com, an Internet-based subsidiary of the well-known Sotheby's auction business. Sotheby's.com provides dealers in collectibles such as art, antiques, and jewelry the opportunity to advertise and sell their products in an on-line auction at the sotheby's.com Web site. Sotheby's.com does not own or take title to the items sold at the auction but does charge the selling dealers a commission for Sotheby's.com services in advertising the goods at the Web site and for taking responsibility for the transaction and credit-card processing. The New York Department of Taxation and Finance ruled that sotheby's.com should be considered neither the vendor in the transaction nor the agent of the selling dealer. Thus, no sales tax is required to be collected by sotheby's.com for on-line auction sales made to New York customers if the selling dealer does not otherwise have nexus with New York. Although this ruling is likely to be followed in some other states, its impact may be limited because New York has an explicit statutory nexus exemption (not generally found in other states) for an entity that accepts orders electronically over the Internet.[78]

In 1996 Vermont issued a ruling on an out-of-state company that maintained a Web mall in California on which certain Vermont retailers sold their products. The California company not only provided a Web site for the Vermont retailers but also acted as their agent in providing design, implementation, support, maintenance, and administrative services on behalf of the Vermont companies. The California company had no physical presence in Vermont. Nonetheless, the Vermont taxing authority ruled that the California company was the agent for the Vermont retailers and was responsible for collecting and remitting sales and use tax to Vermont on sales made by these retailers to Vermont customers.[79]

To date, no similar rulings have appeared in other states. It is unclear whether other states would attempt to impose their jurisdiction over an out-of-state agent that had no physical presence in the state where the Internet retailer had presence. This fact pattern resembles agency nexus in reverse, with the in-state presence of the retailer being used to impose a filing responsibility on the agent.

There is an additional issue with Internet auction houses. Even assuming they are treated as agents, many of the transactions that take place are consumer to consumer, rather than business to consumer. In most jurisdictions consumer-to-consumer transactions are treated as casual and isolated sales and thus exempt from sales and use taxes. However, the number of business-to-consumer transactions over the Internet is likely to increase substantially as some of the United States' 23 million small businesses use the Web auction houses as a convenient means to sell some of their goods and services. It is estimated that business-to-consumer sales will increase from 30 percent of all on-line auctions transaction in 1998 to 66 percent in 2003.[80]

Affiliate Nexus Issues

Another nexus issue related to attributional nexus that may have a significant impact on E-commerce activities is affiliate nexus. The concept of affiliate nexus arises when an out-of-state vendor has no physical presence in the customer's state, but it does have an affiliate, such as a parent, subsidiary, or sister company with retail stores or manufacturing facilities, that is located in the customer's state. The question that surfaces is whether the mere physical presence of the affiliate in the customer's state satisfies constitutional requirements and gives sales and use tax nexus to the out-of-state retailer. Or does the affiliate have to be performing certain functions on behalf of the out-of-state entity to create agency nexus? If so, do these activities have to be equivalent to the nexus-creating activities of an unrelated third-party representative, or is there a lower threshold created by the affiliate relationship?

The issue of affiliate nexus looms large with E-commerce because of the likelihood that so many E-retailers will have existing brick-and-mortar affiliates located in customer states. For instance, most major retailers with stores located in states across the country are either currently involved or plan to be engaged with E-retailing in order to use this rapidly expanding distribution channel. Similarly, a large number of manufacturers are establishing E-retailing operations so as to reach customers directly, instead of relying solely on intermediaries such as distributors and retailers to sell to ultimate customers. Many businesses throughout the world are setting up E-commerce operations because of the widespread perception that failure to at least partially use this new distribution channel will imperil their ability to compete in the new economy.

Indeed, while Web-only retailers such as Amazon.com and eToys have garnered most of the publicity, most on-line sales are made by preexisting businesses. According to a 1998 study by Shop.org, one-third of on-line sales were accounted for by Web-only retailers; the other two-thirds of on-line business-to-consumer sales were accounted for by existing brick-and-mortar retail chains, manufacturers, and mail-order companies. Moreover, the percentage of e business accounted for by existing retailers, manufacturers, and distributors is likely to increase in the near future as large existing companies such as Wal-Mart and Toys "R" Us commit themselves more fully to E-commerce strategies.[81]

Existing entities can establish E-retailing operations as either divisions or separate subsidiaries. To the extent that established companies decide to create separate subsidiaries to manage their E-commerce operations, questions regarding affiliate nexus will abound. For instance, if an Internet subsidiary does not have physical presence in the state of the customer, can it use the in-state operations of its affiliates for furtherance of its Internet-based sales? Can the Internet subsidiary use the existing affiliate for shipping and distribution purposes, for accepting returns at in-state retail stores, for customer service, or for managing common human resource functions? Can the Internet subsidiary share a Web site with its affiliates? Can it share identical trade names, trademarks, or other intellectual property with its affiliates?

To be sure, the issue of affiliate nexus predates the E-commerce era. Mail-order companies frequently had issues concerning possible nexus-creating activities performed by affiliates located in the consumer states. Indeed, as will be discussed subsequently, most of the existing case law on affiliate nexus stems from situations involving existing companies with separate mail-order subsidiaries, such as Saks Fifth Avenue and Bloomingdale's. Many of these independent subsidiaries were established after the U.S. Supreme Court decision in *National Geographic Society v. California State Board of Equalization,* wherein the Court held that a corporate division with physical presence in one state gave nexus to out-of-state mail-order activities of another corporate division, even though the other corporate division had no physical presence in the state and had totally unrelated activities. The Court thus made it clear that sales and use tax nexus is to some degree form driven, that an unrelated division could create nexus for the entire corporation whereas an unrelated subsidiary with the same operations might not.[82]

To address this issue, a number of states enacted statutes stating that nexus could be created for an out-of-state retailer if it had an in-state affiliate, regardless of whether the in-state affiliate performed any activities on behalf of the remote vendor. For instance, the Illinois statute includes within the definition of a retailer maintaining a place of business in this state, "any retailer having or maintaining within this State, directly or by a subsidiary an office . . . or other place of business." Likewise, the Wisconsin nexus regulation provides that "any retailer having any representative . . . operating in Wisconsin under the authority of the retailer or its subsidiary for the purpose of selling, delivering or taking orders for any tangible personal property or taxable services" must register and collect the state's use tax.[83]

The notion of affiliate nexus has been given a certain level of visibility by court cases in Illinois and Tennessee. In a 1970 case, *Readers*

Digest Association, Inc. v. Mahin, the Illinois Supreme Court ruled that the actions of an in-state affiliate could give a sales and use tax collection responsibility to an out-of-state mail-order entity that had no physical presence in the market state. At the time the Illinois statute included within the definition of retailer an entity that had a subsidiary that had a place of business in Illinois. It also included within the definition of retailer, "a retailer that is being owned or controlled by the same interests that own or control any retailer engaging in business in the same or similar line of business in this State." Similarly, in a 1990 Tennessee case, *Pearle Health Services, Inc. v. Taylor,* under a statute similar to the Illinois statue, the court ruled that the in-state presence of a retail subsidiary and franchisees conferred a sales and use tax collection responsibility on an out-of-state parent.[84]

In both cases, however, the courts relied on facts other than the mere presence of the subsidiary in the customer state. In the Illinois case, the court found that the subsidiary's in-state solicitation activities on behalf of the out-of-state parent were enough to impose use tax collection responsibilities on the out-of-state parent even for sales of products unrelated to the subsidiary's solicitation activities. In the Tennessee case, the court focused on some infrequent visits to the state by the out-of-state parent that, in conjunction with the subsidiary's in-state presence, conferred nexus on the out-of-state parent.

Affiliate Nexus Cases with Pro-Taxpayer Decisions

Generally, taxpayers have prevailed in cases brought under the affiliate-nexus theory, especially when the state tax authorities relied solely on the in-state presence of the affiliate without any evidence that the entity performed activities on behalf of the out-of-state affiliate. For instance, in the 1994 California case *Current, Inc. v. State Board of Equalization,* the state court of appeals ruled in favor of the taxpayer and determined that the out-of-state mail-order company did not have nexus with California merely because of the presence of an in-state parent. The California statute imposed a collection responsibility upon "[a]ny retailer owned or controlled by the same interests which own or control any retailer engaged in business in the same or similar line of business in this state."[85]

The court determined that this statutory provision was unconstitutional as applied to an out-of-state subsidiary with no physical presence in state and without any activities performed in the state on its behalf by the in-state parent. The court cited with approval "the fundamental principle of corporate law that the parent corporation and its subsidiary are to be treated as separate and distinct legal persons in the absence of a showing that corporate assets have been intermingled, that the formalities of separate corporate procedure have been ignored, or where the corporation is inadequately financed."[86]

Over the last decade, several other state courts have ruled that the presence of an in-state affiliate with retail stores does not create nexus for an out-of-state mail-order entity. These decisions have been rendered in favor of the taxpayers because the connections between the in-state retail stores and the out-of-state mail-order operations, if any, were de minimis in nature. For instance, in a 1989 Pennsylvania case, *Bloomingdale's By Mail, Ltd. v. Pennsylvania Department of Revenue,* the state court declined to impute the nexus of a parent corporation to its subsidiary. Bloomingdale's By Mail was a mail-order company owned by Federated Dept. Stores, Inc., which also owned various retail store chains, including Bloomingdale's outlets in Pennsylvania. Bloomingdale's By Mail accepted and filled orders for merchandise in Virginia and Connecticut, and the orders were shipped by common carrier into Pennsylvania. The solicitation of Pennsylvania residents occurred solely through catalogs, which were printed and mailed from locations outside of Pennsylvania. According to the court, the mail-order company did not have nexus with Pennsylvania through the parent's retail stores because the stores did not solicit orders on the mail-order company's behalf or act as its agents in any way. In holding for the taxpayer, the court rejected the argument that the in-state stores were agents for the mail-order company based on the occasional acceptance of returns of merchandise purchased from the mail-order entity. The court stated that these activities were "aberrations from normal practice." The court also stated that it was permissible for the mail-order company and the retail stores to use the same advertising themes and motifs.[87]

Similarly, in two cases involving the retailer Saks Fifth Avenue and its mail-order affiliate SFA Folio Collections, Inc., the state courts in Connecticut and Ohio both found in favor of the taxpayer and determined that the in-state retail stores did not create nexus for the out-of-state affiliate. In the 1991 Connecticut case *SFA Folio Collections, Inc. v. Bannon,* the Connecticut Supreme Court declined to impute to the mail-order company the physical presence of Saks Fifth Avenue Stamford, Inc., a sister corporation that operated a retail store in the state. In this case the two corporations had common officers and directors, shared sales and financial data, and used the same trademarks and logos. Furthermore, the mail-order company sent its catalogs to the retail store (primarily for training purposes). Despite these links, the court rejected nexus for the out-of-state mail-order company, ruling that it had a separate corporate existence and the in-state retail stores did not act as agents for the out-of state entity.[88]

In the 1995 case *SFA Folio Collections, Inc. v. Tracy,* the Ohio Supreme Court similarly held for the taxpayer on facts almost identical to those in Pennsylvania. At the time the Ohio statute provided that nexus could be created for an out-of-state retailer if it had "membership in an affiliated group . . . at least one other member of which has substantial nexus with this state.[89] The court applied the U.S. Supreme Court's decision in *Quill,* stating, "*Quill Corp.* requires physical presence in the taxing state for that state to require the vendor to collect use tax. Folio, however, has no physical presence in Ohio; moreover, the parent and subsidiary corporations are separate and distinct legal entities. . . . Thus, to impute nexus to Folio because a sister corporation has a physical presence in Ohio runs counter to federal constitutional law and Ohio corporation law."[90]

Although the U.S. Supreme Court has not yet rendered a decision in an affiliate nexus case, the several state courts that have reviewed the concept have uniformly rejected the notion that the mere presence of an in-state affiliate creates a sales and use tax collection responsibility for an out-of-state entity. These state courts have tended to treat an affiliate as they would any independent third party—looking not at mere presence but at evidence of actual activities conducted on behalf of the out-of-state retailer. In each case the courts held that the in-state affiliate did not act as an agent on behalf of the out-of-state principal. Thus, use tax jurisdiction could not be imposed under an attributional nexus theory.

Indeed, in some judicial precedents that should give some measure of comfort to Internet retailers and their affiliates, the state courts have provided a safe harbor for certain modest links between the in-state and out-of-state companies. Thus, in the Connecticut, Ohio, and Pennsylvania cases just cited, the in-state affiliate was permitted to have certain connections with the out-of-state retailer without crossing the threshold of attributional nexus. These links included common use of trade names, joint advertising campaigns, and *de minimis* levels of other activities such as displaying mail-order catalogs and accepting mail-order returns at the retail locations. These modest links, if adopted by other state courts, could prove important for Internet retailers that will often have some connections with in-state affiliates. For instance, many retail stores now have in-store advertisements that highlight the availability of certain goods through an affiliated Web retailer. Other Internet retailers share trade names and print advertisements with affiliates that operate retail stores. For example, print advertisements for Barnes & Noble state, "Visit the store nearest you or visit bn.com and click the .com to find these featured books fast."[91]

Clearly, corporate form is important in sales and use tax nexus cases. In *SFA Folio Collections, Inc. v. Bannon,* the Connecticut court upheld the legitimacy of a corporate tax minimization strategy in the face of the state's concern that "any retailer with an out-of-state mail-order component could avoid collecting sales and use tax simply by separately incorporating the retail and mail-order businesses." The court concluded that "taxpayers may arrange their affairs to minimize their tax liabilities. Unlike tax evasion, tax avoidance through careful planning of both transactions and corporate structure is a legitimate right of every taxpayer."[92]

Preconditions for Affiliate Nexus

The success of business taxpayers in most affiliate-nexus cases to date does not mean that Internet retailers can totally ignore the market-state activities of affiliates. The U.S. Supreme Court has not yet ruled on this issue, although it has declined to review several of these cases. Thus, it is possible, although unlikely, that state courts in the vast majority of jurisdictions that have not had rendered a judgment on the affiliate-nexus concept could reach a different result than the courts in California, Pennsylvania, Connecticut, and Ohio.

Furthermore, it is clear that, if an in-state affiliate performs certain activities on behalf of the out-of state retailer that help the entity establish and maintain a market in the consumer's state, the more traditional attributional nexus rules will apply. Thus, if an in-state affiliate with retail stores accepts returns on a regular basis for an out-of-state Internet retailer, the latter will likely be attributed with the physical presence of the affiliate. Indeed, California in a 1999 ruling stated that an out-of-state Internet retailer had nexus with the state on the basis on an in-state entity that accepts returns at its in-state stores on behalf of the out-of-state entity.[93] Similarly, if a manufacturing affiliate uses its sales representatives in the market state not only to solicit sales on its own behalf from distributors or retailers but also to solicit sales on behalf of a separately incorporated Internet retailer, then the latter will be deemed to have nexus with the customer state.

In many circumstances the boundary line for affiliate activities that do not create nexus for out-of-state retailers is ambiguous. With the expansion of E-commerce, there is likely to be a myriad of new fact patterns representing small or large overlaps between brick-and-mortar companies and their Web affiliates. These functional overlaps may involve cross marketing of goods, common advertising campaigns, shared customer-service operations or call centers, common use of customer lists, and other shared functions. The extent to which shared functions and cross marketing between in-state affiliates and Internet retailers are permissible without creating nexus for the out-of-state Internet retailer will likely be determined on a case-by-case basis in the state courts.

Massachusetts, for instance, issued a 1999 ruling that an out-of-state mail-order company advertising its products via a wholly owned subsidiary operating a Massachusetts cable television station had nexus with Massachusetts and was required to collect use taxes. Although this ruling, in treating the in-state broadcaster as the agent of the out-of-state retailer, appeared to take a position opposite to the result of the *JS&A Group, Inc. v. State Board of Equalization* case in California, it is distinguishable. Unlike the California case, the Massachusetts case involved an in-state broadcaster that was a wholly owned subsidiary of the out-of-state entity. Moreover, the state relied on the fact that the broadcaster was licensed to broadcast only to an in-state metropolitan area and that the out-of-state retailer dominated the in-state subsidiary's on-air advertising, accounting for over four-fifths of all advertisements. Under these circumstances, the Massachusetts Department of Revenue ruled that the in-state subsidiary's activities were significantly associated with the out-of-state mail-order company's ability to establish and maintain a market in Massachusetts. Thus, the physical presence of the in-state entity was imputed to the out-of-state parent for purposes of determining Massachusetts use tax jurisdiction.[94]

Although the Massachusetts letter ruling is based on a different set of facts than the California court decision, it still represents an instance in which attributional nexus was determined based solely on an in-state affiliate's electronic advertising and solicitation activities on behalf of an out-of-state retailer. In the Massachusetts case, there were no in-person solicitation activities involved. Thus, although this case may be based on a unique set of facts, it signifies the willingness of at least one state to use the affiliate-nexus concept in the generally protected realm of electronic advertising and solicitation. As such, the Massachusetts ruling establishes a precedent that is highly relevant for an Internet retailer that may be using an in-state affiliate to provide Web site or other targeted electronic advertising to local consumers.

Alter-Ego Theory

Finally, if an Internet retailer is not established as an entity that is sufficiently independent of its parent or other affiliates, a state may invoke the alter-ego theory to assert jurisdiction over the out-of-state retailer on the basis that it lacks substance and should be treated as if it is part of the in-state entity.

The Connecticut court in *SFA Folio Collections, Inc. v. Bannon* cited approvingly one principle of corporate law:

[T]he separate corporate entities or personalities of affiliated corporations will be recognized, absent illegitimate purposes, unless: "(a) the business transactions, property, employees, bank and other accounts and records are intermingled; (b) the formalities of separate corporate procedures for each corporation are not observed; . . . (c) the corporation is inadequately financed as a separate unit from the point of view of meeting its normal obligations; . . . (d) the respective enterprises are not held out to the public as separate enterprises; (e) the policies of the corporation are not directed to its own interests primarily but rather to those of the other corporation."[95]

Similarly, a New York state advisory opinion, *Spencer Gifts, Inc.*, set forth a number of factors to be reviewed by the state in determining whether the alter-ego theory would be employed to confer nexus on an out-of-state entity. In rejecting the alter-ego theory in this instance, the New York State Tax Commission stated that the "totality of the circumstances" must be viewed in order to determine whether one affiliated company was so dominated and controlled by its parent that the dominated and controlled company is the alter-ego of the parent. In ruling for *Spencer Gifts, Inc.*, the commission considered the following factors: [96]

- common officers and directors,
- common telephone numbers,
- degree of overlap of personnel,
- amount of business discretion displayed by the corporations,
- whether the entities operated independently of each other,
- whether the parent corporation owned all or most of the stock of the subsidiary,
- whether the corporations sell goods under their own names, and
- whether the corporations hold themselves out to the public as separate and distinct businesses.

Although it is not clear precisely how much independence is required, it is certainly permissible for the Internet subsidiary to use a certain level of services provided by its affiliates. Thus, it is probably acceptable for an affiliate to provide certain services such as human resource management, tax compliance, and shipping and distribution as long as these services are provided to the Internet entity on an arms-length basis. As with all substance-over-form cases, the key is likely to be whether the Internet subsidiary manages its own key operational functions and has a sufficient number of employees so as to be considered a truly independent entity.

Generally, the threshold for satisfying the alter-ego principle is quite high, and thus, most court decisions treat affiliates even with significant overlaps in operations as separate entities.[97] In those instances nexus is conferred upon the out-of-state retailer only if the in-state affiliate acts as an agent of the out-of-state entity. However, there have been a small number of tax cases for which the domination of one entity over another was so great as to satisfy the alter-ego test.[98]

Drop-Shipment States

In some states a sales and use tax collection responsibility can also be created when a *drop shipper* that has nexus in a customer's state ships products directly to consumers on behalf of an out-of-state retailer. A drop-shipment transaction typically involves a sale in which a retailer accepts an order from a consumer, places the order with a third party (manufacturer or wholesaler), and then directs the third party to ship the product directly to the consumer.

Drop shipments may create sales and use tax nexus problems in cases where the retailer has no physical presence in the state in which the customer takes delivery but the manufacturer or wholesaler (the drop shipper) has nexus with that state. Under these circumstances the retailer does not have a sales or use tax collection responsibility in the customer state because it has no physical presence in the state, nor does it have an agent performing any functions on its behalf in the customer state. The drop shipper typically ships the product by common carrier into the customer state and is therefore not treated as the agent of the retailer in the customer state.

However, a significant minority of the states take the position that a drop shipper that has nexus in the customer's state should be treated as the retailer and be required to collect sales or use tax from the ultimate customer (*retail-sales* rule) or from the actual retailer (*wholesale-sales* rule). Among the larger states that impose the retail-sales rule are California,

Massachusetts, and Wisconsin. Among the larger states that impose the wholesale sales rule are Florida and Maryland.

The drop-shipment rule is different than the agency-nexus rule in that the retailer itself does not have nexus because of the actions of the third-party drop shipper. Rather, the manufacturer or distributor that ships the products is generally treated as if it were the retailer or wholesaler of record, and the sales and use tax collection responsibility is imposed on this party.

In practice, however, the drop-shipment rule operates similarly to the attributional-nexus rule. Because the drop shipper does not typically invoice the ultimate consumer and most likely has no knowledge of the retail sales price, this rule frequently compels the retailer to register and collect the sales and use tax, even though the retailer has no physical presence in the market state. Otherwise, the drop shipper is left with sales and use tax exposure if it is audited by the state and determined not to have collected and paid the sales or use tax on the related transactions. Alternatively, in some states the drop shipper may have a responsibility to collect the sales or use tax from the Internet retailer, which in turn may similarly compel the retailer to register and collect the tax from the ultimate consumer.

In most states the drop-shipment rule is not imposed, and neither the drop shipper nor the out-of-state retailer is treated as having a sales or use tax collection responsibility on the transactions. First, the sale from the manufacturer or distributor to the retailer is treated as a sale for resale. These states typically accept either an in-state resale certificate, a multi-state resale certificate, or a resale certificate from the retailer's home state as evidence that the first phase of the transaction is exempt. Second, the sale from the retailer to the ultimate consumer is treated as the taxable sale, but the out-of-state retailer is not required to collect the use tax because it has no physical presence in the customer's state.

Different Drop-Shipment-Rule Approaches

Those states that use the drop-shipment rule to impose a collection responsibility on the manufacturer or distributor use two different approaches to these transactions. In the first approach a state statute may treat a drop-shipment transaction as a taxable wholesale sale from the drop shipper to the retailer. In these states the first phase of the transaction is typically not regarded as a valid sale for resale. The retailer typically cannot provide the drop shipper with a valid resale certificate because the retailer is not registered as a vendor in the market state. For example, the Nebraska statute states, "When company A which is engaged in business in Nebraska . . . delivers property to company C pursuant to a sales agreement between company A and company B which is not engaged in business in this state, company A is required to collect [from] and remit the applicable Nebraska sales tax for company B." States that use this approach impose a sales or use tax on the wholesale price—most likely because the drop shipper does not bill the ultimate consumer and does not know the retail price.[99]

Under the second approach, the drop shipper is treated as if it is the retailer of record and is required to collect the sales or use tax directly from the consumer based on the retail price charged by the retailer to the consumer. For example, Massachusetts defines "retail sale" as the "delivery in the commonwealth of tangible personal property by an owner or former owner thereof, . . . if the delivery is to a consumer . . . pursuant to a retail sale made by a retailer not engaged in business in the commonwealth."[100] The retail sale is considered a retail sale to the person who is making the delivery. The California drop-shipment rule states that, when "tangible personal property is delivered by an owner or former owner thereof . . . pursuant to a retail sale made by a retailer not engaged in business in this state, the person making delivery shall be deemed the retailer of the property . . . [and] shall include the retail selling price of the property in his or her gross receipts or sale price."[101]

In most of the states that impose the drop-shipment rule, it does not matter whether the manufacturer/drop shipper makes shipments of the goods from inside or outside of the customer's state. However, in some states, such as Connecticut and Florida, the manufacturer/drop shipper does not have to collect sales and use tax if it ships the goods from outside the customer's state. Thus, these states use a much more circumscribed drop-shipment rule that is invoked only if the drop shipper both has a physical presence in the market state and ships to the ultimate customer from a distribution center within the market state.

E-Commerce and the Proliferation of Drop Shipments

The drop-shipment scenario is not unique to E-commerce. In fact, this issue has been present for a long time. For instance, California has had a drop-shipment rule since 1939.[102] Nonetheless, the drop-shipment issue has taken on more importance as many states seek to use alternative theories of nexus to circumvent the restrictions imposed by the *Quill* decision.

In addition, E-commerce transactions are much more likely to involve drop shipments than more traditional mail-order sales. A typical mail-order transaction does not involve drop shipments. A vendor such as L.L. Bean or Land's End manufactures its own product and then ships it from one or several distribution centers. Alternatively, the mail-order company outsources the manufacture of the products to third parties but still ships the goods from central distribution centers. In these situations the mail-order company only has a sales or use tax filing responsibility in its headquarter state, the state in which it has distribution facilities, or any other state where it has physical presence.

To be sure, some mail-order companies use drop shippers and must cope with states that have drop-shipment rules. Conversely, many Internet retailers such as Buy.com purchase their products from distributors that do not have physical presence in many states and thus do not create nexus problems for the Internet retailers.

In general, however, E-commerce vendors are much more likely to encounter the drop-shipment problem because of the unique dynamics of the E-commerce business model. First, most start-up dot-com companies do not sell their own products but instead sell the goods and services of many other vendors. A typical dot-com company might sell furniture, computers, household goods, or other products manufactured by dozens of other companies. For operational efficiency reasons, it is likely to be cheaper to have these manufacturers drop ship the product directly to the ultimate consumers. The alternative of establishing a separate distribution center is frequently too expensive for the Internet retailer. Likewise, the purchase of products from a distributor (that might have limited nexus in market states) rather than directly from the manufacturers is frequently not cost effective as it adds another intermediary into the distribution chain.

Second, E-commerce is also leading to a proliferation of manufacturers that are establishing Internet retail operations for making direct sales to customers. If these retail operations are created in a separate subsidiary, the Internet retail affiliate typically uses the drop-shipment model, with products purchased from its manufacturing affiliate for sale and drop shipment to the ultimate customers. To the extent the manufacturing affiliate has physical presence in market states that use the drop-shipment nexus rule—for instance, sales representatives that operate in these states—the manufacturing entity will run afoul of the drop-shipment nexus rules.

Legitimacy of Drop-Shipment Statutes

The legitimacy of the state positions with regard to the drop-shipment rule is unclear. In recent years taxpayers have successfully challenged the drop-shipment rules in several states. For instance, in three states that attempted to tax the first prong of the drop-shipment scenario—the sale from the manufacturer/drop shipper to the retailer—taxpayers have prevailed in the courts or in administrative appeals in having the transaction treated as a legitimate sale for resale. In 1997 a North Carolina court of appeals held for the taxpayers and determined that there was no sales tax imposed on the first phase of the transaction. In *VSA, Inc. v. Faulkner,* a North Carolina wholesaler's drop shipments of products directly to the North Carolina customers of an out-of-state retailer were not taxable under North Carolina law because the state had an exemption for wholesale sales to nonresident retailers. The court ruled that the transfer of title and possession of the goods to the nonresident retailer in North Carolina on a transitory basis did not invalidate the exemption because under the statute the nonresident retailer was considered to be making an exempt purchase for resale as long as it was selling the property outside the state. The court stated the retailer qualified because all of the retailer's activities relating to selling the property occurred outside of North Carolina.[103]

In a similar New York decision, the New York State Tax Commission ruled that the drop-shipment statute should not be enforced because the sale by the drop shipper to the out-of-state retailer was a valid sale for resale followed by a retail sale by an entity without nexus in the state. The commission determined that, even though the resale certificates and affidavits used by the retailer were not in strict compliance with New York sale-for-resale provisions, they did contain sufficient information to satisfy the burden of proof that the sales were for resale.[104]

Finally, in a 1993 decision, *Steelcase, Inc. v. Director, Division of Taxation*, the New Jersey state court ruled that a retailer could use evidence other than an in-state resale certificate to demonstrate that a sale from a drop shipper to the out-of-state retailer was indeed a sale for resale. In this case an out-of-state manufacturer with physical presence in New Jersey dropped shipped goods to the New Jersey customers of a Michigan retailer. While the New Jersey statute required that a New Jersey resale exemption be used to provide proof of an exempt sale for resale, if such a certificate was not available (because the retailer was not registered in the state), the taxpayer could still use other means to establish that the sale was truly a sale for resale.[105]

Each of these three court cases focused only on the issue of whether the first phase of the drop-shipment transaction—the sale from the manufacturer/drop shipper to the out-of-state retailer—was an exempt sale for resale, and each was rendered in favor of the taxpayers based on the specific language in each state's sale-for-resale provision. None of these states had a provision that treated the drop shipper itself as the retailer of record and attempted to tax the de facto sale from the drop shipper to the ultimate consumer.

A Connecticut court case in 1996 did, however, address the application of a more typical drop-shipment statute that treated the drop shipper with physical presence in the customer's state as the retailer with the responsibility to collect the sales and use tax. In this case, *Steelcase, Inc. v. Allan A. Crystal, Commissioner of Revenue Services,* a Michigan manufacturer drop shipped goods to the Connecticut customer of an out-of-state retailer.[106] The manufacturer, had physical presence and was registered as a vendor in Connecticut but shipped the goods on behalf of the retailer from a location outside of Connecticut. The Connecticut statute treated a drop shipper as the retailer: "[T]he delivery in this state of tangible personal property by an owner or former owner thereof or by a factor, if the delivery is to a consumer pursuant to a retail sale made by a retailer not engaged in business in this state, is a retail sale in this state by the person making the delivery."[107]

Although the Connecticut court upheld the drop-shipment statute, it limited its applications to situations wherein the drop shipper not only had presence in the state but actually shipped from a location within the state. The court based its decision on the fact that the contract between the drop shipper and the out-of-state retailer called for title for the goods to be transferred at the time of shipping freight-on-board (FOB) factory. The court concluded that the drop shipper did not make a retail sale in the state subject to sales tax because delivery of the goods took place outside the state. If the drop shipper had shipped from within the state, then delivery would have occurred in Connecticut and the drop shipper would have been treated as the retailer under the drop-shipment statute.[108]

In 1997 a California court also considered the validity of a drop-shipment statute that treated the drop shipper with physical presence in the customer's state as the retailer with responsibility to collect the sales and use tax. In *Lyon Metal Products, Inc. v. State Board of Equalization,* the California Court of Appeals overturned a lower court decision that had declared that the drop-shipment rule was unconstitutional because it allegedly discriminated against interstate commerce. The lower court had ruled that the drop-shipment rule was discriminatory because it was imposed only on out-of-state retailers with no presence in California. The appeals court ruled that there was no discrimination: the tax would have been due either on a sale by the wholesaler: directly to the ultimate customer or on a transaction involving both a wholesaler and a retailer that were outside the state because a use tax would always be owed by the ultimate customer.[109] Because the California case involved a situation in which the wholesaler drop shipped the goods from a California warehouse to the California customer, the California court never had to address the issue of whether the California statute, which is very similar to the Connecticut statute, applied to transactions in which the drop shipment occurs outside of the customer's state.[110]

Although taxpayers have prevailed in several states that attempted to tax the wholesale transaction between the manufacturer/drop shipper and the retailer, it is not clear that taxpayers will prevail in other states that take this position but which have different statutory requirements related to establishing a sale for resale. Likewise, although a taxpayer has succeeded in at least one state (Connecticut) in limiting the application of the drop-shipment rule to a situation where the drop shipper not only has presence in the customer state but also ships the product to the ultimate consumer from a warehouse in that state, it is not clear whether taxpayers will prevail in other states that have similar or different statutory language that treats the drop shipper as the de facto retailer with responsibility to collect the sales and use tax. As with the book club cases previously discussed, state courts often interpret similar statutory language differently, leading to contrary results in court cases.[111]

Thus, it is difficult to predict how existing drop-shipment statutes will be interpreted in the near future. Taxpayers may be successful in some states in overturning the statutes or limiting their application, but they are likely to be unsuccessful in other jurisdictions. As long as the drop-shipment statutes are on the books, taxpayers that ignore them will risk significant tax exposure if they are audited by state tax authorities.

While the state of the law regarding drop-shipment nexus rules may be in flux, it is clear that many E-commerce vendors will encounter difficulties in complying with these statutory provisions. Although the statutory liability may fall on the drop shippers, the ultimate contractual liability may rest with the Internet retailers. If an Internet vendor uses numerous manufacturers to fulfill its orders through drop shipments, it may be difficult to keep track of which drop shippers have nexus in which jurisdictions. Moreover, if an Internet retailer registers in a particular jurisdiction to facilitate sales and use tax compliance on behalf of certain drop shippers, it may adversely affect other drop shippers that do not have nexus in that particular state.

In conclusion, it is likely that the state enforcement of drop-shipment rules will be one of the more contested battlefields of the nexus wars between E-commerce vendors and state governments. For state taxing authorities, these rules are likely to be viewed as a means to limit the adverse effect of the *Quill* decision. For E-retailers the rules are likely to be perceived as arbitrary and difficult to comply with, and it is almost certain that more of these statutes will be challenged by taxpayers on both statutory and constitutional grounds.

Corporate Nexus Issues

Although the focus of this chapter has been primarily on sales and use tax nexus, certain issues related to income tax nexus also need to be discussed in conjunction with E-commerce activities. As already noted, many of the issues related to *de minimis* safe harbors and attributional nexus are the same for purposes of sales and use tax nexus and income tax nexus, except for the added protection for income taxes provided by PL 86-272. However, other issues related to the limitations of PL 86-272 protections, intangible-property presence, and economic presence should be discussed separately in relation to income tax nexus.

Limitations of PL 86-272

For income tax filing purposes, the federal PL 86-272 provides a safe harbor for companies whose physical presence in the market state consists solely of employees or agents soliciting sales of tangible personal property. This federal statute, however, provides no similar protection for in-state solicitation activities related to sales of services or intangible property. Thus, if a company begins to deliver products to customers electronically, it will likely acquire nexus for income tax purposes if it maintains sales representatives in the market states. This result will probably apply to a company involved with digital delivery systems, even if most of its products continue to be delivered by more traditional physical means.

There may, however, be some ambiguity on this issue in those states that treat electronic delivery of products as the sale of tangible personal property for sales and use tax purposes. For instance, many states, including Colorado and Illinois, treat the sale of canned software delivered electronically as the taxable sale of tangible personal property. Although sales and use tax rules do not necessarily apply to income tax issues, some

of these states may be challenged by taxpayers if they prevent corporations from using the PL 86-272 safe harbor, solely because of their delivery of certain products to customers by electronic means. There is also
the possibility that the federal government will clarify or legislatively
change its definition of tangible property to ensure that it applies to all
goods, whether transferred in tangible form or delivered electronically.

A similar scope issue has already arisen with regard to the impact of
PL 86-272 on corporate franchise taxes that are not based on income. In
a 1998 case, North Carolina issued a ruling that PL 86-272 does not
apply to the franchise tax because that federal law only prohibits a state
from imposing an *income tax* on income derived in the state by a corporation if the corporation's only activity in the state is the solicitation of
sales of tangible property. However, in North Carolina and many other
states, the franchise tax is a privilege tax or an excise tax, not a tax on
income. Thus, a corporation that is protected from the payment of income tax under PL 86-272 is not protected from the payment of a franchise tax.[112]

Intangible-Property Presence

The U.S. Supreme Court's decision in *Quill* dealt only with sales and use
tax nexus. Accordingly, it remains unclear whether some form of physical presence is required to establish nexus for corporate income tax purposes or whether a mere economic presence or intangible-property
presence will suffice to establish nexus. This issue has been hotly debated
in the state tax world, but until it is decided by the U.S. Supreme Court,
resolution will remain elusive.

In *Geoffrey, Inc. v. South Carolina Tax Commission* (hereafter referred to
as *Geoffrey*), a 1993 case, the South Carolina Supreme Court held that a
Delaware passive-investment company, whose sole connection with
South Carolina was the licensing of a trademark used in the state, was
subject to South Carolina income tax. In this case, Geoffrey, a fully owned
subsidiary of Toys "R" Us, held the rights to certain intangibles such as the
Toys "R" Us trade name. Geoffrey entered into a license agreement with
its parent to allow the parent to use the Toys "R" Us trade name as well as

other trademarks and trade names in South Carolina and 44 other states. In exchange Toys "R" Us agreed to pay Geoffrey a royalty calculated as a percentage of net sales in a particular jurisdiction. Geoffrey had no other presence in market states such as South Carolina.

In ruling for the state, the South Carolina Supreme Court stated that the taxpayer had purposefully directed its activity at South Carolina's economic forum and thus had satisfied the minimum connection requirements of the Due Process Clause. Additionally, the taxpayer had established a minimum connection with South Carolina through the presence of its intangibles, accounts receivable, and a franchise in the state. The court also held that the *Bellas Hess* and *Quill* physical-presence requirements did not apply in *Geoffrey* because it was not a sales tax case. According to the court, the earning of income from the licensing of intangibles for use in South Carolina met the substantial nexus tests of the Commerce Clause.[113]

Since 1993 a number of states have adopted the *Geoffrey* approach and are pursuing entities that have intangible-property presence in their jurisdictions. Among the major states that have adopted the Geoffrey approach are Florida, Massachusetts, Minnesota, New Jersey, North Carolina, and Virginia. Currently, about one-third of all states are asserting the *Geoffrey* approach to taxing entities that have an intangible-property presence in their jurisdiction.

Arkansas, for example, has stated that holding companies receiving royalty income from an Arkansas business should be filing an Arkansas corporate income tax return. Florida asserts its jurisdiction to tax a company, which licenses an intangible within Florida.[114] Similarly, Massachusetts adopted a policy directive that set forth the conditions under which it would follow the *Geoffrey* approach. The Massachusetts Department of Revenue stated that a foreign corporation's intangible property used within Massachusetts will subject the corporation to the Massachusetts corporate excise if three conditions are met: (1) the intangible property generates, or is otherwise a source of, gross receipts within the state for the corporation, through a license or franchise, (2) the activity through which the corporation obtains such gross receipts from its intangible property is purposeful (e.g., a contract with an in-state company), and (3) the corporation's presence within the state, as indicated by its intangible property and its activities with respect to that property, is more than *de minimis*.[115]

Since the *Geoffrey* decision, many states have issued formal or informal statements asserting that they follow the intangible-property theory in relation to corporate tax nexus. However, few state courts to date have ruled on the legitimacy of these state positions. In addition, the U.S. Supreme Court denied certiorari in the *Geoffrey* case and has not reviewed a case on this issue in the 1990s. Until the Court rules on this subject, the state courts and legislatures are likely to move in different directions in determining whether intangible-property presence creates nexus for income tax purposes. Significant litigation is inevitable because of the financial stakes and the widespread perception within the business community that the *Geoffrey* position will not hold up under the *Quill* precedent.

This issue obviously looms large for the Internet economy because of the pervasiveness of intangibles among E-commerce-type businesses. The intangible-property issue will arise in connection with the use by E-businesses of intellectual property rights such as trade names, trademarks, and patents. It will also come up in conjunction with the widespread use by E-commerce entities of software, music, information, and other products that can be digitized and either delivered electronically to the consumer or accessed by the consumer from a remote location.

It is likely that some states will take the position that the license of these products to a consumer in a market state constitutes the license of an intangible and thus confers nexus under a *Geoffrey* theory. Although the sale of such products with a license maintained by the vendor is widely considered to be a sale, the lease of such products for a fixed period of time is not a sale of the product. Thus, if use of the product located either on the vendor's server or at the customer's location is provided on a per-use or per-time-period basis, a market state could argue that this constitutes the license of an intangible and creates income tax nexus. This is analogous to a nexus theory based on the presence of the vendor's tangible property in the market state, except that it focuses on the intangible nature of the product.

For example, a regulation in Iowa asserts corporate income tax nexus based on the use of intangibles in that state and explicitly includes the licensing of custom software as creating nexus in Iowa. The Iowa regulation sets forth in an example the following:

> G, a corporation with a commercial domicile in State X, earns fees from the licensing of custom computer software. G has no physical presence in Iowa and no other contact with Iowa. G licenses the software to other corporations which do business in Iowa and which use the software in that business in Iowa. Under these circumstances, regardless of whether the fees constitute royalties, or something else, the license fees are earned from intangible personal property with a location or sites in Iowa. Accordingly, G is required to file an Iowa income tax return.[116]

Economic Presence

Along with the assertion of an intangible-property presence theory, several states have also developed theories of economic-presence nexus. Under this theory an out-of-state business is considered to have income tax nexus if it has a certain level of customers or sales within the market state. As with the use of the *Geoffrey* theory, states are adopting this position because of the belief that the *Quill* decision only applies to sales and use taxes, not to income taxes.

Under an economic-presence nexus theory, an out-of-state taxpayer may have nexus with a taxing jurisdiction even without actual physical presence or even intangible-property presence. To satisfy nexus requirements under an economic-presence test, it is sufficient that an out-of-state business seeks commercial exploitation of a market state's consumers through purposeful activities directed toward the market state.

To date, states have only used the economic presence concept to assert nexus with respect to the income taxation of financial institutions. For example, Minnesota, Massachusetts, Tennessee, West Virginia, Kentucky, and Indiana have adopted economic-nexus standards with regard to the taxation of financial institutions.

Nonetheless, it is possible that some states may attempt to extend the use of the economic-presence theory to other service industries or to E-commerce companies that sell digital products. Presumably, states cannot use an economic-presence theory in relation to companies that sell tangible personal property because of the protection of PL 86-272. However, no such protection extends to service businesses or arguably to vendors of goods that are delivered electronically to their customers. Thus, some states will be tempted to tax certain E-commerce businesses without physical presence in their jurisdictions using an economic-presence theory.

The typical economic-presence statute asserts nexus based on the regular performance of services in the market state. According to the Massachusetts statute: "A financial institution has economic presence in Massachusetts if it (1) regularly performs services in the state; (2) regularly engages in transactions with customers in Massachusetts that involve intangible property and result in income flowing to the financial institution from residents of Massachusetts; (3) regularly receives interest income from loans secured by tangible personal or real property in Massachusetts; or (4) regularly solicits and receives deposits from customers in Massachusetts."[117]

Most existing economic-presence statutes have a *de minimis* safe harbor. For instance, the Massachusetts economic-presence statute establishes a rebuttable presumption that an entity is engaged in business in Massachusetts if it has a hundred or more Massachusetts customers, or if the entity has $10 million or more in assets or over $500,000 in receipts attributable to sources within the commonwealth.[118] Similarly, Minnesota and Indiana have nearly identical *de minimis* safe harbor rules. In those states a financial institution is presumed, subject to rebuttal, to regularly solicit business within the state if it conducts activities with 20 or more customers within the state during the taxable year, or if the sum of its assets, including assets arising from loan transactions, and the absolute value of its deposits attributable to the state equal at least $5 million.[119]

Unfortunately, few state courts have yet ruled on the constitutionality of these economic-presence statutes. In the only reported case to date, a Tennessee trial court upheld the Tennessee Department of Revenue's assessment of Tennessee franchise and excise taxes on an out-of-state entity's credit-card business. In this 1998 case, *J.C. Penney National Bank v. Ruth Johnson, Commissioner of Revenue, State of Tennessee,* the court found that the taxpayer had sufficient nexus with Tennessee to satisfy Commerce Clause concerns.[120]

Tennessee has a standard economic-nexus statute as it applies to financial institutions doing business in the state. A financial institution is deemed to be doing business in Tennessee if it has a physical or economic presence in Tennessee. A financial institution has economic presence in Tennessee if it regularly engages in transactions with customers in Tennessee that involve intangible property and result in receipts flowing to the financial institution from within Tennessee, or if it regularly solicits and receives deposits from customers in Tennessee. A financial institution shall be presumed, subject to rebuttal, to be doing business in Tennessee if the sum of its assets and the absolute value of its deposits attributable to sources within Tennessee is $5 million or more.[121]

In *J.C. Penney National Bank v. Ruth Johnson, Commissioner of Revenue, State of Tennessee,* the Tennessee court found that the taxpayer's credit-card activities in Tennessee created a taxable connection with the state. The court rejected the taxpayer's argument that the physical-presence standard set forth in the *Quill* case should apply to franchise and excise taxes. The court nevertheless found that the taxpayer had established substantial nexus with Tennessee via tangible personal property that it owned in the state of Tennessee (i.e., the approximately 17,000 credit cards it had issued to its Tennessee customers). The court found that the number of cards that the contracts specified remained the property of J.C. Penney National Bank was "considerably more than the few diskettes at issue in *Quill*" and exceeded a slightest presence test. Relying on the precedents of *Scripto v. Carson* and *Tyler Pipe Industries, Inc. v. Washington State Department of Revenue,* the court also found that activities performed on behalf of J.C. Penney National Bank by others such as contact lists supplied by in-state stores of an affiliate and other services performed by an affiliated credit-services division were significantly associated with its ability to establish and maintain a market for its sales in Tennessee.[122]

On appeal, the Tennessee Court of Appeals reversed the lower court decision and held for the taxpayers. The court determined that economic presence alone was not sufficient grounds for establishing an out-of-state entity's substantial nexus with the state. In making this determination, the court considered itself bound by the *Quill* decision, at least until such time as the U.S. Supreme Court makes a distinction between the nexus requirements for income taxes and sales and use taxes. The court also held that the presence of thousands of credit cards in Tennessee owned by the out-of-state bank did not constitute physical presence because the cards, in and of themselves, were virtually worthless and really represented an intangible asset. Finally, the court determined that there was no affiliate nexus created by in-state affiliates of the out-of-state bank because these affiliates did not perform any in-state services on behalf of the out-of-state bank.[123]

Thus, as with the determination of the validity of intangible-property-presence statutes, the evaluation of the legitimacy of economic-presence statutes will have to await further state court decisions and ultimately a U.S. Supreme Court decision. In the meantime there is a distinct possibility that some states will extend these statutes to certain E-commerce businesses, at least for income tax nexus purposes. There are many similarities between banks and Internet-related service and digital product companies, particularly in the way they use electronic channels to establish markets in distant states.

Future of Nexus Rules in an E-Commerce Era

The battle between state and local governments and multistate businesses over jurisdiction to tax and nexus issues is a prominent feature of the state and local tax landscape. In an E-commerce era, the ability of vendors in one jurisdiction to sell to customers in multiple jurisdictions without being physically present in the market states virtually guarantees that the economic and political stakes surrounding nexus rules will escalate.

Several possible outcomes need to be considered. First, the U.S. Congress could enact legislation that would provide the states and localities with the authority to implement an expanded duty to collect sales and use taxes based on economic presence alone. Second, the U.S. Congress could move in the opposite direction, either expanding existing nexus safe harbors or altogether exempting from sales and use tax purchases made over the Internet. Third, the states and localities could act on their own and attempt to use existing or revised laws to more vigorously enforce sales or use tax collections related to sales made by remote vendors. Fourth, the status quo may prevail in the short or medium term, with nexus battles continuing to flare up on a number of fronts including *de minimis* issues, attributional nexus, affiliate nexus, drop-shipment issues, and Web site–related issues.

Effort to Expand the Duty to Collect

For several decades state and local governments have sought to expand the duty to collect sales and use taxes to entities that operate in a market state without physical presence. The judicial history of these efforts is symbolized by the U.S. Supreme Court decisions in *Bellas Hess* in 1967 and *Quill* in 1992.

There have also been repeated legislative initiatives by the states and localities to obtain congressional approval for legislation that would allow states to require remote vendors with a certain threshold of sales in a market state to register and collect sales and use taxes. For instance, in the 1990s Senator Dale Bumpers of Arkansas sponsored the Main Street and Consumer Protection Act. The legislation would have permitted states to impose a sales and use tax collection responsibility on any company with U.S. sales revenue of more than $3 million or with in-state sales within a single state of over $100,000. For any state with multiple local rates, the remote vendor would have been able to collect the tax at one standard weighted average of the combined local sales tax rates.[124]

Although federal legislation to expand the duty to collect sales and use taxes has never garnered a majority of either the U.S. Senate or House of Representatives, it has nonetheless remained as a primary political objective of state and local governments. Ironically, one of the principal movers for a federally legislated solution has come from the U.S. Supreme Court, which has otherwise rejected the state's position in the judicial arena.

Although the Supreme Court decision in the *Quill* case was rendered against the position supported by state and local governments, the Court very specifically threw the issue back to Congress for possible resolution. The Court stated:

> This aspect of our decision is made easier by the fact that the underlying issue is not only one that Congress may be better qualified to resolve, but also one that Congress has the ultimate power to resolve. No matter how we evaluate the burdens that use taxes impose on interstate commerce, Congress remains free to disagree with our conclusions. Indeed, in recent years Congress has considered legislation that would overrule the *Bellas Hess* rule. . . . Accordingly, Congress is now free to decide whether, when, and to what extent the States may burden interstate mail-order concerns with a duty to collect use taxes.[125]

The Supreme Court was well aware that the *Bellas Hess* precedent encouraged remote vendors to structure their operations so as to avoid collection responsibilities for sales and use taxes. As the *Quill* court stated, "Indeed, it is not unlikely that the mail-order industry's dramatic growth over the last quarter-century is due in part to the bright-line exemption from state taxation created in *Bellas Hess.*"[126]

However, the Supreme Court was still concerned with the burdens imposed on remote vendors by the complexity of state and local sales and use tax laws. The Court in *Quill* cited approvingly the language in *Bellas Hess,* "that the many variations in rates of tax, in allowable exemptions, and in administrative and record-keeping requirements could entangle [a mail-order house] in a virtual welter of complicated obligations."[127]

Current Political Environment

The interest of state and local governments in federal legislation to expand the duty to collect use taxes on remote sales has accelerated with the rapid expansion of E-commerce. Government officials fear that, if the physical-presence standard is maintained, there will be an escalating erosion of the sales tax base caused by the sharp increase in the number of remote vendors using mail order and Internet channels to reach customers in other jurisdictions. As discussed in chapter 2, the uneasiness of state and local government officials is so great that many organizations that represent their interests, such as the NGA, are at least in principle prepared to do what was previously unthinkable—give up a significant degree of autonomy in local sales tax rates and procedures.

As discussed in chapter 1, the estimates of the potential revenue loss from remote commerce in the United States are highly variable, depending on a number of assumptions about Internet revenue growth, composition of Internet sales, and tax compliance patterns of businesses. One study by Ernst and Young in 1998 estimated revenue losses from Internet remote sales at $170 million compared with revenue losses in that year from remote mail-order sales of $4.5 billion. By comparison, an analysis by Harley Duncan, the executive director of the FTA, looking ahead to the year 2003, estimates state and local tax revenue losses of just over $4 billion from Internet remote sales and about $4.5 billion from mail-order sales. A report by the Center on Budget and Policy Priorities estimates that sales and use tax revenue losses in the year 2003 would be even higher, with about $10 billion from Internet remote sales and about $5 billion from mail-order sales.[128]

The increasing relative importance of remote sales in the age of E-commerce has led to a flurry of political activity aimed at developing solutions to the problems associated with the taxation of E-commerce. These political efforts have focused on a range of issues, foremost of which is whether the duty to collect sales and use taxes should be expanded to encompass entities without physical presence in the market states.

It is clearly too early to predict the outcome of these political initiatives. Despite the bright spotlight shined on nexus issues by the expansion of E-commerce, it is quite possible that the current deadlock between business and state and local government will drag on, a victim of the complexity of the issues and the lack of consensus for any particular set of tax reforms.

For instance, the NTA's Communications and Electronic Commerce Tax Project—a high-level group of government, business, and academic representatives—spent over two years analyzing potential solutions to the E-commerce tax puzzle, without reaching agreement on an expanded duty to collect sales and use taxes. According to the final NTA report issued in September 1999:

> One of the issues addressed by the Project's Steering Committee concerned the possibility of expanding the obligation of some remote sellers to collect sales and use taxes. The Government representatives viewed an expanded duty to collect as necessary to improve the equity, stability and effectiveness of the sales tax and as a major motivation for them to discuss substantial sales and use tax simplification. Business representatives were concerned about the limited scope of tax simplification under consideration and that an agreed-to change in the jurisdictional standard for sales and use tax collection would lead to unintended consequences in the business activity tax nexus area.[129]

The NTA report elaborated on some of the inherent political difficulties of the expanded duty to collect issue:

> While many participants understood the relevance of considering an expanded duty to collect sales and use taxes as part of a simplified tax environment, the discussions did not result in an agreement. Some business representatives were unwilling to agree to an expanded duty to collect sales and use tax until after the main ingredients of sales and use tax simplification were identified, described and agreed to by the Steering Committee. Others felt that the current nexus standards applicable to sales and use tax collection are justified, regardless of the level of simplification achieved. Further, some representatives were concerned that an agreement on an expanded duty to collect sales and use taxes would affect nexus for other types of taxes.[130]

A major subject for discussion within the NTA group was a possible compromise solution involving implementing comprehensive sales and use tax rate and procedures simplification in exchange for a congression-ally enacted expanded duty to collect sales and use tax. However, as was clear from the dialogue that took place during the NTA project, there are significant political obstacles to any such compromise solution.

First, many of the beneficiaries of a more limited duty to collect sales and use tax have little need for sales and use tax simplification because these businesses generally do not collect taxes in the market states in any case. Conversely, many of the companies most desirous of radical sales and use tax simplification have few concerns about an expanded duty to collect because they already have widespread physical presence in the customers' jurisdictions.

Second, many of the potential solutions to the nexus equation are weighed down by the enormity of change required. Most parties agree that it is not possible to enact new nexus standards or sales and use tax procedural rules for just E-commerce. Any nondiscriminatory approach would have to significantly alter the tax landscape for all commerce, a much more daunting undertaking. Moreover, the changes that are being proposed in conjunction with the simplification of sales and use tax law, although widely supported, would still require wrenching adjustments in U.S. federalism on local government autonomy. Finally, there are indus-try segments within E-commerce, such as the telecommunications industry and the Internet access providers, that have their own special set of issues that they would like resolved as part of any global solution.

Third, while it is clear to many observers that the problems associ-ated with remote commerce are increasing in number and complexity, there is also a widely held view that the full manifestation of these prob-lems is still off in the future. Thus, many participants in the public policy debate over the future of state and local sales and use taxation of remote commerce believe that there is no need to rush to judgment, that both government and business can await further development of the Internet before embarking on a course of radical change that might undermine the growth of E-commerce. Indeed, one study by economist Austan Goolsbee suggests that the enforcement of the current sales and use tax laws to all Internet transactions would result in a 24 percent decrease in the number of on-line buyers and a 30 percent decrease in on-line sales.[131]

Fourth, any significant change in the duty to collect sales and use tax rules would require congressional legislation. As is evident from similar congressional battles over the collection of sales and use taxes related to mail-order sales, majority approval of such legislation may be difficult to obtain. Moreover, even if the U.S. Congress were to approve legislation that combined a repeal of the *Quill* doctrine with radical sales and use tax simplification, little change would occur without most states undertaking a substantial revision of their existing state and local fiscal arrangements to eliminate the need for local sales and use taxes.

Federal Advisory Commission on Electronic Commerce

The federal Internet Tax Freedom Act established a federal commission to make recommendations to the U.S. Congress on a range of E-commerce tax-related issues including the jurisdiction to tax (discussed further in chapters 1 and 2). The Advisory Commission on Electronic Commerce includes 19 members: eight representing state and local government, eight representing the private sector, and three representing the federal government. The commission is required by the legislation to issue a report back to Congress by the spring of 2000. The commission reflects the high visibility that the taxation of the Internet has gained in policy circles, with its composition including governors, chief executives, and top executive-branch leaders.

However, the federal Advisory Commission on Electronic Commerce or the U.S. Congress may be hampered by many of the same complexities and political differences that plagued the NTA group and other earlier efforts aimed at revamping both sales and use tax and nexus rules. Not only are there significant disagreements between the business and government sides of the E-commerce taxation debate, but there are also fault lines within each camp. For instance, many mail-order ventures or Internet retailers vigorously oppose any change in the duty-to-collect standard that could entail collections based on economic presence or level of sales in a jurisdiction. Conversely, many brick-and-mortar retail stores or other existing entities already have to collect sales and use taxes on their sales of goods and thus are potentially disadvantaged compared with their direct-marketing competitors. There are some divisions within government groups as well. Most state and local government officials believe that an expansion of the duty to collect sales and use taxes is needed for their fiscal survival in an electronic and information age. Conversely, some government officials, particularly from high-technology states, believe that the Internet should generally remain a tax-free environment so that it can rapidly realize its enormous economic potential.

One of the wild cards in the debate over whether to expand the duty to collect sales and use taxes in relation to remote commerce is the American public. Indeed, national opinion polls taken in the late 1990s indicate that the vast majority of American consumers do not want to have to pay sales or use taxes on purchases made through direct-marketing channels. According to a 1999 poll, 73 percent of those interviewed opposed the imposition of a national sales tax on Internet purchases, compared with only 14 percent that supported such a tax.[132]

While it is difficult to predict the outcome in the political arena, it seems unlikely in the short-term that the U.S. Congress will adopt a far-reaching proposal that would quickly expand the states' authority to require remote vendors to collect sales and use taxes based on an economic presence standard. Certainly, in the year 2000, a presidential election year, it is doubtful that any significant legislation will be enacted by the U.S. Congress on Internet taxation. However, in subsequent years, the political dynamic could change if a compromise is reached between state and local governments and certain business groups that are not necessarily opposed to an extension of the duty to collect sales and use taxes. The compromise could be shaped along the lines previously discussed: a radical simplification of sales and use tax rules and tax rates and other pro-business changes in exchange for the authority to require remote vendors (without physical presence) to collect sales and use tax.

Even if the U.S. Congress does not enact any sweeping measures in the near future, it is likely that pressure will build for some solution as Internet sales increase and existing tax rules result in increased tax litigation, inconsistent treatment of tangible goods and digital products, and significant compliance burdens on businesses in the New Economy. However, any radical revamping of state and local jurisdictional and sales and use tax rules would likely require both Congressional approval and far-reaching state legislation—action steps that are almost certain to slow the process down. Moreover, any approach with a long-term phase-in would be open to Congressional modification or repeal during the intervening years, resulting in a cloud of uncertainty over the final outcome.

An Expansion of Nexus Safe Harbors

Indeed, it is possible that the U.S. Congress could enact changes, that actually extend business safe harbors from nexus rules in certain areas. A probusiness stance would be in keeping with the impetus behind the initial enactment of the Internet Tax Freedom Act. This legislation was enacted not only to prevent discriminatory taxation against E-commerce businesses but also to give the Internet economy a hiatus before extending state tax laws to its activities.

For example, there is considerable business frustration with the current time-consuming battles between the states and the multistate business community over nexus issues. It is not inconceivable that, at the commission's urging, the U.S. Congress would consider enacting laws that provide multistate businesses with more clarity and a broader physical-presence safe harbor than currently exists today. One idea that has support in the business community is to revise PL 86-272 so that it applies to both sales of tangible personal property and to sales of electronic services and digital products.

One of the members of the federal Advisory Commission on Electronic Commerce, Dean Andal, who is the vice chairman of the California State Board of Equalization (the sales tax agency), offered a sweeping proposal in September 1999 to the commission that, if enacted by Congress, would significantly expand the safe harbor for businesses under both income taxes and sales and uses taxes. Andal's proposal would require physical presence as a litmus test under either the income tax (for services as well as property) or the sales or use tax. It would reverse the *Geoffrey* decision, provide a safe harbor for the use of Web sites in the customer's state to take or process orders, and provide a safe harbor for the use of third parties to perform warranty or repair services.[133]

Even if this proposal does not gather significant support, it is quite possible that more modest legislation extending nexus safe harbors could be enacted either at the federal or state-government levels. For instance, given the uncertainty over the effect of an agent's Web site or Web server in a customer state, or of the impact of thousands of affiliates or associates funneling consumers to an out-of-state Web retailer, many jurisdictions may expand safe harbors to provide a more attractive environment for entities that provide third-party services or advertising/marketing links to Web retailers.

Finally, several more far-reaching proposals have been made that would exempt all purchases made over the Internet from sales and use tax. Both Ohio Republican representative John Kasich and Virginia governor James Gilmore, for example, submitted proposals to the Advisory Commission on Electronic Commerce that would prohibit all sales and use taxes on business-to-consumer Internet transactions. Republican presidential candidate John McCain has supported a similar legislative solution. These proposals would move beyond simply relying on jurisdictional constraints to imposing collection duties on remote vendors and would actually eliminate existing taxes on goods or services acquired through E-commerce.

These proposals, however, have already encountered opposition not just from government but also from segments of the business community. The criticism of these proposals is based on the difficulty of limiting the legislative solutions from overreaching into tax categories that were not intended to be exempt. If all Internet purchases were exempt, for instance, then a retail store in a mall could simply set up kiosks inside the store and take orders over the Internet. Similarly, a household could order groceries from peapod.com or webvan.com, or games, movies, books, and music albums from on-line companies such as kozmo.com, and avoid all transactional taxes. Eventually, the sales and use tax base would erode significantly as a majority of purchases made at local retailers could end up exempted from sales and use tax.

Although a blanket exemption for all purchases of digital products not only ordered, but delivered over the Internet would have a more limited impact, it would still reinforce differential tax treatment of similar goods and services, in this case based on the method of delivery. Another proposal for a sales tax exemption for all digitized goods and products and their non-digitized counterparts would eliminate any discriminatory effect, but it could also remove from the tax base a wide range of currently taxable products such as books, movies, software, information and music. Nonetheless, given the complexity of taxing digitized products, there is likely to be considerable support for an exemption, even if temporary, of certain digitized goods and services.

Thus, it is unlikely that the U.S. Congress will enact legislation that exempts Internet purchases of all tangible and intangible property from the sales and use tax. Indeed, the Clinton administration has aligned with state and local government officials to oppose any legislation that would provide a blanket tax exemption for any products purchased over the Internet. A more likely outcome is that Congress will extend the moratorium on sales and use tax on Internet access charges or other limited categories of goods and services.

State Enforcement of Nexus Rules without Federal Intervention

Another possible outcome in the current political environment is that state governments may attempt to enact an expanded duty to collect sales and use taxes without congressional intervention. The U.S. Supreme Court decision in *Quill* focused on the complexity of current state and local sales taxes as a rationale for continuing to require a bright-line physical-presence standard for transactional tax nexus. However, there is a belief among some state tax officials that if they could voluntarily remedy this situation by drastically simplifying state and local sales and use tax rates and procedures, they could win a future test case reasserting the economic-presence nexus theory.

The problem with this approach is that it would require widespread state and local sales and use tax reform, without a guarantee that the courts would ratify state government actions that were not accompanied by congressional resolutions in this area. Moreover, many state and local governments may not be willing to give up their local prerogatives without something concrete in return.

In 1999 the FTA's executive director Harley Duncan discussed this option for the states and localities to create a simplified system on their own initiative and use it as a vehicle for a challenge to the *Quill* decision. Duncan observed that a unilateral approach by the states would be risky: "[I]t's risky because, as lawyers will tell you, the court takes 3 percent of all the cases that get raised to it, and then when you get there, there's at best a 50-50 chance to win." Duncan went on to say, "The 'how,' the vehicle we use, is a lot less important to me now than the 'what.' We can't just look at how to get the expanded duty to collect. We really have to look at ways to make the sales tax simpler."[134]

State-Financed Automated Solutions

In addition to pursuing various nexus theories, the state and local jurisdictions are likely to proactively pursue automated solutions that reduce the compliance burden on remote vendors and encourage them to voluntarily comply with collection rules. There are a number of possible mechanisms now under consideration that could enable remote vendors to use a software system operated by an independent third party to facilitate compliance with state and local sales and use tax laws.

For instance, a broad coalition of state and local government groups made a proposal to the Advisory Commission on Electronic Commerce for a zero-burden streamlined compliance system. This proposal was supported by the so-called Big Seven of state and local government groups, including the National Governors' Association, the National Conference of State Legislatures, the National Association of Counties, the National League of Cities, the U.S. Conference of Mayors, the Council of State Governments, and the International City/County Management Association.[135]

This proposal would create a system funded and certified by state governments that could be used by remote vendors at much lower compliance costs. Government would pay for all the costs of the system, which would be based on a technology-driven solution using a trusted third party (TTP) rather than the vendors for collection of sales and use taxes. For instance, the TTP could be credit-card companies that calculate, collect, and pay over the taxes on behalf of multiple vendors.

The proposal would not require a change in the *Quill* physical-presence standard for nexus. Rather, its aim is to simplify the collection process, lower the cost to vendors, and thus encourage much more widespread compliance by remote Internet vendors that would not otherwise assume a collection responsibility.

If the federal Advisory Commission on Electronic Commerce reaches an impasse or fails to generate substantial state tax reform, the states and localities are likely to accelerate their efforts to create a more user-friendly compliance system with a greater proportion of the compliance costs borne by government. As FTA director Harley Duncan notes:

> A primary ingredient [to the E-commerce issue] is that the states will have to assume greater responsibility for the operation and cost of the tax administration system and correspondingly reduce the burden imposed on sellers of all sorts. In other words, states ought to collectively set certain rules, procedures, and options for sellers and say that if you meet these limited criteria, you are "held harmless" from potential liability for uncollected tax. . . . The key element, however, will be state responsibility for the system and eliminating, to the degree possible, the burden imposed on sellers.[136]

Regardless, any such simplified system will encounter numerous technical and political obstacles and is currently only being discussed on a theoretical basis. Even the government proponents of a TTP system project a timeline of two to five years for implementation of just the first phase of such a streamlined system. It is still too early to determine whether any viable technologically driven and state-financed solutions will emerge.

Origin-State Rule

Some industry representatives have encouraged states to consider a vendor-, or origin-, state approach to sales and use taxation. While the *Quill* decision circumscribed the ability of state and local governments to impose a duty to collect sales and use tax on remote vendors, it did not restrict the state's ability to tax in-state vendors. Although conventional wisdom on taxing E-commerce has focused on destination- or market-state sourcing rules similar to those used with traditional commerce, a vendor-state rule that focuses on sourcing sales to where a vendor is located could overcome the inability of market states to compel a remote vendor to collect sale and use taxes.

According to a 1999 article by Andy Wagner and Wade Anderson, "While no solution is perfect and each solution creates new issues, origin-based taxation would seem to answer the major problems posed by a destination-based tax and would be relatively easy for the states to implement. A seller would only be required to collect tax based on the sales tax law imposed in the seller's location. This would eliminate sellers' concerns over nexus uncertainties, analysis of whether items were taxable or exempt in the various jurisdictions, privacy concerns, and the costs of collection and remittance to hundreds, if not thousands of jurisdiction."[137]

Currently, origin-state rules are used in many jurisdictions for a small number of products, including flowers purchased as gifts, phone cards, and 800 phone calls. These are all products with unique issues that complicate the use of the more traditional destination-state rule.

While an origin-state rule might solve the nexus problem for states by taxing vendors in a location where they have physical presence, this option raises other problems that most likely preclude it from serious consideration in the current political debate. First, there would be problems in identifying the origin state. Although this may appear self-evident, there could be a choice between the state of incorporation of the vendor, the location of the vendor's commercial domicile, the location where the vendor principally manages its E-commerce business, and even the location of the vendor's computer server that hosts the E-commerce business. Moreover, unless states acquire much more uniform rules on sales tax rates and sales tax bases than they currently have, an origin-state rule could lead to a flight of businesses from states that rely more heavily on sales taxes than on other tax types.

Furthermore, applying an origin-state rule initially solely to digital products—given the enormity of change that would be required if it were applied to tangible goods—would create a dual sourcing system that would source sales of digital products differently than tangible goods. Depending on the relative tax rates in the vendor and customer states, this dual system would discriminate against one of the forms of commerce.

Use Tax Enforcement against Consumers

Another approach that states may undertake is to more vigorously enforce use tax self-assessment by businesses and individual consumers. For most Internet transactions, a use tax is due from the consumer even if the vendor does not have the legal duty to collect and pay over the tax. However, particularly with regard to nonbusiness customers, compliance rates are low as most consumers are either unaware of the use tax rules or ignore them with impunity.

Some states have made efforts to more actively enforce the use tax rules within their borders. These efforts have included high-profile audit campaigns aimed at particular industry segments or businesses. The state initiatives have also included measures aimed at nonbusiness customers such as placing a line for use tax payments on personal income tax returns, obtaining customer lists from out-of-state vendors, and sharing information with other states.

There is some indication that more proactive enforcement of the use tax may occur because of increasing state government frustration over the inability to impose a sales and use tax collection responsibility on remote vendors. For instance, in testimony before the federal Advisory Commission on Electronic Commerce, Governor William Janklow of South Dakota stated that, to avoid losing tax dollars to Internet commerce, he would be willing to use South Dakota's State Highway Patrol to pull over delivery trucks, search for packages sent from out-of-state, and have the troopers "follow the packages" to their delivery points to collect the proper taxes.[138]

While these government initiatives have succeeded in increasing or at least maintaining higher self-assessment rates among businesses, they have largely failed to make an appreciable difference among nonbusiness customers. The primary reason is that the taxpaying public is generally opposed to any vigorous efforts to collect use taxes from individuals. Higher audit rates for individuals are typically not cost effective and are widely opposed as akin to a tax increase, which is politically very unpopular.

Continued Enforcement of *De Minimis* and Attributional-Nexus Rules

If neither an expanded duty to collect nor the exemption of all Internet purchases is enacted by the U.S. Congress over the next few years, the strong likelihood is that the status quo will prevail, with continuing skirmishes and battles between government and business over a wide range of nexus-related issues. The current physical-presence standard for sales and use tax nexus has not created a bright-line test but instead has resulted in jurisdictional rules that are frequently ambiguous and inconsistent.

For instance, the absence of clear guidance on what constitutes the *de minimis* safe harbor has led to confusion over what level of physical presence of either people or property is permissible without creating a taxable presence in a market state. Does the substantial-nexus requirement of *Quill* demand substantial physical presence or just more than slightest presence? Do constitutional principles require continuous or permanent physical presence, or is sporadic or transitory presence sufficient? Do both the quality and the quantity of presence in a market state matter?

In addition, the vigorous pursuit by state taxing authorities of agents, affiliates, or other parties whose presence in a market state might be attributed to remote vendors has led to continuous litigation over the proper boundaries of attributional nexus. Do postsale activities by independent third parties create nexus for remote vendors? Are drop-shipment rules valid extensions of state jurisdictional powers? Do Web sites in market states combined with certain third-party transaction processing activities constitute attributional nexus?

The exceedingly slow pace of U.S. Supreme Court decisions on state tax nexus issues virtually guarantees that contentious issues will remain unresolved for years. If MTC *Bulletin 95-1* (on warranty repairs) is any indication, it may be possible to get a significant number of states to simultaneously pursue new, more aggressive nexus positions in advance of Supreme Court decisions on their validity. Similarly, the adoption of *Geoffrey* and economic-presence nexus rules in numerous states indicates that the states are not likely to remain passive and allow remote vendors to avoid income taxation in market states.

Moreover, with the new and evolving business models associated with the Internet, it is frequently difficult to even determine whether the business entity that is interfacing with the ultimate consumers is a retailer, agent, or some other kind of intermediary. In both business-to-business and business-to-consumer models, new intermediaries are being established that will take on a range of responsibilities that may encompass tax calculation and collection for numerous other vendors.

Thus, the current environment, far from being a wholly stable situation, presents a number of challenges for both state governments and multistate businesses as they grope their way through a dizzying array of potential nexus-creating activities. The application of nexus standards to E-commerce transactions is a uniquely difficult undertaking. The Internet opens up possibilities for purposeful direction of economic activity to market states with a wide variety of links between remote vendors and third-party drop shippers, advertisers, hosted Web sites, back-office accounting services, repair services, customer-support services, and telecommunications providers. Although disputes over nexus issues have been a constant in the state tax realm over the last few decades, it is likely that the nexus wars will intensify unless, or until, the duty to collect sales and use taxes is expanded to include entities that operate in a market state without physical presence.

5

Value Added Taxes and E-Commerce

Mike Loten and Jackie Hubbard

Introduction

E-commerce has developed over the last decade as companies have seen the way in which computerization, and the Internet in particular, can significantly accelerate business procedures. It is a truly global business medium, which brings supplier and customer together without actually meeting and without the need for an intermediary.

However, the global nature of the medium and the increase in options for product delivery have created new indirect taxation issues. Some of these tax issues raise practical concerns that businesses involved in electronic activities cannot afford to ignore. For example:

- Should prices be shown as gross or net of tax? This may be a particular concern for U.S. companies accustomed to giving prices net of sales tax, whereas the European public expect to see prices that are inclusive of value-added taxes (VAT).

Mike Loten is a partner and Jackie Hubbard is a manager in Arthur Andersen's Reading, United Kingdom office. Both specialize in value-added taxation services, for U.S. clients. Mike is the Indirect Tax representative on the firm's EMEIA Tax, Legal and Business Advisory E-commerce Task Force, and is a regular speaker on the subject of e-commerce and VAT, both in the U.S. and the U.K.

- Which country's VAT or sales tax should be charged, if any?
- Who should pay any import duties?
- What invoicing requirements exist for different customers in foreign countries?

Noncompliance with legislation and misstatements of tax can result in significant penalties; it is therefore vital at the outset to identify the tax risks and implications of doing business in cyberspace.

Challenging Traditional Taxation

Traditional taxation principles for dealing with international transactions are based on the notion that an identifiable party physically transfers goods to an identifiable customer. Even where several jurisdictions are involved, a system to determine which country has the right to levy tax has generally evolved. Liability to account for VAT is typically influenced by the following:

- the physical location of the goods
- the residence of the seller or buyer
- the nature of the goods or services being transferred

The key difference with cybertransactions is that there may be no transfer of actual goods and/or no obviously identifiable physical location at which that transaction takes place. It may also be difficult to determine the geographic location of one or more parties to the transaction, be it the seller, buyer, or intermediary, or even to establish exactly what is being sold. Any one of these factors may significantly affect how the transaction is taxed.

Cybertransactions do not immediately fit with the traditional concepts of VAT or sales taxes. This problem has forced a drive to achieve a consensus of opinion on the correct VAT or sales tax treatment that remains in line with traditional principles of taxation.

While some transactions via the Internet may be relatively straightforward from a tax perspective, many will not. Consider a French customer visiting the United Kingdom on business who accesses the U.K. Web site of a U.S. company maintained on a German server, and who pays to view the information on screen. This is illustrated in figure 5.1. In this case, not only deciding in which jurisdiction taxes such as VAT should apply but also tracking and auditing the actual transaction may prove difficult. Should VAT be applied where the customer is based (France), where the services are provided (the United Kingdom), where the vendor is based (the United States) or where the server is located (Germany)?

The following questions are fundamental to the imposition of VAT:

- Is it a supply of goods or services?
- On the basis of further categorization of the supply, where does the transaction take place?

Figure 5.1. **A Typical Cybertransaction: Where Is the Tax Due?**

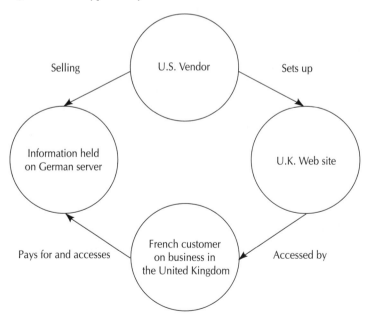

For a sale via the Internet, these seemingly simple questions frequently do not have simple answers—creating enormous potential for the double or nontaxation of transactions.

Types of Transactions

Where the Internet is used simply as a mechanism to solicit and receive customer orders and the product is then physically shipped to the customer, the position is similar to that of traditional mail-order supplies and in theory no additional cyber-related issues arise. This is not to say that there are no new compliance issues relating to the vendor/customer interface. These are considered later in the "Goods" section of this chapter.

Where charges are made for an on-line delivery, there are a number of questions that traditionally determined whether VAT must be charged. The *type* of product has historically determined whether the supply is one of goods or services. For example, traditional VAT principles state that an off-the-shelf software package is a good, whereas customized software specifically designed for the customer is a service. Under current VAT law, the mechanism used to deliver the product to the customer is crucial in deciding the classification for VAT purposes.

However, at the OECD conference in Ottawa on October 8–9, 1998, it was agreed that any supply involving electronic delivery should be treated as a supply of services. The taxation of services is reviewed in "Services," and the specific application of the VAT treatment to cyberactivities is analyzed in "Telecommunications Services" and "Electronic Delivery" later in this chapter.

On a practical note, when doing business the invoice is a crucial document as far as VAT is concerned, because, without the original customer copy, a purchaser cannot claim a VAT credit. Yet cyberspace is a paperless society. Balancing the desire of business to minimize administration with the need for official bureaucracy to have adequate audit controls is proving a difficult task but one which must be addressed. The European Commission's working paper of June 8, 1999 (summarized in "Electronic Delivery"), sets out current official thinking on this issue.

Overview of Value-Added Taxes

Introduction

This section provides a general review of the mechanics of the VAT system, as well as an outline of the system's general principles. It is therefore not specifically focused on E-commerce issues.

The focus of the provisions applicable to these taxes is taken from EU law, but the general principles typically apply to most countries with a VAT or goods and services tax (GST) regime. By the end of 1998, 102 countries had a VAT or GST system in place (see appendix A for a list of the countries), with many more having some other form of cascade indirect tax (see appendix B). Table 5.1 lists all the European Union member states, the name of the VAT system, and their standard VAT rates.

Table 5.1.   **VAT in the European Union**

Country	Tax (in the Original Language)	Standard Rate (%)
Austria	Mehrwertsteuer	20
Belgium	Belasting overde toegevoegde waarde (BTW) / Taxe sur la valeur ajoutée (TVA)	21
Denmark	Merværdiafgift (Moms)	25
Finland	Arvonlisävero (ALV)	22
France	Taxe sur la valeur ajoutée (TVA)	20.6
Germany	Mehrwertsteuer	16
Greece	Φορος Προστιθεμενης Αξιας Foros Prostithemenis Axias	18
Ireland	Value-added tax (VAT)	21
Italy	Imposta sul valore aggiunto (IVA)	20
Luxembourg	Taxe sur la valeur ajoutée (TVA)	15
Netherlands	Belasting over de Toegevoegde Waarde (BTN)	17.5
Portugal	Imposto sobre o valor acrescentado (IVA) (In Azores and Madeira 12 and 4)	17
Spain	Impuesto sobre el valor añadido (IVA)	16
Sweden	Mervärdeskatt (Moms)	25
United Kingdom	Value-added tax (VAT)	17.5

VAT is a tax on turnover and consumption, not a tax on profit. It is charged on transactions (or more strictly, supplies) carried out in the course or furtherance of a business, but it differs from other taxes in one significant way: A purchaser using or intending to use goods or services in the course of his own taxable activities can claim a credit for the VAT paid to his suppliers when accounting to the tax authorities for the VAT he has charged to his customers. Therefore, for the majority of VAT registered businesses, the VAT paid to suppliers should not represent a real cost. A discussion of the exceptions to this rule can be found in "VAT Recovery" later in this section.

Flow of Taxation

Goods and services purchased by a business are known as *inputs;* sales (or supplies) are *outputs.* Input tax is the VAT a business pays on its purchases. Output tax is the VAT it charges its customers.

Each business accounts to the VAT authorities for the output tax charged to customers but is allowed (in principle) to recover its input tax to the extent that the purchases are used for its taxable business activities. The net amount due to the tax authorities in a given period is the difference between input and output tax. If the input tax suffered is greater than the output tax charged, the business will normally be entitled to a repayment of the balance.

Table 5.2 illustrates the way in which VAT is charged on the value-added at each stage of a transaction and ultimately paid by the final consumer. In this example of the production of stationery, the final consumer pays 14,100 (12,000 plus 2,100 irrecoverable VAT). The 2,100 is the total amount of VAT collected in stages by the tax authorities.

What Can be Taxed?

To be within the scope of a VAT charge three conditions must exist:

1. There must be a taxable supply (of either goods or services).
2. The supply must be made by a taxable person.

Table 5.2. **Sample Case of the Collection and Payment of VAT**

	(A) Input VAT Incurred	Net Cost of Onward Supply	(B) Output VAT Charged	(B)–(A) Net VAT Payable
1. Forrester sells timber	—	1,000	175	175
2. Pulp factory buys the timber and produces pulp	175	3,000	525	350
3. Paper factory buys the pulp and sells paper	525	6,000	1,050	525
4. Wholesaler buys and sells the paper	1,050	8,000	1,400	350
5. Retailer buys the paper and sells it to the final consumer	1,400	12,000	2,100	700
				2,100

3. It must be made in the course or furtherance of a business carried out by the taxable person.

Supply

The concept of supply is very widely drawn and includes anything done for a consideration. In a U.K. case, the act of agreeing to take on a property lease, for which a reverse premium was received, was held to involve a supply by the prospective tenant. The consideration may be in money or kind, so barter transactions are included as a common risk area.

A number of transactions, subject to domestic VAT regulations, may be treated as neither a supply of goods nor a supply of services. These include the following:

- the transfer of a business as a going concern (provided certain conditions are satisfied),
- the loss, theft, or destruction of goods (before they have been supplied to the customer), and
- the supply of goods or services within a VAT group registration (where such a concept exists).

Care should be taken in classifying nonsupplies because there are many practical differences in application and interpretation from country to country.

Taxable Supply

All goods and services supplied in the EU are taxable supplies unless specifically classified as exempt or outside the scope of VAT. Examples of goods and services specifically classified as exempt are most supplies in the finance, insurance, education, health, and welfare fields. Many other professional services (i.e., of a lawyer, consultant, solicitor), however, can fall within the taxable-supply (and therefore VAT) regime.

Business

VAT is chargeable if a taxable supply is made by a taxable person in the course or furtherance of any business carried on by him or her. This includes disposals of business assets for private use, for instance the gift of a clock to a retiring employee. A purely private transaction, however, such as the sale of a private car by an individual, is outside the scope of VAT.

Taxable Person

A taxable person is one who is (or should be) registered for VAT. It should be noted that the responsibility and liability to correctly charge VAT on a supply generally rests with the supplier. There are very few exceptions to this rule, and the tax authorities generally only pursue a supplier for failing to charge VAT. The major exceptions are in respect of purchases of imported services (reverse-charge VAT applies) and imports/acquisitions of goods (import VAT/acquisition VAT applies). These will be discussed later in this chapter.

The Rates of Taxation

When considering the VAT implications of a supply, five possible VAT treatments can apply. These are as follows:

1. *Taxable at the standard rate.* All supplies are standard rated unless specifically stated as otherwise in the legislation. All input tax in-

curred in the making of standard-rated supplies is recoverable. Examples of standard-rate supplies are supplies of software products, CDs, adult clothing, and so on.

2. *Taxable at a lower rate.* This rate is typically applied to goods and services used for socially beneficial supplies such as food, books, and domestic power. All input tax incurred in the making of these supplies is recoverable. The minimum reduced rate for domestic supplies in the EU is 5 percent, although the United Kingdom and Republic of Ireland (by special concession) apply a zero rate to certain items. Examples of lower-rate supplies within the EU are sales of children's clothes, some food items, books, and newspapers. The VAT treatment of such supplies may vary from state to state in the EU.

3. *Zero-rated* or *exempt with credit.* These supplies are still classified as taxable even though the supplier does not charge VAT. All input tax incurred in the making of these supplies is recoverable. The zero rate typically applies to exported goods and services.

4. *Exempt.* The supplier does not charge VAT but is unable to claim input tax incurred in making these supplies. Examples of exempt supplies include sales of insurance, financial services, and gambling.

5. *Outside the scope of local VAT.* These supplies are in principle subject to VAT, typically in another country. Input VAT relating to a supply that is outside the scope may or may not be recoverable depending on the specific law applying to that supply. Supplies that fall outside the scope typically include professional services performed for overseas taxable persons.

Most supplies will be deemed to be standard rated unless they specifically qualify for zero rating or exemption. Where a supply could either be zero-rated or exempt, zero rating usually takes priority.

Goods and Services

Once it has been determined that a taxable supply exists and that the supply has been made by a taxable person, the next issue that must be considered is whether the supply is one of goods or of services. A supply of goods is defined in EU law as "the transfer of the right to dispose of tangible property as owner" (Article 5.1, European Commission (EC) 6th VAT Directive). Any supply made for a consideration that is not one of goods qualifies as a supply of services (Article 6.1, EC 6th VAT Directive).

Why does it matter? The simple answer is that different place-, time-, and value-of-supply rules exist for goods and services. For the purposes of this discussion, the place of supply is most important. Specific documentary reporting obligations exist in connection with the intra-EU supply of goods (but not for services). Distinguishing whether a good or a service is being exported is also important when determining what evidence is required to support the zero rating of the supply. In general, more formal documentation is required in respect of exported goods than for exported services.

Guidance on whether an E-commerce sale involves a supply of goods or a supply of services is discussed in more detail in the following two sections of this chapter.

Where a Supply Can Be Taxed

By working through a series of rules, the place of supply can be established. The same principles apply to all supplies made in the EU and are intended to provide against both double taxation and nontaxation. If a trader makes supplies deemed to be taxable in an EU member state, or in a non-EU VAT regime country, a liability to register for VAT in that country/state may arise.

A company does not need a permanent establishment for direct-tax purposes to have a VAT registration liability. For example, a company can be registerable for VAT within a country without having a local establishment because it owns goods located in an EU country or provides services that are deemed to take place there. Both concepts are extremely important when considering sales in an E-commerce environment. If a VAT registration liability has been triggered, failure to register and charge local VAT can result in sometimes punitive penalties being incurred by the business.

For other taxes such as direct corporate taxes, an establishment that gives rise to a taxable presence will generally involve a long-term project typically lasting at least six months and involving numerous personnel working in a particular country. Even then, the existence of a double tax treaty relief may prevent the overseas company from having a taxable presence. For VAT there is no treaty relief whatsoever.

As a general rule it is easier to create nexus for VAT than for other taxes. If a company has a direct-tax presence, it will almost certainly have to be VAT registered. In contrast, a company can be VAT registered in a country without having any liability in respect of corporate direct taxes.[2]

In most cases the vendor will need to charge, collect, and remit the VAT, but in certain specified cases, the tax must be accounted for by the customer. The place of supply is determined firstly by whether the supply involves goods or services, and the specific rules applicable are examined in "Goods" and "Services" later in this chapter.

When and What Tax Is Due to the Revenue

The *time of supply* is known as the tax point and is of great importance for VAT accounting purposes because the tax point determines when the VAT should be paid. There is variation in these rules between EU countries. The following is a discussion of the standard rules applied to the United Kingdom.

In the United Kingdom the general rule is that goods are supplied when they are removed or made available to the customer. This is known as the *basic* tax point. The basic tax point for services is the time that service performance is completed.

The basic tax point is overridden, however, if an *actual* tax point is created by one of the following:

- A tax invoice is issued or a payment is received *before* the basic tax point. The actual tax point is the earlier of the invoice date or the date payment is received.
- A tax invoice is issued within 14 days after the basic tax point. The actual tax point for such a supply is the invoice date.[3]

Other types of tax points occur for imports from outside the EU as well as for acquisitions from other EU member states. When goods are imported into the United Kingdom, a tax point is triggered and VAT becomes due when the goods enter the country. For goods from other EU member states, a tax point is created at the earlier of the following:

- the 15th day of the month following that in which the first removal of the goods occurred, or
- the date of issue of a suitable invoice by the supplier.

Value for Tax Purposes

The value of a supply for VAT purposes will determine how much tax is due (i.e., value times tax rate equals tax due). In general, the consideration paid by the customer will comprise the tax-inclusive value, but there are of course variations and additions to this rule. These rules vary according to whether the supply is one of the following:

- goods,
- services,
- goods acquired from another EU member state, or
- goods imported from outside the EU.

These values will also depend, to some extent, on whether the consideration for the supply is wholly in money.[4]

Imports from non-EU countries

The value of an import for VAT purposes is based on the value used for customs purposes, with the addition of all taxes, duties, and other charges levied outside or, by reason of importation, in the EU.

For example, where a standard-rated item is imported into the United Kingdom from the United States, the following applies:

Value of import	$100.00
Duty @ 10% × 100	10.00
Taxable value	110.00
VAT @ 17.5 × 110	19.25
	129.25

(Note: The standard rate of VAT in the United Kingdom is 17.5 percent.)

VAT Administration

Following VAT registration, or the appointment of a fiscal representative, a business must comply with the VAT accounting requirements of the particular country concerned.[5]

The VAT Return
At the end of each VAT period, businesses must account for any VAT due the tax authorities. Period lengths may range from one month to one year, depending on the nature and size of the business, although in Europe a monthly period is typical. Most VAT returns have to be submitted by the end of the month following the end of the period (i.e., an April return must be submitted—and paid if VAT is due—by May 31).

Accounting Records
The tax authorities require businesses to retain evidence of the VAT paid on purchases and due from or paid by customers. The type and format of records a business is required to keep, and the length of time they must be retained, varies from country to country. For example, in the United Kingdom, a taxable person must keep and preserve its VAT records for a period of six years unless the VAT authorities' approval is obtained for the records to be destroyed (or, for example, transferred to microfiche) at an earlier date. These records should include the VAT account, original purchase invoices, copies of sales invoices, credit and debit notes[6] issued and received, and import and export documentation, including proof of dispatches.

Recovery of VAT through Registration
If a business is required to register for VAT, or registers voluntarily, it must submit a VAT return declaring the tax payable and creditable. As VAT returns have to be submitted fairly frequently, this is a reasonably rapid mechanism for claiming input tax credit.

Recovery of VAT without Registration
VAT-registered businesses established in the EU are entitled to recover VAT incurred in other member states (where they are not registered),

subject to the rules set out in the EC 8th VAT Directive. These regulations apply to all EU member states.[7]

Businesses not established or VAT registered in the EU *may* be able to recover VAT incurred in the EU.[8] Whether a non-EU claimant will be allowed to recover VAT incurred in a given country will depend largely on whether the EU member state requires reciprocal reclaim arrangements in the claimant's country.[9]

Other Points on Tax Credit

Credit for input tax is only available for goods or services used for the purposes of the business. Thus, VAT incurred on personal expenditure cannot be recovered. If goods or services are only partly used for the purposes of the business (e.g., repairs to premises that comprise both a shop and living accommodation), only that proportion relating to business usage will be recoverable.

Input tax is reclaimed on the VAT return for the period to which the expense relates, or in accordance with the specified EC 8th and 13th VAT Directives time limits.[10] It cannot be reclaimed, however, unless valid tax invoices received from suppliers relating to both goods and services, or other acceptable documents, are held. Photocopied invoices, pro forma invoices, or purchase orders do not generally comprise acceptable evidence.[11]

Goods

Introduction

This section focuses on the general rules applicable to the VAT treatment of goods when moved from one territory to another, including the concepts of place of supply and time of supply; sales within a local VAT territory; movement of goods between the EU countries; and imports and exports. In addition to conventional methods of making sales, the treatment should be applied to those goods ordered by electronic means but physically delivered to the customer.

In addition to sales involving a transfer of title, the import of goods into a VAT territory will also be subject to VAT at the time and point of entry irrespective of whether the import involves a sale (at that time or later).

Sale of Goods: A Definition

Article 5.1 of the EC 6th VAT Directive states, " 'Supply of goods' shall mean the transfer of the right to dispose of tangible property as owner." In addition, the following are also treated as supplies of goods:

- producing goods by applying a treatment or process to another person's goods
- the supply of any form of power, heat, refrigeration, or ventilation
- the grant, assignment, or surrender of an interest in fixed property (land)

Place of Supply

Within the VAT system, separate treaties between different countries have not been developed in the same way as they have for direct taxes. Within the EU the VAT legislation relating to place of supply (contained in the EC 6th VAT Directive) has been developed to ensure the harmonization of the 15 VAT regimes coupled with the need to avoid double taxation. In VAT jurisdictions outside the EU, similar principles have been adopted in an attempt to avoid double taxation on cross-border supplies.

For a sale of goods, a vendor must therefore look to the local VAT or sales tax rules in the country for the following information:

- where the goods are when they are dispatched to the customer;
- in circumstances for which the supplier will act as importer of record, the country into which the goods are imported; and
- for goods that must be installed or assembled, the country in which the goods are installed or assembled.

Time of Supply

The time of supply is known as the *tax point* and determines when VAT should be paid. In the United Kingdom, the general rule is that goods are supplied when they are removed or made available to the customer. This is known as the *basic* tax point.

The basic tax point is overridden, however, if an *actual* tax point is created. An actual tax point occurs when either a tax invoice is issued or payment is received *before* the basic tax point. The actual tax point is the earlier of the invoice date or the date payment is received. A further rule states that if a tax invoice is issued within 14 days of the basic tax point, the tax point is the invoice date.

Credit Sales

Where goods are transferred under agreements that expressly contemplate that the property will pass at some point in the future (not later than when the goods are fully paid for), VAT will be due on the full value of the goods at the time of supply. These would include hire purchase agreements, conditional sale agreements, and credit sale agreements.

Sales within a Local VAT Territory

A sale of goods that does not involve a cross-border movement will, of course, be treated as taking place in the country where the goods are located.

EXAMPLE

A company (USCo) purchases a stock of inventory in the United Kingdom (in the EU) and Korea (not in the EU) for sale to U.K. and Korean customers, respectively. The following will occur:

- USCo will pay VAT on the purchase of inventory in the country where the inventory is located at the time the goods are identified as belonging to USCo—Korean and U.K. VAT is charged to USCo.
- USCo will charge Korean and U.K. VAT on sales to Korean and U.K. customers.
- USCo will probably have to VAT register in Korea and the United Kingdom.

Sales within the European Union: The Single Market

The completion of the Single Market on January 1, 1993, and the removal of fiscal frontier controls between EU member states resulted in fundamental changes to the way in which VAT is accounted for on goods moving between the member states.

The Single Market removed the fiscal frontier controls between EU countries. From a VAT and duty perspective, this created a territory in which goods can move freely within the community without border controls applying.

Other than the accounting issues concerning VAT and duties, the main effects of the Single Market on EU tax authorities are as follows:

- increased cooperation between the tax authorities
- greater access to VAT information by the direct tax authorities
- the removal of customs borders and the consequent trade barriers and a reduction in red tape for the business community

Businesses, on the other hand, are now faced with detailed reporting requirements and the need to maintain accurate records. Essentially, the paperwork burden has shifted from the customs borders (import entry forms, etc., traditionally handled by freight agents, shipping departments) to the company accounts department.

Acquisition within the EU

When a company acquires goods from another EU member state (and the goods are dispatched from that other EU member state), it is not charged import VAT at the border but instead must account for what is known as *acquisition tax* on its VAT return.

Whereas import VAT is paid to Customs on entry of the goods (and subsequently reclaimed at a later date through the VAT return), acquisition VAT is paid and reclaimed on the customer's local VAT return. In essence, the customer self-assesses the VAT by calculating the VAT due on the value of the goods. The VAT calculated is declared as output VAT on the return and immediately, on the same return (subject to the usual rules), can be deducted as input VAT. This normally involves no cash flow or absolute cost to the acquirer.

Transporting Own Goods

The movement by a legal entity of its own goods from one EU member state to another may lead to a liability to register for VAT in the recipient country in order to account for acquisition tax. Under the rules previously described, it is necessary for the acquirer to account for acquisition VAT in the member state to which the goods are transferred and (subject to thresholds) to record the acquisition into the country. Any onward sale of the transported goods will be subject to VAT according to the place of supply rules applicable to the terms of the contract. For example, if the goods are not further transported cross border, VAT is due in the country where they are located at the time of the sale.

EU Sales to VAT-Registered Customers

Provided that the vendor obtains and quotes its customer's VAT registration number on the invoice, the vendor is able to zero rate the sale from the country of dispatch. The customer then accounts for acquisition tax in the country of arrival of the goods. The vendor needs to ensure that it records details of these sales to other EU VAT-registered businesses on his European Sales Listing (ESL).

EXAMPLE

DutchCo sells flowers to a Belgian florist (both in the EU). DutchCo asks the florist for its Belgian VAT registration number and then displays this on the invoice. The invoice for the sale can now be zero-rated for Dutch VAT.

When the flowers arrive in Belgium, the florist is required to charge itself Belgian acquisition VAT on the next VAT return it submits. It recovers this acquisition VAT as input VAT on the same return, resulting in a "tax neutral" position for the florist.

Contracts involving the Local Installation or Assembly of Goods

The following is a detailed analysis of what happens from a VAT perspective in situations whereby goods are supplied and installed or assembled at the customer's site.

The VAT treatment of supplies of installed goods between EU countries is the same as that which applies to imports/exports. The vendor transports its own goods cross border and may therefore need to register for VAT in the country of arrival to account for acquisition tax. Some countries waive this rule to allow the customer to account for acquisition tax. The vendor may recover the acquisition VAT it self-accounted for as input tax. When the contract is fulfilled, the vendor must charge local VAT on the sale in the country where the goods are at the time of completion of contract, that is, where they are installed or delivered.

Benefits of up-front planning.   Many businesses undertake contracts to supply and install goods in the EU. These are often high-value onetime projects. In addition, the installation work itself is often subcontracted to a business established in the country in which the goods are to be installed. Such contracts are a good example of how up-front VAT planning can significantly reduce the costs of doing business in the EU.

The issue with supply and install deals from a VAT viewpoint is that they are subject to VAT on the full value of the contracts (i.e., goods and installation services) wherever the goods are installed. This has nothing to do with where the supplier is established or who acts as acquirer. It is quite easy, therefore, for businesses to inadvertently neglect their EU VAT obligations when undertaking supply and install contracts. The consequences of this can be as follows:

- The business fails to register for VAT at the appropriate time (if at all), exposing itself to tax liabilities, with associated penalties and interest charges.
- If installation work has been subcontracted, the subcontractor must charge VAT to the supplier. This will be an extra cost to the supplier unless the company registers for VAT to recover it.

These problems can be avoided in a number of ways. One way, of course, is to recognize these issues in advance and build them into the contractual terms so that there are no surprises for either the customer or the supplier. Alternatively, it is sometimes possible to restructure the contracts so that the supply of the goods is completely separate from the installation service.

Simplification Procedure:
Triangulation (Intra-EU Movements Only)

Triangulation is a simplification procedure applicable to intra-EU supplies of goods involving three parties in a chain whereby the goods move directly from the first person to the last person in the chain (the second person never taking physical possession). Each party must be VAT-registered in different EU member states.

A typical indication that triangulation has taken place is when the invoicing route does not follow the delivery route, as illustrated in figure 5.2. In this example, triangulation takes place because, although the invoicing route is from VendorCo via UKCo to FrenchCo, the goods pass directly from VendorCo to FrenchCo. Clearly, the Internet increases the possibilities for such complex chains of transactions.

Under the normal VAT arrangements for movements of goods between EU member states, the intermediate supplier would have a liability to register for VAT in either the member state of destination or the member state of dispatch (as the intermediate supplier clearly owns the goods in one of the two jurisdictions). This means that suppliers who supply goods in many member states could be liable to register in most of them.

In order to simplify this situation, all member states have agreed to a procedure that allows businesses registered in one member state to avoid having to register purely because of their participation in such triangular transactions.

Figure 5.2. **Example of Triangulation**

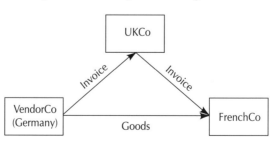

Practical Issues

The supply of goods to another member state can be zero-rated if *all* the following conditions are met:

1. The supplier holds the customers' EU VAT registration number.
2. The goods are removed and documentary evidence obtained within a specified time limit (e.g., three months for the United Kingdom).
3. The supplier holds acceptable commercial evidence showing the goods are removed from the country of dispatch.

If the goods are not removed, or documentary evidence is not obtained within the time limit, the vendor must charge VAT on the supply in the country of dispatch. However, if the supplier subsequently obtains documentary evidence showing that the goods were removed *within* the time limit then zero rating can be reinstated.

Documentary evidence of export.   The specific documentary evidence that is required to demonstrate that the goods have left the country will vary depending on the export medium used. For example, where goods are sent by post, rail, courier, vehicle, air, or sea, different types of document will be supplied to evidence the removal of the goods. The following are some of the most common forms of documentation:

- authenticated seaway bills and airway bills
- international consignment notes
- master airway bills
- bills of lading
- certificates of shipment and official customs documentation (C88s) for non-EU exports

Reporting formalities.   As mentioned previously, the introduction of the Single Market has resulted in increased reporting requirements for businesses. Additional documents (other that the VAT return) to be filed include the following:

1. *Intrastats.* Intrastats record the movements of goods between member states. Separate Intrastat declarations are required for both dis-

patches and acquisitions. In the United Kingdom, businesses with dispatches or acquisitions of goods that exceed £225,000 (from January 1, 1998) must submit Intrastats to the authorities within 10 working days of each month. Noncompliance can lead to legal proceedings. Unlike most VAT penalties in the United Kingdom, noncompliance with Intrastat rules is a criminal, rather than a civil, offense.

2. *European Sales Listings* (ESLs or VIES). All EU businesses that supply goods to VAT-registered customers in the EU and make use of the zero-rating provision (discussed later) are required to submit an ESL. This list summarizes all the sales to VAT-registered customers in other member states. The forms are completed for each calendar quarter and must be submitted within six weeks of the end of the quarter in question.

Specific problems relating to E-commerce.   The Internet provides several specific problems when selling to foreign customers.

- When designing a Web site, for example, attention needs to be given to the issues of correctly displaying prices (i.e., including VAT at the applicable rate) and determining whether VAT invoices will need to be issued, and how these should be formatted.
- On invoicing, the supplier will need to consider how to request VAT numbers from customers elsewhere in the EU so as to zero rate dispatches of goods to those customers.
- When the customers are a mix of registered and unregistered, it will also be difficult to design a pricing system that can inform the customer of the VAT-inclusive price in circumstances where VAT must be charged and collected (nonregistered customers) under different VAT regimes.

EU Sales to Nonbusiness Customers

A liability for the vendor to register for local VAT when selling goods cross border within the EU may be triggered by the taxable status of the customer.

Nonbusiness customers: Distance selling. When goods are sold by a taxable business in one EU country to a person (typically a private individual) who is not registered for VAT, the vendor is required to charge VAT in the country of dispatch under the place of supply rules.

Because the customer cannot provide an EU VAT registration number to the vendor, the supply will initially be subject to VAT in the vendor's country. That is, it cannot be a zero-rated dispatch because the customer is not able to account for acquisition VAT on his or her local VAT return.

However, once the value of these sales to private individuals in the other country exceeds a specific distance sales threshold in that country the supplier becomes liable to register for and charge VAT in that country. The recipient country therefore becomes the place of supply, overriding the normal rules.

Thresholds. Under EU VAT law, the EU member states have a choice of setting their distance-selling thresholds at either 35,000 European currency units (ECU) (about $40,000) or 100,000 ECU (about $110,000) per calendar year. The rates are per sales made to each country. Businesses must keep records monitoring the level of sales to customers in each country and VAT register when sales exceed the distance-selling threshold.

The supplier may, if desired, opt to make the destination country the place of supply before the threshold is reached. This is beneficial if the rate of VAT in the recipient country is lower than that applicable in the vendor's country.[12] (Current distance-selling thresholds are contained in appendix C.)

EXAMPLE

UKCo sells exercise videos to householders (not VAT registered) in the United Kingdom, Austria, and Finland (all in the EU) by mail order.

Sales within the United Kingdom and sales into Finland and Austria below the distance-selling threshold: All sales will be subject to U.K. VAT.

Sales to Finnish nonbusiness customers exceed 35,000 ECU (the distance-selling threshold), but Austrian sales to nonbusiness customers do not exceed 100,000 ECU: UKCo is required to register for Finnish VAT and charge all future sales to its Finnish customers with Finnish VAT, not U.K.VAT. U.K. sales remain subject to U.K.VAT; Austrian sales are also subject to U.K.VAT.

Sales to Austrian and Finnish business customers: UKCo can zero rate these sales provided it quotes the customer's VAT number on the invoice. The sales must be reported on an ESL. If the business customer does not provide its VAT number, U.K.VAT must be charged, and this will not be creditable by the customer.

Imports and Exports

For some vendor companies the Internet has offered a wider international customer base by providing an additional order medium. Electronic ordering may not alter the logistics of delivering the product to the customer, but suppliers do need to consider whether electronic transactions impact their tax liabilities in the context of the wider market that the Internet opens up. For the first time, a vendor may access a market it has not actively sought to target and therefore, a market for which it is not prepared.

Export

To zero rate supplies for export, the exporter must do the following:

- Ensure that the goods are exported within the specified time limits (within three months of the time of supply for direct exports, and within one month for indirect exports).
- Obtain and keep valid commercial evidence of export. The time limits for obtaining this evidence are three months from the time of supply for direct exports and one month from the date of export for indirect exports.

Import VAT

The VAT charged and payable when goods are imported into a country is referred to as *Import VAT* and is usually levied by the tax authority at the port.

When goods are imported into the customs territory of the EU, import VAT applies only once, the VAT rate that is employed depending on which of the 15 EU countries the goods are imported into. As import VAT is usually fully recoverable, importing the goods into a lower VAT-rate country is usually no more than a cash-flow advantage. Duty rates are standard throughout the EU. The value of goods on which VAT is charged is the base cost of the goods plus the incidental expenses of delivering the goods to the border and all customs levies, charges and duties applied.

If the goods are imported by a business customer to be used to make onward sales or for use in its taxable business, then the import VAT can be recovered by the importer of record (customer) as input tax of the business (subject to the normal rules). If the importer of record is a private individual (with no VAT registration) or the goods are not being used for business purposes, they have reached the end-user stage. In line with the philosophy of the VAT system, the customer therefore suffers the import VAT as an irrecoverable cost, ensuring that the foreign goods cannot be purchased at a competitive advantage over locally sold goods.

EXAMPLE

A sale of goods is completed in the United States, and the customer wishes to import the goods into Italy.

The vendor has no VAT liability once the sale is completed (prior to import). Italian Customs will levy VAT and duty on the import of the customer-owned goods. The customer pays the VAT (and offsets it on its Italian VAT return if it is a locally registered business).

Import Administration

Documentation. The normal evidence of the payment of import VAT is the Import VAT Certificate, known in the United Kingdom as the C79 form, which is issued monthly. The C79 is sent to the VAT-registered person whose VAT registration number (plus a three-digit suffix) is shown on import entry. The whole number is referred to as the Trader Unique Reference Number (TURN). The date when the VAT shown on the certificate may be treated as input tax is the accounting date alongside each item rather than the date of issue of the certificate. Equivalent documents exist in other EU member states.

Single Administrative Document.   All goods imported into the EU must be declared using the Single Administrative Document (SAD). As with the C79, equivalent documents exist in other EU member states; C88 is the form used in the United Kingdom. The SAD acts as an import declaration and is used by the tax authorities to collect statistical information. The importer of record must be cited on the SAD.

Importer of record.   The *importer of record* is the person responsible for entering the goods into the relevant EU member state. Often the invoice terms will determine the correct party to list as importer of record. For example, where the delivery terms are delivered duty paid (DDP), an overseas company importing goods will be the importer of record because it is responsible for delivery of the goods to the customer. However, if the delivery terms are free on board (FOB), the consignee is more likely to be the importer of record because it will take responsibility for delivery of the goods into the country in question. This is the more usual route taken when a customer is a business (i.e., VAT-registered) customer. The customer would act as importer of record deducting the import VAT on its local VAT return.

When a vendor imports goods into a VAT jurisdiction in anticipation of needing to fulfil local orders, the vendor is the importer of those goods and should be listed as importer of record on the customs documents. Note that only the person referred to as the importer of record can recover import VAT paid.

Events Occurring after Importation

Determining whether the VAT paid at import is the final level of taxation in the chain of VAT due on the supply of the goods or whether there is an additional local sale of the goods on which VAT is due will be dependent on the terms of the contract. The elements within a contract that determine the time and place of supply of a sale of goods include the following:

- whether the goods are assigned to a customer before transport begins
- whether a company is moving its own stock for logistics purposes
- the delivery terms, e.g., DDP or FOB
- at what point title transfers to the customer
- whether there is any installation element

EXAMPLE

Where goods are sold by a U.S. company to a French customer, French VAT will be due at the point of import into France. The terms of the contract will determine whether the import VAT is chargeable to the French customer who may recover the VAT as import VAT on its French VAT return, or if the import VAT is payable by the U.S. supplier, who must VAT register in France to then sell the goods on to the French customer. Once registered, the U.S. supplier would recover the French import VAT on its French VAT return (subject to the normal rules) and charge French VAT on its supply to the local customer.

Registration liability.   Where the vendor has acted as importer of record, and therefore makes a postimportation sale, it must register for local VAT so that it can issue VAT invoices and collect tax from its customers. The vendor will be entitled to recover the VAT paid at import as input tax relating to its business activities.

VAT recovery.   Making sure the correct party is listed as importer of record ensures that the VAT is recoverable and does not become a cost rolled into the value of the goods.

EXAMPLE

USCo and its products are due to be advertised in the United Kingdom. In anticipation of U.K. orders, USCo sends a container-load of products from the United States to a U.K. warehouse.

USCo pays VAT and duty on the goods when they are retrieved at the U.K. port and retains the customs documents that list USCo as importer of record.

The orders come in as expected, and because USCo will exceed the turnover threshold for registration, it registers for VAT and prints up its invoices displaying all the information required of a VAT invoice and requests the VAT due from the customers.

USCo then completes its VAT return by adding the VAT on sales as output tax and deducting the VAT cost it incurred at import as input tax.

Agents.   If a shipping and forwarding agent is used (and pays the VAT), the import VAT recovery treatment is slightly different. The shipping company cannot recover the tax it has paid on behalf of the importer of record as input tax of its own. The agent must therefore recover the amount paid as import VAT from the importer by treating the tax paid as a disbursement and showing it on the invoice as a separate item from the freight services.

Transfer of Title Qualified by a Specific Action

Contracts will often specify that they are not complete until the vendor fulfills certain obligations and/or the customer approves the goods; for example, the vendor must install the goods or deliver them DDP to the customer. The vendor is therefore responsible for all liabilities associated with the goods until the terms of the contract are fulfilled. The following is a detailed analysis of the VAT issues arising in this scenario.

Import VAT.   Under the contract the vendor is generally the importer of record responsible for the import VAT liability. If the vendor is obliged to pay import VAT but the customer is named as the importer of record, the party listed as importer of record is the *only one* who can recover the import VAT, irrespective of who actually paid it.

Place of supply.   When goods are transported to fulfil a DDP contract, the goods are transported on behalf of the vendor so that it can comply with its contractual obligations. In this situation, when the sale actually takes place (i.e., title officially transfers), the goods are in the customer's country. There is no element of cross-border dispatch relating to the transfer of title itself and therefore the place of supply is "where the goods are when the supply takes place"(Article 8(b), EC 6th VAT Directive), the customer's country.

Installed and assembled goods.   When a vendor has a postimport contractual responsibility to install the goods, there is specific EC legislation relevant to the place of taxation of such supplies. Article 8 of the EC 6th VAT Directive states: "The place of supply of goods shall be deemed to be: (a) in the case of goods dispatched or transported . . . the place where the goods are at the time when dispatch or transport begins. Where the goods are installed or assembled, by or on behalf of the supplier, the place of supply shall be deemed to be the place where the goods are installed or assembled."

The contract is not complete and the supply has not been made until the goods are successfully installed or assembled. It therefore follows that the place of supply should be where the goods are at the time of supply, that is, where they are installed.

Registration liability.   The vendor is obliged to ensure VAT is paid to the authorities on the sale to the customer. To do this the vendor may seek to register for local VAT so that it can collect the VAT due by invoicing its customers for the tax. The VAT on these sales is included on the vendor's VAT return (in the customer's country) as output tax.

In some countries, such as the Netherlands, the vendor may be relieved of the obligation to register for and charge VAT. The obligation to account for VAT can be shifted in local law to the customers (provided certain conditions are met). Note that subcontracting the installation work does not circumvent the vendor's liability to account for VAT on the supply it makes because it is still selling goods for which the place of supply is where they are installed. The VAT the subcontractor charges the vendor on the installation service it provides is, subject to the usual rules, available to the vendor to claim as input tax.

VAT recovery.   If the vendor was listed as importer of record of the goods when they entered the country of import, the VAT paid should be available as input tax to offset against the output tax liability on the supply of the goods.

USCo contracts with its German sister company to supply and install a U.S. manufactured computer-hardware system. GermanyCo does not want to take title to the equipment until USCo proves it is compliant with existing hardware.

USCo is treated as importing its own goods and therefore should be recorded as importer of record into Germany.

The freight forwarder has listed GermanyCo as importer of record by mistake.

GermanyCo agrees with USCo to pay the VAT and then recovers it as input VAT on its German VAT return.

USCo subcontracts the installation work to a German computer specialist.

USCo receives an invoice from the subcontractor that includes German VAT.

GermanyCo confirms the system is compatible and agrees to pay the amount it owes under contract.

Anticipating the sale, USCo registers for German VAT and invoices GermanyCo for the contract value plus VAT.

USCo then submits its first VAT return, including the VAT it charged GermanyCo as output tax and deducting the VAT it paid on the subcontracted services as input tax. The import VAT is not available as USCo's input tax because USCo was not listed as importer of record.

The recovery of this VAT was not lost, however, because GermanyCo was allowed by the authorities to recover the VAT as importer of record even though it did not have title to the goods at the time. (This is not possible in all countries.)

Customs Duty

Introduction

This section focuses on the general provisions applicable to the Customs treatment of goods when moved from one territory to another. In addition to conventional methods of making sales, the treatment discussed can be applied to those goods ordered by electronic means but physically delivered to the customer.

Duty is a substantial bottom-line cost, but it is often unseen and unquantified by importers because it is hidden in the freight costs or costs of sales. Once identified, however, these costs can be managed using different methods.

Customs duty is an indirect tax, but its purpose is less to raise money than to regulate the flow of trade. Customs duty is charged on the value of goods imported into the EU as a single customs territory. It is collected on behalf of the EU by the local country Customs authorities whose procedures are based on European rules in a similar way to VAT legislation within the EU. Unlike VAT, however, it is irrecoverable, and an absolute cost.[13]

The Levying of Duty

The duty is due when goods are entered to free circulation in the EU. This may be at the port or on removal from a customs warehouse. In some cases goods can enter the EU without being declared for free circulation. In such cases they travel under a document known as a T1, which informs the authorities in the countries through which the goods pass that they need to ensure they are either cleared for free circulation or pass through into another country.

How Is Duty Calculated?

Every item that can be traded is classified according to international rules, which allocate a tariff code number. Each tariff code has a corresponding EU duty rate. Where rates are expressed as a percentage of value, the value required is the value in a sale for export from the dispatching country, adjusted to include all incidental logistics expenses up to the place of introduction to the customs territory of the EU. This usually means the port.

What Affects Duty Rates?

The duty rates applicable are affected by the classification and origin of the goods as explained in the following sections.

Classification.   Goods are classified by commodity codes set out in the U.K. Tariff and, inter alia, by general interpretative rules published by the World Customs Organization.

Detailed classification rules mean that product configuration can affect the classification of the good and hence its duty rate. With high-tech products increasingly blurring traditional product distinctions, classification is becoming ever more complex. For example, how should one classify a desktop product that acts as a word processor, fax, photo-copier, desk diary, and alarm clock? The difference in possible duty rates between the lowest and the highest is 3 percent.

If an importer misclassifies, more is at stake than merely duty. The importer may also be prosecuted for evading strict regulations that attach to particular products.[14]

Origin.   Each imported item has an origin. There is extensive legislation on how origin is conferred, and the rules are different for each product.

Consider, for example, a product that was assembled in Thailand from goods sourced equally from Hong Kong, Japan, and the United States. Thailand qualifies for preferential rates, whereas none of the other contributors do. The question is whether the act of assembly of foreign parts confers origin. The answer will depend on the facts in each individual case.

Information Technology Agreement.   Recent discussions of the World Customs Organization (WCO) as part of the World Trade Organization (WTO) have established an agreement between members to reduce duty rates on equipment specific to the information technology community.

The Information Technology Agreement (ITA) was drawn up in Singapore on December 13, 1996. At the conference the participants considered the key role of trade in information technology (IT) products in the development of information industries and in dynamic expansion of the world economy. The aim was to achieve maximum freedom of world trade in IT products and to encourage the continued technological development of the IT industry on a worldwide basis.

The agreement was finalized in March 1997 and the participants agreed on the following:

- Each party's trade regime should evolve in a manner that enhances market-access opportunities for IT products.
- Each participant shall bind and eliminate Customs duties and other duties and charges of any kind through equal rate reduction of Customs duties beginning in 1997 and concluding in 2000.

The ITA covers six main categories of goods:

1. Computers
2. Telecommunications equipment
3. Semiconductors
4. Semiconductor manufacturing equipment
5. Software (only that part of the import classified as goods)
6. Scientific instruments

The ITA provides for the staging of tariff cuts in four equal 25 percent rate reductions: July 1, 1997; January 1, 1998; January 1, 1999; and January 1, 2000 (complete elimination of duties). Some countries, such as the United Kingdom, reduced their duties to zero percent by the second stage.

Since the original agreement was drawn up, there have been proposals issued to expand the classification list, but no agreement has yet been reached.

The agreement provided that the duty elimination would occur providing that participants representing approximately 90 percent of world trade in IT products agreed to participate.[15]

Customs Duty Recovery

Because Customs duty is an irrecoverable cost, it is worth considering planning options designed to reduce duty payments to the minimum required by law. The techniques vary across sectors and by importer, but a typical project will consider the following examples.

Price Unbundling

Price unbundling is the deduction or exclusion for customs purposes of the cost of certain intangibles incorporated in the transaction value or transfer price. Examples include the cost of providing credit terms and damaged stock allowances.

Prior Sales Arrangement

A prior sales arrangement is the use or creation of an earlier transaction in a series of transactions prior to EU importation, which qualifies as a customs value. This technique avoids a duty liability on an intermediary's markup.

Reconfiguration or Reclassification of Goods

Careful use of the classification rules or a commercially insignificant change to design or configuration can have a dramatic impact on the rate at which duty applies. It is surprising how often a fresh eye can identify worthwhile reductions in the duty rate using the approach of reconfiguring or reclassifying goods.

Preferences

The use of smart buying techniques can take advantage of the numerous preferential duty rates (lower rates of duty for buying from a specific origin) or reliefs from duty. The techniques can involve, for example, a modest increase in supplier cost in exchange for a substantial reduction in duty. This can be of special interest to buyers of third-world products.

Duty Reliefs

There are a number of mechanisms under which duty can be suspended and either paid later or not at all. These are briefly explained in this section.

Outward Processing

EU goods are frequently exported for process and subsequently re-turned, perhaps as part of a different product. Outward processing relief avoids Customs duty on the EU element of the inbound product.

Inward Processing

Duty is intended to penalize imported competitor products sold on the EU market. If an imported item is destined for re-export after process-ing, duty and import VAT can be suspended. Many businesses consider the relief difficult to administer, but it can be controlled through simple and effective product tracking systems.

Duty Suspension

Equipment imported into certain countries for the purpose of being leased may benefit from a duty-suspension regime that enables Customs duty to be suspended or reduced on the basis that the equipment will be exported from the country in question at a later date (e.g., South Korea).

It is important to be aware, however, of any extra administration requirements (e.g., putting up a bond for the duty value) or punitive arrangements if the equipment is not subsequently exported (e.g., inter-est on the duty).

Services

Introduction

The VAT treatment for sales of services includes the issues of place of supply, the reverse-charge mechanism, place of establishment of both supplier and customer, and the amendment to Article 9 of the EC 6th VAT Directive. The VAT treatment of services is particularly relevant for E-commerce because of the OECD consensus that electronic products delivered over the Internet should be treated as a supply of services for VAT purposes. As technology develops and a wider variety of products can be transmitted electronically, this view may change, but the conference of OECD countries, the OECD Ministerial Conference in Ottawa, on October 8, 1998, has confirmed this view at least for the time being.

The *basic rule* for the place of supply of services in the EU is that it is supplied and VAT is due in the country where the supplier has established its business or has a fixed establishment from which the service is supplied. Where a supplier has more than one fixed establishment, the supply will be treated as made from the establishment that is most directly involved with supplying the services.

There are, however, exceptions to the basic place-of-supply rules that can result in the tax being levied in a country other than that where the supplier belongs. In practice, the exceptions cover a wide range of services and may also depend on whether the customer is VAT registered. The basic rule is more frequently overridden than applied especially where the sort of services that may be supplied over the Internet are concerned. It is therefore particularly important to establish the nature of the service being supplied up front. Retrospective adjustments to the VAT treatment are not usually a practical solution, especially when the customer is a private individual making a onetime purchase from a Web site.

Place of Taxation of a Sale: The Legislation

Under EU law, the place where a supply is made is the only place where it can be liable to EU VAT. This ensures that a supply is only subjected to EU VAT once. If the place of supply is outside the EU, the supply is said to be outside the scope of EU VAT. The rules determining the place of supply of services within the EU member states are laid out in Article 9 of the EC 6th VAT Directive.

Article 9.1

The basic rule is contained in Article 9.1 of the EC 6th VAT Directive, which states: "The place where a service is supplied shall be deemed to be the place where the supplier has established his business or has a fixed establishment from which the service is supplied or, in the absence of such a place of business or fixed establishment, the place where he has his permanent address or usually resides." A U.K. supplier supplying services covered by Article 9.1 would therefore charge U.K. VAT, irrespective of where the customer is located or where the service is performed. Similarly, a U.S. supplier would not need to charge VAT if it is only established in the United States.

The basic rule in Article 9.1 applies unless the services fall within any of the exceptions detailed in Article 9.2 of the EC 6th VAT Directive. The following sections examine these exceptions in detail.

Article 9.2(a): Services Relating to Land

The place of supply of services relating to land is the country in which the land is situated. Examples include building and construction services and services supplied by architects, surveyors, estate agents, and so on.

Article 9.2(b): Transport Services

The place of supply of transport services is the country in which the transport takes place with regard to the distance traveled under each VAT jurisdiction. International transport services have different place-of-supply rules depending on whether the recipient of the service is VAT registered in a different EU member state than the supplier, and so on.

Article 9.2(c): Services involving Physical Performance

The place of supply of services involving physical performance is the country in which they are actually performed. This includes services relating to the following:

- loading, handling of goods
- valuation of movable tangible property
- work on movable tangible property
- cultural, artistic, sporting, scientific, educational, entertainment, or similar activities, including organizing these activities

It does not matter where the supplier (or recipient) is established or whether the supplier/recipient is VAT registered in a country other than that of the performance of the service. The supply of an Article 9.2(c) service will usually render the supplier liable to VAT register in the country of performance to charge local VAT to the customer. This article applies equally to non-EU-established suppliers.

Note that some countries will allow the customer to self-assess local VAT on Article 9.2(c) services via the reverse-charge mechanism. This only applies when the service is performed in the country where the customer is VAT registered and established. Because the situations wherein this concession applies are strictly limited depending on type of service and the tax status of the recipient, businesses should always take advice before proceeding if they think an Article 9.2(c) service is being provided.

Article 9.2(c) is open to wide interpretation by different taxation authorities. For example, some EU member states treat training services as falling within the provisions of Article 9.2(c) as educational services. The scope offered by such wide interpretation can lead to discussion over issues such as whether television and Web channels may constitute education/entertainment in this context, and if so, where the service would be taxed. It is difficult to come to a definite answer as to the place where education supplied via an interactive telephone channel, for example, would be. Is it where the supplier broadcasts from, where the pupils are, or somewhere in between?

This sort of uncertainty also surrounds services that are increasingly being provided remotely. If a computer system is repaired remotely by a technician in another country, the place of performance of that service cannot be defined easily. Once again, technology is one step ahead of the tax authorities and a clarified and consistent tax treatment may be some years away.

Article 9.2(e)

Article 9.2(e) is of particular importance to businesses dealing in intangibles: "[T]he place where the following services are supplied when performed for customers established outside the Community or for taxable persons established in the Community but not in the same country as the supplier, shall be the place where the customer has established his business [etc.]."

The following services are included in the provisions of Article 9.2(e):

- transfers and assignments of copyrights, patents, licences, trademarks, and similar rights;
- advertising services;
- services of consultants, engineers, consultancy bureaus, lawyers, accountants, and other similar services, as well as data processing and the supplying of information;
- obligations to refrain from pursuing or exercising, in whole or in part, a business activity or a right referred to in Article 9.2(e);
- banking, financial, and insurance transactions including reinsurance, with the exception of the hire of safes;
- the supply of staff;
- the hiring out of movable tangible property, with the exception of all forms of transport;
- telecommunications; and
- the services of agents who act in the name and for the account of another, when they procure for their principal the services referred to in Article 9.2(e).

It must be reiterated that these provisions apply *only* to customers established outside the EU or who are taxable (VAT-registered) persons in other EU member states (from the supplier). Sales to nonbusiness EU customers are not covered by these provisions.

Special provisions in Article 21 of the EC 6th VAT Directive apply to the services listed in Article 9.2(e) relating to which party is liable to pay the VAT due (see table 5.3). Specifically, the burden of accounting for the tax falls to the customer to ensure that VAT is accounted for on supplies made into a country by a nonresident company. This is known as the *tax shift* or *reverse charge*. Such a mechanism was enacted into EU VAT law for two reasons:

1. As a simplification allowing the nonresident supplier to avoid having to register in that country if it is only supplying Article 9.2(e) services.

Table 5.3.   **Article 9(2)(e) Services**

Supplier	Recipient	VAT Due
Non-EU	EU (VAT taxpayer)	Reverse-charge VAT by the customer on its local VAT return.
Non-EU	EU (non-VAT taxpayer)	Either none or for specified services (e.g., telecommunications) the supplier may be required to VAT register in the EU to charge VAT to the customer.
EU	EU (VAT taxpayer)— located in a different EU member state than the supplier	Reverse-charge VAT by the customer on its local VAT return (which must supply its VAT registration number to the supplier).
EU	EU (non-VAT taxpayer) in a different EU member state than the supplier	Supplier charges VAT with regard to the establishment it is making the supply from.
EU	EU—any customer (i.e., including VAT taxpayers) established in the same EU member state as the supplier	Supplier charges VAT with regard to the establishment it is making the supply from.
EU	Non-EU	No VAT charged by the supplier. The customer may be required to account for reverse-charge VAT depending on the VAT regime (if any) of its country.

Note: The issues surrounding the charge to VAT under the provisions of Article 9.2(e) are highly complex. This table should be used as a guide only when users are fully confident they have established a 9.2(e) supply has been made, who the supplier and recipient are, where their establishments are, and where the supplies are made from and to. This table does not cover any VAT charges that may be due in non-EU countries where services are supplied, although it does indicate the main instances where these should be considered.

2.   Because the tax authority is in a better position to audit the resident company and ensure the tax is accounted for.

EXAMPLE 1

A U.S. legal firm, USCo, provides advice to a U.K. company. Should it charge VAT?

The supply of cross-border legal advice is taxable where the recipient belongs, per Article 9.2(e). The service to the U.K. company can be invoiced by the USCo without U.K. VAT because the U.K. company is in a position to apply the reverse charge and account for the VAT due. *Does not charge VAT.*

EXAMPLE 2

A French advertising company is commissioned to produce an advertisement for a U.S. company. Is the supply invoiced with French VAT?

The place of supply of this service is where the customer belongs—the U.S. *No French VAT.*

If the recipient of the service is a nonbusiness person (e.g., a private individual) established in the EU, then Article 9.2(e) does not apply, and the services revert to Article 9.1, being taxed where the supplier belongs.

Liability to Pay the VAT

The system of VAT and the flow of taxation is based on the premise that the supplier is registered for VAT and acts as the collector of the tax. In most cases performing a service that is taxable in a particular country will require the supplier to register for and charge local VAT on the supply.

As previously noted, the exception to this is when a VAT-registered customer imports services to which the provisions of Article 9.2(e) apply. In this case the liability to account for VAT is shifted to the VAT-registered customer. In the EU this is known as the *reverse charge.*

Under the reverse charge, the recipient accounts for output VAT on the value of the imported Article 9.2(e) services received, while at the same time recovering this VAT as input VAT to the extent that it relates to the taxable supplies the recipient makes. Unless the business is one that suffers a restriction on the amount of input tax it can deduct (e.g., financial institutions, charities, local authorities, etc.), the procedure is merely an accounting mechanism that does not generally involve a cash flow or absolute cost to the customer, similar to the acquisition tax arrangements already discussed in the section "Goods."

The Reverse Charge

For the reverse charge to apply, the EU customer must have received a service for the purposes of his or her business. The mechanics of the reverse charge for services are similar to those of acquisition tax for goods; these are also the only two occasions for which tax authorities will pursue the customer (rather than the supplier) for any unpaid VAT.

If the service has been received for nonbusiness purposes, it falls outside the provisions of Article 9.2(e), and the reverse charge cannot be applied. The service is then deemed to have been supplied in the supplier's country under the provisions of Article 9.1. In addition, the local tax authority will require evidence from an EU supplier, typically in the form of an invoice including the customer's VAT number (or other commercial documentation), to show that the customer received the supply in his or her business capacity.

In some countries, such as the Netherlands and Finland, the reverse charge is used for other supplies in addition to those listed in Article 9.2(e), as a simplification procedure to help nonresident suppliers avoid registration.

Antiavoidance

In order to avoid double taxation, nontaxation, or the distortion of competition, a member state has the power to treat the place of supply of services listed in Article 9.2(e) as outside the EU or within its own country, depending on where the services are effectively used and enjoyed. This can be applied in the following situations:

- When tax would otherwise be charged on services used and enjoyed outside the EU.
- When tax would not otherwise be charged on services used and enjoyed inside the EU.

This provision is used in all EU countries for supplies of telecommunications services. The provisions require non-EU telecommunications suppliers to register and charge VAT in all EU member states where they supply services to non-VAT-registered customers. Currently, only France, Denmark, and Italy make extensive use of these antiavoidance rules, although the United Kingdom also applies them for the leasing of tangible property.

Place Where the Supplier/Customer Is Established

The rules of Article 9 in the EC 6th VAT Directive, "Place of Supply of Services," make regular reference to the place of establishment of the parties to the transaction. The definition of *establishment,* or rather the lack of a definition, causes many interpretative problems when determining which country has the right to levy VAT.

Defining the Place of Establishment

The place of belonging of the supplier referred to in Article 9.1 is not extensively defined in EU law. Because the definition is not explicit in its meaning, the U.K. tax authorities have included the following within U.K. VAT law (Section 9.2 of the Value Added Tax Act 1994). This treatment, which is implemented in most VAT regime countries, it is reproduced here:

> The supplier of a service shall be treated as belonging in a country if (a) he has there a business establishment or some other fixed establishment and no such establishment elsewhere; or (b) he has no such establishment (there or elsewhere) but his usual place of residence is there; or (c) he has such establishments both in that country and elsewhere and the establishment of his which is most directly concerned with the supply is there. . . . For the purposes of this section (but not for any other purposes), . . . a person carrying on a business through a branch or agency in any country shall be treated as having a business establishment there.

There is now a body of important case law to assist in determining what constitutes a business establishment in EU VAT law. This case law has determined that a fixed establishment can arise through the following conditions:

1. The vendor has a fixed establishment of a minimum size with the permanent human and technical resources necessary to provide the services.[16]

2. A separate company operating on behalf of the supplier operates as a dependant agent of the supplier.[17]

Future Changes

The European Commission's Working Paper of June 8, 1999, suggests options for future change in the field of indirect tax in connection with E-commerce.[18] This included some radical proposals, including:

- Making Article 9.2(e) a general rule for services, to which the other sections of Article 9.2, plus the concept of taxing where the supplier belongs, will be exceptions.
- Altering Article 9.2(c) to ensure that this only applies where the place of performance is readily identifiable and provides a sensible place of taxation, resolving the difficulties of interpretation for "education" and "entertainment."

Telecommunications Services

Introduction

Tax authorities in most of the world have yet to develop a coherent framework of legislation that is directly applicable to E-commerce. Instead, a pattern has emerged of adapting existing legislation to fit particular types of cybertransactions. This is not a new approach. Most recently, the telecommunications industry has been a prime example of tax legislation trying to keep pace with rapid technology advances.

Telecommunications developments in the fields of technology and competition have tested many of the principles of E-commerce that challenge traditional taxation practices. The legislation that has developed to cope with this dynamic industry is seen to many as the model that will ultimately be applied to E-commerce. This section explores how that legislation has developed and examines the principles that have been extended to cover transactions where historic place of supply rules have been rendered obsolete.

The VAT treatment of telecommunications services has become one of the most complex areas to administer both for taxable persons in the industry and VAT authorities. This complexity is due mainly to the following:

- Major advances in technological and political developments in the telecommunications industry. Many new products have been recently introduced into the European telecommunications marketplace, and there has been significant penetration in (what were) monopoly markets, in particular by U.S. companies.
- The place of the supply rules in Article 9.1 and 9.2 of the EC 6th VAT Directive were simply out of date. They were drafted at a time when cross-border purchase of communication services was not practically possible. As a consequence, the rules have been difficult to apply and interpret in the context of both the telecommunications and E-commerce industries. Moreover, these rules created a pricing disadvantage for EU companies as against non-EU companies.

Since the introduction of the VAT regime in the EU, telecommunications services had been subject to the general VAT rule (Article 9.1 of the EC 6th VAT Directive) regarding the place of supply of services. Consequently, these services were deemed to take place in the country in which the supplier of the services is established. European telecommunications companies therefore had to charge VAT, irrespective of where the customer was established and irrespective of the customer's VAT status. Non-EU telecommunications companies, however, were not required to charge VAT.

The problem of effective taxation of telecommunications services intensified with the development of technical means whereby the supplier could provide the services without the need to have an establishment in the customer's country. This development led to significant VAT revenue losses for member states' public finances and also undermined the competitiveness of European telecommunications companies.

In order to correct the competitive disadvantages as well as budgetary losses, the European Commission agreed to implement significant changes to the place of supply rules that applied to telecommunications services. These are discussed in-depth in the following sections.

VAT Legislation

General Principles regarding Telecommunications Services

In early 1997 the European Commission announced that the VAT treatment of telecommunications services was to be changed and the new legislation was finalized on March 17, 1997. Derogations were granted to all EU member states to implement the changes in their national legislation by no later than July 1, 1997. Some tax authorities (France and Germany) were given approval to implement the rules retroactively to January 1, 1997 (although VAT charges could not be applied in their countries if this led to double taxation). Italy and Austria implemented from April 1, 1997, Belgium from June 1, 1997, and all other EU member states from July 1, 1997.

The changes were introduced on a temporary basis following EU-wide agreement, which was due to expire on December 31, 1999. A permanent change to Article 9 of the EC 6th VAT Directive was required to ensure the changes were permanent.

Accordingly, the Telecommunications Directive was introduced on June 17, 1999.[19] This amends the EC 6th VAT Directive by adding telecommunications services to the list of services normally taxed in the customer's country (listed in "Services" earlier in this chapter).

Establishment

It is worth reiterating that, before the application of the new telecommunications rules for VAT can be determined, the business must have an understanding of where it is established. As discussed at length in "Services," it is possible that a business may be established in more than one country.

To ensure the VAT place-of-supply rules are accurately applied, it is vital to check that all potential establishments have been identified and, if necessary, that it has been determined which establishment is most closely related to the provision of which service.

Place of Supply of Telecommunications Service

As discussed in detail in "Services," the place of taxation of a supply of services varies depending on the type of service being supplied. Telecommunications services were subject to the rules of Article 9.1 of the EC 6th VAT Directive and were therefore taxed according to where the supplier was established. This led to loss of revenue and distortion of competition; thus, by derogation each EU member state was required to add telecommunications services to the list of services to which the Article 9.2(e) rules apply.

Supplies to EU-established business customers or non-EU-established customers. As a consequence of the addition of telecommunications services to Article 9.2(e) of the EC 6th VAT Directive, the place of supply for a customer outside the EU or a VAT-registered trader in the EU is deemed to be where the service is received. An EU business customer is liable to collect and pay the tax under the reverse-charge procedure set out in Article 21 of the EC 6th VAT Directive (and outlined in "Services").

There is, however, a variation to Article 9.2(e) intended to avoid the possibility of distortion to competition arising from the nontaxation or double taxation of these services resulting from the otherwise correct application of Articles 9.2(e). If a service listed in Article 9.2(e) is used and enjoyed in the EU but is treated as supplied outside the EU by the correct application of Article 9.2(e), then Article 9.3(b) of the EC 6th VAT Directive can be used by a member state in its national legislation to bring the supply into the scope of EU VAT: "[T]he place of supply of services, which under this Article would be situated outside the Community, as being within the territory of the county where the effective use and enjoyment of the services takes place within the territory of the country."

This clause in Article 9.3(b) has been *specifically invoked* as a compulsory, rather than permissive, measure in all EU member states for telecommunications services. The implications of the taxable status and place of belonging of suppliers and customers involved in a supply of telecommunications services are detailed in appendixes D and E. Appendix D details the consequences of the telecommunications supplier being established outside the EU, and appendix E details the consequences of the telecommunications supplier being established within the EU.

Accounting for VAT

Where the services fall under the provisions of Article 9.2(e) of the EC 6th VAT Directive because the customer is a VAT-registered business resident in the EU, the services are subject to VAT in the country of the recipient. VAT should be accounted for via the reverse-charge procedure (Article 21.1(b)). (See "Services" for a review of the reverse-charge mechanism.)

Conversely, if the services are provided to a private individual, and Article 9.3(b) applies, the VAT due has to be paid by the supplier because the customer is not VAT registered and therefore is unable to self-account for the local VAT due. This creates an obligation for a non–EU supplier to register for VAT purposes within the EU and to issue invoices plus local VAT.

Where the non–EU supplier renders telecommunications services to private individuals established in different countries, it has a liability to VAT register in each country where the services are provided. For this reason some companies, such as AT&T, have established a company in one EU state to invoice all its EU customers. This allows the supplier to register for and charge only the rate of VAT that is applicable in the EU state where the company is established.

Under the definitive regime, non–EU operators registered in one EU member state would have to charge the state's rate of VAT on all services rendered to EU nonbusiness customers. It might be expected that telecommunications suppliers would opt to establish a company in the member state with the lowest VAT standard rate so that they can charge this rate of VAT to all (or some) EU customers. Table 5.4 indicates which

Table 5.4. **Application of VAT to Telecommunications Services**

Supplier	Recipient	Place of Supply	Party to Account for the VAT
Non EU	EU (VAT taxpayer)	Country of recipient	Recipient
Non EU	EU (non VAT taxpayer)	Country of use	Supplier
EU	EU (VAT taxpayer)	Country of recipient	Recipient
EU	EU (non VAT taxpayer) Or any customer in same country	Country of supplier	Supplier
EU	Non-EU	Country of recipient (per EU law)	Variable—this requires a country-by-country review

party, supplier, or customer is required to account for the VAT on the provision of telecommunications services when either party is established or uses the services within the EU.

Conclusion

It has long been recognized that the application of existing VAT rules to new types of supplies is losing the EU tax revenue and causing a competitive disadvantage for EU businesses in important emerging global industries. In preference to all the changes needed in existing legislation (which itself was only intended to apply until all the member states are fully harmonized under new VAT legislation), it was decided that the European Commission needed a quick and easy solution to the competition problem to bring non-EU telecommunications providers on board and accountable for VAT on their supplies.

Including telecommunications services within the provisions of Article 9.2(e) has addressed many of the inequities regarding the VAT treatment of these services, but it has also generated a host of new questions that have yet to be resolved in practice. In particular:

- How should the telecommunications provider and the tax authorities determine when (and where) the provider needs to register and account for VAT?

- How practical is it for a tax authority to identify a telecommunications provider who should register?
- How will the tax authorities compel telecommunications providers to comply?
- How practical is it for a telecommunications provider to identify what VAT should be charged to a customer (particularly when use and enjoyment principles are involved)?

The European Commission seems to have gone a considerable way to providing a solution that appeases the EU member states and increases VAT revenues, but it remains to be seen if the law is truly workable. The developments in VAT law for telecommunications are instructive with regard to the potential thinking of how VAT may, in due course, be applied to Internet commerce. Some lessons will undoubtedly have been learned, and it will not have escaped notice that the telecommunications industry involves a smaller number of larger players than does the E-commerce industry. It is reasonable to assume that tax compliance is a higher priority for large well-informed and better-resourced telecommunications companies than for smaller E-commerce concerns. It is also considerably easier to police the tax compliance of a small number of multinational companies than it will be to monitor thousands of traders with a business presence on the Internet.

Finally, the EU has concluded it is impractical to attempt to collect tax directly from private purchasers and has not, therefore, gone down the route of adopting a use tax for nonbusiness users.

Electronic Delivery

Introduction

As explained in the earlier VAT sections, whether a supply is one of goods or services is of fundamental importance when determining if and where any VAT is due, as well as in establishing which party is responsible for paying it to the tax authorities. The issue becomes particularly complicated when sales over the Internet are involved.

A Supply of Goods?

Article 5 of the EC 6th VAT Directive defines a supply of goods as follows: " [S]upply of goods' shall mean the transfer of the right to dispose of tangible property as owner." If the sale of a product, fulfilled through on-line delivery, is to qualify as a supply of goods, there must, therefore, be a supply of tangible property, and the right to dispose of this property must have been transferred. It is difficult to see how an on-line delivery can involve a "transfer of the right to dispose of tangible property" and so qualify as a supply of goods under EU law.

Conceptually, many consider that the method of delivery of a product should not alter the tax treatment applying to the sale of that product. This principle has not been adopted for VAT. Indeed the OECD conference in Ottawa in October 1998 concluded that any digital delivery of product must be treated, for VAT purposes, as involving a supply of services.[20] Consequently, where a supply is digitally delivered to a customer established in the EU (or by a supplier established in the EU), the supply is considered to be one of services.

Place of Supply

As discussed previously, Article 9 of the EC 6th VAT Directive determines the place of supply of services. Most items or services capable of being delivered electronically are likely to fall under the specific provisions of Article 9.2(e), although there are exceptions. The place of supply for Article 9.2(e) is as follows:

- Where the customer belongs, when he or she is established (outside the EU or is in business within the EU).
- Where the customer is a private individual and uses the services in a country that has implemented Article 9.3(b) (the use and enjoyment provisions), the supplier needs to register and charge VAT there.

If neither of the above apply, the place of supply will revert to where the supplier belongs. The following section provides examples of how the VAT treatment of a supply can vary depending on where the supplier and customer are established and the business status of the customer.

Provision of information.   Under Article 9.2(e) the supply of electronic information services is listed as one of the services deemed to take place in the country in which the customer is established (provided the customer is either an EU business customer or a non-EU customer). The following is a step-by-step breakdown of the place-of-supply rules as applied to a supply of information services.

Non-EU content provider.   If a non-EU content provider charges for providing information services to a business customer established in the EU, the services are subject to VAT. The VAT due is payable by the customer under the reverse-charge procedure. Consequently, the non-EU company does not have to register for VAT purposes.

If the customer is a private individual or nontaxable entity, the service is deemed to take place in the country of the supplier (Article 9.1), that is, outside the EU. Accordingly, no VAT is charged on these services by supplier or customer. Furthermore, the non-EU company does not have to register for VAT purposes.

However, if the customer makes use of the services in a country that has implemented the provisions of Article 9.3(b), the vendor will be required to register for and charge VAT. Under Article 9.3(b), where such a service is treated as supplied outside the EU by the correct application of Article 9.2(e) but is actually used and enjoyed in the EU, the supply can be brought within the scope of EU VAT. Although only France and Denmark have currently fully implemented the provision, it is open to debate how many other EU member states will follow suit.

Customers established outside the EU are not charged VAT (although there may be VAT consequences in their country if it has a VAT regime).

EU content provider.   If an EU content provider is providing information services, a distinction must be made between the provision of information to a customer established outside the EU and the provision of information to a customer established within the EU.

If the customer is established outside the EU, the service is deemed to take place in the country of the customer. The status of the customer, whether a VAT taxable person or a private person, is irrelevant. As the service is deemed to take place outside the EU, no VAT is applicable.

On the other hand, if the customer is established within the EU, the following applies:

- If the customer is a VAT taxable person in another EU country, the service is subject to VAT in the country in which the customer is established. The VAT due has to be paid by the customer (application of the reverse-charge procedure).
- If the customer is a non-VAT taxable person or resident in the same EU country as the supplier, the service is deemed to take place in the country in which the supplier of the service is established. As a result the EU content provider has to charge its local VAT to such customers.

Internet Access

Internet access is deemed to fall within the definition of *telecommunications services*. As discussed in "Services," telecommunications services fall within the provisions of Article 9.2(e). When provided to nonbusiness customers in the EU (by a non-EU supplier), this will therefore result in VAT registration liabilities for the supplier.

In situations where the Internet service provider supplies other services to the customer as well as access—for example, the provision of information, interactive training, or training materials—the VAT treatment of these services needs to be considered in accordance with the VAT rules pertaining to those services. This has caused difficulties in classifying the supply made by companies such as American Online, Compu Serve and Microsoft Network. Consequently, the scope of Article 9.2(e) has been extended specifically to include the provision of "access to global information networks."

Entertainment and Educational Services

The place of supply of entertainment and educational services is determined by Article 9.2(c): "[T]he place of supply of services relating to: cultural, artistic, sporting, scientific, educational, entertainment or similar activities, including the activities of the organizers of such activities, and where appropriate, supply of ancillary services; . . . shall be the place where those services are physically carried out."

Due to the general way in which Article 9.2(c) is worded, a significant variation in the types of services falling within the provisions of this article exists within the EU member states. Additionally, there may be a conflict with other phrases in Article 9.2, notably "the provision of information" in Article 9.2(e). Is a real-time video or text-based training course provided on-line an educational service or the provision of information? Each member state has applied different interpretations, resulting in a potentially wide variation in treatment.

The main ruling relating to Article 9.2(c) in the United Kingdom is the 1994 VAT tribunal *British Sky Broadcasting, Ltd.* case. Here is a brief summary of the case. British Sky Broadcasting (BSkyB) provided a satellite television service to customers in return for a monthly fee. The company was only established in the United Kingdom, and the case addressed the question of whether U.K. VAT should apply to charges made to customers in Ireland. It was held that, although the services supplied by BSkyB could fall within the general category of entertainment and thus plausibly come within Article 9.2(c), the services did not come within the intended meaning of Article 9.2(c) and that this, being an exception, should be construed strictly. The services supplied by BSkyB were therefore found to fall within Article 9.1 and were subject to U.K. VAT.

Future change?   The working paper produced by the European Commission on June 8, 1999, suggests that part of Article 9.2(c) may need to be amended in the future.[21] It accepts that, for most of the services listed in Article 9.2(c), electronic transmission does not arise or can simply be considered a method of delivery that does not change their essential nature.

The paper also notes, however, that certain of the activities listed in Article 9.2(c) (education, entertainment, etc.) need to be reconsidered, as they could be delivered to paying customers electronically. This may result in the time and place of actual consumption being different from the time and place of performance.

The European Commission's working paper also states that traditional interpretations of the terms used, for example, *cultural, educational,* and *entertainment,* may need to be reconsidered. It specifically raises the question of the difference between "education" and "the supply of information" when these are provided electronically.

The working paper suggests that, where these services are capable of electronic delivery and are so delivered, if supplied for consumption within the EU, they should be taxed within the EU, and where supplied by an EU operator for consumption outside the EU, they should not be taxed. Where supplied by electronic delivery for consumption within the EU, the similar general rules as applied to other services should prevail:

- If to a nontaxable customer within the EU, or a taxable customer in the same member state, Article 9.1 should apply.
- If to a customer outside the EU or a taxable person in another member state, Article 9.2(e) should apply.

Does the Delivery Method Affect the VAT Treatment?

Contrary to the stated intention of the OECD to apply "traditional tax principles to electronic commerce on the basis of neutrality," by the very nature of existing VAT legislation, specific treatment applicable to certain categories of goods cannot apply if the supply is, by virtue of electronic delivery, considered to be a service. A good illustration of this problem is published material.

The Contrast of Electronic Information with Books and Newspapers

There are marked differences in VAT treatment between the provision of information in a printed medium or via the Internet.

- A book or newspaper sold in the United Kingdom is currently zero-rated for VAT purposes, irrespective of whether the purchaser has a business purpose.
- The zero rate applies also when books are sold from the United Kingdom to private persons in other EU member states, although in this case, if a significant number of books are sold in those states, the seller will usually need to register for VAT to account for

distance sales in the target country. (See "Goods" for a review of this requirement.)

- The zero rate only applies to printed matter. It does not apply to a book reproduced on a Web site.[22]

Thus, if a university or bank (with restricted VAT recovery) wishes to read a page from a newspaper, and it is available via the Internet as well as in printed form, it has the choice of whether to access the page on-line or buy the whole newspaper. Purchasing the newspaper will not involve a VAT charge. Any charge for accessing the page on-line will be subject to VAT.

Forexia.   A 1998 U.K. Tribunal decision highlighted the issue of VAT legislation failing to keep abreast of technological change. *Forexia (U.K.) Ltd.* concerned a news digest that, in its printed form, fell clearly within the zero-rating relief available for certain printed matter. The problem was that the document was transmitted to customers by E-mail, fax, and/or by post. The U.K. VAT authorities argued successfully that what was supplied was not zero-rated printed matter (unless it was physically posted) but standard-rated information that the customers could print on their own equipment to turn into the hard-copy document.

In reaching his decision, the Tribunal chairman stated that he arrived at the conclusion that *Forexia*'s supply was standard-rated with great reluctance. He questioned the relevance of rules drafted more than 25 years ago to services that were not widely available then and noted that there was clear distortion of competition introduced by the means of delivery determining the VAT treatment.

Developments: The Political Debate

Introduction

It is widely acknowledged that E-commerce is an area that will experience phenomenal growth in the next few years. For the various players in the E-commerce marketplace this growth results in different problems, opportunities and challenges.

- How do *tax authorities* ensure that E-commerce transactions do not escape the tax net?
- How do *E-commerce vendors* ensure they comply with any VAT requirements that may apply?
- How do E-commerce purchasers know, up front, what (if any) tax they will have to pay, and how?

This section discusses future changes in VAT treatment, including progress made to date, the impetus for change, and a look to the future in light of these questions.

Progress to Date

The VAT issues that arise due to E-commerce transactions have been discussed at length at various forums over the last few years. The main objective of these discussions has been to do the following:

- formulate a consistent treatment to apply to the taxation of all international E-commerce transactions,
- ensure that transactions are taxed once, somewhere (so as to avoid either non- or double taxation), and
- prevent distortions in competition where the same supply is subject to a different tax treatment depending on where the supplier is established.

Such discussions are far from completed; it is certain that as they continue more countries will become involved and new policy will be agreed. In order to facilitate the achievement of the objectives, it is probable that changes will be made to how E-commerce supplies are taxed under existing VAT law. New laws will be written and implemented; indeed, it is difficult to see how the objectives can be achieved by the application of existing VAT law.

The Future

This section gives some indication as to what the future may hold for the taxation of E-commerce supplies. With rapid developments occurring in the E-commerce arena, however, it is difficult to forecast with any accuracy how VAT will be applied to E-commerce transactions made in the 21st century.

Impetus for Change

- The main area of concern to tax authorities is that tax is not being brought to account in their country when they consider it should be.
- The main area of concern to businesses is that another business, by not charging tax, has a commercial advantage.

The most recent example for which the taxation of a supply resulted in both of the above concerns being infringed was the EU VAT treatment of telecommunications services. For once, both the EU tax authorities and a large and powerful sector of the business community (EU telecommunications providers) were in accord that something was needed to level the playing field.

In the case of telecommunications services, it was agreed that a change in the way telecommunications services were taxed under EU VAT law was required. As discussed in "Telecommunications Services," the fix that was implemented was an adaptation of existing VAT rules to achieve a quick result. If it is agreed that the application of traditional place-of-supply rules to E-commerce supplies is unsatisfactory, it is probable that the first thing to be considered will be whether existing VAT law can be changed to provide a satisfactory remedy.

E-commerce is a rapidly expanding area with the capacity for generating high-volume and therefore high-value sales to nonbusiness EU customers. It can only be a matter of time before there is sufficient impetus to be generated among the EU tax authorities and EU Internet service providers to lobby for a change in the way E-commerce sales are taxed. The European Commission (as a separate body to the European Parliament of Member States) has stated that, if the predicted increase in

E-commerce sales to nonbusiness consumers (which are at present not subject to VAT) reaches an economically significant level, it may become necessary to devise mechanisms in conjunction with the business community for taxing such supplies.

Whatever action is taken to regularize the taxation of E-commerce transactions, the European Commission has recognized that the injudicious application of tax could prevent the electronic market from developing to its full potential. The European Commission has stated that, whatever changes are implemented, the EU VAT system must provide the following:

- legal certainty (clear and consistent rules reducing the risk of unforeseen tax liabilities and disputes),
- simplicity (introduction of a common VAT system based on taxation and origin), and
- neutrality (the consequences of taxation should be the same for goods and services whether purchased from within or outside the EU).

If invoking existing law does not work, consideration will have to be given as to whether new laws should be written to cover the taxation of E-commerce transactions. This process would take many years because all EU member states would have to agree to the implementation of any new legislation into their domestic VAT law.

Realistically, therefore, E-commerce transactions will be taxed under existing EU VAT law, adapted to address the concerns primarily of the EU tax authorities as they arise.

Legislation Changes

The EU tax authorities are in the process of reviewing the application of the Article 9 rules of the EC 6th VAT Directive to services provided to non-VAT-registered customers. There is legislation in place in Article 9 (Article 9.3(b)—which can apply to the services listed in Article 9.2(e)) to avoid the possibility of distortion of competition. There has already been increasing use of this measure, for example, for telecommunications.

OECD: Outline Agreement on Taxing E-Commerce

At the OECD Ministerial Conference in Ottawa on October 8, 1998, the Council Ministers of the Member States agreed to work together to develop a common approach to taxing E-commerce and to prevent fiscal discrimination against transactions on the Internet. The framework agreement is intended to do the following:

- Rule out a flat-rate bit tax on all E-commerce transactions.
- Apply traditional tax principles to E-commerce on the basis of neutrality.
- Avoid double taxation on the same transaction by different states.
- Ensure that indirect taxes on E-commerce are levied by reference to the place of consumption rather than the place of production.

The conference also agreed on a division of work on E-commerce tax policy issues among the relevant international organizations:

- tariffs: WTO
- customs procedures: WCO
- value-added tax: EU
- international and direct tax issues: OECD

Certain issues will require detailed work on how to implement these principles, including a satisfactory definition of "place of consumption" for Internet services and the application of the permanent establishment concept, Web sites, and E-commerce. An intensive OECD work program, including joint government and business committees and consultations with non-OECD member states, will endeavor to clarify these issues by the end of 2001.[23]

U.K. Joint Business Brief Pre-Ottawa

A key statement was issued by Customs and Excise and the Inland Revenue in October 1998 in connection with the OECD Conference on E-commerce in Ottawa of that month.[24] It acknowledges that E-commerce has the potential to become one of the greatest economic developments of the 21st century and that tax policy and administration must keep pace with these developments. In this connection a number of broad policy principles have been set out:

- The rules for taxation of E-commerce should seek to be technology neutral so that no particular form of commerce is advantaged or disadvantaged.
- When establishing the treatment of imported supplies for Customs duty purposes, a distinction has to be drawn between goods ordered electronically but delivered by traditional means and direct on-line delivery of digitized products.
- In line with the WTO declaration on global E-commerce, goods ordered and supplied electronically will continue to be treated as services. As such they will be free of import duties but will remain liable to VAT.
- Goods ordered electronically but delivered physically from outside the EU will continue to attract the rate of import duty appropriate to that commodity.
- No additional import duties will be introduced relating to electronic transmissions.

The joint paper on U.K. tax policy summarizes the U.K. government's position as accepting that the following broad principles should apply to the taxation of E-commerce:

- neutrality,
- certainty and transparency,
- effectiveness (the overriding aim should be that the right amount of tax is paid at the right time and in the correct country; as such, the rules will need to be sufficiently flexible to continue to achieve this as technology develops), and
- efficiency.

With specific regard to VAT, the joint paper examines the implications of the development of E-commerce in relation to three broad categories of transaction:

1. A supply of the physical goods to both businesses and private consumers.
2. Business-to-business supplies of services.
3. Business-to-consumer supplies of services and of digitized products.

At present the majority of E-commerce–based supplies fall within the first category. Most of these supplies are business-to-business transactions within a single country. Typically, in these cases the Internet is used solely as a means of communication to place an order. The existing laterals are in general readily applicable to such physical deliveries of goods purchased using electronic means.

The second category of transactions should likewise be capable of accommodation within existing rules. The third category of transactions—supplies of services to private consumers—presents potentially the greatest challenge to effective tax administration. It is, however, also the least developed and so remains relatively insignificant to the tax authorities. Trading models in this sector have been evolving in tandem with technological developments. Satisfactory VAT arrangements for this category of transactions will have to be developed. As yet this has not been done. The United Kingdom is working with all interested parties in this field, including infrastructure providers and software developers to ensure this is put into practice.

E-Commerce: The United Kingdom's Taxation Agenda

Customs and Excise and the Inland Revenue issued a further joint statement in November 1999. The paper sets out the U.K. government's current views on how existing taxation rules could be adapted to cope with the delivery of product and services by electronic means.[25] The paper reiterates some of the statements made in the original joint paper in October 1998, for example, taxation should not be a barrier to growth and the taxation system needs to be clear so business can easily understand its responsibilities in that regard. To enable businesses to trade confidently without fear of double or unintentional taxation, it is recognized that a degree of international cooperation and consensus is required. Both the Inland Revenue and Customs will therefore continue to work toward obtaining international agreement as far as possible.

The following is a brief overview of the VAT issues covered in the paper:

- The existing VAT rules can cope with most cross-border business-to-business sales that involve the electronic delivery or order of goods or services.
- There is also a mechanism for collecting VAT chargeable to private customers where the vendor is established within the EU.
- Difficulties arise where the customer is a private individual and the vendor is not established in the EU.
- The OECD ministers agreed that VAT should be charged where an electronic service is consumed. Consumption, it is proposed, would be the place of establishment for a business customer and the normal residence of the private individual.

This would clearly require some amendment to current EC legislation. At present, most supplies (telecommunications services being the notable exception) of services by non-EU vendors to EU resident private individuals would not be subject to EU VAT. Amending the place of taxation to the place of consumption would bring most non-EU vendors who sell to EU private individuals within the EU VAT net. How this will operate practically remains open to debate.

The paper also suggests that Customs is already considering a potential antiavoidance rule where a business customer is established in one country but consumes the service in another.

- Customs is also looking for ways to improve its service to taxpayers by using the tools and techniques of E-commerce. VAT registration of businesses on-line and the electronic filing of VAT returns are proposed as two ways to help non-U.K.-established businesses in particular to comply with their VAT responsibilities.

European Commission Working Paper

The European Commission's working paper of June 8, 1999, has made the following options for change in the field of indirect tax in connection with E-commerce.

Business-to-business transactions.   As the reverse charge will apply for business-to-business E-commerce transactions, suppliers will need a dependable mechanism to distinguish business from private customers. If it is a business customer, it will also be necessary to ascertain that it holds a valid VAT identification number in another EU country. This information has to be available at the time of transaction.

The proposed Directive on a Common Framework for Electronic Signatures (COM/99/0195) allows for an independent certification process that can include details of VAT registration status. An independent certification process would enable the authenticity of a customer's VAT status to be checked on-line.

The European Commission's working paper suggests two methods of obtaining the verification, either direct from the tax authority or from a "trusted third party." Whether either route or something different is finally implemented, the European Commission acknowledges in its working paper of June 8, 1999, that "tax administrations must accept that they have a role to play in facilitating the availability of the information that is needed to achieve compliance."[26]

Private customers.   When selling to private customers via E-commerce, it is essential that suppliers are able to verify information about the customer. Otherwise, the customer has the power to decide whether to be taxed. The supplier must then develop the ability to compute and collect taxes on the basis of customer location.

Customer location can be verified by intermediaries in the transaction. These could be Internet E-mail providers or payment-system providers such as banks or credit-card companies that hold information about the customer.

Administration.   The European Commission's working paper states that it will be necessary to impose a requirement for non-EU suppliers to register for VAT in the EU when making supplies to private EU customers and to comply with the associated obligations. The question of registration thresholds needs to be addressed to ensure that a onetime sale that is minimal in value does not burden the supplier with an obligation to register for VAT.

The favorable approach would be one that makes the obligations for non-EU suppliers as straightforward as possible. This brings in the favorable idea of creating a single place of registration within the EU and accounting to a single tax administration.

General Principles

The EU has also agreed on a set of general principles that provide a useful foundation of more detailed work in developing systems to cope with this category. In summary, the principles are as follows:

- The focus of activity should be in adapting existing VAT provisions to accommodate E-commerce based on internationally established guidelines. In this context, no new taxes are envisaged at this stage.
- Digitized products supplied by electronic means should be treated for VAT purposes as supplies of services. This is contrary to the OECD's statement that "classification as a good or service should not depend on the means of distribution" (e.g., electronic delivery versus physical delivery).[27]
- The place of taxation of services supplied by electronic means should in principle be the place of consumption.
- The tax system as it applies to such services should be readily enforceable by tax administrations.
- Paperless electronic invoicing should be facilitated for VAT purposes, taking account of the need for adequate controls. International corporations to facilitate such invoicing are essential.
- Compliance with tax rules should be as easy as possible. Businesses should be able to fulfil fiscal obligations by means of electronic declarations and accounting.[28]

The focus of attention for the tax authorities has been on how to tax transactions between businesses in countries outside the EU and private individuals inside the EU. It may be possible for the home country of the business to tax the transaction if it is able to trace the funds accruing to the business. However, if the EU wants its portion, it will have to rely on a level of international cooperation from tax authorities that may be unreasonable.

Summary

The Ottawa Conference may not have provided clear solutions, but it has served to focus attention on several key E-commerce issues:

- The lack of uniformity among tax authorities and their approaches to the indirect taxation of E-commerce must be addressed. The issue of whether a supply is one of goods or services is particularly important (as different VAT rules apply, and only goods are subject to Customs duty).
- Responsibility for correct tax compliance rests principally with suppliers, particularly where sales are being made to private individuals. This means that telecommunications companies selling to private individuals within the EU will become liable to register for VAT.
- Compliance and administration procedures are likely to become increasingly complex and time consuming with many companies facing uncertainty about what VAT (if any) they should be charging.

APPENDIX A

Countries with a VAT System[1]

Country	Standard Rate (%)	Country	Standard Rate (%)
1. Albania	12.5	37. Georgia	20
2. Algeria	21	38. Germany	16
3. Argentina	21	39. Ghana	10
4. Armenia	20	40. Greece	18
5. Austria	20	41. Grenada	15
6. Azerbaijan	20	42. Guatemala	10
7. Bangladesh	15	43. Guinea	18
8. Barbados	15	44. Haiti	10
9. Belarus	20	45. Hungary	25
10. Belgium	21	46. Iceland	24.5
11. Belize	15	47. Indonesia	10
12. Benin	18	48. Ireland	21
13. Bolivia	13	49. Israel	17
14. Brazil	17[2]	50. Italy	20
15. Bulgaria	20	51. Ivory Coast	20
16. Cameroon	18.7	52. Kazakstan	20
17. Chile	18	53. Kenya	18
18. China	17	54. Korea	10
19. Colombia	15	55. Kyrgyzstan	20
20. Congo	18	56. Latvia	18
21. Costa Rica	13	57. Lithuania	18
22. Cote d'Ivoire	20	58. Luxembourg	15
23. Croatia	22	59. Madagascar	20
24. Cyprus	8	60. Mali	15
25. Czech Republic	22[3]	61. Mauritius	15
26. Denmark	25	62. Mexico	15
27. Dominican Republic	8	63. Moldova	20
28. Ecuador	10	64. Mongolia	10
29. El Salvador	13	65. Morocco	20
30. Estonia	18	66. Mozambique	17
31. Fiji	10	67. Nepal	10
32. Finland	22	68. Netherlands	17.5
33. France	20.6	69. Nicaragua	15
34. French Polynesia	2[4]	70. Niger	17
35. Gabon	18	71. Nigeria	5
36. Gaza	17	72. Norway	23

Country	Standard Rate (%)	Country	Standard Rate (%)
73. Papua New Guinea	10	91. Tajikistan	20
74. Paraguay	10	92. Tanzania	20
75. Peru	18	93. Thailand	7[5]
76. Philippines	10	94. Togo	18
77. Poland	22	95. Trinidad & Tobago	15
78. Portugal	17	96. Tunisia	18
79. Romania	22	97. Turkey	17
80. Russia	20	98. Turkmenistan	20
81. Senegal	20	99. Ukraine	20
82. Slovak Republic	23	100. United Kingdom	17.5
83. Slovenia	19	101. Uruguay	23
84. South Africa	14	102. Uzbekistan	20
85. South Korea	10	103. Vanuatu	12.5
86. Spain	16	104. Venezuela	16.5
87. Swaziland	14	105. Vietnam	20
88. Sweden	25	106. Zambia	17.5
89. Switzerland	7.5	107. Zimbabwe	12.5
90. Taiwan	5		

Sources: International VAT Monitor published by IBFD Publications BV; Guides to European Taxation, Volume IV: Value Added Taxation in Europe, published by IBFD Publications BV; and U.S. Department of Commerce Market Access and Compliance Web site, <*http://www.mac.doc.gov*>.

[1] The list is not meant to be exhaustive. Countries change their tax regimes often and sometimes at very short notice. The intention of the above schedule is to give an overall picture of the extent of countries that have a VAT system and how widely the rates of VAT vary between countries are.

[2] Varies between regions.

[3] 22% for goods, 5% for services.

[4] 2% for goods, 3% for services.

[5] 7% rate introduced for a temporary two-year period (April 1, 1999, to March 31, 2001).

The following countries have announced they intend to introduce a VAT system in the future:

- Dominica
- Equatorial Guinea
- India (implementation planned for April 1, 2001)
- Iran
- Macedonia
- Namibia
- Solomon Islands

APPENDIX B
Countries with a Sales Tax or Similar Tax

Country	Tax	Standard Rate (%)
1. Australia	Sales tax	10[1]
2. Bhutan	Sales tax	—
3. Botswana	Sales tax	10
4. Canada	Goods and services tax	7
5. Cape Verde	Consumption tax on nonpriority goods	5–60
6. Dominica	Sales tax[2]	10
7. Egypt	Sales tax	5–25
8. Equatorial Guinea	ICN–turnover tax[3]	—
9. Eritrea	Sales tax	12
10. Ethiopia	Sales tax	12
11. Guyana	Consumption tax	Up to 50
12. Honduras	Sales tax	7
13. India	Sales tax	0–20[4]
14. Jamaica	General consumption tax	12.5
15. Japan	Consumption tax	5
16. Lesotho	Sales tax	10
17. Macedonia	Sales tax on products and services[5]	—
18. Malaysia	Sales tax and services tax	5–15
19. Malta	Excise tax on products (ETP) and excise tax on selective services (ETSS)	5
20. Namibia	General sales tax	10[6]
21. New Zealand	Goods and services tax	12.5
22. Pakistan	Sales tax	15
23. Panama	Sales tax	5
24. Papua New Guinea	Sales tax	10
25. Singapore	Goods and services tax	3
26. Sri Lanka	Goods and services tax	12.5[7]
27. Suriname	General turnover tax	7[8]
28. Yugoslavia	Sales tax	0.6–4

Sources: International VAT Monitor published by IBFD Publications BV; Guides to European Taxation, Volume IV: Value Added Taxation in Europe, published by IBFD Publications BV; and U.S. Department of Commerce Market Access and Compliance website, address <*http://www.mac.doc.gov*>. The list is not meant to be exhaustive.

[1] A GST of 10% has been proposed (to be introduced July 1, 2000).

[2] An introduction of VAT has been announced.

[3] Efforts are underway to replace the ICN by VAT in 1999.

[4] VAT to be introduced in 2001.

[5] VAT to be introduced in 1999.

[6] VAT to be introduced in 1999.

[7] Possibly to be replaced by VAT.

[8] 7% for goods, 5% for services.

APPENDIX C

Distance–Selling Registration Thresholds

Country	Local Currency (approximate)	ECU (European Currency Unit)
Austria	1,400,000	100,000
Belgium	1,500,000	35,000
Denmark	280,000	35,000
Finland	200,000	35,000
France	700,000	100,000
Germany	200,000	100,000
Greece	8,200,000	35,000
Ireland	27,000	35,000
Italy	54,000,000	35,000
Luxembourg	4,200,000	100,000
Netherlands	230,000	100,000
Portugal	6,300,000	35,000
Spain	4,550,000	35,000
Sweden	320,000	35,000
United Kingdom	70,000	100,000

APPENDIX D

Flowchart Detailing the VAT Treatment of Telecommunications Services Supplied by a U.S. Telecommunications Provider

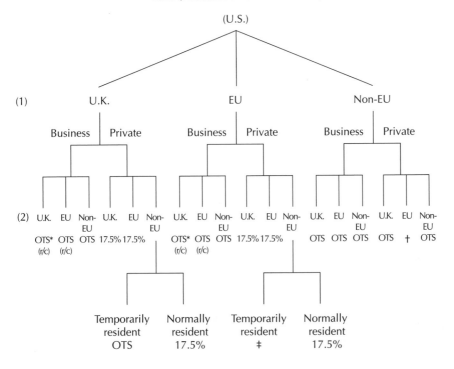

Key:
    (1) Origin of call
    (2) Where customer is established
OTS: Outside the scope of U.K. VAT.
    r/c: Recipient businesses account for VAT under the reverse-charge procedure.
17.5%: Supply subject to U.K. VAT at 17.5%.

* If Telco has both U.K. and U.S. establishments, this is dependent on which of Telco's establishments is most closely related to the supply.

† Normally this would be outside the scope of EU VAT because the call is of non-EU origin, but this will depend upon the local interpretation of Article 9.3(a) (the "use and enjoyment provisions") in the EU country in which the customer belongs.

‡ This supply is taxable in the United Kingdom but would be relieved from U.K. VAT. The EU country where the call originated, however, may try to impose local VAT.

(The VAT treatment of standing charges depends entirely on the place of residence of the customer and whether it is for business or private usage.)

Flowchart Detailing the VAT Treatment of Telecommunications Services Supplied by a U.K. Provider⋆

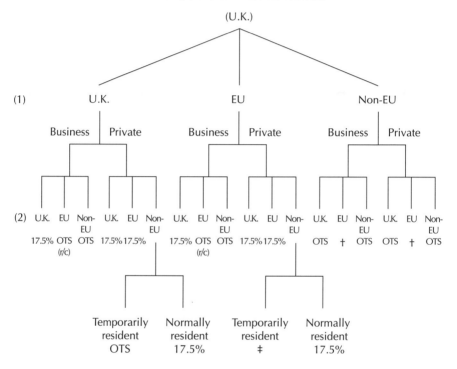

Telco (Telecommunications Provider)

(U.K.)

Key:
(1) Origin of call
(2) Where customer is established
OTS: Outside the scope of U.K. VAT.
r/c: Recipient businesses account for VAT under the reverse-charge procedure.
17.5%: Supply subject to U.K. VAT at 17.5%.

The VAT treatment of standing charges depends entirely on the place of residence of the customer and whether for business or private usage.

† Normally this would be outside the scope of EU VAT because the call is of non-EU origin, but this will depend upon the local interpretation of Article 9.3(a) (the "use and enjoyment provisions") in the EU country in which the customer belongs.

‡ This supply is taxable in the United Kingdom but would be relieved from U.K. VAT. The EU country where the call originated, however, may try to impose local VAT.

APPENDIX F

General Administrative Procedure

An EC 8th VAT Directive Claim

1. **Eligibility**

   Any VAT-registered person in an EU member state may reclaim VAT suffered in another EU member state, subject to a variety of conditions.

   If the taxable person has a place of business or is liable to register for VAT in a particular member state, then the taxpayer should register for VAT in that member state and recover the VAT incurred through the VAT registration accordingly. Applications to recover VAT will be refused where a business has a fixed establishment or a liability to register for VAT in a particular member state.

2. **Nonrefundable VAT**

   (a) **Goods**

   The export of goods from an EU member state to a customer in another member state does not attract a charge to VAT, provided the customer is registered for VAT elsewhere in the EU (and provides the supplier with its VAT registration number). The supply will then be zero-rated. It is clear, therefore, that under the provisions of the EC 8th VAT Directive, recovery of VAT will only apply to delivery of goods within the charging state.

   In addition, VAT may not be reclaimed on goods bought for resale, either within or outside the state, because the entrepreneur will almost certainly be required to register for VAT in respect of the resale. If, on the other hand, goods are purchased as consumables (e.g., stationery) for use within the business, then the VAT incurred may be claimed under the EC 8th VAT Directive.

(b) **Services**

Services is the main area that VAT will be charged to foreign entrepreneurs and where recovery of the tax under the EC 8th VAT Directive will apply.

An 8th Directive may be made in respect of any supplies used in the course or furtherance of a business, subject to the normal rules for claiming input tax in that member state.

The rules for reclaiming input tax on goods and services are slightly different in each member state.

3. **The Application Form**

The application form has a standard layout issued in the language of each member state. Any form may be used, but experience shows that the claim is dealt with more quickly if the own-language version is used. With the exception of the Netherlands and Sweden, which permit the submission of claims in English, the form must be completed in the official language of the member state to which the claim is being made.

4. **Time Limits**

The claim period for reclaims made under the EC 8th VAT Directive is one calendar year. The claim form must be submitted by June 30 of the following year, at the latest. However, some countries allow an extension to this deadline.

Interim claims may be submitted throughout the claim period, but they must be for a period of at least three months.

5. **Claim Thresholds**

Within the rules for time limits, EU member states set a minimum amount that may be reclaimed on each form, which are as follows: interim claims must be for a value of at least 200 ECU; annual claims or claims for the final period in the year must be for a value of at least 25 ECU.

Items issued on earlier interim claims may be included on later claims submitted in the same year.

6. **Repayment Date**

   The length of time taken to repay claims varies in each EU member state.

7. **Supporting Evidence**

   Each claim must be submitted enclosing the following:

   * original invoices;
   * a certificate of VAT status from the applicant's local VAT authority confirming that it is registered for VAT in its home state; and
   * a letter of authority, if a third party is submitting the claim on the claimant's behalf.

   The certificate of VAT status is usually valid for 12 months and should be renewed every year. A separate, original certificate is required for each member state to which a claim is made.

8. **Rejection of Claim**

   If a claim is refused, the appropriate authority should provide an explanation as to why it has been refused. In this situation an appeal may be made. The appeal procedures vary in each member state.

General Administrative Procedure: An EC 13th VAT Directive Claim

The reclaim procedure for recovery of VAT by non-EU businesses is similar to that described above for EU businesses. However, some entrepreneurs will not be eligible to recover VAT in certain members states because some member states specifically reject claims where reciprocal arrangements do not exist.

A non-EU claimant should follow all the recovery procedures as noted for 8th Directive claims with one exception: tax authorities will accept a certificate of taxable status as an alternative to a certificate of VAT status. This certificate should provide evidence that the entrepreneur is a taxable person for business purposes in their own country. For example, the appropriate form in the United States is IRS 6166.

6

Federal and International Income Taxation of E-Commerce

James M. Gannon and Jeffrey A. Weiss

The rise of E-commerce as a commercially feasible medium for conducting all sorts of business across national borders raises numerous international tax issues. Cross-border E-commerce can take on many forms and can involve physical products, intangible property, or services. A sampling of cross-border E-commerce activities includes the sale or lease of physical goods through a Web site on the Internet or directly by ordering through a modem, the provision of services on the Internet (brokerage, ticketing, banking, medical and legal consulting, etc.), the cross-border sale and delivery of intangible digital content (music, video, data, or software), the licensing of the rights to access a database (e.g., providing access to on-line information such as a legal database or electronic medical database), the publication and sale of newspapers, magazines, and other media in electronic format for a subscription fee (or for free, where revenue is earned through advertising), Internet telephony, E-mail services or Internet access, global on-line trading in stocks, bonds,

James M. Gannon is a partner in Arthur Andersen's Office of Federal Tax Services in Washington, D.C. Jeffrey A. Weiss is a senior manager in Arthur Andersen's New York City office. Both specialize in international tax services. Jim leads the eBusiness initiative within Arthur Andersen's Tax and Business Advisory Practice in the United States.

commodities, or other securities, and on-line auctions or barter Web sites for which the site acts as an intermediary for a fee.

Numerous other forms of cross-border electronic businesses will likely be developed in the coming years as bandwidth becomes wider and less costly, computer processing speed become faster, and memory becomes less expensive. The existing set of rules in the international tax area is often ambiguous at addressing these new commercial applications.

The following are some of the principal issues that arise in analyzing cross-border E-commerce:

- Do E-commerce activities rise to the level of a taxable presence, providing a jurisdiction with the right to tax the income?
- Should the income from E-commerce activities be characterized as sales income, rental income, royalty income, or services income?
- What is the manner in which E-commerce revenues, however characterized, should be sourced?
- Should the provision of E-mail, Internet telephony or Internet access be characterized as international telecommunications income?

Because an analysis of the cross-border tax implications of E-commerce involves so many areas of tax law, a basic understanding of U.S. federal rules and a comparison with how other jurisdictions tax international income are needed in order to apply these rules to the various cross-border E-commerce activities.

Introduction to Cross-Border Direct Taxation

Tax jurisdictions rely on a few general principles in their income tax systems. For example, some jurisdictions rely on the principle of imputation, which holds that income earned should only be taxed once. This principle usually provides a tax credit on dividend income at the shareholder level for taxes paid by a corporation with respect to the dividend.

The United States does not have an imputation system, instead subjecting corporate earnings to a second level of tax when already-taxed earnings are distributed to shareholders as dividends.[1]

An important exception to this double-taxation rule for corporate income in the U.S. federal taxation system is with respect to foreign income taxes. The Internal Revenue Code of 1986 (IRC), and the provisions thereunder, provides relief from double taxation by allowing a U.S. taxpayer a credit for foreign taxes paid[2] and, in limited circumstances (for corporations) and subject to limitations discussed in this chapter, to foreign taxes deemed paid.[3] As explained later in this chapter, the U.S. rules that have been developed to avoid the double-taxation result in an international context are complex and do not always achieve their stated goals.

A number of other countries use an exemption system to ensure that foreign income is not subject to double tax. To illustrate the difference between the U.S. foreign tax credit system and an exemption system, suppose that a Dutch corporation (BV) had a wholly owned subsidiary in the United Kingdom (LTD) carrying out active business operations. Earnings of LTD would be subject to U.K. tax at the currently enacted 30 percent tax rate. When LTD distributes its after-tax earnings to BV in the Netherlands as a dividend, it will not be subject to a second level of Dutch tax because the Netherlands has a participation exemption system. This system exempts from Dutch tax income earned outside the Netherlands. If BV had no income other than the dividend from LTD, it would pay a 30 percent income tax on its worldwide income (to the United Kingdom).

Contrast this result with the result under the U.S. foreign tax credit system. Suppose that, instead of being owned by BV, LTD is a wholly owned subsidiary of a U.S. corporation (INC). The earnings of LTD are still subject to a 30 percent tax rate in the United Kingdom, and LTD distributes its after-tax earnings to INC. Under the U.S. foreign tax credit system, the dividend from LTD is not exempt from U.S. federal income tax. Instead, the net dividend received is grossed up by the amount of the underlying 30 percent foreign income taxes paid. The grossed-up earnings are then subject to U.S. tax at full U.S. rates (35 percent for most corporations), and a foreign tax credit, subject to numerous limitation provisions, is permitted for the U.K. tax deemed paid with respect to the income distributed. Assuming that INC has no income other than the dividend from LTD, it will be subject to a U.S. tax of 35 percent on the gross earnings distributed by LTD. INC will also be permitted to claim a foreign tax credit for the foreign income tax paid to the United Kingdom with respect to the dividend income, for a net U.S. tax of 5 percent.

In the first scenario, the worldwide income is taxed at a 30 percent rate, whereas in the second scenario, it would be taxed at a 35 percent rate.[4] Often, however, there are additional tax costs involved in cross-border transactions.

Concepts to Be Explored

Important U.S. international tax concepts that are affected and must be analyzed in E-commerce transactions include taxing jurisdiction, withholding tax obligations and administration, character of income, source of income, and the implications on the foreign tax credit.

In general, a certain base level of activity and physical presence is needed in a jurisdiction before the tax authorities will impose an income tax. The criteria that must be met vary depending on the laws of the taxing jurisdiction. This chapter describes the U.S. criteria for a person to be considered engaged in a U.S. trade or business and the unique issues that arise when the activities in question are digital and the physical presence tenuous. It also discusses the differences between these rules and the rules under which a tax treaty definition of *permanent establishment* is applied to determine whether a jurisdiction has the right to tax. Finally, this chapter examines the unique nature of E-commerce and the level of activity it affords without requiring a physical presence in the traditional sense and whether such activities could rise to the level of a taxable presence under domestic law or international tax treaties.

Withholding taxes are often charged to the recipient of payments when the payee is not a resident of the country of the payor. Withholding taxes are charged on a wide range of cross-border payments; a detailed explanation of these rules is discussed later in this chapter. The rates of withholding tax may vary depending on the characterization of a payment and are generally set by the internal laws of each country. In the United States (that is, for payments from U.S. sources to foreign payees), the withholding tax rate on fixed and determinable annual and periodical income is generally 30 percent absent a bilateral tax treaty providing a lower rate. This rate (established under domestic law) can often be reduced or eliminated by application of a double tax treaty.

As discussed later in this chapter, under most U.S. tax treaties, the character of income has a significant bearing on the withholding tax rate applied. The nature of E-commerce is such that it is often difficult to determine the appropriate character of income for a payment. Character of income is also critical to determining the source of the income, which has implications in the foreign tax credit area and in determining the treaty withholding rate to apply.

Numerous definitions of terms such as *resident, nonresident, fixed place of business,* and so on are important in analyzing E-commerce transactions. For example, for purposes of the source rules, an individual whose tax home (principal place of business) is in the United States is treated as a U.S. resident.[5] A U.S. citizen or resident alien is treated as a U.S. resident if he or she does not have a tax home[6] in a foreign country. A nonresident alien with a tax home in the United States will also be considered a U.S. resident.[7]

While the laws of other countries sometimes look to where an entity is managed and controlled in determining residency, U.S. law treats a corporation, partnership, trust, or estate as a U.S. resident if it is organized under the laws of any state or the District of Columbia.

U.S. Treasury White Paper

In November 1996 the U.S. Treasury issued a paper (White Paper) that addresses some of the policy issues and taxation principles that it believes should apply to the area of E-commerce.[8] The paper advocates the position that the taxation of E-commerce should not produce different results than the taxation of other forms of commerce. In this spirit the White Paper rejects the idea of new or additional taxes on E-commerce.

Rather, it states that the existing rules of taxation should be applied to E-commerce so that it is taxed similarly to other forms of commerce. This position is consistent with the general goal of tax policy that one form of a transaction should not produce significantly different tax results than another form of the transaction that is economically identical.[9]

Significant Issues

The White Paper identifies and addresses some of the significant tax issues affecting E-commerce. Those issues include jurisdiction, classification of income, and tax administration. A brief discussion of these issues follows.

Jurisdiction

The significant issues in taxing E-commerce that are identified by the White Paper include determining which country has taxing jurisdiction over the income produced in an E-commerce transaction. The source of income earned and the residence of the taxpayer earning that income are relevant issues in determining the U.S. tax treatment of the income. A person resident in the United States (a domestic corporation, citizen, or resident alien) is subject to U.S. income tax on worldwide income from all sources. A non-U.S. person, on the other hand, is generally only subject to U.S. income tax on income from U.S. sources. An exception to this general rule allows the United States to tax certain foreign source income effectively connected to a U.S. trade or business of the non-U.S. person.[10] Trade or business income must be effectively connected to a U.S. trade or business before the United States may assert taxing jurisdiction.[11] As discussed later in this chapter, there is a minimal level of connection to the United States that is required to establish a U.S. trade or business.

The White Paper states, correctly, that it is difficult to determine the source of income generated from E-commerce using the existing source rules. The U.S. Treasury believes that this failure of source rules will lead to greater emphasis on residence-based taxation for E-commerce. Thus, the income will be treated as though it is economically derived by the taxpayer's activities in its country of residence. Although the U.S. Treasury's analysis is probably accurate, it opens the door for a taxpayer to move income from E-commerce out of the United States and into low-tax or no-tax jurisdictions, assuming the taxpayer is properly treated as a resident of such a jurisdiction. If taxpayers pursue this type of structuring, it will be interesting to see whether the U.S. Treasury continues to believe that existing rules can adequately be applied to E-commerce transactions.

Classification of Income

The classification of income derived in an E-commerce transaction is a major issue affecting the taxation of that income. The U.S. tax law provides rules for the sourcing of several classes of income. Different classes of income are sourced under different rules (as explained in "Source of Income" later in this chapter). Thus, it is important to determine the proper classification of an item of income so that the appropriate sourcing rule may apply. The White Paper notes that, in an E-commerce transaction, it may be difficult to distinguish different classes of income. For example, a transaction may be a provision of services by means of allowing a customer use software. Suppose a customer receives financial-planning services by accessing software on a Web site that projects her financial position under different investment alternatives. Should the income earned by her based on this software-provided service be classified as services income, or is it licensing income? The answer could yield two very different tax results. The U.S. Treasury explains that this difficulty in classifying income from E-commerce transactions makes source-based taxation difficult to apply.

Tax Administration

The nature of E-commerce transactions gives rise to significant potential issues in respect to tax administration and taxpayer compliance. Much of the paper trail used to document conventional transactions is not present in electronic transactions. This absence of paper documentation presents tax administrators with some potentially difficult issues of determining gross income of a taxpayer engaged in E-commerce.

The potential for intentional underreporting of income also is heightened by E-commerce transactions. This is not a new problem— there exists a sizable underground economy in the United States today. However, this economy is generally dependent on cash or barter transactions. These forms of transactions have problems with inefficiencies because of the requirement to transact with large amounts of currency or with the valuation of bartered goods and services. E-commerce brings with it the potential for transactions to be executed using electronic money. The U.S. Treasury notes that traditional enforcement means could be used to determine gross income in the event of a transaction involving electronic money and physical goods (e.g., tracing inventory movements). As the White Paper points out, however, these methods would be ineffective for transactions involving both electronic cash and electronic goods or services.

The White Paper provided a basis for the discussion and analysis of U.S. tax issues arising in E-commerce. It also has influenced the work of the OECD in this area. However, the White Paper was not intended to resolve the issues in this area and many questions on the proper U.S. taxation of E-commerce transactions remain open.

Interaction of Tax Treaties and Statutory Law

The legal status and interrelationship of treaties and statutory law are derived from the U.S. Constitution. Under the Supremacy Clause of the Constitution, both treaties and federal legislation are the supreme law of the land. Both are supreme above administrative rulings and state or local legislation. In addition, under the Constitution both federal legislation and treaties have equal status in the United States, with their interpretation ultimately residing in the courts.

Treaties and legislation dealing with the same subject are essentially construed as two federal statutes in the same area. Common law principles provide that, if any reasonable construction allows two statutes to be interpreted consistently, they should be so interpreted. Only when consistency is impossible should a later statute be construed as repealing an earlier statute and only to the extent of any inconsistency.

Similar principles have been extended to potential conflicts between statutes and treaties. Whenever possible, treaties and legislation covering the same subject are read in a consistent manner. Should a treaty conflict with an earlier statute, the treaty will prevail. Conversely, a statute will generally (but not always) prevail over a prior treaty. Despite this general rule, it is important to remember that the U.S. Supreme Court has held that "the purpose by statute to abrogate a treaty or any designated part of a treaty, or the purpose by treaty to supersede the whole or a part of an act of Congress, must not be lightly assumed, but must appear clearly and distinctly from the words used in the statute or in the treaty."[12]

Provisions found in the Internal Revenue Code (hereinafter referred to as the Code) and various tax treaties operate to limit potential conflicts between tax treaties and the Code. For example, Article 1(2) of the current U.S. Model Income Tax Treaty provides that "The Convention shall not restrict in any manner any exclusion, exemption, deduction, credit or other allowance now or hereafter accorded (a) by the laws of either Contracting State, or (b) by any other agreement between the Contracting States."[13] This provision, which is found in most U.S. treaties in force, eliminates many situations where conflicts may arise. The savings clause contained in most U.S. tax treaties currently in force also reduces the potential for conflict. This clause, with certain exceptions, generally allows the United States to tax its citizens, residents, and corporations as though the treaty had not come into effect. By restricting the impact of the treaties, the potential for conflicts with the Code is also restricted.

In a similar vein, the Technical and Miscellaneous Reconciliation Act of 1988 (TAMRA) amended IRC § 7852(d)(1) to read as follows: "For purposes of determining the relationship between a provision of a treaty and any law of the United States affecting revenue, neither the treaty nor the law shall have preferential status by reason of its being a treaty or a law." By providing that a treaty provision has the same status as a law, the statute implies that the normal later-in-time rule will apply in the case of an inconsistent statute and treaty. The legislative history of IRC § 7852(d)(1) indicates, however, that income tax treaties should be construed harmoniously to the extent possible with U.S. tax laws. Legislative history notes that canons of construction applied by the courts to the interaction of two statutes enacted at different times should apply in construing the interactions of revenue statutes and treaties enacted and entered into at different times.

IRC § 894(a)(1), which was also amended by TAMRA, provides that the income tax provisions should be applied to any taxpayer with due regard to any treaty obligation of the United States that may apply to such taxpayer. IRC § 894(a)(2) then refers to IRC § 7852(d) to determine the relationship between treaties and the Code. Like IRC § 7852(d), the section adds no operative rules to be applied in determining the relationship of the Code (or other tax law) and a treaty. The conference report to TAMRA indicates that the intent of § 894(a) was to state the constitutional principle that determination of relationships is relevant in determining tax liabilities.

Tax treaties are bilateral agreements entered into by the United States with other countries. They apply to both foreign taxpayers of the treaty country doing business in the United States and to U.S. residents doing business in the treaty country. Tax treaties are designed to encourage trade and business contacts, eliminate taxation when contact is minimal and provide fair division of revenue among countries, eliminate or minimize double taxation, eliminate discriminatory tax treatment, enhance tax administration, and establish grievance procedures.

To eliminate or at least minimize instances of double taxation, tax treaties often provide for a tax credit against home-country taxes for income taxes paid to the treaty partner on income sourced outside the home country. Many times the allowance of such a tax credit in the tax treaty is simply a restatement of the foreign tax credit provisions of the country's internal tax law. The provision may modify the law of the country of residence to provide for consistency with the treaty partner's tax law. The significance of the inclusion of the foreign tax credit in a treaty is threefold:

1. It is a negotiating point permitting the U.S. income taxes that are paid by the other country's taxpayers to be credited by that country, thereby reducing the taxpayer's tax cost of operating in the United States.

2. If foreign tax credit provisions are repealed from the Code, the credit could still be taken under treaty provisions in effect on certain dates.
3. Treaties may allow tax payments that would not otherwise be eligible to be eligible for credit against U.S. tax.

As an alternative to the credit method to eliminate double taxation, some tax treaties use an exemption method. Under the exemption method, the country of residence does not tax the income that, according to the tax treaty, may be taxed by the treaty partner. A full exemption may be given where the country of residence will not consider the subject income at all when computing its tax liability. The country of residence may give an exemption with progression, in that it retains the right to take the subject exempt income into consideration when determining the tax rate imposed on the rest of the income.

The credit provisions of the OECD and United Nations Model tax treaties (in each case Article 23B) deal solely with juridical double taxation, whereby the same income is taxable in the hands of the same person by more than one country. The U.S. Model Tax Treaty (Article 23) is broader, in that its credit provision also provides relief from economic double taxation, where two different persons in the same economic unit (i.e., parent and subsidiary corporations) are taxed in respect to the same income.

Tax credit or exemption provisions do not always ensure that a taxpayer will be free from double taxation. Double taxation or taxation inconsistent with the tax treaty will occur when inconsistent positions are taken by the two taxing jurisdictions. For example, double taxation will result when the two countries disagree as to the determination of residence of the person, source of income and related expenses, character of the income (i.e., dividend versus interest versus royalty payments), or proper allocation of income (i.e., issues such as transfer pricing, management fees, arm's-length interest and royalty payments and allocation of business expenses).

Tax treaties provide for a mutual agreement procedure (Article 25) to resolve these disputes. Under this procedure each country designates a competent authority who will endeavor to resolve the double taxation or taxation inconsistent with the tax treaty by mutual agreement with the competent authority of the treaty partner. The mutual agreement procedure does not obligate the treaty partners to eliminate the double taxation. Rather, they are only obligated to endeavor to relieve the incidence of double taxation. Thus, there may still be double taxation in spite of the mutual agreement procedure.

Engaged in a U.S. Trade or Business: The Standard When There Is No Tax Treaty

Where a tax treaty does not provide a specific standard, the U.S. income tax liability of nonresident alien individuals is determined under IRC § 871 through § 877. The type of income subject to tax, allowable deductions, and the rate of tax depend on whether the taxpayer is engaged in a trade or business in the United States. A nonresident alien who is not engaged in a U.S. trade or business is subject to 30 percent withholding on fixed or determinable annual or periodical (FDAP) income from sources within the United States.[14] The tax is collected through withholding under IRC § 1441(a), although a treaty may reduce the rate. A nonresident alien individual engaged in a trade or business within the United States is subject to U.S. tax on effectively connected income at regular U.S. graduated rates.[15] In computing this tax liability, all effectively connected expenses are deductible if a timely tax return is filed.[16]

Similarly, foreign corporations are subject to U.S. tax.[17] A foreign corporation not engaged in a U.S. trade or business is subject to 30 percent withholding tax on U.S.-source fixed or determinable annual or periodical gains, profits, and income.[18] IRC § 882(a) provides that a foreign corporation engaged in a trade or business in the United States is subject to the ordinary U.S. corporate income tax. If a U.S. tax return is filed in a timely manner, the corporation is entitled to offset its gross income by effectively connected deductions.[19]

The law and regulations do not provide an overall definition of the statutory term *trade or business.* IRC § 864(b) merely states that a trade or business includes the performance of personal services. The rules for determining whether other activities constitute a U.S. trade or business have been developed over the years through court decisions and revenue rulings. Consequently, the determination of a foreign person's income that is effectively connected with the conduct of a U.S. trade or business from U.S. sources may be a matter of professional judgment based on facts and circumstances.

The determination of whether a trade or business exists is measured by relatively objective standards. Engaging in considerable, continuous, and regular activity constitutes a trade or business. The passive collection of income does not constitute a U.S. trade or business.[20] Most cases addressing the presence of a U.S. trade or business have continued to apply this standard. To be a U.S. trade or business, such activity must be conducted in the United States.

Is E-commerce a trade or business? Where is a cyberspace transaction conducted?

E-commerce, if it is considerable, continuous, and regular, probably is a trade or business. It is worth remembering, however, that a single transaction generally does not amount to engaging in a U.S. trade or business.[21] Thus, a single purchase of a product from a foreign company executed by visiting the company's Web site should not result in the foreign company being treated as engaged in a trade or business. Although a casual electronic sale may not constitute a U.S. trade or business, a one-time transaction purposely tailored to produce a single, taxable event has been held to constitute a trade or business. For example, a prize fight,[22] recording session,[23] and horse race[24] were each found to constitute a trade or business in the United States.

The size or success of the transaction is not relevant. The amount of income earned, or loss incurred, is generally held to have no substantial bearing on the question of whether a foreign taxpayer is engaged in a U.S. trade or business. A foreign person may be engaged in a U.S. trade or business whether or not its activities show a profit, as long as the trade or business involves an active pursuit and is continuous or regular. Thus, the following activities have been held to constitute a U.S. trade or business by the courts or in Internal Revenue Service (IRS) rulings:

- sales of goods in the United States[25]
- sales in the United States by salespersons[26]
- sales in the United States through an agent[27]
- technical services in connection with sales of goods[28]
- active management of leased U.S. real estate[29]
- management of rental real estate through an agent[30]
- frequent purchases and sales of real estate[31]

The following activities have been held not to constitute a U.S. trade or business in cases or IRS rulings:

- investigation of business opportunities in the United States[32]
- mere ownership of rental real estate[33]
- ownership of real estate subject to a net lease[34]
- isolated sales of real estate[35]
- holding securities for investment[36]
- occasional sales of securities[37]
- fractional working interest in oil and gas lease held via trust[38]

For an example of the effect of these rules on a foreign corporation, suppose a nontreaty country corporation, ACo, manufactures in its home country and sells its finished goods in the United States. ACo would be considered to be engaged in a U.S. trade or business and would be subject to U.S. tax at graduated rates on the U.S.-source portion of its profit (see source discussion later in this chapter at "Source of Income").

Cyberspace is not a fixed location. It is a place where electrons and data mix and interact. Although tax authorities may take the position that this occurs at the site of the server or the Internet service provider (ISP), such a conclusion would be a practical mistake. Servers can be easily moved to a low- or zero-tax jurisdiction. Once connected to the Internet, a server can be physically located anywhere; there is no reason that it needs to be located within the same country as the site's customers. The key factors in determining the level of speed is the quality of the telecommunications link and the number of "hops" between Internet service providers. Thus, a Web server in Bermuda could easily serve a customer in New York, to the detriment of the U.S. fisc.

It is not at all clear whether a server, which is a machine, can be given the authority to conclude a contract and act on that authority. At the heart of this fundamental question is whether a machine can make decisions or whether the decision is really being made by the individuals who program or authorize the computer. No tax authority, as far as is known, has yet made a determination on this issue.

An additional complication exists when determining and agreeing upon where a contract is concluded in cyberspace. When a sales contract is concluded on-line, it is simply not clear where the contract was concluded for tax purposes. The options are to treat the contract as entered into where the seller is located, where the purchaser is located, or perhaps, where the server is located (if acceptance is only subject to certain specified criteria being met, and the steps for meeting these criteria are automated).

A taxpayer can be treated as engaged in a U.S. trade or business through imputation of the activities of another. Although a foreign individual or corporation may not be present in the United States, a U.S. agent's business activity will be attributable to the foreign person or corporation for purposes of determining whether the foreign individual or corporation is engaged in a U.S. trade or business.[39] The amount of the agent's business undertaken for a foreign individual or corporation necessary to create a U.S. trade or business depends on the facts and circumstances.[40]

Because a corporation is not a natural person, it can act only through agents and employees. Thus, the question may be both one of authority of such agents or employees as well as their U.S. activities. Some measure of affirmative corporate activity is necessary to constitute engaging in or conducting a U.S. trade or business.

Could the licensing by a foreign licensor of software, and the use of that software on-line for a fee by users (licensees) located in the United States, constitute a U.S. trade or business?

The idea of using software on-line is a misnomer. Software can only be used in combination with computer hardware. In situations where the software is not downloaded to a machine in the United States and remains in a foreign country, the program is actually run in the foreign country. The U.S. user may be providing instructions from the United States, but the manipulation and interpretation of those instructions, the calculations performed by the software, and the development of the output all take place where the software is physically located on the machine on which it resides. The Internet merely allows a user in the United States to view the results without traveling to the foreign country. While arguably a small portion of the fee is attributable to the delivery of the output, the important functions for which the user paid the fee occurred outside of the United States. Thus, the use of software on-line for a fee should not constitute a U.S. trade or business.

Is there a withholding tax obligation on this royalty payment?

If the software used on-line resides and is run on a computer located outside of the United States, then the software is used where the calculations are performed (i.e., outside of the United States). Royalties for the use of intangibles in the United States are U.S.-source FDAP[41] income subject to a 30 percent withholding tax (which may be reduced by application of a tax treaty[42]). Royalties for the use of intangibles outside of the United States are foreign-source income and are *not* subject to U.S. withholding. Thus, there should be no withholding tax obligation on royalty payments to a foreign person where the royalty is for the use of the foreign person's software on-line.

Could services performed on behalf of a foreign person in the United States by an ISP rise to the level of an agency relationship that gives rise to a taxing presence (engaged in a U.S. trade or business) for the foreign person?

In the typical ISP arrangement, the ISP performs services, such as providing space on its own or a leased server (for a customer's Web site), access to the Internet (to or from that site), and server maintenance. The ISP typically does not have any other rights or responsibilities with respect to its customer and would almost certainly not be acting as an agent for its customers by actively selling or performing other activities that have been held to constitute a U.S. trade or business. Thus, in the typical ISP arrangement, under existing U.S. rules, the use of a U.S.-based ISP would not give rise to a taxing presence (a U.S. trade or business) for a foreign person.

Although the foregoing fact pattern is typical, it is nonetheless possible for a foreign person and an ISP to arrange their relationship in a manner that is different from the typical ISP/customer relationship. For example, if a contractual arrangement between an ISP and a foreign customer provides the ISP with authority to conclude contracts binding on the foreign person, then the activities of the ISP could be enough to cause the foreign person to be engaged in a U.S. trade or business. A similar result could occur if the foreign person engaged the ISP to maintain a stock of merchandise and to fill orders on its behalf, or to otherwise actively engage in a U.S. trade or business on its behalf. The determination of whether an agent creates a U.S. trade or business for its foreign principal is based on all the facts and circumstances of the situation.[43]

Could a Web site be a fixed place of business?

A fixed place of business is a fixed facility—a place, site, structure, or similar facility—through which a foreign person engages in a trade or business. Here are some examples:

- factory
- store
- workshop
- mine, quarry, or other place of extraction of natural resources[44]

Use of another person's office through which to transact a trade or business on a relatively sporadic or infrequent basis, taking into account the overall needs of the trade or business, will not cause the other person's office to be deemed to be the office of a foreign person.

A foreign corporation is not considered to have a fixed place of business merely because a person controlling that corporation has a fixed place of business from which general supervision is exercised. Further, the law of a foreign country is not controlling in determining whether a foreign person has a fixed place of business in the United States.[45] Provided that the foreign corporation has officers outside the United States that conduct the corporation's day-to-day activity, the fact that management decisions affecting the foreign corporation are made in the United States does not in itself result in the foreign corporation having an office in the United States.[46]

In determining whether a foreign person has a fixed place of business in the United States, a dependent agent's fixed place of business is disregarded unless the agent has the authority to negotiate and conclude contracts in the name of the foreign person and regularly exercises that authority. In most situations an ISP will not have this sort of authority, and thus its fixed place of business should be disregarded in determining whether a foreign person contracting with it for technical services has a fixed place of business in the United States.

Alternatively, a foreign person could have a fixed place of business as a result of a dependent agent's fixed place of business if the dependent agent has a stock of merchandise belonging to the foreign person from which orders are regularly filled on behalf of the foreign person.

A Web site, because it does not fall within the existing definitions, is not a fixed place of business (under existing law). While it is entirely possible that some jurisdiction somewhere in the world may be able to develop an argument that a Web site is a fixed place of business, for this conclusion to be reached in the United States, the definition of the term would need to be broadened.

Could the maintenance and operation of a server in the United States by an ISP that stores digital content on behalf of a foreign person be treated as tantamount to the maintenance of a stock of merchandise?

It is unlikely that, absent legislation to this effect, the maintenance and operation of a server in the United States by an ISP that stores digital content on behalf of a foreign person could be treated as tantamount to the maintenance of a stock of merchandise. Intangibles have never been classified in this manner, and the law has not made this type of analogy before. Even if this position is taken, it would be difficult to argue that an ISP is a dependent agent of a foreign person. An independent agent acting in its ordinary course of business will not create a permanent establishment in the United States for a non-U.S. person. However, in the absence of an income tax treaty, the general U.S. income tax rules would look to an agent's activities to determine whether a non-U.S. person has a U.S. trade or business.[47] It is possible that the non-U.S. person could be considered to be engaged in a U.S. trade or business because of its independent agent and subject to U.S. income tax on its U.S.-source income from the trade or business.

An agent is considered to regularly exercise authority to negotiate and conclude contracts or to fill orders on behalf of a foreign principal only if the authority is exercised with some frequency over a continuous period of time. A dependent agent is any agent other than an independent agent.[48]

An independent agent is a commissioned agent, broker, or other agent of independent status acting in the ordinary course of his business. The determination of whether an agent is an independent agent is made without regard to whether either the agent or the principal owns or controls, or is owned or controlled by, the other. The facts and circumstances must be examined to determine whether an agent is acting in the course of his usual trade or business and in a manner to constitute an independent agent. An independent agent is not treated as a fixed place of business of his principal, irrespective of whether the agent has the authority to negotiate and conclude contracts or maintains a stock of goods from which he regularly fills orders.[49] The fact that a foreign person is related to another person who has a fixed place of business in the United States does not in itself mean that the fixed place of business is attributable to the foreign person.[50]

What other legal precedent is there on this topic? Are there any other analogies that could make the sale of physical goods in the United States by a foreign person through a Web site constitute a trade or business in the United States?

In *Piedras Negras Broadcasting Co. v. Comm'r.,* 43 BTA 297 (1941), it was held that income earned from U.S.-based advertisers for broadcasting commercials over the radio from Mexico into the United States was not and could not be from a trade or business in the United States. All of the equipment used for broadcasting in this case was located in Mexico, and the advertisement contracts were all signed and executed in Mexico. While it is certainly true that the Internet is not the same medium as radio, in many ways sales by nonresidents over the Internet are analogous. The taxpayer in this case also made use of the U.S. postal system for collection of advertising revenues. This was not held to be a close enough connection to the United States to establish a U.S. trade or business. A foreign person transmitting data into the United States could draw a similar conclusion from the use of telecommunications lines in the United States.

Permanent Establishment under a Tax Treaty

Most U.S. tax treaties provide a more narrow definition of activities that give rise to the right to tax than is found in U.S. statutory law. Treaty definitions of permanent establishment typically require more activities, or more physical presence, to rise to the level of taxation.

The OECD Model Treaty defines a permanent establishment as "a fixed place of business through which the business of an enterprise is wholly or partly carried on" in Article 5. Under Article 7 of the Model Treaty, the income that is subject to tax in a host country must be attributable to the permanent establishment's economic activities.

A fixed place of business is required for there to be a permanent establishment (PE). The fixed place of business, however, does not always have to be a fixed place of business of the taxpayer. A foreign person could have a PE under the OECD Model Treaty where she has no fixed place of business, if a dependent agent carries out activities in the country on the foreign person's behalf. Also, an independent agent acting outside of its ordinary course of business could create a PE for its principal. To be characterized as a dependent agent, an agent needs to be dependent both legally and economically.

All of the model tax treaties (OECD, U.S., UN) define the term *permanent establishment* (all in Article 5) to mean a "fixed place of business through which the business of an enterprise is wholly or partially carried on." The model tax treaties go on to state that a permanent establishment includes the following:

- a place of management
- a branch
- an office
- a factory
- a workshop
- a mine, oil or gas well, quarry, or any other place of extraction of natural resources

A fixed place of business such as an office, shop, factory, or mine where the nonresident's trade or business is regularly carried on is a permanent establishment. The fixed place of business can be owned or leased, and it need not be large as long as it is located at a fixed place and lasts a reasonably long time. U.S. Treasury Regulation § 1.864-7(c)(7) prescribes rules for determining whether a nonresident has an office or other fixed place of business in the United States for purposes of computing the effectively connected income of the nonresident. These regulations are closely patterned after the PE rules of income tax treaties, and the United States taxing authorities have traditionally used them in making PE determinations under tax treaties where the term is not defined in the treaty.[51]

Under U.S. Treasury Regulation § 1.864-7(b)(2), a fixed place of business may arise if a nonresident uses the office of another person. The regulations state that such use will not give rise to a fixed place of business if the use is relatively sporadic or infrequent. By implication, regular or frequent use of the office of another person will cause the nonresident to be deemed to have its own fixed place of business in the United States. Also, if a partnership has a PE in the United States, its partners will be deemed to have a permanent establishment in the United States as well.[52]

The OECD Model Tax Treaty in Article 5(3) provides that a "building site or construction or installation project constitutes a permanent establishment only if it lasts more than 12 months." The U.S. Model Tax Treaty Article 5(3) also provides for a similar definition of a permanent establishment. It expands the provision, however, to include an installation or drilling rig or ship used for the exploration or exploitation of natural resources, but only if it lasts more than 24 months, a full 12 months more than the OECD Model Tax Treaty.

The United Nations Model Tax Treaty is similar to OECD's, but it shortens the time period of building site and construction projects to six months (Article 5(3)(a)). The United Nations Model Article 5(3)(b) also provides that "the furnishing of services, including consultancy services, by an enterprise through employees or other personnel engaged by the enterprise for such purpose" will constitute a PE to the extent that the activities of "such nature continue within the country for a period or periods aggregating more than six months within a 12-month period."

The U.S. and OECD Model Treaties in Article 5(4) provide the following examples of situations that do *not* constitute a permanent establishment:

- the use of facilities solely for the purpose of storage, display, or delivery of goods or merchandise belonging to the enterprise,
- the maintenance of a stock of goods or merchandise belonging to the enterprise solely for the purpose of storage, display, or delivery,
- the maintenance of a stock of goods or merchandise belonging to the enterprise for solely the purpose of processing by another enterprise,
- the maintenance of a fixed place of business solely for the purpose of purchasing goods or merchandise, or collecting information for the enterprise, and
- the maintenance of a fixed place of business solely for the purpose of carrying on, for the enterprise, any other activity of a preparatory or auxiliary character.

The U.S. and OECD Model Tax Treaties go on to state that the maintenance of a fixed place of business solely for a combination of the above activities will likewise not constitute a permanent establishment.

When a person acting as a dependent agent has the authority to conclude contracts in the name of an enterprise, and habitually exercises on behalf of an enterprise in the host country, such agency relationship will be deemed to be a PE in the host country in respect of any activities that the dependent agent undertakes for the enterprise. Generally, a subsidiary (not acting as a general agent) located in the host country will not constitute a PE of the parent in the host country.[53]

The nonresident may have a PE if it has within the United States an agent, other than an agent of independent status acting in that capacity, that has and regularly exercises the power to conclude contracts binding on the nonresident. The current position of the U.S. Treasury Department is that the contracting authority referred to in the PE provisions of income tax treaties is the authority to conclude contracts "relating to the essential business operations of the enterprise, rather than ancillary activities."[54] The example of an "ancillary activity" given in the Technical Explanation is the conclusion of a service contract in the name of the nonresident for office equipment used in the agent's office.

There are few decided cases dealing with dependent agents as permanent establishments. *Handfield v. Commissioner,* 23 T.C. 633 (1955), held that a U.S. consignment distributor of a Canadian manufacturer was a permanent establishment under the former United States–Canada treaty in force at that time. The treaty provided that an agent who regularly filled orders from a stock of goods was a PE. This provision is not included in most modern treaties, at least those with major trading partners.

Could the sale of physical goods in the United States via the Internet by a nonresident company with no physical presence in the United States result in a permanent establishment?

The Internet has been described as "a spider's web of connections among hundreds of thousands of computers."[55] It works by allowing a user to access data that resides in memory on a network server. The server could be located anywhere, in any jurisdiction that is attached to the Internet. Data does not necessarily follow the same path from provider to user, instead following the best route available, moving at random between interconnecting computer servers.

The Internet provides customers in a location without company representatives or products a close look at the goods being sold with many of the benefits that traditionally could only be obtained from a physical presence. With the improvement in bandwidth and speed in the coming years, an Internet site will no doubt be able to provide customers with substantially more information on a product than could ever have been offered previously without physical presence in the pre-Internet era. In contrast to a paper catalog and phone bank, an Internet site can provide up-to-date product specifications with graphics, updated price lists, and interactive feedback. It can be customized to customer profiles in a way that a paper catalog cannot. Contracts can even be finalized through secure Internet sites.

In most typical cases, absent any physical presence, the sale of products (tangible or digital) to U.S. customers from outside the United States via a Web site will not result in a U.S. permanent establishment under a treaty analysis.

If there is no physical connection to the United States whatsoever (e.g., if the server is located outside the United States), under existing rules the sale of goods through an Internet site would not result in a PE or a U.S. trade or business. The substance of such a transaction is analogous to a sale via catalog or over the telephone and does not rise to the level of a fixed place of business.

If the server (machinery) on which the Web site resides is physically located in the United States, the foreign corporation may have a PE if it uses its own server and operates and maintains it. Where a treaty based on the OECD Model Treaty is in place, an analogy can be made to commentary on the PE article in the OECD Model Treaty (paragraph 10 of the Commentary on Article 5). The commentary discusses activities conducted through automatic equipment, such as gaming and vending machines and the like, and the circumstances in which these activities could create a PE. The commentary concludes: "A permanent establishment does not exist if the enterprise merely sets up the machines and then leases the machines to other enterprises. A permanent establishment may exist, however, if the enterprise that sets up the machines also operates and maintains them for its own account. This also applies if the machines are operated and maintained by an agent dependent on the enterprise."

From a policy perspective, this conclusion does not appear to be an appropriate answer because servers can be moved too easily. One might come to this conclusion based on an analogy to the foregoing model treaty commentary on automatic machinery and gaming, but this is not the typical situation. Rather than owning and maintaining a server in the

United States, most foreign companies that are merely selling in the United States through an Internet site will contract these services from a third party. Those that do operate and maintain their own servers will likely locate them locally, where they have employees.[56]

The alternative for most sellers would be to lease space on a server from a third party such as an ISP. In most cases an ISP will be independent, a service provider that is contracted with and is not integral to the foreign corporation's business, providing a service similar to that of a phone company or delivery service.

To establish its independence under a tax treaty, an agent must be both economically and legally independent.[57] These are facts and circumstances tests. To be economically independent, an agent has to bear an economic risk separate from the principal. The OECD Model Treaty Commentary further provides: "Business risk refers primarily to risk of loss. An independent agent typically bears risk of loss from its own activities. In the absence of other factors that would establish dependence, an agent that shares business risk with the enterprise, or has its own business risk, is economically independent because its business activities are not integrated with those of the principal."

The OECD Model Treaty Commentary explains that a significant factor in determining legal independence is whether an agent operates under a detailed set of instructions or otherwise falls under the comprehensive control of the principal.

An ISP would not be a dependent agent because it may have thousands of customers and is not economically or legally dependent on any particular principal. Thus, even if the ISP were located in the United States it should not rise to the level of a dependent agent and therefore would not result in the establishment of a permanent establishment for a foreign principal.

If the Web site can be accessed to obtain software, music, or some other digital content or if it can be accessed to obtain data, does this analysis change?

A network server or computer hardware, in conjunction with software that provides users with the ability to download digital data (of whatever form, whether software, music, information, or other content) could be viewed as analogous to a warehouse and delivery system. Applying this analogy, if a Web site is used "solely for the purpose of storage, display, or delivery of goods," it would not rise to the level of a PE. If, however, this analogy takes hold and a sale takes place in the United States, then, depending on the circumstances of the sale, a PE may be found to exist. Existing income tax treaties should protect foreign persons from U.S. tax solely because of the presence of a server in the United States that only delivers digital data. The ability of the server software to perform a credit check and approve the sale to a customer, however, in the United States may cross beyond the threshold of auxiliary and preparatory activities and create a PE in the United States.

For a sale to take place in the United States, title to the digital goods, if treated as inventory property, would have to pass within the United States.[58] In general, under the title passage rule, a sale of property is consummated at the time and the place when the rights, title, and interest of the seller in the property are transferred to the buyer. If an electronic contract specifies that title passes outside of the United States, this may be sufficient (under current law) to avoid the establishment of a PE.

Recent Developments: OECD Draft Proposal

On September 29, 1999, the OECD Working Party No. 1 on Tax Conventions and Related Questions released a draft clarifying Article 5 (the permanent establishment article) of the OECD Model Tax Convention in the context of electronic commerce. The draft paragraphs were intended to clarify the existing commentary and did not address the broader issue of whether changes should be made to the definition of PE or whether the concept itself should be abandoned. The draft paragraphs also did not address the amount of income that should be attributed to E-commerce operations carried out through computer equipment when a PE is found to exist. In addition, no decision was made about where these draft paragraphs should be inserted in the Commentary on Article 5.

The working party draft paragraphs reflect the majority views expressed during a first discussion and are not the official view of the OECD or of any of the OECD member countries.

The first issue in the draft paragraphs was the working party's majority opinion that a distinction should be made between computer equipment, which could constitute a PE, and the data and software used by that equipment. The distinction was viewed as important because an enterprise that operates a server on which a Web site is hosted is often different from the enterprise that carries on business through that Web site. Unless the server itself is deemed to be a fixed place of business of an enterprise, the mere operation of a Web site of an enterprise from a server located in a country cannot constitute a PE of that enterprise in that country.

The second issue that the working party clarified was that it is not relevant whether the equipment used for E-commerce operations in a particular country is or is not operated and maintained by personnel who are residents of that country or visit that country for that purpose because automated equipment that does not require on-site human intervention for its operation may still constitute a PE.

The third issue clarified in the draft was that computer equipment may only constitute a PE if it meets the requirement of being fixed. What matters, according to the working party, is not the possibility of a server being moved, but whether it is in fact so moved. Under this view, in order to constitute a fixed place of business, a server needs to be located at a certain place for a sufficient period of time so as to become fixed within the meaning of paragraph 1 of Article 5.

The fourth issue addressed was a clarification that a PE will generally not be applicable to ISPs as a result of their activities in hosting a Web site of other enterprises on their own servers. While the draft states that this could be the case in very unusual circumstances, it clarifies that paragraph 5 will generally not be applicable because ISPs will not constitute agents of the enterprises to which the Web sites belong. The reason for this conclusion is either that ISPs will not have authority to conclude contracts in the name of these enterprises and will not regularly conclude such contracts or that ISPs will constitute independent agents acting in the ordinary course of their business, as evidenced by the fact that they host the Web sites of many different enterprises. The draft would also clarify that, because the Web site through which an enterprise carries on its business is not itself a "person" as defined in Article 3, paragraph 5 cannot apply to deem a PE to exist by virtue of the Web site being an agent of the enterprise for purposes of that paragraph.

The final issue addressed in the draft clarifies that no PE may be considered to exist where the E-commerce operations carried on through computer equipment located in a country are restricted to the preparatory or auxiliary activities covered by paragraph 4. The draft states that the question of whether particular activities performed through computer equipment fall within paragraph 4 needs to be examined on a case-by-case basis.

Transfer-Pricing Issues

Prior to the 1980s, most of the government's attention directed toward international transactions was focused on U.S. taxpayers doing business abroad. Before the mid 1970s, U.S. investment abroad was clearly more significant than foreign investment in the United States. As foreign investment grew, so did the focus of tax policy makers and administrators. Thus, with 1980 came the Foreign Investment in Real Property Tax Act; 1982 saw § 6038A of the Code and other provisions, and 1986, 1987, 1989, and 1990 brought additional legislation focused on inbound investment.

Section 6038A was added to the Code in 1982 to place reporting requirements for foreign-controlled companies on par with U.S. companies controlled by U.S. persons. Until this time a U.S. subsidiary did not have to separately identify and report transactions with its foreign parent.

Under § 6038A, as originally enacted, only those U.S. companies and foreign companies engaged in a U.S. trade or business that was foreign controlled (i.e., 50 percent or more of combined voting power or total value of shares was owned by a foreign person) were required to comply with the reporting requirements. As foreign investment grew, so did the rules applying to foreign-based multinationals.

Accordingly, the Tax Reform Act of 1986 expanded the types of transactions reported under § 6038A to cover transactions with each foreign person that qualified as a related party. The definition of related party was expanded to include any person that is related to the reporting corporation under § 267(b) or § 707(b)(1) and any other person who is related (within the meaning of § 482) to the reporting corporation.[59]

Between 1986 and 1990, concern that foreign multinationals were not paying their full share of U.S. tax became more public. Numerous articles and IRS reports alleged that foreign multinationals were manipulating fees charged to their U.S. subsidiaries to artificially reduce their income subject to U.S. tax.[60] Congress responded by making substantial changes to § 6038A. The Revenue Reconciliation Act of 1989 significantly expanded the number of corporations required to report related-party transactions by lowering the threshold for reporting corporations to include companies that were at least 25 percent owned by one foreign shareholder.[61] It also expanded the scope of related-party transactions to be reported to include transactions with any 25 percent shareholder and transactions with a party related to a 25 percent shareholder.[62] These changes brought a whole new group of companies, foreign-related parties, and transactions under IRS scrutiny.

The Revenue Reconciliation Act of 1989 also addressed some of the historic problems the IRS has had obtaining information to examine transactions involving foreign-related parties. Under the 1989 act, reporting corporations were required to maintain such records as the IRS prescribes that are related to transactions executed with related parties.[63] The 1989 act also provided that each foreign-related person must designate the reporting corporation as its agent for purposes of service of process in the United States.[64]

The Revenue Reconciliation Act of 1990 extended the enforcement provisions added by the 1989 act to all open years. The IRS can apply these sanctions in connection with requests for information, records, and testimony for taxable years beginning before July 10, 1989. Furthermore, foreign corporations with U.S. branches are subject to the same requirements and sanctions as contained in § 6038A. In addition, § 6038C allows the U.S. Treasury to prescribe in regulations the records that must be retained relating to any item on the foreign corporation's U.S. tax return, not just to transactions with related parties.[65]

A related party is any direct or indirect 25 percent foreign shareholder, or any person who is related within the meaning of § 267(b) and § 707(b)(1) to the reporting corporation or related to a 25 percent foreign shareholder of the reporting corporation. In addition, a related person includes any other person related to the reporting corporation under § 482.[66] Any entity that is controlled by the same interests that controlled the reporting company would be considered to be a related party for purposes of § 6038A. The § 482 regulations specify that the term *controlled* includes "any kind of control, direct or indirect, whether legally enforceable, and however exercisable or exercised. It is the reality of the control which is decisive, not its form or the mode of its exercise."[67]

The largest commercial growth in E-commerce has been the impact the Internet and intranets have had on the internal functioning of businesses. Inventory controls are maintained on-line, and automated ordering systems used by one business unit or a related entity to order parts or materials from another related entity are becoming the norm in many industries. The use of the Internet in this way adds efficiencies and helps fuel global economic growth by cutting costs. It also reduces the amount of paper, which means that the ability of tax authorities to monitor related-party activities and ensure that the arm's-length standard is adhered to can be compromised by the growth of E-commerce. Tax authorities are likely to feel challenged by the practical impact of this growth.

Essentially, the growth of the Internet is making existing pricing problems more difficult by making it harder for tax administrations to identify, trace, and quantify cross-border transactions. Potential problems include the following:

- Tax administrations will have to evaluate the effects of intangibles more often.
- The lack of reliable data will make the transactional approach and the establishment of comparability more difficult.
- Transactions that occurred between associated parties may be more difficult to identify.
- There may be increased difficulties with valuing the contributions of related parties or parts of the same entity where businesses become highly integrated.

- There may be an increasing number of cases highlighting the differing tax treatment between PEs and subsidiaries carrying on economically similar activities.

According to Michael Durst, former director of the IRS's Advanced Pricing Agreement (APA) program, transactions classified as E-commerce could be good candidates for APAs. Because goods and services sold through an electronic medium, for example, the Internet, cross many borders, and the transactions are faster and more complex than in conventional commerce, taxpayers face the risk of double taxation. E-commerce involves activities that take place in a form in which a wide geographic area may be covered. E-commerce APAs might be similar to those negotiated for global trading of financial products, according to Durst.[68]

The Foreign Tax Credit

Since the enactment of the U.S. income tax law, deductions or credits have been allowed for foreign income taxes. Initially, taxpayers were granted a deduction for taxes paid to foreign countries.[69] In 1918 the first predecessor to the present foreign tax credit was enacted to allow taxpayers to credit foreign "income, war profits, and excess profits taxes" instead of deducting such taxes.[70]

The foreign tax credit is based on the following principles:

- The same income should not be taxed more than once.
- The country in which income is earned has the primary right to tax the income.
- The taxpayer's country of residence has a secondary or residual right to tax income earned in a foreign country.

Most foreign countries impose taxes based on the source of income or on the taxpayer's residence or citizenship. Thus, income received from non-U.S. sources will often be taxed by the local jurisdiction. The foreign tax credit is the principal mechanism under U.S. law for mitigating this potential for double taxation.

The foreign tax credit is intended to result in a worldwide effective tax rate on foreign source income equal to the higher of the U.S. rate or the foreign rate. Where the foreign tax rate exceeds the U.S. tax rate, the credit functions to offset only the U.S. tax on the foreign income, making the effective tax rate on foreign source income equal to the foreign tax rate. If the foreign tax rate is less than the U.S. tax rate, the foreign tax credit functions to create neutrality between foreign and domestic investments. This neutrality is achieved by reducing the U.S. tax burden by the total amount of foreign taxes paid or accrued so that there is no additional income tax associated with the foreign investment. In this case the residual tax, equal to the difference between the U.S. tax rate and the foreign tax rate, is paid to the United States.

In addition to the direct tax credit granted to eligible taxpayers, an indirect credit reduces the potential double taxation on dividends from foreign corporations distributed to U.S. corporate shareholders. The availability of the indirect credit is limited to domestic corporations that own 10 percent or more of a foreign corporation when a dividend is received.[71] The U.S. shareholder is deemed to have paid a proportion of the foreign taxes paid or accrued by the foreign corporation in relation to its earnings and profits.

The United States permits a taxpayer to offset foreign income taxes against its U.S. income tax liability, except for certain taxes. This offset is limited to the amount of U.S. tax imposed on foreign source income.[72] By claiming a credit, as opposed to a deduction, for foreign taxes, the U.S. tax on foreign source income is reduced to the extent such income has already been subject to a foreign income tax. The foreign tax credit is allowed against individual and corporate income taxes imposed by chapter 1 of the IRC. The foreign tax credit is not allowed against certain chapter 1 taxes specifically excluded and other taxes enumerated in § 26(b).[73] Thus, the foreign tax credit may not be applied against estate and gift taxes,[74] withholding taxes on amounts paid to nonresident aliens and foreign corporations,[75] employment and self-employment taxes,[76] or excise taxes.[77]

The direct foreign tax credit refers to the credit allowed to a taxpayer for foreign taxes for which the taxpayer is directly liable. Generally, only U.S. citizens and residents and domestic corporations are eligible for the direct credit. Nonresident aliens and foreign corporations are allowed a direct credit for foreign taxes that relate to income effectively connected with the conduct of a U.S. trade or business. In determining who is eligible to claim a direct credit, the focus is on legal liability.

The direct foreign tax credit is relatively simple in its application. The basic theory is that the taxpayer may claim a credit for the foreign taxes for which that taxpayer is directly liable.[78] Typical examples of direct foreign taxes include withholding taxes imposed on interest or dividends received from a foreign person and foreign taxes imposed on income earned by a U.S. company directly through a foreign branch.

There are two issues of concern in analyzing the direct foreign tax credit. The first is whether the taxpayer in question is eligible for the foreign tax credit. There is a broad range of eligible taxpayers that generally are not restricted in their use of the foreign tax credit. However, the particular category of eligibility into which the taxpayer is placed can limit the credit to the taxpayer's allocable share of taxes paid.[79] The second issue is whether the taxpayer is directly liable for the taxes paid. Only the taxpayer on whom the foreign law imposes legal liability for the tax may claim a credit, regardless of the actual source of any remittance.[80]

The indirect foreign tax credit is available to a corporation for a proportionate amount of the taxes paid by a foreign corporation upon the receipt of a dividend from such foreign corporation. The indirect credit extends to foreign taxes imposed on income included in the gross income of a U.S. shareholder under Subpart F and on the portion of a gain that is taxed as dividend income under § 1248 upon the sale of stock in a controlled foreign corporation.[81]

The basic concept of the indirect credit of § 902 is to permit a credit for foreign taxes imposed on foreign subsidiaries. These taxes are deemed paid by the U.S. corporate shareholder upon the receipt of a dividend distribution from a first-, second-, or third-tier subsidiary, provided the requisite ownership threshold is present, and from fourth, fifth, or sixth-tier subsidiaries that are controlled foreign corporations (CFCs). Note that a foreign corporate shareholder may also claim the indirect credit to the extent such foreign corporation has foreign source income effectively connected with a U.S. trade or business.[82]

The purpose of the indirect credit is to provide symmetrical treatment between a foreign branch operation and a foreign subsidiary operation.[83] That is, the indirect credit works to equate the U.S. tax cost imposed on domestic corporations operating abroad through foreign subsidiaries to the U.S. tax burden of domestic corporations with foreign branches. Absent the indirect-credit provisions, a domestic corporation with foreign subsidiaries would receive, in effect, a deduction (rather than a credit) for foreign income taxes paid by those subsidiaries.

Unlike the direct foreign tax credit whereby the foreign taxes are imposed directly on the U.S. taxpayer, the indirect credit applies to the foreign income taxes attributable to the earnings of a foreign corporation. The recipient is deemed to have paid a proportionate share of the taxes paid by the foreign corporation upon the receipt of a dividend.[84] First-tier foreign corporations and second-tier foreign corporations are deemed to have paid the foreign taxes of second- and third-tier foreign corporations, and fourth- and fifth-tier CFCs are deemed to have paid the foreign taxes of fifth- and sixth-tier CFCs, respectively, upon the receipt of a dividend.[85]

Classification of Income

The U.S. taxation of income earned from sources outside the United States, or by non–United States persons from sources within the United States, is dependent on the classification of that income.

Sales versus Rental Income

U.S. tax law looks to the substance of a transaction to determine whether the income is from a sale of an asset or from the rental of that asset. The form of an agreement will not control its U.S. tax treatment. Rather, the characterization of the agreement will depend "upon the intent of the parties as evidenced by the provisions of the agreement, read in the light of the facts and circumstances existing at the time the agreement was executed."[86] Significant facts that would indicate the existence of a sales transaction, rather than a lease, include the following:

- There is transfer of legal title in the subject property from the lessor to the lessee after the required payments are made.
- The level of the rental payments required is substantially similar to the amount that would have to be paid to acquire the subject property.
- The required rental payments substantially exceed the current rental value of the property.
- The lessee has a purchase option with respect to the subject property (or the right to continue using it) that is substantially less than the fair-market value of the property at the time of exercise.
- Some portion of the rental payments is stated to be interest or is substantially equivalent to interest.

Absent other information to the contrary, a sales transaction will be presumed if all required payments under the agreement, including any option to purchase the property, approximates the price that would be required to purchase the property, plus an interest or time value of money factor.[87]

U.S.-source rental income will be subject to gross taxation of 30 percent in the absence of a U.S. trade or business to which the income is attributable.[88] U.S.-source sales income is subject to net basis taxation (gross income less deductions) only to the extent that income is attributable to a U.S. trade or business.[89] Thus, classification of income under transactions similar in form may have a substantial effect on the U.S. taxation of that income.

Sales versus Royalty Income

Much of U.S. tax law in the area of intangible assets was built around the proper tax treatment for transfers of patents. There is a body of court cases addressing sales versus licenses of patents that is substantial. The body of law surrounding other intangibles is less developed. Thus, the principles established for patents have been extended to other intangible assets.

The transfer of all substantial rights in intangible property is a requirement of a sales transaction.[90] Whether all substantial rights in intangible property have been transferred is dependent on all the facts and circumstances. All substantial rights are measured by reference to what the transferor retains, not what it transferred.[91] The same right may be substantial in one case, such that failure to transfer it would preclude sale treatment, and insubstantial in another case. Rights that have been considered substantial include:

- the right to exclude the use of the asset by others,[92]
- the right to a limited geographical use of a patent within the jurisdiction of the approval,[93]
- the transfer for less than the economic life of the intangible asset,[94]
- the right to prevent unauthorized disclosure of the protected property,[95] and
- the right to terminate the agreement at the will of the transferor.[96]

The retention of legal title to a patent to secure performance or payment is not considered a substantial right.[97] Also, the retention of any right not inconsistent with a transfer of ownership in the intangible will not preclude a transfer from being treated as a sales transaction.[98]

The form of payment made for an intangible asset will not be determinative of the classification of the resultant income.[99] However, the form of the consideration will be relevant in determining the source of the income for U.S. tax purposes. The sale of an intangible asset will result in the gross income being sourced similar to royalty income if the payments are contingent upon the use or productivity of the subject intangible asset.[100] This rule stands in contrast to the general rule that sales income is sourced by reference to the residence of the seller.[101]

Services versus Rental Income

In 1984 Congress added § 7701(e) to the Code. The purpose of this section is to establish when income should be treated as rental, as opposed to service, income. The section permits the secretary of the treasury to issue regulations under this section, but no such regulations have been issued. The committee reports to the Deficit Reduction Act of 1984 require that all relevant factors be taken into account in classifying the income. Relevant factors include the following:

- whether the service recipient is in physical possession of the property;
- whether the service recipient is in control of the property;
- whether the contract conveys a significant economic or possessory interest to the service recipient,
- whether the service provider has a substantial risk of lowered profits due to its nonperformance of the services,
- whether the service provider uses the property at the same time to provide services to persons who are not related to the service recipient, and
- whether the total contract price substantially exceeds the rental value of the property.[102]

The presence of these factors would indicate that the arrangement gives rise to income from the leasing of property rather than from the provision of services. While electronic transactions would rarely involve the use of tangible personal property, the question arises whether similar principles could be applied to intangible property. For example, in a case where services are provided over the Internet and such services involve the use of the software of the service provider, the issue is whether the income of the service provider could be classified as royalty income, in part, rather than services income, if the factors noted above were present in the transaction. The United States accords very different tax treatment to services performed outside the United States as compared to royalties for the use of intangible property within the United States. The former is not subject to U.S. tax, whereas the latter is subject to gross basis taxation of 30 percent. The IRS has not attempted to use § 7701(e) principles to treat a service contract as a license of intangible property.

The use of traditional rules for the classification of income is difficult in the area of E-commerce. Some people look to the final regulations addressing the sourcing of software income as a model of the rules that could be applied to E-commerce.

Final Software Regulations

On October 2, 1998, final regulations were published that provide rules for classifying transactions involving computer software.[103] While the regulations are important to software companies, they also have general application. The rules apply to characterize income earned by any person transferring software, whether that person developed the software or purchased the software from a third party and then transferred it to another person.

Many commentators expressed the wish that the software source regulations be expanded in scope to cover other electronic and digitized property. The regulations are based on a consistent analysis of software-related transactions that could well apply to transactions in E-commerce. The U.S. Treasury considered these comments before issuing the final software regulations. In the end, however, it stated that additional guidance would be forthcoming. It is possible that the software source regulations could form the basis for rules addressing the proper source of income derived from transactions in E-commerce.

The software regulations[104] provide rules concerning the characterization of income derived from transactions relating to computer programs. In general, the regulations are effective for transactions occurring pursuant to contracts entered into on or after December 1, 1998. The regulations define a computer program as a series of statements or instructions to be used directly or indirectly on a computer in order to bring about a certain result. A computer program was defined to include any media, user manual, documentation, database, or similar item if it is incidental to the operation of the computer program.

Under the regulations[105] a transaction involving the transfer of a computer program is classified as one of the following:

1. Transfer of a copyright right.
2. Transfer of a copy of the computer program (a copyrighted article).
3. Provision of services relating to the development or modification of a computer program.
4. Provision of know-how relating to computer programming techniques.

The regulations envision that software transactions will generally fall solely into one of these four categories. If a transaction falls into more than one of the categories, then each portion of the transaction is treated as a separate transaction. Any portion of a transaction that is *de minimis* will not be treated as a separate transaction.

A transfer of a computer program is treated as a transfer of a copyright right if a person acquires one or more of the following rights with respect to the transfer:

- the right to make copies of the program for distribution to the public by sale, lease or license,
- the right to prepare derivative computer programs based on the copyrighted computer program,
- the right to make a public performance of the computer program, and/or
- the right to publicly display the computer program.

With respect to the right to make copies for distribution to the public, the final regulations provide that the public does not include a related person or certain persons identified by name or legal relationship to the original transferee.[106]

If a person acquires a computer program but does not acquire any of the copyright rights listed above, and the transaction does not involve provision of more than *de minimis* services or know-how, the transfer is characterized as a transfer of a copyrighted article. The copyrighted article is a copy of a computer program from which the work can be perceived, reproduced, or otherwise communicated. It may be fixed in a magnetic medium, in the main memory or hard drive of a computer, or in any other medium.[107]

The determination of whether a transaction involving the creation or modification of software is a provision of services is based on the facts and circumstances in each case. Factors to be considered are the intent of the parties (evidenced by agreements and contracts) as to which party is to own the intangibles created and the manner in which risk of loss is allocated between the parties. If the developer of the software is not treated as owning rights in what is produced and incurs little or no risk of loss with respect to the development of the software, the regulations treat the developer as receiving services income.[108]

Provision of information with respect to a computer program will not be treated as the provision of know-how for purposes of these rules unless the information is:

- related to programming techniques,
- furnished under conditions preventing unauthorized disclosure that is specifically contracted for between the parties, or
- subject to trade-secret protection.[109]

After classifying software transactions into the foregoing four categories, the related income is further classified to determine characterization and treatment for tax purposes.

The regulations treat the transfer of a copyright right related to software as a sale if, taking into account all facts and circumstances, there has been a transfer of all substantial rights in the copyright. A transaction that is not a transfer of all substantial rights is classified as a license that generates royalty income. This standard requires an analysis of the rights being transferred, taking into account the term of those rights compared to the useful life of the intangible, as well as restrictions on the use and sublicense of the intangible.[110]

A similar analysis is necessary with respect to the treatment of a transfer of a copyrighted article to determine if the transfer is characterized as a sale or a lease that generates rental income. If, taking into account all facts and circumstances, the benefits and burdens of ownership of the copyrighted article have been transferred, the transaction is taxable as a sale. Conversely, if such benefits and burdens are not transferred, the transaction is taxable as a lease.[111]

In analyzing transactions as a sale versus license or sale versus lease, the regulations specify that consideration must be given to the special characteristics of computer programs in transactions that take advantage of those characteristics, such as the ability to duplicate software at a minimal cost. A software transfer in which a person acquires a copy of a computer program on a disk subject to a requirement that the disk be destroyed after a specified period is generally the equivalent of a transaction that requires that the disk be returned after such period. Similarly, a transaction in which a program deactivates itself after a specified period is generally the equivalent of returning the copy. These considerations are relevant in characterizing the length of the term during which the right to use the software is transferred.[112]

In characterizing transfers of computer programs, neither the form adopted by the parties to a transaction nor the classification of the income under copyright law is determinative. Thus, a transfer of software for a onetime payment with restrictions on transfer and reverse engineering may be classified as the sale of a copyrighted article even if the parties characterize it as a license (a shrink-wrap license).[113]

The regulations specify that the classification of a transaction is applied using the principles described previously, irrespective of the physical or electronic medium used to effectuate a transfer of a computer program.[114]

The source of software income affects both U.S. and non-U.S. transferors of software. A U.S. transferor's foreign tax credit limitation is based on the amount of its foreign-source income derived in various categories. A non-U.S. person that transfers software to a U.S. customer may have withholding tax imposed on U.S.-source royalty income.

Once the classification of income from a computer software transaction has been determined, the final regulations provide the following source rules for each category of transaction. The source of income from the license of a copyright right or the lease of a copyrighted article is determined based on the location of the property. Income from the sale of a copyrighted article that was purchased by the seller and is considered inventory in the hands of the seller is sourced where the sale takes place.

The source of income from the sale of a copyrighted article that was manufactured by the seller and is considered inventory in the hands of the seller is allocated between the place of manufacture and the place of sale. The source of income from the sale of a copyrighted article that is not considered inventory in the hands of the seller or the sale of a copyright right is determined based on the residence of the seller. While not specifically provided in the final regulations, income from the provision of services is generally sourced based on where the services are performed. In addition, the source of income from the provision of know-how is generally determined based on the location of the intangible property.

The regulations do not expressly address the application of the characterization rules in the context of qualifying certain software transactions as a sale or lease of export property for purposes of obtaining foreign sales corporation (FSC) benefits. Nevertheless, this characterization regulation would apply in determining whether property is export property under § 927. Under these provisions a sale or lease of a copyrighted article (including mass-marketed computer software), if not accompanied by a right to external reproduction, is export property, subject to other FSC requirements.[115] The regulations characterize certain income as a sale of a copyrighted article, even in cases whereby the software is distributed by an electronic medium. Site licenses with certain restrictions on reproduction and usage may also qualify as a sale or lease of a copyrighted article.[116] The regulation thus appears to allow the treatment of these transactions as transfers of a copyrighted article for FSC purposes.

The treatment of income earned by a CFC under the Subpart F provisions could be altered significantly depending on the character of the income. For example, if a transfer of software by a CFC is treated as a sale of property, the transaction must be analyzed under the foreign base company sales income provisions of § 954(d) and the foreign personal holding company provisions of § 954(c). If the transfer is characterized as a license, the transaction must be reviewed under the foreign personal holding company provisions of § 954(c).

Both of these provisions provide exceptions to Subpart F income (i.e., the foreign base company sales income exception for property subject to manufacturing or substantial transformation and the foreign personal holding company income exception for rents and royalties derived from the active conduct of a business). The exceptions only apply, however, if the CFC satisfies specific criteria related to the particular transaction. The character of the software income is critical to determine which exception to Subpart F income applies and whether the requirements of the exception are met.

The interaction of the regulations and income tax treaties must also be analyzed. Generally, terms not defined in a treaty take their meaning from the internal law of the country imposing the tax. The preamble to the final regulations specifically states that the regulations are intended to apply for purposes of applying and interpreting U.S. tax treaties. Therefore, the treatment of an item of software income may be different under an income tax treaty depending on whether the income is characterized as a sale, lease, license, provision of services, or provision of know-how (see figure 6.1).

Figure 6.1. **Computer Software Transactions: Illustration of Source Rules in Treasury Regulations Section 1.861-18**

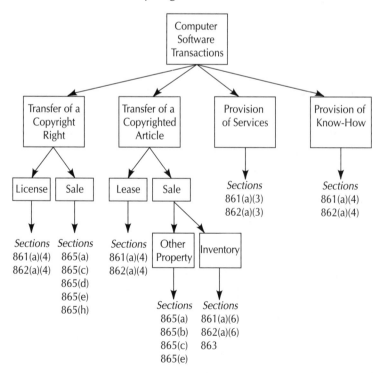

The final regulations have 18 very useful examples of their more general principles. Table 6.1 summarizes these examples.

Source of Income

Determination of the source of income, U.S. or foreign, is critical in deciding the U.S. tax consequences of international transactions. The United States taxes the worldwide income of U.S. citizens (wherever resident), U.S. corporations, and aliens resident in the United States. Relief, via the foreign tax credit, is provided for foreign taxes paid with respect to foreign source income on which U.S. tax is imposed.

Aliens not resident in the United States and foreign corporations are generally taxed on income derived from U.S. sources whether or not connected with the active conduct of a U.S. trade or business. Foreign-source income of nonresident aliens is generally not subject to U.S. tax.

The amount of credit allowed for foreign taxes paid is limited to the U.S. tax due on foreign source taxable income.[117] The amount of the foreign tax credit is limited to the lesser of:

- foreign taxes paid or accrued (plus, in the case of corporate taxpayers, those foreign taxes deemed-paid during the year under § 902), plus any excess credits from other years which are available for credit during the year; or
- section 904(a) limitation:

$$\frac{\text{Foreign-source taxable income}}{\text{Worldwide taxable income}} \times \frac{\text{U.S. tax on worldwide}}{\text{taxable income}} = \frac{\text{Maximum credit}}{\text{for all foreign taxes}}$$

Foreign taxes and foreign-source income are grouped by basket (i.e., active, passive, etc.). The § 904 limitation is applied on a basket-by-basket basis. For U.S. taxpayers the foreign tax credit can be maximized by increasing the amount of income that is treated as foreign source and by decreasing the amount of deductions that must be apportioned to foreign-source income. However, such planning must consider the § 904 limitation as applied to baskets of income.

Table 6.1. **Computer Software Transactions: Summary of Examples in Treasury Regulation Section 1.861-18**

	Transaction	Character of Transaction	Sale/License/ Lease/Service/ Know-How
Example 1	*Shrink-wrap.* Transferee receives shrink-wrap license; perpetual; no reverse engineering; license for use on two computers, but only one at a time; backup copy; ability to sell, but must destroy copies.	Copyrighted article	Sale
Example 2	*Web distribution.* Same as Example 1 except distribution on Web in exchange for a fee; downloaded by transferee; backup copy may be made.	Copyrighted article	Sale
Example 3	*One-week term.* Same as Example 1 but transferee must return program within one week and destroy copies; same result if transferee is required to destroy all copies after one week.	Copyrighted article	Lease
Example 4	*Web distribution with one-week lockup.* Same as Example 2 except at the end of one week, program can no longer be accessed.	Copyrighted article	Lease
Example 5	*Exclusive license to copy and distribute.* Exclusive license for remaining term of the copyright to copy and distribute unlimited copies in a specific country, prepare derivative works, make public performances, and publicly display the program; annual royalty for period the program has commercially exploitable value.	Copyright right	Sale
Example 6	*Nonexclusive license.* Nonexclusive license to reproduce (either directly or through a subcontractor) and distribute in exchange for payment related to number of disks copied and sold; term is less than life of the copyright.	Copyright right	License
Example 7	*Box-top distributor buys/sells disks.* Distributor buys and sells box-top disks covered by shrink-wrap licenses.	Copyrighted article	Sale

Table 6.1. **Continued**

	Transaction	Character of Transaction	Sale/License/Lease/Service/Know-How
Example 8	*Original equipment manufacturer.* Transfer disk to computer manufacturer with nonexclusive right to copy program on hard drive and distribute; term is two years, which is less than the remaining life of the copyright; payment based on number of copies loaded.	Copyright right	License
Example 9	*Shrink-wrap sales to OEM.* Disks are shipped in boxes covered by a shrink-wrap license; loaded on computer; disk transferred with computer; no right to reproduce the software.	Copyrighted article	Sale
Example 10	*Site license.* Transfer of disk with right to load on 50 workstations; internal usage at one location; one-time per-user fee; prohibited from selling disk or any copies; no reverse engineering; perpetual term.	Copyrighted article	Sale
Example 11	*Local area network.* Same as Example 10 except used on a local area network for internal use; one-time fee; transferee is prohibited from selling disk or any copies or reverse engineering; perpetual term.	Copyrighted article	Sale
Example 12	*Renewable monthly term with upgrades; software must be returned on termination.* Same as Example 11, except a monthly fee calculated by reference to the permitted number of users; right to upgrades; agreement may be terminated by either party monthly; if terminated, transferee must return disk and destroy or delete copies; no option to purchase language in agreement; transferor required to provide technical support; monthly fee is not allocated between support and right to upgrades; support expected to be *de minimis.*	Copyrighted article	Lease

Example 13	*Renewable monthly term with upgrades; right to retain latest version on termination.* Same as Example 12 except if agreement terminates, the transferee retains its latest version; no right to sell or transfer a copy.	Copyrighted article	Sale
Example 14	*Site license subject to program modification.* Acquire one copy to be used on 5,000 workstations; transferor agrees to rewrite program to conform to local accounting standards; *de minimis* services needed to rewrite; otherwise, same as site license in Example 10.	Copyrighted article (services are *de minimis*)	Sale
Example 15	*License agreement to create new program.* License agreement for a transferor to write a new program; instructions given by transferee; terminable on a monthly basis; transferor retains payments upon termination; transferee retains rights in any property created; no continuing relationship after completing initial product.	Service	Service
Example 16	*Transfer of noncopyrighted intangibles.* Engineer provides know-how not generally known to computer programmers to more efficiently create computer programs; not copyrightable; trade-secret protection.	Know-how	Provision of know-how
Example 17	*Transfer of development program.* Transfer of disk containing a development program; single fixed payment; development program is used to create other programs; includes libraries of reusable software that serve as general building blocks; libraries can be distributed with programs created with them.	Copyrighted article (copyright rights are *de minimis*)	Sale
Example 18	*Transfer of source and object code.* Transfer of disk containing program's source and object code; license grants right to modify minor errors, make minor adaptations, and recompile modified code; no right to distribute modified code to the public.	Copyrighted article (copyright rights are *de minimis*)	Sale

481

The U.S. income tax liability for nonresident aliens and foreign corporations that is earned in connection with a U.S. trade or business is in general determined based on U.S.-source taxable income.[118] Other U.S.-source income (i.e., not effectively connected) received by a nonresident alien or foreign corporation may be subject to U.S. withholding tax.[119] U.S. withholding tax may be avoided if income received by a foreign corporation or nonresident alien can be treated as foreign-source income.

The U.S. income tax of a foreign corporation or nonresident alien may be minimized by increasing foreign-source income not connected with the U.S. trade or business and increasing expenses allocable against U.S.-source income.

The amount of a CFC's earnings and profits taxable as Subpart F income is determined based on the amount of Subpart F gross income reduced by expenses allocable to such income.[120] To the extent Subpart F income is foreign source, it will increase the taxpayer's foreign tax credit limitation.

The Source Rules

The source-of-income rules are relevant to both U.S. and non-U.S. taxpayers. The U.S. taxpayers are concerned with the source-of-income rules for purposes of determining their foreign tax credit limitation. Non-U.S. taxpayers will generally be subject to U.S. tax on its U.S.-source income. Gross withholding tax of 30 percent is levied on the fixed and determinable annual and period income of a non-U.S. person that is from U.S. sources.[121] No gross withholding tax is assessed on such income from non-U.S. sources. All other income from U.S. sources is generally taxed at a graduated tax rate in the United States.[122] Additionally, a non-U.S. person may have some U.S. income tax liability on its foreign source trade or business income under certain circumstances.[123]

The general source rules are sometimes altered as a result of tax treaties. Treaty provisions relating to source rules are a result of the U.S. Treasury Department's efforts to provide consistent treatment of income between countries, thereby making the foreign tax credit more effective at eliminating double taxation. For example, certain treaties provide that dividends from a treaty partner to a U.S. company will be treated as derived from sources within that country regardless of U.S. tax law (e.g., U.S.–Austria Treaty, Article II(2)(a)). This treaty provision may be in conflict with the U.S. rules for sourcing of dividend payments to the extent that § 904(g) would have treated such income as from U.S. sources.

In general, treaty source rules will prevail over source rules found in the Code, unless the Code provision specifically overrides treaties.[124] In certain instances, where a treaty source rule prevails, the income must be placed in a separate foreign tax credit basket.[125]

Interest Income

Interest income is sourced based on the residence of the obligor. Therefore, interest income on an interest-bearing obligation is classified as income from sources within the United States if received from a resident of the United States, the U.S. government or any of its agencies, a state or any of its political subdivisions, or the District of Columbia.[126] While important generally in international tax planning, the special rules that exist in sourcing interest income will not typically be at issue in a discussion of E-commerce and are not discussed herein.

Dividend Income

The source of dividends is determined by the country in which the paying corporation is incorporated.[127] Thus, dividends paid by a U.S. company are, by definition, U.S. source. However, U.S. withholding tax only applies to dividends paid by a company that meets the 80 percent foreign-business test to the extent of the company's percentage of U.S.-source gross income to total gross income over the three preceding years.[128] If the company had no gross income in the prior three years, the testing period would be the taxable year in which the payment is made.[129]

The so-called 80/20 rules may be altered in the very near future. In any case, these rules and the rules on sourcing of dividend income in general are not discussed herein because the issues are not issues inherent to E-commerce transactions.

Compensation for Personal Services

The general rule for the compensation of personal services is that the source of income for services rendered is determined by the place at which the services are performed.[130] There is only a limited exception to this general rule. The exception provides that services performed in the United States will be treated as foreign source. This exception applies when services are rendered by a nonresident alien temporarily in the United States.[131] To qualify, the compensation paid cannot exceed $3,000. In addition, the services have to be performed as an employee of or under a contract with one of the following:

- a nonresident alien, foreign partnership, or a foreign corporation, not engaged in a trade or business within the United States; or
- an individual who is a citizen or resident of the United States, a domestic partnership, or domestic corporation if such services are performed for a place of business maintained in a foreign country or U.S. possession by such individual, partnership, or corporation.[132]

The exception generally will not apply to foreign persons engaged in E-commerce activities. When services are performed both within and without the United States, the following apportionment rules may be used:

- allocation based on specifically allocable amounts paid; or
- if no accurate allocation can be made, apportionment should be made on a basis that most correctly reflects the proper source of income under the facts and circumstances of the particular case. A time-basis allocation may be appropriate.[133]

The determination of where a service is performed is fundamental to sourcing a service; in the area of E-commerce, there is no clear method to make this determination. Service providers have existed in the E-commerce arena since the medium first became used for commercial purposes and include proprietary on-line networks that provide access to their own content as well as ISPs that provide dial-in access to the Internet. Service providers also include those companies that provide access to proprietary information in their own databases. On-line encyclopedias are proliferating, as are sites that provide users with the ability to play video games against other users located anywhere in the world. Specialty-information databases offer access to information for a fee, such as Lexis/Nexis for tax and legal professionals, various medical databases, and credit-reporting agencies.

The activities of these on-line service providers, if they were performed by human beings, would clearly constitute a service. Because the service is automated, however, it could be argued that what is actually occurring is users being provided with limited use of copyrighted materials. The software regulations (discussed at "Final Software Regulations") provide some guidance on how to characterize and source certain transactions related to software, but expansion of these concepts to other types of E-commerce is not yet provided for in the tax law.

Rents and Royalties

The general rule for rents sources rent derived from the use of tangible property to the country in which that property is located.[134] Similarly, the source of fees (i.e., royalties) derived from the use or right to use intangible property is the country in which the property is used.[135] The software regulations provide additional guidance when the intangible in question is computer software.

International Communications Income

Pursuant to IRC § 863(e)(1)(A), in the case of a U.S. person, 50 percent of international communications income is sourced in the United States and 50 percent of such income is sourced outside the United States. The term *international communications income* includes all income derived from the transmission of communications or data from the United States to any foreign country (IRC § 863(e)(2)). Congress intended that international communications income include income attributable to any transmission between two countries of signals, images, sounds, or data transmitted in whole or in part by buried or underwater cable or by satellite. For example, the term includes income derived from the transmission of telephone calls.[136] The U.S. Treasury has not issued regulations explaining the provisions of IRC § 863(e).

There is quite a bit of uncertainty in this area, and a project is currently underway to provide guidance on some of these issues. The U.S. Treasury recently asked international tax practitioners for comments on issues surrounding a U.S. Treasury project dealing with the sourcing of international communications income. The Treasury noted the increasing importance of global telecommunications systems and also noted that it has the authority to issue regulations under § 863(e). The U.S. Treasury's comments follow an earlier statement terming the sourcing of international communications income an area of "increasing importance." The U.S. Treasury also indicated that a project dealing with the sourcing of international communications income will appear on its 1999 business plan.

One of the areas for which the U.S. Treasury is looking for comments is how they should define international communications income. Other issues cited include the following:

- What effects conversion of transmitted material should have.
- Whether the department should have different rules for communications income solely from within the United States than for income from outside the country.
- How to provide antiabuse rules to curb incentives to move offshore.
- How residence-based rules would treat foreign partnerships receiving U.S.-sourced international communications income, as opposed to U.S. partnerships receiving the same income.

Sale of Personal Property

In general, income from the sale of personal property is sourced based on the residence of the seller.[137] Under this rule income from the sale, exchange, or other disposition of personal property by a U.S. resident will be U.S. sourced. Conversely, income from such a sale by a nonresident is foreign sourced. Specific exceptions to the general rule apply to sales of inventory, depreciable personal property, intangibles, and stock of affiliates. As a result, ordinarily only portfolio stocks, bonds, or other financial instruments fall within the general rule. It should not matter whether the sale of these types of personal property are consummated on the Internet or not.

As noted, an exception to the residence-of-the-seller rule exists for income from the sale of inventory property. Under this exception income from the sale of inventory property is generally sourced based on the title-passage test.[138] If title passes outside of the United States, income from the sale is foreign sourced.[139] If title passes inside the United States, the income from the sale is U.S. sourced.[140]

In general under the title passage rule, a sale of property is consummated at the time when and the place where the rights, title, and interest of the seller in the property are transferred to the buyer. Where bare legal title is retained by the seller, the sale is deemed to have occurred at the time and place of passage to the buyer of beneficial ownership and the risk of loss.

The regulations provide that, if a sales transaction is arranged in a particular manner for the primary purpose of tax avoidance, the substance of the transaction will determine where the sale has occurred. Relevant factors include where negotiations occur, where the agreement is concluded, the location of the property, and the location of the place of payment. Therefore, the sale is treated as having been consummated at the place where the substance of the sale occurred.[141]

In *Liggett Groups, Inc. v. Comm'r.* (*Liggett*), the Tax Court considered whether income from the sale by a U.S. company to its U.S. customers of whisky purchased in the United Kingdom was foreign-source income.[142] The taxpayer received purchase orders from its U.S. customers and placed an order with its supplier in the United Kingdom, who delivered the goods to a ship in the United Kingdom where title passed to the taxpayer. The taxpayer immediately assigned the title to the goods to its customers. The court found that title and risk of loss passed to the U.S. customers from the taxpayer when the goods were placed on the ship in the United Kingdom. The court held that the sales occurred outside the United States and thus generated foreign-source income. The IRS argued that the sale was arranged outside the United States principally for tax avoidance purposes and that the substance of the transaction occurred in the United States. The IRS, in an Action on Decision indicated that it would not appeal or acquiesce to the holding in the case. The IRS indicated that it felt *Liggett* was wrongly decided based on the facts and that the court should have held that such sales generated U.S.-source income. However, the *Liggett* decision continues to be applicable.

Sales of purchased inventory are sourced based solely on the title-passage test.[143] The rules for determining the source of income from the sale of inventory that is manufactured in the United States and sold outside the United States and the sale of inventory manufactured outside the United States and sold in the United States are contained in IRC § 863(b) and § 865(b).

The title-passage test also applies to sales of inventory by nonresidents. Under a special rule, however, income from the sale of inventory attributable to a U.S. office or fixed place of business of a nonresident is generally treated as U.S.-source income, even though title passed outside the United States.[144] Under one exception to this special rule, income attributable to a U.S. office can still be treated as foreign source if the inventory is sold for use outside the United States and an office or other fixed place of business of the taxpayer outside the United States materially participates in the sale.[145]

For depreciable personal property, gain (not in excess of accumulated depreciation) from the sale of depreciable personal property is allocated between U.S. and foreign sources based on the proportion of depreciation deductions previously allowable in computing U.S.-source income and foreign-source income.[146]

Gain in excess of the depreciation recapture is sourced under the title-passage test. If depreciable property (other than certain transportation property as defined in § 168(g)(4)) is used predominantly inside or outside the United States in any taxable year, the depreciation for such year is treated as entirely U.S. or foreign source, as the case may be. However, it should be noted that neither the statute nor the committee reports define the term "predominantly" for this purpose.[147] This rule also applies for sales of depreciable personal property by nonresidents, subject to the office or fixed place of business exception of § 865(e)(2).

Exception for Income from the Sale of Intangible Property

In general, income from the sale of intangible property (e.g., a patent, copyright, secret process or formula, trademark, trade brand, or other like property), to the extent that payment in consideration of the sale is not contingent on productivity, use, or disposition of the intangible, is sourced based on the residence of the seller.[148]

For U.S.-resident sellers, income from the sale of an intangible that is not contingent on the productivity or use of the intangible may be treated as foreign source if the sale is attributable to a fixed place of business outside the United States and a tax of at least 10 percent is actually paid to a foreign country.[149] For nonresidents, income from the sale of intangibles through a U.S. office will be U.S.-source income.[150]

To the extent the sale payments are contingent upon the productivity, use, or disposition of the intangible, the source of the income is determined under the rules applicable to royalties (i.e., where the intangible is used).[151] Any recapture of previously allowed amortization of the intangible is sourced under the depreciation recapture rule discussed previously. The recapture rule applies regardless of whether the sale is contingent on the productivity, use, or disposition of the property.[152]

For noncontingent sales, gain in excess of the recapture amount is sourced under the residence-of-the-seller rule. For contingent sales, the source of all payments will be determined under the recapture rule until the entire recapture amount has been exhausted. Gain in excess of the recapture amount will be sourced as a royalty (i.e., where used).

Notwithstanding any other exceptions, income from the sale of personal property (including inventory, depreciable property, and intangibles) by a nonresident that is attributable to a fixed place of business inside the United States is treated as U.S.-source income[153] except for the following:

- export trade corporations under § 971
- income from the sale of *inventory* for use outside of the United States if an office or fixed place of business of the taxpayer outside the United States materially participates in the sale.

The principles of § 864(c)(5) apply for purposes of determining whether a taxpayer has an office or fixed place of business and whether a sale is attributable to such office or fixed place of business.

Property Manufactured in the United States and Sold outside the United States

IRC § 863(b) and the regulations thereunder provide rules for determining the source of income from the sale of property manufactured in the United States and sold outside or vice versa. The current regulations provide three methods for splitting income from the manufacture and sale of property: (1) the formula method, (2) the independent-price method, and (3) the books-of-account method. These methods attempt to separate the manufacturing profit (sourced based on the location of the property) from the selling (marketing) profit (sourced based on the title-passage test).[154]

The regulations under § 863(b) adopt the formula, or so-called 50/50, method as the primary method for sourcing income from the manufacture of goods within the United States and their sale outside the United States. Taxpayers may elect to use the independent factory price (IFP) method or the books-of-account method of allocating income if either of these methods would give them a favorable result.

To apply the formula method, three steps are required. First, taxable income is split 50/50 into two amounts. These two amounts are deemed to represent the profits resulting from the manufacturing activities and the profits representing the sales activities. Each amount is then apportioned between the United States and foreign source based on a separate formula. U.S.-source manufacturing income is determined by multiplying the 50 percent of taxable income deemed to be a result of manufacturing activities by a ratio of U.S. property divided by worldwide property. U.S.-source selling income is determined by multiplying the 50 percent of taxable income deemed to be a result of the sales activities by a ratio of gross sales in the United States divided by worldwide gross sales.

Total U.S.-source income would be the U.S.-source manufacturing income plus the U.S.-source selling income. Foreign-source taxable income equals total taxable income less U.S.-source income. *Gross sales* for this purpose means only sales of personal property produced in the United States and sold in a foreign country, or produced in a foreign country and sold in the United States. *Property* means only the property used to produce income derived from such sales.

For the most part, application of this formula will result in one-half of the taxpayer's taxable income being U.S.-source, because all property will generally be in the United States and all gross sales will generally be outside the United States.

Once the source of its gross income is determined, the taxpayer must allocate and apportion its expenses, losses, and other deductions separately.[155] Taxpayers using the formula method must apportion expenses

Table 6.2.   **U.S. Sourcing Rules for Various Income Types**

Type of Income	General Sourcing Rule
Interest	Residence of payor
Dividend	Country of incorporation of payor
Personal services	Location of performance
Rent from tangible property	Location in which property is used
Royalty from intangible property	Location in which property is used
International communications income	*U.S. person:* 50% U.S. and 50% foreign *Foreign person:* 100% foreign, unless attributable to U.S. office or place of business
Sale of personal property	Residence of seller
Sale of manufactured personal property	50% to country of title passage and 50% on the basis of the location of manufacturing property
Transportation income	50% to country of origin and 50% to country of destination
Ocean and space income	Residence of taxpayer

allocated to § 863 income on a pro rata basis between U.S. and foreign income.[156]

The sourcing rules in the United States for various types of income are summarized in Table 6.2.

Taxation of E-Commerce in Canada

To date, Canada has not enacted tax rules of specific application to E-commerce or digital transactions. However, in April 1997 the Canadian minister of national revenue established an Advisory Committee on E-Commerce to examine the implications of E-commerce on tax administration.

The committee delivered its report on April 30, 1998, making 72 detailed recommendations in the areas of income tax, commodity taxes, and customs duties and tariffs.[157] Some of those recommendations are outlined below in the context of discussions of the tax issues to which the recommendations relate.

Until such time as the government implements rules dealing specifically with E-commerce (and it is by no means certain that such rules will be perceived as necessary, given that in many areas the committee felt that existing rules and concepts were sufficiently flexible to be used, with some modification, in an E-commerce environment), the existing rules as outlined in this section will continue to be of general application to both traditional and digital transactions, products, and services.

Computation of Taxable Income of a Nonresident Company

A nonresident corporation is taxable in Canada if it is carrying on business in Canada or if it disposes of taxable Canadian property.

Carrying on Business in Canada

The concept of carrying on business in Canada has traditionally centered on the production, manufacture, or construction of goods in Canada. In addition, a provision of the Canadian Income Tax Act deems nonresidents who undertake certain activities in Canada to be carrying on business in Canada. Those activities include soliciting orders or offering anything for sale in Canada through an agent, whether the transaction is to be completed inside or outside Canada, or partly inside and partly outside Canada, or disposing of certain Canadian real property or Canadian resource property.

The growth of E-commerce has increased the difficulty of determining in which jurisdiction a transaction is completed and therefore which country has the right to impose tax on profits earned from that sale. In light of these difficulties, the advisory committee recommended that (1) Revenue Canada, Taxation[158] should issue an interpretation bulletin to clarify its position on the circumstances in which E-commerce activities may constitute carrying on business in Canada,[159] and (2) Revenue Canada should examine the appropriateness of the definition of "carrying on business" under the federal Income Tax Act in an E-commerce environment, including addressing the roles of various E-commerce elements (for example, the location of the file server).

Allocation of Income of Nonresident Companies

Taxable income of a Canadian corporation is allocated, in accordance with income tax regulations, to various provincial jurisdictions, generally based on where the corporation has a permanent establishment. Where a corporation has a permanent establishment in more than one province, taxable income is allocated based on the gross revenue and total salaries and wages attributed to the various jurisdictions. Gross revenue of the corporation is allocated to a PE in accordance with a prescribed set of rules. Gross salaries and wages paid to employees are allocated to the PE to which those employees report.

Regulations provide that, in the case of a corporation that is not resident in Canada, total gross revenue for the year does not include revenue reasonably attributed to a PE outside Canada. Salaries and wages paid to employees of a PE outside Canada are not to be taken into account in applying the regulations.

Transfer Pricing

Canadian earnings may be reduced by the payment of rents, royalties, and management fees to the parent corporation and through the purchase of parent corporation inventory or assets. Canadian tax rules accept these transactions subject to the limitation that the amounts paid must reflect an arm's-length transfer price. In general, Canadian transfer-pricing rules follow the OECD guidelines. The government also imposes a requirement for contemporaneous documentation of the basis for intercompany charges, and significant penalties may be imposed where there are adjustments to transfer prices and the documentation requirements are not met.

The advisory committee recommendations with respect to transfer pricing noted that the ease with which goods and services may be transferred between jurisdictions makes it difficult to determine appropriate transfer-price values. E-commerce will also make it easier to provide services from multiple jurisdictions and will increase the difficulty of determining the source from which services are provided. To address these concerns, the committee (1) recommended that Revenue Canada should examine, in consultation with Canadian business, the application of the transfer-pricing rules to E-commerce transactions and publish the guidelines developed as a result of that study, and (2) stated that there is a need for stronger exchange-of-information and audit agreements and mutual-collection agreements with Canada's trading partners and noted the potential difficulties created for taxpayers by inconsistent approaches to transfer pricing by Canada and the United States.

Withholding Tax on Nonresident, Nonbusiness, or Investment-Type Income

Payments of dividends, interest, rents, royalties, and certain management fees from Canadian sources to nonresidents are subject to Canadian tax. In theory, the liability for this tax is on the nonresident, but in practice, it must be withheld from the payment by the Canadian remitter of the payments.

The basic rate of withholding tax is 25 percent of gross payments. If a tax treaty applies between Canada and the country of residence of the recipient, the treaty will usually specify a lower rate of withholding for various types of payments. For example, the Canada–U.S. Tax Treaty provides for a 10 percent withholding tax rate on interest payments, 15 percent on dividends (reduced to 5 percent where the recipient is a corporate shareholder of 10 percent or more), and 10 percent on certain royalties. Most reasonable management fees are exempt.

Certain royalty payments are exempt from tax, including computer software royalties and royalties paid for the use of, or the right to use, patents and information concerning industrial, commercial, and scientific experience.

The Advisory Committee on E-Commerce noted that, where transactions are carried out in an electronic environment, issues arise both with respect to the characterization of the nature of the transaction and with respect to the location in which a service has been rendered. Both are relevant in determining whether payments in respect of the service are subject to withholding tax. The committee therefore recommended that (1) Revenue Canada and the Department of Finance[160] should examine the appropriateness of revising the applicable sections of the Canadian Income Tax Act to eliminate the withholding requirement on payments for the use of electronic subscriptions and similar transactions, where those transactions are treated as the equivalent to the purchase of tangible goods, and (2) an interpretation bulletin should be issued to clarify the circumstances in which withholdings are applicable as a result of nonresidents providing services through electronic means into Canada.

Digital Commerce Carried On by U.S. Companies with Little Physical Presence in Canada

One of the major provisions contained in most of Canada's tax treaties is that nonresidents who are carrying on business in Canada are subject to tax in Canada only if they earn profits that can be attributed to a permanent establishment. In most treaties, a permanent establishment means a fixed place of business in which the business of the enterprise is wholly or partly carried on. In the context of treaty provisions, E-commerce raises issues as to the relevance of the PE concept. In particular, issues arise relating to what E-commerce components are relevant in determining what constitutes a PE. The advisory committee concluded that current treaties do not provide sufficient direction and definition of the relevant tax concepts to ensure that double taxation does not result. The Committee therefore recommended that (1) Revenue Canada should continue to work with the OECD in addressing E-commerce issues and should in particular continue to participate in OECD discussions on the status of file servers and transaction managers for permanent establishment purposes, and (2) when OECD recommendations with respect to the model treaty are known, the Canadian government should seek to renegotiate Canada's existing tax treaties to incorporate those recommendations.

Comparison of Branch and Subsidiary Taxation

A nonresident investing in Canada, with or without coventurers, must usually decide whether to operate directly in Canada in the capacity of a nonresident person (individual or corporate) or through a Canadian subsidiary corporation. The advantages of operating directly in Canada may include simplicity, although books must be kept on the Canadian enterprise as though it were a separate entity, and the ability to use start-up costs against home-country income tax. The disadvantages are likely to include unlimited liability of the nonresident enterprise in Canadian courts, possible disqualification or disadvantage in regard to certain government grant programs as a source of funding, and perhaps a public-relations drawback in not being regarded as a local enterprise. From a tax point of view, the differences are not great in principle.

Nonresident corporations carrying on business in Canada through either a branch or a controlled subsidiary will be taxed at the prevailing general rates and entitled to the special rates and credits available to Canadian corporations.

After-tax earnings of a Canadian subsidiary corporation may be repatriated to the home country by the payment of dividends, subject to withholding tax, with the rate dependent on the applicable tax treaty. Dividends do not create a tax deduction for the Canadian corporation.

Where a nonresident carries on business in Canada through a branch rather than a subsidiary Canadian corporation, Canada imposes a special branch tax that is intended to match the dividend withholding rate that would be paid if after-tax profits were earned in a subsidiary and paid to a nonresident shareholder. This tax is constructed so that earnings that are reinvested in Canadian assets are not subject to the tax. The Canada–U.S. Tax Treaty provides a measure of protection against branch tax on the first $500,000 accumulated by the Canadian branch of a U.S. corporation.

The advisory committee did not make any recommendations in the area of branch versus subsidiary taxation.

Taxation of E-Commerce in Japan

Japanese direct taxation rules follow a source-based taxation scheme. Because no special rule has been developed for E-commerce, the existing direct-taxation rule will continue being applicable to E-commerce for the time being. Under this basic rule, the tax law provides the rule for sourcing of income by categories of income such as business income, investment income, service fee income, royalty income, and so on. The scope of the taxation for the Japanese-source income of a nonresident company is defined according to its PE status in Japan under the domestic rules. The Corporation Tax Law provides three types of permanent establishments: (1) a branch or similar place of business, (2) a construction site, and (3) a habitual agent. The Corporation Tax Law also provides a so-called force-of-attraction rule. Under this rule a nonresident company that has a Japanese branch may be taxed not only on the Japanese-source income that is attributable to the branch but also on Japanese-source income that is not attributable to the branch. A nonresident company that has an agent PE is also taxed on certain types of Japanese-source income that is not attributable to the activities of the agent PE.

Taxable Income Connected to a Permanent Establishment for a Nonresident Company

The scope of taxation is given by the type of PE that a nonresident company maintains. Two types of PEs are examined here, a nonresident company that has a branch in Japan and a nonresident company that has a habitual agent in Japan. A construction-type PE is not discussed here because it has no application to the nature of E-commerce.

Nonresident Company with a Branch

Due to the force-of-attraction rule under Japanese domestic tax law, a nonresident company with a branch is taxed on all its source income regardless of whether such income is attributable to the activities of the branch. Foreign-source income that is attributable to the branch is not subject to Japanese corporate income taxes under the domestic tax law.

This force-of-attraction rule in Japanese domestic law is superseded by the attributable income rule under most of Japan's existing double-tax treaties. Therefore, a nonresident company is generally not taxed on its industrial or commercial profit from sources in Japan if such income is not attributable to the Japanese branch of the nonresident company.

Nonresident Company with a Habitual Agent

The force-of-attraction rule under the domestic tax laws is also applicable to a nonresident company with a habitual agent in connection with certain types of Japanese-source income, again regardless of whether such income is attributable to the activities of the branch. Such Japanese-source income that is subject to the force-of-attraction rule includes service-fee income and commercial profits. Royalties, dividends, and interest on loans are not subject to the force-of-attraction rule; that is, they are subject to Japanese corporate taxes only if attributable to the activities of the habitual agent.

Allocation of Income of Nonresident Companies

Article 138 of the Corporation Tax Law provides the sourcing rules for income by category of income. Any income that is not defined within a category other than the first category falls within the first category, such that all types of income are subject to the sourcing rules. The first category of income constitutes (1) income from business activities carried out in Japan, (2) income from use, holding, or transfer of an asset that is located in Japan, and (3) incidental income arising in Japan.

Income from business activities carried out in Japan is subject to the following rules:

1. Income from a sale of goods without manufacturing shall be treated as arising in the country where the sale is made.
2. Income from a sale of goods that is manufactured abroad and imported into Japan for sale shall be allocated among countries involved based on an arm's-length principle.
3. Income other than the above (which can be incurred from E-commerce) shall be allocated based on the arm's-length principle.

Income from use, holding, or transfer of an asset that is located in Japan includes the following:

1. Redemption premium on bonds that are issued by the Japanese governments or by domestic corporations.
2. Income from a disposition of a right or license that is granted under Japanese laws. (Note that income from a disposition of intellectual properties for which royalty is paid is also treated as a royalty under the Japanese tax laws.)
3. Income from a sale of securities at a stock exchange in Japan or through a Japanese branch of a dealer or broker.
4. Income from a sale of securities the certificate of which are physically located in Japan at the time of the sale.
5. Income from a sale of Japanese national or local government bonds or Japanese corporation debentures.
6. Income from a sale of substantial shares in a Japanese corporation.
7. Income from a disposal of goodwill related to a business in Japan.
8. Income from a disposition of assets, other than inventories, located in Japan.

Allocation of Specific Types of Income

Specific types of income have allocation rules established in the Japanese tax law, as outlined in the following list:

- Income from personal services that are performed in Japan are allocated to Japan. Personal services include the performance of actors, musicians, artists, athletes, lawyers, CPAs, architects, and so on. It also includes personal services performed based on a special knowledge of scientific technology, business administration, and so on.
- Rental income on immovable property is allocated based on the location of the immovable property.
- Interest on Japanese national or local government bond or Japanese corporation debentures is allocated to Japan.
- Interest on deposits made with a Japanese branch of a banking entity is allocated to Japan.
- If the joint securities investment trust is undertaken by an entity that has a branch in Japan, the profit is allocated to Japan.
- Dividend income received from a Japanese entity is allocated to Japan.
- If the loan is used for the Japanese business operation of the debtor, the interest is allocated to Japan.
- If the intangible property is used for the Japanese business operation of the licensee, the royalty is allocated to Japan.
- If the investment is made for the business operation in Japan, the distribution from Tokumei Kumiai, a form of silent partnership in Japan, is allocated to Japan.

Expenses incurred in connection with these income types are deducted from the reportable income based on a reasonable allocation methodology. The tax laws do not provide any specific methodology, and thus the taxpayer has to prove the reasonableness in the methodology adopted. The tax laws provide that an arm's-length principle be applied to this allocation methodology.

Character of Income of Digital Products and Services

Income from provision of digital products and services can be categorized as either income from a personal service business, royalties, or income from business activities carried out in Japan. Because personal services in this context include personal services performed based on a special knowledge of scientific technology, business administration, and so on, digital services could fall within this category of income. Alternatively, if the digital product is a creation protected by copyright law, the distribution of such a copyrighted product is treated as licensing for which a royalty should be charged and would fall within the royalty category.

The provision of services that do not fall within the definition of a personal services business could also fall within the category of income from business activities. Any sale of a digital product that is not treated as a licensing of intangible property could also fall within the category of income from business activities. An example of this would be income from the sale of packaged software that is not subject to royalty withholding tax.

Transfer-Pricing Issues

No special Japanese transfer-pricing rules have been developed in the area of E-commerce. Japanese tax authorities basically follow the interpretations of the OECD and other authorities on these matters.

Withholding on Nonresident Company, Nonbusiness, or Investment-Type Income

Withholding tax liabilities depend on the type of Japanese-source income under the Japanese Income Tax Law. For the first category of income (i.e., income from business activities carried in Japan, income from use, holding, or transfer of an asset that is located in Japan, and incidental income arising in Japan), the tax law does not impose withholding tax. Income from a sale of immovable properties located in Japan is subject to withholding tax. In addition, the Income Tax Law requires withholding tax on the income from the personal services that are performed in Japan.

Japanese-source income in the following categories is generally subject to withholding tax under the domestic tax laws: rental income on immovable properties located in Japan, interest on bonds, interest on deposits, profits on joint securities investment trust, dividend income, interest on loans, royalties, Tokumei Kumiai income (where the number of investors is 10 or more), and awards, pension income, and similar income.

Withholding tax on any of these categories that also constitutes reportable income of a nonresident company having a PE in Japan can be credited against the final corporation income tax due. Due to the force-of-attraction rule for a branch, all of the nonbusiness or investment-type income from Japanese source is included in the reportable income of the branch. A nonresident company operating through a branch can be exempted from the withholding tax on its income from personal service business, royalty income, rental income on immovable properties located in Japan, interest on loans, and so on, where an appropriate application is filed.

Because royalty, dividend, loan interest, and other nonbusiness income of nonresident companies operating in Japan through a habitual agent are not subject to the force-of-attraction rule, such companies can be exempted from the withholding tax on nonbusiness or investment type income attributable to the activities of its habitual agent. It should also be noted that any Japanese-source income of a nonresident company is not subject to withholding tax if the payment is made by a nonbusiness individual.

Examples of Various Transactions and Their Tax Consequences

EXAMPLE 1

A nonresident company having no branch or agent in Japan sells and delivers a copyrighted digital product to a Japanese company via the Internet. The file transfer is made through a server located in Japan. The Japanese company will use the digital products for its business operation in Japan.

Income under this first example would be categorized as Japanese-source royalty. Currently, there does not appear to be any case law in which a server located in Japan and used for a file transfer is treated as a PE. If it does not constitute a PE, the royalty, as Japanese-source income, will only be subject to withholding tax. Because corporate income tax will not be imposed on the royalty unless the server is treated as a PE, the withholding tax would likely be the final tax.

EXAMPLE 2

A nonresident company having no branch or agent permanent establishment in Japan opens an electronic mall on the Internet that can be accessed from Japan. The nonresident company accepts orders via an independent call center in Japan. The nonresident company maintains inventory at the Japanese warehouse of an independent service provider for filling Japanese orders.

The call center in this second example is not treated as a PE of the nonresident. The warehouse in Japan may be treated as a PE of the nonresident if treaty protection for the independent agent that fills the orders is not available. If a PE is determined to exist, the full sales profit would be subject to Japanese corporate taxes. Because profit from the sale of merchandise is not subject to withholding tax, if a PE is not determined to exist, there would be no Japanese taxes. If the nonresident company has little physical presence in Japan, there would be no right to Japanese corporate taxation on the commercial profit from sale of merchandise under the current tax laws.

If digital content is a creation protected by copyright law, then distribution of such copyrighted content will most likely be treated as licensing for which a royalty should be charged (as long as such a distribution is done legally as a commercial activity). Income from the sale of packaged software is in certain cases treated in practice as the proceeds from sale of copies as if it were tangible property. Although treated this way in practice, such treatment is not well supported in Japanese law, and it is therefore difficult to extend this treatment to sales of digital content. Royalty income of a nonresident company is subject to Japanese withholding tax. If the nonresident company has a PE in Japan, royalty income is also subject to reporting for corporate tax purposes, assuming that the royalty income is attributable to the activities

of a PE. Withholding tax can be credited against the Japanese Corporation Tax due.

A subsidiary is taxed on its worldwide income, with foreign tax
credit available. A branch is taxed on its Japanese source income, with no
foreign tax credit available. No tax is imposed on the remittance of
branch profit to the home office. A subsidiary is taxed on its liquidation
income upon liquidation. The liquidation income is made up of the
unrealized gain on assets upon liquidation. A branch is not required to
report the unrealized gain on branch assets upon branch closing. A nonresident company has to allocate the revenue and the related expenses to
the branch. The transfer-pricing issues in the case of operation through
subsidiaries and the intracompany profit allocation issues in the case of
operation through branches requires the same level of consideration
from a functional analysis standpoint.

Taxation of E-Commerce in the United Kingdom

Taxation of Nonresident Companies

A nonresident company is subject to corporation tax only if it trades in
the United Kingdom through a branch or agency (Section 11 ICTA
[Income and Corporations Taxes Act] 1988), in which case it is taxable
only on the profits attributable to the U.K. operations. If a company is
deemed to be carrying on a trade in the United Kingdom through a
branch or agency and it is also resident in a country with which the
United Kingdom has a double-tax treaty, those activities may not constitute a taxable presence, under the relevant treaty.

Under the OECD Model Tax Treaty, Article 7, for example, a non-
U.K.-resident seller would only be subject to tax in the United Kingdom
if it is trading in the United Kingdom through a PE as defined in Article
5. Essentially a PE requires either (1) a fixed place of business through
which the business of an enterprise is wholly or partly carried on (subject
to exceptions) or (2) a dependent agent who has, and habitually exercises,
an authority to conclude contracts in the name of the nonresident.

Allocation of Income of Nonresident Companies

Domestic Law

Where no treaty exists, U.K. statutory law says little explicitly about the manner in which one should arrive at a measure of taxable profits. The vital question of whether a trade is exercised in the United Kingdom is, therefore, an issue to be determined by case law.

The Inland Revenue begins with the supposition that there is a trade, somewhere worldwide, and asks whether what is done in the United Kingdom amounts to the exercise of the trade in the United Kingdom. Each case is decided on its own facts. However, certain principles have developed in respect of companies selling goods or providing services.

One early case (*Erichsen v Last*) was heard in the Court of Appeal in 1881.[161] The Great Northern Telegraph Company of Copenhagen, a non-U.K.-resident company, owned three cables crossing the North Sea. Messages were collected in the United Kingdom and then transmitted across the cables and thereafter through cables owned by other companies or governments. The company argued that it ought only to be taxed on the profit arising from the relaying of the messages along the main cable because the remaining profits arose from the transmission along other cables that had absolutely nothing to do with the United Kingdom. The courts ruled that, if a company is in the United Kingdom and contracts in the United Kingdom, the profit comes from the contract and should be taxed in the United Kingdom even if the service is partly provided overseas.

Later cases have watered down somewhat this emphasis on the place of contract. Lord Atkin stated in *Smidth & Co v Greenwood*:

It [the place of contract] is obviously a very important element in the enquiry and . . . the contracts in this case were made abroad. But I am not prepared to hold that this test is decisive. I can imagine cases where a contract of resale is made abroad, and yet the manufacture of the goods, some negotiation of the terms, and complete execution of the contract take place here under such circumstances that the trade was in truth exercised here. I think that the question is *where do the operations take place from which the profits in substance arise* [emphasis added]?[162]

The decision in the *Smidth* case, nonetheless, supports the conclusion that, in the case of a merchanting business (buying and selling goods for profit), the trade is normally exercised at the place where the contracts for sale are made—that is where the operations take place from which the profits in substance arise. However, the place of sale, like other elements, can be moved, and therefore, some care needs to be taken. Thus, where contracts are formally made abroad but everything related to the trade takes place in the United Kingdom short of signing a piece of paper, the U.K. Revenue authorities are likely to contend that trading is undertaken in the United Kingdom.

Where services are concerned, greater weight tends to be given to the place where the service is provided. However, there may be more than one part of the trade that can be identified as the profit-producing part. If a product is manufactured in one country and sold in another, the two elements can easily be identified. Difficulty starts to emerge when what is done in the United Kingdom is not clearly identifiable as part of the whole trade in that way. Profits that are attributable to the U.K. activities would then depend on the location of the key profit-generating activities.

Generally, U.K. case law now follows an arm's-length principle in determining the allocation of income and costs under domestic law as well as where a treaty exists (see below). The Inland Revenue manual, *International Tax Handbook,* states, "It is well established that the arm's length principle applies as a matter of law and that this is accepted by taxpayers, tax advisers and the Inland Revenue as the correct basis for taxing nonresidents in the United Kingdom."[163]

Treaty

The majority of nonresidents trading in the United Kingdom are residents of treaty countries. Thus, provided they are trading in the United Kingdom in domestic law terms and have a PE within the treaty's definition, the Business Profits Article of the relevant treaty will determine the measure of their taxable profits.

The Business Profits Article of a treaty based on the OECD Model Tax Treaty provides that, in each contracting state, there shall be attributed to that PE the profits that it might be expected to make if it were a distinct and separate enterprise engaged in the same or similar activities under the same or similar conditions and dealing wholly independently with the enterprise of which it is a PE, i.e., a simple arm's-length rule.

Character of Income of Digital Products and Services

Section 832 ICTA 1988 defines trading as "every trade, manufacture, adventure or concern in the nature of trade." In order to provide guidance on how to interpret this definition, the 1954 Royal Commission on the Taxation of Profits and Income set out badges of trade that can be examined to see if any activity is a trading (i.e., active) activity. These badges include the following:

- subject matter, that is, whether the subject matter under review is commonly held for an enduring benefit or for their intrinsic value or alternatively to be traded;
- way in which asset acquired and held—for example, where an asset is clearly purchased as a fixed asset in an existing trade, its disposal cannot normally be a trading receipt;
- frequency of transactions—for example, transactions that would be treated in isolation as being of a capital nature will be taken to be of a trading nature where their frequency indicates the carrying on of a trade;
- length of ownership—for example, the courts may infer an adventure in the nature of a trade where items purchased are immediately resold, although this is not a cast iron rule; and
- the presence of a profit motive, which is a strong indication that a person is trading.

It is not necessary to show that *all* badges of trade are present for an activity to be assessed as a trade.

Given the profit motive and the nature of E-commerce, it is likely that profits arising in the E-commerce area, assuming that this is a main source of revenue and not merely peripheral to other activities, will be taxed as trading income even if, in some circumstances, the income is characterized as royalty income for withholding tax purposes.

Source of Income of Digital Products and Services

As previously discussed, a number of factors need to be considered in relation to whether a nonresident's income is attributable to the United Kingdom, for example, where the contract is concluded. However, these issues can cause considerable problems when attempting to transport these principles to E-commerce. When a sale is made on-line, for example, it is not clear where the contract for an on-line sale has been made, either for contract law or taxation purposes.

The options are that the contract is made where the seller is located, where the purchaser is located, or perhaps, where the server is located if acceptance of the contract is purely subject to certain specified criteria being fulfilled. Paragraph 177 of the *Inspector's Manual* states: "[I]n general, the place of contract is governed by the place where the acceptance of the offer is received, although it may not be clear which party has made the offer or how acceptance has been conveyed. For instantaneous communication, such as face to face, by telephone, telex or fax then acceptance is received *where the recipient is* [emphasis added]."[164]

In E-commerce the seller's physical location could be selected to obtain preferable tax treatment but may be irrelevant for practical trading purposes. Despite this, taxation based on the seller's location may be the most concrete option available and appears to be the basis used for most current methods of taxation.

"Purchaser's location" could mean the taxable presence of the ultimate end user (that is, taxable in the United Kingdom if the user is a U.K. resident) or the physical location of the end user's personal computer. The increasing use of portable computers, however, means that this latter method could be impossible to monitor and control. For example, if a Japanese resident concludes a purchase contract on-line while on a business trip to the United Kingdom, this method could give the Japanese resident a taxable presence in the United Kingdom.

It is quite possible that more than one server is used in the flow of information, for example, in transferring data from a local server to a central decision-making server. In addition, decisions to accept or reject a sale could be made at both servers, which makes the choice of taxable location difficult, if not impossible.

In any event, the proper analysis should not focus on the mere presence of a server in a particular jurisdiction. If, for example, a nonresident advertises goods for sale on a U.K. server and an overseas customer responds by a telephone call to the nonresident, during which agreement is reached, the contract may technically be made in the United Kingdom even though the nonresident does very little in the United Kingdom. It is not known what view the courts would take of this, although it is not impossible that, while there may be contracts executed in the United Kingdom, there may nevertheless be no trading there.

Until recently, the Inland Revenue has given little guidance in this area. However, in November 1999 it, together with HM Customs and Excise, published a substantial paper entitled "Electronic Commerce: The U.K.'s Taxation Agenda," which clarifies the view of the Inland Revenue in relation to a simple offer to buy by the purchaser and acceptance by the seller. In this case, "where acceptance is communicated instantaneously, the place of contract is generally in the territory to which acceptance is communicated," that is, the territory of the buyer.[165]

Transfer Pricing

As already noted, an arm's-length rule applies to U.K. branches. The basis for calculating the arm's-length rules as they apply to U.K. branches are those set out in the OECD guidelines. These suggest that, in determining an arm's-length price, factors such as the business sector involved, the size of the group, materiality, prevailing practice, and common sense should be taken into account. Nevertheless, some form of study of third-party comparables will be necessary for all but a small minority of cases.

Identifying such a comparable, however, may cause difficulties in the area of E-commerce and requires an assessment of the location of the key profit-generating activities, including where these functions have taken place and how much value was added and where. For example, it may be that the location of the server adds little value and therefore only a small profit needs to be attributed to this function.

A branch is not necessarily required to deem transactions to take place between the PE and head office that do not in fact take place or to attribute a markup to every transaction between head office and the PE. But where goods are transferred between head office and the PE or services are provided by head office or vice versa, the costs or income attributable to the establishment must be arrived at on the arm's-length principle.

Withholding Tax

The United Kingdom, like many other countries, requires tax to be withheld from certain payments, for example, the payment of interest on loans likely to last for a year or more, or from royalties in certain circumstances—that is, payments for the use of, or the right to use, a copyright. Withholding taxes on royalties is 23 percent, although tax treaties between the United Kingdom and the country of the recipient may reduce these rates.

The current rules used to distinguish between such payments and payments for goods and services, from which tax does not usually need to be withheld, were developed in relation to physical products. However, it is increasingly possible for certain products to be transmitted electronically rather than in physical form, such as books and music.

The Inland Revenue has provided little guidance in this area to date and, in its paper "Electronic Commerce: The U.K.'s Taxation Agenda," states that it is currently not always clear whether a payment to view and download copyrighted digitized information is in whole or in part a payment for the use of, or for the right to use, a copyright or is a payment for the purchase of goods or services. The Inland Revenue simply states that it will work with the OECD to obtain an international consensus. It does, however, add that it will be guided by the principle of neutrality—that is, that there should be no difference between a transaction on-line and a similar transaction off-line—and that it will seek to preserve the traditional taxing rights of the United Kingdom.[166]

A further issue arises where computer software is delivered electronically and for which a license fee is payable. Often, the end user obtains one copy of the software delivered through the Internet, with rights of internal reproduction to potentially obtain multiple copies for the end users own use or to sell to other end users.

These transactions also raise questions regarding whether any withholding obligation arises to those individuals or organizations making license-fee payments. In general, it is understood that such payments should not give rise to a withholding tax liability other than potentially where further commercial exploitation takes place. However, this again remains uncertain until some guidance is received from the Inland Revenue.

Examples of Transactions

The following are examples of transactions that may or may not attract United Kingdom withholding tax.

Single On-Line Sale

It is unlikely that payments for a purchase of an individual item via the Web could be considered a copyright royalty. This would indicate that a standard consumer purchase over the Internet would not require individuals to withhold tax.

Multiple On-Line Sales

This situation may be slightly more complex than the single on-line sale. However, if a consumer purchases an item of software for her own use, it would appear that no withholding should be required. If the consumer is a teacher and purchases 20 copies of a software program, delivery could be by means of 20 individual deliveries (off-line or on-line), or could be one copy delivered on-line, with the right for the consumer to make 19 further copies. In either case, the teacher is in substance purchasing 20 copies of a product and, to ensure neutrality with non-E-commerce, the payments should not be considered to be in respect of a copyright, and no withholding tax should be due.

The above example would appear to be different if the copies were, in fact, resold to other consumers, perhaps with some additions to the software, as part of a process of commercial exploitation. Payments would then appear to fall within the definition of "a payment of or on account of a royalty or sum paid periodically for or in respect of a copyright." In this case the position is more analogous to an off-line royalty payment, granting an interest in the copyright rather than a sale of a product. It is understood that withholding tax is required to be paid by the user of the product.

Pay-per-View

Some products are available over the Internet, and their value is in the information they provide rather than the use to which they can be put. Examples of this are newspapers or magazines, historically sold in hard-copy form. Although many newspapers are currently available free over the Internet, it is likely that a charge may be made in the future, and certainly payments are required for similar hard-copy products at present.

For the same reasons stated in the previous section, no withholding should be due because this is simply a means of delivery of the product (via a Web page), and there is no transfer of a right of reproduction for commercial exploitation.

Tax Rules Applicable to Non-U.K. Companies
Engaged in Digital Commerce in the United Kingdom

Traditional U.K. tax law does not easily deal with digital commerce, and there is therefore a great deal of uncertainty in the United Kingdom over when a taxable presence might be established. If the company maintains a server and operates an office with employees undertaking various aspects of the commercial activities in the United Kingdom, then it is understood that general principles can apply to the precise circumstances to determine whether those activities constitute a branch for domestic law or a fixed place of business for the purposes of any double-tax agreement. However, the server is only one factor to be considered in this analysis, and the mere presence of a server should not constitute a PE.

There appears, however, to be considerable uncertainty regarding whether an isolated server situated in the United Kingdom with no other activities and with no employees present in the United Kingdom could constitute a branch or fixed place of business. Even if the server is deemed to be a PE, there is further uncertainty as to whether the company would be able to argue that the server has an auxiliary character and therefore falls within the exemption of paragraph 4 of Article 5 of the OECD Model Convention.

In "Electronic Commerce: The U.K.'s Taxation Agenda," the Inland Revenue raises the issue of whether "a web site on a server is a fixed place through which business in carried on" and states that "it seems clear . . . that some activities (such as advertising) on a web site will not of themselves constitute a permanent establishment since they will fall into the category of preparatory or auxiliary activities."[167] However, the paper provides no conclusions, awaiting guidance from the OECD in the form of an update to the explanatory commentary to the Model Tax Convention.

In October 1999 the OECD Working Party on Tax Conventions released its initial view in this area. The document proposes that a server should create a "fixed place of business" only if the server is located at a certain place for a sufficient period of time. In addition, the OECD agrees that, even if the server is "fixed" and a place of business of the E-commerce enterprise is created, the activities performed may, depending on the facts, be "preparatory or auxiliary" activities, and therefore, there will be no PE.[168] It is expected that the final version of this document will be released in the year 2000.

Treatment of Different Types of Digital Content

For U.K. direct-taxation purposes, the type of digital content is largely irrelevant to the tax treatment of a business operating in the United Kingdom. As previously discussed, any income attributable to the activities performed in the United Kingdom should be treated as trading income and calculated on an appropriate arm's-length basis.

Branch versus Subsidiaries

The choice of entity to use within the United Kingdom should not be dictated solely for taxation purposes, but must be consistent with any regulatory requirements: head office/parent tax considerations, individual and expatriate tax considerations, the need to limit public disclosure of information, and so on. There are currently few tax differences between operating in the United Kingdom as a branch or a subsidiary. The company and branch are taxed at the same rate and on essentially the same basis, although royalty and/or interest payments made directly by a branch to its head office are not normally allowable as deductions from branch profits (although usually allowable against the profits of a subsidiary).

A branch structure usually permits current head-office tax relief for losses incurred by the branch. This relief is automatic by the inclusion of all the branch's income and expenses in the head-office tax computations. If the branch is profitable, however, earnings are immediately taxable both in the United Kingdom and in the head-office country regardless of the level (if any) of distribution of profits. The timing of the availability of foreign tax credits is also inflexible because tax credits may arise in a year when the head office is loss making, and hence the tax credit would not be immediately usable. However, the U.S. check-the-box regulations largely eliminate these differences for U.S. head offices/parents.

Public disclosure of financial information is generally more onerous in the United Kingdom than in the United States. All U.K. incorporated companies are required to make public their company financial statements on an annual basis. Every overseas company that establishes a branch or place of business in the United Kingdom is required to register with the U.K. Registrar of Companies within 30 days of doing so. There is also an annual requirement to file the financial statements of the legal entity of which the branch/place of business is a part with the Registrar of Companies. This filing is open for public inspection.

A U.K. branch is not required to prepare statutory accounts or to perform a statutory audit. However, an audit may be required as part of the head-office company's audit requirements.

Summary of Cross-Border Direct Taxations

The concrete tax rules applying specifically to the direct taxation of E-commerce are few. There is little in the way of new rules or new law to address the proper taxation of E-commerce. Rather, the United States, the OECD, and other countries that have addressed this issue have affirmed the application of existing general principles of taxation to E-commerce.

The historic tax rules applied by developed countries have, as noted in this chapter, focused the incidence of taxation on the source of the income under consideration. The rise of E-commerce produces an environment in which determining the source of the income may be difficult to ascertain. For example, assume a Haven Company has a Web server located in a country that does not have an income tax. A person in the United States accesses the Web site through its own connection with an Internet service provider. That U.S. person buys some financial-planning software of the company and gives the company his credit-card number. All of the credit approval process is automated on the Web server of the Haven Company. The U.S. person receives the software and his credit card is charged for the price of the service. Is the income of Haven Company sourced in the United States (its customer's location) or in the tax haven (its Web server's location)? The answer is essential to the proper taxation of the Haven Company's income.

A source-based tax regime requires the subject income to be properly characterized before it can be properly sourced. The forms of transactions in the E-commerce field add complexity to the proper sourcing of the resulting income. For example, is the downloading and use of a software program for a fee properly classified as a license of the software or as the provision of a service that is facilitated by the use of the software? The classification of the income is fundamental to determining the U.S. tax consequences of the income. Other countries as well will look to the character of the income to ascertain its proper source and then its proper taxation.

As the significance of E-commerce increases, the pressure on the existing source-based tax regimes will be heavy. It would not be inconceivable to witness nations develop specific sourcing rules for E-commerce transactions or to see a migration of tax systems toward a residence-based regime that is less difficult to administer and not dependent on determining source and character of items of income.

The analysis used in transfer pricing could undergo a significant change. Generally, the economic analysis of a typical manufacturer involves segregating its manufacturing and marketing functions from its residual activities and assigning arm's-length returns to each. As sales over the Internet increase, the need for significant sales forces decreases. The value added from marketing functions may also decrease—significantly for Internet-based companies and less so for others. Businesses in general may see a decrease in the returns assigned to marketing activities as the Internet provides an alternative marketing venue. This would result in a lower level of profit that is assigned, under arm's-length principles, to marketing functions and the countries in which the marketing functions occur.

A significant issue for revenue authorities is tax compliance in E-commerce. Payment with electronic funds is akin to payment with cash. There is little in the way of a trail of evidence for the movement of funds electronically over the Internet. Today, the cash economy results in enormous revenue losses to revenue authorities around the world, as potential tax revenues from transactions with no documentation go unreported. An expansion of the use of transactions without a paper trail could compound compliance problems and put greater pressure on the ability to apply existing tax rules to the taxation of non-E-commerce.

The goal of tax neutrality is the proper goal for tax authorities to pursue in their taxation of E-commerce. These transactions should not receive more favorable or less favorable treatment than transactions conducted generally. However, the pursuit of tax neutrality under the existing system may be difficult to achieve. As more transactions occur in E-commerce, experience may point tax authorities toward revising their existing tax regimes to ensure proper administration and compliance.

Notes

Chapter 1

1. U.S. Department of Commerce, *The Emerging Digital Economy II* (Washington, D.C: U.S. Department of Commerce, 1999), 3; "Drawing the Battle Lines," *Wall Street Journal,* September 16, 1996; Peter H. Lewis, "More Users Now Taking Direct Route to the Internet, a Survey Finds," *New York Times,* September 23, 1996; U.S. Government Working Group on Electronic Commerce, *First Annual Report,* <www.ecommerce.gov> (November 30, 1998); U.S. Department of Commerce and U.S. Government Working Group on Electronic Commerce, *The Emerging Digital Economy Report* (Washington, D.C.: U.S. Department of Commerce, April 16, 1998), Chapter 1; Steve Lohr, "Phone Merger Aims to Control Electronic Pipeline of Future," *New York Times,* June 29, 1998; "Beyond the PC," *Business Week,* March 8, 1999, p. 86; Steve Lohr, "Survey Suggests Consumers Are Taking to E-Commerce," *New York Times,* March 22, 1999; "The Internet Age," *Business Week,* October 4, 1999, p. 77.

2. U.S. Department of Commerce, *Emerging Digital Economy II,* 3; U.S. Department of Commerce and U.S. Government Working Group on Electronic Commerce, *Emerging Digital Economy Report;* U.S. Government Working Group on Electronic Commerce, *First Annual Report;* "Amazon.com: The Wild World of E-Commerce," *Business Week,* December 14, 1998, p. 108; *Business Week E.Biz,* March 22, 1999, p. EB 12; NUA studies on world Internet usage, cited in The Internet Economy Indicators, "The Global Internet" <www.internetindicators.com> (June 25, 1999).

3. Robert E. Litan and William A. Niskanen, *Going Digital* (Washington, D.C.: Brookings Institute and the Cato Institute, 1998), 32.

4. U.S. Department of Commerce and U.S. Government Working Group on Electronic Commerce, *Emerging Digital Economy Report,* Chapter 1, p. 2.

5. George Johnson, "Searching for the Essence of the World Wide Web," *New York Times,* April 11, 1999.

6. Nicholas Negroponte, *Being Digital* (New York: Vintage Books, 1995), 12.

7. Shelley Morrisette, William M. Bluestein, and Nicki Maraganore, "Consumer's Digital Decade," <www.forrester.com> (January 1999).

8. U.S. Department of Commerce and U.S. Government Working Group on Electronic Commerce, *Emerging Digital Economy Report,* Chapter 1.

9. "Media Metrix Chronicles the 'History' of the Internet," Media Metrix press release <www.mediametrix.com> (March 18, 1999); NUA study cited at "The Internet Economy Indicators: Facts and Figures," <www.internetindicators.com> (June 25, 1999); "Deloitte Consulting: Ecommerce to Top USD1.1 Trillion by 2002" <www.nua.ie/surveys> (June 23, 1999).

In a 1995 U.S. nationwide survey of software companies, the Internet was not included on virtually any of the companies' top 10 most pressing concerns for the future. In a follow-up 1996 survey, the top two issues were generally the Internet and the software industry's changing business model (primarily in response to the challenge of the Internet). Not surprisingly, in late 1995 William H. Gates, the chairman of Microsoft Corporation, the world's largest software company, announced: "The Internet is the primary driver of all new work we are doing throughout the product line. We are hard core about the Internet." Patrick Porter, "The Net's a Blessing for Some, a Curse for Most," *Massachusetts High Tech,* May 27–June 2, 1996, p. 12 (citing Price Waterhouse Eighth Annual Software Business Practices Survey); Lewis, "More Users Now Taking Direct Route."

10. "Business and the Internet: The Net Imperative," *Economist,* June 26, 1999, p. 34.

11. "Forrester Estimates Worldwide Internet Commerce Will Reach as High as $3.2 Trillion in 2003," Forrester Research press release, <www.forrester.com> (November 5, 1998). Forrester estimated that the low range of worldwide Internet commerce in 2003 would still total almost $1.8 trillion. See also "Business and the Internet," p. 33.

12. Kevin Maney, "As Stock Prices Zoom, Ask Why before You Buy," *USA Today,* July 8, 1998.

13. Steven Syre and Charles Stein, "Taking Measure of the Great Divide," *Boston Globe,* April 13, 1999. By late summer 1999 several of these stocks had dropped by one-quarter or more, demonstrating the volatility of the Internet sector. "USA TODAY Internet 100," *USA Today,* August 9, 1999; Edward Iwata, "The Net at 30," *USA Today,* December 14, 1999.

14. "Call It the Net Effect," *Business Week,* July 12, 1999, pp. 50–51.

15. U.S. Bureau of the Census, *Statistical Abstract of the United States: 1998,* 118th ed. (Washington, D.C.: U.S. Bureau of the Census, 1998), 573, table 915; Lohr, "Phone Merger Aims to Control."

16. International Telecommunication Union, *World Telecommunication Indicators* (Geneva: International Telecommunication Union, 1998), A-7, 79, 83, 85. In 1997 only 47 percent of European businesses had Internet access compared with 61 percent in the United States, only 5.5 percent of European households had Internet access compared with 18 percent in the United States, and only 24 percent of European households had personal computers compared to 46 percent in the United States. See "A High-Tech Europe Is Finally in Sight," *Business Week,* August 31, 1998, p. 122.

17. John Markoff, "Fight of the (Next) Century," *New York Times,* March 7, 1999; Erran Carmel, Jeffrey A. Eisenach, and Thomas M. Lenard, *The Digital Economy*

Fact Book (Washington, D.C.: Progress and Freedom Foundation, 1999), 23; Edward C. Baig, "Surfing with Eye-Opening Ease," *USA Today,* December 29, 1999; "Beyond the PC," pp. 79–88.

18. "Fast Forward: Future Internet," *PC World,* March 1999, pp. 164–66.

19. Cary Lu, *The Race for Bandwidth: Understanding Data Transmission,* (Redmond, Wash.: Microsoft Press, 1998), Chapter 8; U.S. Department of Commerce and U.S. Government Working Group on Electronic Commerce, *Emerging Digital Economy Report,* Chapter 2, p. 2; "Downloading a 'Titanic' File," *USA Today,* October 11, 1999.

20. Christopher Mines, Mary Modahl, and Shar VanBoskirk, "Broadband Hits Home," *Forrester Report,* <www.forrester.com> (August 1998); "Fast Forward: Future Internet," p. 164.

21. "Six Routes to the Internet," *PC World,* March 1999, p. 110.

22. Seth Schiesel, "Cable TV and the Internet, Too," *New York Times,* March 23, 1999, p. C4; Mines, Modahl, and VanBoskirk, "Broadband Hits Home," p. 4.

23. Johnson, "Searching for the Essence," p. 1; Michael Dertouzos, *What Will Be: How the New World of Information Will Change Our Lives* (New York: HarperEdge, 1997), 45–51.

24. Johnson, "Searching for the Essence," p. 1.

25. "Six Routes to the Internet," p. 110; "Filling the Need for Speed," *Business Week,* December 28, 1998, pp. 50–53; "The New Technology: What You Need to Know," *Business Week,* July 6, 1998, p. 28.

26. "The Internet Space Race," *Business Week,* June 1, 1998, p. 48; "Fast Forward: Future Internet," pp. 166–68; Brian E. Taptich, "Star Wars," *Red Herring,* July 1998; G. Christian Hill, "The Spoils of War," *Wall Street Journal,* September 11, 1997; Peter Elstrom, "The Prophet of Telecom," *Business Week,* September 28, 1998, pp. 85–94; In the future, cellular-phone service may also be a source for broadband Internet access. At the present time, however, wireless phone modems tend to provide speeds of only 9.6 kbps. While third generation wireless technology—labeled "3G" by the industry—may provide speeds of 2 mbps, it probably will not be available until at least 2002.

27. "AT&T's Wireless Path to Local Service," *Business Week,* December 28, 1998, p. 53; "Fast Forward: Future Internet," p. 165; John Markoff, "Microsoft Hunts Its Whale, the Digital Set-Top Box," *New York Times,* May 10, 1999.

28. U.S. Government Working Group on Electronic Commerce, *First Annual Report;* U.S. Department of Commerce and U.S. Government Working Group on Electronic Commerce, *Emerging Digital Economy Report,* Chapters 1 and 2; U.S. Bureau of the Census, *Statistical Abstract: 1998,* 573, table 911.

29. U.S. Government Working Group on Electronic Commerce, *First Annual Report;* U.S. Department of Commerce and U.S. Government Working Group on Electronic Commerce, *Emerging Digital Economy Report,* Chapters 1 and 2; U.S. Bureau of the Census, *Statistical Abstract: 1998,* 573, table 911. U.S. Department of Commerce, *Emerging Digital Economy II.*

30. Arthur Andersen, *Net Results 98: Annual Report on the Communications, Media, and Entertainment Industries* (Atlanta, Ga.: Arthur Andersen, 1998), 3–4 (the

Arthur Andersen information-technology category does not include computer hardware and software); International Telecommunication Union, *World Telecommunication Indicators,* A-67 (on worldwide telecommunications spending).

31. University of Texas Center for Research in Electronic Commerce, "The Internet Economy Indicators," <www.internetindicators.com> (October 27, 1999).

32. U.S. Bureau of the Census, *Statistical Abstract: 1998,* 453, table 717; Thomas W. Bonnett, "Is the New Global Economy Leaving State-Local Tax Structures Behind?" *State Tax Notes,* July 13, 1998, p. 116.

33. See generally, Andersen, *Net Results 98,* 3–4 (the Arthur Andersen information-technology category does not include computer hardware and software.); International Telecommunication Union, *World Telecommunication Indicators,* A-67; U.S. Bureau of Census, *Statistical Abstract: 1998,* 571, table 912.

34. "A Cell Phone in Every Pocket," *Business Week,* January 18, 1999, p. 38; Hill, "The Spoils of War," p. R4.

35. Andersen, *Net Results 98,* 11–12; "The New Trailblazers," *Business Week,* April 6, 1998; "From Circuits to Packets," *Economist,* September 13, 1997, p. 25.

36. In Europe, Internet access can be two to four times the cost in the United States because the use of the local network for Internet transmissions is billed based on duration of the calls. See, generally, Frances Cairncross, *The Death of Distance: How the Communications Revolution Will Change Our Lives* (Boston, Mass.: Harvard Business School Press, 1997), Chapter 4.

37. "The New Trailblazers."

38. Cairncross, *Death of Distance,* 59, 76.

39. "Now, Beam Up Some Customers," *Business Week,* December 28, 1998, p. 52.

40. Kevin Maney, "Lights, Camera, Action Broadcast.com," *USA Today,* February 10, 1999, p. B6; Paul Davidson, "RadioNet Set to Blast," *USA Today,* April 28, 1999.

41. David Lieberman, "Movies Soon Could Be Just a Click Away," *USA Today,* May 29, 1998; Negroponte, *Being Digital,* 13.

42. U.S. Bureau of the Census, *Statistical Abstract: 1998,* 585, table 943; "The Emerging Armies of the Web," *Wall Street Journal,* February 11, 1999.

43. Alec Klein, "Will the Future Be Written in E-Ink?" *Wall Street Journal,* January 4, 2000.

44. Carmel, Eisenach, and Lenard, *Digital Economy Fact Book,* 25; Organization of Economic Cooperation and Development, "Measuring Electronic Commerce: International Trade in Software," <www.oecd.org> (April 17, 1998); Denise Caruso, "Educational Technology Recruits a Masterful Marketer of Games to Be Its Leader," *New York Times,* July 29, 1996. On computer games becoming a $2 billion-a-year industry by 2002, see generally, *USA Today,* November 16, 1998.

45. "Net Music Sales to Hit USD4 Billion by 2004," *Financial Times,* May 20, 1999; "Amazon.com," p. 109; "Global Music Growth Slows in First Half of 1998," *Reuters Online News,* October 6, 1998; U.S. Bureau of the Census, *Statistical Abstract:*

1998, 579, table 931; Jon Pareles, "With a Click, a New Era of Music Dawns," *New York Times,* November 16, 1998.

46. Carl Shapiro and Hal R. Varian, *Information Rules: A Strategic Guide to the Network Economy* (Boston, Mass.: Harvard Business School Press, 1999), 78; On the future of digitized music, see generally, Jon Pareles, "Digital Distribution of Music Is Spreading," *New York Times,* July 16, 1998.

47. See generally, Neil Strauss, "Expert to Help Devise Format for Delivering Music on Net," *New York Times,* March 1, 1999; Jon Pareles, "Trying to Get in Tune with the Digital Age," *New York Times,* February 11, 1999.

48. "Amazon.com," p. 109; U.S. Bureau of Census, *Statistical Abstract: 1998,* 579, table 932; 581, table 937; Negroponte, *Being Digital,* 12–13; John W. Wright, ed., *The Universal Almanac 1996* (Kansas City, Mo.: Andrews and McMeel, 1995), 229, n16; *Encyclopedia of Global Industries* (Detroit, Mich.: Gale Research, 1996), 677.

49. Ethan Bronner, "For More Textbooks, a Shift from Printed Page to Screen," *New York Times,* December 1, 1998.

50. U.S. Bureau of the Census, *Statistical Abstract: 1998,* 580, table 934, 579, table 932; Wright, ed., *Universal Almanac 1996,* 227–28; *Encyclopedia of Global Industries,* 705, 712.

51. Evan I. Schwartz, "Advertising Webonomics 101," *Wired,* February 1996.

52. U.S. Bureau of the Census, *Statistical Abstract: 1998,* 572, table 913; *Encyclopedia of Global Industries,* 694, 698.

53. Caruso, "Educational Technology Recruits," p. D5; U.S. Bureau of the Census, *Statistical Abstract: 1998,* 161, table 251 (on higher education spending).

54. Joseph Weber, "School Is Never Out," *Business Week,* October 4, 1999, p. 165.

55. Peter Applebome, "Education.com," *New York Times Education Life,* April 4, 1999, pp. 26, 29.

56. Sarah Lyall, "The British Are Coming," *New York Times Education Life,* April 4, 1999, p. 29.

57. U.S. Bureau of the Census, *Statistical Abstract: 1998,* 511, table 792. Currently, the world's largest banks daily settle accounts by means of about $3 trillion in electronic money transfers. See "How Safe Is the Net?," *Business Week,* June 22, 1998, p. 148.

58. U.S. Department of Commerce and U.S. Government Working Group on Electronic Commerce, *Emerging Digital Economy Report,* Chapter 4.

59. Eric Nee, "Welcome to My Store," *Forbes,* October 19, 1998, p. 143.

60. Denise Caruso, "Get Ready for E-Billing," *New York Times,* November 16, 1998, p. C5; Steve Rosenbush, "More Customers Dialing Web for Phone Billing," *USA Today,* February 25, 1998.

61. Caruso, "Get Ready for E-Billing," p. C5; Steve Rosenbush, "More Customers Dialing Web."

62. U.S. Department of Commerce and U.S. Government Working Group on Electronic Commerce, *The Emerging Digital Economy Report,* Chapter 4, p. 9.

63. "The 21st Century Stock Market," *New York Times,* August 10, 1998; John Tagliabue, "U.S. Online Brokers Eye European Market," *New York Times,* July 20, 1998.

64. U.S. Bureau of Census, *Statistical Abstract: 1998,* 118, table 164.

65. Cairncross, *Death of Distance,* 272.

66. See generally, Steven Levy, "The New Digital Galaxy," *Newsweek,* May 31, 1999.

67. John Dodge, "High-Tech Help for PC Users," *Boston Globe,* April 17, 1996.

68. Tom Lowry, "On-Line Betting Makes March Madness Easy," *USA Today,* March 12, 1999; Steven Crist, "All Bets Are Off," *Red Herring,* July 1998, p. 85.

69. U.S. Bureau of Census, *Statistical Abstract: 1998,* 583–84, tables 940–41; Beth Belton, "U.S. Brings Economy into Information Age," *USA Today,* March 17, 1999; Bruce Orwall and Lisa Bransten, "Caught in the Web," *Wall Street Journal,* March 22, 1999.

70. "Forrester Estimates Worldwide Internet Commerce"; "Business and the Internet."

71. "Forrester Estimates Worldwide Internet Commerce"; "Business and the Internet"; International Data Corporation study cited in "The Internet Age," p. 77.

72. "'Twas the Season for E-Splurging," *Business Week,* January 18, 1999, p. 40; "On-Line Shopping," *USA Today,* March 1, 1999; "Amazon.com," p. 108; Morrisette, Bluestein, and Maraganore, "Consumer's Digital Decade" (on consumer commerce); George Anders, "Click and Buy: Why—and Where—Internet Commerce Is Succeeding," *Wall Street Journal,* December 7, 1998 (on business commerce).

73. University of Texas Center for Research in Electronic Commerce, "The Internet Economy Indicators." For a discussion of the high variation in estimates, see U.S. Department of Commerce, *Emerging Digital Economy II,* i, 5.

74. "Log On, Link Up, Save Big," *Business Week,* June 22, 1998, pp. 134–35 (on EDI). Mail order and other direct marketing to consumers totaled about $87 billion in 1995. See U.S. Bureau of Census, *Statistical Abstract: 1998,* 771, table 1287. While catalogs are the traditional way direct marketers reach the public, television shopping networks have expanded rapidly in recent years. For instance, the Home Shopping Network alone has more than 20 million customer names and credit cards in its files. The two largest home-shopping networks, QVC and Home Shopping Network, sold an estimated $3 billion of goods in 1998. See Ross Kerber, "A Selling Point," *Boston Globe,* March 17, 1999.

75. Cairncross, *Death of Distance,* 27–31, 214.

76. "Two Steps Forward, One Step Back," *Business Week,* August 31, 1998, p. 116.

77. "U.S. Online Business Trade Will Soar to $1.3 trillion by 2003, according to Forrester Research," Forrester Research press release <www.forrester.com> (December 17, 1998); "'Twas the Season for E-Splurging," p. 40; Anders, "Click and Buy." Stephanie Stoughton, "Newest formula for net riches: B2B," *The Boston Globe,* February 10, 2000, page D1.

78. Anders, "Click and Buy"; see also "The 'Click Here' Economy," *Business Week,* June 22, 1998, pp. 124–25.

79. "Log On, Link Up, Save Big," pp. 134–35.

80. "'Twas the Season for E-Splurging," p. 40; "On-Line Shopping"; "Amazon.com," p. 108; Morrisette, Bluestein, and Maraganore, "Consumer's Digital Decade" (on consumer commerce); Anders, "Click and Buy."

81. Seema Williams, "Post-Web Retail" <www.forrester.com> (September 1999); "Peppers and Rogers Group: Direct-to-Consumer Sales to Surge by 2010" <www.nua.ie/surveys> (July 1, 1999); Greg Farrell, "Clicks-and-Mortar World Values Brands," *USA Today,* October 5, 1999.

82. Lohr, "Survey Suggests Consumers Are Taking."

83. Anders, "Click and Buy"; see also "The 'Click Here' Economy," pp. 124–25.

84. See generally, U.S. Bureau of Census, *Statistical Abstract: 1998,* 457, table 723; Nee, "Welcome to My Store," p. 143; "Amazon.com," p. 109; Brad Stone, "Nothing to Sneeze At," *Business Week,* February 15, 1999, p. 60.

85. Steven Levy, "Xmas.com," *Newsweek,* December 7, 1998; "The 'Click Here' Economy," p. 158.

86. Andersen Consulting has estimated that on-line purchase of groceries and other related products could total $85 billion by 2007. See Jared Sandberg, "NoChores.com," *Newsweek,* August 30, 1999, p. 64.

87. "Amazon.com"; "A Real Shot in the Arm for a Virtual Pharmacy," *Business Week,* March 8, 1999, p. 40; "Cyberspace Winners: How They Did It," *Business Week,* June 22, 1998, pp. 154–62; Matthew Mirapaul, "Variety and Prices Draw Music Fans to Web," *New York Times,* July 8, 1998.

88. "eBay vs. Amazon," *Business Week,* May 31, 1999; Tom Lowry, "On-Line Auctioneer eBay Raises Web Site Security," *USA Today,* February 15, 1999; "Cyberspace Winners," p. 154.

89. James L. McQuivey, Kate Delhagen, and Carrie Ardito, "On-Line Retail Strategies," *Forrester Research,* January 1999; U.S. Government Working Group on Electronic Commerce, *First Annual Report,* p. 2.

90. "The 'Click Here' Economy," pp. 122–72. Estimates of potential savings through Web retailing vary widely but are typically in the range of 5 to 15 percent or more compared to traditional retail store sales.

91. Peter de Jonge, "Riding the Wild, Perilous Waters of Amazon.com," *New York Times Magazine,* March 14, 1999; "Amazon.com"; Cynthia Mayer, "Does Amazon = 2 Barnes & Nobles?" *New York Times,* July 19, 1998; "eBay vs. Amazon"; Saul Hansell, "Betting Heavily on Selling Acres of Everything," *New York Times,* November 28, 1999.

92. David Leonhardt, "Lemonade Stands of Electric Avenue," *Business Week E.Biz,* July 26, 1999, p. 64.

93. Steve Lohr, "Looking for Winners in a New Category," *New York Times,* December 23, 1999. The changing business models are intertwined with rapid

advances in technology that also contribute to additional complexity within tax systems. Older technologies such as the single-purpose telephone and the television are in danger of becoming obsolete, replaced by multipurpose handheld computers or Web TVs capable of accessing voice, data, and video. New terminology such as TCP/IP, HTML (hypertext markup language), URL (universal resource locator), VPN (virtual private network), *frame relay, bytes, megabits, digital assistants, Web crawlers, broadband,* and *encryption* is rapidly becoming part of the lexicon. These technological devices and concepts must frequently be understood in order to determine how to adapt traditional global tax systems to the new information-age economy.

94. Kenneth N. Gilpin, "The Internet at Adolescence: A Trillion-Dollar Prodigy," *New York Times,* December 20, 1999.

95. From the European Commission, *Verona Memorandum* (1996), quoted in Richard Doernberg and Luc Hinnekens, *Electronic Commerce and International Taxation* (The Hague: Kluwer Law International, 1999), 23.

96. Committee on Fiscal Affairs, *Organization for Economic Cooperation and Development, Electronic Commerce: A Discussion Paper on Taxation Issues* (Paris: Organization for Economic Cooperation and Development, September, 1998), 18, paragraph 38.

97. U.S. Bureau of Census, *Statistical Abstract: 1998,* 841, table 1365; Organization for Economic Cooperation and Development, *Revenue Statistics of OECD Member Countries* (Paris: Organization for Economic Cooperation and Development, 1996).

98. U.S. Department of the Treasury, *Selected Tax Policy Implications of Global Electronic Commerce* (Washington, D.C.: U.S. Department of Treasury, Office of Tax Policy, November 1996); U.S. Government Working Group on Electronic Commerce, *First Annual Report.*

99. U.S. Government Working Group on Electronic Commerce, *First Annual Report.*

100. Title XI of the *Omnibus Consolidated and Emergency Appropriations Act of 1998,* PL 105-277, October 21, 1998.

101. Title XI of the *Omnibus Consolidated and Emergency Appropriations Act of 1998,* PL 105-277, October 21, 1998.

102. U.S. Bureau of Census, *Statistical Abstract: 1998,* 307, table 499.

103. "Counties, Mayors to File Suit against Internet Commission," *State Tax Notes,* March 8, 1999, pp. 737–39.

104. "Governors Express Concern about Sales Tax Survival in E-Com Age," *State Tax Notes,* March 1, 1999, at 642.

105. "NCSL Tax Panel Offer Input to Federal E-Commerce Panel," *State Tax Notes,* June 7, 1999, p. 1891; David Brunori, "FTA's Harley Duncan on the MTC, Cooperation, E-Commerce," *State Tax Notes,* October 18, 1999, p. 1040.

106. U.S. Government Working Group on Electronic Commerce, *First Annual Report.*

107. U.S. Bureau of Census, *Statistical Abstract: 1998,* 307, table 499. This number includes both general sales taxes and selective sales taxes for utilities, fuel, and so on. The general sales tax amount is about three-quarters of the total.

108. Committee on State Taxation, "Committee on State Taxation's Fifty-State Study and Report on Telecommunications Taxation," *State Tax Notes,* November 22, 1999, p. 1377.

109. Robert J. Cline and Thomas S. Neubig, "The Sky Is Not Falling: Why State and Local Revenues Were Not Significantly Impacted by the Internet in 1998," *State Tax Notes,* June 18, 1999; Advisory Commission on Intergovernmental Relations, "ACIR Releases 1994 Revenue Estimates from Interstate Mail-Order Sales," *State Tax Notes,* August 22, 1994; "State Revenue Losses from E-Commerce Underestimated," *State Tax Notes,* July 26, 1999; Michael Mazerov, Statement of the Center on Budget and Policy Priorities to the Advisory Commission on Electronic Commerce, *State Tax Notes,* September 14, 1999; Mike France, "Commentary: A Web Sales Tax: Not If, but When," *Business Week,* June 21, 1999; Hiawatha Bray, "Rendering unto Caesar," *Boston Globe,* June 24, 1999.

110. Tony Smith, "Email Tax a 'Hoax' Claims US Postal Service," *Register,* June 29, 1999.

111. See the proposals submitted to the Advisory Commission on Electronic Commerce at their Web site, <www.ecommercecommission.org> (December 1999).

112. Curt Anderson, "Panel: E-Commerce Levy Inevitable," *AP on Yahoo.com,* <www.yahoo.com> (June 22, 1999); Dana Blankenhorn, "Get Ready for Internet Sales Taxes," *E Commerce Times,* <www.yahoo.com> (March 16, 1999); Vicky Stamas, "Tax-Free Web Goods May Become Thing of the Past," *Reuters on Yahoo.com,* <www.yahoo.com> (June 24, 1999); Richard Wolffe, "Internet Panel Deeply Divided," *Financial Times at ft.com,* <www.ft.com> (June 22, 1999); Howard Gleckman, "The Net Tax Commission Hits the Ground Arguing," *Business Week Online,* June 28, 1999; "Internet Taxes Not Inevitable," House Majority Leader Dick Armey Web page, <www.freedom.gov/library/technology> (June 28, 1999).

113. Romesh Ratnesar, "A Hex on Your Taxes," *Time,* December 27, 1999, p. 129; see also Richard Wolf, "Income Tax Panel Likely to Deadlock," *USA Today,* December 14, 1999.

114. Advisory Commission on Electronic Commerce, "Issues and Policy Options Paper," Final draft submitted to the commission for the Report Drafting Subcommittee, December 3, 1999. "A Proposal for Internet Tax Reform and Reduction," A 21st Century Approach Presented by the ACEC Business Caucus, February, 2000; "Tech companies outline compromise for Net taxation," *Bloomberg News, www.cnet.com,* January 28, 2000.

Chapter 2

1. National Tax Association, Communications and Electronic Commerce Tax Project, *Final Report* (Washington, D.C., September 7, 1999), p. ii; *Vertex Tax Cybrary,* <http://www.vertexinc.com/taxcybrary20/Sales Tax_Chronicle/taxtrends _tax-facts.hmtl> (November 1999).

2. U.S. Bureau of the Census, *State Government Tax Collections: Fiscal Year 1996–1997* (Washington, D.C.: U.S. Bureau of the Census, 1998); U.S. Bureau of the Census, *Government Finances (1996)* (Washington, D.C.: U.S. Bureau of the Census, 1998). If total state and local taxes are examined, state and local sales tax revenue (from both general and special sales taxes) account for 36 percent of total revenues compared to 32 percent for property tax revenue.

3. John Mikesell, "State Retail Sales Taxes in 1995: The Advantage of a Broad Base," *State Tax Notes,* February 3, 1997.

4. Ibid., pp. 358–59.

5. Ibid., pp. 360–61.

6. Federation of Tax Administrators, *Sales Taxation of Services: 1996 Update,* Research Report no. 143 (Washington, D.C.: Federation of Tax Administrators, April 1997).

7. *Omnibus Consolidated and Emergency Appropriations Act of 1998,* Title XI (PL 105-277).

8. S. 442, 105th Cong., 1st Sess. (1997); H.R. 1054, 105th Cong., 1st Sess. (1997).

9. S. 442, 105th Cong., 1st Sess. (1997); H.R. 1054, 105th Cong., 1st Sess. (1997); *Omnibus Consolidated and Emergency Appropriations Act of 1998,* Title XI, § 1104 (5). Under the *Internet Tax Freedom Act,* the "Internet" is defined as "collectively the myriad of computer and telecommunications facilities, including equipment and operating software, which comprise the interconnected world-wide network of networks that employ the Transmission Control Protocol/Internet Protocol, or any predecessor or successor protocols to such protocol, to communicate information of all kinds by wire or radio."

10. The definition of "Internet access" in the Internet Tax Freedom Act is somewhat ambiguous. Although it may not be the most natural interpretation of this phrase, some taxpayers may take the position that the exemption in the Act covers not just the "transport" over the Internet, but also the "content" if such digitized content is "offered over the Internet." S. 442, 105th Cong., 1st Sess. (1997); H.R. 1054, 105th Cong., 1st Sess. (1997); *Omnibus Consolidated and Emergency Appropriations Act of 1998,* Title XI, § 1104 (3).

11. Mass. Gen. L. ch. 64H, § 1. The actual statutory or regulatory definitions of telecommunications or communications vary from state to state. For instance, in Iowa the regulations state that communication service includes the transmission and receipt of data encoded in computer languages." In Florida the term *telecommunication service* means "Local telephone service, toll telephone service, telegram or telegraph service, teletypewriter or *computer exchange service* [emphasis added]"; Florida Department of Revenue, Technical Assistance Advisement 95A-025R (October 3, 1995).

12. New York State Department of Taxation and Finance, Office of Tax Policy Analysis, *Improving New York State's Telecommunications Taxes: Final Report and Recommendations* (Albany: New York State Department of Taxation and Finance, January 1997), 36.

13. 47 C.F.R. § 64.702(a); Amendment of § 64.702 of the Commission's Rules and Regulations (computer II), 77 Federal Communications Commission 2d.

384 (1980); Multistate Tax Commission (MTC), *Uniform Principles Governing State Transaction Taxation of Telecommunications* (Washington, D.C.: Multistate Tax Commission, 1993); Note that the MTC states that its proposals should not be interpreted as recommending that the taxation of telecommunications should be limited to basic telecommunications, only that its first effort at developing uniformity principles would be limited to such services.

14. As discussed later in the chapter, some states treat such enhanced services not as telecommunications services but as taxable information or computer services. 35 Ill. Comp. Stat.ch. 35, § 2(c); Ind. Code § 6-2.5–4-6; Kan. Stat. Ann. § 79-3603(b)(1).

15. Tenn. Code Ann. § 67-6-102 (29); Tenn. Dept. of Rev., Letter Ruling No. 96-13 (March 21, 1996).

16. In the Matter of the Petition of MCI Telecommunications Corp. for a Declaratory Ruling, Iowa Dept. of Rev. & Fin., No. 94-30-6-0163 (October 28, 1994); In 1999 Iowa passed legislation that exempted Internet access services from taxable communication services. See "Internet Sales Tax Exemption Sent to Governor," *State Tax Notes,* May 24, 1999, p. 1694.

17. S.C. Revenue Ruling 89-14 (July 17, 1989); Mass. Gen. L. ch. 64H, § 1.

18. Some Internet access providers also provide additional services such as design assistance, credit-card processing, site analysis, premium service plans, and so on.

19. *DRS Tax News* (Conn. Dept. of Revenue Services) 8, no. 5 (1996); Texas Code § 151.00394; Texas Code § 151.325.

20. Texas Letter Ruling No. 9503L1343813 (March 15, 1995); *Texas Tax Policy News,* July 1996; Wade Anderson, "The Care and Feeding of the Internet," *State Tax Notes,* May 12, 1997.

21. Florida Technical Assistance Advisement No. 95A-044, (September 22, 1995); "States and Industry Working to Define Tax Policies for Electronic Commerce," *BNA Daily Tax Report,* June 27, 1996.

22. Mass. Gen. L. ch. 64, § 1; Mass. Tech. Info. Release 97-10; Mass. Tech. Info. Release 99-2.

23. Mo. Letter Ruling L9082 (June 28, 1996); Mo. Letter Ruling L9489 (January 17, 1997); Pa. Dept. of Rev., Statement of Policy, 61 Pa. Code, § 60.20 (1997), 27 Pa. Bull. 5432 (1997).

24. Laws of Wash., Chapter 97-304 (1997); Virginia HB 278 (effective July 1, 1998) codified the Virginia rule from: Virginia Ruling of Commissioner, P.D. 97-425, (October 21, 1997).

25. Steve Rosenbush, "PCs Taking Growing Share of Phone Service," *USA Today,* August 20–22, 1999; "The New Trailblazers," *Business Week,* April 6, 1998.

26. Seth Schiesel, "F.C.C. Urges Policy Change in Cyberspace," *New York Times,* April 11, 1998.

27. S. 442, 105th Cong., 1st Sess. (1997); H.R. 1054, 105th Cong., 1st Sess. (1997). *Omnibus Consolidated and Emergency Appropriations Act of 1998,* Title XI, § 1104 (5). See note 9 for the definition of the "Internet" under the *Internet Tax Freedom Act.*

28. 72 P.S. § 7201(rr)(3)(a); 35 Ill. Comp. Stat.ch.35, § 2(c); Ind. Code § 6-2.5-4-6; Kan. Stat. Ann. § 79-3603(b)(1).

29. "The New Trailblazers," p. 96.

30. New York State Department of Taxation and Finance, Office of Tax Policy Analysis, *Improving New York State's Telecommunications Taxes,* 55; New York State Department of Taxation and Finance, TSB-A-99(18)S (April 8, 1999).

31. *Sales Tax Newsletter, New York Office of State Tax Commissioner* 23, no. 1 (1996).

32. Estimates of the sales taxation of the digital economy are based on the author's own research.

33. Minn. Stat. § 297 A.01(g); Tenn. Code Ann. §§ 67-1-102, 67-6-212, 67-6-330, 67-6-402.

34. R.I. Gen. Laws § 44-18-7(J); Wisc. Stat. § 77.52 (12); Wisc. Admin. Code § Tax 11.66(3)(d).

35. Me. Rev. Stat. Ann. § 1752 (17-A), (2-B).

36. See chapter 1.

37. Tex. Tax Code § 151.0033; Tex. Admin. Code tit. 34, § 3.313(a); Fla. Stat. § 212.05(2).

38. Conn. Gen. Stat. § 12-407 (27).

39. There is a large body of rules on issues ancillary to software sales, including the taxation of software installation, modifications, upgrades, maintenance contracts, backup copies, and training.

40. Tex. Tax Code § 151.0031; Tex. Admin. Code, tit. 34, § 3.308(b); Ill. Admin. Code, tit. 86, § 130.1935(a).

41. Conn. Gen. Stat., § 12-407 (2)(i)(A); Conn. Policy Statement 98 (3).

42. Cal. Code Regs., § 1502(f)(1)(D).

43. *Black's Law Dictionary,* 6th ed. (1990), 1456.

44. Cal. Rev. & Tax Code § 6016.

45. S.C. Letter Ruling 96-3 (January 1996). the Tennessee Department of Revenue has similarly ruled that the digital transfer of information over the Internet is not a taxable sale of "tangible personal property." Tenn. Dept. of Rev., Letter Ruling No. 97-51.

46. *Department of Revenue v. Quotron Sys., Inc.,* 615 So.2d 774 (Fla. App. 1993).

47. *South Central Bell Tel. Co. v. Barthelemy,* La. S.Ct., No. 94-C-0499 (October 17, 1994); 637 So. 2d 451 (La. 1994), appeal from Louisiana Court of Appeal, Fourth Circuit (January 27, 1994), affirmed in part, reversed in part, and remanded.

48. Kan. Reg. § 92-19-70; Minn. Stat., § 297A.01; Utah Admin. R. 865-19S-92(B).

49. *American Dist. Tel. Co. v. Porterfield,* 150 Ohio St. 2d 92, 238 N.E.2d 782 (1968).

50. Ala. Reg. 810-6-1-.37(3) and (4).

51. For example, Louisiana taxes custom software as tangible personal property. In 1994 the Louisiana Supreme Court held that custom software created to control call switching was taxable as tangible personal property. The court noted that

"[w]hen stored on magnetic tape, disc, or computer chip, this software, or set of instructions, is physically manifested in machine readable form. . . . The software at issue is not merely knowledge, but rather is knowledge recorded in a physical form which has physical existence, takes up space on the tape, disc, or hard drive, makes physical things happen, and can be perceived by the senses." *South Central Bell Tel. Co. v. Barthelemy,* La. S.Ct., No. 94-C-0499 (October 17, 1994), 637 So. 2d 451 (La. 1994).

52. D.C. Stat., § 47-2001(n)(B); Tex. regulation, Tex. Admin. Code tit. 34, § 3.342.

53. N.Y. Tax Law, § 1105(c)(9). See also Mark S. Klein, TSB-A-93(65)S (December 1993) (investment adviser was subject to sales tax on receipts from the sale of an information service by way of its on-line news service that is not personal or individual in nature); *Quotron Systems, Inc.,* TSB-A-93(61)S (November 1993) (corporation that transmitted financial information to its New York subscribers via leased telephone lines that were linked to its central computer facility was selling a taxable information service).

54. Ohio Rev. Code, § 5739.01(c).

55. Conn. Agencies Regs., § 12-426-27(b)(1). See also Connecticut Department of Revenue, Ruling 93-8 (May 1993). Connecticut is in the process of phasing out its sales and use tax on computer and data-processing services. Beginning with June 30, 1997, the tax rate for such service is being lowered 1 percent per year until July 1, 2002, when such services will become exempt. Conn. Gen. Stat. 12-408(1); Until 1997 the Pennsylvania sales tax was imposed on computer services that were defined as including information retrieval services. Information retrieval services were defined as "providing computer on-line information retrieval services [including but not limited to] . . . data base information retrieval services, on-line information retrieval services, on-line data base information retrieval services or remote data base information retrieval services." However, that legislation was repealed.

56. Iowa Policy letter, July 9, 1999, Tax Research Library Document Link 993300112.

57. Chicago Personal Property Lease Transaction Tax Ordinance.

58. Pennsylvania had a broad category of taxable computer services until the statutory provision was repealed in July, 1997. Under the Pennsylvania statute, taxable computer service included: "The rendition for a consideration of computer programming services; computer-integrated systems design service; computer processing, data processing, data preparation or processing services; information retrieval services; computer facilities management services; or other computer related service."

59. Ill. Admin. Code, tit. 86, § 130.1935(a).

60. Tex. Admin. Code, tit. 34, § 3.308(b)(1).

61. *Hartford Parkview Assoc. Ltd. Partnership v. Groppo,* 558 A.2d 993, 996 (Conn. 1989).

62. *Cummings & Lockwood v. Commissioner of Revenue Services,* Tax Session No. CV-92-0510759 (Conn. Super. Ct. 1994).

63. Connecticut Department of Revenue, Ruling 93-8 (May 1993).

64. *Reuters America Inc. v. Tax Comm'r of Ohio,* No. 92-H-1414 (Ohio Bd. Tax App. 1994).

65. Ibid.

66. Ibid.

67. 72 Ohio St. 3d 222 (Ohio 1995). In *NTN Communications Inc. v. Tax Comm'r of Ohio,* the Ohio Board of Tax Appeals found that the taxpayer, who provided entertainment services involving broadcasts of news, weather, and sports, as well as interactive and noninteractive games to restaurants and bars in Ohio, was providing exempt personal and professional services because the taxpayer employed "cognitive thought to create and update the entertainment broadcast service," No. 93-X-353 (Ohio Bd. Tax App. 1995).

68. Connecticut Department of Revenue, Ruling 96-7 (July 12, 1996); *PNC Bank v. Tracy,* Ohio Bd. Tax App., No. 93-T-1316 (July 7, 1995).

69. Mass. Gen. L., ch. 64H, § 1; N.Y. Tax Law, § 1105(c)(1). Since 1990, New York has clarified the imposition of tax on the electronic furnishing of an information service under another section. N.Y. Tax Law, § 1105(c)(9)(i).

70. Texas Comptroller Ruling No. 9509L1375F11 (September 1995).

71. Texas Comptroller Ruling No. 9604L1408B01 (April 1996).

72. Conn. Gen. Stat., § 12-407 (2)(i)(A), as amended by 1997 Connecticut Public Acts 316, § 6.

73. *DRS Tax News* (Conn. Dept of Rev. Services) 8, no. 1 (1996).

74. CCH, *U.S. Master Sales and Use Tax Guide* (Riverwoods, IL: CCH, 1998), 123–24.

75. N.Y. Tax Law § 1105(c)(3); Conn. Gen. Stat. § 12-407(2)(i)(Q).

76. Steven Levy, "The New Digital Galaxy," *Newsweek,* May 31, 1999.

77. "Selling CDs on Line," *USA Today,* October 4, 1999.

78. S.C. Private Letter Ruling 98-1; *South Central Bell Tel. Co. v. Barthelemy,* La. S.Ct., No. 94-C-0499 (October 17, 1994); 637 So. 2d 451 (La. 1994), appeal from La. Court of Appeal, Fourth Circuit (January 27, 1994), affirmed in part, reversed in part, and remanded.

79. Seth Schiesel, "Time Warner Joins Forces with AT&T," *New York Times,* February 2, 1999; Seth Schiesel, "AT&T Plan Is a Search for Loyalty," *New York Times,* February 11, 1999.

80. Gautam Naik, "How the Cell Phone and Web Contracted an Arranged Marriage," *Wall Street Journal,* October 11, 1999.

81. Jube Shriver, Jr., "FCC Eases Way for Utilities to Enter Telecom," *Boston Globe,* September 13, 1996.

82. Frances Cairncross, *The Death of Distance* (Boston, MA: Harvard Business School Press, 1997), 51, 99.

83. Mass. Dept. of Rev. Regulation, 830 CMR § 64H.1.6 (6)(b). See also Connecticut Department of Revenue, Ruling 91-16 (June 5, 1991).

84. NYCE Corporation (Advisory Opinion), N.Y. Comm. of Tax. & Fin., No. TSB-A-97(86)S (December 29, 1997).

85. Netcom On-Line Communication Services, Inc. (Advisory Opinion), N.Y. Comm. of Tax. & Fin., Nos. TSB-A-97(49)S and TSB-A-97(17)C (July 23, 1997).

86. *Omnibus Consolidated and Emergency Appropriations Act of 1998,* Title XI (PL 105-277).

87. Decision of the Texas Comptroller of Public Accounts, Hearing No. 36,723, (December 3, 1998).

88. Ala. Dept. of Rev., Ruling 94-002.

89. Special Notice, Conn. Dept. of Rev. Services, TSSN-41.

90. *North Dakota Sales Tax Newsletter, Office of State Tax Commissioner* 23, no. 1 (1996).

91. Walter Hellerstein, "Internet Tax Freedom Act Limits States' Power to Tax Internet Access and Electronic Commerce," *Journal of Taxation,* January 1999, p. 6.

92. *Texas Tax Policy News* 6, no. 7 (1996). See also *Connecticut Tax Topics* 3, no. 4 (1996).

93. U.S. Government Working Group on Electronic Commerce, *First Annual Report* (Washington, D.C.: November 30, 1998), 13.

94. Ibid.

95. CCH, *U.S. Master Sales and Use Tax Guide,* 91–92.

96. Conn. Gen. Stat. § 12-412(6).

97. *DRS Tax News* (Conn. Dept. of Rev. Services) 7, no. 4 (1995).

98. N.Y. Tax Law, § 1101(b)(6).

99. Joseph Weber, "School Is Never Out," *Business Week,* October 4, 1999, p. 168.

100. Omnibus Consolidated and Emergency Appropriations Act of 1998, Title XI (PL 105-277), § 1104.

101. Laura Boudette, "German States Forge Ahead in Internet Tax Plan," *ZDNN,* July 30, 1997.

102. Katie Dean, "UN Proposes Global Email Tax," *Wired News,* July 13, 1999; Declan McCullagh, "UN Retreats from Email Tax," *Wired News,* July 16, 1999.

103. "Consuming Movies: Pay TV Eats into Film Spending Cache," *Screen Digest,* January, 1997. Note that these statistics do not include revenues paid by networks or cable stations for non-pay-per-view television or cable showing of movies; David Lieberman, "Movies Soon Could Be Just a Click Away," *USA Today,* May 29, 1998.

104. Based on the author's own research.

105. Charles E. McLure, Jr., "Achieving a Level Playing Field for Electronic Commerce," *State Tax Notes,* June 1, 1998, p. 1770; Raymond J. Ring, Jr., "The Proportion of Consumers' and Producers' Goods in the General Sales Tax," *National Tax Journal* 42, no. 2 (1989): 167–79. Other studies of the proportion of the sales tax paid by businesses range from 18 to 65 percent. However, these figures somewhat overstate the degree of tax pyramiding because some of the output of these businesses is not subject to tax. For instance, a financial-service company may pay taxes on its purchases of computers, but it does not pay sales taxes on its output. See generally, National Tax Association, Communications and Electronic Commerce Tax Project, *Final Report,* 24.

106. CCH, *U.S. Master Sales and Use Tax Guide* 85–86.

107. New York State Department of Taxation and Finance, Office of Tax Policy Analysis, *Improving New York State's Telecommunications Taxes,* (Albany, NY, January 1997) 67–84; Committee on State Taxation, "Committee on State Taxation's Fifty-State Study and Report on Telecommunications Taxation," *State Tax Notes,* November 22, 1999.

108. New York State Department of Taxation and Finance, Office of Tax Policy Analysis, *Improving New York State's Telecommunications Taxes,* 67–84.

109. New Jersey Public Laws, Chapter 26, § 18 (1996).

110. Mass. Gen. L., ch. 64H, § 6(r) and (s); see also *Spectrum Communications Inc. v. State Tax Commission* (1977) A.T.B. No. 73611.

111. 61 Pa. Code § 60.20(b)(6), (e)(1).

112. Connecticut Department of Revenue, Ruling 91-16, (June 5, 1991).

113. *Sales Tax Information Release,* Ohio Department of Taxation, January, 1999; Minnesota Revenue Notice No. 98-03 (March 9, 1998).

114. *Bridge Data Co. v. Director of Revenue,* 794 S.W. 2d 204 (Mo. 1990).

115. N.Y. Tax Law, § 1115(a)(35); L 1999, ch. 407; S. 6110, August 9, 1999. See generally, Marc M. Lewis, "Developers of Software Websites May Qualify under Manufacturing-Type Exemption," *Journal of Multistate Taxation and Incentives,* November–December 1999.

116. *Omnibus Consolidated and Emergency Appropriations Act of 1998,* Title XI (PL 105-277).

117. See generally, McLure, "Achieving a Level Playing Field for Electronic Commerce"; Charles E. McLure, "Achieving Neutrality between Electronic and Nonelectronic Commerce," *State Tax Notes,* July 19, 1999; Robert P. Strauss, "Further Thoughts on State and Local Taxation of Telecommunications and Electronic Commerce," *State Tax Notes,* October 25, 1999.

118. Mass. Regulation, 830 CMR 64H.6.7(3). If, however, a customer takes possession at a vendor's location (instead of having the property shipped to the customer's home address) and subsequently takes the property into the customer's state, then the sale is typically subject to sales tax at the vendor's location.

119. In many digital transactions, such as those involving computer software, there is no technical sale of the product, but rather a license to use the product. However, for sales and use tax purpose, the license to use is generally treated functionally as if it were a sale.

120. Conn. Gen. Stat. § 12-407; Pa. Stat. Ann. § 7504.

121. S.D. Codified Laws Ann., § 10-45-12.3; *In re State & Sales Tax Liability of Quality Serv. Railcar Repair Corp.,* 437 N.W. 2d 209 (South Dakota 1989); N.Y. Tax Law, § 1115(d).

122. Connecticut Policy Statement 98(2).

123. D.C. Mun. Regs. § 475.8; Tex. Admin. Code tit. 34, § 3.330(f). In Pennsylvania, for example, before the repeal of the sales tax on computer services law, the sale of a computer service was subject to tax if the predominate use of the service was in Pennsylvania. Computer services that were delivered to a location in Pennsylvania were presumed to be predominantly used in Pennsylvania.

124. Iowa Regulations , § 701-18.20; Tenn. Dept. of Rev., Letter Ruling No. 96-09 (March, 1996); *Tennessee Tax Quarterly* 16, no.2 (1996); Texas Comptroller of Public Accounts Letter Ruling No. 9711946L (November 26, 1997).

125. Mass. Gen. L., ch. 64H, § 1; Conn. Gen. Stat. § 12-407a; 61 Pa. Code § 60.20(b)(1).

126. *Goldberg v. Sweet,* 488 U.S. 252 (1989).

127. Minn. Stat. § 297A.01; NM. Regs. Sec. 2.1.18.2; *Ragland v. Allen Transformer Co.,* 293 Ark. 601 (1987), *cert. denied* 486 US 1007.

128. Texas Comptroller of Public Accounts Ruling, Microfiche No. 9601L1389G04 (January 1996); Anderson, "Care and Feeding of the Internet," p. 1464.

129. Texas Comptroller of Public Accounts Ruling 9809798L (September 8, 1998).

130. Michigan Regulation R205.80, Rule 30; California Regulation 1571.

131. Walter Nagel, Linda P. Holman, and Douglas A. Richards, "One Approach to State and Local Taxation of Prepaid Calling Cards," *State Tax Notes,* December 16, 1996, p. 1747.

132. Nagel, Holman, Richards, "One Approach to State and Local Taxation," 1747; John McManus, "A Definite Trend: The Changing Sales and Use Taxation of Prepaid Telephone Calling Cards," *State Tax Notes,* October 12, 1998.

133. Laura Blatt, "Is Taxing the Use of Prepaid Telephone Cards a Tough Call?" *CCH State Tax Review,* March 24, 1997, pp. 2–5; New York State Department of Taxation and Finance, Office of Tax Policy Analysis, *Improving New York State's Telecommunications Taxes,* chapter on "Prepaid Phone Cards" (January 1997). According to a survey in Blatt, over two-thirds of the states used the point-of-consumption approach.

134. 61 Pa. Code § 60.20(b)(5); Connecticut Department of Revenue, Ruling 95-10 (August 1995).

135. Excise Tax Bulletin No. 567.08.245, Wash. Dept. of Revenue (December 1994).

136. Data based on the author's own research; see also McManus, "A Definite Trend," p. 968.

137. Ariz. Private Taxpayer Ruling 94-023, Arizona DOR (February 27, 1995); Kan. Stat. Ann, §§ 79-3603(a); 79-3603(u); 79-3602(f); Miss. Code Ann. § 27-65-19(e); Okla. Reg. Rule 710-65-19-331.

138. Ala. Code § 40-23-1(13).

139. Cal. State Board of Equalization, *Tax Information Bulletin,* June 1997.

140. Cairncross, *Death Of Distance,* 127–28.

141. This vendor-state approach is still in keeping with the two-out-of-three test for sourcing sales of telecommunications services: the recipient of the call and the service or billing address are generally located at the vendor's place of business.

142. See generally, "Proposal for Uniform Sourcing for Mobile Telecommunications Transaction Taxes," *State Tax Notes,* September 15, 1997. Congressional legis-

lation may be needed to facilitate a billing-address solution because it may not meet two of the three prongs of the *Goldberg v. Sweet* test.

143. 61 Pa. Code § 60.20, (c)(2).

144. See generally: National Tax Association Communications and Electronic Commerce Tax Project, *Final Report,* 28–48 (section on "Sourcing Transactions for Sales and Use Tax Purposes"); National Tax Association Communications and Electronic Commerce Tax Project, *Final Report: Situs and Sourcing Subcommittee* (Washington, D.C.: National Tax Association, April 10, 1998).

145. National Tax Association, Communications and Electronic Commerce Tax Project, *Final Report,* 28. The NTA project had a prefatory caveat that states: "Nothing is agreed to until everything is agreed to." Thus, this resolution cannot be treated as a definitive statement of the NTA project. Nonetheless, it certainly reflects the general sentiments of the NTA project participants.

146. *Goldberg v. Sweet,* 488 U.S. 252 (1989); *Oklahoma Tax Comm'n v. Jefferson Lines, Inc.,* 115 S. Ct. 1331 (1995). But see *ICC Termination Act of 1995,* PL 104-88 (legislation recently passed by Congress in response to *Oklahoma Tax Comm'n v. Jefferson Lines, Inc,* which among other things included a provision preventing states from levying or collecting taxes on bus fares for interstate travel). Although a state may have the right to tax a particular telecommunications or transportation service, the issue of whether the service provider has sufficient nexus with the state in order to impose a sales/use tax collection responsibility upon the provider must be addressed separately.

147. National Tax Association, Communications and Electronic Commerce Tax Project, *Final Report,* 28–48; National Tax Association Communications and Electronic Commerce Tax Project, *Final Report: Situs and Sourcing Subcommittee.*

148. D.C. Mun. Regs. § 475.8.

149. Ibid.

150. Tex. Admin. Code tit. 34, § 3.342(h).

151. Tex. Admin. Code tit. 34, § 3.342(h)(4).

152. Tex. Admin. Code tit. 34, § 3.342(i).

153. Comeau (Advisory Opinion), Ohio Comm. of Tax. & Fin., TSB-A-90(43)S, Sales Tax (August 20, 1990). See also, Ohio Comm. of Tax. & Fin., *TSB-A-91(1)–(6)S,* Sales Tax.

154. Ohio Reg., Rule 5703-9-46(B)(1).

155. Texas Comptroller of Public Accounts Ruling 9809798L (September 8, 1998).

156. A proposed telecommunications regulation in Massachusetts defines the "use of a telecommunication service" as "[t]he enjoyment of the benefit of the telecommunications service. In general, the benefit of a telecommunications service is enjoyed at the points of origin and termination of the telecommunication." In the proposed regulation, Massachusetts has stated that it will impose a use tax on certain long-distance telephone services such as private leased lines where one end of the transaction occurs in Massachusetts and the state where the "sale" occurs does not

impose a sales tax on such telecommunications services. See Mass. Proposed Reg., 830 CMR 64H.1.6(2), (4)(c).

157. The Information Highway State and Local Tax Study Group, "Supporting the Information Highway: A Framework for State and Local Taxation of Telecommunications and Information Services," *State Tax Notes,* July 3, 1995, p. 57. The wireless telecommunications industry has proposed a similar plan that would resolve the roaming-charges issue already discussed. In late 1997 the industry issued a proposal focused on uniform sourcing rules for mobile-telecommunications transaction taxes. After discussing issues unique to the wireless industry such as roaming charges when initiating calls outside the home carrier geographic area, the paper recommended a quasi-market-state approach to sourcing wireless transactions. Under the proposal mobile-telecommunication charges would be sourced to the location of the customer's state of primary use, as evidenced by the customer's billing address. See "Proposal for Uniform Sourcing For Mobile Telecommunications Transaction Taxes."

158. Interactive Services Association, " Logging On to Cyberspace Tax Policy," *State Tax Notes,* December 20, 1996.

159. Walter Hellerstein, "State Taxation of Electronic Commerce: Preliminary Thoughts on Model Uniform Legislation," *State Tax Notes,* April 28, 1997.

160. National Tax Association, Communications and Electronic Commerce Tax Project, *Final Report,* 28–48; James Eads et al., "National Tax Association Communications and Electronic Commerce Tax Project Report No. 1 of the Drafting Committee," *State Tax Notes,* November 17, 1997; National Tax Association Communications and Electronic Commerce Tax Project, *Final Report: Situs and Sourcing Subcommittee.*

161. For supporters of the vendor state rule, see generally, Terry Ryan and Eric Miethke, "The Seller-State Option: Solving the Electronic Commerce Dilemma," *State Tax Notes,* October 5, 1998; *Digital Products Sourcing for Transaction Tax Purposes,* Report of the CommerceNet Silicon Valley Software Industry Coalition Joint Working Group on Electronic Commerce Taxation, (San Jose, Calif.: Commerce Net, July 20, 1998).

162. Author's own study; National Tax Association, Communications and Electronic Commerce Tax Project, *Final Report,* p. ii; *Vertex Tax Cybrary* <http://www.vertexinc.com/taxcybrary20/Sales Tax_Chronicle/taxtrends_taxfacts.html> (September 1999); Robert J. Cline and Thomas S. Neubig, *Masters of Complexity and Bearers of Great Burdens: The Sales Tax System and Compliance Costs for Multistate Retailers,* <www.ey.com/ecommerce> (September 8, 1999).

163. CCH, *U.S. Master Sales and Use Tax Guide,* 109–18.

164. Ibid.

165. Data regarding state, city and county sales tax rates was also obtained from Vertex, Inc., *Vertex Tax Cybrary* <http://www.vertexinc.com/taxcybrary> (September 1999).

166. James R. Eads, Jr., "Telecommunications Taxation and Electronic Commerce," (paper presented at the Meeting of the Steering Committee of the National

Tax Association Communications and Electronic Commerce Tax Project, Salt Lake City, Utah, April 23, 1998).

167. On the Willis Commission Report, see generally, Kaye Caldwell, "Will the States Repeat Their Major Strategic Error of the Mid-Eighties?" *State Tax Notes,* July 13, 1998, p. 111.

168. *National Bellas Hess, Inc. v. Department of Revenue,* 386 U.S. 753 (1967).

169. Multistate Tax Commission Business Government Dialogue, *Report of the Sales Tax Simplification Planning Committee* (Washington, D.C.: Multistate Tax Commission, October 30, 1997).

170. National Governor's Association Policy, EC-16, *Internet Development Act of 1998.* The document can be found on NGA's Web site, located at <http://www.nga.org/Pubs/Policies/EC/ec16.asp>.

171. Omnibus Consolidated and Emergency Appropriations Act of 1998, Title XI, § 1102(g) (PL 105-277).

172. George Abi-Esher, "NTA Communications and Electronic Commerce Tax Project Endorses One Rate per State on All Commerce," *CCH State Tax Review,* August 24, 1998, p. 16; National Tax Association, Communications and Electronic Commerce Tax Project, *Final Report,* 13–14; National Governor's Association Policy, EC-16, *Internet Development Act of 1998.*

173. *U.S. Bureau of the Census, Statistical Abstract of the United States: 1998,* 118th ed. (Washington, D.C.: U.S. Bureau of the Census, 1998), 307, table 499. This number includes both general sales taxes and selective sales taxes for utilities, fuel, and so on. The general sales tax amount is about three-quarters of the total; John L. Mikesell, "The Future of American Sales and Use Taxation," in David Brunori, ed., *The Future of State Taxation,* (Washington, D.C.: Urban Institute, 1998), 15–16. A less-radical alternative to one rate per state would be to limit the number of tax-rate changes permitted annually. This would involve both limiting the number of tax rate changes that a state or locality may make in a given year and *requiring* a substantial notification period before the changes take effect. Currently, no state has this type of restriction on rate changes.

174. Doug Sheppard, "What Can Be Learned from the NTA's Internet Project," *State Tax Notes,* October 4, 1999, p. 894.

175. See generally, National Tax Association, Communications and Electronic Commerce Tax Project, *Final Report,* 19–27 (section on "Sales and Use Tax Base Issues").

176. See generally, National Tax Association, Communications and Electronic Commerce Tax Project, *Final Report,* 49–71 (section on "Simplification of State and Local Sales and Use Tax Administration"); Multistate Tax Commission, Business Government Dialogue, *Report of the Sales Tax Simplification Planning Committee* (Washington, D.C.: Multistate Tax Commission, October 30, 1997).

177. Multistate Tax Commission Business Government Dialogue, *Report of the Sales Tax Simplification Planning Committee.*

178. Other reforms of the audit-and-appeals process include the following: the development of uniform sampling methodologies for computer-assisted auditing by

state tax auditors; uniform record-keeping rules, particularly with regard to electronic transactions involving EDI, procurement cards, or the Internet; and a uniform statute of limitation for assessments and refunds.

179. Washington Department of Revenue, *Retailers Cost of Collecting and Remitting Sales Tax* (Washington Department of Revenue, 1998).

180. Cline and Neubig, *Masters of Complexity and Bearers of Great Burdens;* Lorrie Jo Brown, "Sales Tax Compliance Costs for E-Tailers Revisited: A Critique of the Ernst and Young Study," *State Tax Notes,* January 24, 2000, p. 315.

181. National Tax Association, Communications and Electronic Commerce Tax Project, Final Report, 49–71 (section on "Simplification of State and Local Sales and Use Tax Administration").

182. *Streamlined Sales Tax System for the 21st Century,* proposal presented to the Advisory Commission on Electronic Commerce (November 1999).

Chapter 3

1. Massachusetts is phasing in the single sales factor for manufacturers and will apply a 100 percent sales factor beginning in 2000. See Mass. Gen. L. ch. 63, § 38; Illinois is phasing in the sales factor and will apply a 100 percent sales factor to all entities beginning in 2000. See Illinois P.A. 90-0613.

2. The typical property factor includes only tangible property such as buildings and equipment. In situations where the property factor also includes intangible property such as intellectual property or loan receivables, the calculation of the property factor can be much more complex. This is evident in the special property-factor apportionment rules applied to financial institutions under the MTC's model apportionment rules for financial institutions. Under these rules, both loan and credit-card receivables are included in the property factor. See generally, Multistate Tax Commission Regulation IV.18(i).

3. *Uniform Division of Income for Tax Purposes Act* (UDITPA) § 15.

4. UDITPA § 16.

5. UDITPA § 17.

6. Cal. Rev. & Tax Code § 25136; Mass. Gen. L. ch. 63, § 38(f); UDITPA § 17. In some states such as Illinois, the all-or-nothing rule is slightly different, with sales sourced to Illinois only if the costs of performance in Illinois exceed the costs of performance outside the state. Ill. Admin. Code tit. 86, § 100.3370(c)(3)(C)(ii).

7. Conn. Gen. Stat. § 12-218(c).

8. Tex. Admin. Code tit. 34 § 3.557(e)(33).

9. Mass. Reg. 830 CMR 63.38.1.

10. Franchise Tax Board, Multistate Audit Technique Manual, June 1995, § 7545.

11. N.Y. Reg. § 4-4.3(a).

12. A similar problem arises with the utilization of the new MTC's financial-institution apportionment rules. Under the property-factor rules for determining

the location of intangible property, loan receivables are sourced to where the preponderance of activities related to the solicitation, investigation, negotiation, approval, and administration of the loan occur. Multistate Tax Commission Regulation § IV.18 (i).

13. Multistate Tax Commission Regulation § IV.17 (3).

14. FTB Notice 97-9, Explanation of the Discussion Draft, Cal. Code of Reg. tit. 18, § 25137-13.

15. CCH, *Multistate Corporate Income Tax Guide (1999)* (Riverwoods, Ill.: CCH, 1999), paragraph 170 (section on "Corporate Income Tax Rate").

16. CCH, *Multistate Corporate Income Tax Guide (1999),* paragraph 146 (section on "Apportionment Formulas").

17. However, the recent MTC regulation on apportionment of income for financial institutions has a throwback rule for the sale of financial services.

18. On the drafters' misgivings on the sourcing rule for services and intangibles, see William J. Pierce, "The Uniform Division of Income for State Tax Purposes," *Taxes* 35 (October, 1957), 747; UDITPA, § 2. This section of the UDITPA states that "[a]ny taxpayer having income from business activity which is taxable both within and without this state, or other than activity as a financial organization or public utility or the rendering of purely personal services by an individual, shall allocate and apportion his net income as provided in this Act." UDITPA § 1(d) defines a "financial organization" as "any bank, trust company, savings bank, industrial bank, land bank, safe deposit company, private banker, savings and loan association, credit union, cooperative bank, investment company, or any type of insurance company." UDITPA § 1(f) defines a "public utility" as "any business entity which owns or operates for public use any plant, equipment, property, franchise, or license for the transmission of communications, transportation of goods or persons, or the production, storage, transmission, sale, delivery, or furnishing of electricity, water, steam, oil, oil products or gas."

19. U.S. Department of Labor, Bureau of Labor Statistics, *Employment and Earnings* (Washington, D.C.: U.S. Department of Labor, September 1997), 41.

20. U.S. Bureau of the Census, *Statistical Abstract of the United States, 1996,* (Washington, D.C.: U.S. Bureau of the Census, 1996), 547; U.S. Department of Commerce, *Historical Statistics of the United States: Colonial Times to 1970,* vol. 2 (Washington, D.C.: U.S. Department of Commerce, 19xx), 957.

21. Seth Godin, ed., *The 1997 Information Please Business Almanac* (Boston, MA: Houghton Mifflin, 1997), 237; Peter Truell, "Buoyant Stock Market Keeps Mergers in Pipeline," *New York Times,* January 5, 1998.

22. In certain states there are also special industry regulations for other service industries. These include construction, franchisors, package delivery, bus lines, leasing and rental enterprises, mail-order businesses and certain other service industries. All of these regulations share in common a focus on market-state rules for sales-factor purposes and an orientation for establishing rules for a single service industry and not for all service businesses.

23. Multistate Tax Commission § IV.18.(i)(1)(d), (g).

24. Multistate Tax Commission § IV.18.(j).

25. Multistate Tax Commission § IV.18.(h).

26. Fla. Rule 12C-1.0155 (2)(g); Kentucky Rev. Stat. § 143.451.6.

27. Mo. Rev. Stat. § 143.451.6.

28. Mass. Regulation, 830 CMR 63.38.1 (9) (d) 3.

29. *Geoffrey Inc. v. South Carolina Tax Commission,* 437 S.E. 2d 13 (S.C. 1993).

30. Multistate Tax Commission § IV.18.(j).

31. Iowa Reg. § 701-54.6(1); Minn. Stat. § 290.191(5)(i), (j); Georgia § 48-7-31(d)(3) (C).

32. Cal. Franchise Tax Board Notice 97-9. See also an analysis of the proposal by its original author in Michael E. Brownell, "California Income and Franchise Tax Issues for Electronic Commerce," *State Tax Notes,* April 28, 1997; Under the draft regulation, subscription-television service would be sourced to the location of the subscriber. This category includes the transmission of video and audio programming by means of cable television services or direct-broadcast satellite service.

33. Cal. Franchise Tax Board Notice 97-9.

34. James H. Peters, "The Undeserved Fate of California's Discussion Draft Regulation 25137-13," *State Tax Notes,* August 17, 1998, pp. 431–33.

35. Peters, "The Undeserved Fate of California's Discussion Draft Regulation 25137-13," p. 433; See *State Tax Notes,* January 27, 1998, p. 241.

36. Brownell, "California Income and Franchise Tax Issues For Electronic Commerce."

37. "Final Report: NTA E-Com Situs and Sourcing Subcommittee," *State Tax Notes,* September 14, 1998. Some of the examples in the California draft regulation read as if they could have been included verbatim in the NTA project's sourcing rules. For instance, Example 5 in the California FTB regulation states: "The taxpayer provides financial information to customers via the taxpayer's terminals at the customer's place of business. The taxpayer charges customers a base fee for the financial information per location and a desk unit related fee. The taxpayer's database and headquarters are in state X. The taxpayer manufactures the terminal equipment in state Y. Customer A has locations both within and without this state. Despite the fact that the taxpayer may have significant costs of performance . . . in state X, or Y, . . . the base fees attributable to Customer A's locations in this state are included in the numerator of the sales factor of this state, because those fees are for providing electronic information at a connection point in this state. The desk unit fee is included in the numerator of the sales factor of this state [as tangible property rented in this state]." See FTB Notice 97-9, Discussion Draft, Section 25137-13 Regulations (c)(4).

38. Research conducted by Arthur Andersen; New York State Department of Taxation and Finance, *Improving New York State Telecommunications Taxes: Final Report and Recommendations,* January 1997; Deborah Bierbaum, David Boughtwood, and Arthur Friedson, "Taxation of Telecommunications: A Review of the States," *State Tax Notes,* December 30, 1996.

39. Research conducted by Arthur Andersen; New York State Department of Taxation and Finance, *Improving New York State Telecommunications Taxes*; Bierbaum, Boughtwood, and Friedson, "Taxation of Telecommunications."

40. New York State Department of Taxation and Finance, *Improving New York State Telecommunications Taxes,* 27, 34.

41. Bierbaum, Boughtwood, and Friedson, "Taxation of Telecommunications," pp. 1893–96.

42. Joan M.Youngman, "Three Questions on the Taxation of Telecommunications Property," *State Tax Notes,* December 30, 1996, p. 1873; Committee on State Taxation, "Committee on State Taxation's Fifty-State Study and Report on Telecommunications Taxation," *State Tax Notes,* November 22, 1999, p. 1380.

43. Richard McHugh, "The Taxation of Telecommunications," in *A Blueprint for Tax Reform,* 763.

44. According to one estimate, in some jurisdictions, nearly three-quarters of all taxes imposed on telecommunications providers are local property taxes. See Youngman, "Three Questions on the Taxation of Telecommunications Property," p. 1877.

45. See generally, Robert L. Bland, "Franchise Fees and Telecommunications Services: Is a New Paradigm Needed?" *State Tax Notes,* February 10, 1997.

46. Mass. Gen. L. ch. 63, § 52A(2).

47. Mass. Gen. L. ch. 63, § 52A(1)(a).

48. Local exchange carriers that lay lines similar to cable television companies, however, have been exempted by the state from paying franchise fees.

49. "Taxation of Telecommunications and Energy in California," *State Tax Notes,* March 18, 1996.

50. McHugh, "Taxation of Telecommunications," 763–67.

51. Committee on State Taxation, "Committee on State Taxation's Fifty-State Study and Report."

52. Ibid.

Chapter 4

1. Even if the provider has no sales tax collection responsibility, the consumer may have a use tax responsibility.

2. Ian Springsteel, "State Taxes: A Guide for the Besieged," *CFO,* August 1996, p. 29.

3. *Complete Auto Transit v. Brady,* 430 U.S. 274 (1976). This decision established a four-prong test for deciding whether a state tax violates the Commerce Clause. In order to pass muster under the Commerce Clause, a state tax must (1) apply to an activity with a substantial nexus with the taxing state, (2) be fairly apportioned, (3) not discriminate against interstate commerce, and (4) be fairly related to the services provided by the state.

4. *Quill Corp. v. North Dakota,* 504 U.S. 298 (1992).

5. Ibid. The Court's ruling in *Quill Corp. v. North Dakota* reaffirmed the portion of its landmark decision in *National Bellas Hess, Inc. v. Department of Revenue,* 386 U.S. 753 (1967), which established a bright-line physical-presence standard under the Commerce Clause that must be met before a state can impose a duty on an out-of-state mail-order seller to collect use tax on purchases from in-state customers. However, the Court overturned its prior decision in *National Bellas Hess, Inc. v. Department of Revenue* to the extent that it indicated that the Due Process Clause requires a seller's physical presence in a state before the seller can be obligated to collect the state's use tax.

6. See *Quill Corp. v. North Dakota; National Bellas Hess, Inc. v. Department of Revenue,* n. 140.

7. 15 U.S.C. § 381(a). See also *William Wrigley, Jr. Co. v. Wisc. Dep't. of Revenue,* 112 S.Ct. 2447 (1992). In this case the Court addressed what constituted "solicitation" and concluded that solicitation covers all activities that are essential to making requests for purchases, as well as all other activities that are entirely ancillary to making such requests. Activities that are "entirely ancillary" are those that serve no purpose apart from their connection to the solicitation of orders. Other activities that a company would engage in anyway, but chooses to allocate to its in-state sales force, are not protected. Providing a car and a stock of free samples to a salesman are examples of entirely ancillary activities under *William Wrigley, Jr. Co. v. Wisc. Dep't. of Revenue.* Repair or service of the company's products, however, is not part of solicitation. The Court also made it clear that the maintenance of an office by a company or its employee does not come within the protection of PL 86-272, even if it is used solely to facilitate requests for purchases.

8. U.S. Bureau of the Census, *Statistical Abstract of the United States: 1998,* 118th ed. (Washington, D.C.: U.S. Bureau of the Census, 1998), 771, table 1287; "Forrester Estimates Worldwide Internet Commerce Will Reach as High as $3.2 Trillion in 2003," Forrester Research press release, <www.forrester.com> (November 5, 1998).

9. "Forrester Estimates Worldwide Internet Commerce"; Seema Williams, "Post-Web Retail," <www.forrester.com/ER/Research/Report> (September 1999); "Business and the Internet: The Net Imperative," *Economist,* June 26, 1999; Lorrie Grant, "Stores with Doors Not Passe," *USA Today,* August 4, 1999; Greg Farrell, "Clicks-and-Mortar World Values Brands," *USA Today,* October 5, 1999.

10. David Leonhardt, "Lemonade Stands of Electric Avenue," *Business Week E.Biz,* July 26, 1999, p. 64.

11. This information is based on data available on the company's respective Web sites or from newspaper accounts.

12. "The Real Internet Revolution," <www.economist.com> (August 29, 1999); Terry Pristin, "Increasingly Traditional Retailers Take That Internet Plunge," *New York Times,* December 25, 1999.

13. "Finding E-Commerce Riches in the Back Office," *Business Week,* July 26, 1999, p. 84; Leslie Kaufman, "Fingerhut Gives Federated Edge in E-Commerce," *New York Times,* July 6, 1999.

14. Bob Tedeschi, "E–Commerce Report," *New York Times*, September 27, 1999. A company could have to pay between $80 million and $100 million to build its own 1 million square foot warehouse.

15. *Quill Corp. v. North Dakota; William Wrigley, Jr. Co. v. Wisc. Dep't. of Revenue.*

16. Office of Texas Comptroller of Public Accounts, Hearing No. 32,349 (January 30, 1995).

17. *Orvis Co., Inc. v. Tax Appeals Tribunal of New York*, 654 NE2d 954 (N.Y. Ct. App. 1995), *cert. denied* 116 S.Ct. 518 (1995); *Vermont Information Processing, Inc. v. Tax Appeals Tribunal*, Docket No. 139 (N.Y. Ct. App. 1995).

18. *Orvis Co., Inc. v. Tax Appeals Tribunal of New York*, *cert. denied; Vermont Information Processing, Inc. v. Tax Appeals Tribunal.*

19. *Brown's Furniture, Inc. v. Wagner*, 665 NE2d 803 (Ill. 1996), *cert. denied*, 117 S.Ct. 175 (1996).

20. *Magnetek Controls, Inc. v. Department of Treasury*, 221 Mich. App 400, 562 NW2d 219 (1997).

21. Ibid.

22. Michigan Department of Treasury, *Revenue Administrative Bulletin 1999-1*, May 12, 1999.

23. Multistate Tax Commission, *State Participant Revised Public Participation Working Group Draft of the Constitutional Nexus Guideline for Application of a State's Sales and Use Tax to an Out-of-State Business*, January 1998 draft (Washington, D.C.: Multistate Tax Commission, January 1998).

24. Ibid.

25. Ibid.

26. *Florida Department of Revenue v. Share International, Inc.*, 676 So.2d 1362 (Fla. 1996) *aff'y* 667 So.2d 226 (Fla. App. 1st Dist. 1995).

27. *Bean v. Pennsylvania*, 516 A.2d 820 (Pa. Comm. Ct. 1986).

28. *Care Computer Systems, Inc. v. Arizona Department of Revenue*, Arizona Board of Tax Appeals, Division Two, No. 1049-93-S, April 4, 1995.

29. *NADA Services Corp.* N.Y. Div. of Tax Appeals, Administrative Law Judge Unit, DTA No. 810592 (February 1, 1996).

30. Ibid.

31. Mass. Gen. L. ch. 64H, § 1; TX Code §151.107(a)(7).

32. Oh. Rev. Code § 5741.01(I)(2), (8).

33. *Tyler Pipe Industries, Inc. v. Washington State Department of Revenue*, 483 U.S. 232 (1987), especially 250–51.

34. Multistate Tax Commission, *State Participant Revised Public Participation Working Group Draft of the Constitutional Nexus Guideline*, January 1998 draft, n. 2.

35. *Bean v. Pennsylvania; NADA Services Corp.; Matthew Bender & Co., Inc. v. Comptroller of the Treasury*, Maryland Court of Special Appeals, No. 1776, June 29, 1989, unreported.

36. *New York Tax Law*, § 208.19.

37. *Quill Corp. v. North Dakota*, n. 8.

38. Texas Decision of the Comptroller of Public Account, Hearing No. 36,237 (July 21, 1998); Kansas Department of Revenue Private Letter Ruling Number P-1998-207 (December 14, 1998).

39. "Court Denies State's Motion to Dismiss AOL Appeal," *State Tax Notes*, November 23, 1998, p. 1319.

40. *Scripto, Inc. v. Carson* 362 U.S. 207, 211, 212 (1960).

41. *Tyler Pipe Industries, Inc. v. Washington State Department of Revenue*, especially 250–51.

42. California State Board of Equalization Ruling 220.0020 (August 29, 1955).

43. *In the Matter of the Appeal of Scholastic Book Clubs, Inc.*, Kansas Supreme Court, No. 75,199 (July 12, 1996); *Scholastic Book Clubs, Inc. v. State Board of Equalization*, California Court of Appeal, First Appellate District, Division Five, No. A040915 (January 30, 1989).

44. *Scholastic Books Clubs v. State of Michigan et. al.*, Michigan Court of Appeals, No. 189386 (May 20, 1997); *Freedom Industries v. Roger W. Tracy, Tax Commissioner of Ohio*, Ohio Board of Tax Appeals, No. 92-C-597 (December 12, 1994); *James Pledger, Director, Department of Finance and Administration v. Troll Book Clubs, Inc.*, Arkansas Supreme Court, No. 93-674 (March 7, 1994).

45. Multistate Tax Commission, *Nexus Bulletin 95-1* (Washington, D.C.: Multistate Tax Commission, December 1995).

46. California State Board of Equalization Regulation 1684.

47. *Furnitureland South, Inc. and Royal Transport, Inc. v. Comptroller*, Maryland Circuit Court for Anne Arundel County, No. C-97-37872 OC (August 13, 1999).

48. *Tyler Pipe Industries v. Washington State Department of Revenue.*

49. "COST Opposes MTC Nexus Bulletin 95-1," *State Tax Notes*, March 25, 1995, pp. 973–77.

50. Multistate Tax Commission, *Nexus Bulletin 95-1*; On activities that fall outside the scope of PL 86-272, see Commonwealth of Massachusetts, 830CMR 63.39.1 (5) (d).

51. Bob Tedeschi, "E-Commerce Report," *New York Times*, December 27, 1999.

52. Illinois Department of Revenue General Information Letter No. 95-0519 (December 29, 1995); Illinois Department of Revenue General Information Letter No. 95-0485 (November 1, 1995); California State Board of Equalization Ruling 220.0010 (July 6, 1977).

53. *Carapace v. Limbach*, Ohio Board of Tax Appeals (May 28, 1993), B.T.A. No. 90-R-825, unreported.

54. Fla. Stat. §§ 212.0596(1), 212.06(2)(C); 35 ILCS §§ 105/2, 105/3-45; 60 Mich. Sta. Ann. §§ 7.555 (2), (3)(1), (4)(b), (5)(a); Ohio Code Ann. §§ 5741.01(E), (H)–(I), 5741.04, 5741.17(A)(1).

55. Calif. Rev. and Tax Code § 6203(c)(2).

56. Indiana Code, § 6-2.5-3-1(c).

57. Multistate Tax Commission, *MTC Constitutional Nexus Guidelines for Application of Sales and Use Tax to an Out-of-State Business,* January 1998 draft (Washington, D.C.: Multistate Tax Commission, January 1998).

58. Greg Farrell, "Ad Rates on Web May Be Pay-per-View," *USA Today,* September 1, 1999.

59. Peter de Jonge, "Riding the Wild, Perilous Waters of Amazon.com," *New York Times Magazine,* March 14, 1999; "AOL Inks Agreement to Promote First USA Credit Cards," *Boston Globe,* February 4, 1999.

60. Jonathan Rosenoer, Douglas Armstrong, and J. Russell Gates, *The Clickable Corporation: Successful Strategies for Capturing the Internet Advantage* (New York: Free Press, 1999), 44–45, 69–70; Steve Rosenbush, "AT&T May Tap AOL to Sell Long-Distance," *USA Today,* March 3, 1999; Steven Levy, "Step Right Up," *Newsweek,* May 25, 1998, p. 80.

61. *Quill Corp. v. North Dakota,* n. 6.

62. Greg Farrell, "Ad Rates on Web."

63. *Internet Tax Freedom Act,* § 1101(a)(2), § 1104 (2)(B).

64. In a New York case, the U.S. District Court ruled that placing an advertisement on a Web site located on a computer server did not establish minimal nexus with New York. In that case, however, the server was located in Missouri and merely accessed by a consumer in New York. *Bensusan Restaurant Corp. v. King,* 96 Civ. 3992 (S.D.N.Y. September 9, 1996).

65. Multistate Tax Commission, *MTC Constitutional Nexus Guidelines for Application of Sales and Use Tax to an Out-of-State Business,* January 1996 draft, November 1996 draft (Washington, D.C.: Multistate Tax Commission, 1996). A similar issue arose regarding whether a telecommunications provider that provided local dial-access service to a customer to enable the customer to access on-line service providers, such as America Online or CompuServe, could be deemed to be creating nexus for these on-line service providers in the states where the telecommunications provider has nexus. The questionable position was that the telecommunications provider acted as an in-state agent or distributor for the on-line service providers in helping them to establish a market in the taxing jurisdiction.

66. Texas Comptroller of Public Accounts LR 9601L1389G04 (January 8, 1996); Wade Anderson, "Care and Feeding of the Internet," *State Tax Notes,* May 12, 1997, p. 1464.

67. Multistate Tax Commission, *Nexus Bulletin 95-1.*

68. California State Board of Equalization Regulation 1684. Indeed there is some ambiguity in the Internet Tax Freedom Act which could be utilized to exempt from agency nexus all market state computer servers with links to out-of-state sellers. See generally: Jerome R. Hellerstein and Walter Hellerstein, *State Taxation, Volume II,* (Boston, Mass.: Warren, Gorham & Lamont, 1999), pages 19-31–19-33.

69. New York Notice TSB-M-97 (January 24, 1997); Oklahoma Regulation 710:65-19-156.

70. 35 ILCS §§ 105/2, 105/3-45.

71. *JS&A Group, Inc. v. State Board of Equalization,* California Court of Appeal, First Appellate District, Division One, No. 1075021 (March 10, 1997).

72. See generally, Leonhardt, "Lemonade Stands of Electric Avenue," pp. 64–66.

73. California State Board of Equalization Regulation 1684.

74. Connecticut Public Statement 98(2).

75. Illinois Department of Revenue General Information Letter No. 95-0519 (December 29, 1995); Illinois Department of Revenue General Information Letter No. 95-0485 (November 1, 1995); California State Board of Equalization Ruling 220.0010 (July 6, 1977).

76. Mass. Gen. L. ch. 64H, § 1.

77. Lorrie Grant, "Going, Going, Gone.com," *USA Today,* May 17, 1999; Tom Lowry, "On-Line Auctioneer eBay Raises Web Site Security," *USA Today,* February 15, 1999.

78. New York State Department of Taxation and Finance, TSB-A-99(49)(S) (November 17, 1999).

79. Vermont Ruling 96-14, Department of Taxes (October 15, 1996).

80. Grant, "Going, Going, Gone.com."

81. Chris Reidy, "Brick-and-Mortar Retailers Rule Net," *Boston Globe,* July 20, 1999.

82. *National Geographic Society v. California State Board of Equalization,* 430 US 551 (1977).

83. Ill. Regulation, § 150.201; Wisc. Reg. § 11.97(3)(d).

84. 35 ILCS 105/2; *Readers Digest Association, Inc. v. Mahin,* 255 N.E.2d 458 (Ill. 1970), *cert. denied,* 399 U.S. 919 (1970); *Pearle Health Services, Inc. v. Taylor,* 799 SW2d 655 (Tenn. 1990).

85. California Revenue and Taxation Code § 6203(g).

86. *Current, Inc. v. State Board of Equalization,* 29 Cal. Rptr. 2d 407, 411 (First District 1994).

87. *Bloomingdale's By Mail, Ltd. v. Pennsylvania Department of Revenue,* 567 A.2d 773 (Pa. Comm. Ct. 1989), *aff'd* 591 A.2d 1047 (1992); *cert. denied,* 112 S. Ct. 2299 (1992).

88. *SFA Folio Collections, Inc. v. Bannon,* 585 A.2d 666 (Conn. 1991), *cert. denied,* 111 S. Ct. 2839 (1991).

89. Ohio Rev. Code § 5741.01(I).

90. *SFA Folio Collections, Inc. v. Tracy,* 652 N.E.2d 693 (Ohio 1995).

91. Barnes & Noble, advertisement in *New York Times,* May 24, 1999.

92. *SFA Folio Collections, Inc. v. Bannon.*

93. California State Board of Equalization Ruling 220.0002, June 2, 1999.

94. Massachusetts Department of Revenue, Letter Ruling 99-1, January 6, 1999.

95. *SFA Folio Collections, Inc. v. Bannon.*

96. *Spencer Gifts, Inc.,* New York State Tax Commission, Petition No. S851028A, TSB-A-86(37)S (September 18, 1986).

97. See generally, *Spencer Gifts, Inc.; G.P. Group, Inc. v. Director of Revenue,* Nos. 91-002180RV and 92-00318RV through 92-00324RV (Missouri Administrative Hearing Commission, February 4, 1986).

98. See generally, *Bottiglieri,* New York TSB-A-88(20)S, (March 2, 1988); *Harfred Operating Corp.,* New York TSB-A-86(28)S (July 18, 1986); *CIT Financial Services Consumer Discount Co. v. Director, Division of Taxation,* 4 N.J. Tax 568 (N.J. Tax. Ct. 1982).

99. Nebraska Regulation 1-006.02.

100. Mass. Gen. L. ch. 64H, § 1.

101. Cal. Rev. and Tax Code § 6007.

102. *Lyon Metal Products, Inc. v. State Board of Equalization,* 58 Cal. App. 4th 906 (Cal. Ct. App. 1997).

103. *VSA, Inc. v. Faulkner,* 485 SE2d 348 (N.C. Ct. App. 1997).

104. *Matter of Steelcase Inc.,* N.Y. State Tax Comm., TSB-H-87(219)S (1988).

105. *Steelcase, Inc. v. Director, Division of Taxation,* New Jersey Tax Court, No. 07-22-2606-90ST (April 5, 1993), 13 N.J. Tax 182.

106. *Steelcase, Inc. v. Allan A. Crystal, Commissioner of Revenue Services,* 238 Conn. 571 (1996).

107. Conn. General Statute, Sec. 12-407(3).

108. Similarly, according to a Florida Technical Assistance Advisement, an out-of-state seller that had no manufacturing facility in Florida, but which registered in the state as a dealer, was not required to collect or remit sales tax on merchandise delivered via common carrier directly to an out-of-state purchaser's Florida customer. Technical Assistance Advisement No.96A-043, Fla. Dept. of Rev. (1996).

109. *Lyon Metal Products, Inc. v. State Board of Equalization.*

110. California defines retail sale as a sale for any purpose other than resale in the regular course of business in the form of tangible personal property:"When tangible personal property is delivered by an owner or former owner, . . . pursuant to a retail sale made by a retailer not engaged in business in this state, the person making the delivery shall be deemed the retailer of that property. He or she shall include the retail selling price of the property in his or her gross receipts or sales price." California Code Sec. 6007.

111. *Pledger v. Troll Book Club; In the Matter of the Appeal of Scholastic Book Clubs, Inc.*

112. North Carolina Department of Revenue Directive CD-98-4 (November 19, 1998).

113. *Geoffrey, Inc. v. South Carolina Tax Commission,* 437 S.E.2d 13 (S.C. 1993), *cert. denied,* 114 S. Ct. 550 (1993).

114. Arkansas Revenue Policy Statement 1995-2; Florida Technical Assistance Advisement No. 95(C)1-008 (August 1995).

115. Mass. DOR Directive 96-2 (1996).

116. Proposed Amendment, N.J.C.A. §§ 18:7-1.6, 1.7, 1.8, 1.9, and 1.10; Iowa Admin. Code, r701-52.1(1)d.

117. Mass. Gen. L. c. 63, § 1-4.

118. Mass. Gen. L. c. 63, § 1 (definition of "engaged in business in the Commonwealth") and § 2.

119. Ind. Code § 6-5.5-3-1 (4), (6), (8),3-4; Minn. Stat. § 290.015, Subd. 1, 2.

120. *J.C. Penney National Bank v. Ruth Johnson, Commissioner of Revenue, State of Tennessee,* Davidson County Chancery Court, No. 96-276-I (October 16, 1998).

121. Tenn. Code § 67-4-806(d)(1), (d)(2).

122. *J.C. Penney National Bank v. Ruth Johnson, Commissioner of Revenue, State of Tennessee.*

123. *J.C. Penney National Bank v. Ruth E. Johnson,* in the Court of Appeals of Tennessee, Appeal No. M1998-00497-COA-R3-CV.

124. *Main Street and Consumer Protection Act of 1995,* S.R. 545; *Main Street and Consumer Protection Act of 1998,* S.R. 1586.

125. *Quill Corp. v. North Dakota,* 318.

126. Ibid., 316.

127. Ibid., n. 6.

128. Robert J. Cline and Thomas S. Neubig, "The Sky Is Not Falling: Why State and Local Revenues Were Not Significantly Impacted by the Internet in 1998," *State Tax Notes,* June 18, 1999; Advisory Commission on Intergovernmental Relations, "ACIR Releases 1994 Revenue Estimates from Interstate Mail-Order Sales," *State Tax Notes,* August 22, 1994, pp. 501–8; "State Revenue Losses from E-Commerce Underestimated," *State Tax Notes,* July 26, 1999, pp. 245–46; Michael Mazerov, Statement of the Center on Budget and Policy Priorities to the Advisory Commission on Electronic Commerce, *State Tax Notes,* September 14, 1999; Mike France, "Commentary: A Web Sales Tax—Not If, but When," *Business Week,* June 21, 1999; Hiawatha Bray, "Rendering unto Caesar," *Boston Globe,* June 24, 1999.

129. National Tax Association, Communications and Electronic Commerce Tax Project, *Final Report* (Washington, D.C.: National Tax Association, September 7, 1999), 17.

130. National Tax Association, Communications and Electronic Commerce Tax Project, *Final Report,* 17.

131. Austan Goolsbee and Jonathan Zittrain, "Evaluating the Costs and Benefits of Taxing Internet Commerce," <www.ecommercecommission.org/document/goolsbee> (May 20, 1999).

132. Richard Wolf, "Opposition to Net Taxes Increases," *USA Today,* September 14, 1999.

133. Dean Andal, *A Uniform Jurisdictional Standard: Applying the Substantial Physical Presence Standard to Electronic Commerce,* proposal presented to the Advisory Commission on Electronic Commerce, <www.ecommercecommission.org/proposal> (September 15, 1999).

134. "NCSL Tax Panel to Offer Input to Federal E-Commerce Panel," *State Tax Notes,* June 7, 1999, p. 1892.

135. *Streamlined Sales Tax System for the 21st Century,* proposal presented to the Advisory Commission on Electronic Commerce (November 1999).

136. David Brunori, "FTA's Harley Duncan on the MTC, Cooperation, E-Commerce," *State Tax Notes,* October 18, 1999, p. 1040.

137. Andy Wagner and Wade Anderson, "Origin-based Taxation of Internet Commerce," *State Tax Notes,* July 15, 1999; See also, Terry Ryan and Eric Miethke, "The Seller-State Option: Solving the Electronic Commerce Dilemma," *State Tax Notes,* October 5, 1998.

138. "NGA Fires Back," *Strategic Technotes News,* coverage of the Advisory Commission on Electronic Commerce, December 14–15, 1999, hearings in San Francisco, Calif., <www.manag.com/technotes/stnews> (January 5, 2000).

Chapter 5

1. Sixth Directive on the harmonization of the laws of the member states relating to turnover taxes—common system of VAT: uniform basis of assessment. (EC Directive 77/388, May 17, 1977).

2. *Interaction of Direct and Indirect Taxes:* Although in the United Kingdom, VAT and direct taxes are administered by different government departments (VAT is administered by Her Majesty's (HM) Customs and Excise whereas the Inland Revenue administers direct taxes), most countries use one authority to administer both direct and indirect taxes. Even where the taxes are administered by different authorities it is increasingly common for the authorities to discuss with each other specific companies and their activities. Performing activities liable to VAT in a country can therefore leave a company open to a review of other potential tax liabilities.

3. In addition, in the United Kingdom, special tax-point rules apply to a number of less-obvious situations. These include some supplies of leases (other than for land and property), goods sold on "sale or return" terms, supplies of power, heat, water and gas, royalty payments, imported services, and services that are supplied on a continuous basis. Even considering the U.K. tax-point rules in isolation, the issue of when any tax should be declared to the Revenue can be problematic. Add into the equation the wide range of rules in other VAT regime countries, and any supply involving more than one country can quickly become highly complex.

4. If the consideration for a supply is wholly in money, its value for VAT purposes is deemed to be the amount of money paid, which is treated as inclusive of VAT. If the consideration is not wholly in money, its value for VAT purposes remains the value of the consideration, inclusive of VAT. When supplies are made to connected parties, the VAT authorities may direct the value to be the open-market value of the goods or services. When the value of a supply is expressed in a foreign currency (e.g., U.S. dollars), the sum should be converted at the market selling rate for that currency, as specified by the tax authorities (e.g., in the national newspapers or by using the monthly rates of exchange published by the VAT authorities).

5. Generally, if a business's taxable supplies exceed the local VAT registration threshold, it will be required to register for VAT in that country. Subsequently, it must comply with all VAT accounting procedures within that country. Alternatively, if a business is making taxable supplies in a particular EU member state, for example, by

making disposals of goods or supplying services within that country, it may engage a fiscal representative to fulfill its VAT registration requirements.

Many countries will not allow an overseas business to register for VAT without a local fiscal representative. Usually, a fiscal representative will be an accountant, lawyer, or freight forwarder already registered for VAT in the country in question. The fiscal representative will be entitled to act on behalf of the business in all VAT matters. It must ensure that the business complies with all obligations relating to VAT and will usually be jointly and severally liable with the business for complying with VAT law.

VAT registration and the appointment of a fiscal representative may not always be necessary. In particular, it is sometimes possible to shift the liability to account for tax to a VAT-registered recipient, for example, when work is carried out on goods. However, where fiscal representation is required, the business must usually complete VAT registration forms and obtain power of attorney to appoint a fiscal representative, as well as supplying other business documentation. It may also be necessary for the business to provide the fiscal representative with a bank guarantee.

It is possible in some countries for a business to voluntarily register for VAT if it can satisfy the tax authorities that it makes taxable supplies or is carrying on a business with the intention to make taxable supplies. A voluntary registration may be advantageous to a business that does not have to declare VAT on its sales (i.e., it makes zero-rated sales) but does incur VAT on its purchases. This type of business will generally be in a net VAT-refund situation if it registered for VAT.

6. To be valid for VAT purposes, a credit or debit note must reflect a genuine mistake or overcharge or an agreed reduction in the value of the supply.

7. Eighth Directive on the harmonization of the laws of the member states relating to turnover taxes—arrangements for the refund of VAT to taxable persons not established in the territory of the country (EC Directive 79/1072, December 6, 1979).

8. The rules governing this are very similar to the EC 8th VAT Directive and are set out in the EC 13th VAT Directive. A brief explanation of the conditions attached to the 8th and 13th Directive refund systems is given in appendix F.

9. The following countries have a VAT or an equivalent system and allow nonresident non-VAT registered entities to recover VAT charged on expenses: Canada, Hungary, Japan, Norway, South Korea, Switzerland. Recovery in a country other than these listed and those in the EU, however, may be possible through registration or fiscal representation.

10. Thirteenth Directive on the harmonization of the laws of the member states relating to turnover taxes—arrangements for the refund of VAT to taxable persons not established in the community territory (EC Directive 86/560, November 17, 1986).

11. Evidence for the recovery of input VAT in the United Kingdom includes the following:

- valid tax invoices received from U.K. suppliers relating to both goods and services
- less-detailed invoices, normally received from retailers, for goods and services of a value not exceeding £100 paid incurred on goods imported from outside the EU
- an invoice in respect of imported services
- an invoice or similar document quoting the customers VAT number from an EU supplier who has used that VAT number to zero rate his or her supply
- authenticated receipts received in respect of building works

The invoice must be correctly addressed to the recipient. Recovery of VAT incurred on importation must sometimes be supported by the official import documents in certain countries. Import VAT can only usually be recovered by the importer of record as named on the import document.

Regarding the recovery of VAT at importation, it is unlikely that a claim for import VAT will made via the 8th and 13th Directives refund scheme. If a business imports goods into a VAT-regime country (in which it is not currently registered), acts as the importer of record, and sells the goods on, it will probably be required to register for VAT in that country. Most import VAT claims will therefore be made via the VAT return mechanism. It is vital that the correct documentation be obtained when goods are imported in order to facilitate the use of Customs duty regimes and properly recover import VAT paid.

When paying and endeavoring to recover import VAT in the EU, the paperwork to be obtained is as follows:

- Copy of C88 (SAD) import document.
- Copy of E2 import document—this is a computer printout issued by the tax authority to accompany the C88. It lists (among other information connected with the shipment) the value of the goods imported, the exchange rate used, any freight charges, and any additional costs. In addition, against each item imported, it lists the Customs duty paid and the import VAT paid. If an import agent is used, the agent receives this document from the tax authority along with a copy of the C88 and should forward this on to the trader.
- Copies of all relevant import documentation (e.g., sea/airway bills, certificates of shipment, consignment notes, etc.).

These items are essential in supporting a claim to recover import VAT.

Irrecoverable Input Tax: The following are considered *irrecoverable input taxes,* for which a taxable person cannot usually reclaim input tax charged to him or her:

- VAT suffered in relation to the making of exempt supplies (subject to *de minimis* limits).

- Goods and services used for nonbusiness purposes.
- Goods and services supplied to other legal entities.
- Automobiles. Most countries have various restrictions on recovery of VAT on the purchase and/or lease of cars.
- Business entertainment. This includes costs incurred on people not directly employed by the taxable person, for example, individuals visiting from an associated company in the United States. Entertainment includes meals, trips to the theater, soccer matches, and so on.
- Hotels. Many countries block VAT recovery on hotel accommodation and related costs.

12. The distance-selling regulations do not apply to those goods subject to excise duty (e.g., tobacco, alcohol, etc.). Such supplies are always taxed in the recipient country, whatever the level of sales.

13. The General Agreement on Tariffs and Trade of October 30, 1947 (GATT) provides for a set of general principles of customs valuation (Article VII). Article VII requires the uniform and consistent adoption of certain methods of customs valuation by all the contracting parties to GATT. It is this article that is embodied in the relevant EU legislation concerning Customs duties. GATT has to some extent been dismantled and replaced by the more all-embracing World Trade Organization (WTO). Established on January 1, 1995, it is the successor to GATT and has a much broader scope in terms of the commercial activity and trade policies to which it applies. A subset of the WTO is the World Customs Organization (WCO). This organization is responsible for implementing and maintaining consistent customs policies in those countries that are members of the WTO. Because the rules governing EU Customs duty stem from Brussels, they apply equally throughout the EU. Thus, any duty saving in importing goods into one EU member state can be replicated in 14 other countries. Differences of interpretation and practice naturally complicate this theory, but it nevertheless holds good in the majority of cases. The law is published in official journals, the most important legislation being Council Regulation EEC no. 2913/92, October 12, 1992 ("The Code"), Commission Regulation EEC no. 2454/93, July 2, 1993 ("The Implementing Regulation"), as amended by Commission Regulation EEC no. 3665/93, Commission Regulation EEC no. 2913/94, Commission Regulation EEC no. 3254/94, and Commission Regulation EEC no. 1762/95. The Code sets out the primary law on which customs planning techniques are based. The Implementing Regulation sets out the basic procedural requirements that must continue to be satisfied when successfully implementing those techniques.

Customs law is directly applicable in all member states requiring no act of Parliament or passing of national law to implement. This is true for all regulations and directives issued concerning Customs duty. Certain administrative procedures, however, may be left to each member state to implement as they see fit.

14. The value of the imported good may not necessarily be the cost, insurance, and freight (CIF) value. Alternatives to such valuation are available. There are six methods of valuing goods at import:

> Method 1. The transaction value of the goods when sold for export to the EU.
>
> Method 2. The transaction value of identical goods imported at around the same time.
>
> Method 3. The transaction value of similar goods imported at around the same time.
>
> Method 4. The resale minus or deductive method.
>
> Method 5. The computed or cost plus method.
>
> Method 6. A flexible approach to the other five methods.

The legislation provides that, where possible, the customs value shall be the transaction value. Only when an acceptable transaction value cannot be established can one of the other customs valuation methods be applied hierarchically, except for methods 4 and 5, which can be transposed.

The transaction value is the total payment made or to be made for the imported good, by the buyer to the seller. The transaction value may require certain additions or deductions in order to arrive at the appropriate customs value. When valuing imported goods, all transport costs to the EU border must be taken into account.

Regarding duty reliefs, inward processing relief (IPR) is a system that allows duty relief on goods imported from non-EU countries, provided those goods are re-exported from the EU at a later stage. Outward processing relief (OPR) allows EU-originating product to be exported for processing and re-imported into the EU without the payment of customs duty and VAT.

OPR is the reverse of IPR, in that the processing occurs outside the EU as opposed to within the EU. As with IPR, authorization must first be obtained from the customs authorities. Other reliefs include end-use relief, -goods relief, sample reliefs, wedding gifts relief, and personal allowances.

15. As of September 30, 1997, the following countries or separate customs territories were participants in the ITA: Australia, Canada, Costa Rica, Czech Republic, El Salvador, Estonia, Hong Kong (China), Iceland, Israel, Indonesia, Japan, Korea, Latvia, Singapore, Slovak Republic, Switzerland, Chinese Taipei, Taiwan, Thailand, Turkey, the United States, Austria, Belgium, Denmark, Finland, France, Germany, Greece, Ireland, Italy, Luxembourg, Netherlands, Portugal, Spain, Sweden, and the United Kingdom.

Collectively, these countries account for approximately 93 percent of world trade in IT products.

16. In regards to human and technical resources, in a 1984 case, *Berkholz,* the European Court of Justice decided that the mere presence of assets, in this case gaming machines, did not create a place of fixed establishment for VAT purposes. The court ruled that for a service to have been supplied from an alternative fixed estab-

lishment the presence of both the human and technical resources necessary for the provision of the service should be permanently present.

The principles of this case were further tested in a 1997 European Court of Justice case, *ARO Leasing BV.* In *ARO Leasing BV,* it was deemed that the appellant did not have a fixed establishment because it did not possess a structure or a level of staffing to a sufficient degree of permanence to provide a framework to draw up agreements or to take management decisions.

Where business is conducted via an agent (i.e., sales are made through the agent), it may not be sufficient to consider the issue of establishment only for the principal. In 1997 the European Court of Justice decided in the case of *C&E Comrs DFDS A/S* that the appellant was deemed to have an establishment in the country where its agent was located because the agent had "the human and technical resources characteristic of a fixed establishment." This conclusion was reached because to do otherwise in the circumstances of this case would have resulted in an irrational VAT treatment.

The issue of the activities of an agent were explored more fully in an earlier decision of the U.K. VAT Tribunal on appeal to the Queens Bench division of the High Court in the United Kingdom (1998) in the case of *The Chinese Channel.* The tribunal looked closely at the services provided by the agent and the extent to which it was deemed to be involved in contributing to the supplies made by its principal to U.K. customers.

As a consequence of the *Chinese Channel* case, businesses must now consider the significance of services provided from any fixed establishment. This will then determine whether the place of supply should be where the fixed establishment is, overriding the service provider's place of belonging.

17. This is a matter of function and substance and not mere legal form; that is, the fact that a subsidiary of a company has its own legal form is not sufficient to establish independence from the parent.

18. "Harmonisation of Turnover Taxes," European Commission Working Party no. 1, Director-General XXI (XXI/99/1201-EN), Brussels, June 8, 1999.

19. Council Directive, June 17, 1999 (99/S9/EC), amending with regard to the VAT arrangements applicable to telecommunications services (EC Directive 77/388/EEC).

20. A summary of the conclusions of the OECD Ministerial Conference on Electronic Commerce held in Ottawa on October 8–9, 1998, can be found on the OECD Web site, <www.oecd.org/daf/fa/e_com/ottawa_pac/.pdf>.

21. "Harmonization of Turnover Taxes."

22. The distance-selling provisions were introduced in order to avoid cross-border shopping for goods wherein a lower rate of tax applies in one state as compared with another. Thus, for example, a U.K. business selling books (a good) to private individuals valued in excess of Fr 700,000 to France in a calendar year will have to register for VAT in France and charge French VAT on its sales.

However, where the text of the book is made available on a Web site for on-line viewing, this is a supply of a service for VAT purposes. Therefore, as the distance-selling provisions do not apply to services, when the customer is a private individual resident in the EU (either in the same member state as the supplier or in a different EU member state), U.K.VAT will be chargeable whatever the value of the sales made by the supplier into a specific country.

23. All the publications relating to the Ottawa conference can be accessed through the OECD Ministerial Conference on Electronic Commerce's Web site, <http://www.ottawaoecdconference.org/english/homepage.html>.

24. "Electronic Commerce U.K. Policy on Taxation Issues, OECD Conference in Ottawa, Canada, 8–9 October 1998," Inland Revenue press release 128/98, October 6, 1998.

25. HM Customs and Excise and Inland Revenue, "Electronic Commerce: The U.K.'s Taxation Agenda," November 1999.

26. "Harmonization of Turnover Taxes."

27. Directorate for Financial, Fiscal, and Enterprise Affairs Committee on Fiscal Affairs, "Electronic Commerce: Taxation Framework Conditions," paper presented at the OECD Ministerial Conference on Electronic Commerce, Ottawa, October 8–9, 1998.

28. Rebecca Allen, "Internet Commerce," *Croner VAT Briefing*, no. 157, October 30, 1998, p. 2.

Chapter 6

1. A significant exception to this general rule in U.S. tax law occurs when the shareholder is another corporation. In these circumstances the dividend-received deduction ensures that income is not taxed a third or fourth time as it is distributed through a chain of corporations. Even with respect to intercorporate dividends, however, double taxation can arise if certain shareholding percentages are not met because the law may provide for only a partial dividend-received deduction.

2. The direct credit provided by Internal Revenue Code § 901.

3. The indirect credit provided by Internal Revenue Code § 902, the mechanics of which are complex and are described later in this chapter.

4. The example is provided for basic illustration purposes only. The actual computation of the deemed paid foreign tax credit would require a calculation of a foreign tax credit limitation. The limitation calculation requires income and expenses to be sourced and assigned to baskets under §§ 861–865 and § 904. In the situation described here, there were no other taxes due on the dividend payments because there is no longer a withholding tax on dividends from the United Kingdom to either the Netherlands or the United States. Effective April 6, 1999, along with the elimination of the United Kingdom's Advanced Corporations Tax and the reduction of the mainstream tax rate on U.K. corporate income from 31 percent to 30 percent, the 5 percent withholding tax on dividends paid from a U.K. subsidiary to its U.S. shareholder was abolished.

5. Internal Revenue Code § 865(g).

6. As defined in Internal Revenue Code § 911(d)(3).

7. Internal Revenue Code § 865(g)(1)(A).

8. "Selected Tax Policy Implications of Global E-Commerce," Department of the Treasury Office of Tax Policy, November 21, 1996.

9. While a general goal of tax policy, U.S. tax law is full of instances in which economically equivalent transactions receive different tax results. For example, consider a corporate reorganization that is tax free under Internal Revenue Code § 368(a)(1)(B) because solely voting stock is used in the exchange. If this transaction is then modified so that a small amount of cash is received in addition to the voting stock, economically, the taxpayer could be in the same position. However, the second transaction results in a recognition event to the taxpayer.

10. Internal Revenue Code § 864(c)(4) and Treas. Reg. § 1.864-5.

11. Internal Revenue Code § 864(c)(1)(B).

12. *U.S. v. Lee Yen Tai,* 185 U.S. 213 (1902).

13. United States Model Income Tax Convention (September 20, 1996).

14. Internal Revenue Code § 871.

15. Internal Revenue Code § 871(b).

16. Internal Revenue Code § 873(a).

17. Under Internal Revenue Code §§ 881–884.

18. Internal Revenue Code § 881(a) and § 1442.

19. Internal Revenue Code § 882(c).

20. This standard was developed by the Second Circuit Court of Appeals in *Pinchot v. Comm'r.,* 113 F.2d 718 (2nd Cir. 1940). The court distinguished between real estate investment and a trade or business of managing real estate noting that a trade or business required considerable, regular, and continuous activity.

21. In *Linen Thread Co. v. Comm'r.,* 14 T.C. 725 (1950), isolated and relatively unplanned sales were held not to constitute a U.S. trade or business. Similarly, in *Continental Trading v. Comm'r.,* 265 F.2d 40 (9th Cir. 1959), the court stated that "in light of the whole enterprise," the U.S. sales were "casual or incidental transactions" not rising to the stature of a trade or business.

22. *Johansson v. U.S.,* 336 F.2d 809 (5th Cir. 1964).

23. *Ingram v. Bowers,* 57 F.2d 65 (2nd Cir. 1932).

24. Rev. Rul. 58-63, 1958-1 C.B. 624, amplified in Rev. Rul. 60-249, 1960-2 C.B. 264.

25. GCM 21219, 1939-1 C.B. 849.

26. Rev. Rul. 56-165, 1956-1 C.B. 849.

27. *Handfield v. Comm'r.,* 23 T.C. 633 (1955).

28. PLR 7739023 (September 29, 1977).

29. GCM 18835, 1937-2 C.B. 141.

30. *de Amodio v. Comm'r.,* 34 T.C. 894 (1960); *Lewenhaupt v. Comm'r.,* 20 T.C. 151 (1953).

31. *Investor's Mortgage Security Co. v. Comm'r.,* 4 T.C.M. 45 (1945).

32. *Abegg v. Comm'r.,* 50 T.C. 145 (1968).

33. *Neill v. Comm'r.,* 46 BTA 197 (1942); *Herbert v. Comm'r.,* 30 T.C. 26 (1958).

34. Rev. Rul. 73-522, 1973-2 C.B. 226.

35. *Pinchot v. Comm'r.*

36. *Higgins v. Comm'r.*, 312 U.S. 212 (1940).

37. *Continental Trading Inc. v. Comm'r.*, 16 T.C.M. 724 (1957), *affd.*, 265 F.2d 40 (9th Cir. 1959).

38. *DiPorta Nova v. U.S.*, 690 F.2d 169 (Ct. Cls. 1982).

39. Rev. Rul. 70-424, 1970-2 C.B. 150.

40. In one case, however, where over 90 percent of the agent's business was for a foreign corporation, the agent was held to be an exclusive agent, and the foreign corporation was deemed to be conducting a U.S. trade or business through the agent. *InverWorld, Inc., et. al., v. Comm'r*, 71 T.C.M. 3231 (1996).

41. Fixed or determinable annual or periodical (FDAP) income includes a number of types of income and is defined in Treas. Reg. § 1.1441-2(a)(1). In defining FDAP income, the regulation states that "other kinds of income are included, as, for instance, royalties."

42. Treas. Reg. § 1.1441-6(a).

43. Treas. Reg. § 1.864-7(a)(2).

44. Treas. Reg. § 1.864-7(b)(1).

45. Treas. Reg. § 1.864-7(a)(3).

46. Treas. Reg. § 1.864-7(c).

47. Rev. Rul. 56-165, 1956-1 C.B. 849.

48. Treas. Reg. § 1.864-7(d)(1).

49. Treas. Reg. § 1.864-7(d)(2).

50. Treas. Reg. § 1.864-7(f).

51. The similarity between the federal regulations and treaty PE rules does not mean that the taxability threshold is the same in both cases. The regulatory definition is used only in determining whether certain classes of income are effectively connected with a U.S. trade or business because they were earned through a U.S. office.

52. *Unger v. U.S.*, 936 F. 2d 1316 (D.C. Cir. 1991); Rev. Rul. 85-60, 1985-1 C.B. 187.

53. *OECD Model Tax Convention on Income and Taxes,* Article 5(5).

54. "Technical Explanation of the United States Model Income Tax Treaty," September 20, 1996, p. 28. See also paragraph 33 of the Commentary on Article 5 of the *OECD Model Tax Convention on Income and Taxes* ("The authority to conclude contracts must cover contracts relating to operations which constitute the business purpose of the enterprise.").

55. From Section 2.4 of the discussion paper "Selected Tax Policy Implications of Global E-Commerce," U.S. Treasury White paper, November 21, 1996.

56. Thus, having no property in the United States and no agent in the United States, they will not have a PE.

57. *OECD Model Tax Convention of Income and Capital,* Article 5(6).

58. Income from the sale of inventory property is generally sourced based on the title passage test pursuant to Internal Revenue Code § 865(b).

59. U.S. Tax Reform Act of 1986, PL No. 99-514, § 1245.

60. See "I.R.S. Investigates Foreign Companies for Tax Cheating," *New York Times,* February 18, 1990; Subcommittee on Oversight, House Ways and Means Committee, Hearings on International Tax Administration Issues, July 10, 1990.

61. Internal Revenue Code § 6038A(a).

62. Internal Revenue Code § 6038A(b)(1), § 6038A(b)(2).

63. Internal Revenue Code § 6038A(a).

64. Internal Revenue Code § 6038A(e).

65. Internal Revenue Code § 6038C(b)(2).

66. Treas. Reg. § 1.6038A-1(d).

67. Treas. Reg. § 1.482-1(a)(3).

68. Bureau of National Affairs, *Daily Tax Report,* no. 128 (July 3, 1997).

69. Revenue Act of 1913, Ch. 16, Secs. IIB, 38 Stat. 49.

70. Revenue Act of 1918, Ch. 18, § 222(a) and § 238(a), 40 Stat. 1057.

71. Internal Revenue Code § 902.

72. Internal Revenue Code § 904.

73. Internal Revenue Code § 901(a).

74. Internal Revenue Code, chapters 11–13.

75. Internal Revenue Code, chapter 3.

76. Internal Revenue Code, chapters 2 and 21–25.

77. Internal Revenue Code, chapter 31–53.

78. Internal Revenue Code § 901.

79. Internal Revenue Code § 901(b)(5).

80. Treas. Reg. § 1.901-2(f)(1).

81. Internal Revenue Code § 960 and Treas. Reg. § 1.1248-1(d).

82. Internal Revenue Code § 906.

83. *Associated Telephone & Telegraph Co. v. U.S.,* 306 F.2d 824 (2nd Cir. 1962), 832.

84. Internal Revenue Code § 902(a).

85. Internal Revenue Code § 902(b).

86. Rev. Rul. 55-540, 1955-2 C.B. 39; see also, *Frank Lyon Company v. U.S.,* 435 U.S. 561.

87. Rev. Rul. 55-540, 1955-2 C.B. 39.

88. Internal Revenue Code § 871(a)(1)(A), § 881(a)(1).

89. Internal Revenue Code § 872(a)(2), § 873, § 882(a).

90. *Hooker Chemical & Plastics Corp. v. U.S.,* 591 F.2d 652 (Ct Cl., 1979); see also, *Pickren v. U.S.,* 378 F.2d 595 (5th Cir. 1967), in which failure to transfer all substantial rights in secret formulas and trade names precluded sale treatment.

91. *Schmitt v. Comm'r.,* 30 T.C. 322 (1964).

92. Rev. Rul 64-56, 1964-1 C.B. 133.

93. Treas. Reg. § 1.1235-2(b)(1)(i).

94. *Pickren v. U.S..*

95. *Stalker Corp. v. Comm'r.,* 209 F. Supp. 30 (1962), 62 2 U.S. Tax Cas. (CCH) 9755.

96. *Taylor-Winfield Corp. v. Comm'r.*, 57 T.C. 205 (1971).

97. Treas. Reg. § 1.1235 2(b)(2)(i).

98. Treas. Reg. § 1.1235 2(b)(2)(ii); *Graham v. Comm'r.*, 26 T.C. 730 (1956).

99. See Rev. Rul. 58-353, 1958 2 C.B. 408, in which payments made for an intangible that were based in part on the sales produced from the use of the intangible asset did not preclude sale treatment. Also, see Treas. Reg. § 1.1235-1(a) with respect to capital gain treatment for transfers of patents.

100. Internal Revenue Code § 865(d).

101. Internal Revenue Code § 865(a).

102. Internal Revenue Code § 7701(e)(1).

103. TD 8785 issued under Internal Revenue Code § 861 (63 F.R. 52971).

104. Treas. Reg. § 1.861-18.

105. Treas. Reg. § 1.861-18(b)(1).

106. Treas. Reg. § 1.861-18(c)(1)(i), § 1.861-18(c)(2).

107. Treas. Reg. § 1.861-18(c)(1)(ii), § 1.861-18 (c)(3).

108. Treas. Reg. § 1.861-18(d).

109. Treas. Reg. § 1.861-18(e).

110. Treas. Reg. § 1.861-18(f)(1).

111. Treas. Reg. § 1.861-18(f)(2).

112. Treas. Reg. § 1.861-18(f)(3).

113. Treas. Reg. § 1.861-18(g)(1).

114. Treas. Reg. § 1.861-18(g)(2).

115. Treas. Reg. § 1.927(a)-1T(f)(3).

116. Treas. Reg. § 1.861-18(h), ex. 10.

117. Internal Revenue Code § 904.

118. Internal Revenue Code § 872, § 882.

119. Internal Revenue Code § 871, § 881.

120. Internal Revenue Code § 954.

121. Internal Revenue Code § 871(a).

122. Internal Revenue Code § 864(c)(3), § 882.

123. Internal Revenue Code § 864(c)(4).

124. See TAMRA § 1012(aa)(3).

125. Internal Revenue Code § 865(h)(1), § 904(g)(10).

126. Internal Revenue Code § 861(a)(1).

127. Internal Revenue Code § 861(a)(2), § 862(a)(2).

128. Internal Revenue Code § 871(i)(2)(B), § 881(d).

129. Internal Revenue Code § 861(c)(1)(C).

130. Internal Revenue Code § 861(a)(3), § 862(a)(3).

131. "Temporarily" would mean for a period or periods not exceeding 90 days during the taxable year.

132. Internal Revenue Code § 861(a)(3).

133. Treas. Reg. § 1.861-4(b).

134. Internal Revenue Code § 861(a)(4), § 862(a)(4).

135. Internal Revenue Code § 861(a)(4), § 862(a)(4).

136. S.R. 313, 99th Cong., 2d sess. 359 (1986).

137. Internal Revenue Code § 865(a).

138. Internal Revenue Code § 865(b).

139. Internal Revenue Code § 862(a)(6).

140. Internal Revenue Code § 861(a)(6).

141. Treas. Reg. § 1.861-7(c).

142. *Liggett Groups Inc. v. Comm'r.*, T.C.M. 1990-18.

143. Internal Revenue Code § 865(b).

144. Internal Revenue Code § 865(e)(2)(A).

145. Internal Revenue Code § 865(e)(2)(b).

146. Internal Revenue Code § 865(c)(1).

147. Internal Revenue Code § 865(c)(3)(B).

148. Internal Revenue Code § 865(d).

149. Internal Revenue Code § 865(e)(1)(A), § 865(e)(1)(B).

150. Internal Revenue Code § 865(e)(2).

151. Internal Revenue Code § 865(d)(1)(B).

152. Internal Revenue Code § 865(d)(4).

153. Internal Revenue Code § 865(e)(2).

154. Treas. Reg. § 1.863-3.

155. Treas. Regs. § 1.861-8T through § 1.861-14T.

156. Research and experimental expenses, however, are allocated under Treas. Reg. § 1.861-17 and not apportioned pro rata under Internal Revenue Code § 863(b).

157. *Electronic Commerce and Canada's Tax Administration: A Report to the Minister of National Revenue from the Minister's Advisory Committee on Electronic Commerce* (Ottawa: Revenue Canada, April 1998).

158. Revenue Canada, Taxation is the department of the federal (national) government charged with responsibility for the administration of federal income tax legislation, which is found, for the most part, in the federal Income Tax Act.

159. Interpretation Bulletins (ITs) are explanatory documents issued by Revenue Canada, outlining the Revenue's interpretation of particular provisions of the Income Tax Act and consequently its assessing policy with respect to those provisions. While ITs do not have the force of law (Revenue's interpretation may, for example, be found to be erroneous by the courts when a particular provision of the Income Tax Act is the subject of litigation), they are useful in determining how Revenue may view a particular transaction or structure on assessment.

160. The Department of Finance is the department of the federal government that has responsibility for the drafting of federal tax legislation, in particular the federal Income Tax Act.

161. *Hermann Gusav Erichsen (Representative of the Great Northern Telegraph Company of Copenhagen) v. W.H. Last (formerly Surveyor of Taxes)*, [1881] 8 Q.B.D. 414, 4 Tax. Cas. 422.

162. *F.L. Smidth & Co. v. F. Greenwood (Surveyor of Taxes)*, [1922] A.C. 417, 127 LT 68, 38 T.L.R. 421, [1921] 3 K.B. 583, [1920] 3 K.B. 275, 8 Tax. Cas. 193.

163. Inland Revenue, *International Tax Handbook,* paragraph 857.

164. *Inspector's Manual,* paragraph 177.

165. HM Customs and Excise and Inland Revenue, "Electronic Commerce: The U.K.'s Taxation Agenda," November 1999, p. 71.

166. Ibid., p. 73.

167. Ibid., pp. 71–72.

168. "The Application of the Permanent Establishment Definition in the Context of Electronic Commerce: Proposed Clarification of the Commentary on Article 5 of the OECD Model Tax Convention," OECD Working Party no. 1 on Tax Conventions and Related Questions, draft discussion document, October 1999.

Index

Italic page numbers refer to illustrations/tables.

A

Advanced Pricing Agreement (APA) program of IRS, 465
Advertising activities protected from creating nexus, 297, 302
Advertising in information-age economy, 26–27
Advertising revenue
  of broadcasters, 239
  income taxation of gross receipts from, 243
  throwback rules for, 244
Advertising spending, Web, 301–302
Advisory Commission on Electronic Commerce (ACEC)
  created under Internet Tax Freedom Act, 56, 191, 347
  proposal to expand nexus safe harbors to, 349
  proposal to extend moratorium on taxation by caucus in, 77
  proposals for rationalizing state sales and use taxes to, 74, 76, 191, 205, 347–350
  zero-burden real-time sales and use tax compliance system proposed to, 202–203, 352
Affiliate nexus, 272, 316–324
  alter-ego theory for, 324–326
  created by brick-and-mortar affiliates of Internet retailers, 310–311, 317, 323
  originating with mail-order companies and existing retailers, 318–321
  preconditions for, 322–324
  safe harbor for, 322
After-sales activities creating attributional nexus, 293–296

Agency (attributional) nexus, 272, 285, 289–334
  created by actions of independent contractors, 293, 295
  enforcing rules for, 356–357
  level of control issue for, 291–293
  local market orientation of third party as creating, 308–310
  marketing activities as creating, 297–299
  presence of third party's server in state not creating, 307
  services of third-party intermediaries in creating, 311–314
  theory of, 289, 291
  types of third-party activity creating, 293–300
Agency, establishing, 291–292, 315
Aggregator sites, 37
All or nothing approach
  to source multiple-user product sale to single jurisdiction, 172–173, 178
  to taxing bundled services, 132–133
Amazon.com
  advertising expenditures of, 301
  estimated sales of, 46
  expenditures for links to, 301
  market valuation of, 46
  on-line inventory of, 43
  publicity for, 317
  stock valuation of, 10
  stock-market valuation of, 11
  use of advantages of Web retailing by, 45–46
Amerestate Inc. v. Tax Commissioner of Ohio, 120

America Online
  marketing rights revenues for, 301–302
  monthly fees for bundled services by, 132
  nexus issues for, 287
  stock-market valuation, 11
Andreessen, Marc, 8
Arm's length accounting rules for multinational operations, 68
ARPANET (DOD), 6–7
AT&T
  aim to reenter local telephone market of, 124–125
  bundling strategy of, 127
  deregulation and divestiture of, 228, 260
  EU operations of, 406
  investment in packet-switching networks of, 99
  purchase of Tele-Communications, Inc. (TCI) by, 124
  services offered by, 125
  state and local tax returns filed annually by, 187
Attributional nexus. See Agency (attributional) nexus
Auction sites, 36
Automated teller machines (ATMs)
  Internet access using, 13
  transaction fees for, 130
Automobile market, on-line vendors for, 42, 44
Automobiles, Internet access using, 13
AutoNation, stores for, 269

B

Bandwidth
  alternative transmissions channels to, 15–19
  defined, 14
  of fiber-optic cable systems for cable television systems, 105
  new methods for expanding, 124, 126
  requirements for digitized music of, 28
  requirements for Web use of, 11, 14–15
Banner ads on Internet, 303
Base-state system for sales tax collection, 201–202
Basic transmission services in telecommunications, 91–92

Bellas-Hess, 188, 302–303, 336, 342–343
Beneficiaries of digitized services, 178–180
Berners-Lee, Tim, 7
Billing address
  market-state approach's use of, 181
  as proxy for state of destination, 165–166, 168
Bit tax, 53, 138
Bits, instantaneous and inexpensive movement of, 5–6
Bloomingdale's By Mail, Ltd. v. Pennsylvania Department of Revenue, 320
Books. See also Electronic books
  delivered electronically, 249
  in information-age economy, 29
  ordered over Internet vs. mail order or bookstore, 135
  purchased at bookstores vs. electronic books
  VAT treatment of electronic information vs., 413–414
Borderless commerce, rise in, 47–48, 60
Brick-and-mortar companies overlapping Web affiliates, 321–323
Brick-and-mortar retail chains
  on-line business-to-consumer sales by, 317, 320–321
  sales and use tax disadvantages for, 347
Brick-and-mortar wholesale clubs, 45
British Sky Broadcasting, Ltd., 412
Broadband connections
  for fast Internet access, 11
  integrated services using, 126
Broadcasting equipment, input exemption for, 143
Broadcasting industries, market-state sourcing for income taxation of, 234–235, 239
Brown's Furniture, Inc. v. Wagner, 274–275
Bundled prices for integrated services, 126, 127
  under Internet Tax Freedom Act, 131–132
Bundled services
  all or nothing approach to taxing, 132–133
  object of transaction approach to taxing, 129–130

separate statement approach to taxing, 130–132
traditional approaches for taxing, 129–133
Bundling
of different service categories, 123–128, 254–255
of Internet access services with voice Internet telephony, 99, 126
of taxable and nontaxable services, 116, 123, 124
of telecommunications services, 99, 100, 124, 132, 254–255
Business and occupation tax on telecommunications, 257
Business models
changing, 50–51
infomediary, 44
Internet, 211–212, 241–242, 357
new, for distance selling, 36–37, 61, 300–302
Business-to-business E-commerce, 40
broadband access overcoming bandwidth inadequacies for, 11, 14
exemption issues for sales and use tax, 268–269
projections of growth of, *38,* 40
sourcing, 165–166
Business-to-consumer E-commerce, 40–42
advantages of, 42–46
by brick-and-mortar retail chains, 317
communication devices for, 11, 14
major categories of, 42
of on-line auctions, 316
projections of growth of, 36, 267
sales and use taxes on, 75
sourcing, 166–167

C

Cable modems, 105–106
speeds of, 124
Cable television service, 103–106
as alternative transmission channel for Internet access, 16, 124
basic, 103
bundled with other integrated services, 125–128
households having, 12
income taxes on, state, 239
pay-per-view channels in, 103, 140–141
premium, 103
sales and use taxes on, state, 104–106
sales tax on, *93,* 104
states taxing, 101, *102*
upheaval in, to include other digital services, 105–106, 124–125
Cable television sets, 12
Cable television station, affiliate nexus between mail-order company and subsidiary, 323–324
California Franchise Tax Board draft regulation on income tax sourcing rules for E-commerce, 242–245, 247
Canadian Income Tax Act, 495
Cellular (cell) telephones
Internet access using, 12
sourcing roaming charges for, 162–163
usage rates of, 6–7
Cellular telephone industry, revamping for wireless channels of, 125
Choice in E-commerce, 43–44
Circuit City, Web purchase pickups from, 269–270
Circuit-switching telephony
distinction between packet-switched telecommunications and, 99–100
Internet telephony vs., 97
Cisco Systems
as primarily virtual corporation, 49
stock-market valuation of, 10–11
Clinton, William (Bill)
balance of tax revenue and Internet vitality stressed by, 66
presidential *Directive on Electronic Commerce* by, 53–54
prevention of discriminatory taxation against E-commerce transactions called for by, 134
Clothing and shoes on-line market, 42
Commerce
borderless (global), 47–48
digital, 48, 55
electronic. *See* E-commerce (electronic-commerce)
real-time, 49–50, 60–61
transition from traditional to electronic, 61–73

Commercial links involving host or third party for Web site creating nexus, 300

Committee on State Taxation (COST) Telecommunications Tax Task Force study, 259

Communications and Electronic Commerce Tax Project (NTA), 58

Communications channels converging in Internet, 5

Communications, falling costs of, 1

Composition of Internet usage, 3–4

Computer bulletin boards, distinguishing between E-mail and access to, 101

Computer facilities management service, taxation of provision of, 115

Computer services
  discriminatory taxation of, 137–138
  information services vs., 118–120
  states taxing, 101, 107, 113–116

Computer software. See Software

Computer time sharing, 115

Consumer information appliances. See also individual devices
  convergence of functionality among various, 13
  global market for, 14
  households owning, 12–14

Consumer purchases over Internet. See Business-to-consumer E-commerce

Consumer-electronics on-line market, 42

Controlled foreign corporations (CFCs), 467–468

Convenience of E-commerce, 42–43

Conventional (physical) delivery
  sales or use taxes on products and services using, 89
  of tangible goods, issues for, 87

Convergence of services following telecommunications deregulation, 128

Core competencies of companies, narrow definition of, 48–49, 67

Corporate income tax rates and apportionment formulas, 223, 242

Corporate intranet
  accessing database on central server via, 169
  impact on functioning of business of, 464

IP for data and nonvoice communications on, 98

software use in multiple jurisdictions via, 170

Corporate nexus. See Income tax nexus, corporate

Corporation Tax Law (Japan), 498

Costs of performance, direct vs. indirect, 216

Cox-Wyden bill. See Internet Tax Freedom Act

Credit-card authorizations, 120

Credit-card companies, billing address information collection by, 168

Cross-border direct taxation, 436–516
  identifying transactions for, 464–465
  summary of, 514–516

Cross-border electronic business, 435–436

Cummings & Lockwood v. Commissioner of Revenue, 119

Current, Inc. v. State Board of Equalization, 319

Customer service, digital delivery of, 34

Customer support, digitalization of, 34–35

Customer-adjustment services, 299

Customization of consumer information in E-commerce, 44–45

Cyberbusinesses, stock-market valuations of, 9–11

D

Data processing services
  states taxing, 115
  Web site design and maintenance considered, 121

Data transmissions, 5

Data-receiving equipment, tax on rental of, 131

Database access as communications subject to sales tax, 92

Databases
  access to, in bundled services, 178–179
  licensing of rights to access, 435
  local-access calls to, 129
  push vs. pull method of information use from, 169

sent electronically to multiple customer sites, 169–170

taxation of electronic transfer of, 112–114, 140

taxation of information access to, 119

De minimis property, 283–289

equipment to facilitate electronic multistate commerce as, 287–289

inventory at distribution and shipping points for, 284–285

leased or licensed, 285–288

De minimis rules, 272–289

applicable to income tax and sales and use tax nexus, 266

continued enforcement of, 356–357

exception for out-of-state corporation to, 273–282

for physical presence in customer jurisdiction, 272, 275, 288

to protect small businesses in E-commerce, 60

De minimis safe harbors, 273–282

boundaries set by states for, 275

broader view of, 276–279

of economic-presence statutes, 339

established by state, 281–282

narrow view of, 273–276

problem in applying, 273

slightest presence test for, 273, 274–275

statutory ambiguity for, 279

variance among states of, 282

Death of distance, 39

Deregulation of industries

growth in multistate economic activity following, 228

not tied to revamping of taxes on industries, 250

Desktop publishing, exemption for equipment used in, 146

Destination rule in sourcing sales and use taxation, 151

Digital cash payments for anonymity, 166

Digital commerce, 48

characterization and sourcing of income from, 55

current taxation of, 87

emergence of, 61

sales and use taxation of, 101–116

Digital economy

preventing discriminatory taxation of, 134

tax issues raised by, 48, 195, 248

Digital manufacturing, decline of exemption for inputs used in, 146–147

Digital products

costs of performance for, 219

delivered on-line to businesses, sourcing of, 165

delivered on-line to nonbusinesses, sourcing of, 166–167

difference in property factor of income apportionment for, 240–241

dual sourcing system for tangible and, 354–355

economic-presence theory for nexus of sellers of, 339

electronic delivery of, 67, 334, 459–460

favorable sales and use tax treatment of, 148

inconsistent treatment of tangible goods and, 77

location of server and Web site as basis for taxing, 110–112, 241

physical goods transformed into, 67

real-time multiple-user access of, 169, 171–174

secondary users or beneficiaries of, 178–180

sourcing of, for income taxes, 212–214

sourcing of, for sales and use taxes, 78, 154, 170–171

states not taxing, 102–103

taxation of, by states, *102,* 123, 350

treated as services, 53

VAT gaps for, 73

Digital revolution in intangible economy for remote commerce, 6

Digital sales

sourcing of, to supplier or consumer's locale, 52–54, 210–211

treated as goods or services, 52

Digital services

added to cable television systems, 105–106

apportioning interstate, 173

bundled, 132

Digital services (*continued*)
  states not taxing, 102–103
  taxation by states of, *102*
  vendor-state rule for sourcing, 154–155
Digital storage sites, outsourced, 170
Digital subscriber lines (DSLs), 125, 126
Digital technology
  fundamental simplification of commerce
    brought by, 5
  future functions of, 13
  usage statistics for, 3–4, 6
Digitized products, complexity of taxing,
    350–351
Direct broadcast satellite (DBS) television,
    141
Direct marketing
  growth of, 1
  impact on sales and use tax collection of
    expanding, 271–272, 347–348
Direct satellite television, 104
Direct taxation, international. *See* Cross-
    border direct taxation
Direct-pay permits for sales and use taxes
  in business-to-business transactions,
    165
  development of uniform procedures for,
    197–198
  for multiple users of digital products,
    174, 176
Directive on a Common Framework for
    Electronic Signatures, 422
Discriminatory taxes, 55
  in absence of uniform sales tax base
    among states, 116
  for E-commerce vs. tangible goods, 89,
    133–141
  for Internet vs. circuit-switching tele-
    phony, 97
Disintermediation, 47
Distance learning, 30–32
  virtual learning centers for, 136–137
Distance selling. *See* Remote selling
Distance-selling registration thresholds,
    428
Distributors
  changes to, 50, 270–271
  Internet retailers as avoiding purchases
    from, 329

Double taxation
  exemption method to eliminate, 445
  indirect credit to reduce, 466
  minimizing, 444
  preventing, 134, 436–437
  in purchases of taxable inputs, 142
  in taxing by vendor- and market-state
    rules, 225
  in taxing inputs and outputs, 145–146
  of telecommunications services for VAT,
    405
Double-weighted sales factors, *223*–224
Drop-shipment nexus rule
  approaches to transactions for, 327–328
  future interpretation of, 333
  legitimacy of state positions toward,
    330–334
  manufacturing affiliates in states using, 330
  sales and use tax collection responsibility
    on manufacturer or distributor under,
    327
Drop shipments, E-commerce transactions
    involving, 329–330, 333
Drop shipper
  fulfillment house distinct from, 284
  nexus issues for, 326–334
  retail-sales rule for, 326–327
  sale to out-of-state retailer by, 330–331
  sales and use tax exposure of, 327
  taxable wholesale sale to retailer from, 328
  treated as retailer or wholesaler of
    record, 327, 328, 331–332
  wholesale-sales rule for, 326–327
drugstore.com, physical presence in Rite
    Aid of, 269
DSL phone lines as alternative transmission
    channel for Internet access, 16–17
Dual sourcing system from origin-state rule
    for digital products, 354–355
Duty, customs. *See* Value-added tax (VAT)
    customs duty

E

E-business defined, 37
EC 6th VAT Directive, 373
  Article 5 of, 409
  Article 9 of, 393, 394–407, 409–413, 417
  Article 21 of, 397

EC 8th VAT Directive Claim, 372, 431–33
EC 13th VAT Directive Claim, 433
E-commerce (electronic-commerce)
    in Canada, taxation of, 492–497
    constraints on growth of, 11–19
    direct vs. indirect, 8
    discriminatory taxes for, 89, 133–141
    drop shipments used for, 329–330
    economic change brought by, 2–3
    E-mail as most common form of, 35
    identifying location for sourcing of, 161
    income taxation of, 2, 207–261, 435–516
    international taxation of, 435–516
    in Japan, taxation of, 497–504
    largest commercial growth in, 464
    multiple or discriminatory taxes prohib-
        ited for, 55
    nascent stages of, 227
    OECD outline agreement on taxing,
        418
    potential of, 8–11, 45
    preferential treatment of, 139–140
    projection of growth of, 37–39
    sales and use taxation of, 81–206
    tax complexity of, 46–60
    tax compromise for, 76
    as trade vs. business, 447–449
    transition from traditional commerce to,
        61–73
    underreporting of income from, 442
    U.K. joint business brief on, 418–420
    U.K. taxation agenda for, 420–421
    in U.K., taxation of, 504–514
    value-added taxes and, 74, 359–433
E-commerce policy, U.S., 53–56
E-mail
    as communications subject to sales tax, 92
    global tax proposed by UN for, 139
    as most common form of E-commerce,
        35
    as taxable telecommunications services,
        95, 100–101
E-purchasing, 40
E-retailers. See Internet retailing
E-trade stock valuation, 10
eBay.com
    inventory for on-line auctions of, 43–44
    stock valuation of, 10

stock-market valuation of, 11
volume of, 315
as Web auction site, 314
Economy
    global. See Global economy
    in information age. See Information-age
        economy
    intangible, 6
    shift from industrial- to information-age, 2
Educational services, electronic, 30–32
    discriminatory taxation of, 136–137
800 numbers, sourcing fees for, 160–161,
    354
Electric companies. See Utilities, power
Electromagnetic communications, sales tax
    exemption for tangible personal prop-
    erty and services used in, 143
Electronic banking services at ATMs, 130
Electronic books, 13, 29
    sales or use tax on tangible books vs.,
        140
Electronic Commerce Working Group, 53
Electronic data interchange (EDI), 39, 40
    taxation of providing, 115
Electronic delivery
    of customer service, 34
    of digital products, 67, 334, 459–460
    of entertainment and educational ser-
        vices, 412
    of manufactured goods, 225–226
    of product repairs, 34, 122–123
    of software, 27, 61–64, 78, 101, 106–112,
        140, 177, 219, 249, 265
Electronic filing of tax return, 131
Electronic information services, 112–114
    defined, 242
    for delivery of magazines and newspa-
        pers, sales tax on, 135–136
    exemption for machinery used in pro-
        viding, 146
    income taxation of gross receipts from,
        243
    in multiple jurisdictions, apportioning,
        174–175
    throwback rules for, 244
Electronic marketing for purchases of on-
    line advertising on Web portals,
    300–301, 306

Electronic Numerical Integrator and Computer (ENIAC), 6
Electronic partnerships for advertising and site links, 300–314
Electronic payment to create anonymous transaction, 166
Electronic service, 108
  defining type of, 121–123
  sourcing rules for, 150, 152
Electronic solicitation, 303
  in-person vs., 311
  remote access to, 304–305
eMachines as virtual corporation, 49
Enhanced services for telecommunications, 90–92
Enterprise resource planning (ERP) software, 50, 111
  automation of corporate functions using, 204
  electronic transmission to central server of, 170
Erichsen v. Last, 505
European Commission plan to tax supplies of E-commerce sales, 416–417
European Commission's Working Paper of June 8, 1999
  Article 9.2(c) changes in, 412
  indirect tax in, 402, 421–423
European Union (EU) VAT systems, 363
  acquisition of goods from another EU member in, 375
  for E-commerce, general principles for, 423–424
  sales of goods within, 374–382
  tax revenue lost on new types of supplies for, 407
  transporting own goods within, 375–376
Excise tax, federal, 75
  on gasoline, 81
  nexus for, 340
  on telecommunications, 81

F

Facsimile (fax) services taxed as telecommunications services, 92, 99, 101

Federation of Tax Administrators (FTA)
  model regulation for direct-pay permits, 197
Fiber transactions, leasing dark and lit, 145
Fiber-optic networks, 126
Financial information, digital transfer of, 109, 178–179
Financial institutions
  economic presence concept to assert nexus for, 338
  market-state sourcing for income taxation of, 230–234
Financial services, digital commerce, 32–33
Flower on-line market, 42
Flowers, rules for gifts of, 155
Food and groceries on-line market, 42, 43
Foreign government initiatives about tax treatment of digital sales, 52–53
Foreign income taxes, 437. See also Cross-border direct taxation
  offset against U.S. income tax, 466
Foreign Investment in Real Property Tax Act (1980), 462
Foreign tax credits, 68, 437–438, 444–445, 465–468
  amount of, calculating, 478
  direct, 467
  eligibility for, 366–467
  indirect, 467–468
  intention of, 465–466
  principles underlying, 465
Forexia (U.K.) Ltd., 414
Forrester Research
  growth of E-commerce and digital technology noted by, 6–7, 9, 37, 126, 267
  growth of Web advertising estimated by, 301
  shipments of Internet retailers estimated by, 270
Franchise fees charged to telecommunications companies, 256–257, 258
Franchise tax, corporate, 335, 340
Fulfillment houses
  inventory at, 284–285
  warranty services through, 295–296
Furnitureland South, Inc. and Royal Transport, Inc. v. Comptroller, 294

G

Gas companies. *See* Utilities, power
Gasoline, federal excises on, 81
Gateway, stores maintained by, 270
Geoffrey, Inc. v. South Carolina Tax Commission, 335–337, 349
Geoffrey nexus rule, 237–238, 336–338, 349, 357
Gift certificate market, 51
Global economy
    Internet as laying foundation of, 1
    trend toward interconnected, 39
Global marketplace
    Internet as transforming, 9
    pace of change caused by Internet and E-commerce in, 2
Global taxation, 1–79
    cutting edge issues of, 60–79
    debate over design of future, 74
Goldberg v. Sweet, 153, 154, 172–173
Governmental units, numerous local, county, and regional, 66
Gross receipts taxes on telecommunications services, 243, 251–253
Growth rate of Internet users and services, 3–4

H

Hambrecht & Quist Internet Index, 10
Handfield v. Commissioner, 457
Handheld computers, 13, 14
Handheld electronic books, 13, 29
Hartford Parkview Ass'n. Ltd. Partnership v. Groppo, 119
Health services, long-distance consulting for, 33–34
Hollow corporation, trend toward, 48–49, 61, 211
Home computers. *See* Personal computers (PCs)
Hypertext Markup Language (HTML) introduced to Internet by Web to create hot links, 7–8, 303

I

IBM stock-market valuation, 11
Import VAT Certificate, 383

Income characterization, 54
Income classification for U.S. taxation
    sales vs. rental, 468–469
    sales vs. royalty, 469–470
    service vs. rental, 470–471
Income from services or intangible property, 47
Income source, U.S. or foreign, 478, 482, 482–492
Income tax compliance rules, adaptation of, 54
Income tax filing responsibility for sale of intangible property, 62
Income tax laws
    imposition of tax under, 438
    need to simplify, 65–66
    taxable connections under federal and international, 72
Income tax nexus, corporate, 61–62, 295, 334–341. *See also* Public Law (PL) 86–272
    economic presence for, 338–341
    intangible-property presence for, 335–338
    sales and use tax nexus vs. 264–266
Income taxation
    apportionment of, 170, 208–229
    based on sales of manufactured goods, 2
    calculated on net income, 82
    corporate, 222–226
    de minimis rules for, 275
    of E-commerce, 54, 67–69, 207–261, 435–516
    harder to apply to vertically integrated businesses, 2
    of Internet, 207–261
Industrial-age economy, shift to information-age economy from, 2
Infomediaries business model, 44
Information about products and services as advantage of E-commerce, 44–45
Information downloads added to cable television systems, 105
Information Highway State and Local Tax Study Group, 180

Information services. *See also* Databases *and*
    Electronic information services
  computer services vs., 118–119
  defined by different statutory languages
    among states, 120–121
  EU VAT rules for charges on, 410–411
  provided on tangible medium, 140
  software vs., 117–118
  sourcing rules for, 153
  sourcing software vs., 176–178
  states taxing, 101
  taxable, determining tax base for,
    130–131
  transmitted electronically, 113, 140
Information Technology Agreement (ITA),
    390–391
Information technology (IT) products,
    390–391
Information-age economy, 19–35
  impact on global commerce and multi-
    jurisdictional taxation of, 78
  market-state sourcing rule adopted in,
    164
  shift from industrial-age economy
    from, 2
Input exemptions from transactional tax
  for digital manufacturing, 146–147
  reform of, 149
  for service industries vs. manufacturing
    or agriculture, 142–146
  vertical vs. horizontal equity for,
    147–148
Intangible property
  applying transactional taxes to, 64–65
  corporate income tax nexus based on
    use of, 335–338
  digital transmissions of electronically
    transmitted software as nontaxable,
    107–108
  electronic transfer of software as sale of,
    62–63
  intellectual property rights as, 337
  license revenue from, 236–239
  licensing of, 335–337
  not protected under PL 86-872, 265
  pervasiveness among E-commerce busi-
    nesses of, 337
  royalties for use of, 450

  transactional tax extended from goods
    to, 139
  VAT directive rules for, 396–397
Integrated voice, data, and video services,
    126
Intellectual property rights as intangible
    property, 337
Interactive games added to cable television
    systems, 105
Interactive Services Association report on
    cybertaxation, 181
Interjurisdictional transactions
  mastery of various tax rules for, 47–48
  treatment of, 52–53
  ways of sourcing goods and services for,
    63
Intermediaries
  duty liability on markup of, 392
  financial, sourcing responsibilities of, 168
  Internet resulting in removal of, 66
  sites for, 36–37
  Web-based, 50, 304, 308
  Web-related functions performed by,
    311–314
Internal Revenue Code of 1986 (IRC,
    Code), 437, 443
Internal Revenue Code Sections
  168(g)(4), 488
  267(b), 463, 464
  482, 463, 464
  707(b)(1), 463, 464
  863, 492
  863(b), 490
  863(e), 486
  863(e)(1)(A), 485
  863(e)(2), 485
  864(b), 446
  864(c)(5), 490
  871–877, 446
  882(a), 446
  894(a)(1), 444
  902, 467, 478
  904(a), 478
  954(c), 476
  954(d), 476
  1248, 467
  1441(a), 446
  6038A, 462–464

6038C, 463
7701(e), 470, 471
7852(d), 444
7852(d)(1), 443–444
International direct taxation, 68–69
International income tax systems, 54
Internet
    advances in computer and communications technology woven in, 6
    barriers of time and geography removed by, 8
    business purchases using. *See* Business-to-business E-commerce
    consumer purchases using. *See* Business-to-consumer E-commerce, E-commerce, Internet retailing, *and* On-line shopping
    defined, 5
    development of, 6–8
    economic change brought by, 2–3
    foundation of global economy laid by, 1
    global taxation in age of, 1–79
    growth rate of, 3–4, 12
    source of vitality of, 5
    state income taxation of, 207–261
    voice traffic conducted over, 69–70, 96–99
Internet access
    access charges for, 128, 153
    added to cable television systems, 105, 124–125
    bundled with other services, 124–128
    defined, 88, 93, 97, 130
    EU VAT for, 411
    Internet telephony sometimes excluded from nontaxable, 98
    statistics for, 51
    taxation of, 92, *93*
    wireless transmissions of, 125
Internet access providers, transport services provided by, 93–94
Internet access services
    agency relationship for, 450–451
    bundled with voice Internet telephony, 99, 126
    cable modems for, 105–106
    income taxation of gross receipts from, 243

Internet Tax Freedom Act limits on taxation of, 88
sales and use taxes for, disputed, 92–96, 101, 105
states imposing sales or use tax on, 93, 94
telecommunications services purchased to provide, 144
throwback rules for, 244
treated as telecommunications services subject to sales tax, 92, *93*
Internet companies not yet profitable, transaction tax on, 82
Internet Development Act of 1998, 59–60
Internet economy
    application of preexisting rules to, 55, 64
    formulation of sourcing rules for, 163–169
    transformation to, 3–19
    trends arising from growth of, 51, 60–61
Internet portal
    electronic marketing for purchases of on-line advertising on, 300–301, 306
    preferential site on, 71
    Web-related services performed on, 313
Internet protocol (IP)
    for data communication on corporate intranet, 98
    for data transfer or voice transmissions over VPNs, 98–99
    for other uses than Web access, 98–99
    for voice calls on regular telephones, 96
Internet retailing
    drop shipment use for, 329–330
    impact of sales and use tax collection on, 346
    independence of parent and affiliates of, 324–326
    metamorphic growth of, 9, 266–269
    on-line advertising for, 300–301
    operational functions performed by third parties in, 270
    organizational structure of companies in, 269–271
    remote commerce expanded by, 1
    traditional industries turned upside down by, 50
    usage rates of, 9

Internet subsidiaries of retailers, 270,
317–318
alter-ego theory for jurisdiction of,
324–326
Internet Tax Freedom Act, 50
Advisory Commission on Electronic
Commerce created under, 56
agents of remote seller under, 304
applicable to state and local sales and use
taxes, 55
discriminatory taxation addressed in,
134, 137–139
extending tax moratorium for, 77
as federal intrusion into state fiscal matters, 59
focus on horizontal equity of, 147
focus on sales and use taxes of, 81
grandfather clause of, 88
impact of, 88–89
Internet access defined in, 97, 130
moratorium terms of, 88, 96, 134–135
multiple taxation of E-commerce prohibited by, 148
sales or use tax on bundled services
under, 131–132
sourcing sales under, 150
taxes not prohibited by, 88–89
Internet telephony, 69–70, 96–99
added to cable television systems, 105
bundled with nonvoice Internet access
services, 99, 126
defined, 96
disputed sales and use taxation of,
97–98
gross receipts taxation for, 253–255
Interstate commerce, taxation of, 57–58,
187–188
Interstate telecommunications
sales tax exclusion for some states for,
101, 105
sales tax on, 93
Intrastate telecommunications, sales tax on,
93, 101
Inventions, pace of technological development measured by adoption rate
of, 4
Inventory levels of E-commerce sites, superior, 43–44

J

J.C. Penney National Bank v. Ruth Johnson, Commissioner of Revenue, State
of Tennessee, 340
Job training, electronic, 30–32
JS&A Group, Inc. v. State Board of Equalization, 309–310, 323
Jurisdiction-to-tax issues for E-commerce,
70–73, 266
Jurisdiction-to-tax rules based on presence
of Web site on server, 137–138
Jurisdictions
market-state, for service industries,
239–240
over foreign companies, 54
over out-of-state companies having trade
names or trademarks in state, 237
right to tax of, 438
for sourcing income tax transactions,
212–229
for sourcing sales tax transactions, 150, 184

L

Leisure-travel bookings on-line market, 42
License revenue from intangible property,
236–238
Liggett Groups, Inc. v. Comm'r., 487
Links
affiliate, 310–311
commercial, 300
for exclusive marketing arrangements,
301–302
Hypertext Markup Language (HTML)
to create, 7–8, 303
revenue from affiliates for, 300–301
L. L. Bean, 277, 282
Local government policy initiatives for
E-commerce, 56–60
Local jurisdictions, local tax rates and sepa-
rate returns for, 82, 185
Lyon Metal Products, Inc. v. State Board of
Equalization, 332

M

Magazines
customized on-line, 29–30
discrimination against electronic delivery
of, 135–136

Mail-order companies
  agency nexus for, 309–310
  goods shipments by, 329
  nexus-creating activities by affiliates of, 318–319, 323–324
  operating in single jurisdiction, 72
  retail stores as not creating nexus for, 320–322
Mail-order sales, 47
  Internet sales to exceed, 267–*268*
  nexus issues in, 265, 271–272, 318, 319–321
  sales and use tax from, 70, 135, 344
  taxation of transaction in state of product receipt for, 151
Managed-compliance audits for determining sales and use tax liability, 199
Manufactured goods delivered electronically, 225–226
Manufacturers transformed into retailers through E-commerce, 50, 330
Manufacturing inputs, preferential sales and use tax treatment of, 148
Manufacturing process, sales tax exemption for products used in, 142–146
Manufacturing-based economy, shift to service-based economy from, 1
Market research for sales into taxing state, 299
Market-state rule to source electronic products, 151–153, 160–161, 164, 180–183, 247
Matthew Bender & Co., Inc. v. Comptroller of the Treasury, 282
MCI WorldCom stock-market valuation, 11
Merger and acquisition activity, U.S., 229
Microsoft Corporation stock-market valuation, 11
Mobility of Internet businesses, 49
Mosaic as first multimedia Web browser, 8
Motion picture industry converging with television industry and Internet, 26
Motion pictures
  inconsistent tax rules based on delivery of, 141
  revenues from theaters, television, video, and pay-per-view for, 140–141

MTC *Nexus Bulletin 95-1,* 293–296, 307, 356
MTC Sales Tax Simplification Planning Committee categories for sales tax reform, 190
Multijurisdictional transactions
  administrative procedures for, 196–200
  apportioning sales and use taxes of multistate , 63, 78, 171–176
Multimedia
  introduced to Internet by Web, 7
  linking data, audio, and video transmissions, 8
Multiple jurisdictions
  administrative procedures for tax filing requirements in, 196–200
  costs of sales and use tax compliance in, 201
  income tax sourcing issues for, 218–221
  in multiple states, sales and use sourcing issues for, 169–180
  in-state, 175
  tax-filing requirements in, 66, 186–187
Multiple tax defined, 148
Multiple-user products, sourcing problems for, 169–180
Multistate Tax Commission (MTC) regulations
  for apportionment of income for broadcasting and publishing industries, 235, 238–239
  for apportionment of income for financial institutions, 230–233
  for apportionment of income for transportation industries, 234
  costs of performance defined in, 218
  for nexus, 275–276, 280–281, 299, 306
Multistate Tax Commission (MTC) task force, 198
Music, taxation for downloading, 13, 28, 123
Music albums, taxation of tangible media vs. electronically delivered, 140, 249
Music industry in information-age economy, 28–29
Mutual-fund industry, market-state sourcing for income taxation of, 233–234

N

National Bellas Hess, Inc. v. Department of Revenue, 188, 302–303, 336, 342–343

National Geographic Society v. California Board of Equalization, 282, 318

National Governors Association (NGA) sales tax legislative proposals, 207

National Tax Association (NTA), Communications and Electronic Commerce Tax Project of

market-state sourcing rule supported by, 164

position regarding expanded duty to collect sales and use tax of, 345–346

simplified sales and use tax system advocated by, 190–192

sourcing sales of multiple-user products examined by, 173–174

state-of-use approach to sourcing advocated by, 181

uniformity efforts for sourcing of, 163, 166–167, 181, 247–248

uniformity efforts for sales tax for taxable goods and services by, 190, 195, 207

Negroponte, Nicholas, 6

News services provided via computer, 120

Newspapers

customized on-line, 29–30

discrimination against electronic delivery of, 135–136

VAT treatment of electronic information vs., 413–414

Nexus, 70–73

affiliate, 272, 310–311, 316–326

agency (attributional), 272, 285, 289–334

of company, 263–357

corporate, 334–341

of drop shippers, 326–334

expanding safe harbors for, 349–351

fulfillment house inventory as creating, 284–285

general principles of, 264–266

income tax, 61–62, 264–266, 295, 334–341

licensed or leased software as creating, 285–286

overlap of sales and use and income tax, 266

physical-presence requirement to create, 302–303, 305, 316–319

sales and use tax, 264–266, 305, 326

semiprocessed goods stored at contractor as creating, 285

substantial, 271, 277, 279–280, 282–283, 289

uncertain, 263, 279

over vendor in customer state, 246

Nexus rules, 137–138. *See also* specific types

continued enforcement of, 356–357

escalating economic and political stakes of, 341

future of, 341–357

Geoffrey, 237–238, 336–337, 357

state enforcement of, 351–356

state/business conflicts over, 264

Nexus standard, 189

900-number services, states taxing, 101

Nokia stock-market valuation, 11

Non-EU vendors, registration as vendors for VAT of, 73

Notes, 513–555

O

Object of the transaction approach, 129–130

Oklahoma Tax Commission v. Jefferson Lines, 172–173

On-line advertising purchased from Web portals, 300–301, 303–304

On-line auction transactions, 314–315

On-line catalogs, 36

On-line selling or retailing. *See* Internet retailing

On-line shopping. *See also* E-commerce *and* Internet retailing

growth of, 8–9, 41

sales categories for, 41–*42*

usage rate of, 7, 40–41

Organization for Economic Cooperation and Development (OECD), 52, 394, 409, 513

Model Tax Convention Article 5, 460–462

Model Treaty Commentary, 459

Model Treaty of, 454–460, 504
outline agreement on taxing E-commerce of, 418
Orvis Co., Inc. v. Tax Appeals Tribunal, 274–275
Outsourcing of computer service functions, 170

P

Packet-switching networks, 99, 126
Packet-switching technology
  for Internet access, 93
  for Internet telephony, 96, 98
  taxation of, 92, 99–100
Pagers, Internet access using, 13
Pay-per-view television, motion picture revenues from, 140–141
Pearle Health Services, Inc. v. Taylor, 319
Performance-based pricing for Web advertising, 304
Permanent establishment (PE)
  in Canada, 493, 496
  defined, 438
  in Japan, 497–498, 502–504
  under OECD Model Tax Convention, 461–462
  under tax treaty, 454–460
  in U.K., 504
Personal computers (PCs)
  households having, 12
  with Internet connections, taxes proposed for, 138
  operations per second performed by, 6
  usage rates of, 6–7, 14
Photography, digital delivery of, 123
Physical-presence threshold for taxation, 137
Piedras Negras Broadcasting Co. v. Comer., 453
Portals, services from, 36
Postal Service, potential lost income from E-mail use to, 73
Pre-paid phone cards, sourcing sales of, 156–159
Presales activities creating attributional nexus, 296–300
Price competition as advantage of E-commerce, 45–46

Priceline.com stock valuation, 10
Private leased lines, data communications over, 99
Private networks, uses of, 98–99
Product choices in E-commerce, wide range of, 43–44
Product fulfillment activities, 299. See also Fulfillment houses
Product repairs, digital delivery of, 34
Professional services, VAT on, 366
Property tax
  difficult to apply to computer-based goods and services, 2
  tax base reliance on, 2
  for telecommunication providers, 255–256, 258
Property transaction transformed into service transaction, 110–111
Public Law (PL) 86–272
  impact on franchise tax of, 335
  no protection for after-sales activities under, 295
  no protection for in-state solicitation activities for sales of services or intangible property, 334
  safe harbor against income tax nexus under, 61–62, 265, 295, 334
  scope issues for, 334–335, 349
Public Utility Commission (PUC) charge, 257
Publishing industries, market-state sourcing for income taxation of, 234–235, 238
Pull method of consumer access to database, 169
Push method of streaming customized information to user's server, 169
Pyramiding of taxes, 141–148
  absence of resale or component-services exemption leading to, 144–145
  on business inputs and outputs, 141–142
  on service provider and retail consumer, 116

Q

Quill Corp. v. North Dakota, 137, 181, 182, 188–189, 347
  licensed or leased software as not creating nexus in, 286

Quill Corp. v. North Dakota (continued)
  limiting impact of, 291, 333
  media advertisements as not creating
    nexus in, 297, 302, 304
  nexus issues for sales or use tax in, 265,
    267, 271, 335, 338, 341–343
  precedent for physical presence from,
    274, 276, 321, 336, 351–353
  slightest presence test for, 273
  staff presence under substantial nexus
    standard of, 272–273, 277

R

Readers Digest Association, Inc. v. Mahin,
  318–319
Real-time approach for sales tax collection,
  202–203
Real-time commerce, 49–50, 60–61
Registration of business for VAT, 371, 377,
  385–387, 422
Remote commerce
  compromise between business and gov-
    ernment over sales and use taxes for, 58
  Internet use causing substantial rise in, 6
  sales and use tax revenue lost from, 71,
    344
Remote selling
  growth of, 1, 35–46
  jurisdiction to tax for, 70
  new business models for, 36–37
  VAT for, 381–382
Remote vendors
  affiliates for, 301, 310–311, 320–321
  agents for, 304
  creating attributional nexus for,
    291–293, 296–300, 308–310
  establishing nexus safe harbors for,
    281–282
  fulfillment house use by, 284–285
  providing market and product perfor-
    mance information to, 299
  responsibility for collecting sales and use
    taxes of, 60, 76, 183, 192, 263,
    266–267, 271
  state tax jurisdiction over, 265
  third-party contractors for operations to
    limit physical presence of, 271,
    299–300

  third-party intermediary services for,
    311–314
  Web site and electronic partnership
    nexus issues for, 300–316
Remote-repair services, 122–123
Resale certificates of transactions exempt
  from sales and use tax, 327, 331
Reuters America Inc. v. Tax Commission of
  Ohio, 120
Revenue Reconciliation Act of 1989, 463
Revenue Reconciliation Act of 1990, 463
Reverse auction sites, 36
Roaming charges, sourcing rules for,
  162–163

S

Sale-for-resale tax exemptions, 144–145,
  327, 330–331, 333
Sales and use tax compliance, 183–204
  complications introduced by multiple
    intrajurisdiction rates to, 184–188
  complications introduced by multiple
    taxing bodies to, 82, 184
  impact of automating sales tax process
    on, 203–204
  reducing burden for remote vendors of,
    352
  reducing costs of, 200–201, 203
  reforms proposed for simplifying,
    191–204
  registration of Internet retailer to facili-
    tate, impact on drop shippers of, 333
  simplifying administrative procedures
    for, 196–200
Sales and use tax rules
  extension to services of tax base for, 64
  nonparity of treating tangible property
    and services under existing, 135
  one rate per state, 167–168, 191–194
  pressure for reform of, 189–191, 346,
    348
  for state and local jurisdictions, 57–59,
    66, 75
  variance among states of, 84
Sales and use tax system
  effort to expand duty to collect under,
    342–351
  fundamental reform of, 200–204

lack of current guidance for, 205–206

Supreme Court restrictions on seller obligations for, 188–189

survival of, 71

trusted third party (TTP) to coordinate collections for, 203, 352

Sales and use taxation of E-commerce, 81–206

for agents of Web mall, 316

apportionment of, 170–171, 173–180

automation of, 50

Internet Tax Freedom Act applicable to, 55, 77

on multiple levels of service or production, 148

remote vendor responsibility for, 60, 183, 192

simplification of, 66, 183–204, 346, 348

software for sales tax administration to facilitate real-time administration for, 202–203

tax compromise for, 76–77

"zero-burden" real-time compliance system for, 50, 75, 202–203

Sales and use taxes, state, 81–89

audits and appeals process for, 198–199

base-state approach to collection of, 201–202

on categories of services involving E-commerce, 87

differences in reliance on, 84

on digital commerce, 101–116

importance in state revenue generation of, 82–83

Internet Tax Freedom Act applied to, 88

real-time approach to collection of, 202–203

reform proposals for collection of, 200–204

reform proposals for filing, 198

revenue losses from mail-order sales for, 344

revenue losses from remote commerce for, 71, 344

states not imposing, 82

on telecommunications, 89–101

voluntary disclosure of previous liabilities for, 199–200

Sales of services or intangible property, 47

Sales, sourcing of, 47

Sales tax. *See* Transactional tax

Sales tax base of states

erosion of, 183, 344

lack of uniform, 116–150

narrowed to exclude electronic and digital products and services, 248

as percentage of total state personal income, 84–85

reform of, 148–150

simultaneous broadening and narrowing of, 148–150

sources of confusion for, 116–123

taxable-service categories for, *85–86*

uniform, 194–196

Sales tax rates for states

proposal for blended, 193

proposal for single, 167–168, 191–194

Satellite services

as alternative transmission channel for Internet access, 17–18

cable television transmission via, 103–104

pay television transmission via, 104

Satellite-television services

expanding market share of, 104, 141

state sales and use taxes on, 104–105

Scripto, Inc. v. Carson, 289–290, 306, 340

Secondary users of digitized products, 178–180

Secure Electronic Transaction (SET) technology, jurisdictional information in, 168

Senate Bill 1433, 75

Separate statement approach, 129, 130–132

Server

access from third-party, 118

consumer, push method of streaming database information to, 169

income tax jurisdiction by location of, 220, 241

jurisdiction for storage of product or service on, 162

leasing space on, 459

maintaining Web site on third-party, 122, 304, 308

maintenance of, considered maintenance of stock of merchandise, 452–453

Server (*continued*)
  for multiple users of digital products,
    alternatives for, 171–172
  sales tax jurisdiction by location of,
    154
  storage of software on third-party, 178
  taxation of transfer of software to,
    110–112
  technology enabling data and software
    storage on remote, 162
  test of permanent establishment using,
    458
  for third-party Web site, 305–307
  vendor, pull method of accessing data-
    base from, 169
Service categories taxes by states, variation
    among, 85
Service industries
  market-state jurisdictions for, 239–240
  market-state sourcing rules for income
    taxation of, 229–238, 245–246
Service-based economy
  growth of, 228–229
  shift from manufacturing-based econ-
    omy to, 1
Services
  communication, 131
  general rule of nontaxability of, 116
  multistate use of, sourcing, 172–178,
    216–229
  not protected under PL 86-872, 265
  repair, 122–123, 152, 154, 299
  sales tax exemption for, in electromag-
    netic communications, 143
  separated into taxable and nontaxable
    transactions, 130–132
  sourcing rules for, 151–161
  transactional tax extended from goods
    to, 139
  transactional tax issues related to,
    64–65
  UDITPA sourcing rules for, 226–229
  variation in state taxation of, *85–86*
  VAT treatment for, 393–402
SFA Folio Collections, Inc. v. Tracy, 321, 322,
    324–325
Shipping functions for Internet retailing,
    270–271

Simplification of sales and use tax system,
    66, 183–204
  hindrances to, 187
  organizations supporting, 190–191
  prior initiatives for, 187–189
  reforms proposed for, 191–204
Single Administrative Document (SAD),
    384
Single Market among EU member states,
    sales within, 374–382
Small businesses in E-commerce
  de minimis rules to protect, 60
  growth of sales over Internet of, 267
Smart cards to purchase goods and services,
    sales and use tax laws for, 159
Smart telephones, 13
Smidth & Co. v. Greenwood, 505–506
Software
  canned vs. custom, 112
  creation of Web site treated as sale of
    custom, 121–122
  custom, electronic transfer of, 101, 106,
    112
  defining, 117–118
  delivered by tangible medium, 102, 116,
    140
  electronic delivery of, 27, 61–64, 78,
    101, 106–112, 140, 177, 219, 249, 265,
    334
  foreign licensor of, 449–450
  information services vs., 117–118,
    176–178
  Information Technology Agreement
    (ITA) for, 391
  in information-age economy, 27
  nexus created from licensed or leased,
    285–287
  remote access from multiple locations of,
    111
  source of income from, 475–476
  tax collection, sales and use, 203–204
  as taxable personal property, 106, 112,
    114
  taxation of sale of, 62–63, 101–102, 107,
    110–112
  transfer of, 472–475
  transfers exempt from state tax for,
    107–108

Software regulations, U.S. Treasury, 472–478

Source-of-income rules, 482
  for compensation for personal services, 484–485
  for dividend income, 483
  exception to, for income from sale of intangible property, 489–490
  for interest income, 483
  for international communications income, 485–486
  for property manufactured in United States and sold outside United States, 490–492
  for rents and royalties, 485
  for sale of personal property, 486–489

Sourcing, 150–183
  default rule for, 166–167
  of digital sales and services, 52–54, 78, 151
  of goods and services in multiple jurisdictions, 63, 169–176, 211
  of income from services to locale of performance, 68
  of income, possibilities for, 54, 67, 210–211
  of income tax, 61
  of software vs. information services, 176–178
  to state level only, 164
  throw-around rule to state of other customers, 167
  throwback rule to state of origin (seller's state) for, 167, 224–225, 353–355

Sourcing rules for income taxes, state
  all-or-nothing, 214–215, 226, 245, 246
  current E-commerce, 238–248
  location of income-producing activity for, 215–226
  market-state, 210, 211, 213, 229–238, 242–249
  mix of market- and vendor-state, 248
  pro rata allocation, 215, 226, 245
  for property factor in apportionment formulas, 240–241
  for sales of digital content, 212–214
  for sales of tangible property, 211–212
  vendor-state, 211, 214–215, 217, 220–222, 227, 229, 231, 233, 236–237, 246–249

Sourcing rules for sales and use taxes, state
  all-or-nothing, 172–173, 178
  apportionment, 170–171, 173–180
  formulation for Internet economy of, 163–169
  market-state (consumer), 151–153, 160–161, 164, 180–183, 247
  origin-state, 353–355
  point-of-consumption approach to, 158
  point-of-sale approach to, 158
  vendor, 153–161
  vendor-state–oriented approach to, 158, 182–183

Sourcing rules for various income types, U.S., 491

South Central Bell Telephone Company v. Barthelmy, 123

Speech-recognition software, 13

Spencer Gifts, Inc., 325

State government policy initiatives for E-commerce, 56–60

State income tax rates, 222–226

State income tax rules, 67
  differences among, 223

State income taxation of Internet, 207–261

State personal income, sales tax base as percentage of, 84–85

State sales or use new taxes on Internet access or on-line services prohibited, 55

State sales tax
  burden of, 83, 186–187, 192
  freedom of states to determine rates and bases of, 83–84
  revenue losses from remote commerce, 71, 344
  total local and, by state, 185

State tax revenue, importance of state-level sales and use taxes for, 83–84, 186

States not imposing state sales and use tax, 82

Statutory language, divergent state interpretations of, 120–121

Steelcase, Inc. v. Allan A. Crystal, Commissioner of Revenue Services, 331–332

Steelcase, Inc. v. Director, Division of Taxation, 331
Stock trades on PC, 13
Stock-market reaction to growth of Internet companies, 9–11
Subscription-based services, 36

T

Tangible goods, tax issues for
delivered by conventional means, 87
discriminatory taxes between
E-commerce and, 89, 133–141
market- or destination-state rule for
interstate, 155
ordered over Internet, 60, 75, 165
Tangible personal property
delivered in digital format, 249
digital transfer of software treated as,
177–178
electronic transmission of information
treated as lease of, 114
electronic transmission of information
treated as sale of, 113–114
general rule of taxability for, 116
market-state rule for income taxation of,
210
sale of canned software transmitted electronically as, 106–110
sale of prepaid phone cards as, 158–159
sales tax exemption for, in electromagnetic communications, 143
tax on digital goods and services as
extension of tax on, 103
tax rules available to businesses engaged
in manufacturing, 62
tax system designed for manufacturers
and vendors of, 61
Tangible property
defined, 108
multiple purchases of, apportionment of
sales tax for, 171
sourcing rules for state income taxation
for sales of, 211–212
Tax bases. See also Sales tax base of states
call for uniform sales and use, 194–196
variations in, 65
Tax enforcement, 53
for nexus rules, 356–357

Tax Reform Act of 1986, 462–463
Tax reform requirements for E-commerce,
75–79
Tax treaties
interaction of statutory law and,
442–446
permanent establishment under,
454–460
standard in absence of, 446–454
Tax-collection process for sales and use
taxes, reform of, 200–204
Taxation implications of E-commerce,
46–60, 347
Taxation principles, traditional, 360–362
Taxation rules
in additional jurisdictions, complexities
of, 47–48
fees for E-commerce during revision of,
73–75
inconsistent, based on method of delivery, 141
international, 53
residence-based, 54, 68
revamping of archaic, 2, 183–204, 259
simplification needed for, 50, 183–204
state and local initiatives for, 56–60
for tangible goods ordered over Internet,
60
undermined by global economic
E-commerce trends, 1
Technical and Miscellaneous Reconciliation Act of 1988 (TAMRA), 443–444
Technological penetration, measuring rates
of, 4
Telecommunications Act of 1996, deregulation of industry by, 127–128, 228,
260
Telecommunications Directive of EC, 404
Telecommunications industry
activities and services of, 250–251
deregulation of, 127–128, 228
destination-based rules for tax sourcing,
180
exemption for equipment used by,
142–143
market-state sourcing for income taxation of, 235–236
nexus issues in, 288

special assessments imposed on, 257

special income taxes for, 249–261

special industry rules for, 69–70, 75, 249–261

Telecommunication lines, leased, 179

Telecommunication services, 89–101

boundaries among categories of taxable, 99–101

bundling of, 99, 100, 124, 132, 254–255

content vs. transport, 100, 117, 254–255

cost-of-performance rules applied to, 219–220

determining taxing jurisdiction for, 153

discriminatory taxation of, 137–138

enhanced services as taxable, 90–92, 124

exemptions for equipment used in, 143

federal excises on, 81

income taxation of, 243, 249–261

in information-age economy, 22–24

as input rather than output, 129

Internet telephony as taxable, 97, 99

Internet-related, gross receipts taxes of, 253–255

interstate provision of, 173

for prepaid phone cards, 157–158

purchased to use in Internet access service, 144

residential, 90

sales or use tax on transmission activities in, 89–90

supplies of, antiavoidance provision for, 400–401

throwback rules for, 244

transmissions as taxable, 90, 100

value-added services in, 91–92, 98, 100–101

VAT treatment of, 402–408, *429–430*

vendors of, 129–130

Telecommunications vendors acting as information providers vs. utilities, 100

Telephone companies. *See* Telecommunication services

Telephone service, 250

bundling of other services with local and long distance, 124–128

leased line, 288

Telephones

households having, 12

Internet telephony using regular, 96

picture, 13

smart, 13, 14

Television services, 251

cable. *See* Cable television services

direct satellite, 104

in information-age economy, 24–26

pay, 104

Television sets

households having, 12

Web, 12, 14

Throwback sales rule to state of origin (seller's state), 167, 224–*225*, 244, 246

Time-limited digital products, nexus for, 287

Toll-free 800 numbers, sourcing rules for, 160–161, 354

Toy on-line market, 42

Trader Unique Reference Number (TURN), 383–384

Training products

computerized, 117–118

discriminatory taxation of Web-based, 136–137

Transactional tax

calculated on gross sales receipts, 82

collection responsibilities for electronically transferred software for, 62

complexity in administering, 82, 183–204

countries with, *427*

difficulty for sales over long distances in applying, 2

discriminatory. *See* Discriminatory taxes

exemptions to, 135–136

issues related to services for, 64–65

lacking on national level in United States, 81

for newspapers and magazines, 135–136

roots of U.S., 139

simplification of tax laws for, 65–66, 183–204

states' reliance on, 84, 194

tax compliance reengineering and automated tax solutions for, 49–50

of telecommunications services, 69, *93*

Transactional tax laws, need to simplify, 65–66

Transactional tax rules based on sales of manufactured goods, 2

Transmission Control Protocol/Internet Protocol (TCP/IP)
as common digital protocol, 7
in packet-switching technology for Internet access, 93

Transmissions in taxing telecommunications services
broad definition of, 92
enhanced services as possibly constituting, 90–91, 100
narrow definition of, 91–92

Transportation, falling costs of, 1

Transportation industry, market-state sourcing for income taxation of, 234

Treasury Regulation Sections
1.861–18, *477, 479–481*
1.864–7(b)(2), 455

Tyler Pipe Industries, Inc. v. Washington State Department of Revenue, 280, 282, 289–291, 294, 296, 306–307, 340

U

Uniform Division of Income for Tax Purposes Act (UDITPA)
residual classification for intangible property of, 213
sales factor defined under, 210
sales of services rules derived from, 210
sourcing rules for services under, 226–229

Uniform multijurisdictional exemption form, 197

Uniform sales tax registration forms, 198

Unit valuation method for assessing property value, 255

United Nations Model Tax Treaty, 456

U.S. Constitution
Commerce Clause of, 188–189, 264–265, 271, 278, 286, 336
Due Process Clause of, 188–189, 264, 305
Supremacy Clause of, 442

U.S. government, development of E-commerce policy by, 53–56

U.S. Model Income Tax Treaty, 443, 445

U.S. resident criteria, 439

U.S. Treasury White Paper, 439–442
classification of income in E-commerce transaction under, 441
documentation of tax administration under, 441–442
jurisdiction in taxing E-commerce under, 440–441

Universal service fund charge, 257

Use tax self-assessment by businesses and consumers, 355–356

Utilities, power
entry into telecommunications fields of, 128
exempted from all-or-nothing cost-of-performance rules under UDITPA, 227
future of taxation for, 259–261
monopoly status of, 250
special taxation of, 250, 258
telecommunications vendors acting as, 100

Utility users tax, 257, 258

V

Valuations of leading Internet companies, 9–11

Value-added network (VAN), states taxing provision of, 115

Value-added services for telecommunications, 91–92, 98, 100–101

Value Added Tax Act 1994, 401

Value-added tax (VAT) customs duty, 388–393
applicable rates for, 390–391
calculating, 389
as indirect cost, 389
levying of, 389–391
outward and inward processing of goods for, 393
preferential rates for, 392
price unbundling of intangibles for, 392
prior sales arrangement for, 392
reconfiguration or reclassification of goods for, 392
recovery of, 391–392

reduction for information technology products of, 390–391

reliefs to suspend, 392–393

Value-added tax invoice, 388

credit, 142, 362

for E-commerce, 380

Value-added tax registration number, 376

of customer held by supplier, 379

Value-added tax return, 371, 383, 385, 388

Value-added tax rules

bases for liability under, 360

importance of mechanism of delivery under, 362

for imposing consumption-based taxes, 142

taxation of E-commerce under, 65, 360

uniformity of, 196

Value-added taxes (VAT), 359–433. *See also* individual types

accounting records required for, 371

actual tax point for, 374

administration of, 371–372

on all E-commerce transactions in Europe and Asia, 74

basic tax point for, 369, 373–374

countries having, *425–426*

credit invoice, 142, 362

defined, 52

delivery method as affecting, 413–414

enforcement issues for, 72–73

in European Union (EU), systems and rates of, *363*

exempt goods and services for, 366, 367

flow of taxation for, 364

for goods, 372–393

growing U.S. interest in, 50

impact of E-commerce on, 52

input, 364, *365,* 372

liability on supplier to pay, 366

lower (reduced) rate for, 367

method of exemption for, 149

national EU, relative simplicity of, 82

net, *365*

nexus for, 369

output, 364, *365*

overview of, 363–372

place of supply for, 368–369, 373, 381

rates of taxation for, 366–367

recovery of, 371–372, 385, 386, 387–388

sample case of collection and payment of, *365*

for services, 393–402

standard rate for, 366–367

to suppliers not considered real cost, 364

supply and install deals for, 376–377

supply of taxable goods or services for, 364–369, 373, 377–378, 408

in tax base of OECD countries, 52–53, 81

tax credit for, 142, 362, 364, 372

as tax on turnover and consumption and not profit, 364

taxable person for, 364, 366

for telecommunications services, 402–408

time of supply for, 369, 373–374

transactions outside scope of, 366, 367

triggering tax point for, 370

value of import for, 370

value of supply for, 370

zero-rated supplies for, 367, 379–382

Value-added taxes (VAT) for E-commerce cybertransactions

adaptation of VAT rules for, 53

E-commerce sale of supply of goods under, 368, 380

E-commerce sale of supply of services under, 368

EC working paper on, 421–423

EU general principles on, 423–424

future of, 416–417

gaps in, for digital goods and services, 73

indirect tax for, 402

jurisdictional issues for, 72, 360–*361*

objectives for, 415

OECD outline agreement on, 418–421

political debate about, 414–424

progress to date on, 415

sold to foreign customers, 380

tracking problems of, 360–*361*

types of transactions for, 362

Value-added taxes (VAT) for electronic delivery, 408–414

of entertainment and educational services, 411–412

of information services, 410–411

Value-added taxes (*continued*)
  of Internet access, 411
  place of supply for, 409–411
  supplies as services for, 409, 410
Value-added taxes (VAT), goods for,
    372–388
  acquisition tax on, 377
  acquisition within EU of, 375
  contracts for local installation or assem-
    bly of, 376–377, 387
  credit sale of, 374
  customer approval of, 386
  customs duty for, 388–393
  European Sales Listings (ESLs, VIES) for,
    380
  export of, 372, 379, 382
  import of, 372, 382–386
  importer of record for, 384
  Intrastats for, 379–380
  place of supply for, 368–369, 373,
    384–385, 386–387
  reexport of, 393
  reporting documents for, 379–380
  sale of, 373, 374–382
  time of supply for, 369, 373–374,
    384–385
  transfer of title qualified by specific
    action of, 386–388
  transporting own, 375–376
  triangulation of, *378*
  zero-rated supply of, 367, 379–382
Value-added taxes (VAT) on services,
    393–402
  antiavoidance for, 400–401
  basic rule for place of supply of,
    394–395
  future changes for, 402
  land, 395
  liability for, 399–401
  physical performance, 395–396
  place of supply of services for, 401–402
  place of taxation of sale of, 394–399
  reverse charge for, 399–400
  transport, 395
Value-added taxes (VAT) on telecommuni-
    cation services, 402–408
  accounting for, 406–*407*
  establishment of business for, 404–405

general principles for, 404
  legislation for, 404–406
  leveling playing field for, 416
  place-of-supply rules for, 405–*407*
  reverse charge for, 406
VAT credit
  claimed by purchaser using goods or ser-
    vices in taxable activities, 364
  for input tax, 372
  invoice required for, 142, 362
Vendor selection of locale, tax disincentives
    for, 182–183, 241–242
Vendor-compensation allowances for col-
    lection and administration of sales tax,
    201
Vendor-state–oriented approach to sourc-
    ing rules, 158, 182–183
Vendors, E-commerce
  parity between tangible product vendors
    and, 180
  identifying state for, 182
Vermont Information Processing, Inc. v. Tax
    Appeals Tribunal, 274
Vertical equity of business inputs to pro-
    duce tangible and electronic goods
    and services, 147–148
Vertically integrated businesses
  income taxation of, 2
  lessening need for, 211–212
  providing both transport and content
    services, 128
Very high speed digital subscriber lines
    (VDSLs), 125
Video on demand, 104, 105
Video programming, 251
Video transmissions, 5
Videotapes of motion pictures, taxation
    rules for, 141
Virtual communities, 36
Virtual corporations, 49
Virtual learning centers, 136–137. *See also*
    Distance learning
Virtual private networks (VPNs), IP for
    data transfer or voice transmissions
    over, 98–99
Voice transmissions, 5
  indistinguishable from data on integrated
    Internet access and telephony, 126

Volume discounts, real-time adjustments for, 45

VSA, Inc. v. Faulkner, 330

W

Web addresses, unknown state of consumer in, 161–162

Web advertisements
  commission sales basis for, 303
  compensation for hits of, 303–304
  exclusive rights deals for, 301–302
  flat-fee payments for, 303
  pay-for-performance standard for, 304
  purchased from Web portals, 300–301

Web auction houses, 301, 314–316

Web browser, Mosaic as first, 8

Web malls
  hosting Web site of out-of-state Internet retailer, 305–306
  jurisdiction of, 307
  protection from treatment as agents of, 308
  purpose of, 301, 306

Web page or site
  affiliate, 301, 310–311
  considered to be fixed place of business, 451–452
  considered to be software, 117
  creation of, defining type of service for, 121–122
  direct marketing through, 271–272
  goods sold by foreign person on, 453–454
  issue of agency nexus created by, 300–316
  issue of taxable connections and physical presence created by, 287–288
  management of consumer sales using, 212, 241
  as permanent establishment, 459–460
  safe harbor for product orders using, 349

shared between Internet affiliates and subsidiaries, 318
third-party, 305–307
third-party host of, 300

Web portal, purchases of on-line advertising from, 300–301

Web site providers as agents for out-of-state Internet vendors, 312

Web television sets (Web TV), 12, 14

Web TV networks, wireless electronic services through, 125

Web-based training, taxation of, 136–137

White Paper. See U.S. Treasury White Paper

Wholesalers, changes to, 50

William Wrigley, Jr. Co. v. Wisc. Dept. of Revenue, 273

Willis Commission report on state taxation of interstate commerce, 187–188

Wireless Application Protocol (WAP), 125

Wireless Internet access, 13

Wireless services, 251
  as alternative transmission channel for Internet access, 17–18

Wireline services, 250, 251

Withholding taxes
  on cross-border payments, 438, 502, 504
  on use of intangibles, 450

World trade statistics, 39

World Wide Web (Web)
  defined, 5
  development by Tim Berners-Lee of, 7
  innovations introduced to Internet by, 7–8
  penetration rate of, 4

Y

Yahoo stock valuation, 10

Z

"Zero-burden" real-time compliance system for sales and use tax collection, 50, 75, 202–203, 352